A book and Web site that work together

bedfordstmartins.com/techcomm

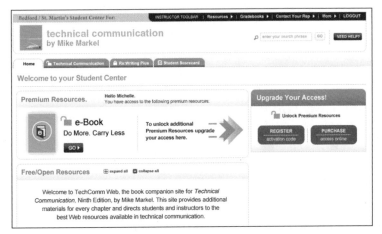

Technical Communication, Ninth Edition, and its companion Web site, TechComm Web <bedfordstmartins.com/techcomm>, are fully integrated and designed to work together. Written by Mike Markel, TechComm Web is updated regularly with new materials.

On TechComm Web

On TechComm Web labels in the margins of the book direct you to a variety of useful free resources on the site that expand the coverage of crucial topics online in formats that are both engaging and interactive.

"I am incredibly grateful for the resources on the Web site and the ways in which they connect to the material in the textbook. I frequently send my students to the Web site for more information about a topic we are discussing, and I use the assignments as well."

—Dan Colson, *University of Illinois, Urbana-Champaign*

NINTH EDITION

Technical Communication

Mike Markel

Boise State University

Bedford/St. Martin's   Boston ◆ New York

For Bedford/St. Martin s

Developmental Editor: Julie Kelly
Editorial Assistant: Melissa Cook
Production Supervisor: Andrew Ensor
Marketing Manager: Molly Parke
Project Management: Books By Design, Inc.
Text Design: Books By Design, Inc.
Cover Design: Donna Lee Dennison
Cover Photo: *Laptop Computer*. Alamy, Ltd.
Composition: Macmillan Publishing Solutions
Printing and Binding: RR Donnelley & Sons Company

President: Joan E. Feinberg
Editorial Director: Denise B. Wydra
Editor in Chief: Karen S. Henry
Director of Marketing: Karen R. Soeltz
Director of Editing, Design, and Production: Marcia Cohen
Assistant Director of Editing, Design, and Production: Elise S. Kaiser
Manager, Publishing Services: Emily Berleth

Library of Congress Control Number: 2008933818

Manufactured in the United States of America.

4   3   2   1   0   9
f   e   d   c   b   a

For information, write: Bedford/St. Martin's, 75 Arlington Street, Boston, MA 02116   (617-399-4000)

ISBN-10: 0-312-48597-2
ISBN-13: 978-0-312-48597-9

Acknowledgments

Figure, p. 1: Copyright © 2008. Reproduced by permission of Alamy Stock Photography. All rights reserved.

Figure, p. 2: Courtesy of Radvision, Inc.

Figure, p. 9: Courtesy of Xerox Corporation.

Figure 1.1, p. 11: Courtesy Segway, Inc.

Acknowledgments and copyrights are continued at the back of the book on pages 738–40, which constitute an extension of the copyright page.

Preface for Instructors

The principles of good technical communication do not change, and *Technical Communication* remains a thorough, accessible introduction to planning, drafting, designing, revising, and testing technical documents. This text continues to offer well-designed, student-friendly coverage of rhetorical, visual, and cross-cultural issues. I have tried to make this new edition reflect the many exciting developments that have occurred in technical communication—and in ways to teach it—in the past few years. Most prominent among these developments is the greatly expanded importance of electronic communication resources, especially the growth of Web 2.0 tools. The ninth edition also shows more explicitly how technical communication in the academy is connected to technical communication in the workplace.

New Chapters

The ninth edition includes two new chapters (with new accompanying cases) that reflect changes in the way we communicate and that respond to requests from many instructors.

- *Chapter 18: Writing Lab Reports.* This chapter greatly expands the book's coverage of an important application that most students use in their academic careers. In addition, it helps students make the transition to writing science and engineering articles on the job.

- *Chapter 22: Connecting with the Public.* This chapter reflects the increasing importance of communicating with various stakeholders, such as customers, vendors, and the general public. The chapter covers presentation applications (brochures, white papers, podcasts, and newsletters) and collaborative applications (blogs, discussion boards, and wikis).

Expanded Coverage

While developing the ninth edition, I reexamined every chapter and relied on the input of fellow technical-communication instructors to inform my decisions about revising the text. Thus, in addition to new chapters and features, the book's coverage has been expanded in the following key areas to reflect a wider range of technical documents and new methods for developing them.

Chapter	What's new
Chapter 1: Introduction to Technical Communication	An expanded discussion of how professionals use the four communication skills in the workplace An increased emphasis on the differences between how audience and purpose are interpreted in academic and workplace settings
Chapter 2: Understanding Ethical and Legal Considerations	An expanded discussion of how the ethical standards of rights, justice, utility, and care can be applied in thinking through ethical conflicts in the workplace New discussions of an employee's obligations to his or her employer, to the public, and to the environment
Chapter 3: Writing Technical Documents	An increased emphasis on the writing process, including a new section on selecting an application, a design, and a delivery method
Chapter 4: Writing Collaboratively	A new discussion of project-management techniques A new discussion of how to participate in a videoconference
Chapter 5: Analyzing Your Audience and Purpose	A new discussion of using the Internet to research your audience
Chapter 6: Researching Your Subject	A new discussion of using Web 2.0 resources to research a subject A new Interactive Sample Document ("Evaluating Information from Internet Sources") A new database research exercise
Chapter 8: Communicating Persuasively	A new Interactive Sample Document ("Analyzing Evidence in an Argument")
Chapter 9: Writing Coherent Documents	An expanded discussion of enhancing coherence in writing titles, headings, lists, and paragraphs An expanded discussion of enhancing coherence through design features
Chapter 10: Writing Effective Sentences	A new Interactive Sample Document ("Revising for Conciseness and Simplicity")
Chapter 11: Designing Documents and Web Sites	A discussion of designing Web sites effectively, highlighting the different ways audiences use paper documents and Web sites A new Interactive Sample Document ("Analyzing a Page Design")
Chapter 12: Creating Graphics	An expanded discussion of how to plan graphics in light of the writer's purpose and the readers' experience An expanded discussion of how to cite graphics appropriately
Chapter 13: Reviewing, Evaluating, and Testing Documents and Web Sites	A substantially updated discussion of revision techniques, usability evaluations, and usability testing, which reflects the increasing importance of ensuring that a document or Web site achieves the writer's purposes and responds to the audience's needs

Chapter 14: Writing Letters, Memos, and E-mails	An expanded discussion of writing effective e-mails
Chapter 15: Preparing Job-Application Materials	A new discussion of the risks and benefits of social-networking Web sites in the job search
	An expanded discussion of techniques for writing effective electronic résumés
Chapter 16: Writing Proposals	An expanded discussion of accommodating readers from other cultures
	A new sample proposal
	A new Interactive Sample Document ("Writing a Project Description")
Chapter 17: Writing Informational Reports	A new emphasis on writing reports with the main purpose of presenting information
	An updated discussion of writing meeting minutes in a tabular format
	A new sample progress report
	A new Interactive Sample Document ("Writing a Persuasive Directive")
Chapter 19: Writing Recommendation Reports	A new emphasis on writing reports with the main purpose of presenting recommendations
	A new sample recommendation report
Chapter 20: Writing Definitions, Descriptions, and Instructions	A new focus on how the techniques of defining and describing complement instructional writing
Chapter 21: Making Oral Presentations	A new approach to writing presentations that uses the claim-and-support structure
	A new Tech Tip on how to create a master page design
	A new Tech Tip on how to set list items to appear and dim
	A new set of presentation graphics to accompany the recommendation report in Chapter 19
	A revised evaluation form for oral presentations
Appendix: Reference Handbook	A new discussion of the IEEE documentation system

Free and Premium Online and Print Resources

Technical Communication offers a wealth of free and premium content that will enhance your teaching experience—and your students' learning experience.

TechComm Web

The TechComm Web site at <bedfordstmartins.com/techcomm> offers access to comprehensive free and premium resources for students and instructors. These resources are fully integrated into the text via cross-references in the margins of the book. Free resources include Interactive Sample Documents, links to additional resources, flash cards, and revised self-study quizzes that reinforce students' understanding of the chapters. Online tutorials on evaluating online sources, creating presentation graphics, using basic document design functions, designing Web sites, and creating effective graphs and charts guide students through some of their most common communication challenges. Instructors can find everything from additional exercises, projects, and cases to sample syllabi, in-class activities, presentation slides that can be adapted for classroom use, and password-protected reading quizzes to download and distribute to students. In addition, TechComm Web offers unique resources for instructors in a series of teaching topics: "Making the Transition from Composition to Technical Communication," "Integrating Technology," "Using *Technical Communication* in Distance Courses," "Addressing Plagiarism," and, new in this edition, "Green Writing," which explains how instructors can model practices and create assignments that help students understand how to reduce their carbon footprints as they write and distribute documents. The *Instructor's Resource Manual*, which includes a chapter-by-chapter teaching guide and advice for using the text and its companion Web site together, can be downloaded from TechComm Web.

Technical Communication e-Book

Our state-of-the-art e-book integrates the complete content of *Technical Communication* with Interactive Sample Documents, tutorials, self-study quizzes, and other valuable resources from TechComm Web. Features of the e-book include flexible navigation; easy-to-use content-management tools such as bookmarking, highlighting, and printing; note-taking functionality for commenting; and a content upload option making the e-book completely customizable. To order *Technical Communication* packaged free with *Technical Communication e-Book*, use ISBN-10: 0-312-56214-4 or ISBN-13: 978-0-312-56214-4. To order *Technical Communication e-Book* by itself, use ISBN-10: 0-312-55534-2 or ISBN-13: 978-0-312-55534-4.

TechCommClass

TechCommClass for *Technical Communication* is a unique online course space shaped by the needs of technical communication students and instructors. In *TechCommClass*, students can read assignments, do their work, and see their grades all in one place, and instructors can easily monitor students' progress and give feedback right away. Along with the *Technical Communication e-Book*, *TechCommClass* comes preloaded with the innovative digital content for which Bedford/St. Martin's is known. To order *Technical Communication* packaged with *TechCommClass*, use ISBN-10: 0-312-56217-9 or ISBN-13: 978-0-312-56217-5.

Document-Based Cases for Technical Communication

Roger Munger, *Boise State University*
With more than 50 examples of documents that students are likely to encounter in the workplace, *Document-Based Cases for Technical Communication*

offers realistic writing tasks based on seven context-rich scenarios. To order *Technical Communication* packaged with *Document-Based Cases for Technical Communication*, use ISBN-10: 0-312-56073-7 or ISBN-13: 978-0-312-56073-7.

ix visual exercises for tech comm

Cheryl E. Ball, *Utah State University*
Kristin L. Arola, *Michigan Technological University*
This CD-ROM introduces the fundamentals of design for technical communication in a medium that extends beyond the printed page. Each of the nine exercises progresses through a three-part sequence, helping students develop a critical vocabulary and method to read and compose all kinds of technical communication. To order *Technical Communication* packaged with *ix visual exercises for tech comm*, use ISBN-10: 0-312-56074-5 or ISBN-13: 978-0-312-56074-5. To order *Technical Communication* packaged with *ix visual exercises for tech comm* and *Document-Based Cases for Technical Communication*, use ISBN-10: 0-312-56072-9 or ISBN-13: 978-0-312-56072-9.

Team Writing

Joanna Wolfe, *University of Louisville*
A print supplement with online videos, *Team Writing* provides guidelines and examples of collaborating to manage written projects by documenting tasks, deadlines, and team goals. Two- to five-minute videos correspond with the chapters in *Team Writing* to give students the opportunity to analyze team interactions and learn about communication styles. Practical troubleshooting tips show students how best to handle specific conflicts within peer groups. To order *Technical Communication* packaged with *Team Writing*, use ISBN-10: 0-312-57560-2 or ISBN-13: 978-0-312-57560-1.

Acknowledgments

All the examples in this book—from single sentences to complete documents—are real. Some were written by my students at Boise State University. Some were written by engineers, scientists, health-care providers, and business-people with whom I have worked as a consultant for more than 30 years. Because much of the information in these documents is proprietary, I have silently changed brand names and other identifying information. I thank the dozens of individuals—students and professionals alike—who have graciously allowed me to reprint their writing. They have been my best teachers.

The ninth edition of *Technical Communication* has benefited greatly from the perceptive observations and helpful suggestions of my fellow instructors throughout the country. Some completed extensive questionnaires about the previous edition; others reviewed the current edition in its draft form. I thank Debra Benedetti, Fairmont State University; Michael A. Bennett, DeVry University (Chicago Campus); Michael J. K. Bokor, Illinois State University;

Lee Brasseur, Illinois State University; Gertrude L. Burge, University of Nebraska; Dan Colson, University of Illinois, Urbana-Champaign; Janice Cooke, University of New Orleans; Lawrence Andrew Cooper Jr., Georgia Institute of Technology; Elizabeth Coughlin, DePaul University; Huey Crisp, University of Arkansas at Little Rock; Paul Dombrowski, University of Central Florida; Jackie Dees Domingue, Blinn College; Michael Fournier, Georgia Institute of Technology; Regina Clemens Fox, Arizona State University; James Frost, University of Illinois, Urbana-Champaign; Mike Garcia, University of New Hampshire; Robert Haynes, Arizona State University; Karen Head, Georgia Tech; Patricia Jenkins, University of Alaska Anchorage; Clinton R. Lanier, University of Memphis; Merton Lee, University of Illinois; Rhonda L. McCaffery, Iowa State University; Susanna J. Paul, University of Maryland; Lynnette Porter, Embry-Riddle Aeronautical University; David Purkiss, University of Texas at Arlington; Cindy Raisor, Texas A&M University; Marcella Reekie, Kansas State University; Benjamin J. Robertson, Georgia Institute of Technology; Derek G. Ross, Texas Tech University; Brandy Lain Schillace, Case Western Reserve University; Stuart Selber, Pennsylvania State University; Karen Stewart, Norwich University; David Tillyer, City College of New York; Stephanie S. Turner, University of Houston–Downtown; Michelle Von Euw, University of Maryland; Sarah Egan Warren, North Carolina State University; Candice Welhausen, University of New Mexico; Laura Muthler White, Pennsylvania State University.

I would like to extend a special thanks to Stuart Selber and his team at Pennsylvania State University—Katherine Cleland, Ryan Croft, Brian Neff, and David Spielman—for their thorough user and student reviews of the *Technical Communication e-Book*. I also thank the following instructors who contributed their insights and suggestions for the *Technical Communication e-Book*: David Adams, University of Maine; Julie Amparano, Arizona State University; Renee Barlow, Indiana University–Bloomington; Jeanelle Barrett, Tarleton State University; Michael A. Bennett, DeVry University (Chicago Campus); Michael J. K. Bokor, Illinois State University; Lee Brasseur, Illinois State University; William Brown, Indiana University–Bloomington; Jennifer Carney, Embry-Riddle Aeronautical University; Joseph Rocky Colavito, Northwestern State University; Rhonda Copeland, Iowa State University; Paul Dombrowski, University of Central Florida; Michael Fournier, Georgia Institute of Technology; James Garcia, Arizona State University; Gretchen Haas, Minnesota State University–Mankato; Lynn Hublou, South Dakota State University; Molly Johnson, University of Houston–Downtown; Susan Katz, North Carolina State University; Eleanor Leo, University of Maine–Augusta; Abigail Mann, Indiana University–Bloomington; Amy Manning, Indiana University–Bloomington; Jason McEntee, South Dakota State University; Chris McKitterick, University of Kansas; Deborah Morton, Texas State University; William Morton, University of Central Florida; Sylvia Pamboukian, Robert Morris University; Paul Pedroza, University of Illinois, Urbana-Champaign; Katie Peebles, Indiana University–Bloomington; Ruth Perkins, Chemeketa Community College; Nicholaus Podsiadlik, Indiana University–Bloomington;

Lynnette Porter, Embry-Riddle Aeronautical University; Marcella Reekie, Kansas State University; Lane Rogers, Indiana University–Bloomington; Gerald Savage, Illinois State University; Jeffry Schantz, University of Akron/Summit College; Brandy Lain Schillace, Case Western Reserve University; Barbara Szubinska, Eastern Kentucky University; Marcy Tanter, Tarleton State University; Shelley Thomas, Weber State University; Stephanie S. Turner, University of Houston–Downtown; Harvey Ussach, Roger Williams University; Sarah Egan Warren, North Carolina State University; Leanne Warshauer, Suffolk County Community College; Peter Wegner, Arizona State University.

I would like to acknowledge three colleagues from Boise State University. Kevin Wilson helped me improve Chapters 9 and 10. Russell Willerton drafted the new Chapter 22 and helped me improve Chapter 13. Roger Munger drafted the new Chapter 18 and helped me strengthen Chapters 4, 6, 12, 16, 17, 19, and 21. He also wrote the new teaching topic, "Green Writing," and several new end-of-chapter cases. In addition, he updated all the Tech Tips and added two. Kevin, Russell, and Roger also helped me with many of the features on TechComm Web, including test questions, flash cards, and the *Instructor's Resource Manual*. In short, the book and the companion Web site are more of a collaborative effort than ever before, a change that has improved their quality significantly. I greatly appreciate their expertise and hard work.

I have been fortunate, too, to work with a terrific team at Bedford/St. Martin's, led by Julie Kelly, an editor of great intelligence, judgment, and energy. Julie has helped me improve the text in many big and small ways. I also want to express my appreciation to Joan Feinberg, Denise Wydra, Karen Henry, and Leasa Burton for assembling the first-class team that has worked so hard on this edition, including Emily Berleth, Melissa Cook, Anna Palchik, Dan Schwartz, Fred Courtright, and Janis Owens, Barbara Jatkola, and Nancy Benjamin of Books By Design. For me, Bedford/St. Martin's continues to exemplify the highest standards of professionalism in publishing. The people there have been endlessly encouraging and helpful. I hope they realize the value of their contributions to this book.

My greatest debt is, as always, to my wife, Rita, who, over the course of many months and nine editions, has helped me say what I mean.

A Final Word

I am more aware than ever before of how much I learn from my students, my fellow instructors, and my colleagues in industry and academia. If you have comments or suggestions for making this a better book, please get in touch with me at the Department of English, Boise State University, Boise, ID 83725. My phone number is (208) 426-3088, or you can send me an e-mail from the companion Web site: <bedfordstmartins.com/techcomm>. I hope to hear from you.

Mike Markel

Introduction for Writers

The ninth edition is organized into five parts, highlighting the importance of the writing process in technical communication and giving equal weight to the development of text and graphics in documents and Web sites.

Part	Coverage
Part One: Understanding the Technical Communication Environment	Provides a basic understanding of important topics in technical communication, including ethical and legal considerations, the role of the writing process in planning and developing technical documents, and the practice of collaborating on documents
Part Two: Planning the Document	Focuses on rhetorical concerns, such as considering audience and purpose, gathering information through primary and secondary research, and planning the organization of documents
Part Three: Developing and Testing the Verbal and Visual Information	Describes communicating persuasively; improving the coherence of text; improving sentence style; drafting, revising, and testing documents and Web sites; and designing documents and Web sites
Part Four: Learning Important Applications	Covers a wide range of types of technical communication: letters, memos, and e-mails; job-application materials, including print and electronic résumés; proposals; informational reports, such as progress and status reports, incident reports, and meeting minutes; lab reports; recommendation reports; definitions, descriptions, and instructions; oral presentations; and applications used in communicating with the public, including brochures, white papers, newsletters, blogs, podcasts, discussion boards, and wikis
Appendix: Reference Handbook	Offers additional help with skimming sources and taking notes; documenting sources using the APA, IEEE, and MLA styles; and editing and proofreading documents
	Provides advice to multilingual writers on cultural, stylistic, and sentence-level communication issues

Technical Communication offers a wealth of support to help you complete your technical communication projects:

In the World chapter openers, made up of current, relevant examples from a wide variety of workplace and technical-communication situations, introduce and reinforce the important themes of the chapter while immediately engaging the reader.

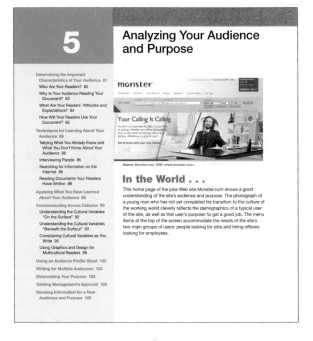

Annotated Examples make it easier for you to learn from the many model documents, illustrations, and screen shots throughout the text.

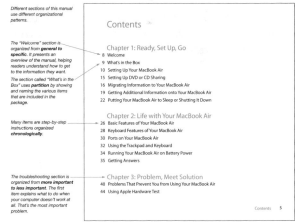

Figure 7.2 **Using Multiple Organizational Patterns in a Single Document**
Source: Apple, Inc., 2008 <http://manuals.info.apple.com/en/MacBook_Air_Users_Guide.pdf>.

Guidelines boxes throughout the book summarize crucial information and provide strategies related to key topics.

Guidelines

Dealing with Copyright Questions

Consider the following advice when using material from another source:

▶ **Abide by the fair-use concept.** Do not rely on excessive amounts of another source's work (unless the information is your company's own boilerplate).

▶ **Seek permission.** Write to the source, stating what portion of the work you wish to use and the publication you wish to use it in. The source is likely to charge you for permission.

▶ **Cite your sources accurately.** Citing sources fulfills your ethical obligation and strengthens your writing by showing the reader the range of your research.

▶ **Consult legal counsel if you have questions.** Copyright law is complex. Don't rely on instinct or common sense.

Ethics Notes in every chapter remind you to think about the ethical considerations and implications of your writing and oral presentations.

Ethics Note

Pulling Your Weight on Collaborative Projects

Collaboration involves an ethical dimension. If you work hard and well, you help the other members of the group. If you don't, you hurt them.

You can't be held responsible for knowing and doing everything, and sometimes unexpected problems arise in other courses or in your private life that prevent you from participating as actively and effectively as you otherwise could. When problems occur, inform the other group members as soon as possible. For instance, call the group leader as soon as you realize you will have to miss a meeting. Be honest about what happened. Suggest ways you might make up for missing a task. If you communicate clearly, the other group members are likely to work with you.

If you are a member of a group that includes someone who is not participating fully, keep records of your attempts to get in touch with that person. When you do make contact, you owe it to that person to try to find out what the problem is and suggest ways to resolve the problem. Your goal is to treat that person fairly and to help him or her do better work, so that the group will function more smoothly and more effectively.

Interactive Sample Documents in every chapter allow you to apply what you have just read as you analyze a real business or technical document.

INTERACTIVE SAMPLE DOCUMENT

Evaluating Information from Internet Sources

The following item appeared in Kaiser Permanente Thrive Exposed, a blog written by Managed Care Watch (2007), which describes itself as follows: "Managed Care Watch is a coalition of concerned consumers and professionals who have come together for the purpose of reforming the HMO and Managed Care industry. All like-minded individuals and organizations are welcome to join us." The item, titled "Another life threatening illness misdiagnosed as psychological problem," begins with the blogger's comments, followed by the text of a newspaper article about the case (see page 132). The questions in the margin ask you to consider the guidelines for evaluating Internet sources (on pages 129–30). E-mail your responses to yourself and/or your instructor on TechComm Web.

Kaiser Permanente Thrive Exposed

One of the more disturbing patterns that has emerged over four years of tracking Kaiser's many misdeeds, is that patients with very real and serious medical problems are often misdiagnosed with mental health issues, leading to much unnecessary suffering, and sometimes death. A few recent examples are the cases of Jupirena Stein, Craig Pazzi, and a woman with West Nile Virus, who was repeatedly told her symptoms were all in her head even after a positive blood test confirmed the infection. For the reason behind this troublesome trend, one need look no further than Kaiser's clinical practice guidelines, where Kaiser doctors are instructed to label anyone with an undiagnosed illness as a psych case.

Update 12/9/07: We have added a scan of *A Secret of Behavioral Health Integration: The Handoff* from "The Collected Papers of Nicholas A. Cummings, Volume I: The Value of Psychological Treatment." In it he describes the process by which Kaiser members are manipulated into accepting mental health treatment for physical illnesses.

The money quote (because it's always about the money at Kaiser):

"Without this seemingly simple touch, patient compliance was not very good, but with this idea of the handoff, compliance jumped to 90 percent. **And the saving in medical costs was tremendous.**"

Cummings developed the Kaiser Behavioral Health Division.

1. Does the author of this blog present himself as an unbiased commentator? In the first paragraph, which comments reveal his perspective on the situation he is describing?

2. As you read the section labeled "Update 12/9/07," what additional information would you like to see to help you understand the validity of the blogger's claims?

3. To what extent does the article from the *Orange County Register*, a newspaper in Orange County, California, lend support to the blogger's claims?

Source: Managed Care Watch, 2007 <www.kaiserthrive.org/2007/12/08/another-life-threatening-illness-misdiagnosed-as-psychological-problem/>.

Tech Tips for using basic software tools give you step-by-step, illustrated instructions on topics such as tracking changes, creating graphics, and modifying templates. Keywords in each Tech Tip help you use the Help menu in your word-processing software to find additional information.

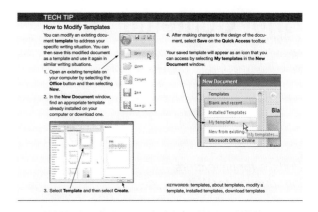

Writer's Checklists summarize important concepts and act as handy reminders as you draft and revise your work.

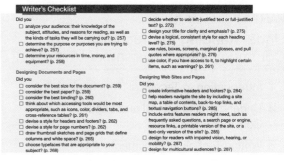

Cases in every chapter present real-world writing scenarios built around common workplace documents that you can critique, download, and revise.

For quick reference, many of these features are indexed on the inside back cover of this book.

For an overview of the numerous resources available to you on TechComm Web, see the inside front cover of this book.

Brief Contents

Preface for Instructors   v
Introduction for Writers   xii

PART 1
Understanding the Technical Communication Environment   1

1 Introduction to Technical Communication   2

2 Understanding Ethical and Legal Considerations   19

3 Writing Technical Documents   41

4 Writing Collaboratively   57

PART 2
Planning the Document   79

5 Analyzing Your Audience and Purpose   80

6 Researching Your Subject   113

7 Organizing Your Information   149

PART 3
Developing and Testing the Verbal and Visual Information   175

8 Communicating Persuasively   176

9 Writing Coherent Documents   198

10 Writing Effective Sentences   221

11 Designing Documents and Web Sites   253

12 Creating Graphics   297

13 Reviewing, Evaluating, and Testing Documents and Web Sites   341

PART 4
Learning Important Applications   361

14 Writing Letters, Memos, and E-mails   362

15 Preparing Job-Application Materials   389

16 Writing Proposals   431

17 Writing Informational Reports   458

18 Writing Lab Reports   478

19 Writing Recommendation Reports   500

20 Writing Definitions, Descriptions, and Instructions   539

21 Making Oral Presentations   578

22 Connecting with the Public   607

APPENDIX
Reference Handbook   629

A Skimming Your Sources and Taking Notes   630

B Documenting Your Sources   637

C Editing and Proofreading Your Documents   683

D Guidelines for Multilingual Writers (ESL)   710

References   725
Selected Bibliography   735
Index   741

Contents

Preface for Instructors   v
Introduction for Writers   xii

PART 1

Understanding the Technical Communication Environment   1

1   Introduction to Technical Communication   2

What Is Technical Communication?   4

Who Produces Technical Documents?   5

Technical Communication and Your Career   6

Characteristics of Technical Documents   6

Addresses Particular Readers   6
Helps Readers Solve Problems   7
Reflects an Organization's Goals and Culture   8
Is Produced Collaboratively   8
Uses Design to Increase Readability   8
■ Interactive Sample Document: Studying How Technical Communication Combines Words and Graphics   9
Consists of Words or Graphics or Both   10

A Look at Three Sample Documents   10

Measures of Excellence in Technical Communication   10

Honesty   10
Clarity   11
Accuracy   12
Comprehensiveness   14
Accessibility   14
Conciseness   14
Professional Appearance   14
Correctness   14

2   Understanding Ethical and Legal Considerations   19

A Brief Introduction to Ethics   20

Your Ethical Obligations   22
Obligations to Your Employer   23
Obligations to the Public   23
Obligations to the Environment   24

Your Legal Obligations   25
Copyright Law   25
Trademark Law   26
■ Guidelines: Determining Fair Use   27
■ Guidelines: Dealing with Copyright Questions   27
■ Ethics Note: Distinguishing Plagiarism from Acceptable Reuse of Information   28
■ Guidelines: Protecting Trademarks   28
Contract Law   29
Liability Law   29
■ Guidelines: Abiding by Liability Laws   30

The Role of Corporate Culture in Ethical and Legal Conduct   31
■ Interactive Sample Document: Analyzing a Code of Conduct   34

Communicating Ethically Across Cultures   35
Communicating with Cultures with Different Ethical Beliefs   35
Communicating with Countries with Different Laws   35

Principles for Ethical Communication   36
Abide by Relevant Laws   36
Abide by the Appropriate Professional Code of Conduct   36
Take Advantage of Your Employer's Ethics Resources   36
Tell the Truth   36
Don't Mislead Your Readers   37
Use Design to Highlight Important Ethical and Legal Information   37
Be Clear   37
Avoid Discriminatory Language   38
Acknowledge Assistance from Others   38

3   Writing Technical Documents   41

Planning   42
Analyzing Your Audience   42
Analyzing Your Purpose   43
Generating Ideas About Your Subject   43
Researching Additional Information   43

Organizing and Outlining Your Document   45
■ Tech Tip: How to Use the Outline View   46
Selecting an Application, a Design, and a Delivery Method   46
Devising a Schedule and a Budget   47

Drafting   47
■ Guidelines: Drafting Effectively   48
Using Templates   48
■ Tech Tip: How to Modify Templates   49
Using Styles   49
■ Interactive Sample Document: Identifying the Strengths and Weaknesses
of a Commercial Template   50
■ Tech Tip: How to Use the Styles Group   51

Revising   51
Studying the Draft by Yourself   52
Seeking Help from Others   52
■ Ethics Note: Acknowledging Reviewers Responsibly   53

Editing   53

Proofreading   53

4   Writing Collaboratively   57

Advantages and Disadvantages of Collaboration   58
Advantages of Collaboration   59
Disadvantages of Collaboration   59

Managing Projects   60
■ Guidelines: Managing Your Project   60

Conducting Meetings   61
Listening Effectively   61
■ Guidelines: Listening Effectively   61
Setting Your Group's Agenda   61
■ Guidelines: Setting Your Agenda   62
■ Ethics Note: Pulling Your Weight on Collaborative Projects   65
Conducting Efficient Face-to-Face Meetings   65
Communicating Diplomatically   65
■ Guidelines: Communicating Diplomatically   67
Critiquing a Group Member's Work   67

Using Electronic Tools in Collaboration   67
■ Guidelines: Critiquing a Colleague's Work   68
Using the Comment, Revision, and Highlighting Features of a Word
Processor   68
■ Tech Tip: How to Use the Review Tab   69
■ Interactive Sample Document: Critiquing a Draft Clearly and Diplomatically   70
Using Groupware   70

Using Videoconferencing Technology   71
■ Guidelines: Participating in a Videoconference   72

Gender and Collaboration   73

Culture and Collaboration   74

PART 2

Planning the Document   79

5   Analyzing Your Audience and Purpose   80

Determining the Important Characteristics of
Your Audience   81
Who Are Your Readers?   82
Why Is Your Audience Reading Your Document?   83
What Are Your Readers' Attitudes and Expectations?   84
How Will Your Readers Use Your Document?   85

Techniques for Learning About Your Audience   86
Tallying What You Already Know and What You Don't Know About
Your Audience   86
Interviewing People   86
Searching for Information on the Internet   86
Reading Documents Your Readers Have Written   88

Applying What You Have Learned About Your Audience   88

Communicating Across Cultures   90
Understanding the Cultural Variables "On the Surface"   92
Understanding the Cultural Variables "Beneath the Surface"   93
Considering Cultural Variables as You Write   95
■ Guidelines: Writing for Readers from Other Cultures   98
■ Ethics Note: Meeting Your Readers' Needs Responsibly   99
Using Graphics and Design for Multicultural Readers   99
■ Interactive Sample Document: Examining Cultural Variables in a Business
Letter   100

Using an Audience Profile Sheet   102

Writing for Multiple Audiences   103

Determining Your Purpose   103

Gaining Management's Approval   104

Revising Information for a New Audience and Purpose   105

6 **Researching Your Subject** **113**

Understanding the Differences Between Academic and Workplace Research 114

Understanding the Research Process 115

Choosing Appropriate Research Methods 116
- Guidelines: Researching a Topic 117

Conducting Secondary Research 119
Understanding the Research Media 120
Using Basic Research Tools 120
Researching Government Information 124
Using Web 2.0 Resources 124
Evaluating the Information 128
- Guidelines: Evaluating Print and Online Sources 129
- Interactive Sample Document: Evaluating Information from Internet Sources 131

Conducting Primary Research 133
Observations and Demonstrations 133
Inspections 133
Experiments 134
Field Research 135
Interviews 136
- Guidelines: Conducting an Interview 136
Inquiry Letters or E-mails 138
Questionnaires 138
- Ethics Note: Reporting and Analyzing Data Honestly 143

7 **Organizing Your Information** **149**

Understanding Three Principles for Organizing Technical Information 150
Analyzing Your Audience and Purpose 150
Using Conventional Patterns of Arrangement 151
Displaying Your Arrangement Prominently 151

Using Basic Patterns of Organizing Information 152
Chronological 154
- Guidelines: Organizing Information Chronologically 155
Spatial 156
- Guidelines: Organizing Information Spatially 156
General to Specific 157
- Guidelines: Organizing Information from General to Specific 157

More Important to Less Important 158
- Guidelines: Organizing Information from More Important to Less Important 158

Comparison and Contrast 159
- Guidelines: Organizing Information by Comparison and Contrast 161
- Ethics Note: Comparing and Contrasting Fairly 162

Classification and Partition 162
- Interactive Sample Document: Comparing and Contrasting Honestly 164
- Guidelines: Organizing Information by Classification or Partition 165

Problem-Methods-Solution 166
- Guidelines: Organizing Information by Problem-Methods-Solution 167

Cause and Effect 167
- Guidelines: Organizing Information by Cause and Effect 169

PART 3
Developing and Testing the Verbal and Visual Information   175

8 Communicating Persuasively   176

Considering the Context of Your Argument 177
Understanding Your Audience's Broader Goals 177
Working Within Constraints 178

Crafting a Persuasive Argument 180
Identifying the Elements of Your Argument 181
Using the Right Kinds of Evidence 182
- Interactive Sample Document: Analyzing Evidence in an Argument 183
Considering Opposing Viewpoints 184
Appealing to Emotions Responsibly 184
Deciding Where to Present Your Claim 185

Avoiding Logical Fallacies 186

Presenting Yourself Effectively 188
- Guidelines: Creating a Professional Persona 189

Using Graphics and Design as Persuasive Elements 189
- Ethics Note: *Seeming* Honest Versus *Being* Honest in Persuasive Writing 191

A Look at Several Persuasive Arguments 191

9 Writing Coherent Documents   198

Writing Coherent Titles 200
Writing Coherent Headings 201
- Guidelines: Revising Headings 203

Writing Coherent Lists   204

Writing Coherent Paragraphs   206

Structuring Paragraphs Clearly   207

■ Ethics Note: Avoiding Burying Bad News in Paragraphs   208

■ Guidelines: Dividing Long Paragraphs   210

Using Coherence Devices Within and Between Paragraphs   211

■ Interactive Sample Document: Identifying the Elements of a Coherent Paragraph   214

Creating a Coherent Design   214

Using Headers and Footers to Enhance Coherence   214

Using Typefaces to Enhance Coherence   215

■ Tech Tip: How to Modify and Create Styles   216

10 Writing Effective Sentences   221

Structuring Effective Sentences   222

Use Lists   222

■ Guidelines: Creating Effective Lists   223

Emphasize New and Important Information   225

■ Tech Tip: How to Create Numbered and Bulleted Lists   226

Choose an Appropriate Sentence Length   227

Focus on the "Real" Subject   228

Focus on the "Real" Verb   229

Use Parallel Structure   230

Use Modifiers Effectively   230

Choosing the Right Words and Phrases   233

Select an Appropriate Level of Formality   233

Be Clear and Specific   234

■ Ethics Note: Euphemisms and Truth Telling   239

Be Concise   239

Use Inoffensive Language   242

■ Interactive Sample Document: Revising for Conciseness and Simplicity   243

■ Guidelines: Avoiding Sexist Language   244

■ Guidelines: Using the People-First Approach   245

Understanding Simplified English for Nonnative Speakers   245

Preparing Text for Translation   246

11 Designing Documents and Web Sites   253

Goals of Document and Web Design   254

Understanding Design Principles   255

Proximity   255

Alignment   255

Repetition   256
Contrast   257

Planning the Design of Documents and Web Sites   257
Analyze Your Audience and Purpose   257
Determine Your Resources   258

Designing Documents   259
Size   259
Paper   259
  ■ Tech Tip: How to Set Up Pages   259
Bindings   260
Accessing Tools   261

Designing Pages   263
Page Layout   263
  ■ Guidelines: Understanding Learning Theory and Page Design   263
Columns   267
  ■ Tech Tip: How to Format Columns   268
Typography   268
  ■ Tech Tip: How to Format Fonts   270
  ■ Ethics Note: Using Type Sizes Responsibly   271
  ■ Tech Tip: How to Modify Line Spacing   274
  ■ Tech Tip: How to Modify Justification   274
Titles and Headings   275
Other Design Features   276
  ■ Tech Tip: How to Create Borders and Screens   278
  ■ Tech Tip: How to Create Text Boxes   278

Analyzing Some Page Designs   279
  ■ Interactive Sample Document: Analyzing a Page Design   283

Designing Web Sites   284
Create Informative Headers and Footers   284
Help Readers Navigate the Site   285
  ■ Guidelines: Making Your Site Easy to Navigate   285
Include Extra Features Readers Might Need   285
Design for Readers with Disabilities   287
Design for Multicultural Audiences   287
  ■ Ethics Note: Designing Legal and Honest Web Pages   288

Designing Web Pages   288
Aim for Simplicity   288
  ■ Guidelines: Designing a Simple Site   289
Make the Text Easy to Read and Understand   289
  ■ Guidelines: Designing Easy-to-Read Text   289
Create Clear, Informative Links   289
  ■ Guidelines: Writing Clear, Informative Links   290

Analyzing Some Web Pages   290

12 Creating Graphics 297

The Functions of Graphics 298

Characteristics of an Effective Graphic 299
- Ethics Note: Creating Honest Graphics 300
- Guidelines: Integrating Graphics and Text 301

Understanding the Process of Creating Graphics 301
Planning Graphics 301
Creating Graphics 304
- Tech Tip: How to Insert and Modify Graphics 305
Revising Graphics 306
Citing Graphics 306

Using Color Effectively 307

Choosing the Appropriate Kind of Graphic 309
Illustrating Numerical Information 312
- Guidelines: Creating Effective Tables 313
- Tech Tip: How to Use Tab Stops 315
- Tech Tip: How to Create Tables 315
- Tech Tip: How to Create Graphics in Excel 317
- Guidelines: Creating Effective Bar Graphs 317
- Tech Tip: How to Use Drawing Tools 321
- Interactive Sample Document: Balancing Clarity and Drama in Graphics 322
- Guidelines: Creating Effective Line Graphs 323
- Guidelines: Creating Effective Pie Charts 324
Illustrating Logical Relationships 325
Illustrating Process Descriptions and Instructions 325
Illustrating Visual and Spatial Characteristics 329
- Guidelines: Presenting Photographs Effectively 329
- Tech Tip: How to Create Screen Shots 331
Showing Motion in Graphics 332
Creating Effective Graphics for Multicultural Readers 333

13 Reviewing, Evaluating, and Testing Documents and Web Sites 341

Understanding Reviewing, Evaluating, and Testing 342

Reviewing Documents and Web Sites 343
Revising 344
Editing 344
- Guidelines: Editing the Draft 344
Proofreading 346

Conducting Usability Evaluations 346

Conducting Usability Tests   349
  The Basic Principles of Usability Testing   350
  Preparing for a Usability Test   350
  Conducting a Usability Test   352
  Interpreting and Reporting the Data from a Usability Test   353
    ▪ Ethics Note: Understanding the Ethics of Informed Consent   354
    ▪ Interactive Sample Document: Obtaining Informed Consent   355

PART 4

Learning Important Applications   361

14   Writing Letters, Memos, and E-mails   362

Understanding the Process of Writing Letters, Memos, and E-mails   363

Selecting a Type of Correspondence   364

Presenting Yourself Effectively in Correspondence   364
  Use the Appropriate Level of Formality   365
  Communicate Correctly   365
  Project the "You Attitude"   366
  Avoid Correspondence Clichés   366
  Communicate Honestly   366
    ▪ Ethics Note: Writing Honest Business Correspondence   368

Writing Letters   368
  Understand the Elements of a Letter   368
  Learn the Format of a Letter   368
  Understand Common Types of Letters   371

Writing Memos   377
    ▪ Guidelines: Organizing a Memo   379

Writing E-mails   379
    ▪ Guidelines: Following Netiquette   380

Writing Business Correspondence to Intercultural Readers   382
    ▪ Interactive Sample Document: Following Netiquette in an E-mail Message   383

15   Preparing Job-Application Materials   389

Understanding the Process of Preparing Job-Application Materials   390

Planning the Job Search   390

Understanding Seven Ways to Look for a Position   393

Understanding the Risks and Benefits of Social-Networking Sites and the Job Search   394

Writing Paper Résumés   395
   Appearance of the Résumé   395
   Content of the Résumé   396
      ■ Ethics Note: Writing Honest Job-Application Materials   399
   Elements of the Chronological Résumé   399
      ■ Guidelines: Elaborating on Your Education   401
   Elements of the Skills Résumé   407

Writing Electronic Résumés   407
   Content of the Electronic Résumé   412
   Format of the Electronic Résumé   413
      ■ Guidelines: Preparing a Text Résumé   413
      ■ Interactive Sample Document: Preparing a Text Résumé   414
      ■ Guidelines: Preparing a Scannable Résumé   415

Writing Job-Application Letters   415
   The Concepts of Selectivity and Development   415
   Elements of the Job-Application Letter   417

Preparing for a Job Interview   422
      ■ Guidelines: Preparing for a Job Interview   423

Writing Follow-up Letters After an Interview   424

16 Writing Proposals   431

Understanding the Process of Writing Proposals   432

The Logistics of Proposals   433
   External and Internal Proposals   433
   Solicited and Unsolicited Proposals   434

The "Deliverables" of Proposals   435
   Research Proposals   436
   Goods and Services Proposals   436

Persuasion and Proposals   437
   Understanding Readers' Needs   437
   Describing What You Plan to Do   438
   Demonstrating Your Professionalism   439
      ■ Guidelines: Demonstrating Your Professionalism in a Proposal   439
      ■ Ethics Note: Writing Honest Proposals   440

Writing a Proposal   440

The Structure of the Proposal   441
   Summary   441
   Introduction   441
      ■ Guidelines: Introducing a Proposal   442
   Proposed Program   442
   Qualifications and Experience   443

Budget   443
Appendices   444
■ Tech Tip: How to Create a Gantt Chart   446

Sample Internal Proposal   447
■ Interactive Sample Document: Writing a Project Description   451

17 Writing Informational Reports   458

Understanding the Process of Writing Informational Reports   459

Writing Directives   461
■ Interactive Sample Document: Writing a Persuasive Directive   462

Writing Field Reports   463
■ Guidelines: Responding to Readers' Questions in a Field Report   464

Writing Progress and Status Reports   464
■ Ethics Note: Reporting Your Progress Honestly   465
Organizing Progress and Status Reports   465
Concluding Progress and Status Reports   466
■ Guidelines: Projecting an Appropriate Tone in a Progress or Status Report   466
Sample Progress Report   466

Writing Incident Reports   472

Writing Meeting Minutes   473

18 Writing Lab Reports   478

Persuasion and Lab Reports   479

Understanding the Process of Writing Lab Reports   480

Understanding the Structure of the Lab Report   481
Title   481
Abstract   482
Introduction   482
■ Guidelines: Writing Equations   483
Materials and Methods   483
Results   484
■ Ethics Note: Presenting Data Honestly   485
Discussion   485
Conclusion   486
Acknowledgments   486
References   486
■ Interactive Sample Document: Evaluating Lab Reports   487
Appendices   488

Understanding the Role of Science and Engineering Articles   489

Sample Lab Report   491

19 Writing Recommendation Reports   500

Using a Problem-Solving Model for Preparing Recommendation Reports   502
   Identify the Problem or Opportunity   502
   Establish Criteria for Responding to the Problem
      or Opportunity   503
   Determine the Options   504
   Study Each Option According to the Criteria   505
   Draw Conclusions About Each Option   506
   Formulate Recommendations Based on the Conclusions   506
      ■ Ethics Note: Presenting Honest Recommendations   507

Writing Recommendation Reports   507
   Writing the Body of the Report   508
      ■ Guidelines: Writing Recommendations   510
   Writing the Front Matter   511
      ■ Tech Tip: How to Format Headers, Footers, and Page Numbers   514
      ■ Tech Tip: How to Create a Table of Contents   514
      ■ Guidelines: Writing an Executive Summary   516
   Writing the Back Matter   516
      ■ Interactive Sample Document: Analyzing an Executive Summary   517

Sample Recommendation Report   518

20 Writing Definitions, Descriptions, and Instructions   539

Writing Definitions   540
   Analyzing the Writing Situation for Definitions   541
   Determining the Kind of Definition to Write   541
      ■ Guidelines: Writing Effective Sentence Definitions   543
   Deciding Where to Place the Definition   547

Writing Descriptions   549
   Analyzing the Writing Situation for Descriptions   549
   Indicating the Nature and Scope of the Description   550
   Introducing the Description Clearly   550
   Providing Appropriate Detail   552
      ■ Guidelines: Providing Appropriate Detail in Descriptions   552
   Concluding the Description   553
   A Look at Sample Descriptions   554

Writing Instructions   558

Designing a Set of Instructions   558
  ■ Guidelines: Designing Clear, Attractive Pages   559
Planning for Safety   560
  ■ Ethics Note: Protecting Your Readers' Safety   561
Drafting Effective Instructions   562
  ■ Guidelines: Drafting Introductions for Instructions   564
  ■ Guidelines: Drafting Steps in Instructions   564
Revising, Editing, and Proofreading Instructions   566
A Look at Sample Instructions   566
  ■ Interactive Sample Document: Presenting Clear Instructions   571

Writing Manuals   572

21 Making Oral Presentations   578

Understanding the Role of Oral Presentations   579

Understanding the Process of Preparing and Delivering an Oral Presentation   580

Preparing a Presentation   580
Analyzing the Speaking Situation   580
Organizing and Developing the Presentation   582
  ■ Guidelines: Introducing a Presentation   583
  ■ Guidelines: Concluding a Presentation   583
Preparing Presentation Graphics   584
  ■ Tech Tip: How to Create a Master Page Design in PowerPoint   588
  ■ Tech Tip: How to Set List Items to Appear and Dim During a Presentation   589
  ■ Interactive Sample Document: Integrating Graphics and Text on a Presentation Slide   594
Choosing Effective Language   594
  ■ Guidelines: Using Memorable Language in Oral Presentations   595
Rehearsing the Presentation   596

Delivering a Presentation   597
Calming Your Nerves   597
  ■ Guidelines: Releasing Nervous Energy   598
Using Your Voice Effectively   598
Using Your Body Effectively   599
  ■ Guidelines: Facing an Audience   599

Answering Questions After a Presentation   600
  ■ Ethics Note: Answering Questions Honestly   600

Sample Evaluation Form   601

22 Connecting with the Public   607

Persuasion and Connecting with the Public   609

Presenting Information to the Public   610

Newsletters   610

■ Guidelines: Designing an Effective Newsletter   611

■ Interactive Sample Document: Evaluating the Design of
a Newsletter   613

Brochures   613

■ Guidelines: Creating a Brochure   614

White Papers   616

■ Guidelines: Writing a White Paper   616

■ Ethics Note: Marketing Your Organization Honestly   618

Podcasts   618

Collaborating with the Public   620

Discussion Boards   620

■ Guidelines: Participating in Discussion Boards   621

Blogs   622

■ Guidelines: Being a Responsible Blogger   622

Wikis   624

■ Guidelines: Using and Participating in Wikis Effectively   625

APPENDIX

Reference Handbook   629

A   **Skimming Your Sources and Taking Notes   630**

Paraphrasing   631
Quoting   633
Summarizing   634

B   **Documenting Your Sources   637**

APA Style   640
IEEE Style   657
MLA Style   665

C   **Editing and Proofreading Your Documents   683**

Grammatical Sentences   684
Punctuation   691
Mechanics   702
Proofreading Symbols and Their Meanings   709

D   Guidelines for Multilingual Writers (ESL)   710

Cultural and Stylistic Communication Issues   710
Sentence-Level Issues   712

References   725
Selected Bibliography   735
Index   741

PART 1   Understanding the Technical Communication Environment

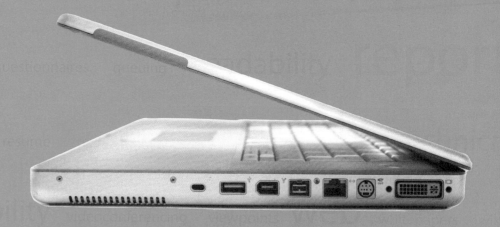

1

Introduction to Technical Communication

What Is Technical Communication? 4

Who Produces Technical
Documents? 5

Technical Communication and
Your Career 6

Characteristics of Technical
Documents 6

Addresses Particular Readers 6

Helps Readers Solve Problems 7

Reflects an Organization's Goals
and Culture 8

Is Produced Collaboratively 8

Uses Design to Increase Readability 8

Consists of Words or Graphics
or Both 10

A Look at Three Sample
Documents 10

Measures of Excellence in Technical
Communication 10

Honesty 10

Clarity 11

Accuracy 12

Comprehensiveness 14

Accessibility 14

Conciseness 14

Professional Appearance 14

Correctness 14

Source: Radvision, 2008 <www.radvision.com/Products/Desktop/CTMPlatform/>.

In the World . . .

Although high-tech tools such as this desktop videoconferencing package from Radvision are becoming more and more important in the workplace, the heart of technical communication remains what it has always been: communicating with people. All technical-communication documents, whether they take the form of e-mails, reports, Web sites, or any of a dozen other forms, are meant to be used by people to help them learn, carry out tasks, and make decisions. This book is about the process of finding and creating technical information and communicating it to others.

A study of more than 100 large American corporations, which together employ some 8 million people, suggests that writing is a more important skill for today's professionals than it has ever been (College Board, 2004, pp. 3–4). Among the major findings of the survey are the following:

- For hiring and promotions, writing is a "threshold skill." If your job-application materials are written poorly, 86 percent of companies surveyed would "frequently" or "almost always" hold it against you. If you somehow got the job, you wouldn't last long enough to be promoted.

- Two-thirds of professionals need strong writing skills in their daily work. Some 80 percent of companies in the service, finance, insurance, and real-estate industries assess applicants' writing during the hiring process. Fifty percent of all companies in all industries consider writing skills in making promotion decisions.

- Half of all companies "frequently" or "almost always" produce reports, memos, and correspondence. Almost 100 percent of companies use e-mail, and more than 80 percent use PowerPoint presentations.

Another study, from the Center for Plain Language (2005), found that up to 40 percent of the cost of managing business and government transactions is due to poor communication. For this reason, employees who communicate well are rewarded. A survey by the Plain English Network (2002) found that 96 percent of the nation's 1,000 largest employers say that employees must have good communication skills to get ahead. Almost 90 percent of more than 800 business-school graduates say that their writing skills have helped them advance more quickly. More than 80 percent of Fortune 400 companies have identified writing skills as their organizations' greatest weakness. Eight major companies, including Nike, put communication skills at the top of the list of traits they look for in employees.

The working world depends on written communication. Within most modern organizations, almost every action is documented in writing, whether on paper or online. Here are a few examples:

- a memo or an e-mail to request information or identify a problem
- a set of instructions to introduce and explain how to carry out a new task
- a proposal to persuade management to authorize a project
- a report to document a completed project
- an oral presentation to explain a new policy to employees

Every organization also communicates with other organizations and often with the public, using materials such as these:

- inquiry letters, sales letters, goodwill letters, and claim and adjustment letters to customers, clients, and suppliers
- Web sites to describe and sell products and to solicit job applications
- research reports for external organizations
- articles for trade and professional journals

WHAT IS TECHNICAL COMMUNICATION?

You can look at technical communication in two ways: as the process of making and sharing information and ideas with others in the workplace, and as a set of applications—the documents you write.

Technical communication is the process of finding and using information and sharing meaning. The brief conversations you have with your colleagues in the hallway, the instant messages you exchange with vendors, the e-mails you send and respond to, the phone calls with your project team—all these are examples of the process of technical communication.

In fact, every professional spends most of every workday using the four communication skills: reading, writing, speaking, and listening. Think of it this way: a professional is a person who communicates with others about a technical subject. An engineer is a person who communicates about engineering. An architect is a person who communicates about architecture. A historian is a person who communicates about history.

Professionals often use these four communication skills to create applications: technical documents and oral presentations. When you make these applications, you are creating, designing, and transmitting technical information so that people can understand it easily and use it safely, effectively, and efficiently. Much of what you read every day—textbooks, phone books, procedures manuals at the office, journal articles, Web sites, owner's manuals—is technical communication. The words and graphics in these documents are meant to help you understand a subject or carry out a task.

The purpose of this book is to help you improve your skills in the process of technical communication (finding information and generating ideas on your own and with others) and in making the applications of technical communication (the e-mails, proposals, reports, and other kinds of documents). The focus of this book is on the techniques skilled communicators use to analyze an audience and a purpose, to create and find the best information on a subject, to arrange the information skillfully to meet the audience's needs and preferences, and to deliver the information effectively using the most appropriate application.

This is certainly not your first writing course, and the principles you have studied in other courses also apply to technical communication. The biggest difference between technical communication and the other kinds of writing you have done is that technical communication has a somewhat different focus on *audience* and *purpose*.

In most of your previous academic writing, your *audience* has been your instructor, and your *purpose* has been to show your instructor that you have mastered some skill or body of information. For instance, in a research paper for a history course, you show your instructor that you have learned important information about the topic and have mastered the process of communicating that information professionally. Typically, you are not trying to create new knowledge or motivate the reader to take a particular action—except to give you an A for that assignment.

By contrast, in technical communication in the workplace, your *audience* will likely include peers and supervisors in your company, and perhaps people outside your company as well. Your *purpose* will likely be to reinforce or change their attitudes toward the subject you are writing about, motivate them to take particular actions, or help them to carry out their own jobs.

> **On TechComm Web**
>
> For a good introduction to technical communication, see Allan Hoffman's article. Click on Links Library for Ch. 1 on <bedfordstmartins.com/techcomm>.

For example, imagine that you are a public-health scientist working for a federal agency. You have just completed a study showing that procyanidins are the main ingredients in red wines that help prevent coronary heart disease. You know that wines from southwestern France and Sardinia have higher concentrations of procyanidins than other wines and that people in these regions generally live longer than people in other parts of the world. You report your methods and findings in a journal article. Your purpose is to communicate this information so that other scientists can follow up on your research by determining, for example, whether there is something about the winemaking process in these regions that makes the wines produced there retain procyanidins, and whether the increased longevity of people in these regions can be linked to drinking local wines. The overall goal of your research is to determine whether it is possible to make the coronary benefits of these red wines available to everyone around the world.

In other words, technical communication responds to the needs of a particular audience and has a clear, specific purpose in the real world.

WHO PRODUCES TECHNICAL DOCUMENTS?

Most technical documents are produced by one of two different categories of people:

- *Technical professionals.* Technically trained individuals, such as engineers and accountants, do a lot of writing, including e-mails, letters, proposals, and reports.

- *Technical communicators.* Technical communicators create manuals, proposals, reports, sales literature, Web sites, letters, journal articles, and speeches. Many technical communicators still call themselves technical writers (or tech writers) even though the term *technical communicator* better reflects the increasing importance of graphics and the use of other media, such as online documentation.

Often, technical professionals and technical communicators work together. For instance, a computer engineer designing a new microchip will draft the specifications for that chip. The technical communicator will study that draft, interview the engineer to resolve any technical questions, and revise the specifications. Those specifications will be included in the company's printed product catalog and Web-based marketing materials.

TECHNICAL COMMUNICATION AND YOUR CAREER

The course you are taking now will help you meet the demands of the working world. In fact, your first step in obtaining a professional position is to write two technical documents—an application letter and a résumé—that will help an organization decide whether to interview you. And once you start work, your supervisors will be looking at your communication skills as well as your technical abilities.

Job ads in newspapers and professional journals suggest that the working world values good communication skills. The following ad from an organization that manufactures medical instruments is typical:

This job ad, as well as many others like it, mentions not only computer skills but also communication skills.

> **Design Assurance Engineer.** Duties include performing electronic/mechanical product, component, and material qualifications. Requires spreadsheet/word-processing abilities and excellent written/oral communication skills. BSEE or biology degree preferred.

▶ **In This Book**
For more about job-application materials, see Ch. 15, p. 390.

According to one survey (College Board, 2004, p. 4), almost half of the largest U.S. companies said that they offer or require training for professionals who cannot write well. The companies reported spending about $900 per employee for writing training. Wouldn't a company rather save that $900? I think so. The facts of corporate life today are simple: if you cannot communicate well, you are less valuable; if you can, you are more valuable.

CHARACTERISTICS OF TECHNICAL DOCUMENTS

Almost every technical document has six major characteristics: it addresses particular readers, helps readers solve problems, reflects an organization's goals and culture, is produced collaboratively, uses design to increase readability, and consists of words or graphics or both.

Addresses Particular Readers

▶ **In This Book**
For more about addressing a particular audience, see Ch. 5, p. 81.

Technical documents address particular readers. For instance, if you are planning to write a proposal for your supervisor, you think about that person's job responsibilities, the level of detail he or she would be interested in reading, and personal factors such as history with the organization and attitudes toward your ideas. These factors help you decide what kind of document to write, how to structure it, how much detail to include, and what sentence style and vocabulary to use.

Even if you do not know your readers personally, you should try to create a profile of them. For example, if readers of your brochure are police officers responsible for purchases, you know that they share a police background and a common responsibility for approving expenditures.

Your writing might also be read by people you never intended as your audience: managers and executives in your organization, or the public or the press. Avoid writing anything that will embarrass you or your organization.

Often, you will write for people from different cultures or whose native language is different from yours. These readers will react differently to the design, organization, and writing style of documents than will people from your own culture. Therefore, you will need to consider these cultural differences as you write.

A good first step is to read a full-length discussion of the topic, such as one or more of the following respected resources:

- Hofstede, G. H. (2003). *Culture's consequences: Comparing values, behaviors, institutions, and organizations across nations* (2nd ed.). Thousand Oaks, CA: Sage.

- Intercultural Communication Institute (http://www.intercultural.org). This nonprofit organization provides a great introduction to the subject, with articles, training, and resource lists.

- Jandt, F. E. (2007). *An introduction to intercultural communication: Identities in a global community* (5th ed.). Thousand Oaks, CA: Sage.

- Lustig, M. W., & Koester, J. (2006). *Intercultural competence: Interpersonal communication across cultures* (5th ed.). Boston: Allyn & Bacon.

- Neuliep, J. W. (2006). *Intercultural communication: A contextual approach* (3rd ed.). Thousand Oaks, CA: Sage.

- Samovar, L. A., Porter, R. E., & McDaniel, E. R. (Eds.). (2006). *Intercultural communication: A reader* (11th ed.). Belmont, CA: Wadsworth.

- Trompernaars, F., & Hampden-Turner, C. (1997). *Riding the waves of culture: Understanding diversity in global business* (2nd ed.). New York: McGraw-Hill.

Helps Readers Solve Problems

Technical documents help readers learn something or carry out a task. For instance, you read your company's employee-benefits manual to help you decide which benefits package you should select. In other words, you read it because you need information to help you analyze a situation and solve a problem.

Reflects an Organization's Goals and Culture

Technical documents further an organization's goals. For example, a state government department that oversees vocational-education programs submits an annual report to the state legislature, as well as a lot of technical information produced for the public: flyers, brochures, pamphlets, radio and television ads, and course materials. These documents help the department secure its funding and reach its audience.

Technical documents also reflect an organization's culture. Some organizations have a rigid hierarchy and expect employees to format their documents in a particular way and to write only to their immediate supervisors and to others on their own level. In other organizations, the culture permits or even encourages employees to make their own decisions on these questions.

Is Produced Collaboratively

Although you will often work alone in writing short documents, you will probably work as part of a team in producing more-complicated documents. Collaboration can range from having a colleague review your two-page memo to working with a team of a dozen technical professionals and technical communicators on a 200-page catalog.

Collaboration is common in technical communication because no one person has all the information, skills, or time to create a large document. Writers, editors, designers, and production specialists work with subject-matter experts—the various technical professionals—to create a better document than any one of them could have created working alone.

Successful collaboration requires interpersonal skills. You have to listen to people with other views and from other business and ethnic cultures, express yourself clearly and diplomatically, and compromise.

In This Book

For more about collaboration, see Ch. 4.

Uses Design to Increase Readability

Technical communicators use design features—typography, spacing, color, special paper, and so forth—to serve three basic purposes:

In This Book

For more about design, see Ch. 11.

- *To make the document look attractive and professional.* If it is attractive and creates a positive impression, you are more likely to accomplish your goal.
- *To help readers navigate the document.* Because a technical document can be long and complicated and most readers want to read only parts of it, design features such as headings, color, and highlighting help readers see where they are and get where they want to be.
- *To help readers understand the document.* If all the safety warnings in a manual appear in a color and size different from the rest of the text, readers will be better able to recognize the importance of the information.

INTERACTIVE SAMPLE DOCUMENT

Studying How Technical Communication Combines Words and Graphics

This is a cover from an eight-page quick-start brochure that accompanies a photo-copier. The questions in the margin ask you to consider how technical communication combines words and graphics. E-mail responses to yourself and/or your instructor on TechComm Web.

Source: Xerox Corporation, 2000.

1. How have the writers used graphic elements in the sentence below the title to emphasize the message in that sentence?

2. In what other ways have the writers used words and graphics to make the document more interesting and appealing to readers?

3. How have the writers used text and graphics to present the tasks that people can accomplish with this machine?

To e-mail your responses to yourself and/or your instructor, click on Interactive Sample Documents for Ch. 1 on <bedfordstmartins.com/techcomm>.

Consists of Words or Graphics or Both

Most technical documents include words and graphics. Graphics help the writer perform five main functions:

In This Book
For more about graphics, see Ch. 12.

- make the document more interesting and appealing to readers
- communicate and reinforce difficult concepts
- communicate instructions and descriptions of objects and processes
- communicate large amounts of quantifiable data
- communicate with nonnative speakers

Technical professionals and technical communicators alike use high-tech tools to produce documents. Although you are unlikely to need to become an expert user of these tools, some of them, such as word processors and spreadsheets, are fundamentally important. You can make the most of these tools by taking advantage of the help they offer.

A LOOK AT THREE SAMPLE DOCUMENTS

Figure 1.1 (page 11), Figure 1.2 (page 12), and Figure 1.3 (page 13) illustrate a number of the characteristics of technical communication discussed in this chapter.

MEASURES OF EXCELLENCE IN TECHNICAL COMMUNICATION

Eight measures of excellence characterize all technical communication: honesty, clarity, accuracy, comprehensiveness, accessibility, conciseness, professional appearance, and correctness.

Honesty

The most important measure of excellence in technical communication is honesty. For three reasons, you have to tell the truth and not mislead the reader:

In This Book
For more about the ethical and legal aspects of technical communication, see Ch. 2.

- *It is the right thing to do.* Technical communication is meant to help people make wise choices as they use the information available in a high-tech culture.
- *If you are dishonest, readers can get hurt.* Misinforming your readers or deliberately omitting important information can defraud, injure, or kill people.
- *If you are dishonest, you and your organization could face serious legal charges.* If a court finds that your document's failure to provide honest, appropriate information caused a substantial injury or loss, your organization might have to pay millions of dollars.

Yes, it's rugged. Yes, it's tough. But equipped with one of our special accessory packages, the Segway x2 is also thoughtful and considerate. Whether you're playing golf, conquering the outdoors, or keeping watch over an expansive and physically demanding territory, an x2 package can make the off-pavement ride more comfortable and enjoyable. Additional accessories are also available for a truly customized Segway experience. See page 22 for more information.

x2 Packages

x2 Golf

Compared to a golf cart, this is a transportation hole-in-one: compact, fun, and easy to maneuver. The x2 Golf package includes low-pressure tires that barely disturb the turf, a scorecard holder, and a bag carrier that automatically positions your clubs upright after you step off.

Scorecard Holder
Accessory Bar
Golf Bag Carrier
LeanSteer Frame Tool-less Height Adjust
Smooth Turf Tires
Golf clubs, bag, balls and tees not included.

20 SEGWAY PRODUCT BROCHURE

Figure 1.1 Product Brochure Showing the Characteristics of Technical Communication
Source: Segway, Inc., 2006 <www.segway.com/downloads/pdfs/2006_Catalog.pdf>.

Characteristics of technical communication:
- **is addressed to particular readers:** *It is addressed to golfers who might be interested in this Segway model.*
- **helps them solve problems:** *It provides information about the features of this Segway model.*
- **reflects an organization's goals and culture:** *It focuses on people of a certain age and income.*
- **consists of both words and graphics:** *The words explain the rationale for the Segway, the larger photo shows the components, and the smaller photo helps the reader see how he or she might look on a Segway.*
- **is produced collaboratively:** *It was created by technical communicators, graphic artists, Web authors, and others.*
- **uses design to increase readability:** *It is neatly organized, with the introductory text about the specialized versions at the top and the particular text and graphics about the golf version at the bottom.*

▶ **On TechComm Web**

To view Fig. 1.1 in context on the Web, click on Links Library for Ch. 1 on <bedfordstmartins .com/techcomm>.

Ethics Note

You will find Ethics Notes throughout this book. These notes describe typical ethical problems involved in technical communication and suggest ways to think about them.

Clarity

Your goal is to produce a document that conveys a single meaning the reader can understand easily. The following directive, written by the British navy (*Technical Communication*, 1990), is an example of what to avoid:

> It is necessary for technical reasons that these warheads should be stored upside down, that is, with the top at the bottom and the bottom at the top. In order that there

Characteristics of technical communication:

- *is addressed to particular readers: It is addressed to software engineers.*
- *helps them solve problems: It provides information they need to determine whether they should read the entire technical report.*
- *reflects an organization's goals and culture: All Sun Microsystems technical reports use the same unadorned design and typography, as well as the Sun logo and other identifying information.*
- *consists of both words and graphics: The logo identifies the report as being the intellectual property of Sun. The textual information helps the reader identify the report and communicate with the authors.*
- *is produced collaboratively: It was created by the authors, with the help of technical communicators.*
- *uses design to increase readability: It is clearly organized, with white space setting off each portion of the page.*

On TechComm Web

To view Fig. 1.2 in context on the Web, click on Links Library for Ch. 1 on <bedfordstmartins.com/techcomm>.

**Web Applications -
Spaghetti Code for the 21st Century**

Tommi Mikkonen and Antero Taivalsaari

SMLI TR-2007-166   June 2007

Abstract:

The software industry is currently in the middle of a paradigm shift. Applications are increasingly written for the World Wide Web rather than for any specific type of an operating system, computer or device. Unfortunately, the technologies used for web application development today violate well-known software engineering principles. Furthermore, they have reintroduced problems that had already been eliminated years ago in the aftermath of the "spaghetti code wars" of the 1970s.

In this paper, we investigate web application development from the viewpoint of established software engineering principles. We argue that current web technologies are inadequate in supporting many of these principles. However, we also argue that there is no fundamental reason for web applications to be any worse than conventional applications in any of these areas. Rather, the current inadequacies are just an accidental consequence of the poor conceptual and technological foundation of the web development technologies today.

Sun
microsystems
Sun Labs
16 Network Circle
Menlo Park, CA 94025

email addresses:
tommi.mikkonen@sun.com
antero.taivalsaari@sun.com

Figure 1.2   Report Page Showing the Characteristics of Technical Communication
Source: Mikkonen & Taivalsaari, 2007 <http://research.sun.com/techrep/2007/smli_tr-2007-166pdf>.

---

may be no doubt as to which is the top and which is the bottom, for storage purposes, it will be seen that the bottom of each warhead has been labeled with the word TOP.

Technical communication must be clear for two reasons:

- *Unclear technical communication can be dangerous.* A carelessly drafted building code, for example, could tempt contractors to use inferior materials or techniques.
- *Unclear technical communication is expensive.* The average cost of a telephone call to a customer-support center is more than $32 (About.com, 2008). Clear technical communication in the product's documentation—its instructions—can greatly reduce the number and length of such calls.

Accuracy

You need to get your facts straight. A slight inaccuracy can confuse and annoy your readers; a major inaccuracy can be dangerous and expensive. In

Figure 1.3   Q&A Showing the Characteristics of Technical Communication
Source: Apple, Inc., 2008 <www.apple.com/iphone/questionsandanswers.html>.

Characteristics of technical communication:
- *is addressed to particular readers: It is addressed to owners and prospective owners of the iPhone.*
- *helps them solve problems: This portion of the Q&A answers general questions about the product. Note the hyperlinks to more information in several of the answers.*
- *reflects an organization's goals and culture: The design and words reflect Apple's emphasis on clean, uncluttered design and functionality.*
- *consists of both words and graphics: The photograph of the iPhone is all readers need to identify the subject.*
- *is produced collaboratively: It was created by a writer, with the help of a photographer, a designer, and a Web specialist.*
- *uses design to increase readability: It is clearly organized, with the questions in boldface for emphasis.*

On TechComm Web

To view Fig. 1.3 in context on the Web, click on Links Library for Ch. 1 on <bedfordstmartins .com/techcomm>.

another sense, accuracy is a question of ethics. Technical documents must be as objective and unbiased as you can make them. If readers suspect that you are slanting information—by overstating or omitting facts—they will doubt the validity of the entire document.

Comprehensiveness

A good technical document provides all the information readers need. It describes the background so that readers unfamiliar with the subject can understand it. It contains sufficient detail so that readers can follow the discussion and carry out any required tasks. It refers to supporting materials clearly or includes them as attachments.

Comprehensiveness is crucial because readers need a complete, self-contained discussion in order to use the information safely, effectively, and efficiently. A document also often serves as the official company record of a project, from its inception to its completion.

Accessibility

▶ In This Book

For more about making documents accessible, see Chs. 9 and 11.

Most technical documents—both in print and online—are made up of small, independent sections. Because few people will read a document from beginning to end, your job is to make its various parts accessible. That is, readers should not be forced to flip through the pages or click links unnecessarily to find the appropriate section.

Conciseness

▶ In This Book

For more about writing concisely, see Ch. 10.

A document must be concise enough to be useful to a busy reader. You can shorten most writing by 10 to 20 percent simply by eliminating unnecessary phrases, choosing short words rather than long ones, and using economical grammatical forms. Your job is to figure out how to convey a lot of information economically.

Professional Appearance

You start to communicate before anyone reads the first word of the document. If the document looks neat and professional, readers will form a positive impression of it and of you. Your documents should adhere to the format standards of your organization or your professional field, and they should be well designed and neatly printed. For example, a letter should follow one of the traditional letter formats and have generous margins.

Correctness

A correct document is one that adheres to the conventions of grammar, punctuation, spelling, mechanics, and usage. Sometimes, incorrect writing can confuse readers or even make your writing inaccurate. The biggest problem, however, is that incorrect writing makes you look unprofessional. If your writing is full of errors, readers will wonder if you were also careless in gathering, analyzing, and presenting the technical information. If readers doubt your professionalism, they will be less likely to accept your conclusions or follow your recommendations.

A technical document is meant to convey information to a particular audience so that they understand something or carry out a task. To accomplish these goals, it must be honest, clear, accurate, comprehensive, accessible, concise, professional in appearance, and correct.

Exercises

 In This Book For more about memos, see Ch. 14, p. 377.

1. **INTERNET EXERCISE** Form small groups to study the following Web page, the Home/Private Users section of the Products portion of the Acer Canada site. Discuss which characteristics of technical communication you see in this example. How effective is this Web page? What changes would you make to improve it? Present your ideas in a brief memo to your instructor.

Source: Acer, Inc., 2008 <www.acer.ca/public/page115.do?sp=page115&stu10.values=30&UserCtxParam=0&GroupCtxParam=0&dctx1=27&CountryISOCtxParam=CA&LanguageISOCtxParam=en&ctx3=32&ctx4=Canada&crc=3481551221>.

2. Locate an owner's manual for a consumer product such as a coffeemaker, bicycle, or hair dryer. In a memo to your instructor, describe and evaluate the manual. To what extent does it meet the measures of excellence discussed in this chapter? In what ways does it fall short? Submit a photocopy of the document (or a representative portion of it) with your memo.

3. **INTERNET EXERCISE** Locate a document on the Web that you believe to be an example of technical communication. Describe the aspects of the document that illustrate the characteristics of technical communication discussed in this chapter. Then evaluate the effectiveness of the document. Write your response in a memo to your instructor. Submit a printout of the document (or a representative portion of it) with your assignment.

Case 1: Judging Entries in a Technical-Communication Competition

▶ In This Book For more about memos, see Ch. 14, p. 377.

Background

The English Department at Bonita Vista High School is sponsoring a technical-communication competition open to all students. The teachers expect the competition to help promote student awareness of the technical-communication profession and to encourage students to develop and showcase their technical-communication skills. The teachers have encouraged students to submit original papers, essays, lab reports, instructions, presentation slides, illustrations, Web sites, and the like on a technical subject of their choice. Students also have been asked to include a brief description of the assignment.

You are one of three judges selected from the community to evaluate entries. The other two judges are named Cheryl and Pat. Cheryl has a bachelor of science degree in Forest Management and works as a natural-resource specialist for the state's Department of Forestry. Pat works as a freelance animator and has 3-D modeling/animation skills. Both have experience creating technical documents or illustrations. You were asked to join the judging panel because you are taking a technical-communication course in college. The panel's task is to evaluate the quality of each submission and to reach a consensus on first-, second-, and third-place winners. A new English teacher, Mr. Insko, is coordinating the competition. He has left the details of how to judge the entries up to the panel.

At your first meeting, Cheryl confesses, "I'm not sure where to begin. The entries are all so different. How are we going to evaluate each entry on its own merits?" She points to three entries spread out on the table (see Documents 1.1–1.3).

Pat admits that she has never served as a judge of a competition. "Look at this entry," she says, pointing to Document 1.1. "The student has a spelling mistake in the first line. Should this entry win an award?"

"Maybe," Cheryl responds. "This entry demonstrates that the student understands the concept of chunking."

"What do you mean by chunking?" Pat asks.

You realize that you all seem to have different ideas of how to define a good technical document. You propose that the panel start by agreeing on some type of scoring or rating sheet with several criteria by which you could judge each entry.

"I agree," Cheryl says. "Each criterion could be worth up to a certain number of points. By totaling the points for each entry, we could determine the awards."

"I like this approach," Pat says. "However, in art school I learned the most from people's comments, not some numeric score. I think it's important that we comment on all the entries. Let's make this a learning experience for the students and not just a 'Who's the Best' contest."

You volunteer to put together a scoring guide that incorporates all of these elements. You explain that you will e-mail your sample scoring guide and a brief explanation of your approach to Cheryl and Pat. You also suggest that the three of you use your scoring guide to judge just these three entries. Based on how well that goes, you'll revise the guide, if necessary, before the panel tackles the two boxes of entries sitting on Mr. Insko's desk.

Your Assignment

1. Create a scoring guide to evaluate the entries. Write a brief memo to the other judges explaining why you think your approach is effective and fair.

2. Using this scoring guide, evaluate Documents 1.1–1.3. Include a one-paragraph comment on each entry.

Under Too Much Pressure?

What is it?

High blood pressure, or hypertension, is when your blood pressure stays too high all the time. Doctors define high blood pressure as 140/90. However, doctors think an adult's blood pressure should be lower than 120/80. The first number (140), or systolic pressure, is your blood pressure when your heart beats. The bottom number (90), or diastolic pressure, is your blood pressure when your heart is at rest.

Am I at risk?

1 in 3 adults have high blood pressure. If you're overweight you are at risk for high blood pressure. Most of us will eventually get high blood pressure or die from heart disease. It's not too early to start worrying. Doctors say that kids as young as 18 are having heart attacks. If your under 18, your blood pressure should be lower than what the table says below.

BOYS	
Age	Blood Pressure
15	131/83
16	134/84
17	136/87

GIRLS	
Age	Blood Pressure
15	127/83
16	128/84
17	129/84

(National Heart, Lung, and Blood Institute)

What are the symptoms?

There are no symptoms so that is why its called the "silent killer."

How do I prevent it?

✓ Get your blood pressure checked regularly
✓ Exercise
✓ Avoid fast food
✓ Lose weight
✓ You shouldn't smoke (or drink☺)
✓ Don't get stressed

CAUTION
HIGH
IN FAT

Allison Sullivan
Health, per. 5

Document 1.1   Entry 001

Student's statement: "For health class, Ms. Ransberg gave us an assignment to create a flyer on a health issue of interest to students. My flyer is on high blood pressure and teenagers."

On TechComm Web

For digital versions of case documents, click on Downloadable Case Documents on <bedfordstmartins.com/techcomm>.

Alexander Luthor
Computer Science, period 2

Java assignment to calculate an integer to an inputted power.

In order to write a program to calculate an integer to an inputted power, I had to figure out how the math is done. Raising an integer to a power is just multiplying that number by itself a certain number of times. In the program, I have the user enter the number and the power. Then the computer has to multiply it out. I did this using a *while loop* so it would be easy to count the number of times the multiplication happened.

```
public class        //starts program – introduces it to compiler
{        /*everything until matching bracket at the end belongs to this class*/
    public static void main(string[]args)
/*describes particular program information. Void – not returning value to anything. Using strings and arguments in the program.*/
    {        //everything until matching closing belongs to this main
        int x,y;              //introduce variables that are integers
        int i=1;              //introduce and make value equal 1
        int power=1;
        x=inInt("Enter base as an integer: ");
/*output " " text and then take value typed on keyboard. Assigns value to variable x and y*/
        y=inInt("Enter exponent as an integer: ");

        while(i<=y)        /*do the following until i value is more than y value*/
        {
            power=power*x;  /*assign a value of power to be itself times x (the number we entered on the keyboard)*/
            i++;            //increase our counter by 1
        }

        system.out.println(+ power);  /*print the final value of power to the computer screen*/
    }
}
```

Document 1.2   Entry 002

Student's statement: "This assignment was to write a program to calculate the power of a number. We had to have the number and power entered from the keyboard and then have the program do the math."

Document 1.3   Entry 003

Student's statement: "The assignment was to explain how to use a feature of Microsoft Word that many students wouldn't already know how to use but would like to. We had to include at least one graphic."

Jonathan O'Toole
English, period 4

Equation Editor in Microsoft Word

The **Equation Editor** in Microsoft Word is an excellent tool to use if a student wants to use his computer for taking notes for math class. A student can take notes on his computer when studying math at home or recopy his handwritten notes from class. If he's a geek, he can bring his computer to class. He can even do his homework on the computer. The **Equation Editor** has hundreds of mathematical symbols and dozens of equation templates for Algebra, Geometry, and Calculus. All a student needs is Microsoft Word.

When a student wants to write an equation, he should pick **Object** from the **Insert** menu. Next, the student should choose the **Create New** tab. Next, he should scroll down the list and select **Microsoft Equation Editor 3.0**. After that, hit **OK**. Now the student is ready to write the equation by picking the symbols he needs for the equation.

This is an **algebra** class example. $x \geq 6$

This is a **geometry** class example (quadratic formula). $x = \dfrac{-b \pm \sqrt{b^2 - 4ac}}{2a}$

This is a **calculus** class example (I think). $\int_{\Pi/2}^{1/2} (1 + \cos \chi) d\chi$

When the student is finished with the equation, he should click somewhere in his Word document.

Understanding Ethical and Legal Considerations

A Brief Introduction to Ethics 20

Your Ethical Obligations 22

Obligations to Your Employer 23

Obligations to the Public 23

Obligations to the Environment 24

Your Legal Obligations 25

Copyright Law 25

Trademark Law 26

Contract Law 29

Liability Law 29

The Role of Corporate Culture in Ethical and Legal Conduct 31

Communicating Ethically Across Cultures 35

Communicating with Cultures with Different Ethical Beliefs 35

Communicating with Countries with Different Laws 35

Principles for Ethical Communication 36

Abide by Relevant Laws 36

Abide by the Appropriate Professional Code of Conduct 36

Take Advantage of Your Employer's Ethics Resources 36

Tell the Truth 36

Don't Mislead Your Readers 37

Use Design to Highlight Important Ethical and Legal Information 37

Be Clear 37

Avoid Discriminatory Language 38

Acknowledge Assistance from Others 38

Source: Yamaha, 2008 <www.yamaha-motor.com/sport/products/modelimagelib/180/9/1/0/image.aspx>.

In the World . . .

Nobody disputes the fact that helmets reduce serious injuries and deaths from motorcycle accidents. But the question of whether to require motorcyclists to wear helmets presents an ethical dilemma. According to the standard of rights, a cyclist should be able to decide; after all, it's his or her head. According to the standard of utility, however, the state should be able to decide, because a severely injured cyclist is often cared for by the state, at a lifetime cost of more than a million dollars. This photograph from the Yamaha Web site shows the riders' helmets. Does the company care about rider safety? Certainly. But the company also cares about product liability. If the company's Web site showed cyclists without helmets, an injured cyclist could sue, claiming that Yamaha suggests it is safe to ride without a helmet.

E thical and legal issues will be all around you in the workplace. For instance, a potential customer might ask you whether the printer your company manufactures is compatible with her computer network. You're not sure, but you say, "I don't see a problem." You have just issued a legally binding warranty. If she buys the printer and it doesn't work with her computer network, your company is liable for breach of contract.

Ethical and legal pitfalls also lurk in the words and graphics of many kinds of formal documents. In writing a proposal, you might be asked to exaggerate or lie about your organization's past accomplishments, pad the résumés of the project personnel, list as project personnel some workers who will not be contributing to the project, or present an unrealistically short work schedule. In drafting product information, you might be asked to exaggerate the quality of products shown in catalogs or manuals or to downplay the hazards of using these products. In creating graphics, you might be asked to hide an item's weaknesses in a photograph by manipulating the photo electronically.

There are many serious ethical and legal issues related to technical communication, and all professionals need a basic understanding of them.

A BRIEF INTRODUCTION TO ETHICS

Ethics is the study of the principles of conduct that apply to an individual or a group. For some people, ethics is a matter of intuition—what their gut feelings tell them about the rightness or wrongness of an act. Others see ethics in terms of their religion or the Golden Rule: treat others as you would like them to treat you. The ethicist Manuel G. Velasquez (2006) outlines four moral standards that are useful in thinking about ethical dilemmas:

- *Rights.* This standard concerns individuals' basic needs and welfare. Everyone agrees, for example, that people have a right to a reasonably safe workplace. When we buy a product, we have a right to expect that the information that accompanies it is honest and clear. However, not everything that is desirable is necessarily a right. For example, in some countries high-quality health care is considered a right. That is, the government is required to provide it, regardless of whether a person can afford to pay for it. In other countries, health care is not considered a right.
- *Justice.* This standard concerns how the costs and benefits of an action or a policy are distributed among a group. For example, the cost of maintaining a highway should be borne, in part, by people who use that highway. However, because everyone benefits from the highway, it is just that general funds also be used. Here's another example: justice requires that people doing the same job receive the same pay, regardless of whether they are male or female, black or white.

- *Utility.* This standard concerns the positive and negative effects that an action or a policy has, will have, or might have on others. For example, if a company is considering closing a plant, the company's leaders should consider not only the money they would save but also the financial hardship of laid-off workers and the economic effects of the closing on the community. One tricky part in thinking about utility is figuring out the time frame to examine. An action can have one effect in the short run—laying off employees can help a company's quarterly balance sheet—and a very different effect in the long run—hurting the company's productivity or the quality of its products.

- *Care.* This standard concerns the relationships we have with other individuals. We owe care and consideration to all people, but we have greater responsibilities to people in our families, our workplaces, and our communities. The closer a person is to us, the more care we owe that person. Therefore, we have greater obligations to members of our family than we do to others in our community.

Although these standards provide a vocabulary for thinking about how to resolve ethical conflicts, they are imprecise, and they often conflict with one another. Therefore, they cannot provide a systematic method of resolving ethical conflicts. Take the case of a job opportunity in your company. You are a member of the committee that will recommend which of six applicants to hire. One of the six is a friend of yours who has recently gone through a divorce and is currently unemployed. He needs the health benefits the job provides because he has a daughter with a chronic condition that requires expensive medications. Unfortunately, you have concluded that he is less qualified for the position than some of the other applicants.

How can the four standards help you think through the situation? According to the *rights* standard, lobbying for your friend or against the other applicants would be wrong, because all applicants have a right to an evaluation process that considers only their qualifications to do the job. Looking at the situation from the perspective of *justice* yields the same conclusion: it would be wrong to tilt the playing field in favor of your friend. From the perspective of *utility*, lobbying for your friend would probably not be in the best interests of the organization, although it might be in his best interests. Only according to the *care* standard does lobbying for your friend seem reasonable.

As you think about this case, you have to consider another related question: should you tell the other people on the hiring committee that one of the applicants is your friend? I think so, because they have a right to know about your personal relationship so that they can better evaluate your contributions to the discussion. You might also want to recuse yourself (that is, not participate in discussing this position), leaving it to the other committee members to decide whether your friendship represents a conflict of interest.

There is one more complication in thinking about this case: Let's say your friend is one of the top two candidates for the job. In your committee, which is made up of seven members, three vote for your friend, but four vote for the other candidate, who currently has a very good job, with excellent benefits. She is a young, dynamic employee with degrees from prestigious universities. In other words, she is likely to be very successful in the working world, regardless of whether she is offered this particular job. Should the fact that your friend's career is in trouble affect your thinking about this problem? Some people would say no: the job should be offered to the most-qualified applicant, end of story. Others would say yes: society does not adequately provide for its less-fortunate members, and because your friend needs the job more than the other top applicant and is almost as qualified as she is, he should be offered the job first. In other words, some people would see this situation as a narrow, technical question of determining the best candidate for the job, whereas others would see it as a much broader social question involving human rights.

Most people do not debate the conflict among rights, justice, utility, and care when they confront a serious ethical dilemma; instead they simply do what they think is right. Perhaps this is good news. However, the depth of ethical thinking varies dramatically from one person to another, and the consequences of superficial ethical thinking can be profound. For these reasons, ethicists have described a general set of principles that can help people organize their thinking about the role of ethics within an organizational context. These principles form a web of rights and obligations that connect an employee, an organization, and the world in which the organization is situated.

For example, in exchange for their labor, employees enjoy three basic rights: fair wages, safe and healthy working conditions, and due process in the handling of matters such as promotions, salary increases, and firing. Although there is still serious debate about the details of employees' rights, such as the freedom from surreptitious surveillance and unreasonable searches in drug investigations, the question almost always concerns the *extent* of employees' rights, not the existence of the basic rights themselves. For instance, ethicists disagree about whether hiring undercover investigators to discover drug users at a job site is an unwarranted intrusion on employees' rights, but there is no debate about the right of exemption from unwarranted intrusion.

YOUR ETHICAL OBLIGATIONS

In addition to enjoying rights, an employee assumes obligations, which can form a clear and reasonable framework for discussing the ethics of technical communication. The following discussion outlines three sets of obligations: to your employer, to the public, and to the environment.

Obligations to Your Employer

You will be hired to further your employer's legitimate aims and to refrain from any activities that run counter to those aims. Specifically, you will have four obligations:

- *Competence and diligence. Competence* refers to your skills; you should have the training and experience to do the job adequately. *Diligence* simply means hard work.

- *Honesty and candor.* You should not steal from your employer. Stealing involves dishonest practices such as embezzlement, "borrowing" office supplies, and padding expense accounts. *Candor* means truthfulness; you should report problems to your employer that might threaten the quality or safety of the organization's products or services.

   A problem involving honesty and candor in research concerns what Sigma Xi, the Scientific Research Society, calls trimming, cooking, and forging (*Honor*, 1986, p. 11). *Trimming* is the smoothing of irregularities to make data look extremely accurate and precise. *Cooking* is retaining only those results that fit the theory and discarding the others. And *forging* is inventing some or all of the data, or even reporting experiments that were never performed. In carrying out research, an employee might feel some pressure to report only positive, statistically significant findings, but he or she must resist this pressure.

- *Confidentiality.* You should not divulge company business outside the company. If a competitor knew that your company was planning to introduce a new product, it might introduce its own version of that product, robbing your company of its competitive advantage. Many other kinds of privileged information—such as quality-control problems, personnel matters, relocation or expansion plans, and financial restructuring—also could be used against a company. A well-known problem of confidentiality involves *insider information*: an employee who knows about a development that will increase the value of the company's stock buys the stock before the information is made public, thus reaping an unfair (and illegal) profit.

- *Loyalty.* You should act in your employer's interests, not your own. Therefore, it is unethical to invest heavily in a competitor's stock, because that could jeopardize your objectivity and judgment. For the same reason, it is unethical to accept bribes or kickbacks. It is unethical to devote considerable time to moonlighting (performing an outside job such as private consulting), because that could lead to a conflict of interest and because the heavy workload could make you less productive in your primary position.

Obligations to the Public

Every organization that offers products or provides services is obligated to treat its customers fairly. As a representative of an organization, and especially as an employee communicating technical information, you will frequently confront ethical questions.

In general, an organization is acting ethically if its products or services are *safe* and *effective*. They must not injure or harm consumers, and they must fulfill their promised functions. However, these commonsense principles provide little guidance in dealing with the complicated ethical problems that routinely arise.

According to the Consumer Product Safety Commission, some 28,000 people in the United States are killed each year as a result of using consumer products and another 33 million are injured. The cost of these accidents is $800 billion a year (U.S. Consumer, 2007, p. 3). Even more commonplace, of course, are product and service failures. For instance, products may be difficult to assemble or operate, they don't do what they are supposed to do, they break down, or they require more-expensive maintenance than indicated in the product information.

Who is responsible for injuries and product failures—the company that produces the product or provides the service, or the consumer who purchases it? In individual cases, blame is sometimes easy to fix. A person who operates a chain saw without reading the safety warnings and without seeking any instruction in how to use it is to blame for any injuries caused by the normal operation of the saw. But a manufacturer who knows that the chain on the saw is liable to break when used under certain circumstances but fails to remedy this problem or warn the consumer is responsible for any resulting accidents.

Unfortunately, such guidelines do not provide a rational theory that can help companies understand how to act ethically in fulfilling their obligations to the public. Most court rulings are based on the premise that the manufacturer knows more about the product than the consumer does and therefore has a greater responsibility to make sure the product complies with all the manufacturer's claims and is safe and effective when used according to the manufacturer's instructions. However, the manufacturer is not liable when something goes wrong that it could not have foreseen or prevented.

Obligations to the Environment

One of the most important lessons we have learned in the past two decades is that we are polluting and depleting our limited natural resources at an unacceptably high rate. Our excessive use of fossil fuels not only deprives future generations of their use but also causes possibly irreversible pollution problems, such as global warming. Everyone—government, business, and individuals—must work to preserve the ecosystem in order to ensure the survival not only of our own species but also of the other species with which we share the planet.

But what does this have to do with you? In your daily work, you probably do not cause pollution or deplete the environment in any extraordinary way.

Yet because of the nature of your work, you will often know how your organization's actions affect the environment. For example, if you work for a manufacturing company, you might be aware of the environmental effects of making or using your company's products. Or you might be asked to help write an environmental impact statement.

As communicators, we should treat every actual or potential occurrence of environmental damage seriously. We should alert our supervisors to the situation and work with them to try to reduce the damage. The difficulty, of course, is that protecting the environment can be expensive. Clean fuels cost more than dirty ones. Disposing of hazardous waste properly costs more (in the short run) than merely dumping it. Organizations that want to cut costs may be tempted to cut corners on environmental protection.

YOUR LEGAL OBLIGATIONS

Although most people believe that ethical obligations are more comprehensive and more important than legal obligations, the two are closely related. Our ethical values have shaped many of our laws. For this reason, professionals should know the basics of four different bodies of law: copyright, trademark, contract, and liability.

Copyright Law

As a student, you are constantly reminded to avoid plagiarism. A student caught plagiarizing would likely fail the assignment or the course or even be expelled from school. If a medical researcher or reporter writing in a journal or newspaper is caught plagiarizing, he or she would likely be fired, or at least find it difficult to publish in the future. But plagiarism is an ethical, not a legal, issue. Although a plagiarist might be expelled from a community, he or she will not be fined or sent to prison.

By contrast, copyright is a legal issue. *Copyright law* is the body of law that relates to the appropriate use of a person's intellectual property: written documents, pictures, musical compositions, and the like. Copyright literally refers to a person's *right* to *copy* the work that he or she has created.

The most important concept in copyright law is that only the copyright holder—the person or organization that owns the work—can copy it. For instance, if you work for IBM, you can legally copy information from the IBM Web site and use it in other IBM documents. This reuse of information is routine in business, industry, and government because it helps ensure that the information a company distributes is both consistent and accurate.

However, if you work for IBM, you cannot simply copy information that you find on the Dell Web site and put it on the IBM site. Unless you obtain written permission from Dell to use its intellectual property, you will be infringing on Dell's copyright.

 On TechComm Web

For more about copyright law, see the U.S. Copyright Office Web site. Click on Links Library for Ch. 2 on <bedfordstmartins .com/techcomm>.

Ⓘ **Attribution.** You stipulate how you want people to give you credit if they copy, distribute, display, or perform your copyrighted work. For example, you might require that another person cite your photograph as "Photo by Jane Curruthers" and include a thumbnail photo of you that you have provided.

Ⓢ **Noncommercial.** You prohibit others from using your work for commercial purposes. For instance, you might permit a nonprofit organization such as the March of Dimes to quote your poem but forbid a commercial publisher to do so.

⚌ **No Derivative Works.** You permit people to copy, distribute, display, and perform your work just as you created it, without making any changes to it. For example, a company can reproduce a computer-based program you have created, but it may not change the background color or any other aspect of the program. In other words, the company may not create a derivative work.

Figure 2.1   Selected Licensing Symbols from Creative Commons

The organization has created a number of symbols to represent rights that copyright owners can retain or surrender.

Source: Creative Commons, 2007 <http://creativecommons.org/about/licenses>.

 **On TechComm Web**

The U.S. Copyright Office Web site describes work made for hire. Click on Links Library for Ch. 2 on **<bedfordstmartins .com/techcomm>.**

Why doesn't the Dell employee who wrote the information own the copyright to that information? The answer lies in a legal concept known as *work made for hire*. Anything written or revised by an employee on the job is the company's property, not the employee's.

Although copyright gives the owner of the intellectual property some rights, it doesn't give the owner all rights. You can place small portions of copyrighted text in your own document without getting formal permission from the copyright holder. When you quote a few lines from an article, for example, you are taking advantage of an aspect of copyright law called *fair use*. Under fair-use guidelines, you have the right to use material, without getting permission, for purposes such as criticism, commentary, news reporting, teaching, scholarship, or research. Unfortunately, *fair use* is based on a set of general guidelines that are meant to be interpreted on a case-by-case basis. Keep in mind that you should still cite the source accurately to avoid plagiarism.

A new trend in copyright is for copyright owners to stipulate which rights they wish to retain and which they wish to give up. You might see references to Creative Commons, a nonprofit organization that provides symbols for copyright owners to use to communicate their preferences. Figure 2.1 shows three Creative Commons symbols.

Trademark Law

On TechComm Web

For more about trademarks, see the U.S. Patent and Trademark Office Web site. Click on Links Library for Ch. 2 on **<bedfordstmartins.com/ techcomm>.**

Companies use *trademarks* and *registered trademarks* to ensure that the public recognizes the name or logo of a product.

- A *trademark* is a word, phrase, name, or symbol that is identified with a company. The company uses the ™ symbol after the product name

responsibility is to resist this pressure, if necessary by going over your supervisor's head.

Don't Mislead Your Readers

A misleading statement—one that invites or even encourages the reader to reach a false conclusion—is ethically no better than lying. Avoid these four common kinds of misleading technical communication:

In This Book

For a more detailed discussion of misleading writing, see Ch. 10, p. 239. For a discussion of avoiding misleading graphics, see Ch. 12.

- *False implications.* If you work for SuperBright and write "Use only SuperBright batteries in your new flashlight," you are implying that only that brand will work. If that is untrue, the statement is misleading. Communicators sometimes use clichés such as *user-friendly, ergonomic,* and *state of the art* to make the product sound better than it is. Use specific, accurate information to back up your claims about a product.

- *Exaggerations.* If you say "Our new Operating System 2500 makes system crashes a thing of the past" but the product only makes them less likely, you are exaggerating. Provide specific technical information on the reduction of crashes. Do not write "We carried out extensive market research" if all you did was make a few phone calls.

- *Legalistic constructions.* It is unethical to write "The 3000X was designed to operate in extreme temperatures, from −40 degrees to 120 degrees Fahrenheit" if the product cannot operate reliably in those temperatures. Although the statement might technically be accurate—the product was *designed* to operate in those temperatures—it is misleading.

- *Euphemisms.* If you refer to someone's being fired, say *fired* or *released,* not *granted permanent leave* or *offered an alternative career opportunity.*

Use Design to Highlight Important Ethical and Legal Information

Courts have found that information that is buried in footnotes or printed in very small type violates a company's obligation to inform consumers and warn them about hazards in using a product. If you want to communicate safety information or other facts that readers need to know, use design features to make that information easy to see and understand. Figure 2.4 on page 38 shows how one company uses design to emphasize important information.

Be Clear

Clear writing helps your readers understand your message easily. Your responsibility is to write as clearly as you can to help your audience understand what you are saying. For instance, if you are writing a product warranty, make it as simple and straightforward as possible. Don't hide behind big words and complicated sentences. Use tables of contents, indexes, and other accessing devices to help your readers find what they need.

In This Book

For techniques for writing clearly, including avoiding offensive language, see Ch. 10.

This portion of a page from a manual written by an aircraft-equipment manufacturer shows the use of color-coded icons to represent warnings, cautions, and notes. Notice that the hottest color, red, represents the most-important information, whereas the coolest color, blue, represents the least-important information.

9.1 OPTIONAL EQUIPMENT

The G1000 provides the display and control interface for the following optional weather and audio entertainment systems:

- L-3 STORMSCOPE® WX-500 Series II Weather Mapping Sensor
- L-3 SKYWATCH® Traffic Advisory System (Model SKY497)
- L-3 SKYWATCH® HP Traffic Advisory System (Model SKY899)
- GDL 69A XM® Radio System
- GWX 68 Weather Avoidance Radar System

WARNING: Do not use any G1000 Weather Data for thunderstorm penetration. Weather Data is approved only for weather avoidance, not penetration.

CAUTION: NEXRAD weather data is intended for long-range planning purposes only. Due to inherent delays and relative age of the data that can be displayed, NEXRAD weather data should not be used for short-range avoidance of weather.

NOTE: The information contained in this Pilot's Guide must be supplemented with detailed information contained in the G1000 Multi Function Display Operation Section. This section assumes the pilot has experience operating the G1000 MFD and is also familiar with the applicable optional equipment User's Guide.

This Section is divided into five parts: 9.1 - Introduction, 9.2 - Stormscope, 9.3 - SKYWATCH, 9.4 - GDL 69A, and 9.5 - GWX 68 Radar.

OPTIONAL EQUIPMENT

Figure 2.4   Using Design to Emphasize Important Information
Source: Garmin, 2005 <www8.garmin.com/manuals/G1000:BeechcraftBaron58_G58_PilotsGuide.pdf>.

Avoid Discriminatory Language

Don't use language that discriminates against people because of their sex, religion, ethnicity, race, sexual orientation, or physical or mental abilities. Employees have been disciplined or fired for sending inappropriate jokes on the company e-mail system. In some cases, employees have even been fired for information posted on their private blogs when that information reflects negatively on the company.

In This Book

For more about citing sources, see Ch. 6, p. 120, and Appendix, Parts A and B.

Acknowledge Assistance from Others

Don't suggest that you did all the work yourself if you didn't. Cite your sources and your collaborators accurately and graciously.

Writer's Checklist

- ☐ Did you abide by relevant laws? (p. 36)
- ☐ Did you abide by the appropriate corporate or professional code of conduct? (p. 36)
- ☐ Did you take advantage of your company's ethics resources? (p. 36)
- ☐ Did you tell the truth? (p. 36)

Did you avoid using
- ☐ false implications? (p. 37)
- ☐ exaggerations? (p. 37)

- ☐ legalistic constructions? (p. 37)
- ☐ euphemisms? (p. 37)

- ☐ Did you use design to highlight important ethical and legal information? (p. 37)
- ☐ Did you write clearly? (p. 37)
- ☐ Did you avoid discriminatory language? (p. 38)
- ☐ Did you acknowledge any assistance you received from others? (p. 38)

Exercises

In This Book For more about memos, see Ch. 14, p. 377.

1. It is late April, and you need a summer job. In a local newspaper, you see an ad for a potential job. The only problem is that the ad specifically mentions that it is "a continuing, full-time position." You know that you will be returning to college in the fall. Is it ethical for you to apply for the job without mentioning this fact? Why or why not? If you feel it is unethical to withhold the information that you plan to return to college in the fall, is there any way you can ethically apply? Be prepared to share your ideas with the class.

2. You serve on the advisory committee of your college's bookstore, which is a private business that leases space on campus and donates 10 percent of its profits to student scholarships. The head of the bookstore wishes to stock Simple Study Guides, a popular series of plot summaries and character analyses of classic literary works. In similar bookstores, the sale of Simple Study Guides yields annual profits of more than $10,000. Six academic departments have signed a statement condemning the idea. Should you support the bookstore head or the academic departments? Be prepared to discuss your answer with the class.

3. **INTERNET EXERCISE** Find an article or advertisement—in a newspaper or magazine or on the Web—that you feel contains untrue or misleading information. Write a memo to your instructor describing the ad and analyzing the unethical techniques. How might the information have been presented more honestly? Include a photocopy or a printout of the ad with your memo.

4. **GROUP EXERCISE** Form small groups. Study the code of conduct of a company or organization in your community. (Many companies and other organizations post their codes on their Web sites.)

- One group member could study the code to analyze how effectively it states the ideals of the organization, describes proper and improper behavior and practices for employees, and spells out penalties.

- Another group member could interview the officer who oversees the use of the code in the organization. Who wrote the code? What were the circumstances that led the organization to write it? Is it based on another organization's code? Does this officer of the organization believe the code is effective? Why or why not?

- A third group member could secure the code of one of the professional groups in the organization's field (search for the code on the Web). For example, if the local organization produces electronic equipment, one professional group would be IEEE. To what extent does the code of the local organization reflect the principles and ideals of the professional group's code?

- As a team, write a memo to your instructor presenting your findings. Attach the local organization's code to your memo.

Case 2: Playing the Name Game

In This Book For more about memos, see Ch. 14, p. 377.

Background

Crescent Energy, an oil-refining corporation based in Riyadh, Saudi Arabia, has issued a request for proposals for constructing an intranet that will link its headquarters with its three facilities in the United States and Europe. McNeil Informatics, a networking consulting company, is considering responding with a proposal. Most of the work will be performed at Crescent's headquarters in Riyadh.

Crescent Energy was established 40 years ago by family members who are related by marriage to the Saudi royal family. At the company headquarters, the support staff and clerical staff include women, most of whom are related to the owners of the company. The professional, managerial, and executive staff is all male, which is traditional in Saudi corporations. Crescent is a large company, with revenues in the billions of dollars.

McNeil Informatics is a small firm (12 employees) established two years ago by Denise McNeil, a 29-year-old computer scientist with a master's degree in computer engineering. She divides her time between working on her MBA and getting her company off the ground. As a result, the company is struggling financially, and she realizes that it must get the Crescent contract to meet its current financial obligations. Her employees include both men and women at all levels. The chief financial officer is a woman, as are several of the professional staff. The technical writer is a man.

Denise traveled to New York from her headquarters in Pittsburgh to attend a briefing by Crescent. All the representatives from Crescent were middle-aged Saudi men; Denise was the only woman among the representatives of the seven companies that attended the briefing. When Denise shook hands with Mr. Fayed, the team leader, he smiled slightly as he mentioned that he did not realize that McNeil Informatics was run by a woman. Denise did not know what to make of his comment, but she got a strong impression that the Crescent representatives felt uncomfortable in her presence. During the break, they drifted off to speak with the men from the other six vendors, leaving Denise to stand awkwardly by herself.

Once back in her hotel room, Denise was still bothered by the Crescent representatives' behavior at the meeting. She thought about the possibility of gender discrimination but decided to bid for the project anyway, because she believed that her company could write a persuasive proposal. McNeil Informatics had done several projects of this type in the past year.

She phoned Josh Lipton, the technical writer, to get him started on the proposal. "When you put in the boilerplate about the company, I'd like you to delete the stuff about my founding the company. Don't say that a woman is the president, okay? And when you assemble the résumés of the project team, I'd like you to use just the first initials, not the first names."

"I don't understand, Denise. What's going on?" Josh asked.

"Well, Crescent looks like an all-male club, very traditional. I'm not sure they would want to hire us if they knew we have a lot of women at the top."

"You know, Denise, there's another problem."

"Which is?"

"I'm thinking of the lead engineer we used in the other networking projects this year."

"Mark Steinberg," she said, sighing. "Do you think this will be a problem?"

"I don't know," Josh said. "I guess we could use another person. Or kind of change his name on the résumé."

"Before we commit more resources to this project, we need to find out if Crescent would act prejudicially. We need more information. Do you have any ideas?"

"Let me think about this a little bit. I'll e-mail you tomorrow morning."

After hanging up with Josh, Denise decided to phone her mentor, Jane Adams. Denise explained what had happened at the meeting with the Crescent representatives and asked, "If I conceal the gender and ethnicity of my employees and never mention I am the company's founder, am I condoning the same types of prejudice that led me to start my own company in the first place, or am I just being a practical businesswoman?"

Jane avoided responding immediately to Denise's question and instead asked for more information: "Besides what happened today, do you have any other evidence that suggests Crescent won't do business with you if you disclose such information in your proposal?"

"I don't know yet. I've asked one of my employees to come up with a research plan. But what if we find out they do business only within the Saudi version of the good-old-boy network?"

"What if you find no signs of antiwomen or ethnic prejudices?" Jane countered.

After a long pause, Denise said, "Either way, I'm not sure what to do."

Your Assignment

1. How should Denise research the situation? In an e-mail to Denise, outline a research strategy to find out more about Crescent's business relationships with non-Arab and female-run vendors.

2. What should Denise do about the fact that the person she wishes to designate as the principal investigator has an ethnic last name that might elicit a prejudiced reaction from Crescent officials? Is Denise's decision to disguise the sex of her employees and to cover up her own role in founding her company justified by common sense, or is it giving in to what she perceives as prejudice? Should she assign someone other than Mark Steinberg to run the project? Should she tailor his name to disguise his ethnicity? If you were Denise's mentor, what advice would you give her? Respond in a 500-word memo to your instructor.

A version of this case first appeared in *Ethics in Technical Communication: A Critique and Synthesis* (Westport, CT: Greenwood, 2001), by Mike Markel.

Writing Technical Documents

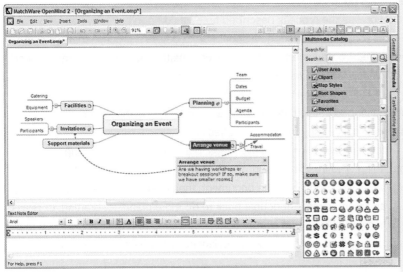

Source: MatchWare, 2008 <www.matchware.com/en/products/openmind/features.htm#MultiMaps>.

In the World...

This is a screen from a program called OpenMind 2, which lets you brainstorm using a variety of visual and verbal designs. Here the writer is creating a cluster diagram that he can save and send to others, who can modify it. The writer can also turn the diagram into presentation slides, timelines, agendas, and many other kinds of applications that can be distributed electronically. Whether you plan on paper, on a whiteboard, or on a computer screen with specialized software like this, brainstorming is a useful technique for generating ideas for any kind of technical document.

Planning 42

Analyzing Your Audience 42

Analyzing Your Purpose 43

Generating Ideas About Your Subject 43

Researching Additional Information 43

Organizing and Outlining Your Document 45

Selecting an Application, a Design, and a Delivery Method 46

Devising a Schedule and a Budget 47

Drafting 47

Using Templates 48

Using Styles 49

Revising 51

Studying the Draft by Yourself 52

Seeking Help from Others 52

Editing 53

Proofreading 53

Just as a mathematician doesn't solve a differential equation by closing her eyes and hoping for inspiration to strike, but instead follows a particular process, a communicator needs to follow a process when he or she writes. This chapter presents such a process, focusing on the techniques and tools that are most useful in writing technical documents.

Should you use the process described here? If you don't already have a process that works for you, yes. But your goal should be to devise a process that enables you to write *effective* documents (that is, documents that accomplish what you want them to) *efficiently* (without taking more time than is necessary). At the end of this chapter, you will find a Writer's Checklist. After you try implementing some of the techniques described in this chapter, you can start to revise the Writer's Checklist to reflect the techniques that you find most effective.

The writing process consists of five steps: planning, drafting, revising, editing, and proofreading. The frustrating part of writing, however, is that these five steps are not linear. That is, you don't plan the document, then check off a box and go on to drafting. At any step, you might double back to do more planning, drafting, or revising. Even when you think you're almost done—when you're proofreading—you might think of something that would improve the planning. That means you need to go back and rethink all five steps.

As you backtrack, you have one eye on the clock, because the deadline is sneaking up on you. Here's a secret: that's the way it is for all writers. A technical writer stops working on a user's manual because she has to get it off to the print shop. An engineer stops working on a set of slides for a conference presentation because it's time to head for the airport.

So when you read about how to write, remember that you are reading about a messy process that goes backward as often as it goes forward and that, most likely, will end only when you run out of time.

PLANNING

Planning, which can take more than a third of the total time spent on a writing project, is critically important for every document, from an e-mail to a book-length manual. Writers sometimes think they should start by thinking about their subject. I think it's best to start by thinking about the audience. Why? Because you need to understand whom you are writing for before you can figure out what you need to say about your subject.

Analyzing Your Audience

If you are lucky, you can talk with your audience before and during your work on the document. These conversations can help you learn what your readers

In This Book

For more about analyzing your audience, see Ch. 5, p. 81.

already know, what they want to know, and how they would like the information presented. You can test out drafts, making changes as you go.

Even if you cannot work with your audience while writing the document, you still need to learn everything you can about them so that you can determine the best scope, organization, and style for your document. Then, for each of your most important readers, try to answer the following three questions:

- *Who is your reader?* Consider factors such as education, job experience and responsibilities, skill in reading English, cultural characteristics, and personal preferences.
- *What are your reader's attitudes and expectations?* Consider the reader's attitudes toward the topic and your message, as well as the reader's expectations about the kind of document you will be presenting.
- *Why and how will the reader use your document?* Think about what the reader will do with the document. This includes the physical environment in which he or she will use it, the techniques he or she will use in reading it, and the tasks the reader will carry out after he or she finishes reading it.

On TechComm Web

For more about analyzing an audience, see Writing Guidelines for Engineering and Science Students. Click on Links Library for Ch. 3 on <bedfordstmartins.com/techcomm>.

Analyzing Your Purpose

You cannot start to write until you can state the purpose (or purposes) of the document. Ask yourself these questions:

- After your readers have read your document, what do you want them to know or to do?
- What beliefs or attitudes do you want them to hold?

A statement of purpose might be as simple as this: "The purpose of this report is to recommend whether the company should adopt a health-promotion program." Although the statement of purpose might not appear in this form in the final document, you need to state it clearly now because it will help you stay on track as you carry out the remaining steps in the writing process.

In This Book

For more about analyzing your purpose, see Ch. 5, p. 103.

Generating Ideas About Your Subject

Generating ideas is a way to start mapping out the information you will need to include in the document, where to put it, and what additional information may be required. Find out what you already know about the topic by using any of the techniques shown in Figure 3.1 on page 44.

Researching Additional Information

Once you have a good idea of what you already know about your topic, you need to obtain the rest of the information you will need. You can find

In This Book

For more about conducting research, see Ch. 6.

and evaluate what other people have already written by reading reference books, scholarly books, and articles in the library. You can also find useful information on the Internet. In addition, you might compile new information by interviewing experts, distributing surveys and questionnaires, making observations, and conducting experiments.

Figure 3.1   Techniques for Generating Ideas About Your Topic

Technique	*Explanation*	*Example*
Asking the six journalistic questions	Asking *who*, *what*, *when*, *where*, *why*, and *how* can help you figure out how much more research you need to do. Note that you can generate several questions from each of the six words.	• *Who* would be able to participate? *Who* would administer it? • *What* would the program consist of?
Brainstorming	Spending 10 or 15 minutes listing short phrases and questions about your subject can help you think of as many ideas as possible that relate to it. Later, when you construct an outline, you will rearrange your list, add new items, and toss out some items.	• Why we need a program • Lower insurance rates • On-site or at a club? • Who pays for it? • What is our liability? • Increase our productivity
Freewriting	Writing without a plan or restrictions—and without stopping—can help you determine what you do and do not understand. One phrase or sentence might spark an important idea.	A big trend today in business is sponsored health-promotion programs. Why should we do it? A number of reasons, including boosting productivity and lowering our insurance premiums. But it's complicated. One problem is that we can actually increase our risk if a person gets hurt. Another is the need to decide whether to have the program—what exactly is the program? Includes smoking cessation, etc.—on-site, by our own employees, or . . .
Talking with someone	Discussing your topic with someone can help you find out what you already know about your topic and can generate new ideas. Simply have the person ask you questions as you speak. Soon you will find yourself in a conversation that will help you make new connections from one idea to another.	You: One reason that we might want to do this is to boost productivity. Bob: What exactly are the statistics on increased productivity? And who has done the studies? Are they reputable? You: Good point. I'm going to have to make a business case that putting money into a program is going to pay off. I need to see whether there are unbiased recent sources that present hard data.

Figure 3.1   (continued)

Technique	Explanation	Example
Clustering	Writing your main idea or question in the middle of the page, then writing second-level and third-level ideas around it can help you expand on your topic.	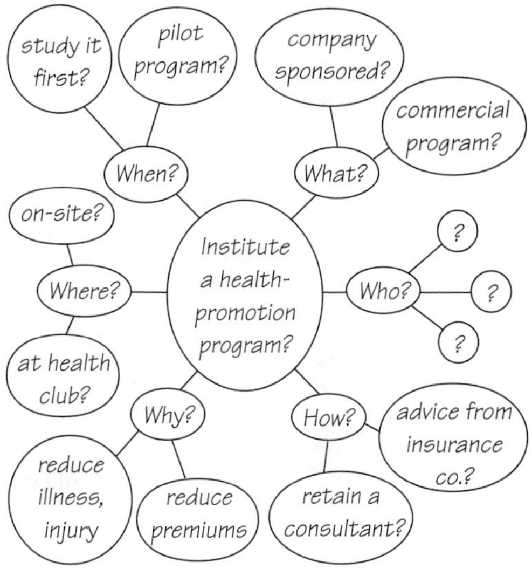 *study it first?* *pilot program?* *company sponsored?* *commercial program?* *When?* *What?* *on-site?* *Institute a health-promotion program?* *?* *Where?* *Who?* *?* *at health club?* *?* *Why?* *How?* *advice from insurance co.?* *reduce illness, injury* *reduce premiums* *retain a consultant?*
Branching	Writing your main idea or question at the top of the page, then writing second-level and third-level ideas below it is another way to help you expand on your topic.	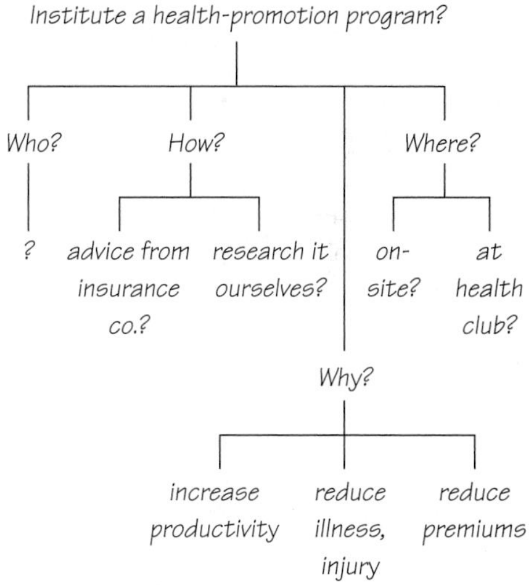 *Institute a health-promotion program?* *Who?* *How?* *Where?* *?* *advice from insurance co.?* *research it ourselves?* *on-site?* *at health club?* *Why?* *increase productivity* *reduce illness, injury* *reduce premiums*

Organizing and Outlining Your Document

Although each document will have its own structure, you can use or adapt existing organizational patterns to your situation. For instance, the comparison-and-contrast pattern might be an effective way to organize a discussion of different health-promotion programs. The cause-and-effect pattern might

On TechComm Web

For more about outlining, see Paradigm Online Writing Assistant. Click on Links Library for Ch. 3 on <bedfordstmartins .com/techcomm>.

How to Use the Outline View

When organizing your document, you can use the **outline view** to examine and revise the structure of your document. To use this view, you must format your document with Word's built-in heading styles or outline levels.

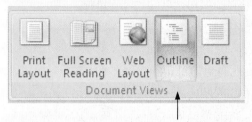

To view the structure of your document, select the **View** tab on the Ribbon and then select **Outline**.

A plus or minus sign indicates whether a heading has any subheadings or text associated with it.

Headings are indented to show subordinate levels.

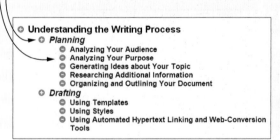

Use the **Outlining** tab to **promote** or **demote** headings or body text; to **move**, **expand**, or **collapse** sections; and to **show levels**.

KEYWORDS: outline view, create a document outline, outline levels

work well for a discussion of the effects that implementing a program might produce.

At this point, your organization is only tentative. When you start to draft, you might find that the pattern you have chosen isn't working well or that you need additional information that doesn't fit into the pattern.

Once you have a tentative plan, write an outline to help you stay on track as you draft. To keep your purpose clearly in mind as you work, you may want to write it at the top of the page before you begin your outline.

Selecting an Application, a Design, and a Delivery Method

Once you have a sense of what you want to say, you need to select an application (the type of document), a design, and a delivery method. You have a number of questions to answer:

- *Is the application already chosen for me?* If you are writing a proposal for the U.S. Department of the Interior, the department will provide its own specifications for how the proposal should look and how it should be delivered. You just need to follow the directions. For most kinds of communication, however, you may need to decide whether to write a set of instructions, a manual, a report, or some other application. Sometimes, you will need to prepare an oral presentation or participate in a phone conference or a videoconference.

- *What do my readers expect?* If your readers expect a written set of instructions, you should provide a set of instructions, unless some other application, such as a report or a manual, is more appropriate. If they expect to see the instructions presented in a simple black-and-white booklet and there is no good reason to design something more elaborate than that, your choice is obvious. For instance, instructions for installing and operating a ceiling fan in a house are generally presented in a small, inexpensive booklet with the pages stapled together. By contrast, readers' expectations regarding instructions for an expensive home-theater system might require you to create a glossy, full-color manual.

- *What delivery method will work best?* Related to the question of readers' expectations is the question of how you will deliver the document to them. For instance, you would likely mail an annual report to your readers and upload it to your company's Web site. You might present routine information to readers through e-mails or in a section of the Web site. You might present industry forecasts in a personal blog or in one sponsored by your employer.

It's important to think about these questions during the planning process because the answers you arrive at will largely determine the scope, organization, style, and design of your document.

Devising a Schedule and a Budget

During the planning stage, you also need to decide when you will need to provide the information and how much you can spend on the project.

For instance, for the project on health-promotion programs, your readers might need a report to help decide what to do before the new fiscal year begins in two months. In addition, they might want a progress report submitted halfway through the project. Making a schedule is often a collaborative process: you meet with your main readers, who tell you when they need the information, and you estimate how long the different tasks will take.

You also need to create a budget. In addition to the time you will need to do the project, you might incur expenses for various parts of the writing process. For example, you might need to travel to visit companies with different kinds of health-promotion programs. You might need to conduct specialized database searches, create and distribute question-naires to employees, or conduct interviews at remote locations. Some projects call for *usability testing*—evaluating prospective users as they try out a system or a document. This testing needs to be included in your budget.

DRAFTING

When you have at least a preliminary outline, it is time to start drafting. Some writers like to draft within the outline created on their word-processing program. Others prefer to place a paper copy of the outline on the desk next to their keyboard.

▶ **In This Book**

For more about progress reports, see Ch. 17, p. 464. For more about project management, see Ch. 4, p. 60.

▶ **In This Book**

For more about usability testing, see Ch. 13, p. 349.

▶ **On TechComm Web**

Purdue University's Online Writing Lab has many instructional handouts covering all aspects of the writing process. Click on Links Library for Ch. 3 on <bedfordstmartins.com/techcomm>.

Guidelines

Drafting Effectively

Try the following techniques when you begin to draft or when you get stuck in the middle of drafting.

▶ **Get comfortable.** Choose a good chair set at the right height for the keyboard and adjust the light so that it doesn't reflect off the screen.

▶ **Start with the easiest topics.** Instead of starting at the beginning of the document, begin with the section you most want to write.

▶ **Draft quickly.** Try to make your fingers keep up with your brain. Turn the phrases from your outline into paragraphs. You'll revise later.

▶ **Don't stop to get more information or to revise.** Set a timer and draft for an hour or two without stopping. When you come to an item that requires more research, skip to the next item. Don't worry about sentence structure or spelling.

▶ **Try invisible writing.** Darken the screen or turn off the monitor so that you can look only at your hardcopy outline or the keyboard. That way, you won't be tempted to stop typing so often to revise what you have just written.

▶ **Stop in the middle of a section.** When you stop, do so in the middle of a paragraph or even in the middle of a sentence. It's easier to resume writing in the middle of an idea than to begin with a new one. This technique will help you avoid writer's block, the mental paralysis that can set in when you stare at a blank page.

Using Templates

In This Book

For more about design, see Ch. 11.

When you draft, you might consider using an existing template or modifying one to meet your needs. Templates are preformatted designs for different applications, such as letters, memos, newsletters, and reports. Templates incorporate the design specifications for the application, including typeface, type size, margins, and spacing. Once you select a template, you just type in the information. Using templates, however, can lead to three problems:

• *They do not always reflect the best design principles.* For instance, most letter and memo templates default to 10-point type, even though 12-point type is easier to read.

• *They bore readers.* Readers get tired of seeing the same designs.

• *They cannot help you answer the important questions about your document.* Although memo templates can help you format information, they cannot help you figure out how to organize and write an effective memo. Sometimes, templates can even send you the wrong message. For example, résumé templates in word processors present a set of headings that might work better for some job applicants than for others.

The more you rely on existing templates, the less likely you are to learn how to use the software to make your documents look professional.

TECH TIP

How to Modify Templates

You can modify an existing document **template** to address your specific writing situation. You can then save this modified document as a template and use it again in similar writing situations.

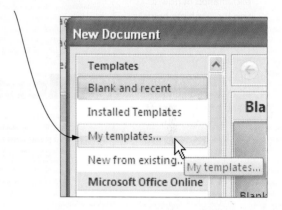

1. Open an existing template on your computer by selecting the **Office** button and then selecting **New**.

2. In the **New Document** window, find an appropriate template already installed on your computer or download one.

3. Select **Template** and then select **Create**.

4. After making changes to the design of the document, select **Save** on the **Quick Access** toolbar.

Your saved template will appear as an icon that you can access by selecting **My templates** in the **New Document** window.

KEYWORDS: templates, about templates, modify a template, installed templates, download templates

Using Styles

Styles are like small templates in that they apply to the design of smaller elements, such as headings. Like templates, styles save you time. For example, as you draft your document, you don't need to add all the formatting each time you want to designate an item as a first-level heading. You can simply place your cursor at the appropriate spot in the text and use the pull-down menu at the top of the screen to select that style. The style will automatically be incorporated into the text.

If you decide to modify a style—by adding italics to a heading, for instance—you need to change it only once; the software will then automatically change every instance of that style in the document. As you create collaborative documents, styles make it easier for collaborators to achieve a consistent look.

INTERACTIVE SAMPLE DOCUMENT
Identifying the Strengths and Weaknesses of a Commercial Template

The following template from Microsoft Word presents one option for writing a memo. The questions in the margin ask you to think about the assumptions underlying this memo. E-mail your responses to yourself and/or your instructor on TechComm Web.

1. How well does the explanation of how to use the template help you understand how to write an effective memo?

2. How well does the template help you understand how to reformat the elements, such as the date?

On TechComm Web

To e-mail your responses to yourself and/or your instructor, click on Interactive Sample Documents for Ch. 3 on <bedfordstmartins.com/techcomm>.

Company Name Here

Memo

To: [Click **here** and type name]
From: [Click **here** and type name]
CC: [Click **here** and type name]
Date: 2/22/2008
Re: [Click **here** and type subject]

_____

How to Use This Memo Template

Select text you would like to replace, and type your memo. Use styles such as Heading 1-3 and Body Text in the Style control on the Formatting toolbar. To save changes to this template for future use, choose Save As from the File menu. In the Save As Type box, choose Document Template. Next time you want to use it, choose New from the File menu, and then double-click your template.

Source: Microsoft, 2007 <http://office.microsoft.com/enus/templates/TC010129271033.aspx?CategoryID=CT101172591033>.

TECH TIP

How to Use the Styles Group

As you draft your document, you can use the **Styles** group to apply styles to elements such as headings, lists, and body text. Using styles helps to ensure consistency and makes it easy to automatically change every instance of a style in your document when you revise.

1. To apply a style, select the text you want to format, then select a style from the **Quick Styles gallery** in the **Styles** group on the **Home** tab.

If you do not see the style you want in the gallery, you may access additional styles by using the up and down arrows.

You may also apply a **Quick Style Set** to your entire document by selecting the **Change Styles** icon.

2. Another way to apply a style is to select the **Styles** dialog box launcher and then select the style you wish to use.

If you do not see the style options you want, select **Options** to display the **Style Pane Options** dialog box.

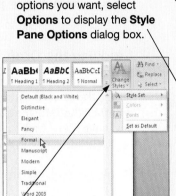

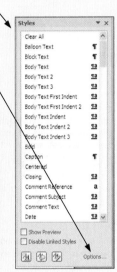

KEYWORDS: styles, quick style, quick styles gallery, change styles, apply a style, apply a different style, styles dialog box launcher, style pane options

REVISING

Revising is the process of looking again at your draft to see whether it works. After you revise, you will carry out two more steps—editing and proofreading—but at this point you want to focus on large questions. Here are the major topics you need to address:

- *Audience.* Has your understanding of your audience changed? Will you be addressing people you hadn't considered before? If so, how will that change what you have to say and how you should say it?

- *Purpose.* Has your understanding of your purpose changed? If so, what changes should you make to the document?

- *Subject.* Has your understanding of the subject changed? Should you change the scope—that is, should you address more topics or fewer? Should you change the organization of the document? Should you present more evidence or different types of evidence?

On the basis of this revision, you might find that you need to make only a few changes, such as adding one or two minor topics. Alternatively, you might need to completely rethink the document.

What is the biggest challenge you will face if you conclude that you need to make major changes to a draft? That's easy to answer: resisting the impulse to talk yourself out of it.

Revising is about looking for ways to improve the document by looking again at the audience, purpose, and subject. There are two major ways to revise: by yourself and with the assistance of others.

Studying the Draft by Yourself

In This Book

For more about improving the effectiveness of revising your draft by yourself, see Ch. 13.

The first step in revision is to read and reread the document, looking for different things each time. For instance, you might read it once just to see whether the information you have presented is appropriate for the audience you have identified. You might read it another time just to see whether each of your claims is supported by appropriate and sufficient evidence.

Seeking Help from Others

In This Book

For more about having another person review your draft, see Ch. 4, p. 68.

For technical documents, it is best to turn to two kinds of people for help. The first kind of people who can help are subject-matter experts (SMEs), who will make sure your facts and explanations are accurate and appropriate. If, for instance, you are writing about fuel-cell automobiles, you could ask an automotive expert to review it. Important documents are routinely reviewed by technical experts before being released to the public.

The second kind of people who can help you revise are actual users of your existing document or prospective users of the next version of the document. These people can help you see problems that you or other knowledgeable readers don't notice. For instance, if you have been studying fuel-cell technologies for a long time in preparing your document, you might take it for granted that everyone knows what a fuel cell is. A prospective user might point out that she doesn't understand the term and that you haven't defined it.

How do you learn from SMEs and from users and prospective users? Here are a few techniques:

In This Book

These techniques, as well as usability testing, are discussed in more detail in Ch. 13.

- surveying, interviewing, or observing readers as they use the existing document
- interviewing SMEs after they have read a draft of the document
- conducting focus groups to learn users' or prospective users' opinions about an existing or proposed document

It is important to revise all drafts, but it is especially important to revise drafts of documents that will be read and used by people from other cultures. If your readers come from another culture, try to have your draft reviewed by

---

Ethics Note

Acknowledging Reviewers Responsibly

When you write on the job, you should take advantage of the expertise of others. It is completely ethical to ask subject-matter experts and people who resemble your intended audience to critique a draft of your document. An ethical question may arise, however, if your reviewer offers detailed comments and suggestions about the draft or sends you a multipage review of the draft, and you use some or many of the ideas. In that case, you should acknowledge the reviewer's contributions. This acknowledgment can take the form of a one- or two-sentence statement of appreciation in the introduction of the document or in a transmittal letter. Or you could write a letter or memo of appreciation to the reviewer; he or she might be able to use such a letter for a future performance evaluation.

---

someone from that culture. That person can help you see whether you have made correct assumptions about how readers will react to your ideas, and whether you have chosen appropriate kinds of evidence and design elements. As discussed in Chapters 11 and 12, people from other cultures might be surprised by some design elements used in reports, such as marginal comments.

EDITING

Having revised the draft and made any changes you wish to its content and organization, you must now turn to editing. Editing is the process of checking the draft to improve its grammar, punctuation, style, usage, diction (word choice), and mechanics (such as use of numbers and abbreviations). You will do most of the editing yourself, but you might also call on assistance from others, especially writers and editors in your organization.

> **In This Book**
> For more about editing for coherence and correctness, see Chs. 9 and 10. For more about correctness, see Appendix, Part C.

The amount of editing required will vary depending on the importance of the document. An annual report, which is perhaps the single most important document that people will read about your organization, should be edited rigorously, because the company wants it to be as close to perfect as possible. A biweekly employee newsletter needs to be edited, but not as rigorously as an annual report. What about the routine e-mails you write every day? You should edit them, too. It's rude not to.

PROOFREADING

Proofreading is the process of checking to make sure you have typed what you meant to type. A sentence such as the following has three errors that you should catch in proofreading:

There are for major reasons we should implementing health-promotion program.

Here they are:

1. "For" is the wrong word. It should be "four."

2. "Implementing" is the wrong verb form. It should be "implement." This mistake is probably left over from an earlier version of the sentence.

3. The article "a" is missing before the phrase "health-promotion program." This is probably just a result of carelessness.

By the way, my spell checker and grammar checker didn't flag any of them. Proofreading is no fun. You're exhausted, and you're thoroughly sick of the document. Proofreading also is probably not the most exciting thing you have ever done. But it is vital to producing a clear, well-written document. Don't insult yourself and your readers by skipping this step. Reread your draft carefully and slowly, perhaps out loud, and maybe get a friend to help. You'll be surprised at how many errors you'll find.

Writer's Checklist

In planning the document, did you

- ☐ analyze your audience? (p. 42)
- ☐ analyze your purpose? (p. 43)
- ☐ generate ideas about your subject? (p. 43)
- ☐ research additional information? (p. 43)
- ☐ organize and outline your document? (p. 45)
- ☐ select an application, a design, and a delivery method? (p. 46)
- ☐ devise a schedule and a budget? (p. 47)

In drafting the document, did you

- ☐ use templates, if appropriate? (p. 48)
- ☐ use styles? (p. 49)

In revising the draft, did you

- ☐ study the draft by yourself? (p. 52)
- ☐ seek help from others? (p. 52)

- ☐ Did you edit the document carefully? (p. 53)
- ☐ Did you proofread the document carefully? (p. 53)

Exercises

In This Book For more about memos, see Ch. 14, p. 377.

1. Read your word processor's online help about using the outline view. Make a file with five headings, each of which has a sentence of body text below it. Practice using the outline feature to do the following tasks:

   a. change a level-one heading to a level-two heading

   b. move the first heading in your outline to the end of the document

   c. hide the body text that goes with one of the headings

2. Your word processor probably contains a number of templates for documents such as letters, memos, faxes, and résumés. Evaluate one of these templates. Is it clear and professional-looking? Does it present an effective design for all users or only for some? What changes would you make to the template to improve it? Write a memo to your instructor presenting your findings.

Case 3: Using Revision Software Effectively

In This Book For more about memos, see Ch. 14, p. 377.

Background

Six months ago, Jim Williams joined the state Department of Environmental Quality (DEQ) as an environmental hydrogeologist. The DEQ enforces various state and federal environmental regulations and laws designed to ensure clean air, water, and land in the state. The DEQ is also responsible for protecting the state's citizens from the adverse health effects of pollution, cleaning up spills and releases of hazardous materials, and managing the proper disposal of hazardous and solid wastes.

Since being hired, Jim has focused on groundwater issues in the state. His fieldwork includes drilling and testing wells and collecting water samples. He also writes numerous reports. Unfortunately, Jim has never considered himself a strong writer. For him, the first draft of a report is the final draft. He would much rather be in the field collecting data than completing reports in the office.

Jim's lack of enthusiasm for writing reports is reflected in the poor quality of his reports and, much to Jim's annoyance, his recent performance review. While going over his latest performance review, Jim's supervisor, Charles Molder, told him, "Writing good, clean, concise reports is a main part of a hydrogeologist's job." He then commented specifically on Jim's poor writing skills and told him bluntly that unless his reports improved, he would be let go. Charles told Jim to spend time revising, editing, and proofreading his report drafts and enlist the help of another hydrogeologist to review his drafts before he submits them. "At the very least," Charles advised, "make use of the spelling and grammar checkers on your computer." Jim left the meeting worried about his job but committed to doing better on his next report.

After drafting a section of a report (Document 3.1), Jim used his word processor's tools to make some revisions (Document 3.2). Then he stopped by your office and asked if you would be willing to take a look at this passage and give him some advice on how to improve it.

Although hydrogeology is not your area of expertise, you agreed to review the passage. After a quick read-through, you told Jim, "This passage doesn't sound like you. The language is awkward, and I noticed several careless mistakes."

"I don't understand," Jim said in frustration. "I used the spelling, grammar, *and* thesaurus tools. I followed all of the advice. Now you're telling me that it *still* has errors?"

"I think I understand what happened," you said. "Let me borrow your original draft as well as this passage, and I'll get back to you tomorrow. I'd like to show you some of the limitations of the software."

Document 3.1
Original Draft of Passage

On TechComm Web

For digital versions of case documents, click on Downloadable Case Documents on <bedfordstmartins.com/techcomm>.

Yearly water quality testing is increasingly popular however less DEQ staff are currently qualified to conduct water quality sampling efforts resulting in a crunch at the years' dead line. In this study, Jim Williams, the principle investigator, collected and reported the data to Walt Shapiro, and he analyzed the data. The water quality sampling schedule took place for a full year to encompass the high flow and base flow for each stream. Its commonly assmed that during a streams high flow it's banks are inaccessible due to safety concerns thus no samples were collected. In one case, the river was not to high to safely access for only too months in the studies time period. The scientists sampling on most of the streams began early May 2004 and continued too late April 2005. Some of the stream's that are impacted and will have state and federal cost share programs on it, will have monitorring continued through an additional year. Samples were collected bi-weekly from April through September, then once a month from October through March, then back to bi-weekly for the remainder of the sampling period. Scientists should analyze samples for total suspended solids, total volatile solids, nitrate + nitrite, ammonia, total nitrogen, total phosphorus, fecal coliform and *E. coli if* you want to cover the major water quality measures. In addition to these analytical tests, on-site field parameters for disolved oxygen, temperature, conductivity total dissolved solids, PH, and discharge are measured, when possible, during each sampling event.

Yearly water quality testing is increasingly popular however; less DEQ staff is currently qualified to conduct water quality sampling efforts resulting in a crunch at the years' dead line. In this study, Jim Williams, the principle investigator, accumulated and accounted the data to Walt Shapiro, and he analyzed the data. The water quality-sampling schedule took place for a full year to encompass the high flow and base flow for each stream. A scientist commonly assumes that during a streams high flow its banks are inaccessible due to safety concerns thus he collects no samples. In one case, the waterway was not too high to safely access for very months in the studies time. The scientists sampling on most of the streams began early May 2004 and continued too late April 2005. Some of the stream's that are impacted and will have state and federal cost share programs on it, will have monitoring continued through an additional year. A scientist collected samples bi-weekly from April through September, then once a month from October through March, then back to bi-weekly for the remainder of the sampling period. Scientists should analyze samples for total suspended solids, total volatile solids, nitrate + nitrite, ammonia, total nitrogen, total phosphorus, fecal coli form and *E. coli if* you want to cover the major water quality measures. In addition to these analytical tests, a scientist measured on-site field parameters for dissolved oxygen, temperature, conductivity total dissolved solids, PH, and discharge, when possible, during each sampling incident.

Your Assignment

1. Download the Microsoft Word file of Document 3.1 from <bedfordstmartins.com/techcomm> or type the passage in a Word document. Using Word's tools, do the following:

   a. Run the passage through the spell checker. Note the limitations of the spell checker.

   b. Run the passage through the grammar checker. Note the limitations of the grammar checker.

   c. Compare the original passage to the revised passage (Document 3.2). Identify places in which Jim used an inappropriate word likely suggested by the thesaurus. Note the limitations of the thesaurus.

   Write Jim a short memo in which you explain the limitations of the tools and suggest how he could use them more effectively.

2. Revise Jim's original passage (Document 3.1) to create a more effective report. Include a memo to Jim explaining your revisions.

Writing Collaboratively

4

Source: Invensys, 2008 <www.infusionecs.com/template.aspx?PageID=19>.

In the World . . .

New technologies such as the InFusion Collaboration Wall make it easy to display and modify numerous screens of data and images. What's the most important element shown in this photograph? Two people talking.

Advantages and Disadvantages of Collaboration 58

Advantages of Collaboration 59

Disadvantages of Collaboration 59

Managing Projects 60

Conducting Meetings 61

Listening Effectively 61

Setting Your Group's Agenda 61

Conducting Efficient Face-to-Face Meetings 65

Communicating Diplomatically 65

Critiquing a Group Member's Work 67

Using Electronic Tools in Collaboration 67

Using the Comment, Revision, and Highlighting Features of a Word Processor 68

Using Groupware 70

Using Videoconferencing Technology 71

Gender and Collaboration 73

Culture and Collaboration 74

People collaborate in writing everything from memos to books. Longer, more complex, or more important documents—such as proposals, reports, manuals, corporate annual reports, and Web sites—are most likely to be written collaboratively.

Figure 4.1 shows three basic patterns of collaboration.

ADVANTAGES AND DISADVANTAGES OF COLLABORATION

As a student, you might have already worked collaboratively on course projects. As a professional, you will work on many more. In the workplace, the stakes might be higher. Effective collaboration can make you look like a star, but ineffective collaboration can ruin an important project—and hurt group members' reputations.

The best way to start thinking about collaboration is to understand its main advantages and disadvantages.

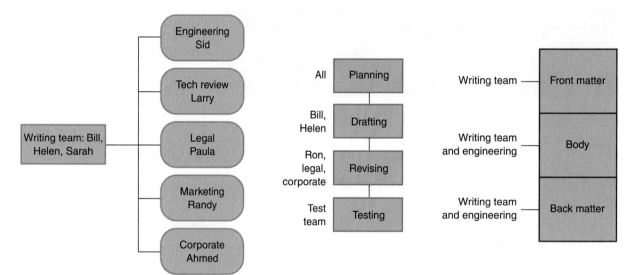

Collaboration based on job specialty. On this team, an engineer is the subject-matter expert, the person in charge of contributing all the technical information; other professionals are in charge of their own specialties. The writing team writes, edits, and designs the document.

Collaboration based on the stages of the writing process. Group members collaborate during the planning stage by sharing ideas about the document's content, organization, and style, then establish a production schedule and an evaluation program. They collaborate less during the drafting stage, because drafting collaboratively is much more time-consuming than drafting individually. During the revising phase, they return to collaboration.

Collaboration based on the section of the document. One person takes responsibility for one section of the document, another person does another section, and so forth. This pattern is common for large projects with separate sections, such as proposals.

Figure 4.1 **Patterns of Collaboration**

Advantages of Collaboration

Writers who collaborate can create a better document and improve the way an organization functions:

- *Collaboration draws on a greater knowledge base.* Therefore, it can be more comprehensive and more accurate than a single-author document.

- *Collaboration draws on a greater skills base.* No one person can be an expert manager, writer, editor, graphic artist, and production person.

- *Collaboration provides a better idea of how the audience will read the document.* Each group member acts as an audience, offering more questions and suggestions than one person could while writing alone.

- *Collaboration improves communication among employees.* Because group members share a goal, they learn about one another's jobs, responsibilities, and frustrations.

- *Collaboration helps acclimate new employees to an organization.* New employees learn how things work—which people to see, which forms to fill out, and so forth—as well as what the organization values, such as the importance of ethical conduct and the willingness to work hard and sacrifice for an important initiative.

Disadvantages of Collaboration

Collaboration can also have important disadvantages:

- *Collaboration takes more time than individual writing.* It takes longer because of the time needed for the collaborators to communicate and because it can be difficult to schedule group meetings.

- *Collaboration can lead to groupthink.* When group members value getting along more than thinking critically about the project, they are prone to *groupthink*. Groupthink, which promotes conformity, can result in an inferior document, because no one wants to cause a scene by asking tough questions.

- *Collaboration can yield a disjointed document.* Sections can contradict or repeat one another or be written in different styles. To prevent these problems, writers need to plan and edit the document carefully.

- *Collaboration can lead to inequitable workloads.* Despite the project leader's best efforts, some people will end up doing more work than others.

- *Collaboration can reduce collaborators' motivation to work hard on the document.* The smaller the role a person plays in the project, the less motivated he or she is to make the extra effort.

- *Collaboration can lead to interpersonal conflict.* People can disagree about the best way to create the document or about the document itself. Such disagreements can hurt the working relationship during the project and long after.

MANAGING PROJECTS

At some point in your academic career, you will likely collaborate on a course project that is just too big, too technical, and too difficult for your group to complete successfully without some advance planning and careful oversight.

Guidelines

Managing Your Project

These seven suggestions can help you keep the project on track.

▶ **Break down a large project into several smaller tasks.** Working backward from what you must deliver to your client or manager, partition your project into its component parts, making a list of the steps you need to take to complete the project. This task is not only the foundation of project management, but it is also a good strategy for determining the resources you will need to complete the project on time. After you have a list of tasks to complete, you can begin to plan your project, assign responsibilities, and set deadlines.

▶ **Plan your project.** Planning allows collaborators to develop an effective approach and reach agreement before investing a lot of time and resources. Planning prevents small problems from becoming big problems with a deadline looming. Effective project managers use planning documents such as *needs analyses*, *information plans*, *specifications*, and *project plans*.

▶ **Create and maintain an accurate schedule.** An accurate schedule helps collaborators plan ahead, allocate their time, and meet deadlines. Update your schedule when changes are made, then place the up-to-date schedule in an easily accessible location (for example, on a project Web site) or e-mail the schedule to each group member. If the group misses a deadline, immediately create a new deadline. Group members should always know when tasks must be completed.

▶ **Put your decisions in writing.** Writing down your decisions and communicating them to all collaborators will help the team remember what was decided. In addition, if questions arise, the team can refer easily to the document and, if necessary, update it.

▶ **Monitor the project.** By regularly tracking the progress of a project, the group can learn what it has accomplished, whether the project is on schedule, and whether any unexpected challenges exist.

▶ **Distribute and act on information quickly.** Acting fast to get collaborators the information they need will help ensure that the group makes effective decisions and makes steady progress toward completing the project.

▶ **Be flexible regarding schedule and responsibilities.** Adjust your plan and methods when new information becomes available or problems arise. When tasks depend on earlier tasks that are delayed or need reworking, the group should be willing to consider revising responsibilities to keep the project moving forward.

▶ **On TechComm Web**

For a discussion of performing a needs analysis, see Saul Carliner's Developer's Toolkit. Click on Links Library for Ch. 4 on <bedfordstmartins.com/techcomm>.

Often, collaborative projects are complex, lasting several weeks or months and involving the efforts of several people at scheduled times so that the project can proceed. For this reason, collaborators need to spend time managing the project to ensure that it not only meets the needs of the audience but also is completed on time and, if appropriate, within budget.

CONDUCTING MEETINGS

Collaboration involves conducting meetings. The following discussion covers five aspects of meetings.

Listening Effectively

Participating in a meeting involves listening and speaking. If you listen carefully to other people, you will understand what they are thinking, and you will be able to speak knowledgeably and constructively. Listening is more than just hearing (receiving and processing sound waves); listening involves understanding what the speaker is saying and interpreting the information.

Guidelines

Listening Effectively

Follow these five steps to improve your effectiveness as a listener.

▶ **Pay attention to the speaker.** Look at the speaker, and don't let your mind wander.

▶ **Listen for main ideas.** Pay attention to phrases that signal important information, such as "What I'm saying is . . ." or "The point I'm trying to make is. . . ."

▶ **Don't get emotionally involved with the speaker's ideas.** Even if you disagree, keep listening. Keep an open mind. Don't stop listening so that you can plan what you are going to say next.

▶ **Ask questions to clarify what the speaker said.** After the speaker finishes, ask questions to make sure you understand. For instance, "When you said that each journal recommends different printers, did you mean that each journal recommends several printers or that each journal recommends a different printer?"

▶ **Provide appropriate feedback.** The most important feedback is to look into the speaker's eyes. You can nod your approval to signal that you understand what he or she is saying. Appropriate feedback helps assure the speaker that he or she is communicating.

Setting Your Group's Agenda

It's important to get your group off to a smooth start. In the first meeting, start to define your group's agenda.

Guidelines

Setting Your Agenda

▶ **Define the group's task.** What document, or "deliverable," will your group submit? Every group member has to agree, for example, that your task is to revise the employee manual by April 10 and that the revision must be no longer than 200 pages. You also need to agree on more-conceptual aspects of the task, including the audience, purpose, and scope of the document.

▶ **Choose a group leader.** This person serves as the link between the group and management. (In an academic setting, the group leader represents the group in communicating with the instructor.) The group leader also keeps the group on track, leads the meetings, and coordinates communication among group members.

▶ **Define tasks for each group member.** As Figure 4.1 on page 58 shows, there are three main ways to divide the tasks. All group members will participate in each phase of the project, and each group member will review the document at every stage. However, each member will have chief responsibility for a task to which he or she is best suited. Group members will likely assume informal roles, too. One person might be good at clarifying what others have said, another at preventing unnecessary arguments, and another at asking questions that force the group to reevaluate its decisions.

▶ **Establish working procedures.** Before starting to work, members need answers—in writing, if possible—to the following questions:

— When and where will we meet?
— What procedures will we follow in the meetings?
— How, and how often, are we to communicate with other group members, including the leader?

▶ **Establish a procedure for resolving conflict productively.** Disagreements about the project can lead to a better product. Give members a chance to express ideas fully and find areas of agreement, then resolve the conflict by a vote.

▶ **Create a style sheet.** If all group members draft using a similar writing style, the document will need less revision. Discuss as many style questions as you can: use of headings and lists, paragraph style and length, level of formality, and so forth. And be sure to use styles, as discussed in Chapter 3.

▶ **Establish a work schedule.** For example, to submit a proposal on February 10, you must complete an outline by January 25, a draft by February 1, and a revision by February 8. These dates are called *milestones.*

▶ **Create evaluation materials.** Group members have a right to know how their work will be evaluated. In college, students often evaluate themselves and other group members. But in the working world, managers are more likely to do the evaluations.

▶ **In This Book**
Fig. 4.2 on p. 63 shows a work-schedule form. Fig. 4.3 on p. 64 shows a group-members evaluation form. Fig. 4.4 on p. 66 shows a self-evaluation form.

Figure 4.2
Work-Schedule Form

WORK-SCHEDULE FORM

Name of Project: *VoIP feasibility study*

Principal Reader: *Joan*

Other Readers: *Carlton, Wendy*

Group Members: *Saada, Larry, Randy, Ahmed*

Type of Document Required: *recommendation report*

Milestones	Responsible Member	Status	Date
Deliver Document	*Saada*		*May 19*
Proofread Document	*all*		*May 18*
Send Document to Print Shop	*n/a*		*n/a*
Complete Revision	*Randy*		*May 17*
Review Draft Elements	*all*	*Done*	*May 16*
Assemble Draft	*Ahmed*	*Done*	*May 13*
Establish Tasks	*Larry*	*Done*	*May 9*

Progress Reports	Responsible Member	Status	Date
Progress Report 3	*n/a*		
Progress Report 2	*n/a*		
Progress Report 1	*Randy*	*Done*	*May 15*

Meetings	Agenda	Location	Date	Time
Meeting 3	*Review final draft*	*Room C*	*May 18*	*3:30*
Meeting 2	*Review draft elements*	*Room B*	*May 16*	*2:00*
Meeting 1	*Kickoff meeting*	*Room C*	*May 9*	*3:00*

Notes

Notice that milestones some-times are presented in reverse chronological order; the delivery-date milestone, for instance, comes first. On other forms, items are presented in normal chronological order.

The form includes spaces for listing the person responsible for each milestone and progress report and for stating the progress toward each milestone and progress report.

 On TechComm Web

For printable versions of Figs. 4.2, 4.3, and 4.4, click on Forms for Technical Communication on <bedfordstmartins.com/ techcomm>.

Figure 4.3
Group-Members
Evaluation Form

GROUP-MEMBERS EVALUATION FORM

Your name: _____ *Mackenzie Hopkins* _____

Title of the project: _____ *4-wheel-drive feasibility report* _____

Date: _____ *October 14, 2008* _____

Instructions

Use this form to evaluate the other members of your group. Write the name of each group member other than yourself in one of the columns, then assign a score of 0 to 10 (0 being the lowest grade, 10 the highest) to each group member for each criterion. Then total the scores for each member. Because each group member has different strengths and weaknesses, the scores you assign will differ. On the back of this sheet, write any comments you wish to make.

Mackenzie gives high grades to Kurt and Amber but low grades to Bob. If Kurt and Amber agree with Mackenzie's assessment of Bob's participation, the three of them should meet with Bob to discuss why his participation has been weak and to consider ways for him to improve.

	Group Members			
Criteria	Kurt	Amber	Bob	
1. Regularly attends meetings	1. 10	1. 9	1. 6	1. ___
2. Is prepared at meetings	2. 9	2. 8	2. 5	2. ___
3. Meets deadlines	3. 9	3. 9	3. 2	3. ___
4. Contributes good ideas in meetings	4. 9	4. 10	4. 9	4. ___
5. Contributes ideas diplomatically	5. 8	5. 9	5. 9	5. ___
6. Submits high-quality work	6. 9	6. 9	6. 7	6. ___
7. Listens to other members	7. 8	7. 10	7. 6	7. ___
8. Shows respect for other members	8. 9	8. 10	8. 6	8. ___
9. Helps to reduce conflict	9. 9	9. 10	9. 5	9. ___
10. Your overall assessment of this person's contribution	10. 9	10. 9	10. 7	10. ___
Total Points	89	93	62	___

> ## Ethics Note
>
> ### Pulling Your Weight on Collaborative Projects
>
> Collaboration involves an ethical dimension. If you work hard and well, you help the other members of the group. If you don't, you hurt them.
>
> You can't be held responsible for knowing and doing everything, and sometimes unexpected problems arise in other courses or in your private life that prevent you from participating as actively and effectively as you otherwise could. When problems occur, inform the other group members as soon as possible. For instance, call the group leader as soon as you realize you will have to miss a meeting. Be honest about what happened. Suggest ways you might make up for missing a task. If you communicate clearly, the other group members are likely to work with you.
>
> If you are a member of a group that includes someone who is not participating fully, keep records of your attempts to get in touch with that person. When you do make contact, you owe it to that person to try to find out what the problem is and suggest ways to resolve the problem. Your goal is to treat that person fairly and to help him or her do better work, so that the group will function more smoothly and more effectively.

Conducting Efficient Face-to-Face Meetings

Human communication is largely nonverbal. That is, people communicate through words but also through the tone, rate, and volume of their speech. They communicate, too, through body language. For this reason, face-to-face discussions provide the most information about what a person is thinking and feeling—and the best opportunity for group members to understand one another.

To help make meetings effective and efficient, group members should arrive on time and stick to the agenda. One group member should serve as secretary by recording the important decisions made at the meeting. At the end of the meeting, the group leader should summarize the group's accomplishments and state the tasks each group member is to perform before the next meeting. If possible, the secretary should give each group member this informal set of meeting minutes.

 **On TechComm Web**

For an excellent discussion of how to conduct meetings, see Matson (1996). Click on Links Library for Ch. 4 on <bedfordstmartins.com/techcomm>.

In This Book

For a discussion of meeting minutes, see Ch. 17, p. 473.

Communicating Diplomatically

Because collaborating can be stressful, it can lead to interpersonal conflict. People can become frustrated and angry with one another because of personality clashes or because of disputes about the project. If the project is to succeed, however, group members have to work together productively. When you speak in a group meeting, you want to appear helpful, not critical or overbearing.

Figure 4.4
Self-Evaluation Form

SELF-EVALUATION FORM

Your name: _Lucas Barnes_   Date: _April 12, 2008_

Title of the project: _digital-camera study progress report_

Instructions

On this form, record and evaluate your own involvement in this project. In the Log section, record the activities you performed as an individual and those you performed as part of the group. For all activities, record the date and the number of hours you spent. In the Evaluation section, write two brief statements, one about aspects of your contribution you think were successful and one about aspects you want to improve.

Log Individual Activities	Date	Number of Hours
Reviewed proposal and analyzed the Simmons article	April 9	1.5
Wrote a draft of the progress report	April 10	2.5
Revised a draft of the progress report	April 11	1

Activities as Part of Group	Date	Number of Hours
Met to discuss test research	April 10	1
E-mailed group and replied to questions about draft	April 11	2.5
Met to discuss revision of progress report	April 11	1.5

Evaluation
Aspects of My Participation That Were Successful

I think I did a good job in reviewing the proposal and critiquing the research. I had the draft ready on time, although there were some rough parts in it. I participated effectively in the group meeting about the revision. I think I'm getting a little better about being less sensitive when the group suggests revisions.

Aspects of My Participation That I Want to Improve in the Future

I still need to get better at completing my work early enough so I can set it aside before getting it out to the other group members. I get embarrassed when they point out superficial mistakes that I should have caught. I need to practice using styles so that my drafts are easier to incorporate into the group's draft. The other members remembered to use them. I didn't.

The evaluation section of the form is difficult to fill out, but it can be the most valuable section for you in assessing your skills in collaborating. When you get to the second question, be thoughtful and constructive. Don't merely say that you want to improve your skills in using the software. Don't just write "None."

Guidelines

Communicating Diplomatically

▶ **Listen carefully, without interrupting.** See the Guidelines box on page 61.

▶ **Give everyone a chance to speak.** Don't dominate the discussion.

▶ **Avoid personal remarks and insults.** Be tolerant and respectful of other people's views and working methods. Doing so is right—and smart: if you anger people, they will go out of their way to oppose you.

▶ **Don't overstate your position.** A modest qualifier such as "I think" or "it seems to me" is an effective signal to your listeners that you realize that everyone may not share your views.

OVERBEARING   My plan is a sure thing; there's no way we're not going to kill Allied next quarter.

DIPLOMATIC   I think this plan has a good chance of success: we're playing off our strengths and Allied's weaknesses.

In the diplomatic version, the speaker calls it "this plan," not "my plan."

▶ **Don't get emotionally attached to your own ideas.** When people oppose you, try to understand why. Digging in is usually unwise—unless it's a matter of principle. Although you may be right and everyone else wrong, it's not likely.

▶ **Ask pertinent questions.** Bright people ask questions to understand what they hear, to connect it to other ideas, and to encourage other group members to examine what they hear.

▶ **Pay attention to nonverbal communication.** Bob might *say* that he understands a point, but his facial expression might show that he doesn't. If a group member looks confused, ask him or her about it. A direct question is likely to elicit a statement that will help the group clarify its discussion.

Critiquing a Group Member's Work

In collaborating, group members often critique notes and drafts written by other group members. Knowing how to do it without offending the writer is a valuable skill.

USING ELECTRONIC TOOLS IN COLLABORATION

Electronic media are useful collaborative tools for two reasons:

- *Face-to-face meetings are not always possible or convenient.* Most electronic media enable people to communicate *asynchronously*. That is, a person can read an e-mail when it is convenient, not when the writer sent it.

- *Electronic communication is digital.* Group members can store and revise comments and drafts, incorporating them as the document develops.

Guidelines

Critiquing a Colleague's Work

▶ **Start with a positive comment.** Even if the work is weak, say "You've obviously put a lot of work into this, Joanne. Thanks." Or, "This is a really good start. Thanks, Joanne."

▶ **Discuss the larger issues first.** Begin with the big issues, such as organization, development, logic, design, and graphics. Then work on smaller issues, such as paragraph development, sentence-level matters, and word choice. Leave editing and proofreading until the end of the process.

▶ **Talk about the document, not the writer.**

RUDE   You don't explain clearly why this criterion is relevant.

BETTER   I'm having trouble understanding how this criterion relates to the topic.

Your goal is to improve the quality of the document you will submit, not to evaluate the writer or the draft. Offer constructive suggestions.

RUDE   Why didn't you include the price comparisons here like you said you would?

BETTER   I wonder if the report would be stronger if we included the price comparisons here.

In the better version, the speaker focuses on the goal—to create an effective report—rather than on the writer's draft. Also, the speaker qualifies his recommendation by saying "I wonder if. . . ." This approach sounds constructive rather than boastful or annoyed.

Using the Comment, Revision, and Highlighting Features of a Word Processor

Word processors offer three powerful features you will find useful in collaborative work:

- The *comment feature* lets a reader add electronic comments to a writer's file.

- The *revision feature* lets readers mark up a text by deleting, revising, and adding words while allowing the writer of the text to keep track of who suggested which changes.

- The *highlighting feature* lets a reader use one of about a dozen "highlighting pens" to call the writer's attention to a particular passage.

TECH TIP

How to Use the Review Tab

When collaborating with others, you can distribute your document to readers electronically so that they can add comments, revise text, and highlight text. You can then review their comments, keep track of who made which suggested changes, compare two versions, and decide whether to accept or decline their changes without ever having to print your document. You can use the **Review** tab to electronically review a document or to revise a document that has already been commented on by readers.

You can access the **Comments**, **Tracking**, **Changes**, and **Compare** groups on the **Review** tab.

1. To **electronically review** a document, highlight relevant text and do the following:

    Select the **New Comment** button in the **Comments** group to write comments in a bubble in the margin.

    Select the **Track Changes** button to distinguish between revised text and original text.

    On the **Home** tab in the **Font** group, select the **Text Highlight** button to emphasize a particular passage.

   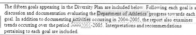
   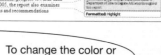

    To change the color or design of comment bubbles or markup, select the **Track Changes** button in the **Tracking** group, then select **Change Tracking Options**. The **Track Changes Options** dialog box will appear.

2. To **revise a document** that has already been commented on by reviewers, you can do the following:

   Use the **Tracking** group to change how the document is **displayed**.

   Select buttons in the **Changes** group to see the **previous** or **next** comment or to **accept** or **reject** a change.

   Select the **Reviewing Pane** button to review all comments and changes.

   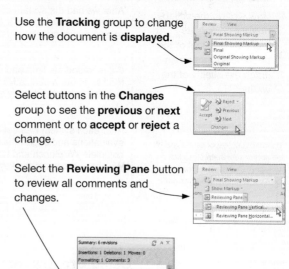

   KEYWORDS: review tab, comments group, tracking group, changes group, compare group

INTERACTIVE SAMPLE DOCUMENT
Critiquing a Draft Clearly and Diplomatically

This is an excerpt from the methods section of a report about computer servers. In this section, the writer is explaining the tasks he performed in analyzing different servers. In a later section, he explains what he learned from the analysis. The comments in the balloons were inserted into the document by the author's colleague.

The questions in the margin ask you to think about techniques for critiquing (as outlined on page 68). E-mail your responses to yourself and/or your instructor on TechComm Web.

1. What is the tone of the comments? How can they be improved?

2. How well does the collaborator address the larger issues?

3. How well does the collaborator address the writing, not the writer?

4. How well do the collaborator's comments focus on the goal of the document, rather than judge the quality of the writing?

On TechComm Web

To e-mail your responses to yourself and/or your instructor, click on Interactive Sample Documents for Ch. 4 on <bedfordstmartins.com/techcomm>.

The first task of the on-site evaluations was to set up and configure each server. We noted the relative complexity of setting up each system to our network.

> **Comment:** Huh? What exactly does this mean?

After we had the system configured, we performed a set of routine maintenance tasks: add a new memory module, swap a hard drive, swap a power supply, and perform system diagnostics.

> **Comment:** Okay, good. Maybe we should explain why we chose these tests.

We recorded the time and relative difficulty of each task. Also, we tried to gather a qualitative feeling for how much effort would be involved in the day-to-day maintenance of the systems.

> **Comment:** What kind of scale are you using? If we don't explain it, it's basically useless.

> **Comment:** Same question as above.

After each system was set up, we completed the maintenance evaluations and began the benchmark testing. We ran the complete WinBench and NetBench test suites on each system. We chose several of the key factors from these tests for comparison.

> **Comment:** Will readers know these are the right tests? Should we explain?

Using Groupware

On TechComm Web

For a tutorial from Microsoft on using Windows Meeting Space, its collaboration tool, click on Links Library for Ch. 4 on <bedfordstmartins.com/techcomm>.

Groupware is software that lets people at the same or different locations plan, draft, revise, and track a document. You may already be familiar with groupware programs such as Lotus Notes or Microsoft Meeting Space. Manufacturers of office suites such as Microsoft and Corel are putting more and more collaboration features in their products.

Team members at different locations can perform seven important collaborative activities:

- *Share files.* Team members can post files to a document library, enabling other team members to view them or download them.

- *Carry out asynchronous discussions.* Team members can carry out discussions by posting comments to a discussion list. All team members can read and download the posts at their convenience.

- *Carry out synchronous discussions.* Using instant messaging, team members can trade text messages in real time.

- *Comment on documents.* Team members can attach comments to files without actually changing the text.

- *Distribute announcements.* Team members can post announcements, such as reminders about deadlines or schedule revisions.

- *Create automated change notifications.* Team members can sign up to be notified by e-mail when a document has been changed.

- *Draw on whiteboards.* Whiteboard software lets people at different locations draw on the screen as if they were all in a room with a whiteboard. Anything drawn on one screen is displayed immediately on every screen. The image can be printed or saved as a file. Figure 4.5 shows a whiteboard screen.

USING VIDEOCONFERENCING TECHNOLOGY

Videoconferencing technology allows two or more people at different locations to see and hear each other, as well as exchange documents, share data

Figure 4.6   A Videoconference on Skype

A camera mounted on top of a computer monitor or a dedicated videoconferencing unit sends a video image from one group of participants to another. Most professional videoconferencing systems let participants display additional "windows" on the monitor.
Source: Skype, 2005 <http://share.skype.com/sites/en/2005/12/skype_20_beta_free_video_calli.html>.

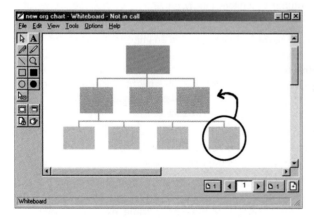

Figure 4.5   A Whiteboard Screen

All the people participating in the whiteboard session see the same screen. Whenever anyone changes anything on his or her screen, all participants see the change on their screens.

on computer displays, and use whiteboards. To carry out a videoconference, one person at each location must have a computer with a Webcam, Internet access, and videoconferencing software. Systems range from simple and inexpensive, such as the Internet-based Skype software, to large, dedicated ones that require extensive electronics, including cameras, servers, and a fiber-optic network or high-speed telephone line. Figure 4.6 on page 71 shows a videoconference.

By reducing the time and costs associated with participants meeting in the same physical location, videoconferencing is increasingly being used in

Guidelines

Participating in a Videoconference

Follow these six suggestions for participating effectively in a videoconference.

▶ **Practice using videoconferencing technology.** For many people, being on camera is uncomfortable, especially the first time. Before participating in a high-stakes videoconference, become accustomed to the camera by participating in a few informal videoconferences.

▶ **Arrange for a person who is experienced with the videoconferencing software to be at each site.** Participants can quickly become impatient or lose interest when someone is fumbling to make the technology work. Each site should have a person who can set up the equipment and troubleshoot if problems arise.

▶ **Organize the room to encourage participation.** If there is more than one person at the site, arrange the chairs so that they face the monitor and camera. Each person should be near a microphone. Before beginning the conference, check that each location has adequate audio and video equipment, as well as access to other relevant technology such as computer monitors. Finally, remember to introduce everyone in the room, even those off camera, to everyone participating in the conference.

▶ **Make eye contact with the camera.** Eye contact is an important element of establishing your professional persona. The physical setup of some videoconferencing technology means you will likely spend most of your time looking at your monitor and not directly into the camera. However, this might give your viewers the impression that you are avoiding eye contact. Make a conscious effort periodically to look directly into the camera when speaking.

▶ **Dress as you would for a face-to-face meeting.** Wearing inappropriate clothing will distract participants and damage your credibility. Avoid brightly colored clothing or clothing that closely matches the color of your skin or hair.

▶ **Minimize distracting noises and movements.** Sensitive microphones can magnify the sound of shuffling papers, fingers tapping on tables, and whispering. Likewise, depending on your position in the picture frame, excessive movements can be distracting.

education, medicine, and business, as well as by the general public. Global businesses, for example, save money on international travel by bringing employees and clients together for videoconferences instead of face-to-face meetings. In addition, more and more people are using this technology to telecommute (work from home).

Before arranging a videoconference, consider the participants' needs and the purpose of your meeting. For example, unless the participants need to see one another or use collaboration features such as whiteboards or file sharing, a teleconference with audio only will most likely meet your needs.

GENDER AND COLLABORATION

Effective collaboration involves two related challenges: maintaining the group as a productive, friendly working unit and accomplishing the task. Scholars of gender and collaboration see these two challenges as representing the feminine and the masculine perspectives.

This discussion should begin with a qualifier: in discussing gender, we are generalizing. The differences in behavior between two men or between two women are likely to be greater than the difference between men and women in general.

The differences in how the sexes communicate and work in groups have been traced to every culture's traditional family structure. As the primary caregivers, women have learned to value nurturing, connection, growth, and cooperation. As the primary breadwinners, men have learned to value separateness, competition, debate, and even conflict (Chodorow, 1978).

For decades, scholars have studied the speech differences between women and men. Women tend to use more qualifiers and "tag" questions, such as "Don't you think?" (Tannen, 1990). Some scholars, however, suggest that women might be using these patterns because it is expected of them and that they use them mainly in groups that include men (McMillan, Clifton, McGrath, & Gale, 1977). Many experts caution against using qualifiers and tag questions, which can suggest subservience and powerlessness.

In collaborative groups, women appear to value consensus and relationships, to show more empathy, and to demonstrate superior listening skills (Borisoff & Merrill, 1987). Women talk more about topics unrelated to the task (Duin, Jorn, & DeBower, 1991), but this talk is central to maintaining group coherence. Men appear to be more competitive and more likely to assume leadership roles. Scholars of gender recommend that all professionals strive to achieve an androgynous mix of the skills and aptitudes commonly associated with both women and men.

CULTURE AND COLLABORATION

Most collaborative groups in industry and in the classroom include people from other cultures. The challenge for all group members is to understand the ways in which cultural differences can affect group behavior. People from other cultures

- might find it difficult to assert themselves in collaborative groups
- might be unwilling to respond with a definite "no"
- might be reluctant to admit when they are confused or to ask for clarification
- might avoid criticizing others
- might avoid initiating new tasks or performing creatively

► In This Book
For more about multicultural issues, see Ch. 5, p. 90.

Even the most benign gesture of friendship on the part of a U.S. student can cause confusion. If a U.S. student casually asks a Japanese student about her major and the courses she is taking, the Japanese student might find the question too personal, but she might consider it perfectly appropriate to talk about her family and her religious beliefs (Lustig & Koester, 2006). Therefore, you should remain open to encounters with people from other cultures without jumping to conclusions about what their actions might or might not mean.

Writer's Checklist

In managing your project, did you

- ☐ break down a large project into several smaller tasks? (p. 60)
- ☐ plan your project? (p. 60)
- ☐ create and maintain an accurate schedule? (p. 60)
- ☐ put your decisions in writing? (p. 60)
- ☐ monitor the project? (p. 60)
- ☐ distribute and act on information quickly? (p. 60)
- ☐ act flexibly regarding schedule and responsibilities? (p. 60)

In your first group meeting, did you

- ☐ define the group's task? (p. 62)
- ☐ choose a group leader? (p. 62)
- ☐ define tasks for each group member? (p. 62)
- ☐ establish working procedures? (p. 62)
- ☐ establish a procedure for resolving conflict? (p. 62)
- ☐ create a style sheet? (p. 62)
- ☐ establish a work schedule? (p. 62)
- ☐ create evaluation materials? (p. 62)

To conduct efficient face-to-face meetings, do you

- ☐ arrive on time? (p. 65)
- ☐ stick to an agenda? (p. 65)
- ☐ make sure that a group member records important decisions made at the meeting? (p. 65)
- ☐ make sure that a group member summarizes your accomplishments and that every member understands what his or her assignment is? (p. 65)

To communicate diplomatically, do you

- ☐ listen carefully? (p. 67)
- ☐ let the speaker finish? (p. 67)
- ☐ let others talk? (p. 67)
- ☐ avoid personal remarks and insults? (p. 67)
- ☐ avoid overstating your position? (p. 67)
- ☐ avoid getting emotionally attached to your own ideas? (p. 67)
- ☐ ask pertinent questions? (p. 67)
- ☐ pay attention to body language? (p. 67)

In critiquing a group member's draft, do you

- ☐ start with a positive comment? (p. 68)
- ☐ discuss the larger issues first? (p. 68)
- ☐ talk about the writing, not the writer? (p. 68)
- ☐ focus on the group's document, not on the group member's draft? (p. 68)

If appropriate, do you

- ☐ use the comment, revision, and highlighting features of a word processor? (p. 68)
- ☐ use groupware? (p. 70)

In participating in a videoconference, did you

- ☐ practice using videoconferencing technology? (p. 72)
- ☐ arrange for a person experienced with the videoconferencing software to be at each site? (p. 72)
- ☐ organize the room to encourage participation? (p. 72)
- ☐ make eye contact with the camera? (p. 72)
- ☐ dress as you would for a face-to-face meeting? (p. 72)
- ☐ minimize distracting noises and movements? (p. 72)

Exercises

In This Book For more about memos, see Ch. 14, p. 377.

1. Experiment with the comment, revision, and highlighting features of your word processor. Using online help if necessary, learn how to make, revise, and delete comments; make, undo, accept, and reject revisions; and add and delete highlights.

2. **INTERNET EXERCISE** Using a search engine, find free videoconferencing software on the Internet. Download the software, install it on your computer at home, and learn how to use it.

3. You have probably had a lot of experience working in collaborative teams in previous courses or on the job. Brainstorm for five minutes, listing some of your best and worst experiences participating in collaborative teams. Choose one positive experience and one negative experience. Think about why the positive experience went well. Was there a technique that a team member used that accounted for the positive experience? Think about why the negative experience went poorly. Was there a technique or action that accounted for the negative experience? How might the negative experience have been prevented or fixed? Be prepared to share your responses with the class.

4. **INTERNET EXERCISE** Your college or university wishes to update its Web site to include a section called "For Prospective International Students." Along with members of your group, first determine whether your school already has information of particular interest to prospective international students. If it does, write a memo to your instructor describing and evaluating the information. Is it accurate? Comprehensive? Clear? Useful? What kinds of information should be added to the site to make it more effective?

If the school's site does not have this information, perform the following two tasks:

- *Plan.* What kind of information should it include? Does some of this information already exist, or does it all have to be created from scratch? For example, can you create a link to information on how to obtain a student visa, or does this information not exist on the Web? Write an outline of the main topics that should be covered.

- *Draft.* Write the following sections: "Where to Live on or near Campus," "Social Activities on or near Campus," and "If English Is Not Your Native Language." What graphics could you include? Are they already available? What other sites should you link to for these three sections?

In a memo, present your suggestions to your instructor.

Case 4: Handling Interpersonal Conflict

▶ **In This Book** For more about claims and persuasion, see Ch. 8. For more about memos, see Ch. 14, p. 377.

Background

Your company, Green Flag Solutions, provides a wide range of e-commerce and Web site–development solutions to the motor-sports industry. Brooks, a company offering specialized automotive parts to racing teams, has sent out a request for proposals to develop an e-catalog of its products. Colby Larson, Green Flag Solutions' Vice President of Development, has assigned you to an interdisciplinary team responsible for responding to this request. The other members of the team are Allison and Ken. Allison is a software engineer; Ken is a customer sales representative; you are a Web designer.

At your first group meeting, you choose Allison as the team leader. As the company's top software engineer, she has had a lot of experience working collaboratively and is happy to take on the task of supervising your team's work. The first meeting, to discuss the proposal, is scheduled for 11 A.M. Monday in the company's conference room.

It is 11:15 Monday, and Ken has not arrived for the meeting. Neither Allison nor you have heard from him. At 11:30, you and Allison decide to phone Ken on his cell phone. There is no answer.

You and Allison are angry that Ken hasn't arrived or left a message. The two of you are unwilling to start work on the project without him. You decide to cancel the meeting. Allison says that she will call him later that afternoon.

At about 3 P.M., you get a call from Allison. She received a phone message from Ken (Document 4.1) sent to her at 10:50 A.M. She just spoke with Ken, who has agreed to meet the next day at 3 P.M. in the conference room. Is that okay with you? Allison says that Ken has agreed to bring to the meeting marketing information on companies that might be bidding against Green Flag Solutions. She asks you to bring a summary of the e-catalog requirements the team's proposal must address. You agree and write the time in your appointment book.

The next day, at 3:15 P.M., Ken rushes into the room. "Sorry I'm late," he says with a smile. You and Allison give him a cold look. Allison begins the discussion.

"Okay, we each agreed to bring information to the meeting today. Ken, what have you got?"

"That was for today? I'm really sorry. I just didn't get to it. Don't we already have something similar from the, um, Lindt Motors proposal we sent off earlier this year?"

Allison stares at Ken for a second or two and turns to you. You read your summary of e-catalog requirements. Then Allison outlines a possible strategy for meeting the client's needs. You and Allison agree that the team needs some rough cost estimates for the proposed solution. Allison asks Ken to bring the cost estimates to the next meeting. While the group sets a time for the next meeting and decides on an agenda, Ken answers two phone calls on his cell phone. When the meeting concludes, Ken quickly leaves with his cell phone to his ear. At 5:15, Allison sends an e-mail reminder (Document 4.2) to both of you.

At the next meeting, Allison and you are left waiting for Ken again. After 15 minutes, Allison decides to check her e-mail. She finds that Ken sent her an e-mail message (Document 4.3) just before midnight the previous night.

"I'm not happy with what I see developing with Ken," she says. "We're going to be slowed down if he doesn't come to the meetings or prepare. I'm tempted to send him an e-mail right now telling him to get with the program. Do you think we should?"

"Let's take a few hours to cool down and think about what's happening before we do anything," you reply. "I'll send you an e-mail when I get back from lunch."

Your Assignment

1. How should you respond to Allison? Should you merely hope that Ken starts to participate more responsibly? Is there some way to delegate tasks that will motivate Ken to participate more actively? Should you and Allison go ahead with the project, letting Ken participate when he chooses to? Should Allison talk with him? Should both of you talk with him together? Write Allison an e-mail suggesting how to address the conflict.

2. Ken doesn't respond well to your latest communication, and you and Allison decide to discuss the matter with Colby Larson. What should you say to her? How should you prepare, and what sort of documentation should you collect? How will you support your claims? In a memo to Colby, explain the situation and request her advice in resolving the team's conflict.

Document 4.1
Message Left by Ken

"Hey, Allison, I'm busy with Michael Glenn at Racing Solutions. He seems real interested in talking about our e-commerce services, especially our work for Blanchard Custom Wheels. Sorry I can't make it today. Talk to you when I'm back in the office."

Document 4.2
Allison's E-mail Reminder

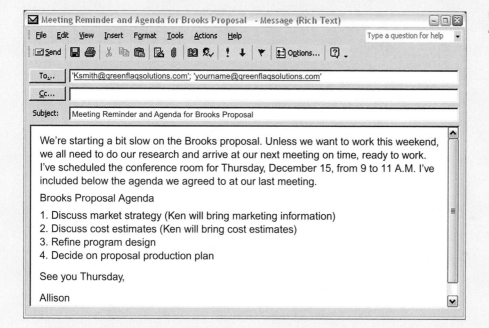

Meeting Reminder and Agenda for Brooks Proposal - Message (Rich Text)

File   Edit   View   Insert   Format   Tools   Actions   Help   Type a question for help

Send

To...   'Ksmith@greenflagsolutions.com'; 'yourname@greenflagsolutions.com'

Cc...

Subject: Meeting Reminder and Agenda for Brooks Proposal

We're starting a bit slow on the Brooks proposal. Unless we want to work this weekend, we all need to do our research and arrive at our next meeting on time, ready to work. I've scheduled the conference room for Thursday, December 15, from 9 to 11 A.M. I've included below the agenda we agreed to at our last meeting.

Brooks Proposal Agenda

1. Discuss market strategy (Ken will bring marketing information)
2. Discuss cost estimates (Ken will bring cost estimates)
3. Refine program design
4. Decide on proposal production plan

See you Thursday,

Allison

Document 4.3
Ken's E-mail Reply

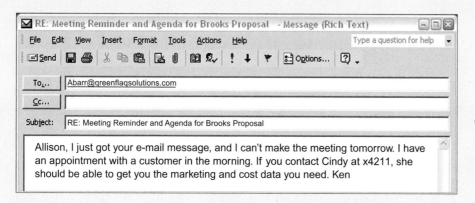

RE: Meeting Reminder and Agenda for Brooks Proposal - Message (Rich Text)

File   Edit   View   Insert   Format   Tools   Actions   Help   Type a question for help

Send

To...   Abarr@greenflagsolutions.com

Cc...

Subject: RE: Meeting Reminder and Agenda for Brooks Proposal

Allison, I just got your e-mail message, and I can't make the meeting tomorrow. I have an appointment with a customer in the morning. If you contact Cindy at x4211, she should be able to get you the marketing and cost data you need. Ken

On TechComm Web

For digital versions of case documents, click on Downloadable Case Documents on <bedfordstmartins.com/techcomm>.

PART 2 Planning the Document

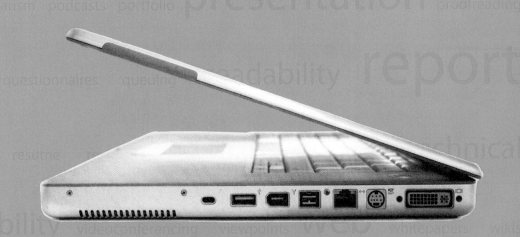

Analyzing Your Audience and Purpose

**Determining the Important
Characteristics of Your Audience** 81

Who Are Your Readers? 82

Why Is Your Audience Reading Your
Document? 83

What Are Your Readers' Attitudes and
Expectations? 84

How Will Your Readers Use Your
Document? 85

**Techniques for Learning About Your
Audience** 86

Tallying What You Already Know and
What You Don't Know About Your
Audience 86

Interviewing People 86

Searching for Information on the
Internet 86

Reading Documents Your Readers
Have Written 88

**Applying What You Have Learned
About Your Audience** 88

Communicating Across Cultures 90

Understanding the Cultural Variables
"On the Surface" 92

Understanding the Cultural Variables
"Beneath the Surface" 93

Considering Cultural Variables as You
Write 95

Using Graphics and Design for
Multicultural Readers 99

Using an Audience Profile Sheet 102

Writing for Multiple Audiences 103

Determining Your Purpose 103

Gaining Management's Approval 104

**Revising Information for a New
Audience and Purpose** 105

Source: Monster.com, 2008 <www.monster.com>.

In the World . . .

This home page of the jobs Web site Monster.com shows a good understanding of the site's audience and purpose. The photograph of a young man who has not yet completed his transition to the culture of the working world cleverly reflects the demographics of a typical user of the site, as well as that user's purpose: to get a good job. The menu items at the top of the screen accommodate the needs of the site's two main groups of users: people looking for jobs and hiring officers looking for employees.

The key concept in technical communication is that audience and purpose determine everything about how you communicate on the job. Nurses need to communicate information to both doctors and patients. They use different language with these two audiences and have different goals in relaying information to them. Sales managers need to communicate information about their products to potential clients. They communicate the same information differently to other sales representatives whom they're training to work with them. To create effective technical communication, you must consider your different audiences and purposes and present information in different ways.

What can go wrong when you don't analyze your audience? McDonald's found out when it printed take-out bags decorated with flags from around the world. Among the flags was that of Saudi Arabia, which contains excerpts from the Koran. This was extremely offensive to the Saudis, who considered it sacrilegious to throw out the bags because they contained scripture. Sales went way down.

Understanding your audience and purpose will help you meet your readers' needs—and your own. Audience and purpose are not unique to technical communication. When a classified ad describes a job, for example, audience and purpose are clear:

AUDIENCE	prospective applicants
PURPOSE	to describe the job opening and motivate qualified persons to apply

Once you have identified the two basic elements of your writing situation, you must analyze each of them before deciding what to say and how to say it.

Throughout this chapter, I will refer to your *reader* and your *document*. But all of the information refers as well to oral presentations, which are the subject of Chapter 21.

DETERMINING THE IMPORTANT CHARACTERISTICS OF YOUR AUDIENCE

When you analyze your audience, you are trying to learn about their technical background and knowledge, their reasons for reading or listening to you, their attitudes and preferences, and how they will use the information.

Who Are Your Readers?

For each of your most important readers, consider six factors:

- *The reader's education.* Think not only about the person's degree but also about when the person earned the degree. A civil engineer who earned a BS in 1989 has a much different background from a person who earned the same degree in 2009. Also consider formal and informal course work the person has completed while on the job.

  Knowing your reader's educational background helps you determine how much supporting material to provide, what level of vocabulary to use, what kind of sentence structure and length to use, what types of graphics to include, and whether to provide such formal elements as a glossary or an executive summary.

- *The reader's professional experience.* A nurse with a decade of experience might have represented her hospital on a community committee to encourage citizens to give blood and also might have contributed to the planning for the hospital's new delivery room. In short, her range of experience might have provided several areas of competence or expertise that you need to consider as you plan the document's content and style.

- *The reader's job responsibility.* Consider the reader's major job responsibility and how your document will help him or her carry it out. For example, if you are writing a feasibility study on ways to cool the air for a new office building and you know that your reader, an upper-level manager, has to worry about utility costs, you should explain how you are estimating future utility costs.

- *The reader's personal characteristics.* The reader's age might suggest how he or she will read and interpret your document. A senior manager at age 60 is probably less interested in tomorrow's technology than a 30-year-old manager is. Does your reader have any other personal characteristics you should consider, such as impaired vision, that would affect the way you write and design your document?

- *The reader's personal preferences.* One person might hate to see the first-person pronoun *I* in technical documents. Another might find the word *interface* distracting when the writer isn't discussing computers. Try to accommodate as many of your reader's preferences as you can.

- *The reader's cultural characteristics.* Knowing your reader's cultural characteristics can help you appeal to his or her interests and avoid being confusing or offensive. As discussed later in this chapter (page 92), cultural characteristics can affect virtually every aspect of a reader's comprehension of a document and perception of the writer.

Why Is Your Audience Reading Your Document?

For each of your most important readers, consider why he or she is reading your document. Some communicators find it helpful to classify readers into categories—such as primary, secondary, and tertiary—each of which identifies a reader's distance from the writer. Here are some common descriptions of three categories of readers:

- A *primary audience* consists of people close to the writer who use the document in carrying out their jobs. For example, they might include the writer's team members, who assisted in conducting an analysis of a new server configuration for the Information Technology Department; the writer's supervisor, who reads it to decide whether to authorize its main recommendation to adopt the new configuration; an executive, who reads it to determine how high a rank the server project should have on the company's list of projects to fund; and a business analyst, who reads it in determining how the organization can pay for it.

- A *secondary audience* consists of people more distant from the writer who need to stay aware of developments in the organization but who will not directly act on or respond to the document. Examples include managers of other departments who are not directly involved in the project but who need to be aware of its broad outlines and representatives of the Marketing Department or Legal Department, who need to check that the document conforms to the company's standards and practices, as well as to relevant legal standards, such as antidiscrimination or intellectual-property laws.

- A *tertiary audience* consists of people even farther removed from the writer who might take an interest in the subject of the document. Examples include interest groups, such as environmental groups or other advocacy organizations; local, state, and federal government officials; and, if the report is made public, the general public. Even if the report is not intended to be distributed outside the organization, given today's climate of information access and the ease with which documents can be distributed, chances are good that it will be published.

Regardless of whether you classify your readers using a scheme such as this, think hard about why the most important audience members will be reading your document. Don't be content to list only one purpose. Your direct supervisor, for example, might have several purposes that you need to keep in mind:

- to learn what you have accomplished in the project
- to determine whether to approve any recommendations you present
- to determine whether to assign you to a follow-up team that will work on the next stage of the project
- to determine how to evaluate your job performance next month

On TechComm Web

For more about audience analysis, see Writing Guidelines for Engineering and Science Students. Click on Links Library for Ch. 5 on <bedfordstmartins.com/techcomm>.

You will use all of this information about your audience later as you determine how to write your document or plan your presentation. Make sure to write it down so that you can refer to it later.

What Are Your Readers' Attitudes and Expectations?

In thinking about the attitudes and expectations of each of your most important readers, consider these three factors:

- *Your reader's attitude toward you.* Most people will like you if you are hardworking, intelligent, and cooperative. Some won't. If a reader's animosity toward you is irrational or unrelated to the current project, try to earn that person's respect and trust by meeting him or her on some neutral ground, perhaps by discussing other, less volatile projects or some shared interest, such as gardening, skiing, or science-fiction novels.

- *Your reader's attitude toward the subject.* If possible, discuss the subject thoroughly with your reader to determine whether he or she is positive, neutral, or negative toward it. Here are some basic strategies for responding to different attitudes.

If . . .	Try this . . .
Your reader is neutral or positively inclined toward your subject	Write the document so that it responds to the reader's needs; make sure that vocabulary, level of detail, organization, and style are appropriate.
Your reader is hostile to the subject or your approach to it	• Find out what the objections are, then answer them directly. Explain why the objections are not valid or are less important than the benefits. • Organize the document so that your recommendation follows your explanation of the benefits. This strategy encourages the hostile reader to understand your argument rather than to reject it out of hand. • Avoid describing the subject as a dispute. Seek areas of agreement and concede points. Avoid trying to persuade readers overtly; people don't like to be persuaded, because it threatens their egos. Instead, suggest that some new facts need to be considered. People are more likely to change their minds when they realize this.
Your reader was instrumental in creating the policy or procedure that you are arguing is ineffective	In discussing the present system's shortcomings, be especially careful if you risk offending one of your readers. When you address such an audience, don't write "The present system for logging customer orders is completely ineffective." Instead, write "While the present system has worked well for many years, new developments in electronic processing of orders might enable us to improve logging speed and reduce errors substantially."

- *Your reader's expectations about the document.* Think about how your reader expects to see the information treated in terms of scope, organizational pattern, and amount of detail. Consider, too, the application. If your reader expects to see the information presented as a memo, use a memo unless some other format would clearly work better.

How Will Your Readers Use Your Document?

In thinking about how each of your most important readers will use your document, consider the following three factors:

- *The way your reader will read your document.* Will he or she
  — file it?
  — skim it?
  — read only a portion of it?
  — study it carefully?
  — modify it and submit it to another reader?
  — try to implement recommendations?
  — use it to perform a test or carry out a procedure?
  — use it as a source document for another document?

  If only 1 of your 15 readers will study the document for detailed information, you don't want the other 14 people to have to wade through that information. Therefore, put it in an appendix. If you know that your reader wants to use your status report as raw material for a report targeted to a higher-level reader, try to write it so that it requires little rewriting. Use the reader's own writing style and give the reader the electronic file so that your report can be merged with the new document without requiring rekeying.

- *Your reader's reading skill.* Consider whether you should be writing at all, or whether it would be better to do an oral presentation or use computer-based training. If you decide to write, consider whether your reader can understand how to use the type of document you have selected, handle the level of detail you will present, and understand your graphics, sentence structure, and vocabulary.

- *The physical environment in which your reader will read your document.* Often, technical documents are formatted in a special way or constructed of special materials to improve their effectiveness. Documents used in poorly lit places might be printed in larger-than-normal type. Some documents might be used on ships, on aircraft, or in garages, where they might be exposed to water, wind, or grease. You might have to use special waterproof bindings, oil-resistant or laminated paper, coded colors, or unusual-size paper.

▷ **In This Book**

For more about designing a document for use in different environments, see Ch. 11, p. 258.

TECHNIQUES FOR LEARNING ABOUT YOUR AUDIENCE

To learn about your audience, figure out what you already know and what you don't know, interview people, learn about them by searching on the Internet, and read documents they have written.

Tallying What You Already Know and What You Don't Know About Your Audience

Start by asking yourself what you already know about your most important readers: their demographic factors, such as age, education, and job responsibilities; their expectations and attitudes toward you and the subject; and the ways they will use your document. List the important factors you don't know. That is where you will concentrate your energy.

Interviewing People

For each of your most important readers, make a list of people who you think have known the reader and his or her work the longest or who are closest to the reader on the job. These people might include those who joined the organization at about the same time your reader did, people who work in the same department as your reader, and people in other organizations who have collaborated with your reader.

    Prepare a few interview questions that are likely to elicit information about your reader and his or her preferences and needs. Then conduct informal interviews in person or on the phone.

▶ **In This Book**
For a discussion of interviewing, see Ch. 6, p. 136.

Searching for Information on the Internet

The Internet is your best source of information about people you don't know personally. Let's say you work for a company that offers customized training courses, and you have been invited to make a sales presentation about your company's services to the Vice President of Human Resources at Micron Technology. You learn that this person is Pat Otte. You have never heard of Pat Otte; you don't even know whether Pat is a man or a woman.

    Start by searching for "Pat Otte" on the Internet using a search engine. First, make sure you find the right Pat Otte. You are not interested in the award-winning eight-ball player from Jefferson County, Wisconsin; the Site Director for the Washington, D.C., metropolitan area; or the 16-year-old Led Zeppelin fan from Bristol, England. You are looking for the Pat Otte who is listed on the Micron Technology site, as shown in Figure 5.1.

Pat Otte

Vice President of Human Resources

Pat Otte is Vice President of Human Resources. Mr. Otte joined Micron in 1987 and has served in various positions of increasing responsibility, including Production Manager in several of Micron's fabrication facilities, Operations Manager for Micron Technology Italia S.r.l. and, most recently, Site Director for Micron's 300mm fabrication facility in Manassas, Virginia. Mr. Otte holds a Bachelor of Science degree from St. Paul Bible College in Minneapolis, Minnesota.

Figure 5.1   Corporate Profile of an Executive
Source: Micron Technology, Inc., 2008 <www.micron.com/about/executives/officers/otte>.

From just this entry, you can learn quite a few things about Pat Otte:

- He is a man.
- He has more than 20 years of experience with Micron.
- Although he is now the Vice President of Human Resources, based in the company's Boise, Idaho, headquarters, he has considerable technical background at Micron, having been Production Manager at several of the company's fabrication plants.
- He worked for a time at a Micron facility in Italy and at one in Manassas, Virginia.

From Zoom Information, Inc. (<www.zoominfo.com>), you learn that Mr. Otte has a master's degree from Boise State University. From a news item from Virginia Tech, you learn that he represented Micron when the company donated $750,000 to fund that university's Micron Technology Semiconductor Processing Laboratory. From Old Dominion University, you learn that he represented the company in discussions with the engineering college at that university to strengthen ties between the two organizations. From Invest in Italy, you learn that in 1996 he attended the "Log On to Italian Opportunities in IT" workshop on Italian investment opportunities in information technology. You could learn more from other business sites, and Mr. Otte even has a page on Facebook.

Based on 10 minutes of research, you know three important things about Pat Otte:

- He is a talented, hardworking executive with a long track record at Micron.

- He is very interested in higher education and its relationship to his industry.
- He has international work experience.

How might you use this information in planning your presentation? I can think of four things to consider:

- Without a doubt, he is busy and influential. Prepare and rehearse the presentation carefully.
- Because of his technical knowledge of the industry, you can discuss your technical courses. He will understand you.
- He already knows why industry relies on educated workers. Don't go on and on about that topic. But because your company offers training courses, not university courses, you should anticipate that he might question whether training is as effective as education.
- Because he has lived and worked overseas, he probably understands the value of knowing more than one language. Be sure not to overlook your company's language courses in your presentation.

Reading Documents Your Readers Have Written

Try to find some documents that each of your most important readers has written. These can tell you a lot about what the reader likes to see in a document, including everything from design, organization, and development to style, vocabulary, and level of detail.

APPLYING WHAT YOU HAVE LEARNED ABOUT YOUR AUDIENCE

As we saw in the preceding section, you can use what you know about your audience to tailor your communication to their needs and preferences. If your most important reader does not understand the details of DRAM technology, you cannot use concepts and vocabulary related to that field. If she always includes a one-page summary at the beginning of her documents, consider whether that will work for you. If his paragraphs always start with a clear topic sentence, yours should, too.

Figure 5.2 on pages 89–90 shows some of the ways writers have applied what they know about their audiences in creating text for their documents. Figure 5.3 on page 91 shows how writers use verbal and visual techniques to meet the needs, interests, and attitudes of their audiences.

Figure 5.2   Using Text to Appeal to Readers' Needs, Interests, and Attitudes

About CamCamX

A 6x2 live video mixer that uses the native 4:2:2 YUV color space of video. A 2-up side by side configuration allows you to prepare a second source (QuickTime movie, still picture, camera) off-screen while the other source is live. Then, when you're ready, just slide the cross-fader to switch inputs. It's just like a DJ mixer, for video. Designed for live performances, you can also record your live video mix directly into **iMovie HD** or other QuickTime enabled camera recording applications.

Under Tiger, CamCamX also virtualizes the iSight or webcam in your MacBook/Mac so you can use all your favorite camera applications AT THE SAME TIME. Works with PhotoBooth (Tiger), Skype, Yahoo Messenger, Flash Chat-enabled web sites, DotMatrix (input or output), Qamera (input), iMovie HD, and many more. . . .

In this brief description of a video software project, the writer uses highly technical vocabulary and concepts. A reader who is thinking about downloading this software would understand this passage.

Source: Apple, Inc., 2008 <www.apple.com/downloads/macosx/video/camcamx.html>.

What about officer accountability in deploying TASER ECDs?

We have pioneered accountability with our built-in dataport microchip system which provides the exact time, date, and duration of field uses by law enforcement officers. This data objectively corroborates an officer's report of any TASER use incident. We also provide a higher level of accountability with our new TASER CAM accessory that creates an audio/visual digital MPEG 4 recording of all TASER system uses. Imagine having video of the suspect's actions as well as the officer's verbal commands whenever a TASER system is activated. It comes down to safety, effectiveness, and accountability, which no other tool of this type can match.

In this excerpt from an FAQ from Taser, a maker of stun guns, the writer is addressing high-level police officers who are responsible for ordering police equipment. The writer explains that the product provides a record of its use by officers, thus answering one question the reader might have about the controversial product.

Source: Taser International, Inc., 2008 <www.taser.com/research/Pages/LawEnforcementFAQs.aspx>.

Figure 5.2 (continued)

This fall the Foundation is co-sponsoring the first and only major scientific symposium exclusively focused on therapeutics development for PD. It will bring together top PD researchers for strategic assessment of next steps toward improved therapeutics.

The conference is just one example of what we call "funding for patient impact"—four words that get at the heart of how the Foundation goes about its business every day.

This phrase encompasses the rigorous assessment we conduct before spending a single dollar, to ensure every penny you contribute has the greatest chance to speed development of treatments that can affect patients' everyday lives. It includes the prioritization we build into our selection process, because there's no shortage of research into interesting questions about PD, but we are here to answer the crucial questions. It is shorthand for every system and safeguard we've put in place in our short history for targeting resources toward our one definition of success: better treatments and a cure for Parkinson's.

We're so grateful for the continued commitment of you, our supporters and friends, and we take our accountability to you seriously. I hope you'll browse this newsletter and read about more of the ways we're pressing forward toward the impact whose urgency is so clear to us, to you and to the millions of people whose lives are touched by Parkinson's.

Source: Michael J. Fox Foundation for Parkinson's Research, 2007 <www.michaeljfox.org/newsletters/Fall%202007%20FINAL.pdf>.

This statement, from the Michael J. Fox Foundation for Parkinson's Research newsletter, is addressed to donors and potential donors.

The purpose is to show that the organization takes its responsibilities seriously, that it is co-sponsoring a scientific conference about Parkinson's disease (PD), and that it uses a rigorous selection process in funding research to achieve its goal: better treatments and a cure for PD.

Notice that the writer concludes with a statement of appreciation to those who support the organization.

COMMUNICATING ACROSS CULTURES

Our society and our workforce are becoming increasingly diverse, both culturally and linguistically, and businesses are exporting more and more goods and services. As a result, technical communicators and technical professionals often communicate with nonnative speakers of English in the United States and abroad and with speakers of other languages who read texts translated from English into their own languages.

The economy of the United States depends on international trade. In 2006, the United States exported more than $1.4 trillion worth of goods and services (U.S. Census, 2007, p. 786). Also in 2006, direct investment abroad by U.S. companies totaled more than $2.6 trillion (U.S. Census, 2007, p. 793). In addition, the population of the United States itself is truly multicultural. Each year, the United States admits more than a million immigrants (U.S. Census, 2007, p. 8). In 2005, 12.4 percent of the U.S. population was foreign-born, and of those, 22.2 percent had entered the country since the year 2000 (U.S. Census, 2007, p. 42).

Effective communication requires an understanding of culture: the beliefs, attitudes, and values that motivate people's behavior.

Source: Netflix, Inc., 2008 <www.netflix.com/HowItWorks>.

This screen shows a good understanding of the typical Netflix user. This user, a general reader, wants to understand how the service works. The simple graphics, accompanied by brief textual comments, are clear and unintimidating. Notice that the screen clearly shows that there are two ways to get movies.

This screen from National Geographic is part of an educational unit for adults. Here the organization presents the first question in its quiz about "Going Green."

Note that the text in pale green introduces the quiz by explaining that the reader can make a difference.

Responding to the question is easy. The reader simply selects one of the two buttons.

The green color scheme reinforces the message of the educational unit.

Source: National Geographic Society, 2008 <http://green.nationalgeographic .com/environment/global-warming/quiz-going-green.html?nav=FEATURES>.

This screen from the Forums page of Linux.com appeals to the interests of its readers.

The table provides the sort of information readers want: the name and description of each forum the organization sponsors, the number of topics discussed, the number of comments ("posts") received, and when the most recent comment was posted.

Icons provide additional information about each forum.

Readers who are interested in the open-source operating system Linux are likely comfortable with this highly informative and well-organized design.

Figure 5.3   Using Verbal and Visual Techniques to Appeal to Readers' Needs, Interests, and Attitudes
Source: Linux.com, 2008 <www.linux.com/forums>.

Understanding the Cultural Variables "On the Surface"

Communicating effectively with people from another culture requires understanding a number of cultural variables that lie on the surface. You need to know, first, what language or languages to use. You also need to be aware of political, social, religious, and economic factors that can affect how readers will interpret your documents. Understanding these factors is not an exact science, but it does require that you learn as much as you can about the culture of those you are addressing.

A brief example: An American manufacturer of deodorant launched an advertising campaign in Japan in which a cute octopus applied the firm's product under each of its eight arms. But the campaign failed, because in Japan an octopus has eight *legs*, not eight arms (Bathon, 1999).

In *International Technical Communication*, Nancy L. Hoft (1995) describes seven major categories of cultural variables that lie on the surface:

- *Political.* This category includes trade issues and legal issues (for example, some countries forbid imports of certain foods or chemicals) and laws about intellectual property, product safety, and liability.

- *Economic.* In many developing countries, most people cannot afford personal computers.

- *Social.* This category covers many issues, including gender and business customs. In most Western cultures, women play a much greater role in the workplace than they do in many Middle Eastern and Asian cultures. Business customs—including forms of greeting, business dress, and gift giving—vary from culture to culture.

- *Religious.* Religious differences can affect diet, attitudes toward individual colors, styles of dress, holidays, and hours of business.

- *Educational.* In the United States, 40 million people are only marginally literate. In other cultures, that rate can be much higher or much lower. In some cultures, classroom learning with a teacher is considered the most acceptable way to study. In others, people tend to study on their own.

- *Technological.* If you sell high-tech products, you need to know whether your readers have the hardware, the software, and the technological infrastructure to use them.

- *Linguistic.* In some countries, English is taught to all children starting in grade school. In other countries, English is seen as a threat to the national language. In many cultures, the orientation of text on a page and in a book is not from left to right.

In addition to these basic differences, you need to understand dozens of other factors. For instance, the United States is the only major country that has not adopted the metric system. Americans also use periods to separate whole numbers from decimals, and commas to separate thousands from hundreds. Much of the rest of the world reverses this usage.

| UNITED STATES | 3,425.6 |
| EUROPE | 3.425,6 |

In the United States, the format for writing out and abbreviating dates is different from that of most other cultures.

UNITED STATES	March 2, 2009	3/2/09
EUROPE	2 March 2009	2/3/09
JAPAN	2009 March 2	09/3/2

These cultural variables are important in an obvious way: you can't send a fax to a person who doesn't have a fax machine. However, there is another set of cultural characteristics—those beneath the surface—that you also need to understand.

Understanding the Cultural Variables "Beneath the Surface"

Scholars of multicultural communication have identified a number of cultural variables that are less obvious than those discussed in the previous section but just as important. Table 5.1 on page 94, based on an excellent article by Tebeaux and Driskill (1999), explains six key variables and how they are reflected in technical communication.

As you consider this set of cultural variables, keep four points in mind:

- *Each variable represents a spectrum of attitudes.* Terms such as *high context* and *low context*, for instance, represent the two endpoints on a scale. Many cultures occupy a middle ground.

- *The six variables do not line up in a clear pattern.* Although Table 5.1 suggests in various places that several of the variables correlate—for example, individualistic cultures tend to see a great distance between business life and personal life—in any one culture, the six variables do not form a consistent pattern. For example, the dominant culture in the United States is highly individualistic rather than group oriented, but only about midway along the scale of attitudes toward accepting uncertainty.

- *Different organizations within the same culture can vary greatly.* For example, one software company in Germany might have a management style that does not tolerate uncertainty, whereas another software company in Germany might have a management style that tolerates a lot of uncertainty.

- *An organization's cultural attitudes are fluid, not static.* How organizations operate is determined not only by the dominant culture but also by its own people. As new people join an organization, its culture changes. The IBM of 1989 is not the IBM of 2009.

For you as a communicator, this set of variables offers no answers. Instead, it offers a set of questions. You cannot know in advance the attitudes of the people in an organization. You have to interact with them for a long time before you can reach even tentative conclusions. The value of being

Table 5.1 Cultural Variables "Beneath the Surface"

Variable	Explanation	How this variable is reflected in technical communication
Focus on individuals or groups	Some cultures, especially in the West, value individuals more than groups. The typical employee doesn't see his or her identity as being defined by the organization. Other cultures, particularly in Asia, value groups more than individuals. The typical employee sees himself or herself first as a member of the organization rather than as an individual who works there.	Communication addressed to people from individualistic cultures focuses on the writer's and reader's needs rather than on those of the two organizations. Writers use the pronoun *I* rather than *we*. Letters are addressed to the principal reader and signed by the writer. Communication addressed to people from group-oriented cultures focuses on the organization's needs by emphasizing the benefits to be gained by the two organizations through a cooperative relationship. Writers emphasize the relationship between the writer and reader rather than the specific technical details of the message. Writers use *we* rather than *I*. They might address letters "Dear Sir" and use the organization's name, not their own, in the complimentary close.
Distance between business life and private life	In some cultures, especially in the West, people separate their business lives from their private lives. When the workday ends, they are free to go home and spend their time as they wish. In other cultures, particularly in Asia, people see a much smaller distance between their business lives and their private lives. Even after the day ends, they still see themselves as employees of the organization. Cultures that value individualism tend to see a great distance between business life and private life. Cultures that are group oriented tend to see a smaller distance between business life and private life.	Communication addressed to people from cultures that see a great distance between business life and private life focuses on the technical details of the communication, with relatively little reference to personal information about the writer or the reader. Communication addressed to people from cultures that see a smaller distance between business life and private life contains much more personal information—about the reader's family and health—and more information about, for example, the weather and the seasons. The goal is to build a formal relationship between the two organizations. Both the writer and the reader are, in effect, on call after business hours and are likely to transact business during long social activities such as elaborate dinners or golf games.
Distance between ranks	In some cultures, the distance in power and authority between workers within an organization is small. This small distance is reflected in a close working relationship between supervisors and their subordinates. In other cultures, the distance in power and authority between workers within an organization is great. Supervisors do not consult with their subordinates. Subordinates use formal names and titles—"Mr. Smith," "Dr. Jones"—when addressing higher-ranking people. Cultures that focus on individualism and that separate business and private lives tend to have a smaller distance between ranks.	In cultures with a small distance between ranks, communication is generally less formal. Informal documents (e-mails and memos) are appropriate, and writers often sign their documents with their first names only. Keep in mind, however, that many people in these cultures resent inappropriate informality, such as receiving letters or e-mails addressed "Dear Jim" if they have never met the writer. In cultures with a great distance between ranks, communication is generally formal. Writers tend to use their full professional titles and to prefer formal documents (such as letters) to informal ones (such as memos and e-mails). Writers make sure their documents are addressed to the appropriate person and contain the formal design elements (such as title pages and letters of transmittal) that signal their respect for their readers.

Table 5.1 (continued)

Variable	Explanation	How this variable is reflected in technical communication
Nature of truth	Some cultures feel that truth is a universal concept. An action is either wrong or right. There are no exceptions. If facts are presented clearly and comprehensively, all reasonable readers will understand them in the same way. Other cultures think that truth is a more complex and relative concept and that reasonable people can have different perspectives on complex ethical issues.	In cultures that take a universal approach to truth, such as the United States, documents tend to be comprehensive and detailed. They spell out the details of the communication, leaving nothing to interpretation. In cultures that take a relative view of truth, documents tend to be less detailed and less conclusive. Discussions might seem vague, as if the writer is unwilling to reach a clear conclusion.
Need to spell out details	Some cultures value full, complete communication. The written text must be comprehensive, containing all the information a reader needs to understand it. These cultures are called *low context.* Other cultures value documents in which some of the details are merely implied. This implicit information is communicated through other forms of communication that draw upon the personal relationship between the reader and the writer, as well as social and business norms of the culture. These cultures are called *high context.* Low-context cultures tend to be individualistic; high-context cultures tend to be group oriented.	In low-context cultures, writers spell out all the details. Documents are like contracts in that they provide the specific information that indicates the rights and responsibilities of both the writer and the reader and explain procedures in great detail. In high-context cultures, writers tend to omit information that they consider obvious because they don't want to insult readers. For example, a manual written for people in a high-context culture might not mention that a remote control for a television set requires batteries, because everyone knows that a remote control needs a power source.
Attitudes toward uncertainty	In some cultures, people are comfortable with uncertainty. They communicate less formally and rely less on written policies. In many cases, they rely more on a clear set of guiding principles, as communicated in a code of conduct or a mission statement. In other cultures, people are uncomfortable with uncertainty. Businesses are structured formally, and they use written procedures for communicating.	In cultures that tolerate uncertainty, written communication tends to be less detailed. Oral communication is used to convey more of the information that is vital to the relationship between the writer and the reader. In cultures that value certainty, communication tends to be detailed. Policies are lengthy and specific, and forms are used extensively. Everyone knows what he or she is supposed to do, and there is a wide distance between ranks.

aware of the variables is that they can help you study the communications from people in that organization and become more aware of underlying values that affect how they will interpret your documents.

Considering Cultural Variables as You Write

The challenge of communicating effectively with a person from another culture is that you are communicating with a person, not a culture. You cannot be sure which cultures have influenced that person (Lovitt, 1999). For example, a 50-year-old Japanese-born manager for the computer manufacturer Fujitsu in Japan has been shaped by the Japanese culture, but he also has been influenced by the culture of his company and of the Japanese computer industry in general. It is also likely that he has worked outside Japan for several years and has absorbed influences from another culture.

A further complication is that when you communicate with a person from another culture, to that person *you* are from another culture, and you cannot know how much that person is trying to accommodate your cultural patterns. As Bell (1992) points out, the communication between the two of you is carried out in a third, hybrid culture. When you write to a large audience, the complications increase. A group of managers for Fujitsu represents a far more complex mix of cultural influences than one manager for Fujitsu.

No brief discussion of cultural variables can answer questions about how to write for a particular multicultural audience. You need to study your readers' culture and, as you plan the document, seek assistance from someone native to the culture who can help you avoid blunders that might confuse or offend your readers.

▶ **On TechComm Web**

For a discussion of communication practices in China, see Coggin, Coggin, and Li's "Living and Working in China: Understanding Communication Requirements." Click on Links Library for Ch. 5 on <bedfordstmartins.com/ techcomm>.

Start by reading some of the basic guides to communicating with people from other cultures, then study guides to the particular culture you are investigating. In addition, numerous Web sites provide useful guidelines that can help you write to people from another culture. Here, for instance, is an excerpt from a guide to writing letters to Japanese readers (Anderson School, 2002):

> A Japanese letter is the reverse of one in the West, in the sense that you proceed first from the general to the specific. You need to begin with the social niceties, with small talk about the weather, the holidays, or some seasonal reference. Include at least a paragraph of such material before getting to the heart of the correspondence. You may begin the business section with a phrase such as: "We are so happy that your business is becoming even more prosperous," and then state your business in a "soft" manner. Even then, do not be overly direct or assertive. Use phrases like: "I am not sure . . ."; "I wonder if . . ."; "I hope this is not too bold a request but. . . ." Also include some sort of reference to the personal, trusting relationship you have both put so much effort into, and how you desire its continuance. Your letter should end with a closing general phrase at the bottom, followed by the date. The date is given in the reverse order of dates in the West: the year, the month, and then the day.

If possible, study the documents written by people in your audience. If you don't have access to these, try to locate documents written in English by people from that culture. Figure 5.4 shows several excerpts from documents that provide useful glimpses into cultural variables.

Excerpt	Commentary
From a Japanese electronics company (Sugimoto, 2008)	
The FDK Group manufactures and markets innovative products for the global electronics industry, from materials to electronic modules to high performance batteries. To do this we have merged our original materials technology, cultivated for decades, with the latest cutting edge technology.	Notice how the writer describes his company in terms of its long history and its cutting-edge technology. In Japan, a long history suggests trustworthiness.
As we build the New FDK, we do our utmost to develop new and more effective technologies and products in order to earn high marks and total satisfaction from our customers. A significant component of this effort is new product and technology development and production innovation. . . .	He emphasizes the concept of total customer satisfaction.
In recognition of the importance of the global environment, we place environmental issues high on our list of priorities and strive for positive activity in this area throughout the entire Group.	Here he describes his company's commitment to the global environment. This focus emphasizes the Japanese concept of living in harmony with the physical environment.
This year marks the 57th anniversary of the founding of the company. I expect our business to create success for our customers by ensuring total satisfaction with our products and support. In this way The FDK Group will contribute to the growth and success of the whole electronics industry.	Again he emphasizes customer satisfaction and the long history of the company. Through the company's commitment to quality, the "whole electronics industry" will succeed.
From "Salient Features of the Indian Railways" (Indian Railways, 2008)	
India is a land of diverse culture and Indian Railways play a key role in not only meeting the transport needs of the country, but also in binding together dispersed areas and promoting national integration. Truly, Indian Railways have emerged as the sinews of the Indian economy and have reached out to bring together the great Indian family.	The statement begins by stressing the cultural value of the services offered by the Indian rail system, called "the sinews of the Indian economy." Throughout this statement, the writer stresses the role of the rail system in serving the nation's needs.
Indian Railways have been the prime movers to the nation and have the distinction of being one of the largest railway systems in the world under a single management. Railways being the more energy efficient mode of transport are ideally suited for movement of bulk commodities and for long distance travel. As compared to road transport, the railways have a number of intrinsic advantages.	The writer refers with pride to the fact that "Indian Railways have been the prime movers to the nation."
Railways are five to six times more energy efficient, four times more efficient in land use and significantly superior from the standpoints of environment impact and safety. Indian Railways, therefore, rightly occupy pride of place in the growth and development of the nation.	The writer presents an argument that railways are the most energy-efficient transportation mode. Even this technical argument ends with the statement that the "Indian Railways . . . rightly occupy pride of place in the growth and development of the nation."
	To someone from the United States, these references to the pride of the rail system might sound insincere and self-serving. To an Indian audience, with its long history of honoring service, these references are perfectly appropriate.

Figure 5.4   Passages Reflecting Cultural Variables

Excerpt	Commentary
From the head of the Patent Office in Finland (Enäjärvi, 2007)	
The National Board of Patents and Registration (NBPR) continued to develop its various functions in the year under review. These included the upgrading of the Enterprises and Corporations Line information services, further promotion of growing PCT activity, and enhancing the role of civic activities. Our successful domestic projects Innofinland, Innoschool and Innoint found a parallel in the Ideapilot project, particularly among SMEs. This project is being realized in cooperation with the World Intellectual Property Organization, WIPO, and numerous domestic interest groups. . . .	Although this Finnish manager's use of English does not sound exactly like a native speaker's, his strategy sounds very much like that used in the United States. He reports the accomplishments of his organization.
We did not succeed in reaching our results targets as well as in preceding years, owing primarily to sizable development projects and variations in consumer demand. Nevertheless, the entire personnel of the NBPR deserve warm thanks for a job well done. The positive feedback from clients, the international ISO 9001:2000 certificate granted for the PCT examination work, and the Gender Equality Award presented to the NBPR testify to the quality of our work. We also take this opportunity to thank our interest groups in both the public and private sector for their excellent cooperation.	He offers an explanation for the fact that his organization did not meet its targets. He ends on a positive note, citing successes and graciously thanking his fellow Finnish citizens for their cooperation.

Figure 5.4 (continued)

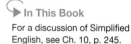

In This Book

For a discussion of Simplified English, see Ch. 10, p. 245.

Guidelines

Writing for Readers from Other Cultures

The following eight suggestions will help you communicate more effectively with multicultural readers:

▶ **Limit your vocabulary.** Every word should have only one meaning, as called for in Simplified English and in other basic-English languages.

▶ **Keep sentences short.** There is no magic number, but try for an average length of no more than 20 words.

▶ **Define abbreviations and acronyms in a glossary.** Don't assume that your readers know what a *GFI* (ground fault interrupter) is, because the abbreviation is derived from English vocabulary and word order.

▶ **Avoid jargon unless you know your readers are familiar with it.** For instance, your readers might not know what a *graphical user interface* is.

▶ **Avoid idioms and slang.** These terms are culture specific. If you tell your Japanese readers that your company plans to put on a *full-court press*, most likely they will be confused.

▶ **Use the active voice whenever possible.** The active voice is easier for nonnative speakers of English to understand than the passive voice.

▶ **In This Book**
For more about voice, see Ch. 10, p. 234.

▶ **Be careful with graphics.** The garbage-can icon on the Macintosh computer does not translate well, because garbage cans have different shapes and can be made of different materials in other countries.

▶ **Be sure someone from the culture reviews your document.** Even if you had help in planning the document, have it reviewed before you publish and distribute it.

▶ **In This Book**
For more about graphics, see Ch. 12.

Ethics Note

Meeting Your Readers' Needs Responsibly

A major theme of this chapter is that effective technical communication meets your readers' needs. What this theme means is that as you plan, draft, revise, and edit, you should always be thinking of who your readers are, why they are reading your document, and how they will read the document. For example, if your readers include many nonnative speakers of English, you need to adjust your vocabulary, sentence structure, and other textual elements so that they can understand your document easily. If your readers will be seated at computer terminals as they use your document, you should choose a page size that lets them place the document next to their terminals.

Meeting your readers' needs does *not* mean writing a misleading or inaccurate document. If your readers want you to slant the information, omit crucial data, or downplay bad news, they are asking you to act unethically. You are under no obligation to do so. For more information on ethics, see Chapter 2.

Using Graphics and Design for Multicultural Readers

One of the challenges in writing for people from another culture is that they are likely to be nonnative speakers of English. One way to overcome the language barrier is to use effective graphics and design the document effectively.

However, the use of graphics and design can differ from culture to culture. A business letter written in Australia uses different-size paper and a different format than a similar letter in the United States. An icon for a file folder in a software program made in the United States could confuse European readers, who use a different size and shape for file folders in offices (Bosley, 1999). A series of graphics arranged left to right could confuse readers from the Middle East, who read from right to left. For this reason, you should study samples of documents written by people from the culture you are addressing to learn the important differences.

▶ **In This Book**
For more about design for multicultural readers, see Ch. 11, p. 287. For more about graphics for international readers, see Ch. 12, p. 333.

INTERACTIVE SAMPLE DOCUMENT
Examining Cultural Variables in a Business Letter

These two versions of the same business letter were written by a sales manager for an American computer company. The first letter was addressed to a potential customer in the United States; the second version was addressed to a potential customer in Japan. The questions in the margin ask you to think about how the cultural variables affect the nature of the evidence, the structure of the letters, and their tone (see pages 93–99). E-mail your responses to yourself and/or your instructor on TechComm Web.

Server Solutions
Cincinnati, OH 46539

Nadine Meyer
Director of Marketing

July 3, 2009

Mr. Philip Henryson, Director of Purchasing
Allied Manufacturing
1321 Industrial Boulevard
Boise, ID 83756

Dear Mr. Henryson:

Thank you for your inquiry about our PowerServer servers. I'm happy to answer your questions.

The most popular configuration is our PowerServer 3000. This model is based on the Intel® Xeon processor, ServerSure High-End UltraLite chipset with quad-peer PCI architecture, and embedded RAID. The system comes with our InstallIt system-management CD, which lets you install the server and monitor and manage your network with a simple graphical interface. With six PCI slots, the PowerServer 3000 is equipped with redundant cooling as well as redundant power, and storage expandability to 950 GB. I'm taking the liberty of enclosing the brochure for this system to fill you in on the technical details.

The PowerServer 3000 has performed extremely well on a number of industry benchmark tests. I'm including with this letter copies of feature articles on the system from *PC World*, *InternetWeek*, and *Windows Vista Magazine*.

It would be a pleasure for me to arrange for an on-site demo at your convenience. I'll give you a call on Monday to see what dates would be best for you. In the meantime, please do not hesitate to get in touch with me directly if you have any questions about the PowerServer line.

I look forward to talking with you next week.

Sincerely,

Nadine Meyer

Nadine Meyer
Director of Marketing

Attachments:
    "PowerServer 3000 Facts at a Glance"
    "Another Winner from Server Solutions"
    "Mid-Range Servers for 2009"
    "Four New Dual-Processor Workhorses"

Mr. Kato Kirisawa, Director of Purchasing
Allied Manufacturing
3-7-32 Kita Urawa
Saitama City, Saitama Pref. 336-0002
Japan

Server Solutions
Cincinnati, OH 46539

Nadine Meyer
Director of Marketing

Dear Sir:

It is my sincere hope that you and your loved ones are healthy and enjoying the pleasures of summer. Here in the American Midwest, the warm rays of the summer sun are accompanied by the sounds of happy children playing in the neighborhood swimming pools. I trust that the same pleasant sounds greet you in Saitama City.

Your inquiry about our PowerServer 3000 suggests that your company is growing. Allied Manufacturing has earned a reputation in Japan and all of Asia for a wide range of products manufactured to the most demanding standards of quality. We are not surprised that your company requires new servers that can be expanded to provide fast service for more and more clients.

For more than 15 years, Server Solutions has had the great honor of manufacturing the finest computer servers to meet the needs of our valued customers all over the world. We use only the finest materials and most innovative techniques to ensure that our customers receive the highest-quality, uninterrupted service that they have come to expect from us.

One of my great pleasures is to talk with esteemed representatives such as yourself about how Server Solutions can help them meet their needs for the most advanced servers. I would be most gratified if our two companies could enter into an agreement that would be of mutual benefit.

Sincerely,

Nadine Meyer

Nadine Meyer
Director of Marketing

Attachments:
 "PowerServer 3000 Facts at a Glance"
 "Another Winner from Server Solutions"
 "Mid-Range Servers for 2009"
 "Four New Dual-Processor Workhorses"

2009 July 3

1. How does the difference in the salutation (the "Dear . . ." part of the letter) reflect a cultural difference?

2. Does the first paragraph have any function beyond delaying the discussion of business?

3. What is the function of telling Mr. Kirisawa about his own company? How does this paragraph help the writer introduce her own company's products?

4. To a reader from the United States, the third paragraph would probably seem thin. What aspect of Japanese culture makes it effective in the context of this letter?

5. Why doesn't the writer make a more explicit sales pitch at the end of the letter?

 On TechComm Web

To e-mail your responses to yourself and/or your instructor, click on Interactive Sample Documents for Ch. 5 on <bedfordstmartins.com/ techcomm>.

USING AN AUDIENCE PROFILE SHEET

To help you analyze your audience, fill out an audience profile sheet, as shown in Figure 5.5, for each primary and secondary reader (assuming, of course, that there are just a few readers).

Figure 5.5   An Audience Profile Sheet

Assume that you work in the drafting department of an architectural engineering firm. You know that the company's computer-assisted design (CAD) software is out-of-date and that recent CAD technology would make it easier and faster for the draftspersons to do their work. You want to persuade your company to authorize buying a CAD workstation that costs about $4,000. To do so, you fill out an audience profile sheet for your primary reader, Harry Becker, the manager of your company's Drafting and Design Department.

AUDIENCE PROFILE SHEET

Reader's Name: Harry Becker

Reader's Job Title: Manager, Drafting and Design Department

Kind of Reader: Primary __X__ Secondary ____

Education: BS, Architectural Engineering, Northwestern, 1989. CAD/CAM Short Course, 1989; Motivating Your Employees Seminar, 1991; Writing on the Job Short Course, 1994

Professional Experience: Worked for two years in a small architecture firm. Started here 16 years ago as a draftsperson. Worked his way up to Assistant Manager, then Manager. Instrumental in the Wilson project, particularly in coordinating personnel and equipment.

Job Responsibilities: Supervises a staff of 12 draftspersons. Approves or denies all requests for capital expenditures over $2,000 coming from his department. Works with employees to help them make the best case for the purchase. After approving or denying the request, forwards it to Tina Buterbaugh, Manager, Finance Dept., who maintains all capital expenditure records.

Personal Characteristics: N/A

Personal Preferences: Likes straightforward documents, lots of evidence, clear structure. Dislikes complicated documents full of jargon.

Cultural Characteristics: Nothing of note.

Attitude Toward the Writer: No problems.

Attitude Toward the Subject: He understands and approves of my argument.

Expectations About the Subject: Expects to see a clear argument with financial data and detailed comparisons of available systems.

Expectations About the Document: Expects to see a report, with an executive summary, of about 10 pages.

Reasons for Reading the Document: To offer suggestions and eventually approve or deny the request.

Way of Reading the Document:
Skim it ____   Study it __X__ Read a portion of it ____   Which portion? ____
Modify it and submit it to another reader ____
Attempt to implement recommendations ____
Use it to perform a task or carry out a procedure ____
Use it to create another document ____
Other ____   Explain. ____

Reading Skill: Excellent

Reader's Physical Environment: N/A

On TechComm Web

You should modify this form to meet your own needs and those of your organization. For a downloadable version of Fig. 5.5, click on Forms for Technical Communication on <bedfordstmartins.com/techcomm>.

Contents

Foreword		v
Preface		vii
Summary for Policymakers	←	1
Technical Summary		19
1	Historical Overview of Climate Change Science	93
2	Changes in Atmospheric Constituents and Radiative Forcing	129
3	Observations Atmospheric Surface and Climate Change	235
4	Observations Changes in Snow, Ice and Frozen Ground	337
5	Observations Ocean Climate Change and Sea Level	385
6	Palaeoclimate	433
7	Coupling Between Changes in the Climate System and Biogeochemistry	499
8	Climate Models and Their Evaluation	589
9	Understanding and Attributing Climate Change	663
10	Global Climate Projections	747
11	Regional Climate Projections	847
Annex I:	Glossary	941
Annex II:	Contributors to the IPCC WGI Fourth Assessment Report	955
Annex III:	Reviewers of the IPCC WGI Fourth Assessment Report	969
Annex IV:	Acronyms	981
Index		989

This table of contents shows the organization of a modular document.

Few readers will want to read the whole document—it's almost 1,000 pages long.

Most readers will want to read the 18-page summary for policymakers.

Some readers will want to read selected sections of the technical summary or "annexes" (appendices).

Figure 5.6   Table of Contents for a Modular Report
Source: Solomon et al., 2007, p. xix.

WRITING FOR MULTIPLE AUDIENCES

Many documents of more than a few pages are addressed to more than one reader. Often, multiple audiences consist of people with widely different backgrounds, needs, and attitudes.

If you think your document will have a number of readers, consider making it *modular*: break it up into components addressed to different readers. A modular report might contain an executive summary for managers who don't have the time, knowledge, or desire to read the whole report. It might also contain a full technical discussion for expert readers, an implementation schedule for technicians, and a financial plan in an appendix for budget officers. Figure 5.6 shows the table of contents for a modular report.

DETERMINING YOUR PURPOSE

Once you have identified and analyzed your audience, it is time to examine your purpose. Ask yourself this: "What do I want this document to accomplish?" When your readers have finished reading what you have written, what do you want them to *know* or *believe*? What do you want them to *do*? Your writing should help your readers carry out a task, understand a concept, or hold a particular belief.

In defining your purpose, think of a verb that represents it. (Sometimes, of course, you have several purposes.) The following list presents verbs in two categories: those used to communicate information to your readers and those used to convince them to accept a particular point of view.

Communicating Verbs

describe	explain	inform
illustrate	review	outline
authorize	define	summarize

Convincing Verbs

assess	request	propose
recommend	forecast	evaluate

This classification is not absolute. For example, *review* could in some cases be a *convincing verb* rather than a *communicating verb*: one writer's review of a complicated situation might be very different from another's.

Here are a few examples of how you can use these verbs to clarify the purpose of your document (the verbs are italicized).

- This report *describes* the research project intended to determine the effectiveness of the new waste-treatment filter.
- This letter *authorizes* the purchase of six new laptops for the Jenkintown facility.
- This memo *recommends* that we revise the Web site as soon as possible.

Sometimes, your real purpose differs from your expressed purpose. For instance, if you want to persuade your reader to lease a new computer system rather than purchase it, you might phrase the purpose this way: to *explain the advantages of leasing over purchasing.* As I mentioned earlier, many readers don't want to be *persuaded* but are willing to learn new facts or ideas.

GAINING MANAGEMENT'S APPROVAL

After you have analyzed your audience and purpose, consider gaining the approval of management before you proceed. The larger and more complex the project and the document, the more sense it makes to be sure that you are on the right track before you invest too much time and effort.

For example, you are planning a CAD equipment project. You already know your audience and purpose, and you are drafting a general outline in your mind. But before you actually start to write an outline or gather the information you will need, spend another 10 or 15 minutes making sure your primary reader agrees with your thinking. You don't want to waste days or even weeks working on a document that won't fulfill its purpose. If you have misunderstood what your supervisor wants, it is far easier to fix the problem at this early stage.

Your statement can also serve another purpose: if you want your reader's views on which of two strategies to pursue, you can describe each one and ask your reader to state a preference.

What application should you use? It doesn't matter. You can write an e-mail or a memo, as long as you clearly and briefly state what you are trying to do. Here is an example of the statement you might submit to your boss about the CAD equipment.

Juan:

Please tell me if you think this is a good approach for the proposal on CAD equipment.

The purpose of the memo

Outright purchase of the complete system will cost more than $1,000, so you would have to approve it and send it on for Tina's approval. (I'll provide leasing costs as well.) I want to show that our CAD hardware and software are badly out-of-date and need to be replaced. I'll be thorough in recommending new equipment, with independent evaluations in the literature, as well as product demonstrations. The proposal should specify what the current equipment is costing us and show how much we can save by buying the recommended system.

A statement of the audience for the proposal

A statement of the purpose, followed by early statements of the scope of the document

I'll call you later today to get your reaction before I begin researching what's available.

A statement of how the writer intends to follow up on this memo

Renu

Once you have received your primary reader's approval, you can feel confident about starting to gather information.

REVISING INFORMATION FOR A NEW AUDIENCE AND PURPOSE

Chapter 2 introduced the concept of boilerplate information: standard text or graphics that are plugged into various documents (see page 25). But not all information can be standardized and distributed in one form. In other words, one size doesn't necessarily fit all. Most of the time, you need to revise information to accommodate a new audience and purpose.

Figure 5.7 on page 106 shows the first few paragraphs of a press release from Ford Motor Company (2007).

Figure 5.8 on page 107 is an excerpt from Autoblog. The writer is reporting on an interview he conducted with Ford and Microsoft representatives.

A press release is a statement distributed by a company to the news media to promote a new product or development at the company. The company hopes the news media will print the release, thereby publicizing the product or development. Notice the marketing spin in the title of the press release. The writer is trying to attract potential customers, especially young people.

Press releases often include quotations from company officers that highlight the features or benefits of the new product or development.

FORD TEAMS UP WITH MICROSOFT TO DELIVER SYNC; IN-CAR DIGITAL SYSTEM EXCLUSIVE TO FORD

DETROIT, Mich., Jan. 7, 2007—Ford Motor Company today announced the launch of a new factory-installed, in-car communications and entertainment system that is designed to change the way consumers use digital media portable music players and mobile phones in their vehicles.

The Ford-exclusive technology based on Microsoft Auto software, called Sync, provides consumers the convenience and flexibility to bring into their vehicle nearly any mobile phone or digital media player and operate it using voice commands or the vehicle's steering wheel or radio controls.

Ford owners will not need to worry about whether their car or truck is compatible with the latest phone or music player that hits the market. Sync seamlessly integrates the vehicle with the popular portable electronic devices of today and is upgradeable to support the devices and services of tomorrow.

"Sync is what today's generation and today's drivers demand in connectivity," says Derrick Kuzak, group vice president, product development, Ford Motor Company. "Not only does it offer hands-free phone operation and iPod®, Zune or MP3 player connectivity, it's built on a software platform that is upgradeable and will allow us to offer new features by simply upgrading the software."

Sync offers consumers two ways to bring electronic devices into their Ford, Lincoln and Mercury vehicles and operate them seamlessly through voice commands or steering wheel controls:
- Bluetooth, for wireless connection of phones and phones that play music.
- A USB 2.0 port for command and control and charging of digital media players—including the Apple iPod and Microsoft Zune—as well as PlaysForSure music devices and most USB media storage devices. Supported formats include MP3, AAC, WMA, WAV and PCM.

Figure 5.7   Press Release
Source: The Ford Motor Company, 2007 <http://media.ford.com/newsroom/release_display.cfm ?release=25168>.

At Ford's recent 2008 product information event, the Blue Oval showed that it's catching up to the competition on many fronts, including powertrains, interior quality, and overall refinement. The fact is, the folks over in Dearborn *are* playing catch-up vs. the competition, and in some ways Ford has a lot of work ahead of it. One area where the automaker's been lacking was with regards to iPod compatibility and integration in its vehicles, but with Microsoft's Sync technology rolling out for 2008, Ford's ready to jump to the head of the class.

The writer begins by placing the Sync technology in the context of other attempts by Ford to improve its products.

We sat down with representatives from Ford and Microsoft during our recent trip to Dearborn, and we got an in-depth walkthrough of Ford's multimedia initiative. Sync integrates MP3 players and Bluetooth phones into the stereo system to give drivers greater flexibility to their digital assets. One very exciting aspect of Sync is that high-end stereo and nav systems aren't needed to use the technology. Sync will be standard on all Lincoln models and available as an option on most Fords and Mercurys for MY 2008. During our demo, we saw a Zune player (like we said, it's Microsoft) plugged into the audio jack inside the armrest storage area, plus a Blackberry device connected via Bluetooth, all running through the stereo. . . .

This paragraph draws on information from the press release and from the writer's discussion with company representatives.

Songs, artists, and genre can be selected off the MP3 player by voice command via the "Push to Talk" button on the steering wheel controls. This feature worked very well, . . . but if you ask for a song or artist that doesn't reside on your MP3 player, Sync gives you the song or artist that sounds most like the one you asked for. We'd have preferred it if Sync came up with nothing vs. a guess that's likely wrong. Due to shortcomings of Bluetooth technology, Sync had trouble accessing MP3 music from phones, but the folks at Microsoft say that a fix is on the way.

The writer diverges from the press release in pointing out shortcomings of the product. That's his job: to determine how well the technology really works.

Figure 5.8   Article Based on a Press Release

Source: Shunk, 2007 <www.autoblog.com/2007/07/04/video-live-from-dearborn-microsoft-and -ford-demo-sync>.

Writer's Checklist

Following is a checklist for analyzing your audience and purpose. Remember that your document might be read by one person, several people, a large group, or several groups with various needs.

In analyzing your audience, did you consider the following questions about your most important readers?

☐ What is your reader's educational background? (p. 82)

☐ What is your reader's professional experience? (p. 82)

☐ What is your reader's job responsibility? (p. 82)

☐ What are your reader's personal characteristics? (p. 82)

☐ What are your reader's personal preferences? (p. 82)

☐ What are your reader's cultural characteristics? (p. 82)

☐ Why is the reader reading your document? (p. 83)

☐ What is your reader's attitude toward you? (p. 84)

☐ What is your reader's attitude toward the subject? (p. 84)

☐ What are your reader's expectations about the subject? (p. 84)

☐ What are your reader's expectations about the document? (p. 85)

☐ How will your reader read your document? (p. 85)

☐ What is your reader's reading skill? (p. 85)

☐ What is the physical environment in which your reader will read your document? (p. 85)

In learning about your reader, did you:

☐ tally what you already know and what you don't know about him or her? (p. 86)

☐ interview people? (p. 86)

☐ search for information on the Internet? (p. 86)

☐ read documents your reader has written? (p. 88)

In planning to write for an audience from another culture, did you consider the following cultural variables:

☐ political? (p. 92)

☐ economic? (p. 92)

☐ social? (p. 92)

☐ religious? (p. 92)

☐ educational? (p. 92)

☐ technological? (p. 92)

☐ linguistic? (p. 92)

In planning to write for an audience from another culture, did you consider the other set of cultural variables:

☐ focus on individuals or groups? (p. 94)

☐ distance between business life and private life? (p. 94)

☐ distance between ranks? (p. 94)

☐ nature of truth? (p. 95)

☐ need to spell out details? (p. 95)

☐ attitudes toward uncertainty? (p. 95)

In writing for a multicultural audience, did you

☐ limit your vocabulary? (p. 98)

☐ keep sentences short? (p. 98)

☐ define abbreviations and acronyms in a glossary? (p. 98)

☐ avoid jargon unless you know that your readers are familiar with it? (p. 98)

☐ avoid idioms and slang? (p. 99)

☐ use the active voice whenever possible? (p. 99)

☐ use graphics carefully? (p. 99)

☐ have the document reviewed by someone from the reader's culture? (p. 99)

☐ Did you fill out an audience profile sheet for your primary and secondary audiences? (p. 102)

☐ Did you consider your purpose in writing and express it in the form of a verb or verbs? (p. 104)

☐ Did you get management's approval of your analysis of audience and purpose? (p. 104)

Exercises

 In This Book For more about memos, see Ch. 14, p. 377.

1. **INTERNET EXERCISE** Choose a 200-word passage from a technical article related to your major course of study and addressed to an expert audience. (You can find a technical article on the Web by using a directory search engine such as Yahoo!, selecting a subject area such as "science," and then selecting "journals." In addition, many federal government agencies publish technical articles and reports on the Web.) Rewrite the passage so that it is clear and interesting to the general reader. Submit the original passage to your instructor along with your revision.

2. The following passage is an advertisement from a translation service. Revise the passage to make it more appropriate for a multicultural audience. Submit the revision to your instructor.

   If your technical documents have to meet the needs of a global market but you find that most translation houses are swamped by the huge volume, fail to accommodate the various languages you require, or make your deadlines, where do you turn?

Well, your search is over. Translations, Inc., provides comprehensive translations in addition to full-service documentation publishing.

We utilize ultrasophisticated translation programs that can translate a page in the blink of an eye. Then our crack linguists comb each document to give it that personalized touch.

No job too large! No schedule too tight! Give us a call today!

3. **INTERNET EXERCISE** Audience is your primary consideration in many types of nontechnical writing. Choose a one- or two-page magazine advertisement or Web site for an economy car, such as a Kia, and one for a luxury car, such as a Mercedes. In a memo to your instructor, contrast the audiences for the two ads according to age, sex, economic means, hobbies, interests, and leisure activities. In contrasting the two audiences, consider the explicit information in the ads—the writing—as well as the implicit information—hidden persuaders such as background scenery, color, lighting, angles, and the situation portrayed by any people photographed. Keep in mind that your purpose is to contrast the two audiences, not merely to describe the content of the ad or its design. Submit color photo-

copies or the original ads from the magazines or sites along with your memo.

4. **GROUP/INTERNET EXERCISE** Form small groups and study two Web sites that advertise competing products. For instance, you might choose the Web sites of two car manufacturers, two television shows, or two music publishers. Have each person in the group, working *alone*, compare and contrast the two sites according to these three criteria:

a. the kind of information they provide: hard, technical information or more emotional information

b. the use of multimedia such as animation, sound, or video

c. the amount of interactivity they invite—that is, the extent to which you can participate in activities while you visit the site

After each person has separately studied the sites and taken notes about the three points, come together as a group. Allow each person to share his or her findings, then discuss the differences as a group. Which aspects of these sites caused the most differences in the group members' reactions? Which aspects seemed to elicit the most consistent reactions? In a brief memo to your instructor, describe and analyze how the two sites were perceived by the different members of the group.

Case 5: Planning an Apology to a Customer from the People's Republic of China

 In This Book For more about letters of complaint and adjustment, see Ch. 14, p. 377. For more about interviews, see Ch. 6, p. 136.

Background

You work in the Marketing Department at Zander Instruments, a manufacturer of scientific measurement instruments used in the pharmaceutical, chemical, and semiconductor industries. Your latest product is an x-ray scanner used by airlines to inspect cargo pallets to be sure they contain the cargo listed on the cargo manifest and do not contain illegal drugs or other contraband.

After a negotiation that lasted more than four months, your company signed a contract to supply 15 of these devices, at a total cost of over $2 million, to China Air, on

July 1. In the contract, you agreed to provide complete product documentation, including operating and routine-maintenance instructions, in Modern Chinese, the written language used in the People's Republic of China.

It is July 14. Today you received a letter (Document 5.1) from Haiwang Guo, Director of Operations for China Air, who is unhappy that, although the shipment of scanners arrived on July 1, the Chinese documentation was missing. You call Pablo Hidalgo, the head of the Documentation Department.

China ★ Air

17th floor, United Centre, No. 93
Queensway, Hong Kong

Haiwang Guo
Director of Operations, China Air

[your name]
Director of Far East Marketing
Zander Instruments
9500 Zelzah Avenue
Northridge, CA 91324

Dear [your name]:

I hope that cool ocean breezes greet your summer season and your family enjoys health and happiness. The new cooperation between Zander Instruments and China Air will be a major boost to our cargo network and improve our distribution ability as we move into the future.

China Air wishes to thank you for your role in establishing a prosperous relationship between our companies. I appreciate the management of your company seeing the value of our two organizations working together and I recommit to you my desire on behalf of my company.

In January 2009, your company contracted to supply China Air 15 x-ray scanners on July 1, 2009. The scanners arrived on July 1 with only English documentation. China Air had been very much busy planning a ceremony at its Hong Kong headquarters in preparation for the installation of the scanners at five major airports. The missing documentation resulted in China Air canceling the ceremony on July 3.

It is hoped that Zander Instruments understands the urgency in the request by China Air to supply the Chinese documentation for the scanners and looks forward to providing China Air with an answer just as soon as possible.

May you be lucky, safe, and sound this season, and may our goodwill reach everyone.

Sincerely,

Haiwang Guo

Haiwang Guo
Director of Operations, China Air

2009 July 10

▶ On TechComm Web

For digital versions of case documents, click on Downloadable Case Documents on <bedfordstmartins.com/techcomm>.

Document 5.1 **Letter from China Air's Director of Operations**

FOR IMMEDIATE RELEASE

CHINA AIR ANNOUNCES JOINT VENTURE WITH ZANDER INSTRUMENTS

HONG KONG, June 1, 2009 /XFNHK-ChinaNet/ —

China Air today announced that it will install state-of-the-art cargo scanners at the five major airports the airline serves. Supplied by Zander Instruments (United States), the new scanners will allow the airline to more efficiently inspect cargo pallets. To celebrate this new business relationship between China Air and Zander Instruments, China Air's Director of Operations, Haiwang Guo, announced today that the company will hold a ceremony at its Hong Kong headquarters to celebrate the purchase and installation of the new scanners. The ceremony will illustrate China Air's management spirit of "safety first and customers highest."

About China Air:

China Air, formally known as China Northern, was founded in 1995. It is one of only six air-lines in mainland China not directly controlled by the Civil Aviation Administration of China (CAAC). China Air began its operations with one Boeing jet. Since then, China Air has grown gradually. In the end of 2007, it offered its quality services with 4 aircrafts to 5 destinations with a total of 150 skillful employees. Following the successful expansion of its domestic cargo service in 2008, China Air is now ready to spread its wings into domestic skies as a new alter-native cargo carrier.

    For more information, contact:

        Haiwang Guo, Director of Operations, China Air
        E-mail: hw@china-air.com
        Web: www.china-air.com

# # #

Document 5.2   China Air Press Release

"The Chinese documentation was delayed because of translation problems," Pablo explains. "Several of our graph-ics with text needed translating, and we didn't allow for text expansion during translation. We had to revise the layout on several pages—"

"When will the documentation be ready?" you interrupt.

"It will be available by next week."

You next talk to Paula Tiller, Zander's President, to discuss the situation. "I can understand why Haiwang is unhappy. The company planned for a big ceremony. Here's the press release," Paula says, handing you a sheet of paper (Document 5.2).

After some more discussion, Paula says that she wants you to arrange for the documentation to be hand-delivered to Haiwang Guo, complete with a letter of apology. "I'm counting on you to convey our sincerest apologies and to keep China Air as one of our clients," she concludes.

Your Assignment

1. You decide that the first step is to interview a knowledge-able person from the People's Republic of China to learn what you can about how formal apologies are handled there. A friend of yours, Jun Xiaoyan, in Zander's Research and Development Department, is from China. You think he might be willing to sit down with you for 15 or 20 minutes. Write a set of questions you would like to ask your friend before apologizing to Haiwang Guo. For each question, write a brief paragraph explaining how the answer to the question might help you complete an appropriate letter of apology to China Air. For example, you might want to know whether the letter should be highly formal in its vocabulary.

2. Jun Xiaoyan contacts you before your meeting and suggests that you bring along a rough draft of your apology letter. "It will give us something specific to work with," he says. Based on what you already know about inter-cultural communication, draft a letter of apology to China Air. Include in the margins any specific questions you want to ask Jun about your letter.

Researching Your Subject

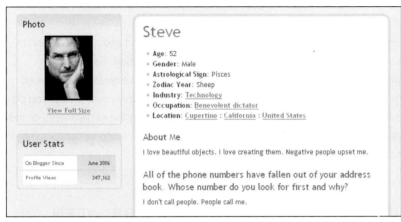

Photo	Steve	

Photo

View Full Size

User Stats

On Blogger Since	June 2006
Profile Views	247,162

Steve

- **Age**: 52
- **Gender**: Male
- **Astrological Sign**: Pisces
- **Zodiac Year**: Sheep
- **Industry**: Technology
- **Occupation**: Benevolent dictator
- **Location**: Cupertino : California : United States

About Me

I love beautiful objects. I love creating them. Negative people upset me.

All of the phone numbers have fallen out of your address book. Whose number do you look for first and why?

I don't call people. People call me.

Source: Forbes.com, 2008 <www.blogger.com/profile/15043759939497216186>.

In the World . . .

This is a portion of the profile page from the blog The Secret Diary of Steve Jobs. If you are researching Steve Jobs or Apple, you're likely to stumble upon this blog. And stumble you will, because the blog is a parody written by Daniel Lyons, an editor at *Forbes* magazine who is now known as the Fake Steve Jobs. The real Steve Jobs, by the way, is a fan of the Fake Steve Jobs.

Understanding the Differences Between Academic and Workplace Research 114

Understanding the Research Process 115

Choosing Appropriate Research Methods 116

Conducting Secondary Research 119

Understanding the Research Media 120

Using Basic Research Tools 120

Researching Government Information 124

Using Web 2.0 Resources 124

Evaluating the Information 128

Conducting Primary Research 133

Observations and Demonstrations 133

Inspections 133

Experiments 134

Field Research 135

Interviews 136

Inquiry Letters or E-mails 138

Questionnaires 138

In the workplace, you will conduct research all the time. A buyer for a clothing retailer might need to determine whether a new line of products would be successful in his store. A civil engineer might need to decide whether to replace her company's traditional surveying equipment with GPS-based gear. A pharmacist might need to find out what medication a patient is taking and find information on potentially harmful drug interactions.

This chapter focuses on conducting primary research and secondary research. *Primary research* involves creating technical information yourself. *Secondary research* involves collecting information that other people have already discovered or created. This chapter presents secondary research first. Only rarely would you do primary research before doing secondary research. To design the experiments or the field research that goes into primary research, you need a thorough understanding of the information that already exists about your subject.

UNDERSTANDING THE DIFFERENCES BETWEEN ACADEMIC AND WORKPLACE RESEARCH

Although *academic research* and *workplace research* can overlap, in most cases they differ in their goals and methods.

In *academic research*, your goal is to find information that will help answer a scholarly question: "What would be the effect on the balance of trade between the United States and China if China lowered the value of its currency?" "At what age do babies learn to focus on people's eyes?" Academic research questions are often more abstract than applied. That is, they get at the underlying principles of a phenomenon. Academic research usually requires extensive secondary research: reading scholarly literature in academic journals and books. If you do primary research, as scientists do in labs, you do so only after doing extensive secondary research.

In *workplace research*, your goal is to find information to help you answer a practical question, usually one that involves the organization you work for: "Should we stay with our distributed printing configuration or adopt a centralized configuration?" "What would be the advantages and disadvantages if our company adopted a European-style privacy policy for customer information?" Because workplace research is often focused on improving a situation at a particular company, it calls for much more primary research. You need to learn about your own company's processes and how the people in your company would respond to your ideas.

Regardless of whether you are conducting academic or workplace research, the basic research methods—primary and secondary research— are fundamentally the same, as is the goal: to answer questions.

UNDERSTANDING THE RESEARCH PROCESS

When you need to perform research, you want the process to be effective and efficient. That is, you want the information you find to answer the questions you need to answer. And you don't want to spend any more time than is necessary getting that information. To meet these goals, you have to think about how the research relates to the other aspects of the overall project. Figure 6.1 provides an overview of the research process.

Figure 6.1
An Overview of the Research Process

Analyze Your Audience

Who are your most important readers? What are their personal characteristics, their attitudes toward your subject, and their motivations for reading? If you are writing to an expert audience that might be skeptical about your message, you need to do a lot of research to gather the evidence for a convincing argument. See Ch. 5.

Analyze Your Purpose

Why are you writing? Understanding your purpose helps you understand the types of information readers will expect. Think in terms of what you want your readers to know, believe, or do after they finish reading your document. See Ch. 5.

Analyze Your Subject

What do you already know about your subject? What do you still need to find out? Using techniques such as freewriting and brainstorming, you can determine those aspects of the subject you need to investigate. See Ch. 3.

Visualize the Deliverable

What application will you need to deliver: a proposal, a report, a Web site? What kind of oral presentation will you need to deliver? See Ch. 3.

Work Out a Schedule and a Budget for the Project

When is the deliverable—the document or the presentation—due? Do you have a budget for phone calls, database searches, or travel to libraries or other sites? See Ch. 3.

Determine What Information Will Need to Be Part of That Deliverable

Draft an outline of the contents, focusing on the kinds of information readers will expect to see in each part. See Ch. 3.

Figure 6.1 (continued)

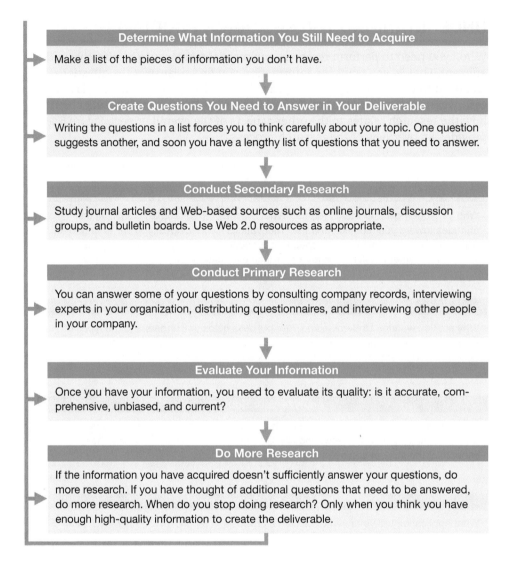

Determine What Information You Still Need to Acquire

Make a list of the pieces of information you don't have.

Create Questions You Need to Answer in Your Deliverable

Writing the questions in a list forces you to think carefully about your topic. One question suggests another, and soon you have a lengthy list of questions that you need to answer.

Conduct Secondary Research

Study journal articles and Web-based sources such as online journals, discussion groups, and bulletin boards. Use Web 2.0 resources as appropriate.

Conduct Primary Research

You can answer some of your questions by consulting company records, interviewing experts in your organization, distributing questionnaires, and interviewing other people in your company.

Evaluate Your Information

Once you have your information, you need to evaluate its quality: is it accurate, comprehensive, unbiased, and current?

Do More Research

If the information you have acquired doesn't sufficiently answer your questions, do more research. If you have thought of additional questions that need to be answered, do more research. When do you stop doing research? Only when you think you have enough high-quality information to create the deliverable.

CHOOSING APPROPRIATE RESEARCH METHODS

Once you have determined the questions you need to answer, think about the various research techniques you can use to answer them. Different research questions require different research methods.

For example, your research methods for finding out how a current situation is expected to change would be different from your research methods for finding out how well a product might work for your organization. That is, if you want to know how outsourcing will change the computer-support industry over the next 10 to 20 years, you might search for long-range predictions in journal articles and magazine articles and on reputable Web sites. You might also see if experts have made forecasts on blogs. By contrast, if you want to figure out whether a specific scanner will produce the quality of scan that you need and will function reliably, you might read product reviews on reputable Web sites and study discussion lists, observe the use of the product or service at a vendor's site, schedule product demos at your site, follow up by interviewing others in your company, and perform an experiment in which you try two different scanners and then analyze the results.

Choosing research methods means choosing the ways in which you'll conduct your research. Start by thinking about the questions you need to answer:

- *What types of research media might you use?* Should you look for information in books, journals, and reports or online on Web sites, discussion boards, and blogs?

- *What types of research tools might you use?* Are these media best accessed via online catalogs, reference works, indexes, or abstract services?

- *What types of primary research might you conduct?* Should you use observations, demonstrations, inspections, experiments, interviews, questionnaires, or other field research?

You are likely to find that your research plan changes as you conduct your research. You might find, for instance, that you need more than one method to get the information you need, or that the one method you thought would work doesn't. Still, having a plan can help you discover the most appropriate methods more quickly and efficiently. The advice in Figure 6.2 provides a good starting point.

In addition to planning, researching a subject requires perseverance, organization, and judgment.

Guidelines

Researching a Topic

Follow these three guidelines as you gather information to use in your document.

▶ **Be persistent.** Don't be discouraged if a research method doesn't yield useful information. Even experienced researchers fail at least as often as they succeed. Be prepared to rethink how you might find the information. Don't hesitate to ask reference librarians for help or to post questions on online discussion groups.

▶ **Record your data carefully.** Prepare the materials you will need to write your document. Write information down, on paper or online. Record interviews (with the respondents' permission). Cut and paste the URLs of the sites you visit into your notes. Bookmark sites so you can return to them easily.

▶ **Triangulate your research methods.** *Triangulating* your methods means using more than one or two sources. If a manufacturer's Web site says that a printer produces 17 pages per minute, an independent review in a reputable journal also says 17, and you get 17 in a demo at your office with your documents, the printer probably will produce 17 pages per minute.

Figure 6.2   Research Questions and Methods

Type of question	*Example of question*	*Appropriate research technique*
What is the theory behind this process or technique?	How do greenhouse gases contribute to global warming?	**Encyclopedias**, **handbooks**, and **journal articles** present theory. Also, you can find theoretical information on **Web sites** from reputable professional organizations and universities. Search using keywords such as "greenhouse gases" and "global warming."
What is the history of this phenomenon?	When and how did engineers first try to extract shale oil?	**Encyclopedias** and **handbooks** present history. Also, you can find theoretical information on **Web sites** from reputable professional organizations and universities. Search using keywords such as "shale oil" and "petroleum history."
What techniques are being used now to solve this problem?	How are companies responding to the federal government's new laws on health-insurance portability?	If the topic is recent, you will have better luck using digital media such as **Web sites** and **Web 2.0 resources** than using traditional print media. Search using keywords and tags such as "health-insurance portability." Your search will be most effective if you use the "official" terminology in your search, such as "HIPAA" for the health-insurance law.
How is a current situation expected to change?	What changes will outsourcing cause in the computer-support industry over the next 10 to 20 years?	For long-range predictions, you can find information in **journal articles** and **magazine articles** and on reputable **Web sites**. Experts might write forecasts in **blogs**.
What products are available to perform a task or provide a service?	Which vendors are available to maintain our company's Web site?	For current products and services, search **Web sites** and **blogs**. Reputable vendors—manufacturers and service providers—have sites describing their offerings. But be careful not to accept vendors' claims. Even the specifications they provide might be exaggerated.
What are the strengths and weaknesses of competing products and services?	Which portable GPS product is the lightest?	Search for benchmarking articles by experts in the field, such as a **journal article**—either in print or on the Web—about camping and outfitting that compares the available GPS products according to reasonable criteria. Also check **online discussion groups** for reviews and **blogs** for opinions. If appropriate, do **field research** to answer your questions.
Which product or service do experts recommend?	Which four-wheel-drive SUV offers the best combination of features and quality for our needs?	Experts write **journal articles** and **magazine articles** and sometimes **blogs**. Often, they participate in **online discussion groups**. Sometimes, you can **interview** them, in person or on the phone, or write **inquiry letters**.
What are the facts about how we do our jobs at this company?	Do our chemists use gas chromatography in their analyses?	Sometimes, you can **interview** a person, in person or on the phone, to answer a simple question. To find out how much money the company spends on utilities, contact the Operations or Accounting Department.

Figure 6.2 (continued)

Type of question	Example of question	Appropriate research technique
What can we learn about what caused a problem in our organization?	What caused the contamination in the clean room?	You can **interview** personnel who were closest to the problem and **inspect** the scene to determine the cause of the problem.
What do our personnel think we should do about a situation?	Do our quality-control analysts think we need to revise our sampling quotient?	If there are only a few personnel, **interview** them. If there are many, use **questionnaires** to get the information more quickly.
How well would this product or service work in our organization?	Would this scanner produce the quality of scan that we need and interface well with our computer equipment?	Read product reviews on reputable **Web sites**. Study **discussion lists**. **Observe** the use of the product or service at a vendor's site. Schedule product **demos** at your site. Follow up by **interviewing** others in your company to get their thinking. Do an **experiment** in which you try two different solutions to a problem, then analyze the results.

If you are doing research for a document that will be read by people from other cultures, think about what kinds of evidence your readers will consider appropriate. In many non-Western cultures, tradition or the authority of the person making the claim can be extremely important— more important than the kind of scientific evidence that is favored in Western cultures.

And don't forget that all people pay particular attention to information that comes from their own culture. If you are writing to European readers about telemedicine, for instance, try to find information from European authorities and about European telemedicine. This information will interest your readers and will likely reflect their cultural values and expectations.

CONDUCTING SECONDARY RESEARCH

Even though workplace research often focuses on primary research, you will almost always need to do secondary research as well. Some topics call for research in a library. You might need specialized handbooks or access to online subscription services that are not freely available on the Internet. As a college student, you do most of this research in one of the libraries on campus. As a working professional, you might find most of the information in your organization's information center. An *information center* is the organization's library, a resource that collects different kinds of information critical to the organization's operations. Large organizations have specialists who can answer research questions or get articles or other kinds of data to you. Often, however, you can do much or even most of your research on the Internet.

Understanding the Research Media

Today, most technical information is distributed not only in print but also through digital media accessible on the Internet. You will probably use information published in five major media, as described in Figure 6.3.

Using Basic Research Tools

There is a tremendous amount of information in the different media. The trick is to learn how to find what you want. This section discusses five basic research tools.

Online Catalogs   An online catalog is a database of books, microforms, films, compact discs, phonograph records, tapes, and other materials. In most cases, an online catalog lists and describes the holdings at one particular library or a group of libraries. Your college library has an online catalog of its holdings. To search for an item, consult the instructions for searching, which explain how to limit your search by characteristics such as type of media, date of publication, and language. The instructions also explain how to use punctuation and words such as *and*, *or*, and *not* to focus your search effectively.

Reference Works   Reference works include general dictionaries and encyclopedias, biographical dictionaries, almanacs, atlases, and dozens of other general research tools. These print and online works are especially useful when you begin a research project because they provide an overview of the subject and often list the major works in the field.

How do you know if there is a dictionary of the terms used in a given field? The following reference books—the guides-to-the-guides—list the many resources available:

- Lester, R. (Ed.). (2005–2007). *The new Walford guide to reference resources.* London: Facet.

- Rasmussen, K. G. (2004). *The Prentice-Hall writer's guide to research and documentation.* East Rutherford, NJ: Prentice Hall.

- Hacker, D. *Research and documentation online.* <http://dianahacker.com/resdoc>.

- Palmquist, M. *The Bedford researcher.* <http://bedfordresearcher.com/links/disciplines>.

On TechComm Web

For links to these and other reference sources, click on Links Library for Ch. 6 on <bedfordstmartins.com/techcomm>.

Print

Books, journals, reports, and other documents will continue to be produced in print because printed information is portable and you can write on it. For documents that do not need to be updated periodically, print remains a useful and popular medium. To find it, you will continue to use online catalogs, as you do now.

Online Databases

Most libraries—even many public libraries—subscribe to services, such as LexisNexis, ProQuest, InfoTrac, and EBSCOhost, that provide access to large databases of journal articles, conference proceedings, newspapers, and other documents.

Web Sites

The good news is that there are billions of pages of information on the Web. The bad news is that there are billions of pages of information on the Web.

Online Discussion Groups

There are two major forums for online discussions: Usenet newsgroups and electronic mailing lists.

- *Usenet newsgroups*, sometimes called *bulletin boards*, publish e-mail messages sent by members of the group. Newsgroups give participants an opportunity to discuss issues, ask questions, and get answers. Usenet consists of thousands of newsgroups organized according to nine basic categories, including computer science, science, recreation, and business. In a Usenet newsgroup, mail is not sent to individual computers, but is stored on databases, which you then access.
- *Electronic mailing lists* are like newsgroups in that they publish e-mail messages sent by members. The basic difference is that mailing lists send e-mail messages to every person who subscribes. The mail comes to you; you don't go to it, as you do with a newsgroup.

Web 2.0 Resources

Web 2.0 resources include online resources such as blogs, podcasts, and social-networking sites. Although many *blogs* (Weblogs) are personal diaries that are of little or no value to a researcher, many others are useful. Scientists, engineers, journalists, corporate leaders, and other professionals publish blogs that can help you understand topics being discussed by professionals in your field. *Podcasts*—downloadable audio files playable on Apple iPods and similar audio players—are another increasingly popular means of disseminating information. When you use blogs, podcasts, and social-networking sites, be sure to verify the authority of the information source and search for more formal versions of the information presented in edited media such as reputable newspapers and journals.

Figure 6.3   Five Major Information Media

On TechComm Web

The Internet Public Library Reference Center is an excellent source on all aspects of Internet research. Click on Links Library for Ch. 6 on <bedfordstmartins.com/techcomm>.

On TechComm Web

For sites that list newsgroups and discussion boards, click on Links Library for Ch. 6 on <bedfordstmartins.com/techcomm>.

To find information on the Web, use a library Web site or search engine and go to its "reference" section. There you will find numerous sites that contain links to excellent collections of reference works online, such as the Best Information on the Net, CyberStacks^SM, and the Internet Public Library.

Periodical Indexes   Periodicals are excellent sources of information because they offer recent, authoritative discussions of limited subjects. The biggest challenge in using periodicals is identifying and locating the dozens of relevant articles that are published each month. Although only half a dozen major journals might concentrate on your field, a useful article might appear in one of hundreds of other publications. A periodical index, which is simply a list of articles classified according to title, subject, and author, can help you determine which journals you want to locate.

There are periodical indexes in all fields. The following brief list gives you a sense of the diversity of titles:

- *Applied Science & Technology Index*
- *Business Periodicals Index*
- *Readers' Guide to Periodical Literature*
- *Engineering Index*

You can also use a directory search engine. Many directory categories include a subcategory called "journals" or "periodicals" listing online and printed sources.

Once you have created a bibliography of printed articles you want to study, you have to find them. Check your library's online catalog, which includes all the journals your library receives. If your library does not have an article you want, you can use one of two techniques for securing it:

- *Interlibrary loan.* Your library finds a library that has the article. That library photocopies the article and sends it or faxes it to your library. This service can take more than a week.

- *Document-delivery services.* If you are in a hurry, you can log on to a document-delivery service, such as Ingenta, which searches a database of 23 million articles in 31,000 periodicals. If the company has the article, it faxes it to you or makes an electronic copy available. These companies charge a fee for this service.

Newspaper Indexes   Many major newspapers around the world are indexed by subject. The three most important indexed U.S. newspapers are the following:

- *The New York Times.* Perhaps the most reputable U.S. newspaper for national and international news.
- *The Christian Science Monitor.* Another highly regarded general newspaper.
- *The Wall Street Journal.* The most authoritative news source on business, finance, and the economy.

On TechComm Web

For links to online newspapers, click on Links Library for Ch. 6 on <bedfordstmartins.com/ techcomm>.

Many newspapers are now available on the Web and can be searched electronically, although sometimes they charge for archived articles. Keep in mind that the print version and the electronic version of a newspaper can vary greatly. If you wish to cite a quotation from an article in a newspaper, the print version is the preferred one.

Abstract Services   Abstract services are like indexes but also provide abstracts: brief technical summaries of the article. In most cases, reading the abstract will enable you to decide whether to seek out the full article. The title of an article alone is often a misleading indicator of its content.

Some abstract services, such as *Chemical Abstracts*, cover a broad field, but many are specialized rather than general. *Adverse Reaction Titles*, for instance, covers research on the subject of adverse reactions to drugs. Figure 6.4 shows an abstract from ARTbibliographies Modern.

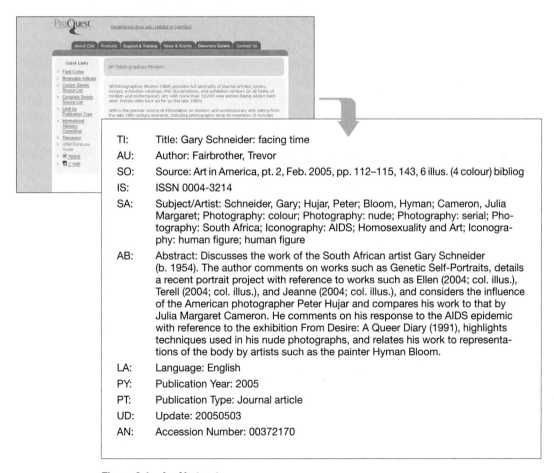

▶**In This Book**
For more about abstracts, see Ch. 18, p. 482.

Figure 6.4   An Abstract
Source: CSA Illumina, 2008 <www.csa.com/factsheets/artbm-set-c.php>.

Researching Government Information

The U.S. government is the world's biggest publisher. In researching any field of science, engineering, or business, you are likely to find that a federal agency or department has produced a relevant brochure, report, or book.

Government publications are not usually listed in the indexes and abstract journals. The *Monthly Catalog of United States Government Publications*, available on paper, on CD, and on the Web, provides extensive access to these materials.

Printed government publications are usually cataloged and shelved separately from other kinds of materials. They are classified according to the Superintendent of Documents system, not the Library of Congress system. A reference librarian or a government documents specialist at your library can help you use government publications.

You can also access many government sites and databases on the Internet. For example, if your company wishes to respond to a request for proposals (RFP) published by a federal government agency, you will find that RFP on a government site. The major entry point for federal government sites is USA.gov (<www.usa.gov>), which links to hundreds of millions of pages of government information and services. It also features tutorials, a topical index, online transactions, and links to state and local governments.

Using Web 2.0 Resources

Commentators are now using the terms *Web 2.0* and *World Live Web* to refer to a new generation of interactive Internet-based services such as wikis, social-networking sites, blogs, social-bookmarking sites, and folksonomies (collaboratively created labels used to describe Web 2.0 content). Web 2.0 resources enable people to collaborate, share, link, and generate content in ways that traditional Web sites offering static content cannot.

The result is an Internet that can harness the collective intelligence of people around the globe. *Wikis*, for example, allow people to create documents collaboratively by easily adding, removing, and revising content. *Blogs* enable people to publish their opinions quickly and easily to create online diaries or columns.

The ease and speed of posting new content, as well as the lack of formal review of the content, creates challenges for people who do research on the Internet. Everyone using Web 2.0 resources must be extra cautious.

The following discussion explains tagged content, social-bookmarking sites, and RSS feeds.

Tagged Content   Tags are descriptive keywords people use to categorize and describe content such as blog entries, videos, podcasts, audio files, and images they post to the Internet. Tags can be one-word descriptors without spaces or punctuation (such as "sandiegozoo") or multiword descriptors (such as "San Diego Zoo"). A tag for a photo posted on the Web might be as

On TechComm Web

For links to the *Monthly Catalog*, to USA.gov, and to other government information, click on Links Library for Ch. 6 on <bedfordstmartins.com/techcomm>.

In This Book

For more about RFPs, see Ch. 16, p. 434.

On TechComm Web

For an excellent guide to using government information, see Patricia Cruse and Sherry DeDecker's "How to Effectively Locate Federal Government Information on the Web." Click on Links Library for Ch. 6 on <bedfordstmartins.com/techcomm>.

simple as "grizzly." A more descriptive tag might be "grizzlycubs" or "Alaska bears." One challenge in using tagged content is that searching for "San Diego Zoo" might generate different results than searching for "sandiegozoo." Trying multiple variations of a key phrase will help you locate more material.

Tags help people find content similar to what they are posting and to search for content based on the tags associated with the content. Figure 6.5 shows the results of a search for photos tagged with "Iceland" on a photo-sharing Web site.

Figure 6.5   Search Results for Photos Tagged with "Iceland"
Source: Flickr, 2008
<www.flickr.com/photos/tags/iceland>.

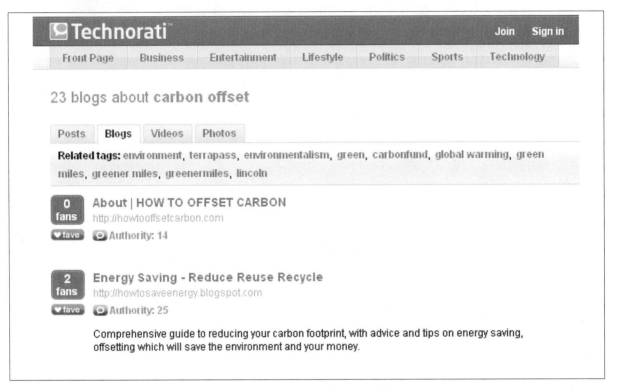

Figure 6.6   Search Results for Blogs Tagged with "Carbon Offset"

Tabs allow readers to search for posts, blogs, videos, and photos tagged with "carbon offset."
Related tags help readers locate additional content associated with "carbon offset." For
example, a researcher might want to search for "green miles" or "carbonfund." The "Authority"
link allows readers to view reactions to a blog posting.
Source: Technorati, 2008 <http://technorati.com/blogs/tag/carbon+offset>.

When you search for tagged content, you need to predict how the content might be tagged. For example, when searching for an image, the image might include tags related to the type of image (such as "photo"), style ("landscape"), location ("Belize"), or a person's name ("Roger"). Figure 6.6 shows the search results for blogs tagged with "carbon offset" on Technorati, a site that currently tracks 112.8 million blogs and more than 250 million pieces of tagged social media.

Social-Bookmarking Sites   Social-bookmarking sites such as Del.icio.us allow you to manage and share your bookmarks and to access them from any computer with Internet access. Because people use tags to organize and remember their bookmarks, you can use social-bookmarking sites to search for tagged bookmarks relevant to your research needs. Figure 6.7 shows a list of bookmarks tagged with "pesticide."

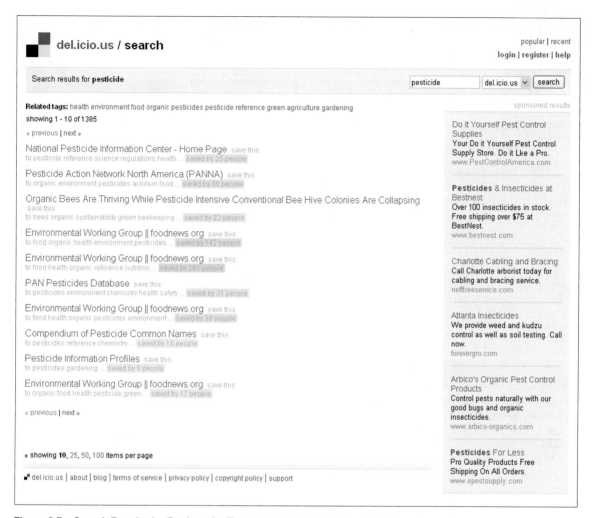

Figure 6.7   Search Results for Bookmarks Tagged with "Pesticide"

This site allows users to see how many other people saved a bookmark listed in the search results. By selecting a related tag, you can view other potentially relevant bookmarks. A bookmark saved by many people might be useful. However, you are responsible for evaluating the credibility of each site you use in your research.

Source: Del.icio.us, 2008 <http://del.icio.us/search/?fr=del_icio_us&p=pesticide&type=all>.

RSS Feeds   Repeatedly checking for new content on many different Web sites can be a time-consuming and haphazard way to research a topic. *RSS* (short for *rich site summary* or *really simple syndication*) *technology* allows readers to check just one place (such as a software program running on their computer or some e-mail programs) for alerts to new content posted on selected Web sites.

Figure 6.8   Web Site Offering RSS Feeds

This page shows how to use RSS feeds on USA.gov, the gateway to information from the U.S. government.
Source: U.S. General Services, 2008 <www.usa.gov/rss/index.shtml>.

Readers use a special type of software program called an *RSS aggregator* to be alerted by *RSS feeds* (notifications of new or changed content) from Web sites of interest to them. RSS aggregators allow readers to organize RSS feeds and monitor new content on Web sites without having to visit each site separately. Figure 6.8 shows a Web site that offers RSS feeds.

Evaluating the Information

You've taken notes, paraphrased, and quoted material from your secondary research. Now, with more information than you can possibly use, you try to figure out what it all means. You realize that you still have some questions, that some of the information is incomplete, some contradictory, and some just unclear. There is no shortage of information; the challenge is to find the right information. Look for information that is accurate, unbiased, comprehensive, appropriately technical, current, and clear.

- *Accurate.* You are researching whether your company should consider flextime scheduling. You start by determining the number of employees

In This Book

For more about taking notes, paraphrasing, and quoting, see Appendix, Part A.

who might be interested in flextime. If you estimate that number to be 500 but it is in fact closer to 50, you will waste time doing an unnecessary study.

- *Unbiased.* You want sources that have no financial stake in the project. A private company that transports workers in vans is likely to be a biased source because it wants your business.

- *Comprehensive.* You want information from different kinds of people—in terms of gender, cultural characteristics, and age—and from people representing all views of the topic.

- *Appropriately technical.* Good information is sufficiently detailed to respond to the needs of your readers, but not so detailed that they cannot understand it. For the study of flextime, you need to find out whether opening your building an hour earlier and closing it an hour later will significantly affect your utility costs. You can get this information by interviewing people in the Operations and Security Departments. You will not need to do a detailed inspection of all the utility records of the company.

- *Current.* If your information is 10 years old, it might not accurately reflect today's situation.

- *Clear.* You want information that is easy to understand. Otherwise, you'll waste time figuring it out, and you might misinterpret it.

The most difficult kind of material to evaluate is information from the Internet, because it often appears on the Internet without passing through the formal review procedure used for books and professional journals.

On TechComm Web

For links to sources on finding and evaluating Internet information, click on Links Library for Ch. 6 on <bedfordstmartins .com/techcomm>.

Guidelines

Evaluating Print and Online Sources

Criteria	For printed sources	For online sources
Authorship	Do you recognize the name of the author? Does the source describe the author's credentials and current position? If not, can you find it in a who's who or by searching for other books or other journal articles by the author?	If you do not recognize the author's name, is the site mentioned on another reputable site? Does the site contain links to other reputable sites? Does it contain biographical information—the author's current position and credentials? Can you use a search engine to find other references to the author's credentials? Be especially careful with unedited sources such as Wikipedia; some articles in it are authoritative, but others are not. Be careful, too, with blogs, some of which are written by disgruntled former employees with an ax to grind.

On TechComm Web

Evaluating sources is easier if you start searching from a reputable list of links, such as that of the WWW Virtual Library, sponsored by the World Wide Web Consortium. Click on Links Library for Ch. 6 on <bedfordstmartins.com/techcomm>.

Criteria	For printed sources	For online sources
Publishing body	What is the publisher's reputation? A reliable book is published by a reputable trade, academic, or scholarly publisher; a journal is sponsored by a professional association or university. Are the editorial board members well-known? Trade publications—magazines about a particular industry or group—often promote the interests of that industry or group. For example, information in trade publications for loggers or environmentalists might be biased. If you doubt the authority of a book or journal, ask the reference librarian or a professor.	Can you determine the publishing body's identity from headers or footers? Is the publishing body reputable? If the site comes from a personal account on an Internet service provider, the author might be writing outside his or her field of expertise. Many Internet sites exist largely for public relations or advertising. For instance, Web sites of corporations and other organizations are unlikely to contain self-critical information. For blogs, examine the *blogroll*, a list of links to other blogs and Web sites. Credible blogs are likely to link to blogs already known to be credible. If a blog links only to friends, blogs hosted by the same corporation, or blogs that share the same beliefs, be very cautious.
Knowledge of the literature	Does the author appear to be knowledgeable about the major literature? Is there a bibliography? Are there notes throughout the document?	Analyze the Internet source as you would any other source. Often, references to other sources will take the form of links.
Accuracy and verifiability of the information	Is the information based on reasonable assumptions? Does the author clearly describe the methods and theories used in producing the information, and are they appropriate to the subject? Has the author used sound reasoning? Has the author explained the limitations of the information?	Is the site well constructed? Is the information well written? Is it based on reasonable assumptions? Are the claims supported by appropriate evidence? Has the author used sound reasoning? Has the author explained the limitations of the information? Are sources cited? Online services such as BlogPulse help you evaluate how active a blog is, how the blog ranks compared to other blogs, and who is citing the blog. Active, influential blogs that are frequently linked to and cited by others might be more likely to contain accurate, verifiable information.
Timeliness	Does the document rely on recent data? Was the document published recently?	Was the document created recently? Was it updated recently? If a site is not yet complete, be wary.

INTERACTIVE SAMPLE DOCUMENT
Evaluating Information from Internet Sources

The following item appeared in Kaiser Permanente Thrive Exposed, a blog written by Managed Care Watch (2007), which describes itself as follows: "Managed Care Watch is a coalition of concerned consumers and professionals who have come together for the purpose of reforming the HMO and Managed Care industry. All like-minded individuals and organizations are welcome to join us." The item, titled "Another life threatening illness misdiagnosed as psychological problem," begins with the blogger's comments, followed by the text of a newspaper article about the case (see page 132). The questions in the margin ask you to consider the guidelines for evaluating Internet sources (on pages 129–30). E-mail your responses to yourself and/or your instructor on TechComm Web.

One of the more disturbing patterns that has emerged over four years of tracking Kaiser's many misdeeds, is that patients with very real and serious medical problems are often misdiagnosed with mental health issues, leading to much unnecessary suffering, and sometimes death. A few recent examples are the cases of Jupirena Stein, Craig Pazzi, and a woman with West Nile Virus, who was repeatedly told her symptoms were all in her head even after a positive blood test confirmed the infection. For the reason behind this troublesome trend, one need look no further than Kaiser's clinical practice guidelines, where Kaiser doctors are instructed to label anyone with an undiagnosed illness as a psych case.

Update 12/9/07: We have added a scan of *A Secret of Behavioral Health Integration: The Handoff* from "The Collected Papers of Nicholas A. Cummings, Volume I: The Value of Psychological Treatment." In it he describes the process by which Kaiser members are manipulated into accepting mental health treatment for physical illnesses.

The money quote (because it's always about the money at Kaiser):

"Without this seemingly simple touch, patient compliance was not very good, but with this idea of the handoff, compliance jumped to 90 percent. **And the saving in medical costs was tremendous.**"

Cummings developed the Kaiser Behavioral Health Division.

Source: Managed Care Watch, 2007 <www.kaiserthrive.org/2007/12/08/another-life-threatening-illness-misdiagnosed-as-psychological-problem>.

1. Does the author of this blog present himself as an unbiased commentator? In the first paragraph, which comments reveal his perspective on the situation he is describing?

2. As you read the section labeled "Update 12/9/07," what additional information would you like to see to help you understand the validity of the blogger's claims?

3. To what extent does the article from the *Orange County Register,* a newspaper in Orange County, California, lend support to the blogger's claims?

Kaiser to pay $1.8 million in malpractice case

45-year-old man was not diagnosed with cerebral bleeding and later suffered permanent brain damage.

BY COURTNEY PERKES

The Orange County Register

Kaiser Permanente will pay $1.8 million to the family of a Huntington Beach man who suffered a brain aneurysm after his headache was wrongly attributed to grief.

In 2005, 45-year-old Ted Blackwell visited a Kaiser clinic in Orange County with a headache and neck pain. According to the binding arbitration document, doctors attributed his symptoms to grief over the death of his brother eight days earlier.

He received an injection and was sent home.

Blackwell returned to the clinic two days later, still in pain. According to the document, his daughter requested a CT scan because of her father's disorientation but doctors decided that wasn't necessary.

Two days later, Blackwell collapsed and underwent surgery at Hoag Hospital for bleeding in his brain. He suffered permanent brain damage and is unable to work, according to his attorney James McElroy of Del Mar.

Jim Anderson, a spokesman for Kaiser, expressed sympathy to Blackwell, but added "we thought differently in this or we wouldn't have taken it to arbitration."

The award, decided by arbitrator Robert Devich, covers pain and suffering and lost wages, but the bulk is for around-the-clock supervision for the rest of Blackwell's life.

In California, malpractice judgments are capped at $250,000 for pain and suffering. Additional monetary damages result from loss of wages and need for ongoing care.

Contact the writer: 714-796-3686 or cperkes@ocregister.com

Source: OC Register <www.ocregister.com/life/blackwell-pain-brain-1937851-kaiser-days>.

On TechComm Web

To e-mail your responses to yourself and/or your instructor, click on Interactive Sample Documents for Ch. 6 on <bedfordstmartins.com/techcomm>.

A general principle for using any information you find on the Internet—and this goes double for information from Web 2.0 resources—is to be extremely careful. Because content is unlikely to have been reviewed before being published on a Web 2.0 site, use one or more trusted sources to confirm the information. Some instructors do not allow their students to use blogs or wikis, including Wikipedia. Check with your instructor about his or her policies.

CONDUCTING PRIMARY RESEARCH

Although the library and the Internet offer a wealth of secondary sources, in the workplace you will often need to conduct primary research to acquire new information. There are seven major categories of primary research: observations and demonstrations, inspections, experiments, field research, interviews, inquiry letters or e-mails, and questionnaires.

Observations and Demonstrations

Observations and demonstrations are two common forms of primary research. When you *observe*, you simply watch some activity to understand some aspect of it. For instance, if you are trying to determine whether the location of the break room on a factory floor is interfering with the work on the floor, you could observe the situation, preferably at different times of the day and on different days of the week. If you saw workers distracted by people moving in and out of the room or by sounds made in the room, you would record your observations by taking notes, taking still pictures, or videotaping the events. An observation might lead to other forms of primary research. You might, for example, follow up by interviewing some employees who might help you understand what you have observed.

When you witness a *demonstration* (or *demo*), you are watching someone carry out a process. For instance, if your company is considering purchasing a mail-sorting machine, you could arrange to visit a manufacturer's facility, where technicians would show how the various machines work. If your company is considering a portable machine, such as a laptop computer, the manufacturer or dealer could bring its product(s) to your facility.

When you observe a situation or witness a demo, prepare beforehand. Write down the questions you need answered or the points you want to investigate. Prepare interview questions in case you have a chance to speak with someone. Think about how you are going to incorporate the information you acquire into the document you will write. Finally, bring whatever equipment you will need (pen and paper, computer, camera, audio recorders, etc.) to the site of the observation or demo.

Inspections

Inspections are like observations, but you participate more actively. For example, a civil engineer can determine what caused the crack in a foundation by inspecting the site: walking around, looking at the crack, photographing it and the surrounding scene, picking up the soil. An accountant can determine the financial health of an organization by inspecting its financial records, perhaps performing calculations and comparing the data she finds with other data.

These professionals are applying their knowledge and professional judgment as they inspect a site, an object, or a document. Sometimes, inspection techniques are more complicated. A civil engineer inspecting foundation cracking might want to test his hunches by taking soil samples back to the lab and studying them.

When you carry out an inspection, do your homework beforehand. Think about how you will use the data in your document: will you need photographs, video files, or computer data? Then prepare the materials and equipment you'll need to capture the data.

Experiments

Learning to conduct the many kinds of experiments used in a particular field can take months or even years. This discussion is a brief introduction.

In many cases, conducting an experiment involves four phases:

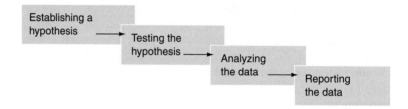

- *Establishing a hypothesis.* A hypothesis is an informed guess about the relationship between two factors. In a study relating gasoline octane and miles per gallon, a hypothesis might be that a car will get 10 percent better mileage with 89 octane gas than with 87 octane.

- *Testing the hypothesis.* Usually, you need an experimental group and a control group. These two groups would be identical except for the condition you are studying: in the above example, the gasoline. The control group would be a car running on 87 octane. The experimental group would be an identical car running on 89 octane. The experiment would consist of driving the two cars on an identical course at the same speed—preferably in some sort of controlled environment—over a given distance, such as 1,000 miles. Then you would calculate the miles per gallon. The results would either support or refute your original hypothesis.

- *Analyzing the data.* Do your data show a correlation—one factor changing along with another—or a causal relationship? For example, we know that sports cars are involved in more fatal accidents than sedans, but we don't know whether the car or the way it is driven is the important factor.

- *Reporting the data.* When researchers report their findings, they explain what they did, why they did it, what they saw, what it means, and what ought to be done next.

▶ **In This Book**

For more about reports, see Chs. 17–19.

Field Research

Whereas an experiment yields quantitative data that can be measured, most field research is qualitative. It yields data that cannot be measured or, at least, cannot be measured as precisely as experimental data. Often in field research, you seek to understand the quality of an experience. For instance, you might want to understand how a new seating arrangement might affect group dynamics in a particular classroom. You could design a study in which you observed and recorded the class and interviewed the students and instructor about their reactions. Then you could do the same in a traditional classroom and compare the results.

Some kinds of studies have both quantitative and qualitative elements. In the case of classroom seating arrangements, you could include some quantitative measures, such as the number of times students talked with each other. You could also distribute questionnaires to elicit the opinions of the students and the instructor. If you used these same quantitative measures on enough classrooms, you could gather valid quantitative information.

When you are doing quantitative or qualitative studies on the behavior of animals—from rats to monkeys to people—try to minimize two common problems:

- *The effect of the experiment on the behavior you are studying.* In studying the effects of the classroom seating arrangement, minimize the effects of your own presence. For instance, make sure that the camera is placed unobtrusively and that it is set up before the students arrive, so they don't see the process. Still, anytime you bring in a camera, you can never be sure that what you witness is typical.

- *Bias in the recording and analysis of the data.* Bias can occur because researchers want to confirm their hypotheses. In an experiment to determine whether word processors help students write better, the researcher might see improvement where other people don't. For this reason, the experiment should be designed so that it is *double-blind.* That is, the students doing the writing shouldn't know what the experiment is about so they won't change their behavior to support or negate the hypothesis. And the data being analyzed should be disguised so that researchers don't know whether they are examining the results from the control group or the experimental group. If the control group wrote in ink and the experimental group used word processors, for example, the control group's papers should be formatted on a word processor so that all the papers look identical.

Conducting an experiment or field research is relatively simple; the hard part is designing your study so that it accurately measures what you want it to measure.

Interviews

Interviews are extremely useful when you need information on subjects that are too new to have been discussed in the professional literature or are inappropriate for widespread publication (such as local political questions).

In choosing a respondent—a person to interview—answer three questions:

- *What questions do you want to answer?* Only after you answer this question can you begin to search for a person who can provide the information.

- *Who could provide this information?* The ideal respondent is an expert willing to talk. Unless the respondent is an obvious choice, such as the professor carrying out the research you are studying, use directories, such as local industrial guides, to locate potential respondents.

- *Is the person willing to be interviewed?* On the phone or in writing, state what you want to ask about. The person might not be able to help you but might be willing to refer you to someone who can. Explain why you have decided to ask him or her. (A compliment works better than admitting that the person you really wanted to interview is out of town.) Explain what you plan to do with the information, such as write a report or give a talk. Then, if the person is willing to be interviewed, set up an appointment at his or her convenience.

Guidelines

Conducting an Interview

Preparing for the interview

▶ **Do your homework.** If you ask questions that are already answered in the professional literature, the respondent might become annoyed and uncooperative.

▶ **Prepare good questions.** Good questions are clear, focused, and open.

— Be clear. The respondent should be able to understand what you are asking.

UNCLEAR Why do you sell Trane products?

CLEAR What are the characteristics of Trane products that led you to include them in your product line?

The unclear question can be answered in a number of unhelpful ways: "Because they're too expensive to give away" or "Because I'm a Trane dealer."

— Be focused. The question must be narrow enough to be answered briefly. If you want more information, you can ask a follow-up question.

On TechComm Web

For an excellent discussion of interview questions, see Joel Bowman's *Business Communication: Managing Information and Relationships*. Click on Links Library for Ch. 6 on <bedfordstmartins.com/techcomm>.

UNFOCUSED	What is the future of the computer industry?
FOCUSED	What will the American chip industry look like in 10 years?

— Ask open questions. Your purpose is to get the respondent to talk. Don't ask a lot of questions that have yes or no answers.

CLOSED	Do you think the federal government should create industrial partnerships?
OPEN	What are the advantages and disadvantages of the federal government's creating industrial partnerships?

▶ **Check your equipment.** If you will be taping the interview, test your tape recorder or video camera to make sure it is operating properly.

Beginning the interview

▶ **Arrive on time.**

▶ **Thank the respondent for taking the time to talk with you.**

▶ **State the subject and purpose of the interview and what you plan to do with the information.**

▶ **If you wish to tape the interview, ask permission.**

Conducting the interview

▶ **Take notes.** Write down important concepts, facts, and numbers, but don't take such copious notes that you are still writing when the respondent finishes an answer.

▶ **Start with prepared questions.** Because you are likely to be nervous at the start, you might forget important questions. Have your first few questions ready.

▶ **Be prepared to ask follow-up questions.** Listen carefully to the respondent's answer and be ready to ask a follow-up question or request a clarification. Have your other prepared questions ready, but be willing to deviate from them if the respondent leads you in unexpected directions.

▶ **Be prepared to get the interview back on track.** Gently return to the point if the respondent begins straying unproductively, but don't interrupt rudely or show annoyance. Do not say "Whoa! I asked about layoffs in this company, not in the whole industry." Rather, say "On the question of layoffs at this company, do you anticipate . . . ?"

Concluding the interview

▶ **Thank the respondent.**

▶ **Ask for a follow-up interview.** If a second meeting would be useful, ask to arrange it.

▶ **Ask for permission to quote the respondent.** If you think you might want to quote the respondent by name, ask for permission now.

After the interview	▶ **Write down the important information while the interview is fresh in your mind.** (This step is unnecessary, of course, if you have recorded the interview.) If you will be printing a transcript of the interview, make the transcript now.
	▶ **Send a brief thank-you note.** Within a day or two, send a note that shows you appreciate the respondent's courtesy and that you value what you have learned. In the note, confirm any previous offers you have made, such as sending the respondent a copy of your final document.

When you wish to present the data from an interview in a document you are preparing, include a transcript of the entire interview or an excerpt from the interview. It is generally best to present an entire transcript in an appendix so that readers can refer to it but are not slowed down when reading the body of the document. You might decide to present brief excerpts from the interview in the body of the document as evidence supporting points you make.

Figure 6.9 is from a transcript of an interview with an attorney specializing in information technology. The interviewer was a student who was writing about legal aspects of software ownership.

Inquiry Letters or E-mails

A useful alternative to a personal interview is an inquiry letter or e-mail. Most large organizations make it more convenient for you to e-mail than to send a letter (look for the "Contact Us" link on the site). Many people prefer to receive e-mail inquiries because it is easier to hit the Reply button than to create a letter. However, letters are more formal than e-mails and therefore might be more appropriate if the topic is important (concerning personnel layoffs, for instance) or related to safety.

In This Book
For more about inquiry letters, see Ch. 14, p. 371.

If you are lucky, your respondent will provide detailed and helpful answers. However, the respondent might not clearly understand what you want to know or might choose not to help you. Although the strategy of the inquiry letter is essentially that of a personal interview, inquiry letters can be less successful, because the recipient has not already agreed to provide information and might not respond. Also, a written inquiry, unlike an interview, gives you little opportunity to follow up by asking for clarification.

Keep a copy of the e-mail or letter that you send. You might need to include it in an appendix if you include the recipient's reply in your document.

Questionnaires

Questionnaires enable you to solicit information from a large group of people. You can send questionnaires through the mail, e-mail them, or present

Figure 6.9   Excerpt from an Interview

Interview Transcript, Page 1

Q. Why is copyright ownership important in marketing software?

A. If you own the copyright, you can license and market the product and keep other people from doing so. It could be a matter of millions of dollars if the software is popular.

Q. Shouldn't the programmer automatically own the copyright?

Notice how the student prompts the attorney to expand her answers.

A. If the programmer wrote the program on personal time, he or she should and does own the copyright.

Q. So "personal time" is the critical concept?

A. That's right. We're talking about the "work-made-for-hire" doctrine of copyright law. If I am working for you, anything I make under the terms of my employment is owned by you.

Q. What is the complication, then? If I make the software on my machine at home, I own it; if I'm working for someone, my employer owns it.

Notice how the student responds to the attorney's answers, making the interview more of a discussion.

A. Well, the devil is in the details. Often terms of employment are casual, or there is no written job description or contract for the particular piece of software.

Q. Can you give me an example of that?

A. Sure. There was a 1992 case, *Aymes v. Bonelli*. Bonelli owned a swimming pool and hired Aymes to write software to handle record keeping on the pool. This was not part of Bonelli's regular business; he just wanted a piece of software written. The terms of the employment were casual. Bonelli paid no health benefits, Aymes worked irregular hours, usually unsupervised—Bonelli wasn't a programmer. When the case was heard, the court ruled that even though Bonelli was paying Aymes, Aymes owned the copyright because of the lack of involvement and participation by Bonelli. The court found that the degree of skill required by Aymes to do the job was so great that, in effect, he was creating the software by himself, even though he was receiving compensation for it.

Q. How can such disagreements be prevented? By working out the details ahead of time?

A. Exactly. The employer should have the employee sign a statement that the project is being carried out as work made for hire and should register the copyright with the U.S. Copyright Office in Washington. Conversely, employees should try to have the employer sign a statement that the project is not work made for hire and should try to register the copyright themselves.

Q. And if agreement can't be reached ahead of time?

A. Then stop right there. Don't do any work.

them as forms on a Web site. Unfortunately, questionnaires rarely yield completely satisfactory results, for three reasons:

- *Some of the questions will misfire.* Respondents will misinterpret some of your questions or supply useless answers.
- *You won't obtain as many responses as you want.* The response rate will almost never exceed 50 percent. In most cases, it will be closer to 10 to 20 percent.

- *You cannot be sure the respondents are representative.* People who feel strongly about an issue are much more likely to respond than are those who do not feel strongly. For this reason, you need to be careful in drawing conclusions based on a small number of responses to a questionnaire.

When you send a questionnaire, you are asking the recipient to do you a favor. Your goal should be to construct questions that will elicit the information you need as simply and efficiently as possible.

Asking Effective Questions　　To ask effective questions, follow two suggestions:

- *Use unbiased language.* Don't ask "Should U.S. clothing manufacturers protect themselves from unfair foreign competition?" Instead, ask "Are you in favor of imposing tariffs on men's clothing?"
- *Be specific.* If you ask "Do you favor improving the safety of automobiles?" only an eccentric would answer no. Instead, ask "Do you favor requiring automobile manufacturers to equip new cars with electronic stability control, which would raise the price by an average of $300 per car?"

Table 6.1 explains common types of questions used in questionnaires. Include an introductory explanation with the questionnaire. This explanation should clearly indicate who you are, why you are writing, what you plan to do with the information, and when you will need it.

Table 6.1 Common Types of Questions Used in Questionnaires

Type of question	Example	Comments
Multiple choice	Would you consider joining a company-sponsored sports team? Yes ____ No ____	The respondent selects one of the alternatives.
Likert scale	The flextime program has been a success in its first year. strongly disagree __ __ __ __ __ __ strongly agree	The respondent ranks the degree to which he or she agrees or disagrees with the statement. Using an even number of possible responses (six, in this case) increases your chances of obtaining useful data. With an odd number, many respondents choose the middle response.
Semantic differentials	simple __ __ __ __ __ __ difficult interesting __ __ __ __ __ __ boring	The respondent registers a response along a continuum between a pair of opposing adjectives. Usually, these questions measure a person's feelings about a task, an experience, or an object. As with Likert scales, an even number of possible responses yields better data.
Ranking	Please rank the following work schedules in order of preference. Put a 1 next to the schedule you would most like to have, a 2 next to your second choice, and so on. 8:00–4:30 _____　9:00–5:30 _____ 8:30–5:00 _____　flexible _____	The respondent indicates a priority among a number of alternatives.

Table 6.1 (continued)

Type of question	Example	Comments
Short answer	What do you feel are the major advantages of the new parts-requisitioning policy? 1. _____ 2. _____ 3. _____	The respondent writes a brief answer using phrases or sentences.
Short essay	The new parts-requisitioning policy has been in effect for a year. How well do you think it is working? _____ _____ _____ _____ _____ _____	Although an essay question can yield information you never would have found using closed-ended questions, you will receive fewer responses because they require more effort. Also, essays cannot be quantified precisely, as the data from the other types of questions can.

Testing the Questionnaire   Before you send out *any* questionnaire, show it and the accompanying letter or memo to a few people who can help you identify any problems. After you have revised the materials, test them on people whose backgrounds are similar to those of your real respondents. Revise the materials a second time and, if possible, test them again. Once you have sent the questionnaire, you cannot revise it and resend it to the same people.

▶ **In This Book**

For more about testing documents, see Ch. 13, p. 349.

Administering the Questionnaire   Determining who should receive the questionnaire can be simple or difficult. If you want to know what the residents of a particular street think about a proposed construction project, your job is easy. But if you want to know what mechanical-engineering students in colleges across the country think about their curricula, you will need background in sampling techniques to isolate a representative sample.

Make it easy for respondents to present their information. For mailed questionnaires, include a self-addressed, stamped envelope.

Figure 6.10 on page 142 shows a sample questionnaire.

Presenting Questionnaire Data in Your Document   To decide where and how to present the data that you acquire from your questionnaire, think about your audience and purpose. Start with this principle: important information is presented and analyzed in the body of a document, whereas less-important information is presented in an appendix (a section at the end of the document that only some of your audience will read). Most often, some version of the information appears in both places, but in different ways.

**Figure 6.10
Questionnaire**

September 6, 2009

To: All employees
From: William Bonoff, Vice President of Operations
Subject: Evaluation of the Lunches Unlimited food service

As you may know, every two years we evaluate the quality and cost of the food service that caters our lunchroom. We would like you to help in our evaluation by sharing your opinions about the food service. Please note that your responses will remain anonymous. Please drop the completed questionnaires in the marked boxes near the main entrance to the lunchroom.

1. Approximately how many days per week do you eat lunch in the lunchroom?
   0 _____   1 _____   2 _____   3 _____   4 _____   5 _____

2. At approximately what time do you eat in the lunchroom?
   11:30–12:30 _____   12:00–1:00 _____   12:30–1:30 _____   varies _____

3. A clean table is usually available.
   strongly disagree _____ _____ _____ _____ _____ _____ strongly agree

4. The Lunches Unlimited personnel are polite and helpful.
   strongly disagree _____ _____ _____ _____ _____ _____ strongly agree

5. Please comment on the quality of the different kinds of food you have eaten in the lunchroom.
   a. Daily specials
      excellent _____   good _____   satisfactory _____   poor _____
   b. Hot dogs and hamburgers
      excellent _____   good _____   satisfactory _____   poor _____
   c. Other entrées
      excellent _____   good _____   satisfactory _____   poor _____

6. What *foods* would you like to see served that are not served now?
   _____
   _____
   _____

7. What *beverages* would you like to see served that are not served now?
   _____
   _____
   _____

8. Please comment on the prices of the foods and beverages served.
   a. Hot meals (daily specials)
      too high _____   fair _____   a bargain _____
   b. Hot dogs and hamburgers
      too high _____   fair _____   a bargain _____
   c. Other entrées
      too high _____   fair _____   a bargain _____

9. Would you be willing to spend more money for a better-quality lunch if you thought the price was reasonable?
   yes, often _____   sometimes _____   not likely _____

10. On the other side of this sheet, please provide whatever comments you think will help us evaluate the catering service.
   _____

Thank you for your assistance.

Likert-scale questions 3 and 4 make it easy for the writer to quantify data about subjective impressions.

Short-answer questions 6 and 7 are best for soliciting ideas from respondents.

If you think your questionnaire data are relatively unimportant, present the questionnaire in an appendix. If you can, present the respondents' data—the answers they provided—in the questionnaire itself, as shown here.

1. Approximately how many days per week do you eat lunch in the lunchroom?

   0 **12** 1 **16** 2 **18** 3 **12** 4 **9** 5 **4**

2. At approximately what time do you eat in the lunchroom?

   11:30–12:30 **3** 12:00–1:00 **26** 12:30–1:30 **7** varies **23**

If you think your questionnaire data are relatively important, present the full data in an appendix and interpret selected data in the body of the document. For instance, you might want to devote a few sentences or paragraphs to the data for one of the questions. The following example shows how one writer might discuss the data from question 2.

> Question 2 shows that 26 people say that they use the cafeteria between noon and 1:00. Only 10 people selected the other two times, 11:30–12:30 and 12:30–1:30. Of the 23 people who said they use the cafeteria at various times, we can conclude that at least a third—some 8 people—use it between noon and 1:00. If this assumption is correct, some 34 people (26 + 8) use the cafeteria between noon and 1:00. This would explain why people routinely cannot find a table during the noon hour, especially between 12:15 and 12:30. To alleviate this problem, we might consider asking department heads not to schedule meetings between 11:30 and 1:30, which would make it easier for their people to choose one of the less-popular times.

The body of a document is also a good place to discuss important non-quantitative data. For example, you might wish to discuss and interpret several representative textual answers to open-ended questions.

If you think your reader will benefit from analyses of the data, present such analyses. For instance, you could calculate the percentage for each response: for question 1, "12 people—16 percent—say they do not eat in the cafeteria at all." Or you could present the percentage in parentheses after each number: "12 (16%)."

Ethics Note

Reporting and Analyzing Data Honestly

When you put a lot of time and effort into a research project, it's frustrating when you can't find the information you need, or when the information you find doesn't help you say what you want to say. As discussed in Chapter 2, your challenge as a professional is to tell the truth.

If the evidence suggests that the course of action you propose won't work, don't omit that evidence or change it. Rather, try to figure out the discrepancy between the evidence and your proposal. Present your explanation honestly.

If you can't find reputable evidence to support your claim that this device works better than that one, don't just keep silent and hope your readers won't notice. Explain why you think the evidence is missing and how you propose to follow up by continuing your research.

If you make an honest mistake, you are a person. If you cover up a mistake, you're a dishonest person. If you get caught fudging the data, you could be an unemployed dishonest person. If you don't get caught, you're still a smaller person.

Writer's Checklist

Did you

- ☐ determine the questions you need to answer in your document? (p. 114)
- ☐ choose appropriate secondary-research methods to answer those questions, including, if appropriate,
  - ☐ online catalogs? (p. 120)
  - ☐ reference works? (p. 120)
  - ☐ periodical indexes? (p. 122)
  - ☐ newspaper indexes? (p. 122)
  - ☐ abstract services? (p. 123)
  - ☐ government information? (p. 124)
  - ☐ Web 2.0 resources? (p. 124)
- ☐ choose appropriate primary-research methods to answer those questions, including, if appropriate,
  - ☐ observations and demonstrations? (p. 133)
  - ☐ inspections? (p. 133)
  - ☐ experiments? (p. 134)
  - ☐ field research? (p. 135)
  - ☐ interviews? (p. 136)
  - ☐ inquiry letters or e-mails? (p. 138)
  - ☐ questionnaires? (p. 138)

In evaluating information, did you carefully assess

- ☐ the author's credentials? (p. 129)
- ☐ the publishing body? (p. 130)
- ☐ the author's knowledge of literature in the field? (p. 130)
- ☐ the accuracy and verifiability of the information? (p. 130)
- ☐ the timeliness of the information? (p. 130)

- ☐ Did you appropriately present and analyze the information you acquired? (p. 143)

Exercises

⟿ In This Book For more about memos, see Ch. 14, p. 377.

1. **INTERNET EXERCISE** Use a search engine to find at least 10 Web sites about some key term or concept in your field, such as "genetic engineering," "hospice care," or "fuzzy logic." For each site, write a brief paragraph explaining why it would or would not be a credible source of information for a research report.

2. **INTERNET EXERCISE** Using a search engine, answer the following questions. Provide the URL of each Web site you mention. If your instructor requests it, submit your answers as an e-mail to him or her.

   a. What are the three largest or most important professional organizations in your field? For example, if you are a construction-management major, your field is construction management, civil engineering, or industrial engineering.

   b. What are three important journals read by people in your field?

   c. What are three important online discussion lists or bulletin boards read by people in your field?

   d. What are the date and location of an upcoming national or international professional meeting for people in your field?

   e. Name and describe, in one paragraph for each, three major issues being discussed by practitioners or academics in your field. For instance, nurses might be discussing the effect of managed care on the quality of medical care delivered to patients.

3. Revise the following interview questions to make them more effective. In a brief paragraph for each, explain why you have revised it as you have.

   a. What is the role of communication in your daily job?

   b. Do you think it is better to relocate your warehouse or go to just-in-time manufacturing?

   c. Isn't it true that it's almost impossible to train an engineer to write well?

   d. Where are your company's headquarters?

   e. Is there anything else you think I should know?

4. Revise the following questions from questionnaires to make them more effective. In a brief paragraph for each, explain why you have revised it as you have.

   a. Does your company provide tuition reimbursement for its employees? Yes_____ No_____

   b. What do you see as the future of bioengineering?

c. How satisfied are you with the computer support you receive?

d. How many employees work at your company?

5–10____   10–15____   15 or more____

e. What kinds of documents do you write most often?

Memos____   Letters____   Reports____

5. **GROUP/INTERNET EXERCISE** Form small groups and brainstorm a list of tags that might be helpful to locate content on the World Live Web that would be useful for someone who is researching how to select a wide-screen television. Go to a World Live Web site such as Del.icio.us.com or Technorati.com and have each group member search using a different tag. Evaluate the content available on the first five items listed in the search results. Next, select a related tag listed in the search results. Evaluate the relevance of the resulting items to the research topic. Compare your findings with those of other group members. Which tags seemed to generate the most useful content? Present your findings in a memo to your instructor.

6. **GROUP/INTERNET EXERCISE** Form small groups and describe and evaluate your college or university's Web site. A different member of the group might carry out each of the following tasks:

- In an e-mail to the site's Webmaster, ask questions about the process of creating the site. For example, how involved with the content and design of the site was the Webmaster? What is the Webmaster's role in maintaining the site?

- Analyze the kinds of information the site contains and determine whether the site is intended primarily for faculty, students, alumni, legislators, or prospective students.

- Determine the overlap between information on the site and information in printed documents published by the school. In those cases in which they overlap, is the information on the site merely a duplication of the printed information, or has it been revised to take advantage of the unique capabilities of the Web?

In a memo to your instructor, present your findings and recommend how the site might be improved.

Case 6: Choosing an Appropriate Primary-Research Method

▶ In This Book   For more about memos, see Ch. 14, p. 377.

Background

You are part of a five-person documentation group for Intelliplay, a video game–development company. Intelliplay develops entertainment software for personal computers and advanced game systems. The company's documentation group is responsible for writing the brief player manuals shipped with the games. These player manuals, each about five small pages long, cover topics such as system requirements, installation, game controls, game rules, play options, and technical support.

Intelliplay is developing a game tentatively titled Stomp, Crunch, and Munch, in which players control giant monsters similar to those popularized by Hollywood's B movies of the 1950s and 1960s. The object of the game is for a monster to destroy as much of a city as possible while avoiding the military forces sent to protect the city. Players can select single-player or multiplayer mode. Multiplayer mode allows each of several players to control a monster or military unit and play on a LAN (local area network) or the Internet. Currently, the documentation team is writing the instructions for the multiplayer mode.

A recently hired colleague, David Vidinah, walks into your office and confides, "I can't seem to get much help." He explains that he is writing a section on how to host a multiplayer game over the Internet. He e-mailed a message (Document 6.1) to Intelliplay's president, Erik Warden, and the four other game developers. Only Erik and two of the game developers, Sonja Morganfeld and Matt Giller, replied to David. Since being hired, David has had little interaction with Erik and has never spent much time talking with the game developers. David knows that Sonja is a new mother just back from maternity leave and works part-time. He frequently sees Matt shooting baskets or playing game prototypes with other employees, including people from the documentation group.

"I'm confused," David says. "Erik implied I did something wrong, and the game developers basically ignored me. What responses I did get were contradictory or not very helpful. What's going on?"

You offer to take a look at David's message and the replies (Documents 6.2–6.4) and get back to him the next day.

Document 6.1 E-mail
Message Requesting Help

On TechComm Web

For digital versions of case
documents, click on Downloadable Case Documents on
<bedfordstmartins.com/
techcomm>.

The e-mail message (Document 6.1) reads:

To... Erik Warden; Game Development Team
Cc...
Subject: Questions

I want to get the multiplayer section done and start my weekend and I have just a few questions that I thought you could help me with.

In multiplayer mode, can more than one monster have the same special abilities (fire, radioactive breath, flight, slime, etc.)? What happens if two players select the same monster type while in multiplayer mode?

Do players have to enter a name for the game they are hosting? Can I enter "Dave's Game"? What about "Dave's #!%* Cool Monster Brawl to the Death III"?

When I want to join a multiplayer game, I scroll through a list of available multiplayer games and select one? I sometimes get a dialog box. What am I doing wrong?

After selecting a multiplayer game, I enter the "Monsters Lair" and wait for other players to join before starting the game. How do you think I should describe the "Monsters Lair" to players?

I was also wondering why the Super-Colossal Amoeba monster isn't harmed by electricity. Since normal one-celled animals are harmed by electricity, shouldn't a giant one-celled animal also be damaged by electricity? Also, why is the Giant Radioactive Bug harmed by radiation?

Thanks! David

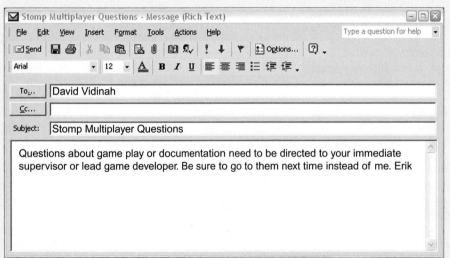

Document 6.2 E-mail
Reply from the Company
President

The reply (Document 6.2) reads:

To... David Vidinah
Cc...
Subject: Stomp Multiplayer Questions

Questions about game play or documentation need to be directed to your immediate supervisor or lead game developer. Be sure to go to them next time instead of me. Erik

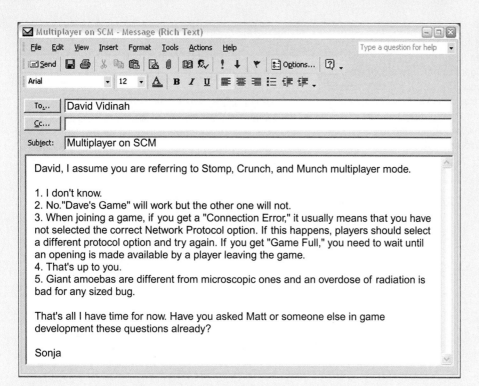

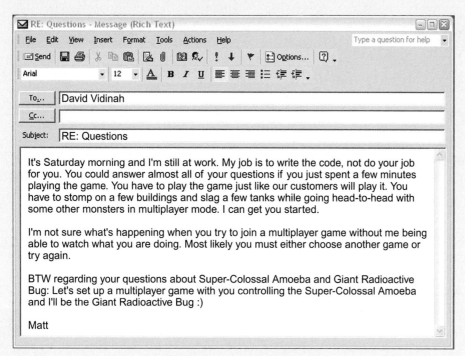

Your Assignment

1. Examine David's request for help (Document 6.1) and the responses he received from the company president (Document 6.2) and the game developers (Documents 6.3 and 6.4). What can you infer about the relationship each wants to have with David? How do you think each wants to communicate with him? Write David an e-mail explaining why you think he didn't get the help he wanted and what he should do next.

2. Who are the appropriate people for David to contact with his questions, and what is the best way to approach each of them? Write David an e-mail telling him whom he should contact and how he should approach each of them.

3. Think about what steps David needs to take and what materials he needs to create to get answers to his questions. Create the materials that will enable him to finish the documentation for the game's multiplayer mode.

Organizing Your Information

Source: Gore, 2006 <www.read-the-truth.com>.

In the World . . .

Al Gore's book and documentary *An Inconvenient Truth* is an argument arranged according to causal analysis: human activities have caused potentially catastrophic climate change. Gore uses many other organizational patterns to present his case. This photograph of the border between Haiti and the Dominican Republic contrasts the forest conservation policies of the two countries.

Understanding Three Principles for Organizing Technical Information 150

Analyzing Your Audience and Purpose 150

Using Conventional Patterns of Arrangement 151

Displaying Your Arrangement Prominently 151

Using Basic Patterns of Organizing Information 152

Chronological 154

Spatial 156

General to Specific 157

More Important to Less Important 158

Comparison and Contrast 159

Classification and Partition 162

Problem-Methods-Solution 166

Cause and Effect 167

Before you can draft a document, you need to organize the information that will go into it. If you're a new employee at a publishing company writing your first trip report, how should you organize it? If you're a police officer writing an accident report or a lawyer working on a nondisclosure agreement, how do you find out how to organize that document, and how much freedom do you have to change the organization? Talk with an experienced co-worker, who probably can help you understand the organization's policies and culture. Your goal is to organize your document to reflect your audience, purpose, and subject. This chapter presents techniques for organizing technical documents so that they meet your readers' needs.

At this point, you should know for whom you are writing and why, and you have done most of your research. Now it is time to start organizing the information that will make up the body of your document.

UNDERSTANDING THREE PRINCIPLES FOR ORGANIZING TECHNICAL INFORMATION

Follow these three principles in organizing your information:

- Analyze your audience and purpose.
- Use conventional patterns of organization.
- Display your organizational pattern prominently.

Analyzing Your Audience and Purpose

▶ In This Book

For more about audience and purpose, see Ch. 5.

Although you have thought about your audience and purpose as you have planned and researched your subject, your initial analyses of audience and purpose are likely to change as you continue. Therefore, it is useful to review your assessment of audience and purpose before you proceed.

Will your audience like the message you will present? If so, announce your main point early in the document. If not, consider an organizational pattern that presents your important evidence before your main message. Is your audience used to seeing a particular organizational pattern in the kind of document you will be writing? If they are, you will probably want to use that pattern, unless you have a good reason to use a different one.

What is your purpose in writing the document? Do you want your audience to understand a body of information or to accept a point of view and perhaps act on it? One purpose might call for a brief report without any appendices; the other might require a detailed report, complete with appendices.

If you are addressing people from other cultures, remember that organizational patterns can vary from culture to culture. If you can, study documents written by people from the culture you are addressing to see whether they favor an organizational pattern different from the one you are considering. Consider, for example, these four factors:

- *Does the text follow expected organizational patterns?* For example, part of this chapter discusses general-to-specific organization. Does the text you are studying present the specific information first?

- *Do the introductions and conclusions present the kind of information you would expect?* In the United States, main findings are often presented in the introduction. In other cultures, the main findings are not presented until late in the document.

- *Does the text appear to be organized linearly?* Is the main idea presented first in a topic sentence or thesis statement? Does supporting information follow? In some cultures, main ideas are withheld until the end of the paragraph or document.

- *Does the text use headings?* If so, does it use more than one level?

If documents from the culture you plan to address are organized very differently from those you're used to seeing, take extra steps to ensure that you don't distract readers by using an unfamiliar organizational pattern.

Using Conventional Patterns of Arrangement

This chapter presents a number of conventional patterns of arrangement, such as the chronological pattern and the spatial pattern. You should begin by asking yourself whether a conventional pattern for presenting your information already exists. Using a conventional pattern makes things easier for you as a writer and for your audience.

For you, a conventional pattern serves as a template or checklist, helping you remember which information to include and where to put it. In a proposal, for example, you include a budget, which you put near the end or in an appendix. For your audience, a conventional pattern makes your document easier to read and understand. Readers who are familiar with proposals can find the information they want because you have put it where others have put similar information.

Does this mean that technical communication is merely the process of filling in the blanks? No. You need to assess the writing situation continuously as you work. If you think you could communicate your ideas better by modifying a conventional pattern or by devising a new pattern, do so. However, you gain nothing if an existing pattern would work just as well.

Displaying Your Arrangement Prominently

Make it easy for your readers to understand the overall arrangement of your information. Displaying your arrangement prominently involves three main steps:

- *Creating a detailed table of contents.* If your document has a table of contents, include at least two levels of headings to help readers find the information they seek.

In This Book

For more about tables of contents, see Ch. 19, p. 512. For more about headings and topic sentences, see Ch. 9, pp. 201 and 207.

- *Using headings liberally.* Headings break up the text, making your page more interesting visually. They also communicate the subject of the section, improving readers' understanding.
- *Using topic sentences at the beginning of paragraphs.* The topic sentence announces the main point of a paragraph and helps readers understand the details that follow.

▶ On TechComm Web

For a discussion of organizing information, see Paradigm Online Writing Assistant. Click on Links Library for Ch. 7 on <bedfordstmartins.com/techcomm>.

USING BASIC PATTERNS OF ORGANIZING INFORMATION

Every argument calls for its own organizational pattern. Figure 7.1 explains the relationship between the organizational pattern and the kind of information you are presenting.

Figure 7.1　Organizational Patterns and the Kinds of Information You Want to Present

If you want to . . .	Consider using this organizational pattern	For example . . .
Explain events that occurred or might occur, or tasks readers are to carry out	**Chronological** (p. 154). Most of the time, you present information in chronological order. Sometimes, however, you use reverse chronology.	You describe the process you used to diagnose the problem with the accounting software. Or, in a job résumé, you describe your more-recent jobs before your less-recent ones.
Describe a physical object or scene, such as a device or a location	**Spatial** (p. 154). You choose an organizing principle such as top to bottom, east to west, or inside to outside.	You describe the three buildings that will make up the new production facility.
Explain a complex situation, such as the factors that led to a problem or the theory that underlies a process	**General to specific** (p. 157). You present general information first, then specific information. Understanding the big picture helps readers understand the details.	You explain the major changes in and the details of the law mandating the use of the new refrigerant in cooling systems.
Present a set of factors	**More important to less important** (p. 158). You discuss the most-important issue first, then the next-most-important issue, and so forth. In technical communication, you don't want to create suspense.	When you launch a new product, you discuss market niche first, competition second, and pricing third.

Figure 7.1 (continued)

If you want to . . .	Consider using this organizational pattern	For example . . .
Present similarities and differences between two or more items	**Comparison and contrast** (p. 159). You choose from one of two patterns: (1) discuss all the factors related to one item, then all the factors related to the next item, and so forth; (2) discuss one factor as it relates to all the items, then another factor as it relates to all the items, and so forth.	You discuss the strengths and weaknesses of three companies bidding on a contract your company is offering.
Assign items to logical categories or discuss the elements that make up a single item	**Classification and partition** (p. 162). Classification involves placing items in categories. Partition involves breaking a single item down into its major elements.	You group the motors your company manufactures according to the fuel they burn: gasoline or diesel. Or you explain how each major component of one of your motors operates.
Discuss a problem you encountered, the steps you took to address the problem, and the outcome or solution	**Problem-methods-solution** (p. 166). You can use this pattern in discussing the past, the present, or the future. Readers understand this organizational pattern because everyone uses it every day in his or her normal routine.	In describing how your company is responding to a new competitor, you discuss the problem (the recent loss in sales), the methods (how you plan to examine your product line and business practices), and the solution (which changes will help your company remain competitive).
Discuss the factors that led to (or will lead to) a given situation, or the effects that a situation led to or will lead to	**Cause and effect** (p. 167). You can start from causes and speculate about effects, or start with the effects and work backward to determine the causes.	Sales of one of your products have dipped in the past year. You want to discuss factors that you think contributed to the sales dip.

Long, complex arguments often require several organizational patterns. For instance, one part of a document might be a causal analysis of the problem you are writing about, whereas another might be a comparison and contrast of two options for solving that problem. Figure 7.2 on page 154, an excerpt from a user's manual, shows how different organizational patterns might be used in a single document.

Different sections of this manual use different organizational patterns.

*The "Welcome" section is organized from **general to specific**. It presents an overview of the manual, helping readers understand how to get to the information they want.*

*The section called "What's in the Box" uses **partition** by showing and naming the various items that are included in the package.*

*Many items are step-by-step instructions organized **chronologically**.*

*The troubleshooting section is organized from **more important to less important**. The first item explains what to do when your computer doesn't work at all. That's the most important problem.*

Contents

Chapter 1: Ready, Set Up, Go

8   Welcome
9   What's in the Box
10 Setting Up Your MacBook Air
15 Setting Up DVD or CD Sharing
16 Migrating Information to Your MacBook Air
19 Getting Additional Information onto Your MacBook Air
22 Putting Your MacBook Air to Sleep or Shutting It Down

Chapter 2: Life with Your MacBook Air

26 Basic Features of Your MacBook Air
28 Keyboard Features of Your MacBook Air
30 Ports on Your MacBook Air
32 Using the Trackpad and Keyboard
34 Running Your MacBook Air on Battery Power
35 Getting Answers

Chapter 3: Problem, Meet Solution

40 Problems That Prevent You from Using Your MacBook Air
44 Using Apple Hardware Test

Contents   5

Figure 7.2   Using Multiple Organizational Patterns in a Single Document
Source: Apple, Inc., 2008 <http://manuals.info.apple.com/en/MacBook_Air_Users_Guide.pdf>.

Chronological

The chronological—or time-line—pattern commonly describes events. In an *accident report*, you describe the events in the order in which they occurred. In the background section of a *report*, you describe the events that led to the present situation. In a *reference manual*, you explain how to carry out a task by describing the steps in sequence.

Figure 7.3 shows a passage arranged chronologically.

Guidelines

Organizing Information Chronologically

▶ **Provide signposts.** If the passage is more than a few hundred words long, use headings. Choose words such as *step*, *phase*, *stage*, and *part*, and consider numbering them. Add descriptive phrases to focus readers' attention on the topic of the section:

> Phase One: Determining Our Objectives
>
> Step 3: Installing the Lateral Supports

At the paragraph and sentence levels, transitional words such as *then*, *next*, *first*, and *finally* help your readers follow your discussion.

▶ **Consider using graphics to complement the text.** Flowcharts, in particular, help you emphasize chronological passages for all kinds of readers, from the most expert to the general reader.

▶ **Analyze events where appropriate.** When you use chronology, you are explaining what happened in what sequence, but you are not necessarily explaining why or how an event happened or what it means. For instance, the largest section of an accident report is usually devoted to the chronological discussion, but the report is of little value unless it explains what caused the accident, who bears responsibility, and how such accidents can be prevented.

In This Book
For more about transitions, see Ch. 9, p. 211.

In This Book
For more about graphics, see Ch. 12.

Steps to a Safe Workplace	In Spanish

Basic steps to a safe workplace for your employees

Step 1: Follow WISHA's Safety and Health Core Rules.

Step 2: Build a safety program.

Step 3: Display the required Labor & Industries (L&I) posters.

Step 4: Find other rules that apply to your workplace such as:
- ○ Industry specific rules like Agriculture, Logging, Construction, or Sawmills.
- ○ Hazard specific rules such as Confined Spaces.
- ○ Machine specific rules such as Portable Power Tools or Machine Safety.

Note: For small non-manufacturing businesses, the Safety & Health Core Rules may cover everything you need.

Step 5: Find other programs that apply to your workplace.
- ○ Rules Requiring Training or Written Plans
- ○ Additional Program Requirements

Step 6: Get required L&I certifications and licenses.

Step 7: Request assistance, if needed, from L&I.

In this chronological passage, links to expanded discussions are presented in blue.

Figure 7.3   Information Organized Chronologically
Source: Washington State Department of Labor and Industries, 2008 <www.lni.wa.gov/Safety/Basics/Steps/default.asp>.

Spatial

The spatial pattern is commonly used to describe objects and physical sites. In an *accident report*, you describe the physical scene of the accident. In a *feasibility study* about building a facility, you describe the property on which it potentially would be built. In a *proposal* to design a new microchip, you describe the layout of the new chip.

Guidelines

Organizing Information Spatially

▶ **Provide signposts.** Help your readers follow the argument by using words and phrases that indicate location (*to the left*, *above*, *in the center*) in headings, topic sentences, and support sentences.

▶ **Consider using graphics to complement the text.** Diagrams, drawings, photographs, and maps clarify spatial relationships.

▶ **Analyze events where appropriate.** A spatial arrangement doesn't explain itself; you have to do the analysis: a diagram of a floor plan cannot explain why the floor plan is effective or ineffective.

Figure 7.4 shows the use of both chronological and spatial organization of information.

This screen from the Metropolitan Museum of Art's "How Van Gogh Made His Mark" Web feature is organized using both chronological and spatial organization.

The four phases of the artist's life are presented in the places where he worked. Phase 5 represents the artist's enduring legacy, which is worldwide.

▶ On TechComm Web

To view Fig. 7.4 in context on the Web, click on Links Library for Ch. 7 on <bedfordstmartins .com/techcomm>.

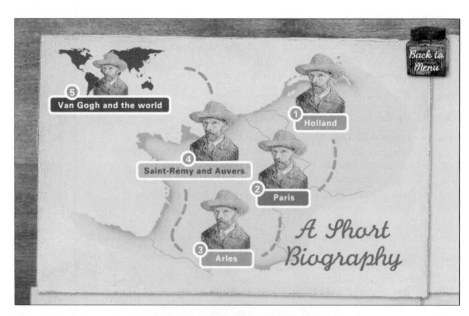

Figure 7.4   Information Organized Chronologically and Spatially
Source: Metropolitan Museum of Art, 2008 <www.metmuseum.org/explore/van_gogh/menu.html>.

General to Specific

The general-to-specific pattern is used when readers need a general understanding of a subject before they can understand and remember the details. For example, in a *report*, you include an executive summary—an overview for managers—before the body of the report. In a set of *instructions*, you provide general information about the necessary tools and materials and about safety measures before providing the step-by-step instructions. In a *memo*, you present the background information before going into the details.

Guidelines

Organizing Information from General to Specific

▶ **Provide signposts.** Explain that you will address general issues first and then move on to specific concerns. If appropriate, incorporate the words *general* and *specific* or other relevant terms in the major headings or at the start of the text for each item you are describing.

▶ **Consider using graphics to complement the text.** Diagrams, drawings, photographs, and maps help your readers understand the general or fine points of the information.

Figure 7.5 is an example of information organized from general to specific.

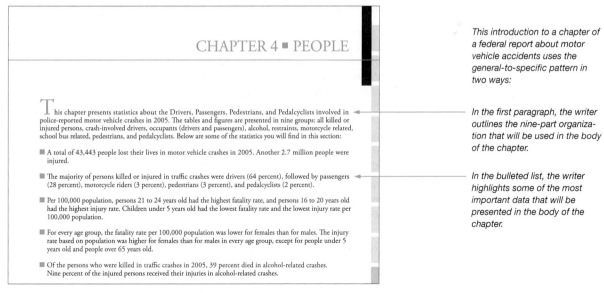

This introduction to a chapter of a federal report about motor vehicle accidents uses the general-to-specific pattern in two ways:

In the first paragraph, the writer outlines the nine-part organization that will be used in the body of the chapter.

In the bulleted list, the writer highlights some of the most important data that will be presented in the body of the chapter.

Figure 7.5   Information Organized from General to Specific
Source: National Highway Traffic Safety Administration, 2007
<www-nrd.nhtsa.dot.gov/pdf/nrd-30/NCSA/TSFAnn/TSF2005.pdf>.

More Important to Less Important

The more-important-to-less-important pattern recognizes that readers often want the bottom line—the most important information—first. For example, in an *accident report*, you describe the three most-important factors that led to the accident before describing the less-important factors. In a *feasibility study* about building a facility, you present the major reasons that the site is appropriate, then the minor reasons. In a *proposal* to design a new microchip, you describe the major applications for the new chip, then the minor applications.

For most documents, a more-important-to-less-important pattern works well because readers want to get to the bottom line as soon as possible. For some documents, however, other patterns work better. People who write for readers outside their own company often reverse the more-important-to-less-important pattern because they want to make sure their audience reads the whole discussion. This pattern is also popular with writers who are delivering bad news. For instance, if you want to justify recommending that your organization *not* go ahead with a popular plan, the reverse sequence lets you explain the problems with the popular plan before you present the plan you recommend. Otherwise, readers might start to formulate objections before you have had a chance to explain your position.

Guidelines

Organizing Information from More Important to Less Important

▶ **Provide signposts.** Tell your readers how you are organizing the passage. For instance, in the introduction of a proposal to design a new microchip, you might write, "The three applications for the new chip, each of which is discussed below, are arranged from most important to least important."

In assigning signposts, be straightforward. If you have two very important points and three less-important points, present them that way: group the two very important points and label them, as in "Major Reasons to Retain Our Current Management Structure." Then present the less-important factors as "Other Reasons to Retain Our Current Management Structure." Being straightforward makes the material easier to follow and enhances your credibility.

▶ **Explain why one point is more important than another.** Don't just say that you will be arranging the items from more important to less important. Explain why the more-important point is more important.

▶ **Consider using graphics to complement the text.** Diagrams and numbered lists often help to suggest levels of importance.

Figure 7.6 shows the more-important-to-less-important organizational structure.

2007 Performance Highlights

In 2007, we intensified our efforts to reduce the hazards from imported consumer goods. In the summer of 2007, a number of imported products made in China, including painted toys and children's jewelry, were found to contain lead. We worked with industry to recall those toys already in the marketplace and prevent others from entry into the U.S. In September 2007, we made an important breakthrough with the Chinese government when we hosted the 2nd Biennial U.S.-Sino Product Safety Summit. At this Summit, CPSC reached agreement with our Chinese counterpart agency, the General Administration of Quality Supervision, Inspection, and Quarantine, that the Chinese government would take immediate action to eliminate the use of lead paint on Chinese manufactured toys exported to the U.S. This was an important signal that the Chinese government is serious about working with CPSC to keep dangerous products out of American homes. CPSC staff is also following up to assure that this commitment is fully implemented.

The writer begins with the most-important activity: responding to the highly publicized problem of unsafe imported consumer goods.

To combat the problem further, we worked with the Chinese government to improve import safety. The Chinese government agreed to: (1) increase inspections; (2) take specific steps to assist CPSC in tracing imported products with identified safety problems to Chinese firms; (3) exchange technical personnel with CPSC; (4) establish regular and systematic exchanges of information with CPSC about emerging product safety issues; and (5) attend CPSC-led training activities on the content of U.S. product safety standards and the importance of adhering to all those standards.

The start of paragraph two—"To combat the problem further"—shows that the writer is discussing a less-important follow-up activity.

We are also working at home to improve import safety. In 2007, we:
- Facilitated the translation of the summary provisions of nearly 300 U.S. safety standards into Chinese so that Chinese manufacturers would understand U.S. product safety standards requirements when manufacturing various products;
- Worked with Customs to improve CPSC's electronic data exchange and our capabilities to identify, track, and stop hazardous products from entering the U.S.;
- Cross-trained other federal agencies working at the ports to identify hazardous imported products;
- Identified and implemented methods to decrease the time to test samples of imported products containing lead; and
- Established an Import Safety Initiative.

The third paragraph, about activities that the organization is "also" working on, collects a number of even less-important activities.

In general, technical communication presents more-important information before less-important information.

Figure 7.6   Information Organized from More Important to Less Important
Source: U.S. Consumer Product Safety Commission, 2007 <www.cpsc.gov/cpscpub/pubs/reports/2007par.pdf>.

Comparison and Contrast

Typically, the comparison-and-contrast pattern is used to describe and evaluate two or more items or options. For example, in a *memo*, you compare and contrast the credentials of three finalists for a job. In a *proposal* to design a new microchip, you compare and contrast two different strategies for designing the chip. In a *feasibility report* describing a legal challenge that your company faces, you compare and contrast several options for responding.

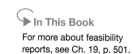

In This Book

For more about feasibility reports, see Ch. 19, p. 501.

The first step in comparing and contrasting two or more items is to determine the *criteria*: the standards or needs you will use in studying the items. For example, a professional musician who plays a piano in restaurants might be looking to buy a new portable keyboard. She might compare and contrast available instruments using the number of keys as one criterion. For this person, 88 keys would be better than 64. Another criterion might be weight. A keyboard that weighs 25 pounds would be better than one that weighs 46 pounds.

Almost always, you will need to consider several or even many criteria. Start by deciding whether a criterion represents a necessary quality or merely a desirable one. In studying keyboards, for instance, the number of keys might be a necessary quality. If you need an 88-key instrument to play your music, you are not going to consider any instruments without 88 keys. The same thing might be true of touch-sensitive keys. But a MIDI interface might be less important, a merely desirable quality; you would like MIDI capability, but you would not eliminate an instrument from consideration just because it doesn't have MIDI.

Two typical patterns for organizing a comparison-and-contrast discussion are *whole-by-whole* and *part-by-part*. The following table illustrates the difference between them. In this table, two printers—Model 5L and Model 6L—are being compared and contrasted according to three criteria: price, resolution, and print speed.

The whole-by-whole pattern provides a coherent picture of each option: the 5L and the 6L. This pattern works best if your readers need an overall assessment of each option or if each option is roughly equivalent according to the criteria.

Whole-by-whole	Part-by-part
Model 5L • price • resolution • print speed	Price • Model 5L • Model 6L
Model 6L • price • resolution • print speed	Resolution • Model 5L • Model 6L Print Speed • Model 5L • Model 6L

The part-by-part pattern lets you focus your attention on the criteria. If, for instance, Model 5L produces much better resolution than Model 6L, the part-by-part pattern reveals this difference more effectively than the whole-by-whole pattern does. The part-by-part pattern is best for detailed comparisons and contrasts.

You can have it both ways. If you want to use a part-by-part pattern to emphasize particular aspects, you can begin the discussion with a general description of the various items. Once you have chosen the overall pattern—whole-by-whole or part-by-part—you can decide how to organize the second-level items. That is, in a whole-by-whole passage, you have to sequence the "aspects"; in a part-by-part passage, you have to sequence the "options."

Figure 7.7 shows a comparison-and-contrast passage organized according to the whole-by-whole pattern.

Guidelines

Organizing Information by Comparison and Contrast

▶ **Establish criteria for the comparison and contrast.** Choose criteria that are consistent with the needs of your audience.

▶ **Evaluate each item according to the criteria you have established.** Draw your conclusions.

▶ **Organize the discussion.** Choose either the *whole-by-whole* or *part-by-part* pattern or some combination of the two. Then organize the second-level items.

▶ **Consider using graphics to complement the text.** Graphics can clarify and emphasize comparison-and-contrast passages. Diagrams, drawings, and tables are common ways to provide such clarification and emphasis.

Searching on the Internet today can be compared to dragging a net across the surface of the ocean. While a great deal may be caught in the net, there is still a wealth of information that is deep and, therefore, missed. The reason is simple: Most of the Web's information is buried far down on dynamically generated sites, and standard search engines never find it.

Traditional search engines create their indices by spidering or crawling surface Web pages. To be discovered, the page must be static and linked to other pages. Traditional search engines cannot "see" or retrieve content in the deep Web—those pages do not exist until they are created dynamically as the result of a specific search. Because traditional search engine crawlers cannot probe beneath the surface, the deep Web has heretofore been hidden.

Deep Web sources store their content in searchable databases that only produce results dynamically in response to a direct request. But a direct query is a "one at a time" laborious way to search. BrightPlanet's search technology automates the process of making dozens of direct queries simultaneously using multiple-thread technology and thus is the only search technology, so far, that is capable of identifying, retrieving, qualifying, classifying, and organizing both "deep" and "surface" content.

This passage from BrightPlanet compares and contrasts searching the surface Web and searching the deep Web.

The first paragraph uses a metaphor of dragging a net to introduce the main difference between the surface Web and the deep Web.

The two remaining paragraphs are organized according to the whole-by-whole pattern. The first of the two paragraphs is devoted to traditional search engines that search the surface Web. The second highlights the company's new search engine, which searches the deep Web.

Figure 7.7 Information Organized by Comparison and Contrast
Source: Based on Bergman, 2004 <www.brightplanet.com/technology/deepweb.asp>.

Ethics Note

Comparing and Contrasting Fairly

Because the comparison-and-contrast organizational pattern is used frequently in evaluating items, it appears often in product descriptions as part of the argument that one company's products are better than a competitor's. There is nothing unethical in this. But it is unethical to misrepresent items, such as when a writer portrays his or her own product as better than it is or a competitor's as worse than it is. Obviously, lying about a product is unethical.

But some practices are not so easy to characterize. For example, your company makes laptop computers, but your chief competitor's model has a longer battery life than yours. In comparing and contrasting the two laptops, are you ethically obligated to mention battery life? No, you are not. If readers are interested in battery life, they are responsible for figuring out what your failure to mention battery life means and for seeking further information from other sources. If you do mention battery life, you must do so honestly, using industry-standard techniques for measuring it. You cannot measure your laptop's battery life under one set of conditions and your competitor's under another set.

Classification and Partition

Classification is the process of assigning items to categories. For instance, all the students at a university could be classified by sex, age, major, and many other characteristics. You can also create subcategories within categories, such as males and females majoring in business.

Classification is common in technical communication. In a *feasibility study* about building a facility, you classify sites into two categories: domestic and foreign. In a *journal article* about ways to treat a medical condition, you classify the treatments as surgical and nonsurgical. In a description of a major in a *college catalog*, you classify courses as required or elective.

Partition is the process of breaking a unit into its components. For example, a home-theater system could be partitioned into the following components: TV set, amplifier, peripheral devices such as a CD player, and speakers. Each component is separate, but together they form a whole system. Each component can, of course, be partitioned further.

Partition is used in descriptions of objects, mechanisms, and processes. In an *equipment catalog*, you use partition to describe the major components of one of your products. In a *proposal*, you use partition to present a detailed description of an instrument being proposed for development. In a *brochure*, you describe how to operate a product by describing each of its features.

In Figure 7.8, a discussion of the Saffir-Simpson Hurricane Scale, the writer uses classification effectively in introducing categories of hurricanes to a general audience.

The Saffir-Simpson Hurricane Scale

The Saffir-Simpson Hurricane Scale is a 1–5 rating based on the hurricane's present intensity. This is used to give an estimate of the potential property damage and flooding expected along the coast from a hurricane landfall. Wind speed is the determining factor in the scale, as storm surge values are highly dependent on the slope of the continental shelf and the shape of the coastline, in the landfall region. Note that all winds are using the U.S. 1-minute average.

Category One Hurricane:

Winds 74–95 mph (64–82 kt or 119–153 km/hr). Storm surge generally 4–5 ft above normal. No real damage to building structures. Damage primarily to unanchored mobile homes, shrubbery, and trees. Some damage to poorly constructed signs. Also, some coastal road flooding and minor pier damage. Hurricane Lili of 2002 made landfall on the Louisiana coast as a Category One hurricane. Hurricane Gaston of 2004 was a Category One hurricane that made landfall along the central South Carolina coast.

Category Two Hurricane:

Winds 96–110 mph (83–95 kt or 154–177 km/hr). Storm surge generally 6–8 feet above normal. Some roofing material, door, and window damage of buildings. Considerable damage to shrubbery and trees with some trees blown down. Considerable damage to mobile homes, poorly constructed signs, and piers. Coastal and low-lying escape routes flood 2–4 hours before arrival of the hurricane center. Small craft in unprotected anchorages break moorings. Hurricane Frances of 2004 made landfall over the southern end of Hutchinson Island, Florida, as a Category Two hurricane. Hurricane Isabel of 2003 made landfall near Drum Inlet on the Outer Banks of North Carolina as a Category Two hurricane.

Category Three Hurricane:

Winds 111–130 mph (96–113 kt or 178–209 km/hr). Storm surge generally 9–12 ft above normal. Some structural damage to small residences and utility buildings with a minor amount of curtainwall failures. . . .

Category Four Hurricane:

Winds 131–155 mph (114–135 kt or 210–249 km/hr). Storm surge generally 13–18 ft above normal. More extensive curtainwall failures with some complete roof structure failures on small residences. Shrubs, trees, and all signs are blown down. Complete destruction of mobile homes. . . .

Category Five Hurricane:

Winds greater than 155 mph (135 kt or 249 km/hr). Storm surge generally greater than 18 ft above normal. Complete roof failure on many residences and industrial buildings. Some complete building failures with small utility buildings blown over or away. All shrubs, trees, and signs blown down. Complete destruction of mobile homes. . . .

This classification system from the National Weather Service begins with an introductory statement that serves as an advance organizer explaining why the determining factor of each category is wind speed, not property damage.

The description of each category includes the same information: wind speed, typical property damage, and examples of recent hurricanes that fall within the category.

Figure 7.8   Information Organized by Classification
Source: National Weather Service, 2007 <www.nhc.noaa.gov/aboutsshs.shtml>.

INTERACTIVE SAMPLE DOCUMENT
Comparing and Contrasting Honestly

This comparison-and-contrast table is from the Web site of the manufacturer of an orthodontic product called Invisalign. The questions in the margin ask you to think about the ethics of the table. E-mail your responses to yourself and/or your instructor on TechComm Web.

1. Is it unethical for the company to present the column on its product before the columns on metal braces and veneers?

2. Some of the criteria, such as "removable," are based on factual claims. That is, the three technologies are either removable or not. But some of the other criteria are based on opinions, not facts. Identify one criterion that is based on opinions, then determine whether the use of that criterion in the table is fair.

3. Is the criterion "No metal or brackets to irritate your mouth" a fair criterion to present in this table? Why or why not?

4. The text above the table discusses the average treatment time for Invisalign. Why isn't that criterion included in the table itself? Is it unethical not to include it in the table?

On TechComm Web

To e-mail your responses to yourself and/or your instructor, click on Interactive Sample Documents for Ch. 7 on <bedfordstmartins.com/techcomm>.

Is Invisalign for Me?

» **Product Comparison**

🖶 *Printer Friendly*

Find Experienced Invisalign Doctors in Your Area

Learn More »

The Invisalign technology has allowed me to have discreet and effective orthodontic treatment.
-Allison, Ozawkie, KS

Product Comparison Chart

Take a look at the chart below to see how Invisalign compares to other treatment options. Considering that the average treatment time for an Invisalign patient is generaly about a year, the choice is clear—Invisalign.

	Invisalign®	Metal Braces	Veneers
How Does It Work?	Invisalign® uses a series of clear removable aligners to straighten your teeth without metal wires or brackets.	Metal braces use wires and brackets to pressure your teeth into straighter alignment.	Laminates that are bonded to teeth to cover up imperfections.
Invisible	Yes	No	n/a
Removable	Yes	No	n/a
Comfortable	Yes	No	n/a
No metal or brackets to irritate your mouth	Yes	No	n/a
Does not require grinding to remove tooth enamel	Yes	Yes	No
Does not require costly replacement	Yes	n/a	No
Able to brush and floss normally during treatment	Yes	No	n/a

Source: Invisalign, 2005 <www.invisalign.com/generalapp/us/en/for/compare.jsp>.

Guidelines

Organizing Information by Classification or Partition

▶ **Choose a basis of classification or partition that fits your audience and purpose.** If you are writing a warning about snakes for hikers in a particular state park, your basis of classification will probably be whether the snakes are poisonous. You will describe all the poisonous snakes, then all the nonpoisonous ones.

▶ **Use only one basis of classification or partition at a time.** If you are classifying graphics programs according to their technology—paint programs and draw programs—do not include another basis of classification, such as cost.

▶ **Avoid overlap.** In classifying, make sure that no single item could logically be placed in more than one category. In partitioning, make sure that no listed component includes another listed component. Overlapping generally occurs when you change the basis of classification or the level at which you are partitioning a unit. In the following classification of bicycles, for instance, the writer introduces a new basis of classification that results in overlapping categories:

— mountain bikes
— racing bikes
— touring bikes
— ten-speed bikes

The first three items share a basis of classification: the general category of bicycle. The fourth item has a different basis of classification: number of speeds. Adding the fourth item is illogical because a particular ten-speed bike could be a mountain bike, a racing bike, or a touring bike.

▶ **Be inclusive.** Include all the categories necessary to complete your basis of classification. For example, a partition of an automobile by major systems would be incomplete if it included the electrical, fuel, and drive systems but not the cooling system. If you decide to omit a category, explain why.

▶ **Arrange the categories in a logical sequence.** Use a reasonable plan: chronology (first to last), spatial development (top to bottom), importance (most important to least important), and so on.

▶ **Consider using graphics to complement the text.** Organization charts are commonly used in classification passages; drawings and diagrams are often used in partition passages.

Figure 7.9 is an example of partition. For more examples of partition, see Chapter 20, which includes descriptions of objects, mechanisms, and processes (page 549).

This "What's in the Box" page from a user's manual for a camera partitions the kit into its components. The manual then discusses each of the components.

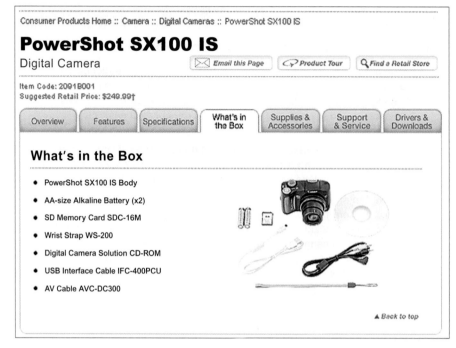

Consumer Products Home :: Camera :: Digital Cameras :: PowerShot SX100 IS

PowerShot SX100 IS
Digital Camera

Email this Page　　Product Tour　　Find a Retail Store

Item Code: 2091B001
Suggested Retail Price: $249.99†

| Overview | Features | Specifications | What's in the Box | Supplies & Accessories | Support & Service | Drivers & Downloads |

What's in the Box

- PowerShot SX100 IS Body
- AA-size Alkaline Battery (x2)
- SD Memory Card SDC-16M
- Wrist Strap WS-200
- Digital Camera Solution CD-ROM
- USB Interface Cable IFC-400PCU
- AV Cable AVC-DC300

▲ Back to top

Figure 7.9　Information Organized by Partition
Source: Canon U.S.A., Inc., 2008 <www.usa.canon.com/consumer/controller?act =ModelInfoAct&fcategoryid=144&modelid=15672#BoxContentsAct>.

Problem-Methods-Solution

The problem-methods-solution pattern reflects the logic used in carrying out a project. The three components of this pattern are simple to identify:

- *Problem.* A description of what was not working (or not working effectively) or what opportunity exists for improving current processes.
- *Method.* The procedure performed to confirm the analysis of the problem, solve the problem, or exploit the opportunity.
- *Solution.* The statement of whether the analysis of the problem was correct or what was discovered or devised to solve the problem or capitalize on the opportunity.

The problem-methods-solution pattern is common in technical communication. In a *proposal*, you describe a problem in your business, how you plan to carry out your research, and how your deliverable (an item or a report) can help solve the problem. In a *completion report* about a project to improve a manufacturing process, you describe the problem that motivated the project, the methods you used to carry out the project, and the findings: the results, conclusions, and recommendations.

Guidelines

Organizing Information by Problem-Methods-Solution

▶ **In describing the problem, be clear and specific.** Don't write "Our energy expenditures are getting out of hand." Instead, write "Our energy usage has increased 7 percent in the past year, while utility rates have risen 11 percent." Then calculate the total increase in energy costs.

▶ **In describing your methods, help your readers understand what you did and why you did it that way.** You might need to justify your choices. Why, for example, did you use a *t*-test in calculating the statistics in an experiment? If you can't defend your choices, you lose credibility.

▶ **In describing the solution, don't overstate.** Avoid overly optimistic claims, such as "This project will increase our market share from 7 percent to 10 percent within 12 months." Instead, be cautious: "This project could increase our market share from 7 percent to 10 percent." That way, you won't be embarrassed if things don't turn out as well as you had hoped.

▶ **Choose a logical sequence.** The most common sequence is to start with the problem and conclude with the solution. However, different sequences work equally well as long as you provide a preliminary summary to give readers an overview and use headings or some other design elements (see Chapter 11) to help readers find the information they want. For instance, you might want to put the methods last if you think your readers already know them or are more interested in the solution.

▶ **Consider using graphics to complement the text.** Graphics, such as flowcharts, diagrams, and drawings, can clarify problem-methods-solution passages.

The example of the problem-methods-solution argument in Figure 7.10 on page 168 is from the federal Energy Star program.

Cause and Effect

Technical communication often involves cause-and-effect discussions. Sometimes, you will reason forward, from cause to effect: if we raise the price of a particular product we manufacture (cause), what will happen to our sales (effect)? Other times, you will reason backward, from effect to cause: productivity went down by 6 percent in the last quarter (effect); what

This case study from the federal government's Energy Star program begins with the problem faced by a family that had just moved into a house.

Here are the methods: the steps the family took to try to solve the problem.

Here the writer presents the solution to the problem.

Although this structure— from problem to methods to solution—is probably the easiest to understand, writers can begin with the solution, then present the problem and methods.

Dealing with Dust in Georgia
Suwanee, Georgia

When the Milewskys moved into their home in December 2004, they noticed hot and cold spots throughout. They both suffered from nasal congestion and sinus infections due to high levels of dust in the house.

To counter the dust problem, the Milewskys contacted two contractors participating in the Southface Home Performance with ENERGY STAR program. Homescan and Climatrol, respectively, performed diagnostic testing and retrofit work on their home. Homescan found that the furnace needed repair and service (in fact, a sealing had been inadvertently left off the bottom of the furnace causing insulation to be sucked into the furnace and ductwork, thereby contributing to dusty conditions). Also, ductwork throughout the home was found to be very leaky. According to Tom Milewsky, "There were holes big enough to put your arm in."

After servicing and repairing the furnace, the technician installed a new sealing plate. This instantly led to a better supply of air throughout the Milewsky home. The attic was sealed to prevent any insulation or dust from intruding into the living areas. Insulation was also blown into the spaces behind interior walls and chases that had previously been empty cavities.

Tom noted "there is very little dust in the house." He expects to see a positive impact on his heating and cooling costs. "You can already feel the difference in the house. Air and heat are being distributed nicely."

Tom views the home assessment and energy efficiency improvements as a "no-brainer." The family received a rebate for the assessment fee from their utility Jackson EMC. Tom also wrote a letter to his homeowner's warranty company explaining the work Climatrol had completed on the home. The warranty company sent Tom a check to cover a portion of the work. In the end, the family received about half of the project costs from these rebates, nearly $1,000.

The Home Performance with ENERGY STAR program is available in 12 states. Benefits of the program include:

- Up to 30% Savings on Energy Bills
- A Quieter, More Comfortable Living Environment
- Improved Air Quality
- Greater Home Durability with Lower Maintenance

Figure 7.10   Information Organized by the Problem-Methods-Solution Pattern
Source: Energy Star, 2007 <www.energystar.gov/ia/home_improvement/Case_Georgia2.pdf>.

factors led to this decrease (causes)? Cause-and-effect reasoning, therefore, provides a way to answer the following two questions:

- What will be the effect(s) of X?
- What caused X?

Arguments organized by cause and effect are common in technical communication. In an *environmental impact statement*, you might argue that a proposed construction project would have three important effects on the ecosystem. In the recommendation section of a *report*, you might argue that a recommended solution would improve operations in two major ways. In a *memo*, you might describe a new policy, then explain the effects you anticipate the policy will have.

Cause-and-effect relationships are difficult to describe because there is no scientific way to determine causes or effects. You draw on your common sense and your knowledge of your subject. When you try to determine, for example, why the product you introduced last year failed to sell, you start with the obvious possibilities: the market was saturated, the product was of low quality, the product was poorly marketed, and so forth. The more you know about your subject, the more precise and insightful your analysis will be.

A causal discussion can never be certain. You cannot *prove* why a product failed in the marketplace. But you can explain why you think the causes or effects you are identifying are the most plausible ones. For instance, to make a plausible case that the main reason is that the product was poorly marketed, you can show that, in the past, your company's other unsuccessful products were marketed in similar ways and that your company's successful products were marketed in other ways.

Figure 7.11 on page 170 illustrates an effective cause-and-effect argument.

Guidelines

Organizing Information by Cause and Effect

▶ **Explain your reasoning.** To support your claim that the product was marketed poorly, use specific facts and figures: the low marketing budget, delays in beginning the marketing campaign, and so forth.

▶ **Avoid overstating your argument.** For instance, if you write that Steve Jobs, the co-founder of Apple, "created the computer revolution," you are claiming too much. It is better to write that Steve Jobs "was one of the central players in creating the computer revolution."

▶ **Avoid logical fallacies.** Logical fallacies, such as hasty generalizations or post hoc reasoning, can undermine your discussion.

▶ **Consider using graphics to complement the text.** Graphics, such as flowcharts, organization charts, diagrams, and drawings, can clarify and emphasize cause-and-effect passages.

▶ **In This Book**
For more about logical fallacies, see Ch. 8, p. 186.

In this excerpt from a summary of several research studies, the author identifies two major effects—an increased risk of traffic accidents and snarled traffic—that result when people use cell phones while driving.

The result of one cause can be the cause of another effect. For instance, an increased risk of traffic accidents and snarled traffic are the reasons (cause) that many states and some countries have banned the use of cell phones while driving (effect).

Drivers on Cell Phones Kill Thousands, Snarl Traffic

Finally, empirical proof you can blame chatty 20-somethings for stop-and-go traffic on the way to work.

A new study confirms that the reaction time of cell phone users slows dramatically, increasing the risk of accidents and tying up traffic in general, and when young adults use cell phones while driving, they're as bad as sleepy septuagenarians.

"If you put a 20-year-old driver behind the wheel with a cell phone, their reaction times are the same as a 70-year-old driver who is not using a cell phone," said University of Utah psychology professor David Strayer. "It's like instantly aging a large number of drivers."

The study was announced today and is detailed in the winter issue of the quarterly journal *Human Factors*.

Cell phone distraction causes 2,600 deaths and 330,000 injuries in the United States every year, according to the journal's publisher, the Human Factors and Ergonomics Society.

The reason is now obvious: Drivers talking on cell phones were 18 percent slower to react to brake lights, the new study found. In a minor bright note, they also kept a 12 percent greater following distance. But they also took 17 percent longer to regain the speed they lost when they braked. That frustrates everyone.

"Once drivers on cell phones hit the brakes, it takes them longer to get back into the normal flow of traffic," Strayer said. "The net result is they are impeding the overall flow of traffic."

Figure 7.11 A Discussion Organized by the Cause-and-Effect Pattern
Source: Britt, 2005 <www.livescience.com/technology/050201_cell_danger.html>.

Writer's Checklist

Did you

- [ ] analyze your audience and purpose? (p. 150)
- [ ] consider using a conventional pattern of arrangement? (p. 151)
- [ ] display your organization prominently by
  - [ ] creating a detailed table of contents? (p. 151)

- [ ] using headings liberally? (p. 152)
- [ ] using topic sentences at the beginning of your paragraphs? (p. 152)

The following checklists cover the eight organizational patterns discussed in this chapter.

Chronological and Spatial
Did you

- ☐ provide signposts, such as headings or transitional words or phrases? (p. 155)
- ☐ consider using graphics to complement the text? (p. 155)
- ☐ analyze events where appropriate? (p. 155)

General to Specific
Did you

- ☐ provide signposts, such as headings or transitional words or phrases? (p. 157)
- ☐ consider using graphics to complement the text? (p. 157)

More Important to Less Important
Did you

- ☐ provide signposts, explaining clearly that you are using this organizational pattern? (p. 158)
- ☐ explain why the first point is the most important, the second is the second most important, and so forth? (p. 158)
- ☐ consider using graphics to complement the text? (p. 158)

Comparison and Contrast
Did you

- ☐ establish criteria for the comparison and contrast? (p. 161)
- ☐ evaluate each item according to the criteria you have established? (p. 161)
- ☐ organize the discussion by choosing a structure—whole-by-whole or part-by-part—that is most appropriate for your audience and purpose? (p. 161)
- ☐ consider using graphics to complement the text? (p. 161)

Classification and Partition
Did you

- ☐ choose a basis of classification or partition that is consistent with your audience and the purpose of the document? (p. 165)
- ☐ use only one basis at a time? (p. 165)
- ☐ avoid overlap? (p. 165)
- ☐ include all the appropriate categories? (p. 165)
- ☐ arrange the categories in a logical sequence? (p. 165)
- ☐ consider using graphics to complement the text? (p. 165)

Problem-Methods-Solution
Did you

- ☐ describe the problem clearly and specifically? (p. 167)
- ☐ if appropriate, justify your methods? (p. 167)
- ☐ avoid overstating your solution? (p. 167)
- ☐ arrange the discussion in a sequence consistent with the audience and purpose of the document? (p. 167)
- ☐ consider using graphics to complement the text? (p. 167)

Cause and Effect
Did you

- ☐ explain your reasoning? (p. 169)
- ☐ avoid overstating your argument? (p. 169)
- ☐ avoid logical fallacies? (p. 169)
- ☐ consider using graphics to complement the text? (p. 169)

Exercises

1. **INTERNET EXERCISE** Using a search engine, find the Web site of a company that makes a product used by professionals in your field. (Personal computers are a safe choice.) Locate three discussions on the site. For example, there will probably be the following: a passage devoted to ordering a product from the site (using a chronological pattern), a description of a product (using a partition pattern), and a passage describing why the company's products are superior to those of its competitors (using a comparison-and-contrast argument). Print a copy of the passages you've identified.

2. For each of the lettered topics that follow, identify the best organizational pattern for a discussion of the subject. For example, a discussion of distance education

and on-campus courses could be organized using the comparison-and-contrast pattern. Write a brief explanation about why this would be the best organizational pattern to use. (Use each of the organizational patterns discussed in this chapter at least once.)

a. how to register for courses at your college or university

b. how you would propose reducing the time required to register for classes or to change your schedule

c. the current price of gasoline

d. advances in manufacturing technology

e. a student organization on your campus

f. the tutorials that come with two different software programs

g. MP3 players

h. increased security in airports

i. the room in which you are sitting

j. a guitar

k. cooperative education and internships for college students

l. digital and film photography

m. how to prepare for a job interview

3. Write a 500-word discussion of one of the lettered topics in Exercise 2. If appropriate, include graphics. Preface your discussion with a sentence explaining the audience and purpose of the discussion.

Case 7: Organizing a Document

▶ **In This Book** For more about memos, see Ch. 14, p. 377.

Background

"One of the first items on my agenda is to write an internship handbook," Georgia McCallum told the group seated around the conference table. This was the first meeting of the Internship Working Group. Georgia, the newly hired university internship director, had assembled the group to review current practices for academic internships and to create reasonable, consistent university-wide standards for academic internships. Attending the meeting were Professors Leandra Lucas and Rick Burtt. Leandra serves as the internship coordinator for the School of Engineering; Rick coordinates internships for the Department of Kinesiology. You were invited to participate as a student representative.

"One of the things I learned when I interviewed all the internship coordinators this fall was that internship standards tend to be set by individual departments," Georgia explained. "I also learned that new internship coordinators don't have much guidance or resources. They don't know what options they have in regard to working with student interns and the sponsoring organizations. The result is an inconsistent internship experience for students and confused sponsoring organizations."

"I agree," you said. "When I interned at KBCI-TV, I had to write a learning agreement, keep a learning log, submit weekly progress reports, and complete a self-evaluation. I even think my internship coordinator met with my supervisor at KBCI once or twice. Another intern from a different department only had to write a one-page report at the end of the semester."

"My point exactly. Should both students earn the same amount of academic credit?" Georgia asked the group.

"With the number of interns I supervise each semester," Rick said, "I couldn't possibly maintain that level of contact with the interns and their supervisors."

"That's why I think we should establish some basic requirements, such as number of hours worked per credit hour, and leave the details up to the individual internship coordinators," Leandra added.

"Didn't the Office of the Registrar already establish that an intern must work 50 hours per credit hour of the internship?" Rick asked.

"I worked only 45 hours per credit—"

"See," Georgia interrupted, "that's what I see as the role of this internship handbook: to outline the basic requirements for internships offered through the university and then to provide resources for providing high-quality internship experiences for our students."

"I think the handbook also needs to address some of the issues raised by the employers who responded to the internship survey we conducted last summer, especially those responses relating to how we could improve the college internship program," Leandra added. She pointed to a page from the survey report listing some of the employer comments (Document 7.1).

Responses to Open-ended Question Number 3

Question number 3 asked employers, "In what ways could our college internship program be improved?" A total of 213 comments were received. Comments were placed in five categories: collaboration and teamwork, planning, student expectations, procedures for matching interns with sponsoring organizations, and miscellaneous comments.

Collaboration and Communication

Nearly half of the comments focused on the topic of collaboration and communication (97 of 213). Following are representative examples of comments in this category:

> I'm tired of being the one that always comes to campus. I think the professors should visit the employer.

> Better supervision by faculty. My intern's faculty supervisor took no interest in her and never tried to contact me.

> We offer several internships a semester, and it seems like I'm always filling out something different for each intern. Get your act together and have a single set of internship requirements!

> I believe it would be better if the faculty supervisor was available to help the intern if he or she had questions about how to do something.

> I want to be able to contact professors if I have questions.

> Let employers know what we are expected to do—paperwork, meetings, etc.

> Better communication. When we have to hire an intern from among several applicants, I would like the faculty supervisor to provide some input.

> The intern supervisor should work more closely with the employer and the intern.

Document 7.1   Employer Responses to Survey Question

On TechComm Web

For digital versions of case documents, click on Downloadable Case Documents on <bedfordstmartins.com/techcomm>.

"Absolutely," Georgia agreed. "The employers had some great ideas. I think faculty would be really receptive to their ideas."

"So this handbook is for faculty internship coordinators?" Rick asked.

"Yes. I also want to give this handbook to sponsoring organizations. I think it would be great if the handbook was reorganized and made available to students as well." Georgia paused after looking at the group's concerned faces. "I know this sounds like an ambitious undertaking with only a few weeks left in the semester, but I already have an outline developed for faculty coordinators and sponsoring organizations," she explained as she distributed the outline (Document 7.2).

After a few minutes, Leandra asked Georgia, "How do you want us to help?"

"This is a very rough draft and needs lots of work. It's all subject to change. I was hoping that each of you could take a look at the outline and let me know if the organization makes sense to you and whether I should change or add topics. I'd also like your advice on how to reorganize the material for students."

Your Assignment

1. Download Document 7.2 from <bedfordstmartins.com/techcomm> and study it in Word's outline view. Then reorganize the outline to make it more logical based on your study of Chapter 7 and your understanding of the

- **Basic Internship Information**
  - *Getting Involved*
  - *Department Requirements for Internship Programs*
  - *Concluding Thoughts*
- **The Roles of the Faculty Member and Student Intern**
  - *The Role of the Student Intern*
    - Intern Responsibilities
    - The Student Release Form
    - Activity Log
    - Guidelines for Learning Agreements
  - *The Learning Agreement*
  - *The Student Release Form*
  - *Interacting with your Student Interns*
    - Communicating with Interns
      - **Phone**
      - **E-mail**
      - **Site visits**
  - *Placing Students in Internships*
- Site Visits
- The Learning Agreement
- **The Role of the Agency Supervisor**
  - *Legal Issues Concerning Internships*
    - Sponsoring Organization Responsibilities
  - *Getting Involved*
  - *Interacting with Your Intern*
  - *The Learning Agreement*
- **Evaluation of Interns**
  - *Evaluation Methods*
    - Intern Self-Evaluation
    - Reflective Journals
    - Agency Supervisor's Evaluation
- **Legal Matters**
  - *The Student Release Form*
- **University Policy Statement on Academic Internships and Rationale for Policy**
- **Index**

Document 7.2 Outline of Internship Handbook

author's purpose and audiences. Create an outline for faculty coordinators and sponsoring organizations, then create a different outline for student interns. Keep in mind that your outlines might incorporate several different patterns of organization. If appropriate, add or delete topics.

2. Write Georgia a memo in which you explain why your approaches are the best ones to use. Attach your revised outlines.

PART 3 Developing and Testing the Verbal and Visual Information

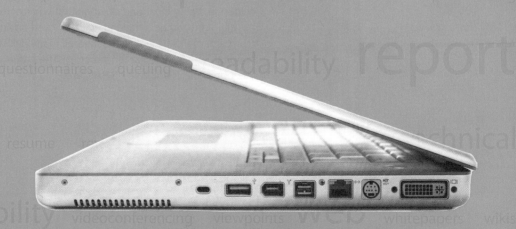

8

Communicating Persuasively

Considering the Context of Your
Argument 177

Understanding Your Audience's
Broader Goals 177

Working Within Constraints 178

Crafting a Persuasive Argument 180

Identifying the Elements of Your
Argument 181

Using the Right Kinds
of Evidence 182

Considering Opposing
Viewpoints 184

Appealing to Emotions
Responsibly 184

Deciding Where to Present
Your Claim 185

Avoiding Logical Fallacies 186

Presenting Yourself Effectively 188

Using Graphics and Design as
Persuasive Elements 189

A Look at Several Persuasive
Arguments 191

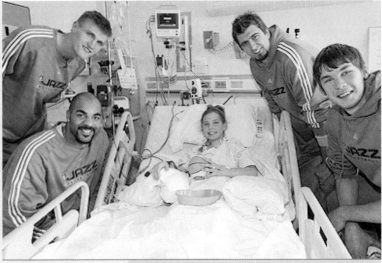

Spirit of Giving   Holiday Cheer   All-Star Drive

During the holiday season, NBA players spent time reaching out to local communities. Baron Davis, Shawn Marion, Kevin Garnett, Kobe Bryant and more discuss the importance of giving back and making holiday wishes come true!

Source: NBA Media Ventures, LLC, 2008 <www.nba.com/nba_cares>.

In the World . . .

Technical communication, like any other kind of writing, calls for making persuasive claims and supporting them effectively. Some forms of evidence are so clear and obvious that you immediately understand the claim the writer is making, without even having to read it. Here, four members of the Utah Jazz basketball team visit with a patient in a hospital. The five smiles tell the story. The name of the Web site where this photograph appears? NBA Cares.

I t is a mistake to think that technical communication is only about facts. Certainly, facts are important. But communication is about determining which facts are appropriate, describing the context that helps people understand what those facts mean, and presenting a well-reasoned argument about those facts. Your job as a communicator is to convince a reader of a viewpoint—about what factors caused a situation, for example, or what a company ought to do to solve a problem. If you are lucky, you will be reinforcing a viewpoint the reader already has. Sometimes, however, you will want to change the reader's mind. Regardless, you are presenting an *argument*: an arrangement of facts and judgments about some aspect of the world.

CONSIDERING THE CONTEXT OF YOUR ARGUMENT

An argument can be as short as a sentence or as long as a multivolume report. It can take many forms, including oral communication. And it can discuss almost any kind of issue. Here are some examples:

- *from a description of a construction site:*

    Features A, B, and C characterize the site.

- *from a study of why a competitor is outselling your company:*

    Company X's dominance can be attributed to four major factors: A, B, C, and D.

- *from a feasibility study considering four courses of action:*

    Alternative A is better than alternatives B, C, or D.

- *from a set of instructions for performing a task:*

    The safest way to perform the task is to complete task A, then task B, and so on.

Before you can develop an effective argument, you must understand your audience's broader goals and work within constraints.

Understanding Your Audience's Broader Goals

When you analyze your audience, consider the values that motivate them. Certainly, most people want the company they work for to prosper, but they are also concerned about their own welfare and interests within the company. Your argument is most likely to be effective if it responds to three goals that most people share: security, recognition, and personal and professional growth.

Security   People resist controversial actions that might hurt their own interests. Those who might lose their jobs will likely oppose an argument that their division be eliminated, even if there are many valid reasons to support

On TechComm Web

For an excellent discussion of persuasion, see Business Communication: Managing Information and Relationships. Click on Links Library for Ch. 8 on <bedfordstmartins.com/techcomm>.

the argument. Another aspect of security is workload; most people will resist an argument that calls for them to work more.

Recognition   People like to be praised for their hard work and their successes. Where appropriate, be generous in your praise. Similarly, people hate being humiliated in public. Therefore, allow people to save face. Avoid criticizing their actions or positions and speculating about their motivations. Instead, present your argument as a response to the company's present and future needs. Look ahead, not back, and be diplomatic.

Personal and Professional Growth   People want to develop and grow on the job and in their personal lives. In an obvious way, this means that they want to learn new skills and assume new duties. This desire is also reflected in efforts to improve how the organization treats its employees and customers, relates to the community, and coexists with the environment. Your argument will be more persuasive if you can show how the recommended action will help your organization become an industry leader, reduce environmental pollution, or help needy people in your city. We want to be associated with—and contribute to—organizations that are good at what they do and that help us become better people.

Figure 8.1, from the employment section on the Microsoft Web site, profiles an employee who the company believes reflects the personality and character of those who work at Microsoft.

Working Within Constraints

In planning a persuasive document, you need to work within the constraints that shape your environment on the job. As a student, you routinely work within constraints: the amount of information you can gather for a paper, the required length and format, the due date, and so forth. In business, industry, and government, similar constraints play a role.

Ethical Constraints   Your greatest responsibility is always to your own sense of what constitutes ethical behavior. Being asked to lie or mislead directly challenges your ethical standards, but in most cases, you have options. Some organizations and professional communities have a published code of conduct. In addition, many large companies have ombudspersons, who use mediation to help employees resolve ethical conflicts.

▶In This Book
For more about ethical and legal constraints, see Ch. 2.

Legal Constraints   Abide by all applicable laws on labor practices, environmental issues, fair trade, consumer rights, and so forth. If you think the action recommended by your supervisor might be illegal, meet with your organization's legal counsel and, if necessary, attorneys outside the organization.

Political Constraints   Don't spend all your energy and credibility on a losing cause. If you know that your proposal would help the company but that

Employee Profile

Corey
Business Development
Manager

Go Back

"I've been with Microsoft 11 years, and I'm chiefly responsible for developing an end-to-end strategy for non-government organizations (NGOs), in terms of how we respond to their services, sales and support needs."

Campus Life
"I work remotely—either from my home office or from satellite Microsoft offices—and my boss lives in Belgium. I travel about 60 percent of the time, and the opportunity to see the world has helped me broaden my personal outlook and my business perspective. I get to see how my colleagues and Microsoft are shaping and changing the world."

Fueling the Fire
"My job affords me the opportunity to effectively change the world. That might sound a like a cliché, but I really think the work we are doing is contributing to that and how NGOs engage to meet their missions. The opportunity to contribute in a significant way over the years has been inspiring."

Opening Doors
"I walked in here on a one-day temp assignment 11 years ago. I've had many supportive managers over the years, who recognized my talent and made certain that I had the tools and resources to contribute in a significant way to this company. A benefit has never been denied for my professional development. I've seen a significant amount of personal and professional growth, and it's awesome to think about it in those terms: It started with a one-day assignment."

On the Job
"There are many opportunities here to be entrepreneurial: to have a great idea, get support for it and then be given the latitude, autonomy and flexibility to get the job done. There are great opportunities afforded at Microsoft for an individual to be involved and engaged in community outreach, giving you the wonderful experience of connecting your personal passions to the workplace."

By profiling employee Corey in the employment section of the Microsoft Web site, the company hopes to encourage like-minded people to apply for positions at Microsoft.

Personal and professional growth, as well as the ability to change the world, are the themes of this passage. Corey has the opportunity at Microsoft to grow professionally by taking on new challenges and accepting new responsibilities, and he feels that the company appreciates his efforts.

On TechComm Web

To view Fig. 8.1 in context on the Web, click on Links Library for Ch. 8 on <bedfordstmartins .com/techcomm>.

Figure 8.1   Appealing to an Audience's Broader Goals
Source: Microsoft, 2008 <http://members.microsoft.com/careers/epdb/profileDetailPage.aspx?profileID=90>.

management disagrees with you or the company can't afford to approve it, consider what you might achieve through some other means, or scale back the idea. Two big exceptions to this rule are matters of ethics and matters of safety. As discussed in Chapter 2, ethical and legal constraints may mean that compromise is unacceptable.

Informational Constraints   The most common informational constraint you might face is that the information you need is not available. You might want your organization to buy a piece of equipment, for example, but you can't find unbiased evidence that would convince a skeptical reader.

What do you do? You tell the truth. Explain the situation, weighing the available evidence and carefully noting what is missing. If you unintentionally suggest that your evidence is better than it really is, you will lose your most important credential: your credibility.

▶ In This Book

For more about collaboration, see Ch. 4.

Personnel Constraints   The most typical personnel constraint you might face is a lack of access to as many collaborators as you need. In such cases, present a persuasive proposal to hire the personnel you need. However, don't be surprised if you have to make do with fewer people than you want.

Financial Constraints   Financial constraints are related to personnel constraints: if you had unlimited funds, you could hire all the personnel you need. But financial constraints can also affect other kinds of resources: you might not be able to print as many copies of the document as you want, or you might need to settle for black and white instead of full color.

▶ In This Book

For more about scheduling, see Ch. 3, p. 47.

Time Constraints   Start by determining the document's deadline. (Sometimes a document will have several intermediate deadlines.) Then create a schedule. Keep in mind that tasks almost always take longer than estimated. And when you collaborate, the number of potential problems increases, because when one person is delayed, others may lack the necessary information to proceed, causing a logjam.

Format and Tone Constraints   You will be expected to work within one additional set of constraints:

- *Format.* Format constraints are limitations on the size, shape, or style of a document. For example, your reader might like to see all tables and figures presented at the end of the report. If you are writing to someone in your own organization, follow the format constraints described in the company style guide, if there is one, or check similar documents to see what other writers have done. Also ask more-experienced co-workers for their advice. If you are writing to someone outside your organization, learn what you can about that organization's preferences.

- *Tone.* When addressing superiors, use a formal, polite tone. When addressing peers or subordinates, use a less formal tone but be equally polite.

CRAFTING A PERSUASIVE ARGUMENT

Persuasion is important, whether you wish to affect a reader's attitude or merely present information clearly. To make a persuasive case, you must identify the elements of your argument, use the right kinds of evidence, consider opposing viewpoints, appeal to emotions responsibly, and decide where to state your claim.

Identifying the Elements of Your Argument

A persuasive argument has three main elements:

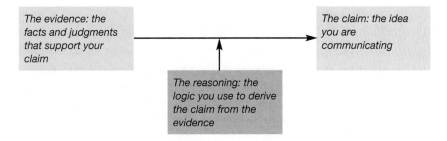

The *claim* is the conclusion you want your readers to accept. For example, your claim might be that your company should institute flextime, a scheduling approach that gives employees some flexibility in when they begin and end their workdays. You want your readers to agree with this idea and to take the next steps toward instituting flextime.

The *evidence* is the information you want your readers to consider. For the argument about flextime, the evidence might include the following:

- The turnover rate of our female employees is double that of our male employees.

- At exit interviews, 40 percent of our female employees under the age of 38 state that they quit so that they can be home for their school-age children.

- Replacing a staff-level employee costs us about one-half the employee's annual salary; replacing a professional-level employee costs a whole year's salary.

- Other companies have found that flextime significantly decreases turnover among female employees under the age of 38.

- Other companies have found that flextime has additional benefits and introduces no significant problems.

The *reasoning* is the logic you use to connect the evidence to your claim. In the discussion of flextime, the reasoning involves three links:

- Flextime appears to have reduced the turnover problem among younger female employees at other companies.

- Our company is similar to these other companies.

- Flextime, therefore, is likely to prove helpful at our company.

Using the Right Kinds of Evidence

People most often react favorably to four kinds of evidence:

- *"Commonsense" arguments.* Here, *commonsense* means "Most people would think that. . . ." The following sentence presents a commonsense argument that flextime is a good idea:

  > Flextime makes sense because it gives people more control over how they plan their schedules.

  A commonsense argument says, "I don't have hard evidence to support my conclusion, but it stands to reason that. . . ." In this case, the argument is that people like to have as much control over their time as possible. If your audience's commonsense arguments match yours, your argument is likely to be persuasive.

- *Numerical data.* Numerical data—statistics—are generally more persuasive than commonsense arguments.

  > Statistics drawn from the personnel literature (McClellan, 2008) show that, among Fortune 500 companies, flextime decreases turnover by 25 to 35 percent among female employees younger than 38.

  Notice that the writer states that the study covered many companies, not just one or a handful. If the sample size were small, the claim would be much less persuasive. (The discussion of logical fallacies later in this chapter explains such *hasty generalizations*.)

- *Examples.* An example makes an abstract point more concrete and therefore more vivid and memorable.

  > Mary Saunders tried for weeks to arrange for child care for her two preschoolers that would enable her to start work at 7 A.M., as required at her workplace. The best she could manage was having her children stay with a non-licensed provider. When conditions at that provider led to ear infections in both her children, Mary decided that she could no longer continue working.

  Examples are often used along with numerical data. The example gives the problem a human dimension, but the argument also requires numerical data to show that the problem is part of a pattern, not a coincidence.

- *Expert testimony.* A message from an expert is more persuasive than the same message from someone without credentials. A well-researched article on flextime written by a respected business scholar in a reputable business journal is likely to be persuasive. When you make arguments, you will often cite expert testimony from published sources or interviews you have conducted.

▶ In This Book
For advice on evaluating information from the Internet, see Ch. 6, p. 128.

INTERACTIVE SAMPLE DOCUMENT
Analyzing Evidence in an Argument

In this excerpt from "Web Site Lets People Offer Microloans to Borrowers Worldwide," the writer describes Kiva.org, a Web site that facilitates microloans. The questions in the margin ask you to consider the evidence presented in the excerpt. E-mail your responses to yourself and/or your instructor on TechComm Web.

Jaime Acosta, a college student and baker from Houston, last year loaned some money to Eleuterio Salazar Segura, a store owner in Mexico who wanted to purchase merchandise for his store. After Salazar repaid his loan in full, Acosta then loaned to Penina Mataoa, a tailor in Samoa. "I care about the well-being of others around the world. With all the resources that we have, extreme poverty should not exist," Acosta said.

Acosta made his loans through Kiva.org, a nonprofit microlending Web site. Kiva—which means "unity" or "agreement" in Swahili—is the brainchild of Matt and Jessica Flannery, who got the idea while Jessica Flannery was consulting on microfinance in East Africa a few years ago. Kiva is "all about connecting people" and "connecting lenders with micro-businesses online," Matt Flannery wrote in his blog.

Thanks to Kiva, Chiyenure Uwobodo, a Nigerian mother of four, was able to borrow $250 to expand her beauty salon business. And Grace Ayaa, a mother of four in Uganda, borrowed $475 for a refrigerator to store the peanut butter she was making until she could sell it, and to buy packing materials. She was able to save enough from her increased income to buy a small piece of land and begin building a home for her family. . . .

"Kiva is about empowering the poor through loans," Fiona Ramsey, a Kiva volunteer, said in an interview.

Kiva did not invent microfinance—the supply of loans, savings, and other small-scale financial services to the poor—but its creation of an online marketplace for lenders and borrowers is innovative enough to have led to explosive growth of over 30 percent per month since the Web site's founding in 2005. Based on the recommendations of an international panel of judges, the Tech Museum of Innovation presented Kiva with an economic development award on November 7 at a ceremony in San Jose, California.

"Kiva's mission is about connecting people through lending for the sake of alleviating poverty, but an important part of this is connecting people," said Ramsey. "We want to create ways where people in the developing and the developed world can connect with each other . . . in a way that is different and not in a beneficiary-benefactor relationship, but a partnership relationship."

1. What kind of evidence is presented in the first three paragraphs of this excerpt? Why did the writer use that form of evidence at the start of the article?

2. What kind of evidence is presented in paragraph 4?

3. What kind of evidence is presented in paragraph 5?

4. The final paragraph, about connections between people, does not present evidence to clarify its claim. What kinds of evidence might support the claim?

 **On TechComm Web**

To e-mail your responses to yourself and/or your instructor, click on Interactive Sample Documents for Ch. 8 on <bedfordstmartins.com/techcomm>.

Source: Thomas, 2007 <www.america.gov/st/washfile-english/2007/December/
200712111708191CJsamohT0.2462274.html>.

Considering Opposing Viewpoints

When you present an argument, you need to address opposing points of view. If you don't, your opponents will simply conclude that your argument is flawed because it doesn't address problems that they think are important. In meeting the skeptical or hostile reader's possible objections to your case, you can use one of several tactics:

- *The opposing argument is based on illogical reasoning or on inaccurate or incomplete facts.* You can counter the argument that flextime increases utility bills by citing unbiased research studies showing that it does not.

- *The opposing argument is valid but less powerful than your own.* If you can show that the opposing argument makes sense but is outweighed by your own argument, you appear to be a fair-minded person who understands that reality is complicated. You can counter the argument that flextime reduces carpooling opportunities by showing that only 3 percent of your employees use carpooling and that three-quarters of those employees favor flextime anyway because of its other advantages.

- *The two arguments can be reconciled.* If an opposing argument is not invalid or clearly inferior to your own, you can offer to study the situation thoroughly to find a solution that incorporates the best from each argument. For example, if flextime might cause serious problems for your company's many carpoolers, you could propose a trial period during which you would study several ways to help employees find other carpooling opportunities. If the company cannot solve the problem, or if most of the employees prefer the old system, you will switch back to it. This proposal can remove much of the threat posed by your ideas.

When you address an opposing argument, be gracious and understated. Focus on the argument, not on the people who oppose you. If you embarrass or humiliate them, you undermine your own credibility and motivate your opponents to continue opposing you.

There is no one best place to address opposing arguments. In general, however, if you know that important readers hold opposing views, address those views relatively early. Your goal is to show *all* your readers that you are a fair-minded person who has thought carefully about the subject and that your argument is stronger than the opposing arguments.

Appealing to Emotions Responsibly

Writers sometimes appeal to their readers' emotions. Writers usually combine emotional appeals with appeals to reason. For example, an argument that we ought to increase foreign aid to drought-stricken African countries

Figure 8.2 An Argument That Uses an Emotional Appeal
Source: KentuckyFriedCruelty.com, 2008 <www.kentuckyfriedcruelty.com>.

This document from People for the Ethical Treatment of Animals (PETA) relies on emotion in describing what it calls the "abuses" of KFC. The bulk of the passage details the physical suffering endured by the chickens. To the extent that readers are moved emotionally by these descriptions, the argument will be persuasive.

The passage also uses another strategy: the celebrity of the people supporting the message. This strategy is a weak form of the argument from authority (see Table 8.1 on p. 186).

might describe (and present images of) the human plight of the victims but also include reason-based arguments about the extent of the problem, the causes, the possible solutions, and the pragmatic reasons we might want to increase foreign aid.

When you use emotional appeals, do not overstate or overdramatize them, or you will risk alienating readers. Try to think of additional kinds of evidence that will also help support your claim. Figure 8.2 shows a brief argument that relies on an emotional appeal.

Deciding Where to Present Your Claim

In most cases, the best place to state your claim is at the start of the argument. Then provide the evidence and, if appropriate, the reasoning. Sometimes, however, it is more effective to place the claim *after* the evidence and the reasoning. This indirect structure works best if a large number of readers oppose your claim. If you present your claim right away, these readers might become alienated and stop paying attention. You want a chance to present your evidence and your reasoning without causing this kind of undesirable reaction.

 On TechComm Web

For exercises on logical fallacies, see Writing Guidelines
for Engineering and Science
Students. Click on Links
Library for Ch. 8 on
<bedfordstmartins.com/
techcomm>.

AVOIDING LOGICAL FALLACIES

A logical fallacy—a mistake in reasoning—can undercut the persuasiveness of your writing. An example is if someone says, "Antidepressants are a scam. I know that because Tom Cruise says so, and he's a world-famous actor." Although it is true that Tom Cruise is a world-famous actor, it does not follow that what he thinks about antidepressants is true just because he says so. Table 8.1 explains some of the most common logical fallacies.

Table 8.1 Common Logical Fallacies

Fallacy	Explanation	Example and comment
Ad hominem argument; also called *argument against the speaker*	An argument against the writer, not against the writer's argument	"Of course Matthew wants us to buy more computers—he's a computer geek." The fact that Matthew is a "computer geek" doesn't necessarily mean that his argument for buying more computers is unwise.
Argument from ignorance	An argument that a claim is true because it has never been proven false, or false because it has never been proven true	"Nobody has ever proven that global warming is occurring. Therefore, global warming is a myth." The fact that a concept has not yet been proven does not necessarily mean that it is false. Perhaps the measurement techniques are insufficiently precise or not yet available.
Appeal to pity	An argument based on emotion, not reason	"We shouldn't sell the Ridgeway division. It's been part of the company for over 40 years." The fact that the division has long been a part of the company is not in itself a good reason to retain it.

Table 8.1 (continued)

Fallacy	Explanation	Example and comment
Argument from authority	An argument that a claim is valid because the person making the claim is an authority	"According to world-renowned climatologist Dr. William Smith, global warming is definitely a fact." Even if Dr. Smith is a recognized authority in this field, saying that global warming is a fact is not valid unless you present a valid argument to support it.
Circular argument; also called *begging the question*	An argument that assumes what it is attempting to prove	"HP is more successful than its competitors because of its consistently high sales." Because "more successful" means roughly the same thing as achieving "consistently high sales," this statement says only that HP outsells its competitors. The writer needs to explain *why* HP outsells its competitors and is therefore more successful.
Either-or argument	An argument that poses only two alternatives when in fact there might be more	"If we don't start selling our products online, we're going to be out of business within a year." This statement does not explain why these are the only two alternatives. The company might improve its sales by taking measures other than selling online.
Ad populum argument; also called *bandwagon argument*	An argument that a claim is valid because many people think it is or act as if it is	"Our four major competitors have started selling online. We should, too." The fact that our competitors are selling online is not in itself an argument that we should sell online, too.

Table 8.1   (continued)

Fallacy	Explanation	Example and comment
Hasty generalization; sometimes called *inadequate sampling*	An argument that draws conclusions based on an insufficient number of cases	"The new Tata is an unreliable car. Two of my friends own Tatas, and both have had reliability problems." Before reaching any valid conclusions, you would have to study a much larger sample and compare your findings with those for other cars in the Tata's class.
Post hoc reasoning (the complete phrase is *post hoc, ergo propter hoc*)	An argument that claims that because A precedes B, A caused B	"There must be something wrong with the new circuit breaker in the office. Ever since we had it installed, the air conditioners haven't worked right." Maybe the air conditioners are malfunctioning because of the circuit breaker, but the malfunctioning might have other causes.
Oversimplifying	An argument that omits important information in establishing a causal link	"The way to solve the balance-of-trade problem is to improve the quality of the products we produce." Although improving quality is important, international trade balances are determined by many factors, including tariffs and currency rates, and therefore cannot be explained by simple cause-and-effect reasoning.

PRESENTING YOURSELF EFFECTIVELY

A big part of presenting yourself effectively is showing that you know the appropriate information about your subject. However, you also need to come across as a professional.

Guidelines

Creating a Professional Persona

Your *persona* is how you appear to your readers. Demonstrating the following characteristics will help you establish an attractive professional persona.

▶ **Cooperativeness.** Make clear that your goal is to solve a problem, not advance your own interests.

▶ **Moderation.** Be moderate in your judgments. The problem you are describing will not likely spell doom for your organization, and the solution you propose will not solve all the company's problems.

▶ **Fair-mindedness.** Acknowledge the strengths of opposing points of view, even as you offer counterarguments.

▶ **Modesty.** If you fail to acknowledge that you don't know everything, someone else will be sure to volunteer that insight.

The following paragraph shows how a writer can demonstrate the qualities of cooperativeness, moderation, fair-mindedness, and modesty:

This plan is certainly not perfect. For one thing, it calls for a greater up-front investment than we had anticipated. And the return on investment through the first three quarters is likely to fall short of our initial goals. However, I think this plan is the best of the three alternatives for the following reasons. . . . Therefore, I recommend that we begin planning immediately to implement the plan. I am confident that this plan will enable us to enter the flat-screen market successfully, building on our fine reputation for high-quality advanced electronics.

In the first three sentences, the writer acknowledges the problems with his recommendation.

The use of "I think" adds an attractive modesty; the recommendation might be unwise.

The recommendation itself is moderate; the writer does not claim that the plan will save the world.

In the last two sentences, the writer shows a spirit of cooperativeness by focusing on the company's goals.

USING GRAPHICS AND DESIGN AS PERSUASIVE ELEMENTS

Graphics and design are fundamentally important in communicating persuasively because they help you convey both technical data and non-technical information. Figure 8.3 on page 190 shows a typical combination of verbal and visual techniques used to make a persuasive argument on a corporate Web page.

Photographs can be used to convey technical evidence, as shown in Figure 8.4 on page 190.

If you are writing a persuasive passage to a reader from another culture, keep in mind that cultures differ significantly not only in matters

The opening page from the "Officer Candidate's Guide to the U.S. Marine Corps" uses words and graphics to tell a story.

The text refers to the proud history of the Marine Corps, asking readers to consider whether they have the qualities necessary to be a leader in the U.S. Marines.

In the main image, the photo of an officer in dress uniform, the focus is on the sparkling white gloves and the ornamental sword, both of which allude to the long, distinguished history of the Marine Corps.

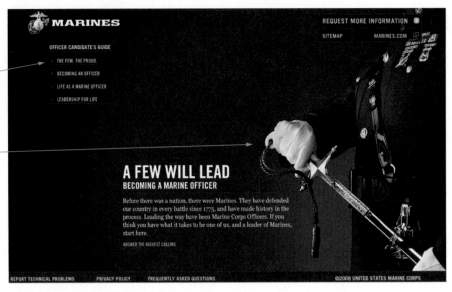

Figure 8.3   Verbal and Visual Techniques in Persuasion
Source: U.S. Marine Corps, 2008 <http://officer.marines.com>.

In a report on a crash test, this photograph is used to illustrate the following sentence: "Smeared greasepaint shows where the driver dummy's head was protected from being hit by hard structures by the side curtain airbag."

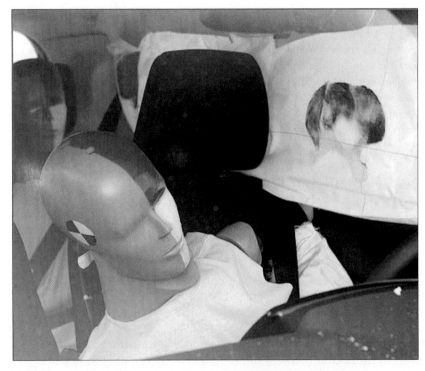

Figure 8.4   A Photograph Used to Provide Technical Information
Source: Insurance Institute for Highway Safety, 2008 <www.iihs.org/ratings/rating.aspx?id=867>.

> ## Ethics Note
>
> ### *Seeming* Honest Versus *Being* Honest in Persuasive Writing
>
> The young actor asks the old actor, "What's the key to great acting?" The old actor replies, "Sincerity. Once you learn how to fake sincerity. . . ." Any discussion of image and persuasion has to address the question at the heart of this old joke. Does a writer have to *be* cooperative to *appear* cooperative?
>
> Well, not really. There are tricks for appearing cooperative, and they can work for a while. But the easiest way to *appear* honest and cooperative is to *be* honest and cooperative. As suggested in Chapter 2, you need to tell the truth and not mislead your readers. As suggested in Chapter 4, you need to be cooperative, diplomatic, and constructive. And as suggested in this chapter, you need to remember people's broader goals: to protect their own security, to achieve recognition, and to learn and grow in their personal and professional lives.

such as business customs but also in their most fundamental values. These differences can affect persuasive writing. Culture determines two factors:

- *What makes an argument persuasive.* Statistics and experimental data are fundamental kinds of evidence in the West, but testimony from respected authority figures can be much more persuasive in the East.

- *How to structure an argument.* In a Western culture, the claim is usually presented up front. In an Eastern culture, it is likely to be delayed or to remain unstated but implied.

When you write for an audience from another culture, use two techniques:

- Study that culture and adjust the content, structure, and style of your arguments.

- Include in your budget the cost of having your important documents reviewed and edited by a person from the target culture. Few people are experts on cultures other than their own.

A LOOK AT SEVERAL PERSUASIVE ARGUMENTS

The following examples of technical communication show how the persuasive elements of an argument differ depending on a writer's purpose.

Figure 8.5 on page 192 presents two paragraphs from a student's job-application letter.

A student writer uses specific examples to persuade a prospective employer.

Without making her claim explicit, the writer presents evidence that she is hardworking and lets the prospective employer draw his or her own conclusions.

In listing some of the training courses she has taken, the writer supports an earlier claim that her broad background might be of use to her next employer.

> At Western State University, I have earned 87 credits toward a degree in Technical Communication. I have been a full-time student (no fewer than 12 credit hours per semester) while working full-time for the Northwest Watershed Research Center. The four upper-division courses I am taking this semester, including Advanced Technical Communication and Technical Editing, are required for the BA in Technical Communication.
>
> In addition to my formal education, I have completed 34 training courses on the job. These courses have included diverse topics such as financial management, the Fair Labor Standards Act, the Americans with Disabilities Act, career-development opportunities in public affairs, and software applications such as MS Office, Quark XPress, and RoboHelp.

Figure 8.5   Persuading a Prospective Employer

Figure 8.6, a statement from General Electric (GE) about its Ecomagination program, illustrates an effective use of tone and evidence.

Figure 8.7, from a product description, uses text and photographs effectively to present persuasive arguments.

Published on GE's Web site, this statement claims that the company's Ecomagination policy is both environmentally and financially responsible.

The photograph of a field of sunflowers has been edited to suggest an earlier era.

Against this backdrop, the high-tech, energy-efficient locomotive suggests that the company's environmental awareness will help sustain the natural world.

Figure 8.6   Persuading Investors and the General Public
Source: General Electric, 2008 <http://ge.ecomagination.com/site/index.html#vision/intro>.

Honeywell Active Alert® analyzes the behavior of individuals and vehicles to provide real-time alarms and search tools that enhance manned and unmanned video surveillance systems.

This unique, patented software automatically:

* Distinguishes between humans, vehicles and other objects.
* Tracks up to 20 targets in each camera view.
* Reports more than 35 actionable events and behaviors.
* Delivers real-time alarms, local voice/visual notification, relay closure for integration with alarm panels, e-mail, cell-phone text messages, and Remote Network Client.
* Offers data mining capabilities to enable end users to spot trends and modify operations to maximize security.

Key Features:

* Enables user-defined event and alarm settings for each camera view.
* Remote Client allows full distributed system access regardless of location.
* Powerful search tools offer an instantaneous method of searching and locating incident video captured by digital video recorders and network video recorders. By combining user-friendly smart indexing with interactive retrieval tools, Active Alert enables rapid search, review and filtering of selected video incidents.
* Flexible query system allows the user to specify a combination of alarm or event types, object types or cameras, within any target time range.

Sample Applications:

Perimeter Protection

Restricted Area

Loitering

Abandoned Object

The Active Alert family includes:

* **Active Alert® Base:** Identifies and classifies the most common user-defined events and behaviors, and provides basic perimeter intrusion detection.

* **Active Alert® Standard:** All the benefits of Active Alert Base, plus tracking of up to 20 objects in a scene and automatically alarming on more than 35 different events, incidents and behaviors.

* **Active Alert® Premium:** All the benefits of Active Alert Standard, plus additional analytics for high-risk facilities and locations such as abandoned object, removed object and possible theft functionality.

* **People Counter:** Powerful traffic flow measurement with real-time or periodic reporting.

* **Smart Impressions®:** Smart video solutions optimize operations by analyzing individual customer and vehicular activities and traffic patterns.

This page from a Honeywell brochure presents a number of persuasive arguments.

The large text presents a general description of what the system does.

Smaller text describes what the software does and its key features.

Two other arguments are presented on this page:
* *The large photo and its text show different versions of the system.*
* *The set of small photos shows sample applications for the system.*

Figure 8.7   Using Text and Graphics to Present Persuasive Arguments
Source: Honeywell International, Inc., 2008 <www.honeywellvideo.com/products/ias/va/160966.html>.

Writer's Checklist

In analyzing your audience, did you consider the broader goals of

- ☐ maintaining security? (p. 177)
- ☐ achieving recognition? (p. 178)
- ☐ growing personally and professionally? (p. 178)

In planning, did you consider the following constraints:

- ☐ ethical? (p. 178)
- ☐ legal? (p. 178)
- ☐ political? (p. 178)
- ☐ informational? (p. 179)
- ☐ personnel? (p. 180)
- ☐ financial? (p. 180)
- ☐ time? (p. 180)
- ☐ format and tone? (p. 180)

In crafting a persuasive argument, did you

- ☐ use the three-part structure of claim, evidence, and reasoning? (p. 181)
- ☐ choose the appropriate kinds of evidence? (p. 182)
- ☐ consider opposing viewpoints? (p. 184)
- ☐ appeal to emotions reasonably? (p. 184)
- ☐ decide where to present the claim? (p. 185)

In writing the argument, did you avoid the following logical fallacies:

- ☐ ad hominem argument? (p. 186)
- ☐ argument from ignorance? (p. 186)
- ☐ appeal to pity? (p. 186)
- ☐ argument from authority? (p. 187)
- ☐ circular argument? (p. 187)
- ☐ either-or argument? (p. 187)
- ☐ *ad populum* argument? (p. 187)
- ☐ hasty generalization? (p. 188)
- ☐ post hoc reasoning? (p. 188)
- ☐ oversimplifying? (p. 188)

In drafting your argument, did you create a persona that is

- ☐ cooperative? (p. 189)
- ☐ moderate? (p. 189)
- ☐ fair-minded? (p. 189)
- ☐ modest? (p. 189)

- ☐ In addressing a multicultural audience, did you consider what types of evidence and what argument structures would be most effective? (p. 191)

Exercises

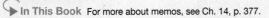

In This Book For more about memos, see Ch. 14, p. 377.

1. **INTERNET EXERCISE** Visit the Web site of a car manufacturer, such as Ford (<www.ford.com>) or Mercedes-Benz (<www.mbusa.com>). Identify the major techniques of persuasion used in the words and graphics on the site. For example, what claims are made? What types of evidence are used? Is the reasoning sound?

2. For each of the following items, write one paragraph identifying the logical flaw:

   a. The election couldn't have been fair—I don't know anyone who voted for the winner.

   b. It would be wrong to prosecute Allied for age discrimination; Allied has always been a great corporate neighbor.

   c. The decrease in smoking can be attributed to increased restrictions on smoking in public.

   d. Bill Jensen's proposal to create an on-site day-care center is just the latest of his harebrained ideas.

   e. Since the introduction of cola drinks at the start of the twentieth century, cancer has become the second-greatest killer in the United States. Cola drinks should be outlawed.

   f. If mutual-fund guru Peter Lynch recommends this investment, I think we ought to buy it.

   g. We should not go into the flash-memory market; we have always been a leading manufacturer of DRAM.

   h. The other two hospitals in the city have implemented computerized patient record keeping; I think we need to do so, too.

   i. Our Model X500 didn't succeed because we failed to sell a sufficient number of units.

j. No research has ever established that Internet businesses can earn money; they will never succeed.

3. **GROUP/INTERNET EXERCISE** Form groups of two for this research project on multicultural communication styles. Have each person in the group secure a document written in English by a person working in a company or government agency outside the United States, then follow these steps:

   a. Using a search engine, enter the name of a country and the word *business*. For example, enter "Nicaragua business." Find the Web site of a business, then print out the "About the Company" page or some similar page, such as "Mission" or "Projects." Or enter the name of a country and the word *government*, such as "Nicaragua government." Find a government agency that has published a report that is available on the Internet. Print several pages of the report.

   b. On your copy of the pages you have printed, disguise the country of origin by blacking out the name of the company or government agency and any other information that would indicate the country of origin.

   c. Exchange pages with the other person in your group. Study your partner's pages. Do the pages show a different strategy of persuasion than you would expect from a writer in the United States? For instance, does the writer support his or her claims with the kind of evidence you would expect to see in the United States? Is the organization of the information as you would expect it to be in the United States? Does the writer create a persona as you would expect to see in the United States?

   d. Meet with your partner and explain to him or her what you see in the pages that is similar or different from what you would expect if the document came from the United States. Ask your partner whether he or she saw the same things. Present your findings in a memo to your instructor.

Case 8: Being Persuasive About Privacy

▶ **In This Book** For more about memos, see Ch. 14, p. 377.

Background

You and the other members of your group are in the Department of Corporate Communications at Blanchard Ag-Supply, an agricultural seed company. Your company specializes in developing, breeding, processing, packaging, and distributing a variety of forage and cool-season turfgrass seeds to clients in North America, Australia, and Europe. Forage crops represent a major feed component in the diets of animals that graze or eat hay. Turfgrass seeds are used for home lawns, sports fields, golf courses, and decorative landscaping. Blanchard Ag-Supply relies heavily on its Web site to conduct its global business. This Web site includes the company's privacy statement (Document 8.1).

Although you knew your company posted a privacy statement on its Web site, you had never taken the time to read it until you received a series of e-mails forwarded to you by your supervisor, Andrea Dugan. Earlier today, Andrea stopped you in the hallway and said, "I'm caught in the middle of an argument between Lance Bulos in Marketing and Burt Christensen in Legal. Burt wants us to revise the company's privacy statement; Lance doesn't think the statement needs any revision. With their permission, I just forwarded you the e-mail messages Burt forwarded to me. I want your help." (See Documents 8.2 and 8.3.)

"Sure, what sort of help do you need?"

"Right from the first paragraph, where it says we want to balance our company's need to be competitive and our customers' right to privacy, something seems off. Would you mind studying the statement and getting back to me on whether it has any problems?" Andrea asked.

"I'll get back to you in a day or two."

Your Assignment

1. Identify those elements of persuasion in Document 8.1 that are used effectively and those that are used ineffectively, then write a memo responding to Andrea's request.

2. Later, Andrea stops by your office. "It looks like we need to revise the privacy statement," she tells you. "You've read the e-mails from Burt and Lance. I'd like you to recommend an approach to fixing the statement and show me a draft of your revision." Write Andrea a memo in which you recommend how to fix the statement. Include a revised privacy statement that reflects your recommendations.

Blanchard Ag-Supply Privacy Statement

At Blanchard Ag-Supply, we want our customers to always be aware of any information we collect, how we use it, and under what circumstances, if any, we release it. Blanchard Ag-Supply's goal is to balance the realities of conducting business in a competitive global market with your right to control how your personal information is used. We want our customers to be offered the products that best meet their needs. As a result, we collect personal information to personalize your visit and to develop and offer competitively priced products and services.

The collection of personal information

We respect each customer's right to personal privacy and online security. We may request such personally identifiable information as first and last name, e-mail address, street address, and phone number from our visitors to process and fulfill orders for products or services. Blanchard Ag-Supply uses this information to make sure you find the right product or service at the right price. Blanchard Ag-Supply may also use this information to provide advertisements about goods and services of value to you.

You may visit our site without divulging any personal information. However, if you choose not to reveal some identifying information, Blanchard Ag-Supply cannot guarantee that we can provide the highest-quality service tailored to your specific needs.

Blanchard Ag-Supply also collects information such as demographic data and browsing patterns automatically each time you visit our site. Such data collection requires no effort on your part and allows Blanchard to better serve you during your current and subsequent visits.

Disclosure to Blanchard Ag-Supply team members

Our goal is satisfied customers. To this end, if Blanchard feels that you would benefit from services or products offered by Blanchard Ag-Supply team members, Blanchard may share information with these third parties. If you receive marketing materials not meeting your current business needs from our team members, please contact them directly.

Blanchard Ag-Supply reserves the right to change the way we use your personal information and to change, modify, or update this privacy statement at any time without notice. Blanchard recommends you read this privacy statement each time you visit our site.

Document 8.1   Privacy Statement Posted on Blanchard Ag-Supply's Web Site

 On TechComm Web For digital versions of case documents, click on Downloadable Case Documents on <bedfordstmartins.com/techcomm>.

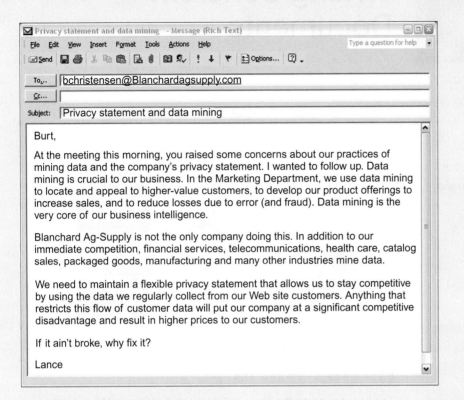

Privacy statement and data mining - Message (Rich Text)

File   Edit   View   Insert   Format   Tools   Actions   Help   Type a question for help

Send

To...   bchristensen@Blanchardagsupply.com

Cc...

Subject: Privacy statement and data mining

Burt,

At the meeting this morning, you raised some concerns about our practices of mining data and the company's privacy statement. I wanted to follow up. Data mining is crucial to our business. In the Marketing Department, we use data mining to locate and appeal to higher-value customers, to develop our product offerings to increase sales, and to reduce losses due to error (and fraud). Data mining is the very core of our business intelligence.

Blanchard Ag-Supply is not the only company doing this. In addition to our immediate competition, financial services, telecommunications, health care, catalog sales, packaged goods, manufacturing and many other industries mine data.

We need to maintain a flexible privacy statement that allows us to stay competitive by using the data we regularly collect from our Web site customers. Anything that restricts this flow of customer data will put our company at a significant competitive disadvantage and result in higher prices to our customers.

If it ain't broke, why fix it?

Lance

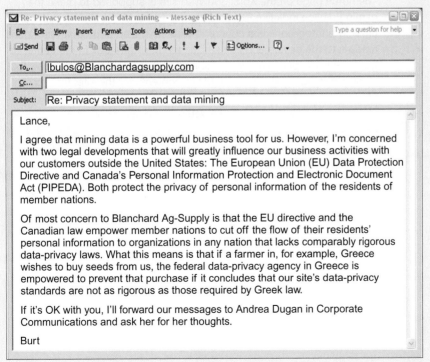

Re: Privacy statement and data mining - Message (Rich Text)

File   Edit   View   Insert   Format   Tools   Actions   Help   Type a question for help

Send

To...   lbulos@Blanchardagsupply.com

Cc...

Subject: Re: Privacy statement and data mining

Lance,

I agree that mining data is a powerful business tool for us. However, I'm concerned with two legal developments that will greatly influence our business activities with our customers outside the United States: The European Union (EU) Data Protection Directive and Canada's Personal Information Protection and Electronic Document Act (PIPEDA). Both protect the privacy of personal information of the residents of member nations.

Of most concern to Blanchard Ag-Supply is that the EU directive and the Canadian law empower member nations to cut off the flow of their residents' personal information to organizations in any nation that lacks comparably rigorous data-privacy laws. What this means is that if a farmer in, for example, Greece wishes to buy seeds from us, the federal data-privacy agency in Greece is empowered to prevent that purchase if it concludes that our site's data-privacy standards are not as rigorous as those required by Greek law.

If it's OK with you, I'll forward our messages to Andrea Dugan in Corporate Communications and ask her for her thoughts.

Burt

9

Writing Coherent Documents

Writing Coherent Titles 200

Writing Coherent Headings 201

Writing Coherent Lists 204

Writing Coherent Paragraphs 206

Structuring Paragraphs Clearly 207

Using Coherence Devices Within and
Between Paragraphs 211

Creating a Coherent Design 214

Using Headers and Footers to
Enhance Coherence 214

Using Typefaces to Enhance
Coherence 215

Source: Microsoft, 2008 <www.xbox.com/en-US/hardware/?WT.svl=nav>.

In the World . . .

The home page on the Xbox 360 Web site is supposed to make the gaming device look like fun, and it does. But underneath the cool colors and photographs is a coherent, well-organized page that introduces readers to the device and its uses. Inside the white box in the center of the screen is a photo of the console and the controller. To the right, four smaller photographs act as a table of contents for the site: first you choose the right console, then you get into the games, and then you start playing online; finally, when you're not playing games, you have a digital amplifier to power your home-theater system. Using the Xbox might be "extreme fun," as the home page says, but making the page coherent and easy to navigate was extreme hard work.

A coherent document flows smoothly from one part to the next, enabling readers to concentrate on understanding the information it contains. An incoherent document is harder to read; readers can easily misunderstand the information or become confused, unable to determine how a particular point relates to one that precedes it.

Should you worry about coherence when you draft or when you revise and edit? Because many writers need to concentrate fully on making the information clear and accurate when they draft, they concentrate on coherence only after they have a complete draft. More-experienced writers automatically incorporate these coherence techniques into the drafting process. Whatever approach you use, make sure the document is coherent before it gets to your readers.

In looking for problems that need fixing, most writers look for the largest, most important problems first, then work on the smaller, less important ones. That way, they don't waste time on awkward paragraphs they might eventually decide to throw out. They begin revising by considering the document as a whole (for organization, development, and content), saving the sentence-level concerns (such as grammar, punctuation, and spelling) for later.

For example, you might look through the document and answer questions such as these:

- Have you left out anything in turning your outline into a draft?
- Have you included all the elements your readers expect to see?
- Is the document organized logically?
- Does the document contain sufficient and appropriate evidence?
- Is your reasoning valid and persuasive?
- Do you come across as reliable, honest, and helpful?
- Are all the elements presented consistently?
- Is the emphasis appropriate throughout the document?

Perhaps the best way to check your whole document for coherence is to study the outline view of the document. Figure 9.1 on page 200 shows how the outline view gives you a bird's-eye view of the text.

In addition to making sure the whole document is coherent, you also need to focus on the most important structural components of the document: titles, headings, lists, and paragraphs.

In This Book

For more about planning, drafting, revising, editing, and proofreading a document, see Ch. 3.

In This Book

For more about revising for coherence, see Ch. 13, p. 344.

On TechComm Web

For more advice on revising the whole document, see Purdue University's Online Writing Lab handouts on revising. Click on Links Library for Ch. 9 on <bedfordstmartins.com/techcomm>.

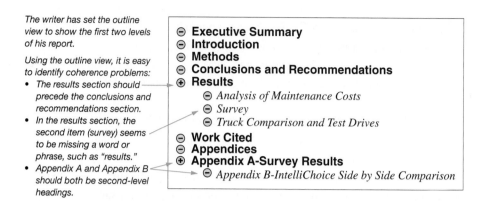

The writer has set the outline view to show the first two levels of his report.

Using the outline view, it is easy to identify coherence problems:

- *The results section should precede the conclusions and recommendations section.*
- *In the results section, the second item (survey) seems to be missing a word or phrase, such as "results."*
- *Appendix A and Appendix B should both be second-level headings.*

⊖ **Executive Summary**
⊖ **Introduction**
⊖ **Methods**
⊖ **Conclusions and Recommendations**
⊕ **Results**
    ⊖ *Analysis of Maintenance Costs*
    ⊖ *Survey*
    ⊖ *Truck Comparison and Test Drives*
⊖ **Work Cited**
⊖ **Appendices**
⊕ **Appendix A-Survey Results**
    ⊖ *Appendix B-IntelliChoice Side by Side Comparison*

Figure 9.1   Studying the Coherence of a Document Using the Outline View

WRITING COHERENT TITLES

The title is crucial because it is your first chance to define the subject and purpose of the document for your readers, giving them their first clue about whether the document contains the information they need. The title is an implicit promise to your readers: "This document is about Subject A, and it was written to achieve Purpose B." Everything else that follows has to relate clearly to the subject and purpose defined in the title. If it doesn't, either the title is misleading or the document has failed to make good on the promise the title makes.

You might want to put off giving a final title to your document until you have completed the document, as you cannot be sure that the subject and purpose you established during the planning stages will not change. However, you should jot down a working title before you start drafting to give you a sense of direction, then come back to revise it later. Be sure to give yourself a strong sense of direction by defining in the working title not only the subject of the document but also its purpose. The working title "Snowboarding Injuries" is okay, but "How to Prevent Snowboarding Injuries" is better because it helps keep you focused on your purpose.

An effective title is precise. For example, if you are writing a feasibility study on the subject of offering free cholesterol screening at your company, the title should contain the key terms *cholesterol screening* and *feasibility*. The following title would be effective:

    Offering Free Cholesterol Screening at Thrall Associates: A Feasibility Study

If your document is an internal report discussing company business, you might not need to identify the company. In that case, the following would be clear:

    Offering Free Cholesterol Screening: A Feasibility Study

Or you could present the purpose before the subject:

    A Feasibility Study of Offering Free Cholesterol Screening

Avoid using general terms, such as *health screening* for *cholesterol screening* or *study* for *feasibility study*; the more precise your terms, the more useful your readers will find the title. An added benefit of using precise terms is that your document can be more accurately and effectively indexed in electronic databases and online libraries, increasing the chances that someone researching your subject will be able to find and retrieve the document.

Before settling on a particular title, test its effectiveness by asking "Will readers be able to paraphrase the title in a clear, meaningful sentence?" For instance, "A Feasibility Study of Offering Free Cholesterol Screening to Employees of Thrall Associates" could be paraphrased as "This document reports on a study conducted to determine whether it is feasible to offer free cholesterol screening for employees of Thrall Associates."

But notice what happens when the title is incomplete: "Free Cholesterol Screening." With only those three words to go on, readers will know that the document has something to do with free cholesterol screening, but is the writer recommending that screening be instituted or discontinued? Or is the writer reporting on how well an existing screening program is working?

Clear, comprehensive titles tend to be long. If you need eight or ten words to say what you want to say about your subject and purpose, use them.

WRITING COHERENT HEADINGS

Headings are lower-level titles for the sections and subsections in a document. Although they are used only sometimes in traditional academic writing, they are used frequently in almost every kind of technical document.

Headings do more than announce the subject that will be discussed in the document. Collectively, they create a *hierarchy of information*, dividing the text into major sections and subdividing those sections into subsections. In this way, coherent headings communicate to readers the relative importance and generality of the information that follows, helping readers recognize major sections as *primary* (likely to contain more-important and more-general information) and subsections as *secondary* or *subordinate* (likely to contain less-important and more-specific information).

Coherent, well-designed headings communicate this relationship not only through their content but also through their design. For this reason, you should make sure that the design of a primary heading (sometimes referred to as a *level 1 heading, 1 heading,* or *A heading*) clearly distinguishes it from a subordinate heading (a *level 2 heading, 2 heading,* or *B heading*) and that the design of the subordinate heading clearly distinguishes it from an even more subordinate heading (a *level 3 heading, 3 heading,* or *C heading*).

The headings used in this book illustrate this principle, as does the following example. Notice that this example uses both typography and indentation to distinguish one level of heading from another and to communicate visually how information at one level logically relates to information at other levels.

► **In This Book**

For more about how to format headings, see Ch. 11, p. 275.

Level 1 Heading
Level 2 Heading
Level 3 Heading

Because a heading is a type of title, much of the advice about titles in the previous section also applies to headings. For instance, a clear, informative heading is crucial because it announces the subject and purpose of the discussion that follows, just as a title does for the whole document. Announcing the subject and purpose in a heading helps readers understand what they will be reading or, in some cases, whether they need to read it at all. For the writer, a heading eliminates the need for awkward transitional sentences such as "Let us now turn to the advantages of the mandatory enrollment process" or "The next step in replacing the saw blade is to remove the arbor nut from the driveshaft."

Effective headings can help both readers and writer by forecasting not only the subject and purpose of the discussion that follows but also its scope and organization. When readers encounter the heading "Three Health Benefits of Yoga: Improved Muscle Tone, Enhanced Flexibility, Better Posture," they know (or can reasonably assume) that the discussion will consist of three parts and is likely to begin with muscle tone, followed by flexibility and posture.

Because a heading introduces text that discusses or otherwise elaborates on the subject defined by the heading, you should avoid using back-to-back headings:

3. Approaches to Neighborhood Policing
3.1 Community Policing
According to the COPS Agency (a component of the U.S. Department of Justice), "Community policing focuses on crime and social disorder." . . .

What's wrong with back-to-back headings? First, they're illogical. If your document contains a level 1 heading, you have to say something at that level before jumping to the discussion at level 2. Second, back-to-back headings distract and confuse readers. The heading "3. Approaches to Neighborhood Policing" announces to readers that you have something to say about neighborhood policing—but you don't say anything. Instead, the subordinate heading announces to readers that you now have something to say about community policing.

To avoid confusing and frustrating readers, separate the headings with text, as in this example:

3. Approaches to Neighborhood Policing

Over the past decade, the scholarly community has concluded that community policing offers significant advantages over the traditional approach based on patrolling in police cars. However, the traditional approach has some distinct strengths. In the following discussion, we define each approach and then explain its advantages and disadvantages. Finally, we profile three departments that have successfully made the transition to community policing while preserving the major strengths of the traditional approach.

3.1 Community Policing

According to the COPS Agency (a component of the U.S. Department of Justice), "Community policing focuses on crime and social disorder." . . .

The text after the heading "3. Approaches to Neighborhood Policing," called an *advance organizer*, indicates the background, purpose, scope, and organization of the discussion that follows. Advance organizers improve coherence by giving readers an overview of the discussion before they encounter the details in the discussion itself.

Guidelines

Revising Headings

▶ **Avoid long noun strings.** The following example is ambiguous and hard to understand:

> Proposed Production Enhancement Strategies Analysis Techniques

Is the heading introducing a discussion of techniques for analyzing strategies that have been proposed? A discussion that proposes using certain techniques to analyze strategies? Readers shouldn't have to ask such questions. Adding prepositions makes the heading clearer:

> Techniques for Analyzing the Proposed Strategies for Enhancing Production

This heading announces more clearly that the discussion describes techniques for analyzing strategies, that those strategies have been proposed, and that the strategies are aimed at enhancing production. It's a longer heading than the original, but that's okay. It's also much clearer.

▶ **Be informative.** In the preceding example, you could add information about how many techniques will be described:

> Three Techniques for Analyzing the Proposed Strategies for Enhancing Production

You could go one step further by indicating what you wish to say about the three techniques:

> Advantages and Disadvantages of the Three Techniques for Analyzing the Proposed Strategies for Enhancing Production

Again, don't worry if the heading seems too long; clarity is more important than conciseness.

▶ **Use a grammatical form appropriate to your audience.** The question form works well for less-knowledgeable readers (Benson, 1985) or for nonnative speakers:

> What Are the Three Techniques for Analyzing the Proposed Strategies for Enhancing Production?

The "how to" form is best for instructional material, such as manuals:

> How to Analyze the Proposed Strategies for Enhancing Production

The gerund form (*-ing*) works well for discussions and descriptions of processes:

> Analyzing the Proposed Strategies for Enhancing Production

▶ **Avoid back-to-back headings.** Use advance organizers to separate the headings.

In This Book
For more about noun strings, see Ch. 10, p. 238.

WRITING COHERENT LISTS

In This Book

For a discussion of lists at the sentence level, see Ch. 10, pp. 222–25.

Lists are another feature of technical communication that distinguishes it from academic writing. While academic writing typically consists of conventional paragraphs, technical documents often contain paragraphs in list format, as shown in Figure 9.2. The following discussion explains the advantages of turning traditional paragraphs into lists.

Lists are especially well suited for conveying information that can be itemized or expressed in a sequence. If, for example, you are discussing three physical conditions that frequently lead to patients' developing adult-onset diabetes, you have an opportunity to structure that discussion as three paragraphs in list format. A similar opportunity arises if you are describing the operation of a four-stroke gasoline engine; not only can the strokes be itemized, but they also occur in sequence (*intake, compression, ignition, exhaust*).

Why use a list format instead of traditional paragraphs? Lists add a visual dimension to the text, making it easier for readers to understand the discussion and making it easier for writers to express ideas clearly and coherently.

Turning the paragraph into a list forces the writer to create headings that sharply focus each bulleted entry.

By deleting the wordy topic sentences from the paragraph version, the writer saves space. The list version of the passage is not significantly longer than the paragraph version, despite the indentations and extra white space.

Paragraph format	List format
Currently, there are three conceptions of the relation between engineering as a profession and society as a whole.	Currently, there are three conceptions of the relation between engineering as a profession and society as a whole:
The first conception is that there is no relation. Engineering's proper regard is properly instrumental, with no constraints at all. Its task is to provide purely technical solutions to problems.	• *There is no relation.* Engineering's proper regard is properly instrumental, with no constraints at all. Its task is to provide purely technical solutions to problems.
The second conception is that engineering's role is to protect society. It must be concerned, as a profession, with minimizing the risk to the public. The profession is to operate on projects as presented to it, as an instrument; but the profession is to operate in accordance with important safety constraints, which are integral to its performing as a profession.	• *The engineer's role is to protect society.* Engineering is concerned, as a profession, with minimizing the risk to the public. The profession is to operate on projects as presented to it, as an instrument; but the profession is to operate in accordance with important safety constraints, which are integral to its performing as a profession.
The third conception is that engineering has a positive social responsibility to try to promote the public good, not merely to perform the tasks that are set for it, and not merely to perform those tasks such that risk is minimized or avoided in performing them. Rather, engineering's purpose as a profession is to promote the social good.	• *The engineer's role is to promote the public good.* Engineering has a positive social responsibility to try to promote the public good, not merely to perform the tasks that are set for it, and not merely to perform those tasks such that risk is minimized or avoided in performing them. Rather, engineering's purpose as a profession is to promote the social good.

Figure 9.2   Paragraph Format and List Format
Source: Based on Cohen & Grace, 1994.

For readers, the chief advantage of a list is that it makes the information easier to read and remember. Readers see the overall structure of the discussion—often at a single glance—before they read the details. Once they start reading the list, they can more easily follow the discussion because the design of the discussion mirrors the logic. For example, a list-format discussion of the four stages of mitosis (*prophase, metaphase, anaphase, telophase*) is arranged in the order in which the stages occur and uses bullets or numbers to distinguish one stage from another. As a result, readers are able to navigate the discussion easily and confidently, if only because they can tell at a glance where the discussion of one phase ends and the discussion of the next phase begins. Reaching the end of the list, they know without having to read further that they have arrived at the end of the discussion.

For you as a writer, turning paragraphs into lists has four advantages:

- *It forces you to look at the big picture.* In drafting a document, it is easy to lose sight of the information outside the paragraph you are working on. Turning traditional paragraphs into lists expands your perspective beyond a single paragraph. By looking for opportunities to create lists as you revise, you not only focus on the key idea in each paragraph but also consider how that key idea relates to the key ideas of other paragraphs. Revising this way increases your chances of noticing that an important item is missing or that an item is unclear. It also increases the chances that you'll think more deeply about how items and key ideas are related to one another.

- *It forces you to examine the sequence.* As you turn some of your paragraphs into lists, you get a chance to reconsider whether the sequence of the information is logical. Sometimes, the visual dimension that lists add to the text will reveal an illogical sequence that you might have overlooked in traditional paragraphs.

- *It forces you to create a helpful* lead-in, *or introduction to the list.* Every list requires a lead-in; without one, readers are left to guess at how the list relates to the discussion and how the items in the list relate to one another. In the lead-in, you can add a number signal that further forecasts the content and organization of the material that follows:

    Auto imports declined last year because of four major factors:

    You can add the same kind of number signal in a traditional paragraph, but you are less likely to think about adding one if you are not focusing on creating a list.

- *It forces you to tighten and clarify your prose.* When you make a list, look for a word, phrase, or sentence that identifies each item. Your focus shifts from weaving sentences together in a paragraph to highlighting key ideas, thereby giving you an opportunity to critically consider those key ideas and revise accordingly.

In This Book
For advice on writing effective lead-ins, see Ch. 10, p. 224.

In many other cultures, headings and lists are considered too informal for some documents. To address this cultural difference, try to find samples written by people from the culture you are addressing to examine their use of headings and lists. Consider the following questions in studying documents from other cultures:

- *How does the writer make the information accessible?* That is, how does the writer help readers easily find the information they need without having to flip through pages or click links unnecessarily?
- *How does the writer show the relationship among types of information?* Are they grouped, highlighted, listed, set off by headings, or set in a typeface different from the typefaces used for other types of information? When conveying information that lends itself to being itemized or sequenced, what form does the itemization or sequencing take?
- *How does the writer communicate to readers the organization of the document?* This includes both the document as a whole and the parts making up the whole.
- *How does the writer make transitions from one subject to another?* As noted earlier, a heading eliminates the need for awkward transitional sentences such as "Let us now turn to the advantages of the mandatory enrollment process." In some cultures, however, the heading would be considered awkward and possibly brusque, informal, or disrespectful.

WRITING COHERENT PARAGRAPHS

There are two kinds of paragraphs: body paragraphs and transitional paragraphs.

A *body paragraph*, the basic unit for communicating information, is a group of sentences (or sometimes a single sentence) that is complete and self-sufficient and that contributes to a larger discussion. In an effective paragraph, all the sentences clearly and directly articulate one main point, either by introducing the point or by providing support for it. In addition, the whole paragraph follows logically from the material that precedes it.

A *transitional paragraph* helps readers move from one major point to another. Like a body paragraph, it can consist of a group of sentences or be a single sentence. Usually, it summarizes the previous point, introduces the next point, and helps readers understand how the two are related.

The following example of a transitional paragraph appeared in a discussion of how a company plans to use this year's net proceeds.

The first sentence contains the word *then* to signal that it introduces a summary.

Our best estimate of how we will use these net proceeds, then, is to develop a second data center and increase our marketing efforts. We base this estimate on our current plans and on projections of anticipated expenditures. However, at this time we cannot precisely determine the exact cost of these activities. Our actual expenditures may exceed what we've predicted, making it necessary or advisable to reallocate the net proceeds within the two uses (data center and marketing) or to use portions of the net proceeds for other purposes. The most likely uses appear to be reducing short-term debt and addressing salary inequities among software developers; each of these uses is discussed below, including their respective advantages and disadvantages.

The final sentence clearly indicates the relationship between what precedes it and what follows it.

Structuring Paragraphs Clearly

Most paragraphs consist of a topic sentence and supporting information.

The Topic Sentence   The topic sentence states, summarizes, or forecasts the main point of the paragraph. With that in mind, you should put the topic sentence up front. Technical communication should be clear and easy to read, not suspenseful. If a paragraph describes a test you performed, include the results of the test in your first sentence:

> The point-to-point continuity test on Cabinet 3 revealed an intermittent open circuit in the Phase 1 wiring.

Then go on to explain the details. If the paragraph describes a complicated idea, start with an overview. In other words, put the "bottom line" on top:

> Mitosis is the usual method of cell division, occurring in four stages: (1) prophase, (2) metaphase, (3) anaphase, and (4) telophase.

Notice how difficult the following paragraph is to read:

DRAFT   A solar panel affixed to a satellite in distant geosynchronous orbit receives about 1,400 watts of sunlight per square meter. On Earth, cut this number in half, due to the day/night cycle. Cut it in half again because sunlight hits Earth obliquely (except exactly on the equator). Cut it in half again due to clouds and dust in the atmosphere. The result: eight times the amount of sunlight falls on a solar panel in sun-synchronous orbit than falls on the same size area on Earth.

Putting the bottom line on top makes the paragraph much easier to read, as illustrated by the following revision:

REVISION   Eight times the amount of sunlight falls on a solar panel in distant geosynchronous orbit than falls on the same size area on Earth. A solar panel affixed to a satellite in sun-synchronous orbit receives about 1,400 watts of sunlight per square meter. On Earth, cut this number in half, due to the day/night cycle. Cut it in half again because sunlight hits Earth obliquely (except exactly on the equator). Cut it in half again due to clouds and dust in the atmosphere.

Make sure each of your topic sentences relates clearly to the organizational pattern you are using. In a discussion of the physical condition of a building, for example, you might use a spatial pattern and start a paragraph with the following topic sentence:

> On the north side of Building B, water damage to about 75 percent of the roof insulation and to the insulation in some areas in the north wall indicates that the roof has been leaking for some time. The leaking has contributed to. . . .

Your next paragraph should begin with a topic sentence that continues the spatial organizational pattern:

> On the east side of the building, a downspout has eroded the lawn and has caused a small silt deposit to form on the neighboring property directly to the east. Riprap should be placed under the spout to. . . .

The phrase "On the east side of the building" signals to readers that you are done discussing the condition of the building's north side and are now discussing the condition on its east side. Also notice that the phrase signals to readers that the discussion is following the points of the compass in a clockwise direction, further emphasizing the spatial pattern. Readers can reasonably assume that the next two parts of the discussion will be about the south side of the building and the west side, in that order.

Similarly, if your first topic sentence is "First, we need to . . . ," your next topic sentence should reflect the chronological pattern: "Second, we should. . . ." (Of course, sometimes well-written headings can make such references to the organizational pattern unnecessary, as when headings are numbered to emphasize that the material is arranged in a chronological pattern.)

Ethics Note

Avoiding Burying Bad News in Paragraphs

The most emphatic location in a paragraph is the topic sentence, usually the first sentence in the paragraph. The second most emphatic location is the end of the paragraph. Do not bury bad news in the middle of the paragraph, hoping readers won't see it. It would be misleading to structure a paragraph like this:

The writer has buried the bad news in a paragraph that begins with a topic sentence that appears to suggest good news. The last sentence, too, suggests good news.

> In our proposal, we stated that the project would be completed by May. In making this projection, we used the same algorithms that we have used successfully for more than 14 years. In this case, however, the projection was not realized, due to several factors beyond our control. . . . We have since completed the project satisfactorily and believe strongly that this missed deadline was an anomaly that is unlikely to be repeated. In fact, we have beaten every other deadline for projects this fiscal year.

A more forthright approach would be as follows:

Here the writer forthrightly presents the bad news in a topic sentence.

> We missed our May deadline for completing the project. Although we derived this schedule using the same algorithms that we have used successfully for more than 14 years, several factors, including especially bad weather at the site, delayed the construction. . . .

Then he creates a separate paragraph with the good news.

> However, we have since completed the project satisfactorily and believe strongly that this missed deadline was an anomaly that is unlikely to be repeated. . . . In fact, we have beaten every other deadline for projects this fiscal year.

The Supporting Information   The supporting information makes the topic sentence clear and convincing. Sometimes a few explanatory details provide all the support needed. At other times, however, this part of the paragraph must clarify a difficult thought or defend a controversial one, requiring substantial supporting information. How much supporting information to provide also depends on whom you're writing to (audience) and what you are trying to accomplish (purpose). Readers knowledgeable about your subject may require little supporting information compared to less-knowledgeable readers. Likewise, you may need to provide little supporting information if your purpose is merely to document a controversial point of view rather than persuade your readers to agree with it. In deciding such matters, your best bet is to be generous with supporting information. Paragraphs with too little support are far more common than paragraphs with too much.

Supporting information is most often developed using the basic patterns of organization discussed in Chapter 7, and it usually fulfills one of these five roles:

- It defines a key term or idea included in the topic sentence.
- It provides examples or illustrations of the situation described in the topic sentence.
- It identifies causes: factors that led to the situation.
- It defines effects: implications of the situation.
- It supports the claim made in the topic sentence.

Joseph Williams (2006), a respected authority on style, says that writers should think of writing a topic sentence as making a promise to readers. At the very least, when you write a topic sentence that says "Within five years, the City of McCall will need to upgrade its wastewater-treatment facilities because of increased demand from a rapidly rising population within city limits," you are implicitly promising readers that the paragraph will be not only about wastewater-treatment facilities but also about the logical relationship between a rapidly rising population and the need to upgrade the facilities—specifically, that one causes the other. If your paragraph fails to discuss these things, it fails to deliver on the promise you made with the topic sentence. If the paragraph discusses these things but also goes on to speculate about the price of concrete over the next five years, it is delivering on promises that the topic sentence never made. As Williams points out, both situations result in a paragraph gone astray.

Paragraph Length   How long should a paragraph be? In general, 75 to 125 words are enough for a topic sentence and four or five supporting sentences. Long paragraphs are more difficult to read than short paragraphs because they require more focused concentration. They can also intimidate some readers, who then skip over them.

Don't let arbitrary guidelines about length take precedence over your own analysis of the audience and purpose. You might need only one or two sentences to introduce a graphic, for example. Transitional paragraphs are also likely to be quite short. If a brief paragraph fulfills its function, let it be. Do not combine two ideas in one paragraph simply to achieve a minimum word count.

You may need to break up your discussion of one idea into two or more paragraphs. An idea that requires 200 or 300 words to develop should probably not be squeezed into one paragraph.

Body paragraphs and transitional paragraphs can both consist of a single sentence. However, you should view your single-sentence paragraphs with suspicion, for they are likely to need revision. Sometimes, the idea in that single sentence belongs with the paragraph immediately before it or immediately after it, or in another paragraph elsewhere in the document. Other times, the idea needs to be developed into a paragraph of its own. And still other times, the idea doesn't belong in the document at all.

Guidelines

Dividing Long Paragraphs

Here are three techniques for dividing long paragraphs.

Technique	Example
Break the discussion at a logical place. The most logical place to divide this paragraph is at the introduction of the second factor. Because the paragraphs are still relatively long, this strategy works best for skilled readers.	High-tech companies have been moving their operations to the suburbs for two main reasons: cheaper, more modern space and a better labor pool. A new office complex in the suburbs will charge from one-half to two-thirds of the rent charged for the same square footage in the city. And that money goes a lot further, too. The new office complexes are bright and airy; new office space is already wired for computers; and exercise clubs, shopping centers, and even libraries are often on-site. The second major factor attracting high-tech companies to the suburbs is the availability of experienced labor. Office workers and middle managers are abundant. In addition, the engineers and executives, who tend to live in the suburbs anyway, are happy to forgo the commuting, the city wage taxes, and the noise and stress of city life.
Make the topic sentence a separate paragraph and break up the supporting information. This revision is easier for all readers to understand because the brief paragraph at the start clearly introduces the information. In addition, each of the two main paragraphs now has a clear topic sentence.	High-tech companies have been moving their operations to the suburbs for two main reasons: cheaper, more modern space and a better labor pool. First, office space is a bargain in the suburbs. A new office complex will charge from one-half to two-thirds of the rent charged for the same square footage in the city. And that money goes a lot further, too. The new office complexes are bright and airy; new office space is already wired for computers; and exercise clubs, shopping centers, and even libraries are often on-site. Second, experienced labor is plentiful. Office workers and middle managers are abundant. In addition, the engineers and executives, who tend to live in the suburbs anyway, are happy to forgo the commuting, the city wage taxes, and the noise and stress of city life.

Use a list.

This is the easiest of the three versions for all readers because of the extra visual cues provided by the list format.

High-tech companies have been moving their operations to the suburbs for two main reasons:

- *Cheaper, more modern space.* Office space is a bargain in the suburbs. A new office complex will charge anywhere from one-half to two-thirds of the rent charged for the same square footage in the city. And that money goes a lot further, too. The new office complexes are bright and airy; new office space is already wired for computers; and exercise clubs, shopping centers, and even libraries are often on-site.

- *A better labor pool.* Office workers and middle managers are abundant. In addition, the engineers and executives, who tend to live in the suburbs anyway, are happy to forgo the commuting, the city wage taxes, and the noise and stress of city life.

Using Coherence Devices Within and Between Paragraphs

In a coherent paragraph, ideas are linked clearly and logically. Parallel ideas are expressed in parallel grammatical constructions. Even if the paragraph already moves smoothly from sentence to sentence, you can emphasize the coherence by adding transitional words and phrases, repeating key words, and using demonstrative pronouns followed by nouns.

Adding Transitional Words and Phrases Transitional words and phrases help readers understand a discussion by explicitly stating the logical relationship between two ideas. Table 9.1 lists the most common logical relationships between two ideas and some of the common transitions that express those relationships.

Transitional words and phrases benefit both readers and writers. When a transitional word or phrase explicitly states the logical relationship between two ideas, readers don't have to guess at what that relationship might be. As a writer, using transitional words and phrases forces you to think more deeply about the logical relationships between ideas than you might otherwise.

Table 9.1 Transitional Words and Phrases

Relationship	*Transition*
addition	also, and, finally, first (second, etc.), furthermore, in addition, likewise, moreover, similarly
comparison	in the same way, likewise, similarly
contrast	although, but, however, in contrast, nevertheless, on the other hand, yet
illustration	for example, for instance, in other words, to illustrate
cause-effect	as a result, because, consequently, hence, so, therefore, thus
time or space	above, around, earlier, later, next, to the right (left, west, etc.), soon, then
summary or conclusion	at last, finally, in conclusion, to conclude, to summarize

To better understand how transitional words and phrases benefit both readers and writers, consider the following pairs of sentences:

WEAK	Demand for flash-memory chips is down by 15 percent. We have laid off 12 production-line workers.
IMPROVED	Demand for flash-memory chips is down by 15 percent; *as a result*, we have laid off 12 production-line workers.
WEAK	The project was originally expected to cost $300,000. The final cost was $450,000.
IMPROVED	The project was originally expected to cost $300,000. *However*, the final cost was $450,000.

The next sentence pair differs from the others in that the weak example does contain a transitional word, but it's a weak transitional word:

WEAK	According to the report from Human Resources, the employee spoke rudely to a group of customers waiting to enter the store, *and* he repeatedly ignored requests from co-workers to unlock the door so the customers could enter.
IMPROVED	According to the report from Human Resources, the employee spoke rudely to a group of customers waiting to enter the store; *moreover*, he repeatedly ignored requests from co-workers to unlock the door so the customers could enter.

In the weak version, *and* implies simple addition: the employee did this, and then he did that. The improved version carries a stronger connotation, adding to simple addition the idea that refusing to unlock the door compounded the employee's rude behavior, elevating it to something more serious. By using *moreover*, the writer is saying that it was bad enough that the employee spoke rudely to customers, but he *really* crossed the line when he refused to open the door.

Whichever transitional words and phrases you use, place them as close as possible to the beginning of the second idea. As shown in the previous examples, the link between two ideas should be near the start of the second one, to provide context for it. Consider the following example:

> The vendor assured us that the replacement parts would be delivered in time for the product release. The parts were delivered nearly two weeks after the product release, however.

The idea of the second sentence stands in contrast to the idea of the first sentence, but readers don't see the transitional word until the end of the second sentence. Put the transition at the start of the second idea, where it will do the most good.

You should also use transitional words to maintain coherence *between* paragraphs, just as you use them to maintain coherence *within* paragraphs. The link between two paragraphs should be near the start of the second paragraph.

Repeating Key Words   Repeating key words—usually nouns—helps readers follow the discussion. In the following example, the first version could be confusing:

UNCLEAR	For months, the project leaders carefully planned their research. The cost of the work was estimated to be more than $200,000.
	What is the work: the planning or the research?
CLEAR	For months, the project leaders carefully planned their research. The cost of the research was estimated to be more than $200,000.

From a misguided desire to be interesting, some writers keep changing their important terms. *Plankton* becomes *miniature seaweed*, then *the ocean's fast food*. Avoid this kind of word game; it can confuse readers.

Of course, too much repetition can be boring. You can vary nonessential terms as long as you don't sacrifice clarity.

| SLUGGISH | The purpose of the new plan is to *reduce* the *problems* we are seeing in our accounting operations. We hope to see a *reduction* in the *problems* by early next quarter. |
| BETTER | The purpose of the new plan is to *reduce* the *problems* we are seeing in our accounting operations. We hope to see an *improvement* by early next quarter. |

Using Demonstrative Pronouns Followed by Nouns   Demonstrative pronouns—*this, that, these,* and *those*—can help you maintain the coherence of a discussion by linking ideas securely. In almost all cases, demonstrative pronouns should be followed by nouns rather than stand alone in the sentence. In the following examples, notice that a demonstrative pronoun by itself can be vague and confusing.

UNCLEAR	New screening techniques are being developed to combat viral infections. *These* are the subject of a new research effort in California.
	What is being studied in California: new screening techniques or viral infections?
CLEAR	New screening techniques are being developed to combat viral infections. *These techniques* are the subject of a new research effort in California.
UNCLEAR	The task force could not complete its study of the mine accident. *This* was the subject of a scathing editorial in the union newsletter.
	What was the subject of the editorial: the mine accident or the task force's inability to complete its study of the accident?
CLEAR	The task force failed to complete its study of the mine accident. *This failure* was the subject of a scathing editorial in the union newsletter.

INTERACTIVE SAMPLE DOCUMENT
Identifying the Elements of a Coherent Paragraph

The following paragraph is taken from a report published by a water company. In this paragraph, the writer is describing how he decided on a method for increasing the company's business within his particular branch. (The sentences are numbered.)

The questions in the margin ask you to think about the qualities of coherent paragraphs (as outlined on pages 206–14). E-mail your responses to yourself and/or your instructor on TechComm Web.

1. In what ways does the topic sentence function as it should?

2. Identify the transitional words or phrases. How are they used effectively?

3. Identify the repeated key words. How effectively does the writer use key words?

4. Identify the demonstrative pronouns followed by nouns. How effectively does the writer use them?

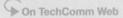 On TechComm Web

To e-mail responses to yourself and/or your instructor, click on Interactive Sample Documents for Ch. 9 on <bedfordstmartins .com/techcomm>.

> (1) We found that the best way to improve the Montana branch would be to add a storage facility to our existing supply sources. (2) Currently, we can handle the average demand on a maximum day; the storage facility will enable us to meet peaking requirements and fire-protection needs. (3) In conducting our investigation, we considered developing new supply sources with sufficient capacity to meet current and future needs. (4) This alternative was rejected, however, when our consultants (Smith and Jones) did groundwater studies that revealed that insufficient groundwater is available and that the new wells would have to be located too far apart if they were not to interfere with each other.

Even when the context is clear, a demonstrative pronoun used without a noun might interrupt the readers' progress by referring them back to an earlier idea.

INTERRUPTIVE	The law firm advised that the company initiate proceedings. This caused the company to search for a second legal opinion.
FLUID	The law firm advised that the company initiate proceedings. *This advice* caused the company to search for a second legal opinion.

CREATING A COHERENT DESIGN

So far, this chapter has focused on making the words in your document coherent. You should also make sure the design of your document is coherent. Focus on the design of headers and footers and of the typefaces in the document.

Using Headers and Footers to Enhance Coherence

Headers and footers, which appear at the tops and bottoms of pages, contain information that helps readers navigate the document. This information

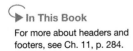 In This Book

For more about headers and footers, see Ch. 11, p. 284.

PERFORMANCE SECTION • *STRATEGIC GOAL 5: ECONOMIC PROSPERITY AND SECURITY* |

FY 2004 PERFORMANCE ACCOUNTABILITY REPORT | 173

Figure 9.3 Headers and Footers Enhance Coherence

Headers and footers help make documents coherent. The header on this page contains the appropriate section and subsection titles. The footer contains the document title and appropriate page number.
Source: U.S. Agency for International Development, 2005 <www.usaid.gov/policy/par04/performance.pdf>.

might include page number, chapter or section title and number, and document title. You can create headers and footers using your word-processing software. Figure 9.3 shows a header and a footer in a report.

Using Typefaces to Enhance Coherence

Using different typefaces is one way to create visual distinctions throughout your document. Visually distinct headings help to keep readers oriented as they navigate the document, reminding them where they are in the discussion. For similar reasons, body text should be visually distinct from headings, and both should be visually distinct from headers and footers. Using different typefaces **consistently** is one way to add coherence to a document.

As discussed in Chapter 3, the best way to make sure you use typefaces consistently is to use *styles* in your word-processing software. In simple terms, a style is a set of formatting instructions that you can apply to all headings or other design elements that you want to look alike. Because you create a style only once and then apply it to any number of headings or other design elements, you're far more likely to format these items consistently than if you were to format each one individually.

Styles also speed up the process of changing the appearance of headings and other design elements. As you revise, you might notice that two levels of headings are insufficiently distinct. You can easily use the styles function to change the design of one of those headings so it is distinct and therefore does a better job of helping readers follow the discussion and understand where they are in the document. In addition, you can create new styles to ensure consistency when, for instance, you subdivide a subsection of a document or introduce bulleted lists into the discussion.

In This Book
For more about typefaces, see Ch. 11, p. 268.

TECH TIP

How to Modify and Create Styles

As you write, you can modify and create styles to address your specific writing situation using the **Styles** group.

1. To modify a style, select the style in the **Styles** group on the **Home** tab you wish to modify. Select **Modify** from the drop-down menu that appears.

Use the **Modify Style** dialog box to make changes.

Additional formatting options for elements such as font, paragraph, and numbering are available by selecting the **Format** button.

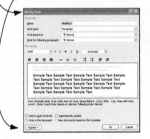

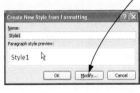

2. To create a new style, apply the desired character formatting to some text or the paragraph formatting to a paragraph. Next, select the desired text or paragraph and then right-click on the selected text. Choose **Styles** and then **Save Selection as a New Quick Style**.

Use the **Create New Style from Formatting** dialog box to name your new style. Apply additional formatting to the style by selecting the **Modify** button.

3. You can also create a new style by selecting the **Styles** dialog box launcher and then selecting the **New Style** button. Use the dialog box that appears to create a new style.

KEYWORDS: styles group, quick styles, create new quick styles, modify styles, new styles

Writer's Checklist

Did you revise the title so that it

- [ ] clearly refers to your audience and the purpose of your document? (p. 200)
- [ ] is sufficiently precise and informative? (p. 200)

Did you revise the headings to

- [ ] avoid long noun strings? (p. 203)
- [ ] be informative? (p. 203)
- [ ] use the question form for less-knowledgeable readers? (p. 203)

- [ ] use the "how to" form in instructional materials, such as manuals? (p. 203)
- [ ] use the gerund form (-*ing*) to suggest a process? (p. 203)
- [ ] avoid back-to-back headings by including an advance organizer? (p. 203)

- [ ] Did you look for opportunities to turn traditional paragraphs into lists? (p. 204)

Did you revise your paragraphs so that each one

- ☐ begins with a clear topic sentence? (p. 207)
- ☐ has adequate and appropriate support? (p. 209)
- ☐ is not too long for readers? (p. 209)
- ☐ uses coherence devices such as transitional words and phrases, repetition of key words, and demonstratives followed by nouns? (p. 211)

- ☐ Did you use headers and footers to help enhance coherence? (p. 214)
- ☐ Did you use typefaces in the body text and headings to enhance coherence? (p. 215)

Exercises

1. The following titles fall short of incorporating the advice found in this chapter. Write a one-paragraph evaluation of each title. How clearly does the title indicate the subject and purpose of the document? In what ways does it fall short of incorporating the advice in this chapter about titles? On the basis of your analysis, rewrite each title.

   a. Recommended Forecasting Techniques for Haldane Company

   b. A Study of Digital Cameras

   c. Agriculture in the West: A 10-Year View

2. The following headings fall short of incorporating the advice found in this chapter. Write a one-paragraph evaluation of each heading. How clearly does the heading indicate the subject and purpose of the text that will follow it? In what ways does it fall short of incorporating the advice in this chapter about headings? On the basis of your analysis, rewrite each heading to make it clearer and more informative. Invent any necessary details.

   a. Multigroup Processing Technique Review Board Report Findings

   b. The Great Depression of 1929

   c. Intensive-Care Nursing

3. Revise the following passage (based on Snyder, 1993) using a list format. The subject is *bioremediation*: the process of using microorganisms to restore natural environmental conditions.

   Scientists are now working on several new research areas. One area involves using microorganisms to make some compounds less dangerous to the environment. Although coal may be our most plentiful fossil fuel, most of the nation's vast Eastern reserve cannot meet air-pollution standards because it emits too much sulfur when it is burned. The problem is that the aromatic compound dibenzothiothene (DBT) attaches itself to hydrocarbon molecules, producing sulfur dioxide. But the Chicago-based Institute of Gas Technology last year patented a bacterial strain that consumes the DBT (at least 90 percent, in recent lab trials) while leaving the hydrocarbon molecules intact.

   A second research area is the genetic engineering of microbes in an attempt to reduce the need for toxic chemicals. In 1991, the EPA approved the first genetically engineered pesticide. Called Cellcap, it incorporates a gene from one microbe that produces a toxin deadly to potato beetles and corn borers into a thick-skinned microbe that is hardier. Even then, the engineered bacteria are dead when applied to the crops.

   A third research area is the use of microorganisms to attack stubborn metals and radioactive waste. Microbes have been used for decades to concentrate copper and nickel in low-grade ores. Now researchers are exploiting the fact that if certain bacteria are given special foods, they excrete enzymes that break down metals and minerals. For example, researchers at the U.S. Geological Survey found that two types of bacteria turn uranium from its usual form—one that easily dissolves in water—into another one that turns to a solid that can be easily removed from water. They are now working on doing the same for other radioactive waste.

4. Provide a topic sentence for each of the following paragraphs:

   a. _____. The goal of the Web Privacy Project is to make it simple for users to learn the privacy practices of a Web site and thereby decide whether to visit the site. Site owners will electronically "define" their privacy practices according to a set of specifications. Users will enter their own preferences through settings on their browsers. When a user attempts to visit a site, the browser will read the site's practices. If those practices match the user's preferences, the user will seamlessly enter the site. However, if the site's practices do not match the user's preferences, the user will be asked whether he or she wishes to visit the site.

b. _____. The reason for this difference is that a larger percentage of engineers working in small firms may be expected to hold high-level positions. In firms with fewer than 20 engineers, for example, the median income was $62,200. In firms of 20 to 200 engineers, the median income was $60,345. For the largest firms, the median income was $58,600.

5. The following paragraph was written by the contractor for a nuclear power plant. The audience is a regulator at the Nuclear Regulatory Commission (NRC), and the purpose of the paragraph is to convince the regulator to waive one of the regulations. In this paragraph, transitional words and phrases have been removed. Add an appropriate transition in each blank space. Where necessary, add punctuation.

As you know, the current regulation requires the use of conduit for all cable extending more than 18 inches from the cable tray to the piece of equipment. _____ conduit is becoming increasingly expensive: up 17 percent in the last year alone.

_____ we would like to determine whether the NRC would grant us any flexibility in its conduit regulations. Could we _____ run cable without conduit for lengths up to 3 feet in low-risk situations such as wall-mounted cable or low-traffic areas? We realize _____ that conduit will always remain necessary in high-risk situations. The cable specifications for the Unit Two report to the NRC are due in less than two months; _____ we would appreciate a quick reply to our request, because this matter will seriously affect our materials budget.

6. In each of the following exercises, the second sentence begins with a demonstrative pronoun. Add a noun after the demonstrative to enhance coherence.

a. The Zoning Commission has scheduled an open hearing for March 14. This _____ will enable concerned citizens to voice their opinions on the proposed construction.

b. The university has increased the number of parking spaces, instituted a shuttle system, and increased parking fees. These _____ are expected to ease the parking problems.

c. Congress's decision to withdraw support for the supercollider in 1994 was a shock to the U.S. particle-physics community. This _____ is seen as instrumental in the revival of the European research community.

Case 9: Writing Guidelines About Coherence

On TechComm Web For digital versions of case documents, click on Downloadable Case Documents on <bedfordstmartins.com/techcomm>.

Background

You are a public-information officer recently hired by the Agency for Healthcare Research and Quality (AHRQ). One of your responsibilities is to make sure that your agency's public information on the Web is clear and accurate. Your supervisor, Paloma Martinez, has asked you to write a set of guidelines for physicians and other researchers who write the articles you put on your site. You ask her why she thinks they need guidelines. "Their writing is factually correct," Paloma replies, "but because they are taking excerpts from longer, more scientific studies, their documents can be choppy. They need to be smoothed out."

"Do you have examples, both good and bad?" you ask. Paloma directs you to two AHRQ "Focus on Research" fact sheets highlighting AHRQ research projects and findings. "This is a good sample of how to write to the general reader," she tells you, pointing at the HIV disease fact sheet (Document 9.1). "This other one just doesn't seem to flow smoothly." (See Document 9.2.)

Your Assignment

1. Study the two fact sheets, noting the different techniques the writer used to achieve coherence in Document 9.1 and the areas that could be improved in Document 9.2. Focus on the titles, the headings, and the paragraphs. Write a brief set of guidelines using excerpts from these samples to illustrate your advice.

2. Using your guidelines, revise Document 9.2.

AHRQ Focus on Research: HIV Disease

Scope of the Problem

About 40,000 Americans were infected with HIV in 2000. Despite progress in treating HIV disease, the costs are high—$18,300 per year for each patient—and disparities in mortality and care of HIV patients remain:

- Four of every 10 HIV patients are black. Nearly 1 in 5 is Hispanic.
- Blacks are over 1.5 times more likely than whites to die from HIV/AIDS.
- More than $7 billion is spent each year by Medicaid, Medicare, the Department of Veterans Affairs, and the Ryan White CARE Act to treat people with HIV disease.
- Around 44 percent of HIV patients depend on Medicaid, or Medicaid combined with Medicare, to pay for HIV treatment. Six percent depend on Medicare alone.
- One in 5 HIV patients is uninsured.

Background

The Agency for Healthcare Research and Quality (AHRQ) supports research on improving the quality of health care, reducing cost, enhancing patient safety, and broadening access to and use of essential services. Part of AHRQ's goal in studying HIV is to learn more about access to health care for people living with the disease as well as the benefits and risks of new treatments.

AHRQ's mission in examining what works and what does not work in health care includes not only translating research findings into better patient care but also providing public policymakers and other health care leaders with information needed in making critical health care decisions. By disseminating the results of its research on HIV, AHRQ aims to ensure that health care needs of the diverse populations with HIV are effectively met.

Impact of AHRQ Research

AHRQ research informs the health care system about costs, access, and outcomes of different approaches to HIV care. The contributions of two major research studies, HIV Cost and Services Utilization Study (HCSUS) and Comprehensive Health Enhancement Support System (CHESS), are discussed below.

HIV Cost and Services Utilization Study (HCSUS)

As the first major research effort to collect information on a nationally representative sample of HIV patients, HCSUS examined many aspects of care and quality of life for HIV patients. These aspects include access and costs of care, use of services, unmet needs for medical and nonmedical services, social support, satisfaction with medical care, and knowledge of HIV therapies. The following two findings from HCSUS have informed the health care system:

- People with HIV who have case managers to help them obtain and coordinate care are more likely to be meeting their needs for income assistance, home care, and emotional counseling. HIV patients with case managers are also 1.5 times more likely than those without this support to be following at least two HIV drug regimens.
- Blacks are 65 percent less likely than whites to receive new antiretroviral drug therapies even when severity levels of HIV disease are similar.

Comprehensive Health Enhancement Support System (CHESS)

CHESS is a computer-based system developed with AHRQ support that gives people with HIV access to information, expert advice, and support from other patients. Using CHESS not only helps HIV patients keep track of their condition and alert their doctors when they are having problems, but it also has helped lower their average treatment costs by $400 a month.

Current Projects

AHRQ is currently funding two major projects:

- *HIV Research Network.* AHRQ and three other agencies in the Department of Health and Human Services are sponsors of this network that collects information on persons with HIV disease from providers who specialize in HIV care. The purpose of the data is to provide policymakers and others with timely information about the cost, quality, and access to care for persons with HIV.
- *Medication Errors in HIV Patients.* Researchers at the University of Illinois at Chicago are designing and testing a computerized system that integrates genotype resistance test results with patients' medication data. The goal is to reduce antiretroviral prescribing errors and improve doctors' selection of drugs.

Document 9.1 *HIV Disease* Fact Sheet
Source: Based on Agency for Healthcare Research and Quality, March 2002 <www.ahrq.gov/news/focus/fochiv.htm>.

AHRQ Focus on Research: Health Care for Women

In 1900, the leading causes of death among U.S. women included infectious diseases and complications of pregnancy and childbirth. Today, other health problems and chronic conditions face women. Heart disease is the number one killer of women in the United States. Approximately 185,000 new cases of breast cancer are diagnosed among U.S. women each year, and nearly 45,000 women die from the disease. Each year, about 600,000 women have a hysterectomy. By age 60, more than one-third of U.S. women have had a hysterectomy. Costs associated with hysterectomy are estimated at $5 billion per year. An estimated 4 million women a year are victims of domestic violence.

Finally, by age 65, half of all women have two or more chronic diseases. These illnesses occur most often in minority and low-income women.

AHRQ Research

The Agency for Healthcare Research and Quality (AHRQ) supports research on all aspects of women's health care, including quality, access, cost, and outcomes. A priority is given to identify and reduce disparities in the health care of minority women, address the health needs of women living in rural areas, and care for women with chronic illness and disabilities.

This important information is brought to the attention of policymakers, health care providers, and consumers who can make a difference in the quality of health care women receive. This agency serves as a catalyst for change by promoting the results of research findings and incorporating those findings into improvements in the delivery and financing of health care.

Impact

AHRQ funded the development of two software tools, now standard features on hospital electrocardiograph machines, that have improved diagnostic accuracy and dramatically increased the timely use of "clot-busting" medications in women having heart attack. Women treated in emergency rooms (ERs) are less likely to receive life-saving medication for heart attack.

Older black women are least likely to be referred for cardiac catheterization. A survey of physician referral practices found that blacks and women, particularly older black women, were much less likely to be referred for cardiac catheterization than whites and men. This stimulated new research to examine why these disparities in health care occur and to evaluate interventions to reduce them.

Poor and minority women have fewer mammograms than other women. AHRQ-funded researchers have used less traditional approaches, such as providing information through churches, to increase mammography screenings. Over the past two decades, AHRQ has been a co-sponsor of research that supported mobile mammography screening vans. This intervention has also increased access to mammography for poor and minority women.

Outpatient mastectomies have increased over the last decade. Several key factors influence whether a woman gets a complete mastectomy in the hospital or in an outpatient setting: the State where she lives and who is paying for it. According to an AHRQ study, women in New York were more than twice as likely, and in Colorado nearly nine times as likely, as women in New Jersey to have an outpatient complete mastectomy.

Most patients are satisfied with the results of hysterectomy. According to a Maryland study, 96 percent of women interviewed at 1 and 2 years after hysterectomy surgery said the problems or symptoms they experienced before the surgery were completely or mostly resolved.

Fibroid tumors are the most common reason for hysterectomy for women. AHRQ studies have found that black women at any age who have uterine fibroids are more likely to have them surgically removed than are white or Hispanic women with fibroids. To date, only limited evidence shows that drugs and other nonsurgical treatments are effective in avoiding or postponing the need for a hysterectomy.

Initiatives

Clinical preventive services are the focus of the U.S. Preventive Services Task Force (USPSTF), an independent panel of experts in primary care and prevention whose work is supported by AHRQ. They are updating its recommendations for preventive interventions on many conditions affecting women. For example, the USPSTF recently recommended screening mammography, with or without clinical breast examination, every 1 to 2 years for women ages 40 or older. Second, heart disease is the subject of an unprecedented long-term public-private sector collaboration to clarify which diagnostic and therapeutic interventions are most effective for women, as well as evaluate strategies to improve outcomes for older women. Finally, domestic violence is the second leading cause of death among women of child bearing age. A new 5-year effort supported by AHRQ will assess and compare health care intervention models for screening and treatment of domestic violence victims.

Document 9.2   *Health Care for Women* **Fact Sheet**
Source: Based on Agency for Healthcare Research and Quality, March 2002 <www.ahrq.gov/news/focus/focwomen.htm>.

Writing Effective Sentences

Structuring Effective Sentences 222

Use Lists 222

Emphasize New and Important Information 225

Choose an Appropriate Sentence Length 227

Focus on the "Real" Subject 228

Focus on the "Real" Verb 229

Use Parallel Structure 230

Use Modifiers Effectively 230

Choosing the Right Words and Phrases 233

Select an Appropriate Level of Formality 233

Be Clear and Specific 234

Be Concise 239

Use Inoffensive Language 242

Understanding Simplified English for Nonnative Speakers 245

Preparing Text for Translation 246

Source: Chacón and Davis, 2006.

In the World . . .

The title of this book refers to the controversy about whether people who enter the United States unlawfully should be considered "illegal immigrants" or "undocumented aliens." The authors make their perspective clear in the title and the subtitle: *No One Is Illegal: Fighting Racism and State Violence on the U.S.–Mexico Border*. Word choice matters.

Managers in business, industry, and government think that it's important to write accurate, clear, concise, and forceful sentences. If a sentence doesn't say what its writer intended, misunderstandings can occur, and misunderstandings cost money. More important, the ability to write well—sentence by sentence—reflects positively on you and on your organization. If you write well, you sound like a professional; you sound like someone worth reading. Regardless of your field, you will be judged by how well you can construct sentences.

People read technical communication to learn how to carry out a task, to keep abreast of developments, or to gather information. In other words, they read it to get a job done. To help them, make your sentences clear, concise, and easy to understand.

STRUCTURING EFFECTIVE SENTENCES

Good technical communication consists of clear, correct, and graceful sentences that convey information without calling attention to themselves. When sentences in a technical document call attention to themselves, readers are distracted from *what* is being said by *how* it is being said. This section consists of seven principles for structuring effective sentences.

Use Lists

Many sentences in technical communication are long and complicated:

> We recommend that more work on heat-exchanger performance be done with a larger variety of different fuels at the same temperature, with similar fuels at different temperatures, and with special fuels such as diesel fuel and shale-oil-derived fuels.

Here, readers cannot concentrate fully on the information because they are trying to remember all the "with" phrases following "done." If they could *see* how many phrases they have to remember, their job would be easier:

> We recommend that more work on heat-exchanger performance be done
>
> - with a larger variety of different fuels at the same temperature
> - with similar fuels at different temperatures
> - with special fuels such as diesel fuel and shale-oil-derived fuels

In this version, the arrangement of the words on the page reinforces the meaning. The bullets direct readers' eyes to three items in a series, and the fact that each item begins at the same left margin helps, too.

If you don't have enough space to list the items vertically, or if you are not permitted to do so, number the items within the sentence:

> We recommend that more work on heat-exchanger performance be done (1) with a larger variety of different fuels at the same temperature, (2) with similar fuels at different temperatures, and (3) with special fuels such as diesel fuel and shale-oil-derived fuels.

Guidelines

Creating Effective Lists

▶ **Set off each listed item with a number, a letter, or a symbol (usually a bullet).**

— Use numbered lists to suggest sequence (as in the steps in a set of instructions) or priority (the first item being the most important). Using numbers helps readers see the total number of items in a list (as in the "Seven Warning Signs of Cancer" from the American Cancer Society). For sublists, use lowercase letters:

1. Item
   a. subitem
   b. subitem

2. Item
   a. subitem
   b. subitem

— Use bullets to avoid suggesting either sequence or priority, such as for lists of people (everyone except number 1 gets offended). For sublists, use dashes.

- Item
  – subitem
  – subitem

— Use an open (unshaded) box (☐) for checklists.

▶ **Break up long lists.** Because most people can remember only 5 to 9 items easily, break up lists of 10 or more items.

In This Book

For more about designing checklists, see Ch. 12, p. 326.

Original list	*Revised list*
Tool kit:	Tool kit:
• handsaw	• Saws
• coping saw	– handsaw
• hacksaw	– coping saw
• compass saw	– hacksaw
• adjustable wrench	– compass saw
• box wrench	• Wrenches
• Stillson wrench	– adjustable wrench
• socket wrench	– box wrench
• open-end wrench	– Stillson wrench
• Allen wrench	– socket wrench
	– open-end wrench
	– Allen wrench

▶ **Present the items in a parallel structure.** A list is parallel if all the items take the same grammatical form. For instance, in the following parallel list, each item is a verb phrase.

In This Book

For more about parallelism, see p. 230.

Nonparallel	Parallel
Here is the sequence we plan to follow:	Here is the sequence we plan to follow:
1. construction of the preliminary proposal	1. write the preliminary proposal
2. do library research	2. do library research
3. interview with the Bemco vice president	3. interview the Bemco vice president
4. first draft	4. write the first draft
5. revision of the first draft	5. revise the first draft
6. preparing the final draft	6. prepare the final draft

▶ **Structure and punctuate the lead-in correctly.** A *lead-in* introduces a list. As noted in Chapter 9, every list requires a lead-in; without one, readers are left to guess at how the list relates to the discussion and how the items in the list relate to each other. Although standards vary from organization to organization, the most common lead-in consists of a grammatically complete clause followed by a colon, as shown in the following examples:

> Following are the three main assets:

> The three main assets are as follows:

> The three main assets are the following:

If you cannot use a grammatically complete lead-in, use a dash or no punctuation at all:

> The committee found that the employee
> - did not cause the accident
> - acted properly immediately after the accident
> - reported the accident according to procedures

▶ **Punctuate the list correctly.** Because rules for punctuating lists vary, you should find out whether people in your organization have a preference. If not, punctuate lists as follows:

— If the items are phrases, use a lowercase letter at the start. Do not use a period or a comma at the end. The white space beneath the last item indicates the end of the list.

> The new facility will offer three advantages:
> - lower leasing costs
> - shorter commuting distance
> - larger pool of potential workers

— If the items are complete sentences, use an uppercase letter at the start and a period at the end.

> The new facility will offer three advantages:
> - The leasing costs will be lower.
> - The commuting distance for most employees will be shorter.
> - The pool of potential workers will be larger.

— If the items are phrases followed by complete sentences, use an initial upper-case letter and a final period. Begin the complete sentences with an upper-case letter and end them with a period. Use italics to emphasize the main idea in each bullet point.

The new facility will offer three advantages:
- *Lower leasing costs.* The lease will cost $1,800 per month; currently we pay $2,300.
- *Shorter commuting distance.* Our workers' average commute of 18 minutes would drop to 14 minutes.
- *Larger pool of potential workers.* In the past decade, the population has shifted westward to the area near the new facility. As a result, we would increase our potential workforce in both the semiskilled and managerial categories.

— If the list consists of two kinds of items—phrases and complete sentences—punctuate both with uppercase letters and periods.

The new facility will offer three advantages:
- Lower leasing costs.
- Shorter commuting distance. Our workers' average commute of 18 minutes would drop to 14 minutes.
- Larger pool of potential workers. In the past decade, the population has shifted westward to the area near the new facility. As a result, we would increase our potential workforce in both the semiskilled and managerial categories.

In most lists, the second and subsequent lines, called *turnovers*, align under the first letter of the first line, highlighting the bullet or number to the left of the text. This *hanging indentation* helps readers see and understand the organization of the passage.

Emphasize New and Important Information

Sentences are often easier to understand and more emphatic if new information appears at the end. For instance, if your company has labor problems and you want to describe the possible results, structure the sentence like this:

Because of the labor problems, we anticipate a three-week delay.

In this case, the three-week delay *is the new information.*

If your readers already expect a three-week delay but don't know the reason for it, reverse the structure:

We anticipate the three-week delay in production because of labor problems.

Here, labor problems *is the new and important information.*

TECH TIP

How to Create Numbered and Bulleted Lists

To structure and emphasize information in your document, you can format text in a numbered or bulleted list. You can create a list by selecting either the **Numbering** or **Bullets** button in the **Paragraph** group or by applying a list style using the **Styles** group.

Highlight the text you wish to include in a list, then select either the **Numbering** or **Bullets** button in the **Paragraph** group.

You can modify, format, and customize your list by using the drop-down menu on the **Numbering** or **Bullets** button.

If you wish to apply the same list style consistently throughout your document and make it easy to modify the style, you can apply a list style to highlighted text by selecting the **Styles** dialog box launcher and then selecting the list style you wish to use.

If you do not see the style options you want, select **Options** to display the **Style Pane Options** dialog box.

KEYWORDS: lists, bullets, numbering

Try not to end the sentence with qualifying information that blunts the impact of the new information.

| WEAK | The joint could fail under special circumstances. |
| IMPROVED | Under special circumstances, the joint could fail. |

Put orienters to time and space at the beginning of the sentence, where they can provide context for the main idea of the sentence.

Since the last quarter of 2008, we have experienced an 8 percent turnover rate in personnel assigned to the project.

On the north side of the building, water from the leaking pipes has damaged the exterior siding and the drywall on some interior walls.

Choose an Appropriate Sentence Length

Sometimes sentence length affects the quality of the writing. In general, an average of 15 to 20 words is effective for most technical communication. A series of 10-word sentences would be choppy. A series of 35-word sentences would probably be too demanding. And a succession of sentences of approximately the same length would be monotonous.

In revising a draft, use your software to compute the average sentence length of a representative passage.

On TechComm Web

For more about varying sentence length, search for "sentence variety" in Guide to Grammar & Writing. Click on Links Library for Ch. 10 on <bedfordstmartins.com/techcomm>.

Avoid Overly Long Sentences   How long is too long? There is no simple answer, because ease of reading depends on the vocabulary, sentence structure, and sentence length; the reader's motivation and knowledge of the topic; and the purpose of the communication.

Often, a draft will include sentences such as the following:

> The construction of the new facility is scheduled to begin in March, but it might be delayed by one or even two months by winter weather conditions, which could make it impossible or nearly impossible to begin excavating the foundation.

To avoid creating such long sentences, express one idea clearly and simply before moving on to the next idea. For instance, to make this difficult 40-word sentence easier to read, divide it into two sentences:

> The construction of the new facility is scheduled to begin in March. However, construction might be delayed until April or even May by winter weather conditions, which could make it impossible or nearly impossible to begin excavating the foundation.

As discussed in the Guidelines box on page 223, sometimes an overly long sentence can be fixed by creating a list.

Avoid Overly Short Sentences   Just as sentences can be too long, they can also be too short and choppy, as in the following example:

> Customarily, environmental cleanups are conducted on a "time-and-materials" (T&M) basis. Using the T&M basis, the contractor performs the work. Then the contractor bills for the hours worked and the cost of equipment and materials used during the work. With the T&M approach, spending for environmental cleanups by private and government entities has been difficult to contain. Also, actual contamination reduction has been slow.

The problem here is that the sentences are choppy and contain too little information, calling readers' attention to how the sentences are constructed rather than to what the sentences say. In cases like this, the best way to revise is to combine sentences:

> Customarily, environmental cleanups are conducted on a "time-and-materials" (T&M) basis: the contractor performs the work, then bills for the hours worked and the cost of equipment and materials. With the T&M approach, spending for environmental

cleanups by private and government entities has been difficult to contain, and contamination reduction has been slow.

Another problem with excessively short sentences is that they needlessly repeat key terms. Again, consider combining sentences:

SLUGGISH	I have experience working with various microprocessor-based systems. Some of these microprocessor-based systems include the T90, RCA 9600, and AIM 7600.
BETTER	I have experience working with various microprocessor-based systems, including the T90, RCA 9600, and AIM 7600.

Focus on the "Real" Subject

On TechComm Web

For more about using "real" subjects, see the e-handout on revising prose from the Writing Center @ Rensselaer. Click on Links Library for Ch. 10 on <bedfordstmartins.com/techcomm>.

The conceptual, or "real," subject of the sentence should also be the grammatical subject. Don't disguise or bury the real subject in a prepositional phrase following a weak grammatical subject. In the following examples, the weak subjects obscure the real subjects. (The grammatical subjects are italicized.)

WEAK	The *use* of this method would eliminate the problem of motor damage.
STRONG	This *method* would eliminate the problem of motor damage.
WEAK	The *presence* of a six-membered lactone ring was detected.
STRONG	A six-membered lactone *ring* was detected.

In revising a draft, look for the real subject (the topic) and ask yourself if the sentence would be more effective if the real subject was also the grammatical subject. Sometimes, all that is necessary is to ask yourself this question: what is the topic of this sentence? The author of the first example above wasn't trying to say something about *using* a method; she was trying to say something about the method itself. Likewise, in the second example, it wasn't the *presence* of a lactone ring that was detected; rather, the lactone ring itself was detected.

Another way to make the subject of the sentence prominent is to reduce the number of grammatical expletives. *Expletives* are words that serve a grammatical function in a sentence but have no meaning. The most common expletives are *it is*, *there is*, *there are*, and related phrases.

WEAK	There is no alternative for us except to withdraw the product.
STRONG	We have no alternative except to withdraw the product.
WEAK	It is hoped that testing the evaluation copies of the software will help us make this decision.
STRONG	We hope that testing the evaluation copies of the software will help us make this decision.

**In This Book**

For more about using the passive voice, see p. 234.

The second example uses the expletive *it is* with the passive voice. The problem is that the sentence does not make clear who is doing the hoping.

Expletives are not errors. Rather, they are conversational expressions that can clarify meaning by emphasizing the information that follows.

WITH THE EXPLETIVE	It is hard to say whether the recession will last more than a few months.
WITHOUT THE EXPLETIVE	Whether the recession will last more than a few months is hard to say.

The second version is harder to understand because the reader has to remember a long subject ("Whether the recession will last more than a few months") before getting to the verb ("is"). Fortunately, you can revise the sentence in other ways to make it easier to understand and to eliminate the expletive.

I don't know whether the recession will last more than a few months.

Nobody knows whether the recession will last more than a few months.

Use the search function of your word processor to locate both weak subjects (usually they precede the word *of*) and expletives (search for *it is*, *there is*, and *there are*).

Focus on the "Real" Verb

A "real" verb, like a "real" subject, should stand out in every sentence. A common problem in technical communication is the inappropriate use of a *nominalized* verb—a verb that has been changed into a noun, then coupled with a weaker verb. *To install* becomes *to effect an installation*; *to analyze* becomes *to conduct an analysis*. Notice how nominalizing the verbs in the following sentences makes them both awkward and unnecessarily long. (The nominalized verbs are italicized.)

WEAK	Each *preparation* of the solution is done twice.
STRONG	Each solution is prepared twice.
WEAK	*Consideration* should be given to an *acquisition* of the properties.
STRONG	We should consider acquiring the properties.

Like expletives, nominalizations are not errors. In fact, many common nouns are nominalizations: *maintenance*, *requirement*, and *analysis*, for example. In addition, nominalizations often effectively summarize an idea from a previous sentence (in italics in the following example).

Congress recently passed a bill that restricts how high-definition television (HDTV) can be marketed to consumers. The new *legislation* could delay our *entry* into the HDTV market. This *delay* could cost us millions.

Some software programs search for common nominalizations. With any word processor, however, you can identify most of them by searching for character strings such as *tion*, *ment*, *sis*, *ence*, *ing*, and *ance*, as well as the word *of*.

Use Parallel Structure

On TechComm Web

For interactive exercises on parallelism and other topics discussed in this chapter, click on Re:Writing, then Exercise Central on <bedfordstmartins .com/techcomm>.

A sentence is parallel if its coordinate elements follow the same grammatical form: for example, all the clauses are either passive or active, all the verbs are either infinitives or participles, and so on. Parallel structure creates a recognizable pattern, making a sentence easier for readers to follow. Nonparallel structure creates no such pattern, distracting and possibly confusing readers. For example, the verbs in the following sentence are nonparallel because they do not use the same verb form. (The verbs are italicized.)

NONPARALLEL	Our present system *is costing* us profits and *reduces* our productivity.
PARALLEL	Our present system *is costing* us profits and *reducing* our productivity.
NONPARALLEL	The compositor *should follow* the printed directions; *do not change* the originator's work.
PARALLEL	The compositor *should follow* the printed directions and *should not change* the originator's work.

When using parallel structure, make sure that parallel items in a series do not overlap, causing confusion or even changing the meaning of the sentence:

CONFUSING	The speakers will include partners of law firms, businesspeople, and civic leaders.
	"Partners of" appears to apply to "businesspeople" and "civic leaders," as well as to "law firms." That is, "partners of" carries over to the other items in the series. The following revision solves the problem by rearranging the items so that "partners of" can apply only to "law firms."
CLEAR	The speakers will include businesspeople, civic leaders, and partners of law firms.
CONFUSING	We need to buy more lumber, hardware, tools, and hire the subcontractors.
	The writer has linked two ideas inappropriately. The first idea is that we need to buy three things: lumber, hardware, and tools. The second is that we need to hire the subcontractors. Hiring is not in the same category as the items to buy. In other words, the writer has structured and punctuated the sentence as if it contains a four-item series when in fact it contains a three-item series followed by a second verb phrase.
CLEAR	We need to buy more lumber, hardware, and tools, and we need to hire the subcontractors.

Use Modifiers Effectively

Modifiers are words, phrases, and clauses that describe other elements in the sentence. To make your meaning clear, you must indicate whether a modifier provides necessary information about the word or phrase it refers to (its *referent*) or whether it simply provides additional information. You must also clearly identify the referent.

Distinguish Between Restrictive and Nonrestrictive Modifiers   As the term implies, a *restrictive modifier* restricts the meaning of its referent; it provides information that readers need to identify the referent and is, therefore, crucial to understanding the sentence. Notice that restrictive modifiers—italicized in the following examples—are not set off by commas:

> The airplanes *used in the exhibitions* are slightly modified.

> *The modifying phrase "used in the exhibitions" identifies which airplanes the writer is referring to. Presumably, there are at least two groups of airplanes: those used in the exhibitions and those not used. The restrictive modifier tells readers which of the two is being discussed.*

> Please disregard the notice *you recently received from us.*

> *The modifying phrase "you recently received from us" identifies which notice. Without it, the sentence could be referring to one of any number of notices.*

In most cases, the restrictive modifier doesn't require a relative pronoun, such as *that* or *which*. If you choose to use a pronoun, however, use *that* or *who* (for a person):

> The airplanes *that* are used in the exhibitions are slightly modified.

A *nonrestrictive modifier* does not restrict the meaning of its referent: that is, readers do not need the information to identify the referent. If you omit the nonrestrictive modifier, the basic sentence retains its primary meaning. If you use a relative pronoun, choose *which* (*who* or *whom* for a person).

> The Hubble telescope, *intended to answer fundamental questions about the origin of the universe*, was last repaired in 2002.

Here, the basic sentence is "The Hubble telescope was last repaired in 2002." Removing the modifier doesn't change the meaning of the basic sentence.

> When you arrive, go to the Registration Area, *which is located on the second floor.*

Here, the basic sentence is "When you arrive, go to the Registration Area." Again, removing the modifier doesn't change the meaning of the basic sentence.

Be sure to use commas to separate a nonrestrictive modifier from the rest of the sentence. In the first example, a pair of commas separates the nonrestrictive modifier from the rest of the sentence. In that respect, the commas function much like parentheses, indicating that the modifying information is parenthetical. In the second example, the comma indicates that the modifying information is tacked on at the end of the sentence as additional information.

Avoid Misplaced Modifiers   The placement of the modifier often determines the meaning of the sentence, as the placement of *only* illustrates in the following sentences.

Only Turner received a cost-of-living increase last year.

Meaning: Nobody else received one.

Turner received *only* a cost-of-living increase last year.

Meaning: He didn't receive a merit increase.

Turner received a cost-of-living increase *only* last year.

Meaning: He received a cost-of-living increase as recently as last year.

Turner received a cost-of-living increase last year *only*.

Meaning: He received a cost-of-living increase in no other year.

Misplaced modifiers—those that appear to modify the wrong referent—are a common problem. Usually, the best solution is to place the modifier as close as possible to its intended referent.

MISPLACED	The subject of the meeting is the future of geothermal energy *in the downtown Webster Hotel.*
CORRECT	The subject of the meeting *in the downtown Webster Hotel* is the future of geothermal energy.

A *squinting modifier* falls ambiguously between two possible referents, so readers cannot tell which one is being modified:

UNCLEAR	We decided *immediately* to purchase the new system.
	Did we decide immediately, or did we decide to make the purchase immediately?
CLEAR	We *immediately* decided to purchase the new system.
CLEAR	We decided to purchase the new system *immediately*.

A subtle form of misplaced modification can also occur with correlative constructions, such as *either . . . or, neither . . . nor,* and *not only . . . but also:*

MISPLACED	The new refrigerant *not only* decreases energy costs *but also* spoilage losses.

Here, the writer is implying that the refrigerant does at least two things to energy costs: it decreases them and then does something else to them. Unfortunately, that's not how the sentence unfolds. The second thing the refrigerant does to energy costs never appears.

CORRECT	The new refrigerant decreases *not only* energy costs *but also* spoilage losses.

Here, the phrase "decreases not only" implies that at least two things will be decreased, and as the sentence develops that turns out to be the case.

"Decreases" applies to both "energy costs" and "spoilage losses." Therefore, the first half of the correlative construction follows "decreases." Note that if the sentence contained two different verbs, the first half of the correlative construction should precede the verb:

> The new refrigerant *not only* decreases energy costs *but also* reduces spoilage losses.

Avoid Dangling Modifiers   A dangling modifier has no referent in the sentence and can therefore be unclear:

DANGLING   Trying to solve the problem, the instructions seemed unclear.

This sentence says that the instructions are trying to solve the problem. To correct the problem, rewrite the sentence, adding the clarifying information either within the modifier or next to it:

CORRECT   As I was trying to solve the problem, the instructions seemed unclear.

CORRECT   Trying to solve the problem, I thought the instructions seemed unclear.

Sometimes, you can correct a dangling modifier by switching from the *indicative mood* (a statement of fact) to the *imperative mood* (a request or command):

DANGLING   To initiate the procedure, the Begin button should be pushed.
                  (*indicative mood*)

CORRECT   To initiate the procedure, push the Begin button. (*imperative mood*)

CHOOSING THE RIGHT WORDS AND PHRASES

This section discusses four principles that will help you use the right words and phrases in the right places: select an appropriate level of formality, be clear and specific, be concise, and use inoffensive language.

Select an Appropriate Level of Formality

Although no standard definitions of levels of formality exist, most experts would agree that there are three levels:

INFORMAL   The Acorn 560 is a real screamer. With 3.8 GHz of pure computing power, it slashes through even the thickest spreadsheets before you can say 2 + 2 = 4.

MODERATELY   With its 3.8 GHz microprocessor, the Acorn 560 can handle even
FORMAL   the most complicated spreadsheets quickly.

HIGHLY FORMAL   With a 3.8 GHz microprocessor, the Acorn 560 is a high-speed personal computer appropriate for computation-intensive applications such as large, complex spreadsheets.

Technical communication usually requires a moderately or highly formal style.

To achieve the appropriate level and tone, think about your audience, your subject, and your purpose:

- *Audience.* You would probably write more formally to a group of retired executives than to a group of college students. You would likewise write more formally to the company vice president or to people from most other cultures than to your co-workers.
- *Subject.* You would write more formally about a serious subject—safety regulations or important projects—than about plans for an office party.
- *Purpose.* You would write more formally in a report to shareholders than in a company newsletter.

In general, it is better to err on the side of formality. Avoid an informal style in any writing you do at the office, for two reasons:

- *Informal writing tends to be imprecise.* In the example "The Acorn 560 is a real screamer," what exactly is a "screamer"?
- *Informal writing can be embarrassing.* If your boss spots your e-mail to a colleague, you might wish it didn't begin "What up, dawg?"

▶ In This Book

For more about writing for a multicultural audience, see Ch. 5, p. 98.

Be Clear and Specific

Follow these seven guidelines to make your writing clear and specific:

- Use the active voice and the passive voice appropriately.
- Be specific.
- Avoid unnecessary jargon.
- Use positive constructions.
- Avoid long noun strings.
- Avoid clichés.
- Avoid euphemisms.

▶ On TechComm Web

For more about choosing an appropriate voice, see "The Passive Engineer" by Helen Moody. Click on Links Library for Ch. 10 on <bedfordstmartins.com/techcomm>.

Use Active and Passive Voice Appropriately   In a sentence using the active voice, the subject performs the action expressed by the verb: the "doer" of the action is the grammatical subject. By contrast, in a sentence using the passive voice, the recipient of the action is the grammatical subject. Compare the following examples (the subjects are italicized):

ACTIVE   *Dave Brushaw* drove the launch vehicle.

The doer of the action is the subject of the sentence.

PASSIVE   The launch *vehicle* was driven by Dave Brushaw.

The recipient of the action is the subject of the sentence.

In most cases, the active voice works better than the passive voice because it emphasizes the *agent* (the doer of the action). An active-voice sentence also is shorter because it does not require a form of the verb *to be* and the past participle, as a passive-voice sentence does. In the active version of the example sentence, the verb is "drove" rather than "was driven," and "by" is unnecessary.

The passive voice, however, is generally better in these four cases:

- When the agent is clear from the context:

    Students are required to take both writing courses.

    The context makes it clear that the college sets the requirements.

- When the agent is unknown:

    The comet was first referred to in an ancient Egyptian text.

    We don't know who wrote this text.

- When the agent is less important than the action:

    The documents were hand-delivered this morning.

    It doesn't matter who the messenger was.

- When a reference to the agent is embarrassing, dangerous, or in some other way inappropriate:

    Incorrect figures were recorded for the flow rate.

    It might be unwise or tactless to specify who recorded the incorrect figures. Perhaps it was your boss. However, it is unethical to use the passive voice to avoid responsibility for an action.

In This Book

For more about ethics, see Ch. 2.

The passive voice can also help maintain the focus of your paragraph.

Local area networks (LANs) offer three major advantages. First, they are inexpensive to run. Second, they can be expanded easily. . . .

Some people believe that the active voice is inappropriate because it emphasizes the person who does the work rather than the work itself, making the writing less objective. In many cases, this objection is valid. Why write "I analyzed the samples for traces of iodine" if there is no ambiguity about who did the analysis or no need to identify who did it? The passive focuses on the action, not the actor: "The samples were analyzed for traces of iodine." But if in doubt, use the active voice.

Other people argue that the passive voice produces a double ambiguity. In the sentence "The samples were analyzed for traces of iodine," readers are not quite sure who did the analysis (the writer or someone else) or when it was done (during the project or sometime previously). Identifying the actor can often clarify both ambiguities.

The best approach is to recognize that the two voices differ and to use each one where it is most effective.

In This Book

For more about the use of the passive voice in lab reports, see Ch. 18, p. 484.

Many grammar checkers can help you locate the passive voice. Some will advise you that the passive is undesirable, almost an error, but this advice is misleading. Use the passive voice when it works better than the active voice for your purposes.

Any word processor allows you to search for the forms of *to be* used most commonly in passive-voice expressions: *is*, *are*, *was*, and *were*. You can also search for *ed* to isolate past participles (for example, *purchased*, *implemented*, and *delivered*), which appear in most passive-voice constructions.

Be Specific   Being specific involves using precise words, providing adequate detail, and avoiding ambiguity.

- *Use precise words.* A Ford Focus is an automobile, but it is also a vehicle, a machine, and a thing. In describing the Focus, *automobile* is better than the less specific *vehicle*, because *vehicle* can also refer to pickup trucks, trains, hot-air balloons, and other means of transport. As words become more abstract—from *machine* to *thing*, for instance—the chances of misunderstanding increase.

- *Provide adequate detail.* Readers probably know less about your subject than you do. What might be perfectly clear to you might be too vague for them.

VAGUE	An engine on the plane experienced some difficulties.
	Which engine? What plane? What kinds of difficulties?
CLEAR	The left engine on the Martin 411 temporarily lost power during flight.

- *Avoid ambiguity.* Don't let readers wonder which of two meanings you are trying to convey.

AMBIGUOUS	After stirring by hand for 10 seconds, add three drops of the iodine mixture to the solution.
	After stirring the iodine mixture or the solution?
CLEAR	Stir the iodine mixture by hand for 10 seconds. Then add three drops to the solution.
CLEAR	Stir the solution by hand for 10 seconds. Then add three drops of the iodine mixture.

If you don't have the specific data, you should approximate—and clearly tell readers that you are doing so—or explain why the specific data are unavailable and indicate when they will be available:

The fuel leakage is much greater than we had anticipated; we estimate it to be at least five gallons per minute, not two.

The fuel leakage is much greater than we had anticipated; we expect to have specific data by 4 P.M. today.

Avoid Unnecessary Jargon   Jargon is shoptalk. To the general reader, *ATM* means automated (or automatic) teller machine; to an electrical engineer, it means asynchronous transfer mode; to a math teacher, it means Association of Teachers of Mathematics. Jargon is often ridiculed; many dictionaries define it as "writing that one does not understand" or "nonsensical, incoherent, or meaningless talk." However, jargon is useful in its proper sphere. For one thing, jargon enables members of a particular profession to communicate clearly and precisely with one another.

That said, using unnecessary jargon is inadvisable for four reasons:

- *It can be imprecise.* If you ask a co-worker to review a document and provide *feedback*, are you asking for a facial expression, body language, a phone call, or a written evaluation?
- *It can be confusing.* If you ask a computer novice to *cold swap the drive*, he or she might have no idea what you're talking about.
- *It is often seen as condescending.* Readers may think you're showing off— displaying a level of expertise that excludes them. If readers feel alienated, they will likely miss your message.
- *It is often intimidating.* Readers might feel inadequate or stupid because they don't know what you're talking about. Obviously, this reaction undermines communication.

If you are addressing a technically knowledgeable audience, it's acceptable to use jargon recognized in that field. However, keep in mind that technical documents often have many audiences in addition to the primary audience. When in doubt, forgo the jargon and use more-common expressions or simpler terms.

Use Positive Constructions   The term *positive construction* has nothing to do with being cheerful. It indicates that the writer is describing what something is instead of what it is not. In the sentence "I was sad to see this project completed," "sad" is a positive construction. The negative construction would be "not happy."

Here are a few more examples of positive and negative constructions:

> ▶ **On TechComm Web**
>
> For advice on positive constructions, *see A Plain English Handbook*, by the Securities and Exchange Commission. Click on Links Library for Ch. 10 on <bedfordstmartins.com/ techcomm>.

Positive Construction	Negative Construction	Positive Construction	Negative Construction
most	not all	inefficient	not efficient
few	not many	reject	cannot accept
on time	not late, not delayed	impossible	not possible
positive	not negative		

Readers understand positive constructions more quickly and more easily than negative constructions. Consider the following examples:

DIFFICULT	Because the team did not have sufficient time to complete the project, it was not surprising that it was not able to prepare a satisfactory report.
SIMPLER	Because the team had too little time to complete the project, it produced an unsatisfactory report.

Avoid Long Noun Strings   A noun string contains a series of nouns (or nouns, adjectives, and adverbs), all of which modify the last noun. For example, in the phrase *parking-garage regulations*, the first two words modify *regulations*. Noun strings save time, and if your readers understand them, they are fine. It is easier to write *passive-restraint system* than *a system that uses passive restraints*.

Hyphens can clarify noun strings by linking words that go together. For example, in the phrase *flat-panel monitor*, the hyphen links *flat* and *panel*. Together they modify *monitor*. In other words, it is not a *flat panel* or a *panel monitor*, but a *flat-panel monitor*. However, noun strings are sometimes so long or so complex that hyphens can't ensure clarity. To clarify a noun string, untangle the phrases and restore prepositions, as in the following example:

▶ In This Book
For more about hyphens, see Appendix, Part C.

UNCLEAR	preregistration procedures instruction sheet update
CLEAR	an update of the instruction sheet for preregistration procedures

Noun strings can sometimes be ambiguous—they can have two or more plausible meanings, leaving readers to guess at which meaning you're trying to convey.

AMBIGUOUS	The building contains a special incoming materials storage area.
	What's special? Are the incoming materials special? Or is the area they're stored in special?
UNAMBIGUOUS	The building contains a special area for storing incoming materials.
UNAMBIGUOUS	The building contains an area for storing special incoming materials.

An additional danger is that noun strings can sometimes sound pompous. If you are writing about a simple smoke detector, there is no reason to call it a *smoke-detection device* or, worse, a *smoke-detection system*.

Avoid Clichés   Good writing is original and fresh. Rather than use a cliché, say what you want to say in plain English. Instead of writing "thinking outside the box," write "thinking creatively." Other clichés include *pushing the envelope*; *mission critical*; *paradigm shift*; *at the end of the day*; and *been there, done that*. The best advice is to avoid clichés. If you are used to hearing or reading a phrase, don't use it.

Compare the following cliché-filled sentence and its plain-English translation:

TRITE — Afraid that we were between a rock and a hard place, we decided to throw caution to the wind with a grandstand play that would catch our competition with its pants down.

PLAIN — Afraid that we were in a difficult position, we decided on a risky, aggressive move that would surprise our competition.

Avoid Euphemisms   A euphemism is a polite way of saying something that makes people uncomfortable. For instance, a near miss between two airplanes is officially an "air proximity incident." The more uncomfortable the subject, the more often people resort to euphemisms. Dozens of euphemisms deal with drinking, bathrooms, sex, and death. David Lord (as quoted in Fuchsberg, 1990) lists 48 euphemisms for firing someone, including these:

personnel-surplus reduction

workforce-imbalance correction

degrowing

indefinite idling

corporate downsizing

dehiring

decruiting

redundancy elimination

career-change-opportunity creation

Be Concise

The following five principles promote concise technical communication:

- Avoid obvious statements.
- Avoid filler.
- Avoid unnecessary prepositional phrases.
- Avoid wordy phrases.
- Avoid fancy words.

Avoid Obvious Statements   Writing can become sluggish if it overexplains. The italicized words in the following example are sluggish:

SLUGGISH
: The market for *the sale of* flash memory chips is dominated by *two chip manufacturers*: Intel and Advanced Micro Systems. These *two chip manufacturers* are responsible for 76 percent of the $1.3 billion market *in flash memory chips* last year.

IMPROVED
: The market for flash memory chips is dominated by Intel and Advanced Micro Systems, two companies that claimed 76 percent of the $1.3 billion market last year.

Avoid Filler   In our writing, we sometimes use filler, much of which is more suited to speech. Consider the following examples:

basically	kind of
certain	rather
essentially	sort of

Such words are common in oral communication, when you have to think on your feet, but they are meaningless in writing.

BLOATED
: *I think that*, *basically*, the board felt *sort of* betrayed, *in a sense*, by the *kind of* behavior the president displayed.

BETTER
: The board felt betrayed by the president's behavior.

But modifiers are not always meaningless. For instance, it might be wise to use *I think* or *it seems to me* to show that you are aware of other views.

BLUNT
: Next year we will face unprecedented challenges to our market dominance.

LESS BLUNT
: In my view, next year we will face unprecedented challenges to our market dominance.

Of course, a sentence that sounds blunt to one reader can sound self-confident to another. As you write, keep your audience's preferences and expectations in mind.

Other fillers include redundant expressions, such as *collaborate together*, *past history*, *end result*, *any and all*, *still remain*, *completely eliminate*, and *very unique*. Say it once.

REDUNDANT
: This project would not have succeeded if not for the *hard work and considerable effort* of *each and every one* of the auditors assigned to the project.

BETTER
: This project would not have succeeded if not for the *hard work* of *every one* of the auditors assigned to the project.

Avoid Unnecessary Prepositional Phrases   A prepositional phrase consists of a preposition followed by a noun or a noun equivalent, such as *in the summary, on the engine,* and *under the heading.* Unnecessary prepositional phrases, often used along with abstract nouns and nominalizations, can make your writing long and boring.

LONG   The increase *in* the number *of* students enrolled *in* the materials-engineering program *at* Lehigh University is suggestive *of* the regard *in* which that program is held *by* the university's new students.

SHORTER   The growth of Lehigh University's materials-engineering program suggests that the university's new students consider it a good program.

Avoid Wordy Phrases   Wordy phrases also make writing long and boring. For example, some people write *on a daily basis* rather than *daily.* The long phrase may sound more important, but *daily* says the same thing more concisely. Table 10.1 lists common wordy phrases and their more concise equivalents.

Compare the following wordy sentence and its concise translation:

WORDY   I am of the opinion that, in regard to profit achievement, the statistics pertaining to this month will appear to indicate an upward tendency.

CONCISE   I think that this month's statistics will show an increase in profits.

Table 10.1 Wordy Phrases and Their Concise Equivalents

Wordy phrase	*Concise phrase*	*Wordy phrase*	*Concise phrase*
a majority of	most	in the event that	if
a number of	some, many	in view of the fact that	because
at an early date	soon	it is often the case that	often
at the conclusion of	after, following	it is our opinion that	we think that
at the present time	now	it is our recommendation that	we recommend that
at this point in time	now	it is our understanding that	we understand that
based on the fact that	because	make reference to	refer to
check out	check	of the opinion that	think that
despite the fact that	although	on a daily basis	daily
due to the fact that	because	on the grounds that	because
during the course of	during	prior to	before
during the time that	during, while	relative to	regarding, about
have the capability to	can	so as to	to
in connection with	about, concerning	subsequent to	after
in order to	to	take into consideration	consider
in regard to	regarding, about	until such time as	until

Table 10.2 Fancy Words and Their Plain Equivalents

Fancy word	Plain word	Fancy word	Plain word
advise	tell	herein	here
ascertain	learn, find out	impact (verb)	affect
attempt (verb)	try	initiate	begin
commence	start, begin	manifest (verb)	show
demonstrate	show	parameters	variables, conditions
due to	because of	perform	do
employ (verb)	use	prioritize	rank
endeavor (verb)	try	procure	get, buy
eventuate	happen	quantify	measure
evidence (verb)	show	terminate	end, stop
finalize	end, settle, agree, finish	utilize	use
furnish	provide, give		

Avoid Fancy Words　Writers sometimes think they will impress their readers by using fancy words—*utilize* for *use*, *initiate* for *begin*, *perform* for *do*, *due to* for *because of*, and *prioritize* for *rank*. In technical communication, plain talk is best. Compare the following fancy sentence with its plain-English version:

FANCY　　　　The purchase of a database program will enhance our record-maintenance capabilities.

PLAIN　　　　Buying a database program will help us maintain our records.

Table 10.2 lists commonly used fancy words and their plain equivalents.

Use Inoffensive Language

Writing to avoid offense is not merely a matter of politeness; it is also a matter of perception. Language reflects attitudes, but it also helps form attitudes. Writing inoffensively is one way to break down stereotypes.

Use Nonsexist Language　Sexist language suggests that some kinds of work are appropriate for women and some kinds for men. Policy manuals that consistently use *she* to refer to administrative assistants suggest that most or all administrative assistants are female. Manuals that use *he* to refer to engineers suggest that most engineers are male. In this way, sexist language stereotypes people. In almost all cases of sexist language, women are assigned to duties and jobs that are less prestigious and lower paid than those to which men are assigned.

On TechComm Web

For more about nonsexist language, see Jenny R. Redfern's essay. Click on Links Library for Ch. 10 on <bedfordstmartins.com/techcomm>.

INTERACTIVE SAMPLE DOCUMENT
Revising for Conciseness and Simplicity

The following passage is from a request for proposals published by the National Science Foundation. (Sentence numbers have been added here.) The questions in the margin ask you to think about word choice (as discussed on pages 239–42). E-mail your responses to yourself and/or your instructor on TechComm Web.

1. Grants.gov, part of the President's Management Agenda to improve government services to the public, provides a single Government-wide portal for finding and applying for Federal grants online.

2. Proposals submitted via Grants.gov must be prepared and submitted in accordance with the *NSF Grants.gov Application Guide*, available through Grants.gov as well as on the NSF website at: http://www.nsf.gov/bfa/dias/policy/docs/grantsgovguide.pdf.

3. The Grants.gov Application Guide contains important information on:

   - general instructions for submission via Grants.gov, including the Grants.gov registration process and Grants.gov software requirements;
   - NSF-specific instructions for submission via Grants.gov, including creation of PDF files;
   - grant application package instructions;
   - required SF 424 (R&R) forms and instructions; and
   - NSF-specific forms and instructions.

4. Upon successful insertion of the Grants.gov submitted proposal in the NSF FastLane system, no further interaction with Grants.gov is required.

5. All further interaction is conducted via the NSF FastLane system.

Source: National Science Foundation, 2008 <www.nsf.gov/pubs/policydocs/pappguide/nsf08_1/gpg_1.jsp#IA1>.

1. This passage contains many prepositional phrases. Identify two of them. For each one, is its use justified, or would the sentence be easier to understand if the sentence were revised to eliminate it?

2. Part of this passage is written in the passive voice. Select one sentence in the passive voice that would be clearer in the active voice and rewrite it in the active voice.

3. This passage contains a number of examples of fancy words. Identify two of them. How can they be translated into plain English?

On TechComm Web

To e-mail your responses to yourself and/or your instructor, click on Interactive Sample Documents for Ch. 10 on <bedfordstmartins.com/techcomm>.

Guidelines

Avoiding Sexist Language

▶ **Replace male-gender words with non–gender-specific words.** *Chairman*, for instance, can become *chairperson* or *chair*. *Firemen* are *firefighters*, and *policemen* are *police officers*.

▶ **Switch to a different form of the verb.**

| SEXIST | The operator must pass rigorous tests before he is promoted. |
| NONSEXIST | The operator must pass rigorous tests before being promoted. |

▶ **Switch to the plural.**

| NONSEXIST | Operators must pass rigorous tests before they are promoted. |

Some organizations accept the use of plural pronouns with singular nouns, particularly in memos and other informal documents:

> If an employee wishes to apply for tuition reimbursement, they should consult Section 14.5 of the Employee Manual.

Careful writers and editors, however, resist this construction because it is grammatically incorrect (it switches from singular to plural). In addition, switching to the plural can make the sentence unclear:

UNCLEAR	Operators are responsible for their operating manuals.
	Does each operator have one operating manual or more than one?
CLEAR	Each operator is responsible for his or her operating manual.

▶ **Switch to *he or she*, *he/she*, *s/he*, or *his or her*.** *He or she*, *his or her*, and related constructions can be awkward, especially if overused, but at least they are clear and inoffensive.

▶ **Address readers directly.** Use *you* and *your*, or the understood *you* (as in "[You] enter the serial number in the first text box").

▶ **Alternate *he* and *she*.** The language scholar Joseph Williams (2006) and many other language authorities recommend alternating *he* and *she* from one paragraph or section to the next.

In This Book

For books about nonsexist language, see the Handbooks for Grammar and Style in the Selected Bibliography, p. 735.

You can use your word processor to search for *he*, *man*, and *men*, the words and parts of words most often associated with sexist writing. Some grammar checkers identify common sexist terms and suggest alternatives. But use your common sense. You don't want to produce a sentence like this one from a benefits manual: "Every employee is responsible for the cost of his or her gynecological examination."

Use Inoffensive Language When Referring to People with Disabilities
One in six Americans—some 50 million people—has a physical, sensory, emotional, or mental impairment that interferes with daily life (U.S. Census, 2006). In writing about people with disabilities, use the "people-first" approach: treat the person as someone with a disability, not as someone defined by that disability. The disability is a condition the person has, not what the person is.

Guidelines

Using the People-First Approach

When writing about people with disabilities, follow these guidelines, which are based on Snow (2008).

▶ **Refer to the person first, the disability second.** Write "people with mental retardation," not "the mentally retarded."

▶ **Don't confuse *handicap* with *disability.*** *Disability* refers to the impairment or condition; *handicap* refers to the interaction between the person and his or her environment. A person can have a disability without being handicapped.

▶ **Don't refer to victimization.** Write "a person with AIDS," not "an AIDS victim" or "an AIDS sufferer."

▶ **Don't refer to a person as "wheelchair-bound" or "confined to a wheelchair."** People who use wheelchairs to get around are not confined.

▶ **Don't refer to people with disabilities as "abnormal."** They are atypical, not abnormal.

UNDERSTANDING SIMPLIFIED ENGLISH FOR NONNATIVE SPEAKERS

Because English is the language of more than half of the world's scientific and technical communication, millions of nonnative speakers of English read technical communication in English. To address the information needs of such readers, many companies and professional associations have created versions of Simplified English. Each version consists of a basic set of grammar rules and a vocabulary of about 1,000 words, each of which has only one meaning: for instance, *right* is the opposite of *left*; it does not mean *correct*. Each version of Simplified English is made for a specific discipline. For example, ASD Simplified English is intended for aerospace workers.

 **On TechComm Web**

For more about Simplified English, see Userlab's manual on Simplified English. Click on Links Library for Ch. 10 on <bedfordstmartins.com/techcomm>.

Here is an example of original text and its Simplified English equivalent:

ORIGINAL	Before filling the gas tank, it is necessary to turn off the propane line to the refrigerator. Failure to do so significantly increases the risk of explosion.
SIMPLIFIED ENGLISH	Before you pump gasoline into the gas tank, turn off the propane line to the refrigerator. If you do not turn off the propane line, it could explode.

For more on Simplified English, see Userlab (2004).

PREPARING TEXT FOR TRANSLATION

As discussed in Chapter 5, more and more organizations prepare their documents and Web sites not only in English but also in other languages. Although you won't have to do the translating yourself, you should be aware of some simple steps you can take to make it easier for someone else to translate your writing. Luckily, most of these steps are the same ones you use to make your writing clear and easy to read in English.

- *Use short sentences.* Try for an average of no more than 20 words.
- *Use the active voice.* The active voice ("You should do this procedure after the engine has run for 100 hours") is easier to translate than the passive voice ("This procedure should be done after the engine has run for 100 hours").
- *Use simple words.* Translators will find it easier to translate *do* than *perform.*
- *Include a glossary.* If you need to use technical terms, define them in a glossary.
- *Use words that have only one meaning.* Write "This is the correct valve," not "This is the right valve," because *right* could also mean "the one on the right side."
- *Use pronouns carefully.* Don't write "Matthews phoned Hawkins to ask if he was scheduled to speak at the meeting." The translator might not know which person *he* refers to. Instead, write "Matthews phoned Hawkins to ask if Hawkins was scheduled to speak at the meeting."
- *Avoid jokes, puns, and culture-bound references.* Humor doesn't translate well. If you refer to a box of computer pointing devices as "a box of mice," the translator might translate the words literally because the device (a mouse) is not known by that name everywhere. Also avoid other culture-bound references, such as sports metaphors (*hat trick* or *grand slam*) or references to national heroes or holidays (*George Washington* or *Fourth of July*).

On TechComm Web

For more about preparing text for translation, see George Rimalower's essay "Crossing Borders—Tips for Preparing Your Writing for Subsequent Translation." Click on Links Library for Ch. 10 on <bedfordstmartins.com/techcomm>.

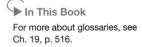
In This Book

For more about glossaries, see Ch. 19, p. 516.

Writer's Checklist

Lists

☐ Is each list of the appropriate kind: numbered, lettered, bulleted, or checklist? (p. 223)

☐ Does each list contain an appropriate number of items? (p. 223)

☐ Are all the items in each list grammatically parallel? (p. 223)

☐ Is the lead-in to each list structured and punctuated properly? (p. 224)

☐ Are the items in each list punctuated properly? (p. 224)

Sentences

☐ Are the sentences structured with the new or important information near the end? (p. 225)

☐ Are the sentences the appropriate length: neither long and difficult to understand nor short and choppy? (p. 227)

☐ Does each sentence focus on the "real" subject? (p. 228)

☐ Have you reduced the number of expletives used as sentence openers? (p. 228)

☐ Does each sentence focus on the "real" verb, without weak nominalizations? (p. 229)

☐ Have you eliminated nonparallelism from your sentences? (p. 231)

☐ Have you used restrictive and nonrestrictive modifiers appropriately? (p. 231)

☐ Have you eliminated misplaced modifiers, squinting modifiers, and dangling modifiers? (p. 232)

Words and Phrases

Did you

☐ use active and passive voice appropriately? (p. 234)

☐ use precise words? (p. 236)

☐ provide adequate detail? (p. 236)

☐ avoid ambiguity? (p. 236)

☐ avoid unnecessary jargon? (p. 237)

☐ use positive rather than negative constructions? (p. 237)

☐ avoid long noun strings? (p. 238)

☐ avoid clichés? (p. 238)

☐ avoid euphemisms? (p. 239)

☐ avoid stating the obvious? (p. 240)

☐ avoid filler? (p. 240)

☐ avoid redundancy? (p. 240)

☐ avoid unnecessary prepositional phrases? (p. 240)

☐ use the most concise phrases? (p. 241)

☐ avoid fancy words? (p. 242)

☐ use nonsexist language? (p. 242)

☐ use the people-first approach in referring to people with disabilities? (p. 245)

☐ write in such a way that it will be easy to translate? (p. 246)

Exercises

 In This Book For more about memos, see Ch. 14, p. 377.

NOTE: In completing the following exercises, pay close attention to what you are being asked to do, and do only as much revising as is necessary. Take special care not to change the meaning of the original material.

1. Refer to the advice on pages 222–25 and rewrite each of the following sentences in the form of a list.

a. The causes of burnout can be studied from three perspectives: physiological—the roles of sleep, diet, and physical fatigue; psychological—the roles of guilt, fear, jealousy, and frustration; environmental—the role of the physical surroundings at home and at work.

b. There are several problems with the online registration system used at Dickerson University. First, lists of closed sections cannot be updated as often as necessary. Second, students who want to register in a closed section must be assigned to a special terminal. Third, the computer staff is not trained to handle student problems. Fourth, the Computer Center's own terminals cannot be used on the system; therefore, the university has to rent 15 extra terminals to handle registration.

2. The following sentences might be too long for some readers. Refer to the advice on pages 227–28 and break each sentence into two or more sentences.

   a. If we get the contract, we must be ready by June 1 with the necessary personnel and equipment to get the job done, so with this in mind a staff meeting, which all group managers are expected to attend, is scheduled for February 12.

   b. Once we get the results of the stress tests on the 125-Z fiberglass mix, we will have a better idea of where we stand in terms of our time constraints, because if the mix isn't suitable we will really have to hurry to find and test a replacement by the Phase 1 deadline.

   c. Although we had a frank discussion with Backer's legal staff, we were unable to get them to discuss specifics on what they would be looking for in an out-of-court settlement, but they gave us a strong impression that they would rather settle out of court.

3. The following examples contain choppy, abrupt sentences. Refer to the advice on pages 227–28 and combine sentences to create a smoother style.

   a. I need a figure on the surrender value of a policy. The number of the policy is A4399827. Can you get me this figure by tomorrow?

   b. The program obviously contains an error. We didn't get the results we anticipated. Please ask Paul Davis to test the program.

   c. The supervisor is responsible for processing the outgoing mail. He is also responsible for maintaining and operating the equipment.

4. In the following sentences, the "real" subjects are buried in prepositional phrases or obscured by expletives. Refer to the advice on pages 228–29 and revise the sentences so that the real subjects appear prominently.

   a. There has been a decrease in the number of students enrolled in our training sessions.

   b. It is on the basis of recent research that I recommend the new CAD system.

   c. The use of in-store demonstrations has resulted in a dramatic increase in business.

5. In the following sentences, unnecessary nominalization obscures the "real" verbs. Refer to the advice on page 229 and revise the sentences to focus on the real verbs.

   a. Pollution constitutes a threat to the Wilson Wildlife Preserve.

   b. Evaluation of the gumming tendency of the four tire types will be accomplished by comparing the amount of rubber that can be scraped from the tires.

   c. Reduction of the size of the tear-gas generator has already been completed.

6. Refer to the advice on page 230 and revise the following sentences to eliminate nonparallelism.

   a. The next two sections of the manual discuss how to analyze the data, the conclusions that can be drawn from your analysis, and how to decide what further steps are needed before establishing a journal list.

   b. With our new product line, you would not only expand your tax practice, but your other accounting areas as well.

   c. Sections 1 and 2 will introduce the entire system, while Sections 3 and 4 describe the automatic application and step-by-step instructions.

7. Refer to the advice on pages 230–33 and revise the following sentences to correct punctuation or pronoun errors related to modifiers.

   a. You press the Greeting-Record button to record the greeting which is stored on a microchip inside the machine.

   b. This problem that has been traced to manufacturing delays, has resulted in our losing four major contracts.

   c. Please get in touch with Tom Harvey who is updating the instructions.

8. Refer to the advice on pages 232–33 and revise the following sentences to eliminate the misplaced modifiers.

   a. Over the past three years we have estimated that eight hours per week are spent on this problem.

   b. Information provided by this program is displayed at the close of the business day on the information board.

   c. The computer provides a printout for the Director that shows the likely effects of the action.

9. Refer to the advice on page 233 and revise the following sentences to eliminate the dangling modifiers.

   a. By following these instructions, your computer should provide good service for many years.

   b. To examine the chemical homogeneity of the plaque sample, one plaque was cut into nine sections.

   c. The boats in production could be modified in time for the February debut by choosing this method.

10. Refer to the advice on pages 233–34 and revise the following informal sentences to make them moderately formal.

  a. The learning modules were put together by a couple of profs in the department.

  b. The biggest problem faced by multimedia designers is that users freak if they don't see a button—or, heaven forbid, if they have to make up their own buttons!

  c. If the University of Arizona can't figure out where to dump its low-level radioactive waste, Uncle Sam could pull the plug on millions of dollars of research grants.

11. Refer to the advice on pages 234–36 and rewrite the following sentences to remove inappropriate use of the passive voice.

  a. Most of the information you need will be gathered as you document the history of the journals.

  b. Mistakes were made.

  c. Come to the reception desk when you arrive. A packet with your name on it can be picked up there.

12. Refer to the advice on pages 239–42 and revise the following sentences to remove the redundancies.

  a. In grateful appreciation of your patronage, we are pleased to offer you this free gift as a token gesture of our gratitude.

  b. An anticipated major breakthrough in storage technology will allow us to proceed ahead in the continuing evolution of our products.

  c. During the course of the next two hours, you will see a demonstration of our improved speech-recognition software, which will be introduced for the first time in November.

13. Refer to the advice on page 236 and revise the following sentences by replacing the vague elements with specific information. Make up any reasonable details.

  a. The results won't be available for a while.

  b. The fire in the lab caused extensive damage.

  c. A soil analysis of the land beneath the new stadium revealed an interesting fact.

14. Refer to the advice on page 237 and revise the following sentences to remove unnecessary jargon.

  a. We need to be prepared for blowback from the announcement.

  b. The perpetrator was apprehended and placed under arrest directly adjacent to the scene of the incident.

  c. The mission-critical data on the directory will be migrated to a new server on Tuesday.

15. Refer to the advice on pages 237–38 and revise the following sentences to convert the negative constructions to positive constructions.

  a. Williams was accused by management of filing trip reports that were not accurate.

  b. We must make sure that all our representatives do not act unprofessionally toward potential clients.

  c. The shipment will not be delayed if Quality Control does not disapprove any of the latest revisions.

16. Refer to the advice on page 238 and rewrite the following sentences to eliminate the long noun strings, which general readers might find awkward or difficult to understand.

  a. The Corporate-Relations Committee meeting location has been changed.

  b. The research team discovered a glycerin-initiated, alkylene-oxide-based, long-chain polyether.

  c. We are considering purchasing a digital-imaging-capable, diffusion-pump-equipped, tungsten-gun SEM.

17. Refer to the advice on pages 238–39 and revise the following sentences to eliminate clichés.

  a. We hope the new program will positively impact all our branches.

  b. If we are to survive this difficult period, we are going to have to keep our ears to the ground and our noses to the grindstone.

  c. If everyone is on the same page and it turns out to be the wrong page, you're really up a creek without a paddle.

18. Refer to the advice on page 239 and revise the following sentences to eliminate euphemisms.

  a. Downsizing our workforce will enable our division to achieve a more favorable cash-flow profile.

  b. Of course, accident statistics can be expected to show a moderate increase in response to a streamlining of the training schedule.

  c. The economically disadvantaged purchase fewer large watercraft than do the more affluent.

19. Refer to the advice on page 240 and revise the following sentences to eliminate the obvious material.

   a. To register to take a course offered by the university, you must first determine whether the university will be offering that course that semester.

   b. The starting date of the project had to be postponed for a certain period of time due to a delay in obtaining the necessary authorization from the Project Oversight Committee.

   c. After you have installed DataQuick, please spend a few minutes responding to the questions about the process, then take the card to a post office and mail it to us.

20. Refer to the advice on page 240 and revise the following sentences to remove meaningless filler.

   a. It would seem to me that the indications are that the project has been essentially unsuccessful.

   b. For all intents and purposes, our company's long-term success depends to a certain degree on various factors that are in general difficult to foresee.

   c. The presentation was generally well received for the most part, despite the fact that we received a rather small number of comment cards.

21. Refer to the advice on pages 240–41 and revise the following sentences to eliminate unnecessary prepositional phrases.

   a. The complexity of the module will hamper the ability of the operator in the diagnosis of problems in equipment configuration.

   b. The purpose of this test of your aptitudes is to help you with the question of the decision of which major to enroll in.

   c. Another advantage of the approach used by the Alpha team is that interfaces of different kinds can be combined.

22. Refer to the advice on pages 239–42 and revise the following sentences to make them more concise.

   a. The instruction manual for the new copier is lacking in clarity and completeness.

   b. The software packages enable the user to create graphic displays with a minimum of effort.

   c. We remain in communication with our sales staff on a daily basis.

23. Refer to the advice on page 242 and revise the following sentences to eliminate the fancy words.

   a. This state-of-the-art soda-dispensing module is to be utilized by the personnel associated with the Marketing Department.

   b. It is indeed a not insupportable inference that we have been unsuccessful in our attempt to forward the proposal to the proper agency in advance of the mandated date by which such proposals must be in receipt.

   c. Deposit your newspapers and other debris in the trash receptacles located on the station platform.

24. Refer to the advice on pages 242–44 and revise the following sentences to eliminate the sexism.

   a. Each doctor is asked to make sure he follows the standard procedure for handling Medicare forms.

   b. Policemen are required to live in the city in which they work.

   c. Professor Harry Larson and Ms. Anita Sebastian— two of the university's distinguished professors— have been elected to the editorial board of *Modern Chemistry.*

25. Refer to the advice on pages 242–45 and revise the following sentences to eliminate the offensive language.

   a. This year, the number of female lung-cancer victims is expected to rise because of increased smoking.

   b. Mentally retarded people are finding greater opportunities in the service sector of the economy.

   c. This bus is specially equipped to accommodate the wheelchair-bound.

26. **GROUP EXERCISE** Form small groups. Have one person in the group distribute a multipage document that he or she has written recently, either in this class or in another. Have each member annotate a copy of this document according to the principles of sentence effectiveness discussed in this chapter. Then have each group member write a summary statement about the document, highlighting its effective techniques of sentence construction and possible improvements. Meet as a group, study these annotated documents, and write a memo to your instructor describing the sentence features cited by more than one group member, as well as those aspects cited by only one group member. Overall, what are the basic differences between the group members' annotations and summary statements? Do you think that, as a general practice, it would be worthwhile to have a draft reviewed and annotated by more than one person? What have you learned about the usefulness of peer review?

Case 10: Preparing Products for the Global Marketplace

 In This Book For more about memos, see Ch. 14, p. 377.

Background

MetraPark Fitness Solutions is known in the U.S. commercial and corporate fitness industries for producing durable fitness machines based on highly regarded research in biomechanics, physiology, and anatomy. Now the company has decided to market its fitness equipment to commercial gyms in Europe. You were hired two weeks ago to take charge of the company's documentation needs. Up to that time, the design engineers had been responsible for writing the product descriptions.

"Fifteen thousand dollars?" asks Rex Bookwalter, your new boss. You have just shown Rex a translation company's bid to translate your product descriptions into German, Spanish, French, and Italian.

"Yes, that quote is for translating 31 product descriptions into four different languages," you answer.

"Why can't we just use our existing English-language descriptions?"

"The first step toward breaking into the European market is translating our promotional literature. Recent e-commerce research suggests that consumers are three times more likely to buy online on a Web site written in their native language."

"What about translating our products into just one other language—say, German?"

"That would certainly save us money in the short term," you explain. "However, we could reach nearly 90 percent of Europe's online population if we went with German, Spanish, French, and Italian. In the long run, reaching a broader customer base might be a better business strategy."

"Okay, but why is it so expensive to translate these product descriptions? They're not that long or complicated."

"Depending on the language, we're paying the translation company 20 to 30 cents per word—"

"*Per word?* Let me take a look at one of those product descriptions."

You hand Rex the product description for the MFS Leg Extension machine (Document 10.1). After about five minutes, he hands the description back to you and says, "We can do better. Rewrite this description so it's not so long and boring."

MFS® LEG EXTENSION
Product # : 08281967
Price: $3,999

At MFS, we let a muscle's function dictate the design of our equipment. That's why our machines provide the correct resistance in every position. MFS Leg Extension is no exception. Designed for novice and expert users, the MFS Leg Extension provides both superior biomechanics and greater results than ever before.

Document 10.1   Product Description for the MFS Leg Extension Machine

 **On TechComm Web**
For digital versions of case documents, click on Downloadable Case Documents on <bedfordstmartins.com/techcomm>.

Proven Biomechanics

Most conventional exercise machines in addition to free weights provide only linear (or straight up and down) resistance. The problem caused by this fact is that all movement in the human body involves rotation around an axis (or joint). Take, for example, the common bicep curl with free weights (see Figure 1). Although the weight moves in a rotary fashion as a lifter performs a bicep curl, gravity causes the resistance to be linear. The end result is the weight being the heaviest at 90 degrees but almost no effective resistance at the start or end of his motion. The lifter is always limited in his training by how much weight he can lift in the weakest position.

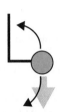
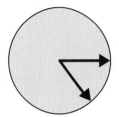
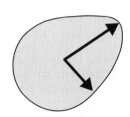

Figure 1. *Rotary Movement versus Linear Resistance*

Figure 2. *Traditional Pulley*

Figure 3. *MFS Cam*

Other types of commercial exercise machines that typically employ round pulleys are not any more efficient. Due to the fact that the strength of your muscle varies as it progresses through its range of motion, it requires variable resistance: lower resistance in weaker positions and higher in your stronger positions. The effective lever arm of round pulleys never changes during the time that the muscle moves through the exercise (see Figure 2). Therefore, the resistance is completely out of whack with the actual strength curve of your muscle, and you waste your time, energy, and money.

The legendary MFS cam, backed by years of research in the fields of biomechanics, physiology, and anatomy, is a proven method of varying resistance during rotary movement around a joint. By varying the radius of the cam, the changes in the effective lever are produced (see Figure 3). The shape of the MFS cam is determined by exacting research on the specific muscle group's strength curve being targeted in the exercise. The end result is that you get the correct resistance in every position. Engineered to be safe, each MFS machine is efficient and functional when utilized.

Superior Features

MFS exercise machines are the only equipment that is designed with the structural functions of the human muscle in mind, as well as a user's comfort and safety. Features include friction-free bearings, easy-to-access weight stacks, quick-set seat adjustments, oversized movement-arm roller pad, detailed instructions on the placard, range-limiting device, and an integrated seat belt for the stability and the safety of handicapped users.

Built-Tough™ Construction

MFS exercise machines feature Built-Tough™ construction features such as rubber footplates and bumpers for quiet operation and wear reduction, bent-steel tubing with exceptional durability, integral bearings and cables, and wear covers that are replaceable.

Product Specs

Weight Stack: 320 lb. (145 kg), **Footprint:** 46" (117 cm) W x 48" (123 cm) L x 58" (147 cm) H, **Weight:** 670 lb. (305 kg)

Your Assignment

1. Using the techniques explained in this chapter, revise Document 10.1 to make the description more concise and easier to translate.

2. Use the Internet to research strategies for preparing text for translation. Write a memo to company employees in which you provide guidelines for writing documents that will be easy to translate.

Designing Documents and Web Sites

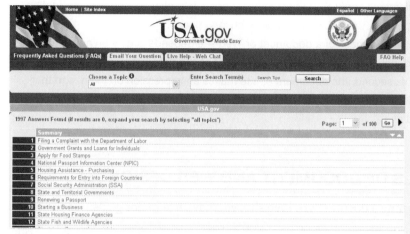

Source: U.S. General Services, 2008 <http://answers.usa.gov/cgi-bin/gsa_ict.cfg/php/enduser/std_alp.php?p_sid=KTOOiSBh>.

In the World . . .

This is the top portion of the "Frequently Asked Questions" page of USA.gov, the federal government's Web portal. But there's a problem: this page links to answers for 1,997 questions. Unfortunately, with that many questions, you'll have to wade through quite a few until you find the one you want. As you can see, they're not grouped by category (questions about taxes, veterans' affairs, and so forth), and they're not even alphabetized. But there is a way to sift through the questions more efficiently. If you can find the "Choose a Topic" window, you can at least find the right category. But in the "Laws, Legislation and Court" category, for example, there are 261 questions, and they're not alphabetized either. This is a design problem.

Goals of Document and
  Web Design 254

Understanding Design Principles 255
  Proximity 255
  Alignment 255
  Repetition 256
  Contrast 257

Planning the Design of Documents
  and Web Sites 257
  Analyze Your Audience
    and Purpose 257
  Determine Your Resources 258

Designing Documents 259
  Size 259
  Paper 259
  Bindings 260
  Accessing Tools 261

Designing Pages 263
  Page Layout 263
  Columns 267
  Typography 268
  Titles and Headings 275
  Other Design Features 276

Analyzing Some Page Designs 279

Designing Web Sites 284
  Create Informative Headers and
    Footers 284
  Help Readers Navigate the Site 285
  Include Extra Features Readers Might
    Need 285
  Design for Readers with
    Disabilities 287
  Design for Multicultural
    Audiences 287

Designing Web Pages 288
  Aim for Simplicity 288
  Make the Text Easy to Read and
    Understand 289
  Create Clear, Informative Links 289

Analyzing Some Web Pages 290

In our visual culture, technical communication is designed. *Design* refers to the physical appearance of documents and their pages, as well as to the appearance of Web sites and their pages. For printed documents, design features include the binding, page size, typography, and use of color. For Web sites, many of the same design elements apply, but other elements come into play, too, such as navigation bars, hyperlinks, and tables of contents on long pages.

The effectiveness of a document or Web site depends largely on how well it is designed, because readers *see* the document or site before they actually *read* it. In less than a second, the document or site makes an impression on them, and that impression might determine how well they read it—or even whether they decide to read it at all.

GOALS OF DOCUMENT AND WEB DESIGN

In designing a document or Web site, you have five major goals:

- *To make a good impression on readers.* Your document or site should reflect your own professional standards and those of your organization.

- *To help readers understand the structure and hierarchy of the information.* As readers navigate a document or site, they should know where they are and how to get where they are headed. They should also be able to see the hierarchical relationship between one piece of information and another.

- *To help readers find the information they need.* Usually, people don't read printed technical documents from cover to cover. Design elements (such as tabs, icons, and color), page design, and typography help readers find the information they need—quickly and easily. On Web sites, helping readers find information is critical, because they can see only the page that is currently displayed on the screen.

- *To help readers understand the information.* Effective design can clarify information. For instance, designing a set of instructions so that the text describing each step is next to the accompanying graphic makes the instructions easier to understand. A Web site where the main sections are clearly displayed on a navigation bar is easier to understand than one that doesn't have this feature.

- *To help readers remember the information.* An effective design helps readers create a visual image of the information, making it easier to remember. Text boxes, pull quotes, and similar design elements help readers remember important explanations and passages.

UNDERSTANDING DESIGN PRINCIPLES

To design effective documents and Web sites, you need to understand a few basic design principles. The following discussion is based on Robin Williams's *The Non-Designer's Design Book*, second edition (Berkeley, CA: Peachpit Press, 2004), which describes four principles of design: proximity, alignment, repetition, and contrast.

Proximity

The principle of proximity is simple: group related items together. If two items appear close to each other, readers will interpret them as related to each other. If they are far apart, readers will interpret them as unrelated. Text describing a graphic should be positioned close to the graphic. Figure 11.1 shows the proximity principle.

Alignment

The principle of alignment is that you should consciously place text and graphics on the page so that readers can understand the relationships among these elements. Figure 11.2 shows how alignment works to help organize information.

On TechComm Web

Also see Roger C. Parker's design site and John Magnik's essays on design and typography. Click on Links Library for Ch. 11 on <bedfordstmartins.com/techcomm>.

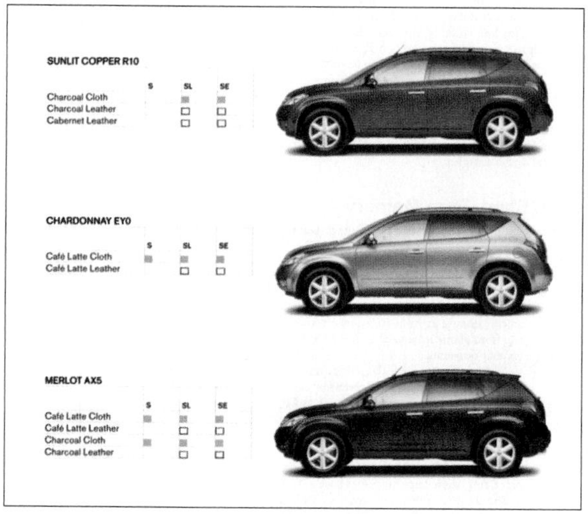

Figure 11.1   Effective Use of Proximity

Text and graphics are clearly related by the principle of proximity. The fabric options are placed near the car to which they refer.
Source: Nissan, 2004.

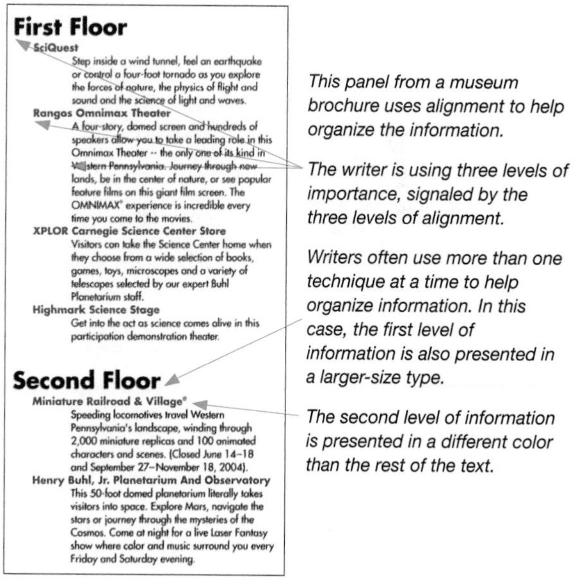

This panel from a museum brochure uses alignment to help organize the information.

The writer is using three levels of importance, signaled by the three levels of alignment.

Writers often use more than one technique at a time to help organize information. In this case, the first level of information is also presented in a larger-size type.

The second level of information is presented in a different color than the rest of the text.

Figure 11.2   Effective Use of Alignment
Source: Carnegie Science Center, n.d.

Repetition

The principle of repetition is that you should treat the same kind of information in the same way to create consistent patterns. For example, all first-level headings should have the same typeface, type size, and spacing above and below. This repetition signals a connection between headings, making the content easier to understand. Other elements that are used to create consistent visual patterns are colors, icons, rules, and screens. Figure 11.3 shows an effective use of repetition.

This page shows repetition used effectively as a design element.

Different colors, typefaces, and type sizes are used for the headings, figures, and definitions in the margin. For instance, the two graphics use the same beige background and the same typeface, style, and color for the titles and captions.

In the main text, the two headings and subheadings use the same typeface, size, and color.

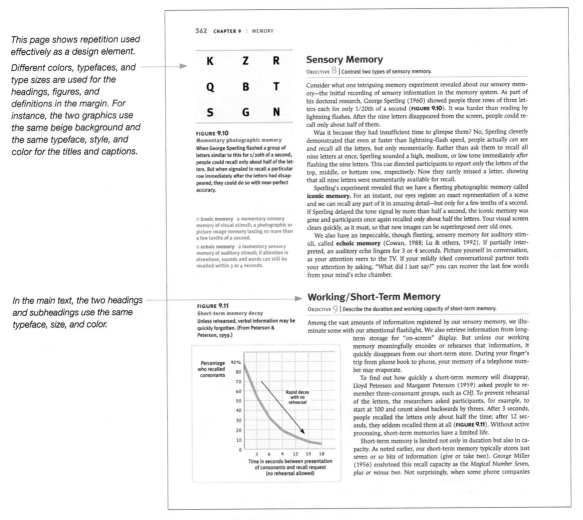

Figure 11.3   Effective Use of Repetition
Source: Myers, 2007, p. 362.

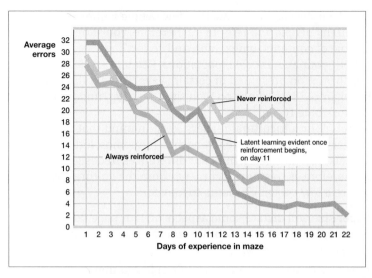

Figure 11.4   Effective Use of Contrast

Because the three data lines intersect, using a different color for each one enables readers to understand the information better than using one color would.
Source: Myers, 2007, p. 334.

Contrast

The principle of contrast works in several different ways in technical documents and Web sites. For example, black print is easiest to see against a white background; larger letters stand out among smaller ones; information printed in a color, such as red, grabs readers' attention better than information printed in black. Figure 11.4 shows an effective use of contrast.

PLANNING THE DESIGN OF DOCUMENTS AND WEB SITES

The first step in designing a technical document or Web site is planning. Analyze your audience and purpose, then determine your resources.

Analyze Your Audience and Purpose

Consider factors such as the audience's knowledge of the subject, their attitudes, their reasons for reading, the way they will be using the document, and the kinds of tasks they will perform. For instance, if you are writing a benefits manual for employees, you know that few people will read it from start to finish but many people will refer to it. Therefore, you should build in accessing tools: table of contents, index, tabs, and so forth.

Think, too, about your audience's expectations. Readers expect to see certain kinds of information presented in certain ways. Try to fulfill those expectations. For example, hyperlinks on Web sites are often underscored and presented in dark blue type.

In This Book

For more about analyzing your audience, see Ch. 5. For more about tables of contents, see Ch. 19, p. 512.

If you are writing for multicultural readers, keep in mind that many aspects of design vary from one culture to another. In memos, letters, reports, and manuals, you may see significant differences in design practices. The best advice, therefore, is to study documents from the culture you are addressing. Here are a few design elements to look for:

- *Paper size.* Paper size will dictate some aspects of your page design. If your document will be printed in another country, find out about standard paper sizes in that country.

On TechComm Web

View Ichimura's essay online. Click on Links Library for Ch. 11 on <**bedfordstmartins.com/ techcomm**>.

- *Typeface preferences.* One survey (Ichimura, 2001) found that readers in the Pacific Rim prefer sans-serif typefaces in body text, whereas Western readers prefer serifs. (Typography is discussed later in this chapter.)
- *Color preferences.* In China, for example, red suggests happiness, whereas in Japan it suggests danger.
- *Text direction.* If some members of your audience read right to left but others read left to right, you might arrange your graphics vertically, from top to bottom; everybody reads from top to bottom. Or you might use Arabic numerals to indicate the order in which items are to be read (Horton, 1993).

Analyze your purpose or purposes. For example, imagine that you run a dental office and you want to create a Web site. The first question is, What is the purpose of the site? It's one thing to list your hours and provide directions to your office, but do you also want patients to be able to schedule or change appointments? Ask you a question? Find high-quality dental information on your site? Each of these purposes affects the site design.

In This Book

For more about analyzing your purpose, see Ch. 5, p. 103.

Determine Your Resources

Think about your resources of time, money, and equipment. Short, informal documents and Web sites are usually produced in-house; more-ambitious projects are often subcontracted to professionals. If your organization has a technical-publications department, consult the people there about scheduling and budgeting.

In This Book

For information on designing Web sites and pages, see pp. 284 and 288.

- *Time.* What is your schedule? A sophisticated design might require professionals at service bureaus and print shops, and their services could require weeks. Creating even a simple design for a site could require many hours.

- *Money.* Can you afford professional designers, print shops, and Web developers? Most managers would budget thousands of dollars to design an annual report but not an in-house newsletter.
- *Equipment.* Complex designs require graphics and Web software, as well as layout programs. A basic laser printer can produce attractive documents in black and white, but you need a more expensive printer for high-resolution color.

DESIGNING DOCUMENTS

Before you design individual pages for a printed document, design the whole document. You want the different elements to work together to accomplish your objectives. Consider these four elements in designing the whole document: size, paper, bindings, and accessing tools.

Size

Size refers to two aspects of document design: page size and page count.

- *Page size.* Think about the best page size for your information and about how the document will be used. For a procedures manual that will sit on a shelf most of the time, three-hole 8.5 × 11-inch paper is a good choice. For a software tutorial that will fit easily on a desk while the reader works at a keyboard, consider a 5.5 × 8.5-inch size. Paper comes precut in a number of standard sizes, such as 4.5 × 6 inches and 6 × 9 inches. Although paper can be cut to any size, nonstandard sizes are more expensive.
- *Page count.* Because paper is expensive and heavy, you want as small a number of pages as possible, especially if you are printing and mailing many copies. And there is a psychological factor, too: people don't want to spend a lot of time reading technical communication. Therefore, if you can design the document so that it is 15 pages long rather than 30—but still attractive and easy to read—your readers will appreciate it.

Paper

Paper is made not only in different standard sizes but also in different weights and with different coatings.

The most widely used paper is the relatively inexpensive stock used in photocopy machines and laser printers. Others include bond (for letters and memos), book paper (a higher grade

---

that permits better print resolution), and text paper (an even higher grade used for more-formal documents such as announcements and brochures).

Most paper comes coated or uncoated. The coating, which increases strength and durability, provides the best print resolution. However, some glossy coated papers produce a glare. To deal with this problem, designers often choose paper with a slight tint.

Work closely with printing professionals. They know, for example, about UV-coated paper, which greatly reduces fading, and about recycled paper, which is constantly improving in quality and becoming less expensive.

Bindings

Although documents of a few pages can be attached with a paper clip or a staple, longer documents require more-sophisticated binding techniques. Table 11.1 illustrates and describes the four types of bindings commonly used in technical communication.

**On TechComm Web**

For more on bindings, see Jacci Howard Bear's Binding Decisions. Click on Links Library for Ch. 11 on <bedfordstmartins.com/ techcomm>.

Table 11.1 Common Types of Bindings

	**Loose-leaf binders.** Loose-leaf binders are convenient when pages must be added and removed frequently. A high-quality binder can cost as much as several dollars.
	**Ring or spiral binders.** The wire or plastic coils or combs that hold the pages together let you open the document on a desk or even fold it over so that it takes up the space of only one page. Print shops can bind documents of almost any size in plastic coils or combs for about a dollar each.
	**Saddle binding.** The document is opened to its middle pages, and large staples are inserted from the outside. Saddle binding is impractical for large documents.
	**Perfect binding.** Pages are glued together along the spine edge, and a cover is attached. Perfect binding, used in book publishing, produces the most formal appearance, but it is relatively fragile, and the open document usually does not lie flat.

Accessing Tools

In a well-designed document, readers can easily find the information they seek. Most accessing tools use the design principles of repetition and contrast to help readers navigate the document. Table 11.2 explains six common kinds of accessing aids.

Table 11.2 Typical Accessing Aids

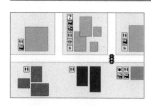

Icons. Icons are pictures that symbolize actions or ideas. An hourglass or a clock tells you to wait while the computer performs a task. Perhaps the most important icon is the stop sign, which alerts you to a warning. Icons depend on repetition: every time you see the warning icon, you know what kind of information the writer is presenting.

Don't be too clever in thinking up icons. One computer manual uses a cocktail glass about to fall over to symbolize "tip." This is a bad idea, because the pun is not functional: when you think of a cocktail glass, you don't think of a tip for using computers. Don't use too many different icons, or your readers will forget what each one represents.

The icons in the legend help readers understand where various resources and facilities are located in the area.

Source: Kittery Outlets, 2005.

Color. Perhaps the strongest visual attribute is color (Keyes, 1993). Use color to draw attention to important features of the document, such as warnings, hints, major headings, and section tabs. But use it sparingly, or it will overpower everything else in the document.

Color exploits the principles of repetition (every item in a particular color is logically linked) and contrast (items in one color contrast with items in another color).

Use color logically. Third-level headings should not be in color, for example, if first- and second-level headings are printed in black.

Using different-colored paper for each section of a document is another way to simplify access.

In This Book

For more about using color, see Ch. 12, p. 307.

On TechComm Web

Color Vision Simulator, from Vischeck, lets you see what graphics look like to people with different color disabilities. Click on Links Library for Ch. 11 on <bedfordstmartins.com/techcomm>.

Here the color red is used to emphasize the title of the feature, the heading for each letter, the erratum box, and the reference to more letters on the journal's Web site.

Source: *Discover,* 2005.

Table 11.2 (continued)

Dividers and tabs. You are already familiar with dividers and tabs from loose-leaf notebooks. A tab provides a place for a label, which enables readers to identify and flip to a particular section. Sometimes dividers and tabs are color-coded. Tabs work according to the design principle of contrast: the tabs literally stick out.

Read . . .	To learn to . . .
Ch. 1	connect to the router
Ch. 2	set up a firewall

Cross-reference tables. These tables, which exploit the principle of alignment, refer readers to related discussions.

▶ **On TechComm Web**

For more about headers and footers, see the Document Design Tutorial on <bedfordstmartins.com/techcomm>.

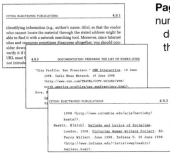

Headers and footers. Headers and footers help readers see where they are in the document. In a book, for example, the headers on the left-hand pages might repeat the chapter number and title; those on the right-hand pages might contain the most recent first-level heading. Sometimes writers build other identifying information into the headers. For example, your instructor might ask you to identify your assignments with a header like the following: "Smith, Progress Report, English 302, page 6." Headers and footers work according to the principle of repetition: readers learn where to look on the page to see where they are.

Source: Microsoft, 2001.

Page numbering. For one-sided documents, use Arabic numerals in the upper right corner. (The first page of most documents is unnumbered.) For two-sided documents, put the page numbers near the outside margins.

Complex documents often use two number sequences: lowercase Roman numerals (i, ii, and so on) for front matter and Arabic numerals for the body. The title page is unnumbered; the page following it is ii.

Appendices are often paginated with a letter and number combination: Appendix A begins with page A-1, followed by A-2, and so on; Appendix B starts with page B-1 and so on.

Sometimes documents list the total number of pages in the document (so recipients can be sure they have all of them). The second page is "2 of 17," and the third page is "3 of 17."

Documents that will be updated are sometimes numbered by section: Section 3 begins with page 3-1, followed by 3-2; Section 4 begins with 4-1. This way, a complete revision of one section does not affect the page numbering of subsequent sections.

Source: Gibaldi, 1999.

DESIGNING PAGES

A page of technical communication is effectively designed if readers can recognize a pattern, such as where to look for certain kinds of information.

Page Layout

Every page has two kinds of space: white space and space devoted to text and graphics. The best way to design a page is to make a grid—a drawing of

On TechComm Web

For information on design principles and software, see the discussion about desktop publishing at About.com. Click on Links Library for Ch. 11 on <bedfordstmartins.com/techcomm>.

Guidelines

Understanding Learning Theory and Page Design

In designing the page, create visual patterns that help readers find, understand, and remember information. Three principles, the results of research into how people learn, can help you design effective pages: chunking, queuing, and filtering.

- **Chunking.** People understand information best if it is delivered to them in chunks—small units—rather than all at once. For single-spaced type, chunking involves double-spacing between paragraphs, as shown in Figure 11.5.

During the 18th century, there were many wars in Europe caused by the ambition of various kings to make their domains larger and to increase their own incomes. King Louis XIV of France had built up a very powerful kingdom. Brave soldiers and skillful generals spread his rule over a great part of what is Belgium and Luxemburg, and annexed to the French kingdom the part of Germany between the Rhine River and the Vosges (Vo_zh) Mountains.
Finally, the English joined with the troops of the Holy Roman Empire to curb the further growth of the French kingdom, and at the battle of Blenheim (1704), the English Duke of Marlborough, aided by the emperor's army, put an end to the further expansion of the French.
The 18th century also saw the rise of a new kingdom in Europe. You will recall that there was a county in Germany named Brandenburg, whose count was one of the seven electors who chose the emperor. The capital of this county was Berlin. It so happened that a number of Counts of Brandenburg, of the family of Hohenzollern, had been men of ambition and ability. The little county had grown by adding small territories around it. One of these counts, called "the Great Elector," had added to Brandenburg the greater part of the neighboring county of Pomerania. His son did not have the ability of his father, but was a very proud and vain man.
He happened to visit King William III of England, and was very much offended because during the interview, the king occupied a comfortable arm chair, while the elector, being simply a count, was given a chair to sit in which was straight-backed and had no arms. Brooding over this insult, as it seemed to him, he went home and decided that he too should be called a king. The question was, what should his title be. He could not call himself "King of Brandenburg," for Brandenburg was part of the Empire, and the emperor would not allow it. It had happened some one hundred years before, that, through his marriage with the daughter of the Duke of Prussia, a Count of Brandenburg had come into possession of the district known as East Prussia, at the extreme southeastern corner of the Baltic Sea.
The son of this elector who first called himself king had more energy and more character than his father. He ruled his country with a rod of iron, and built up a strong, well-drilled army. He was especially fond of tall soldiers, and had agents out all over Europe, kidnapping men who were over six feet tall to serve in his famous regiment of Guards. He further increased the size of the Prussian kingdom.
His son was the famous Frederick the Great, one of the most remarkable fighters that the world has ever seen. This prince had been brought up under strict discipline by his father. The old king had been insistent that his son should be no weakling. It is told that one day, finding Frederick playing upon a flute, he seized the instrument and snapped it in twain over his son's shoulder.
The young Frederick, under this harsh training, became a fit leader of a military nation. When his father died and left him a well-filled treasury and a wonderfully drilled army, he was fired with the ambition to spread his kingdom wider. Germany, as has been said, was made up of a great many little counties, each ruled by its petty prince or duke, all owing homage, in a general way, to the ruler of Austria, who still was supposed to be the head of the Holy Roman Empire.
This empire was not a real nation, but a collection of many different nationalities which had little sympathy with each other. The ruler of Austria was also king of Bohemia.

a. Without chunking

France in the 18th Century

During the 18th century, there were many wars in Europe caused by the ambition of various kings to make their domains larger and to increase their own incomes. King Louis XIV of France had built up a very powerful kingdom. Brave soldiers and skillful generals spread his rule over a great part of what is Belgium and Luxemburg, and annexed to the French kingdom the part of Germany between the Rhine River and the Vosges (Vo_zh) Mountains.

Finally, the English joined with the troops of the Holy Roman Empire to curb the further growth of the French kingdom, and at the battle of Blenheim (1704), the English Duke of Marlborough, aided by the emperor's army, put an end to the further expansion of the French.

Prussia

The 18th century also saw the rise of a new kingdom in Europe. You will recall that there was a county in Germany named Brandenburg, whose count was one of the seven electors who chose the emperor. The capital of this county was Berlin. It so happened that a number of Counts of Brandenburg, of the family of Hohenzollern, had been men of ambition and ability. The little county had grown by adding small territories around it. One of these counts, called "the Great Elector," had added to Brandenburg the greater part of the neighboring county of Pomerania. His son did not have the ability of his father, but was a very proud and vain man.

He happened to visit King William III of England, and was very much offended because during the -interview, the king occupied a comfortable arm chair, while the elector, being simply a count, was given a chair to sit in which was straight-backed and had no arms. Brooding over this insult, as it seemed to him, he went home and decided that he too should be called a king. The question was, what should his title be. He could not call himself "King of Brandenburg," for Brandenburg was part of the Empire, and the emperor would not allow it. It had happened some one hundred years before, that, through his marriage with the daughter of the Duke of Prussia, a Count of Brandenburg had come into possession of the district known as East Prussia, at the extreme southeastern corner of the Baltic Sea.

The son of this elector who first called himself king had more energy and more character than his father. He ruled his country with a rod of iron, and built up a strong, well-drilled army. He was especially fond of tall soldiers, and had agents out all over Europe, kidnapping men who were over six feet tall to serve in his famous regiment of Guards. He further increased the size of the Prussian kingdom.

His son was the famous Frederick the Great, one of the most remarkable fighters that the world has ever seen. This prince had been brought up under strict discipline by his father. The old king had

b. With chunking

Figure 11.5 Chunking

Chunking emphasizes units of related information. Note how the use of headings creates clear chunks of information.

▶ **Queuing.** Queuing refers to creating visual distinctions to indicate levels of importance. More-emphatic elements—those with bigger type or boldface type—are more important than less-emphatic ones. Another visual element of queuing is alignment. Designers start more-important information closer to the left margin and indent less-important information. (An exception is titles, which are often centered in reports in the United States.) Figure 11.6 shows queuing.

▶ **Filtering.** Filtering is the use of visual patterns to distinguish various types of information. Introductory material might be displayed in larger type, and notes might appear in italics, another typeface, or a smaller size. Figure 11.7 shows filtering.

limits for "hardship" reasons; and the definition of "work" is somewhat flexible, as up to 30% of recipients can count education or job-skills training as work.

Supplemental Security Income (SSI) SSI is a program that provides cash welfare to the aged, blind, and disabled. Essentially, the job of SSI is to fill holes that are left by the incomplete nature of two of our major social insurance programs, Social Security and disability insurance (DI). Some individuals who have not worked enough in the past may not qualify for benefits under either of these social insurance programs, so they qualify for SSI: for example, a young person who has never worked and is disabled in a car accident would not qualify for DI, but he can receive SSI. Indeed, a large share of the SSI caseload is youth, due to a 1990 court decision that qualified youth with learning disabilities as disabled for SSI purposes. This decision led to a rise in the number of youths on the program from under 300,000 in 1990 to over 800,000 in just four years.[9] This rapid rise in enrollment highlights the problems in truly defining disability, particularly in a population such as children. SSI is not very widely known, nor is it debated with the ferocity of TANF, but it is in fact a bigger program, with expenditures of $31.6 billion in 2002.[10]

In-Kind Programs
Along with these two cash programs, there are four major types of in-kind benefits provided to the poor in the United States.

Food Stamps The food stamps program traditionally provided vouchers to individuals that they could use to pay for food at participating retailers. These vouchers have been replaced by debit card–like systems where individuals are issued a card for a certain value of food, which is drawn down as they make purchases.

Food stamps is a national program, with spending of $24.1 billion in 2002.[11] Households composed entirely of TANF, SSI, or other state cash welfare recipients are automatically eligible for food stamps; otherwise, monthly cash income is the primary eligibility determinant. Households without elderly or disabled members must have income below 130% of the poverty line to receive food stamps, and the amount of the food stamp benefit falls as income rises. In addition, able-bodied adults are required to register for work and be willing to take any job offered; if they violate these conditions, the welfare agency may discontinue benefits for one to six months. Finally, many noncitizens are ineligible: permanent residents must have been in the United States for at least five years to receive food stamps.

Medicaid We discussed the Medicaid program extensively in the previous chapter, but it is worth remembering that this is by far the largest categorical welfare program in the United States, with expenditures of $250 billion in 2003.

[9] See Garrett and Glied (2000) for a discussion of this change.
[10] U.S. House of Representatives Committee on Ways and Means (2004), Section 3.
[11] U.S. House of Representatives Committee on Ways and Means (2004), Section 15.

Figure 11.6   Queuing
Source: Gruber, 2005, p. 461.

Throughout the book from which this page was excerpted, different kinds of information are designed to be easy for the reader to identify.

Figures are presented with a tan screen behind them. The figure number, preceded by a red square, is set in a different typeface than the body text. The figure title, also set in a different typeface, and caption are presented against a gray screen.

Definitions appear in the margin, set off with faint red rules.

This page shows four queuing techniques to distinguish the more-important heading from the less-important headings:

- *Color. The more-important heading is presented in a warmer color, the rust, which stands out more than the cooler blue.*
- *Size. The more-important heading is larger than the other headings.*
- *The heading's placement on the line. The more-important heading is on its own line, giving it more emphasis than the run-in headings.*
- *Line spacing. The more-important heading has more space above it.*

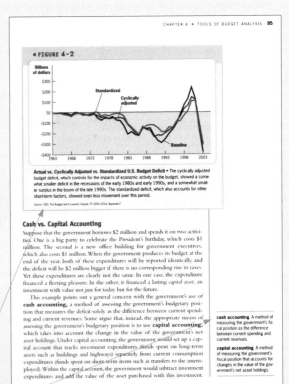

CHAPTER 4 • TOOLS OF BUDGET ANALYSIS   95

■ FIGURE 4-2

Actual vs. Cyclically Adjusted vs. Standardized U.S. Budget Deficit • The cyclically adjusted budget deficit, which controls for the impacts of economic activity on the budget, showed a somewhat smaller deficit in the recessions of the early 1980s and early 1990s, and a somewhat smaller surplus in the boom of the late 1990s. The standardized deficit, which also accounts for other short-term factors, showed even less movement over this period.
Source: CBO, *The Budget and Economic Outlook, FY 2005–2014,* Appendix 7.

Cash vs. Capital Accounting
Suppose that the government borrows $2 million and spends it on two activities. One is a big party to celebrate the President's birthday, which costs $1 million. The second is a new office building for government executives, which also costs $1 million. When the government produces its budget at the end of the year, both of these expenditures will be reported identically, and the deficit will be $2 million bigger if there is no corresponding rise in taxes. Yet these expenditures are clearly not the same. In one case, the expenditure financed a fleeting pleasure. In the other, it financed a lasting *capital asset,* an investment with value not just for today but for the future.

This example points out a general concern with the government's use of **cash accounting,** a method of assessing the government's budgetary position that measures the deficit solely as the difference between current spending and current revenues. Some argue that, instead, the appropriate means of assessing the government's budgetary position is to use **capital accounting,** which takes into account the change in the value of the government's net asset holdings. Under capital accounting, the government would set up a capital account that tracks investment expenditures (funds spent on long-term assets such as buildings and highways) separately from current consumption expenditures (funds spent on short-term items such as transfers to the unemployed). Within the capital account, the government would subtract investment expenditures and add the value of the asset purchased with this investment.

cash accounting A method of measuring the government's fiscal position as the difference between current spending and current revenues.

capital accounting A method of measuring the government's fiscal position that accounts for changes in the value of the government's net asset holdings.

Figure 11.7   Filtering
Source: Gruber, 2005, p. 95.

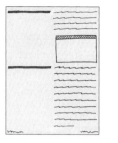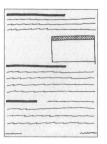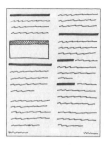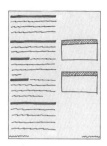

Figure 11.8   Thumbnail Sketches

what the page will look like. In making a grid, you decide how to use white space and determine how many columns to have on the page.

Page Grids   As the phrase suggests, a *page grid* is like a map on which you plan where the text, the graphics, and the white space will go. Many writers like to begin with a *thumbnail sketch*, a rough drawing that shows how the text and graphics will look on the page. Figure 11.8 shows several thumbnail sketches for a page from the body of a manual.

Experiment by sketching the different kinds of pages of your document: body pages, front matter, and so on. When you are satisfied, make page grids. You can use either a computer or a pencil and paper, or you can combine the two techniques.

Figure 11.9 shows two simple grids: one using picas (the unit that printing professionals use, which equals one-sixth of an inch) and one using inches.

Create different grids until the design is attractive, meets the needs of your readers, and seems appropriate for the information you are conveying. Figure 11.10 on page 266 shows some possibilities.

White Space   Sometimes called *negative space*, white space is the area of the paper with no writing or graphics: the space between two columns of text, the space between text and graphics, and, most obviously, the margins.

On TechComm Web

For more about page layout, see the Document Design Tutorial on <bedfordstmartins.com/techcomm>.

Figure 11.9   Sample Grids Using Picas and Inches
Source: Kerman & Tomlinson, 2004, p. 388.

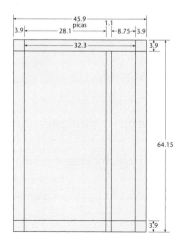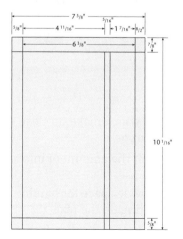

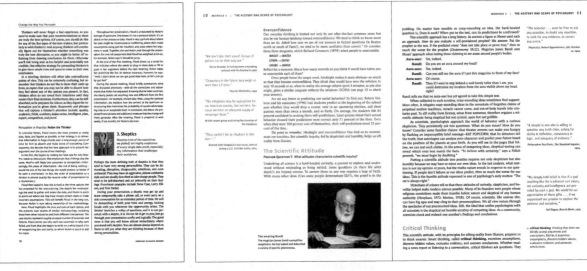

a. Double-column grid
Source: Williams & Miller, 2002, p. 70.

b. Two-page grid, with narrow outside columns for notes
Source: Myers, 2003, pp. 10–11.

c. Three-panel brochure
Source: Norman Rockwell Museum, 2005.

Figure 11.10   Popular Grids

Margins, which make up close to half the area on a typical page, serve four main purposes:

- They limit the amount of information on the page, making it easier to read and use.

- They provide space for binding and allow readers to hold the page without covering up the text.

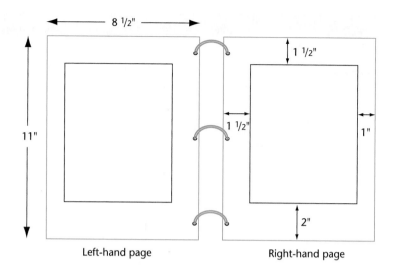

Figure 11.11 Typical Margins for a Document That Is Bound Like a Book

Increase the size of the margins when the subject becomes more difficult or when your readers become less knowledgeable about it.

- They provide a neat frame around the type.
- They provide space for marginal glosses. (Marginal glosses are discussed later in this chapter.)

Figure 11.11 shows common margin widths for left-hand and right-hand pages.

White space can also set off and emphasize an element on the page. For instance, white space around a graphic separates it from the text and draws readers' eyes to it. White space between columns helps readers read the text easily. And white space between sections of text helps readers see that one section is ending and another is beginning.

Columns

Many workplace documents have multiple columns. A multicolumn design offers three major advantages:

- Text is easier to read because the lines are shorter.
- Columns allow you to fit more information on the page, because many graphics can fit in one column or extend across two or more columns. In addition, a multicolumn design can contain more words on a page than a single-column design.
- Columns let you use the principle of repetition to create a visual pattern, such as text in one column and accompanying graphic in an adjacent column.

TECH TIP

How to Format Columns

A multicolumn design allows you to fit more text on a page, create easier-to-read pages, and use more options when sizing graphics. To divide your document into multiple columns, use the **Columns** drop-down menu in the **Page Setup** group.

In the **Page Setup** group, select **Columns**.

You can use **preset** layouts.

You can also control the **number of columns** and specify the **width** and **spacing** yourself by using the **Columns** dialog box.

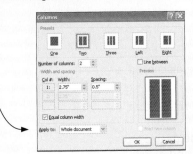

When you divide your document into columns, text flows from the bottom of one column to the top of the next column.

If you want to end a column of text in a specific location or create columns of equal length, you can use the **Breaks** drop-down menu to insert a **column break**. This action will move the following text to the next column.

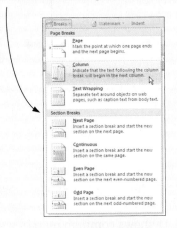

KEYWORDS: columns, breaks, column break, page setup group

Typography

Typography, the study of type and the way people read it, encompasses typefaces, type families, case, and type size, as well as the white space of typography: line length, line spacing, and justification.

Typefaces   A typeface is a set of letters, numbers, punctuation marks, and other symbols, all bearing a characteristic design. There are thousands of typefaces, and more are designed every year. Figure 11.12 shows three contrasting typefaces.

As Figure 11.13 illustrates, typefaces are generally classified into two categories: *serif* and *sans serif*.

Most of the time, you will use a handful of standard typefaces such as Times New Roman and Arial, which are included in your software and which your printer can reproduce.

On TechComm Web

See John Magnik's Typography 1st for information on typography and design. Click on Links Library for Ch. 11 on <bedfordstmartins.com/ techcomm>.

> This paragraph is typed in French Script typeface. You are unlikely to see this style of font in a technical document because it is too ornate and too hard to read. It is better suited to wedding invitations and other formal announcements.
>
> This paragraph is Times Roman. It looks like the kind of type used by the *New York Times* and other newspapers in the nineteenth century. It is an effective typeface for text in the body of technical documents.
>
> This paragraph is Univers, which has a modern, high-tech look. It is best suited for headings and titles in technical documents.

Figure 11.12   Typefaces

Serif typefaces are often considered easier to read because the serifs — the short extensions on the letters — encourage the movement of readers' eyes along the line.

The effect of serifs on readability might differ from culture to culture, because if you see one kind of type often, you become used to it and read it quickly and easily.

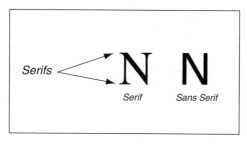

Sans-serif typefaces are harder on readers' eyes because the letters are less distinct from one another than they are in a serif type-face. However, sans-serif typefaces are easier to read on the screen because the letters are simpler.

Sans-serif typefaces are used mostly for short documents and for headings.

Figure 11.13   Serif and Sans-Serif Typefaces

Type Families   Each typeface belongs to a family of typefaces, which consist of variations on the basic style, such as italic and boldface. Figure 11.14, for example, shows Helvetica.

Be careful not to overload your text with too many different members of the same family. Used sparingly and consistently, however, they can help you with filtering: calling attention to various kinds of text, such as warnings and notes. Use italics for book titles and other elements, and use boldface for emphasis and headings. However, you can live a full, rewarding life without ever using outlined or shadowed versions.

On TechComm Web

For more about typography, see the Document Design Tutorial on <bedfordstmartins.com/techcomm>.

Helvetica Light	*Helvetica Bold Italic*
Helvetica Light Italic	**Helvetica Heavy**
Helvetica Regular	***Helvetica Heavy Italic***
Helvetica Regular Italic	Helvetica Regular Condensed
Helvetica Bold	*Helvetica Regular Condensed Italic*

Figure 11.14   Helvetica Family of Type

TECH TIP

How to Format Fonts

To improve the readability of your document, you can use the **Font** group to specify typographical elements such as typeface, type style and size, color, character spacing, and text effects.

In the **Font** group menu, use the **Font** dialog box launcher to display the **Font** dialog box.

You can change the appearance of a typeface by checking **Effects** boxes.

You can also specify basic font formatting such as typeface, type size, bold, italic, and underlining by using drop-down menus and buttons in the **Font** group.

KEYWORDS: font group, font, font style

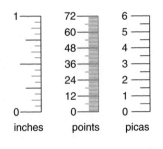

Individual variations are greater in lowercase words

THAN THEY ARE IN UPPERCASE WORDS.

Figure 11.15   Individual Variations in Lowercase and Uppercase Type

Lowercase letters are easier to read than uppercase because the individual variations from one letter to another are greater.

Case   To make your document easy to read, use uppercase and lowercase letters as you would in any other kind of writing (see Figure 11.15).

The average person requires 10 to 25 percent more time to read text using all uppercase letters than to read text using both uppercase and lowercase. In addition, uppercase letters take up as much as 35 percent more space than lowercase letters (Haley, 1991). And if the text includes both cases, readers will find it easier to see where new sentences begin (Poulton, 1968).

Type Size   Type size is measured with a unit called a *point*. There are 12 points in a *pica* and 72 points in an inch. In most technical documents 10-, 11-, or 12-point type is used for the body of the text:

Using Type Sizes Responsibly

Text set in large type contrasts with text set in small type. It makes sense to use large type to emphasize headings and other important information. But be careful with small type. It is unethical (and, according to some court rulings, illegal) to use excessively small type (6 points or smaller) to disguise information that you *don't* want to stand out. When you read the fine print in an ad for cell-phone service, you get annoyed when you figure out that the low rates are guaranteed for only three months or that you are committing to a long-term contract. You *should* get annoyed. It's annoying. Don't do it.

This paragraph is printed in 10-point type. This size is easy to read, provided it is reproduced on a high-quality ink-jet printer or laser printer.

This paragraph is printed in 12-point type. If the document will be read by people over age 40, 12-point type is a good size because it is more legible than a smaller size.

This paragraph is printed in 14-point type. This size is appropriate for titles or headings.

Type sizes used in other parts of the document include the following:

footnotes	8- or 9-point type
indexes	2 points smaller than body text
slides or transparencies	24- to 36-point type

In general, aim for at least a 2- to 4-point difference between the headings and the body. Too many size variations, however, suggest a sweepstakes advertisement rather than serious text.

Line Length The line length most often used on an 8.5 × 11-inch page—about 80 characters—is somewhat difficult to read. A shorter line of 50 to 60 characters is easier, especially in a long document (Biggs, 1980).

Line Spacing Sometimes called *leading* (pronounced "ledding"), *line spacing* refers to the white space between lines or between a line of text and a graphic. If lines are too far apart, the page looks diffuse, the text loses coherence, and readers tire quickly. If lines are too close together, the page looks crowded and becomes difficult to read. Some research suggests that smaller type, longer lines, and sans-serif typefaces all benefit from extra line spacing. Figure 11.16 on page 272 shows three variations in line spacing.

---

a. Excessive line spacing

Aronomink Systems has been contracted by Cecil Electric Cooperative, Inc.

(CECI) to design a solid waste management system for the Cecil County

plant, Units 1 and 2, to be built in Cranston, Maryland. The system will consist

of two 600 MW pulverized coal-burning units fitted with high-efficiency elec-

trostatic precipitators and limestone reagent FGD systems.

b. Appropriate line spacing

Aronomink Systems has been contracted by Cecil Electric Cooperative, Inc.
(CECI) to design a solid waste management system for the Cecil County
plant, Units 1 and 2, to be built in Cranston, Maryland. The system will
consist of two 600 MW pulverized coal-burning units fitted with high-
efficiency electrostatic precipitators and limestone reagent FGD systems.

c. Inadequate line spacing

Aronomink Systems has been contracted by Cecil Electric Cooperative,
Inc. (CECI) to design a solid waste management system for the Cecil
County plant, Units 1 and 2, to be built in Cranston, Maryland. The system
will consist of two 600 MW pulverized coal-burning units fitted with high-
efficiency electrostatic precipitators and limestone reagent FGD systems.

Figure 11.16   Line Spacing

Line spacing is usually determined by the kind of document you are writing. Memos and letters are single-spaced; reports, proposals, and similar documents are often double-spaced or one-and-a-half-spaced.

Figure 11.17 shows how line spacing can be used to distinguish one section of text from another and to separate text from graphics.

Justification   Justification refers to the alignment of words along the left and right margins. In technical communication, text is often *left-justified* (also called *ragged right*). Except for paragraph indentations, the lines begin along a uniform left margin but end on an irregular right border. Ragged right is most common in word-processed text (even though word processors can justify the right margin).

In *justified* text, also called *full-justified text*, both the left and right margins are justified. Justified text is seen most often in formal documents, such as books. The following passage (U.S. Department of Agriculture, 2002) is presented first in left-justified form and then in justified form:

The line spacing between two sections should be greater than the line spacing within a section.

Line spacing separates the text from the graphic.

This page uses no extra line spacing between single-spaced paragraphs. Instead, it uses paragraph indents. This format can make the page look dense and uninviting.

DNA AND ITS ROLE IN HEREDITY 217

third of the original ³²P—and thus, presumably, one-third of the original DNA. Because DNA was carried over in the virus from generation to generation but protein was not, a logical conclusion was that the hereditary information of the virus is contained in the DNA.

The Hershey–Chase experiment convinced most scientists that DNA is the carrier of hereditary information.

The Structure of DNA

As soon as scientists were convinced that the genetic material was DNA, they began efforts to learn its precise, three-dimensional chemical structure. In determining the structure of DNA, scientists hoped to find the answers to two questions: how DNA is replicated between nuclear divisions, and how it causes the synthesis of specific proteins. Both expectations were fulfilled.

X-ray crystallography provided clues to DNA structure

The structure of DNA was deciphered only after many types of experimental evidence and theoretical considerations were combined. The crucial evidence was obtained by X-ray crystallography (Figure 11.4). Some chemical substances, when they are isolated and purified, can be made to form crystals. The positions of atoms in a crystalline substance can be inferred from the pattern of diffraction of X-rays passed through it. Even today, however, this is not an easy task when the substance is of enormous molecular weight.

In the early 1950s, even highly talented X-ray crystallographers could (and did) look at the best available images from DNA preparations and fail to see what they meant. Nonetheless, the attempt to characterize DNA would have been impossible without the crystallographs prepared by the English chemist Rosalind Franklin. Franklin's work, in turn, depended on the success of the English biophysicist Maurice Wilkins, who prepared a sample containing very uniformly oriented DNA fibers. These DNA preparations provided samples for diffraction that were far better than previous ones.

11.5 Chargaff's Rule In DNA, the total abundance of purines is equal to the total abundance of pyrimidines.

The chemical composition of DNA was known

The chemical composition of DNA also provided important clues about its structure. Biochemists knew that DNA was a polymer of nucleotides. Each nucleotide of DNA consists of a molecule of the sugar deoxyribose, a phosphate group, and a nitrogen-containing base (see Figures 3.24 and 3.25). The only differences among the four nucleotides of DNA are their nitrogenous bases: the purines adenine (A) and guanine (G), and the pyrimidines cytosine (C) and thymine (T).

In 1950, Erwin Chargaff at Columbia University reported some observations of major importance. He and his colleagues found that DNA from many different species—and from different sources within a single organism—exhibits certain regularities. In almost all DNA, the following rule holds: The amount of adenine equals the amount of thymine (A = T), and the amount of guanine equals the amount of cytosine (G = C) (Figure 11.5). As a result, the total abundance of purines (A + G) equals the total abundance of pyrimidines (T + C). The structure of DNA could not have been worked out without this information, now known as Chargaff's rule, yet its significance was overlooked for at least three years.

Watson and Crick described the double helix

The solution to the puzzle of the structure of DNA was accelerated by model building: the assembly of three-dimensional representations of possible molecular structures using known relative molecular dimensions and known bond angles. This technique, originally exploited in structural stud-

11.4 X-Ray Crystallography Revealed the Basic Helical Structure of the DNA Molecule The positions of atoms in a purified chemical substance can be inferred by the pattern of diffraction of X-rays passed through it, although the task requires tremendous skill.

Figure 11.17 Line Spacing Used to Distinguish One Section from Another
Source: Purves, Sadava, Orians, & Heller, 2004, p. 217.

We recruited participants to reflect the racial diversity of the area in which the focus groups were conducted. Participants had to meet the following eligibility criteria: have primary responsibility or share responsibility for cooking in their household; prepare food and cook in the home at least three times a week; eat meat and/or poultry; prepare meat and/or poultry in the home at least twice a week; and not regularly use a digital food thermometer when cooking at home.

We recruited participants to reflect the racial diversity of the area in which the focus groups were conducted. Participants had to meet the following eligibility criteria: have primary responsibility or share responsibility for cooking in their household; prepare food and cook in the home at least three times a week; eat meat and/or poultry; prepare meat and/or poultry in the home at least twice a week; and not regularly use a digital food thermometer when cooking at home.

Notice that the space between words is uniform in left-justified text.

In justified text, the spacing between words is irregular, slowing down the reader. Because a big space suggests a break between sentences, not a break between words, readers can become confused, frustrated, and fatigued.

Notice that the irregular spacing not only slows down reading but also can create "rivers" of white space. Readers are tempted to concentrate on the rivers running south rather than on the information itself.

TECH TIP

How to Modify Line Spacing

When designing a page, you can adjust the white space between lines of text and before or after each paragraph by using the **Paragraph** dialog box and the **Line spacing** drop-down menu.

In the **Paragraph** group, use the **Paragraph** dialog box launcher to display the **Paragraph** dialog box.

In the **Paragraph** dialog box, you can change the **spacing before** and **after** paragraphs.

You can also specify the **line spacing**, the space between lines of text.

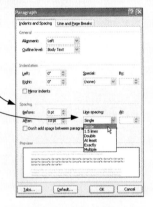

You can select **preset** line-spacing options by using the **Line spacing** drop-down menu in the **Paragraph** group.

TECH TIP

How to Modify Justification

To increase the readability of your document, you can specify the alignment of words along the left and right margins by using the **Paragraph** dialog box or use buttons in the **Paragraph** group.

To modify justification using the **Paragraph** dialog box, select the **Paragraph** dialog box launcher.

You can specify that lines begin along a left margin or right margin, are centered on the page, or are justified.

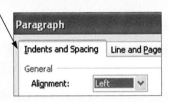

To modify justification using buttons in the **Paragraph** group, select one of the following buttons:

To left-align text

To right-align text

To center text

To justify text

Full justification can make the text harder to read in one more way. Some word processors and typesetting systems automatically hyphenate words that do not fit on the line. Hyphenation slows down and distracts readers. Left-justified text does not require as much hyphenation as full-justified text.

Titles and Headings

Titles and headings should stand out visually on the page because they present a new idea.

Titles   Because a title is the most important heading in a document, it should be displayed clearly and prominently. If it is on a cover page or a title page, use boldface in a large size, such as 18 or 24 points. If it also appears at the top of the first page, make it slightly larger than the rest of the text—perhaps 16 or 18 points for a document printed in 12 point—but smaller than it is on the cover or title page. Many designers center titles on the page between the right and left margins.

In This Book

For more about titling your document, see Ch. 9, p. 200.

Headings   Readers should be able to tell when you are beginning a new topic. The most effective way to distinguish one level of headings from another is to use size variations (Williams & Spyridakis, 1992). Most readers will notice a 20 percent size difference between a first-level heading and a second-level heading. Boldface also sets off headings effectively. The *least* effective way to set off headings is underlining, because the underline obscures the *descenders*, the portions of letters that extend below the body of the letters, such as in *p* and *y*.

In This Book

For more about using headings, see Ch. 9, p. 201.

In general, the more important the heading level, the closer it is to the left margin: first-level headings usually begin at the left margin, second-level headings are often indented one-half inch, and third-level headings are often indented an inch. Indented third-level headings can also be run into the text.

In designing headings, use line spacing carefully. A perceivable distance between a heading and the text increases the impact of the heading. Consider these three examples:

On TechComm Web

For more about designing headings, see the Document Design Tutorial on <bedfordstmartins.com/techcomm>.

Summary

In this example, the writer has skipped a line between the heading and the text that follows it. The heading stands out clearly.

Summary
In this example, the writer has not skipped a line between the heading and the text that follows it. The heading stands out, but not as emphatically.

Summary. In this example, the writer has begun the text on the same line as the heading. This run-in style makes the heading stand out the least.

Other Design Features

Table 11.3 shows five other design features that are used frequently in technical communication: rules, boxes, screens, marginal glosses, and pull quotes.

Table 11.3 Rules, Boxes, Screens, Marginal Glosses, and Pull Quotes

Two types of rules are used here: the vertical rules to separate the columns, and the blue horizontal rules to separate the items. Rules enable you to fit a lot of information on a page, but when overused they make the page look cluttered.

Rules. A *rule* is a design term for a straight line. Using the drawing tools in a word processor, you can add rules. Horizontal rules can separate headers and footers from the body of the page or divide two sections of text. Vertical rules can separate columns on a multicolumn page or identify revised text in a manual. Rules exploit the principles of alignment and proximity.

Source: Institute, 2005, p. 43.

Boxes. Adding rules on all four sides of an item creates a box. Boxes can enclose graphics or special sections of text, or form a border for the whole page. Boxed text is often positioned to extend into the margin, giving it further emphasis. Boxes exploit the principles of contrast and repetition.

Source: Valley, 2005, p. 61.

Table 11.3 (continued)

The use of three different colors of screens clearly distinguishes the three sets of equations.

Source: Purves et al., 2004, p. 466.

Screens. The background shading behind text or graphics for emphasis is called a *screen*. The density can range from 1 percent to 100 percent; 5 to 10 percent is usually enough to provide emphasis without making the text illegible. You can use screens with or without boxes. Screens exploit the principles of contrast and repetition.

This author uses marginal glosses for presenting definitions of key words.

Source: Myers, 2003, p. 603.

Marginal glosses. A marginal gloss is a brief comment on the main discussion. Marginal glosses are usually set in a different typeface—and sometimes in a different color—from the main discussion. Although marginal glosses can be helpful in providing a quick overview of the main discussion, they can also compete with the text for readers' attention. Marginal glosses exploit the principles of contrast and repetition.

This pull quote is placed in the margin, but it can go anywhere on the page, even spanning several columns or the whole page.

Source: Roark et al., 2005, p. 115.

Pull quotes. A pull quote is a brief quotation (usually just a sentence or two) that is pulled from the text and displayed in a larger type size, and usually in a different typeface and enclosed in a box. Newspapers and magazines use pull quotes to attract readers' attention. Pull quotes are inappropriate for reports and similar documents because they look too informal. They are increasingly popular, however, in newsletters. Pull quotes exploit the principles of contrast and repetition.

TECH TIP

How to Create Borders and Screens

To emphasize page elements by enclosing them in a box or including background shading, use the **Borders and Shading** dialog box.

To create a **border** around a page element or an entire page, select the area you want to format and then select **Page Borders** in the **Page Background** group.

Select the **Borders** or **Page Border** tab.

You can specify the type of border, line style, color, and line width.

To create **shading**, also called a screen, select the area you want to format and then select **Page Borders** in the **Page Background** group.

Select the **Shading** tab.

You can specify the color within the box as well as the style of the pattern.

KEYWORDS: borders, page borders, shading, page background group

TECH TIP

How to Create Text Boxes

To emphasize graphics or special sections of text or to position such elements independently of your margins, use the **Text Box** feature in the **Text** group.

To **create** a text box, select **Draw Text Box** from the **Text Box** drop-down menu.

Click and drag your cursor to create your text box.

Click inside the text box and begin typing text.

You can select the text box and move it around the page.

You can also insert a **built-in** text box from the **Text Box** drop-down menu.

To **format** your text box, select the box and then select the **Text Box Styles** dialog box launcher.

This action launches the **Format Text Box** dialog box, which enables you to specify design elements such as fill color, border style, box size, and internal margins, as well as the wrapping style of the surrounding text.

After selecting the text box, you can also use buttons on the **Format** tab to specify design elements such as fill color, line color, font color, line style, shadow style, and 3-D style.

KEYWORDS: text box

ANALYZING SOME PAGE DESIGNS

Figures 11.18–11.21 on pages 279–82 show typical page designs used in technical documents. These figures illustrate the concepts discussed in this chapter.

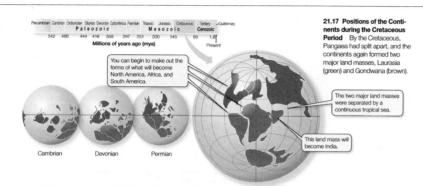

21.17 **Positions of the Continents during the Cretaceous Period**   By the Cretaceous, Pangaea had split apart, and the continents again formed two major land masses, Laurasia (green) and Gondwana (brown).

You can begin to make out the forms of what will become North America, Africa, and South America.

The two major land masses were separated by a continuous tropical sea.

This land mass will become India.

Cambrian   Devonian   Permian

evolved. Dinosaur lineages evolved into predators that walked on two legs and large herbivores that walked on four legs (**Figure 21.16**). Several groups of mammals first appeared during this time. Plant evolution continued with the emergence of the flowering plants that dominate Earth's vegetation today.

THE CRETACEOUS (145–65 MYA)   By the early **Cretaceous** period, Laurasia was completely separate from Gondwana, which was beginning to break apart. A continuous sea encircled the tropics (**Figure 21.17**). Sea levels were high, and Earth was warm and humid. Life proliferated both on land and in the oceans. Marine invertebrates increased in diversity and in number of species. On land, dinosaurs continued to diversify. The first snakes appeared during the Cretaceous, but the modern groups with the most species resulted from a later radiation. Early in the Cretaceous, flowering plants began the radiation that led to their current dominance on land. Fossils of the earliest known flowering plants, dated at 124 million years ago, were recently discovered in Liaoning Province in northeastern China (**Figure 21.18**). By the end of the period, many groups of mammals had evolved. Most of them were small, but one species recently discovered in China, *Repenomamus giganticus*, was large enough to capture and eat young dinosaurs.

As described earlier in this chapter, another meteorite-caused mass extinction took place at the end of the Cretaceous period. In the seas, many planktonic organisms and bottom-dwelling invertebrates became extinct. On land, all animals larger than about 25 kilograms in body weight apparently became extinct. Many species of insects died out, perhaps because the growth of their food plants was greatly reduced following the impact. Some species survived in the northern parts of North America and Eurasia, areas that were not subjected to the devastating fires that engulfed most low-latitude regions.

The modern biota evolved during the Cenozoic era

By the early **Cenozoic** era (65 mya), the positions of the continents resembled those of today, but Australia was still attached to Antarctica, and the Atlantic Ocean was much narrower. The Cenozoic era was characterized by an extensive radiation of mammals, but other groups were also undergoing important changes.

Flowering plants diversified extensively and came to dominate world forests, except in cool regions. Mutations of two genes in one group of plants allowed them to use atmospheric N_2 directly by forming symbioses with a few species of nitrogen-fixing bacteria (see Section 36.4). The evolution of this symbiosis between certain early Cenozoic plants and these specialized bacteria was

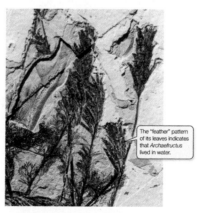

The "feather" pattern of its leaves indicates that *Archaefructus* lived in water.

21.18 **Flowering Plants of the Cretaceous**   These fossils of *Archaefructus* are the earliest known examples of flowering plants, the type of plants most prevalent on Earth today.

Figure 11.18   A Two-Column Design
Source: Sadava, Heller, Orians, Purves, & Hillis, 2008, p. 477.

This page from a textbook was designed to use space efficiently.

The two-column format is economical because a lot of words fit on a page and because it lets the designer use narrow or wide graphics without wasting space.

This page from a corporate white paper uses an effective one-column design.

Many designers today use a narrow column on the outside margin for brief comments or graphics.

Note that the main column is relatively narrow. Rather than fill up the whole page, which would lead to a long line length and a dense appearance, the designer has opted for a less intimidating look, with plenty of white space.

lacks the ability to interact with voice and its input is limited to the 12 keys on most mobile phones.

Convergence and Multimodality

The convergence of mobile phones and computer technology is helping to validate the need for multimodal-enabled devices

Today, the trend toward converging many different technologies has produced powerful new mobile devices. Many of today's mobile personal digital assistants (PDAs) provide the benefits of mobile phones and computers such as larger, color displays. These devices are pointing toward a future where mobile devices will provide powerful network services. This will be further enhanced by new, soon-to-be-released, Class A mobile devices that enable simultaneous voice and data communications channels, helping to bring multimodality into the mainstream.

A royalty-free, platform-independent standard is being developed that will allow multimodal telephony-enabled access to information, applications and web services from mobile devices and wireless PDAs. The Speech Application Language Tags (SALT) Forum, founded by Comverse, Microsoft, Intel, Philips, Cisco and SpeechWorks, is developing the SALT standard, a protocol that extends existing mark-up languages such as HTML, XHTML and XML. SALT will let users interact with an application using speech, a keypad, a mouse or a stylus and it will produce data as synthesized speech, audio, plain text, motion video or graphics. Each of these modes will be able to be used independently or concurrently.

Multimodality in Action

Multimodal applications will combine powerful forms of user input and data output to help network operators deliver new services. The key options are:

- **Speech Input**: Using speech recognition technology, users will be able to search for information (such as the name of an airport), navigate within and between applications, fill in data fields and perform other hands-free functions.
- **Keypad Input**: Using the navigation capabilities of their mobile devices (arrows, joysticks, stylus, keypad, touch-screen, etc.) users will be able to make selections, enter numbers such as a password or PIN, and perform a wide range of other functions.

Comverse White Paper: Multimodality: The Next Wave of Mobile Interaction   Page 6

Figure 11.19   One-Column Design
Source: Stelzner, 2008 <www.stelzner.com/PDF/Comverse-MultiModality.pdf>.

The box is a three-column design. Notice that the photograph in the box does not align exactly with the columns. The blue box and the blue headings give the box unity. Notice that the typeface for the text within the box is sans serif, whereas the typeface in the text below it is serif. This contrast helps readers distinguish the two main components of the page.

BIOLOGICAL MOTIVATION   **309**

CRITICAL THINKING 8.1

Has Evolution Programmed Us to Overeat?

Consider this fact. Numerous correlational studies of humans and experiments with rodents and Rhesus monkeys have consistently come to the same conclusion: Eating a restricted but balanced diet produces a variety of health benefits and promotes longevity (e.g., Barzilai & Gupta, 1999; Cefalu & others, 1997; Weindruch, 1996). So if eating a calorically restricted but balanced diet confers numerous health benefits and promotes longevity, *why do so many people overeat?*

University of British Columbia psychologists John P. J. Pinel, Sunaina Assanand, and Darrin R. Lehman (2000) believe that the evolutionary perspective provides several insights. For animals in the wild, food sources are often sporadic and unpredictable. When animals do find food, competition for it can be fierce, even deadly. If an animal waited to eat until it was hungry and its energy reserves were significantly diminished, it would run the risk of starving or falling prey to another animal.

Thus, the eating patterns of many animals have evolved so that they readily eat even if not hungry. Overeating when food is available ensures ample energy reserves to survive times when food is *not* available.

For most people living in food-abundant Western societies, foraging for your next meal is usually about as life-threatening as waiting your turn in the Taco Bell drive-

through lane. According to Pinel and his colleagues, people in food-rich societies do *not* eat because they are hungry or because their bodies are suffering from depleted energy resources. Rather, we are enticed by the anticipated pleasure of devouring that SuperSize burrito or calzone. In other words, we are motivated to eat by the *positive incentive value* of highly palatable foods.

When a food with a high positive incentive value is readily available, we eat, and often overeat, until we are satiated by that specific taste, which is termed *sensory-specific satiety*. Should another food with high positive incentive value become available, we continue eating and overconsume (Raynor & Epstein, 2001). As noted in the text, this is referred to as the *cafeteria diet effect*. From the evolutionary perspective, there is adaptive pressure to consume a

variety of foods. Why? Because consuming a varied diet helps promote survival by ensuring that essential nutrients, vitamins, and minerals are obtained.

But unlike our ancient ancestors scrounging through the woods for seeds, fruits, and vegetables to survive, today's humans are confronted with foraging for burgers, cheese fries, and Oreo McFlurries. Therein lies the crux of the problem. As Pinel and his colleagues (2000) explain, "The increases in the availability of high positive-incentive value foods that have occurred over the past few decades in industrialized nations—increases that have been much too rapid to produce adaptive evolutionary change—have promoted levels of ad libitum consumption that are far higher than those that are compatible with optimal health and long life."

Critical Thinking Questions

■ Look back at the section on motivation theories. How might each theory (instinct, drive, incentive, arousal, and humanistic) explain the behavior of overeating?

■ How might the insights provided by the evolutionary explanation be used to resist the temptation to overeat?

The main text is a one-column design, with a wide margin for definitions.

The "SuperSize It" Syndrome: Overeating   In the last two decades, average daily caloric intake has increased nearly 10 percent for men and 7 percent for women (Koplan & Dietz, 1999). Every day, we are faced with the opportunity to overeat at all-you-can-eat brunches, pizza buffets, and fast-food restaurants that offer to "SuperSize" your portions for only a few cents more.

The Cafeteria Diet Effect: Variety = More Consumed   If variety is the spice of life, it's also a sure-fire formula to pack on the pounds. Offered just one choice or the same old choice for a meal, we consume less. But when offered a variety of highly palatable foods, such as at a cafeteria or an all-you-can-eat buffet, we consume more (Zandstra & others, 2000). This is sometimes called the **cafeteria diet effect** (Raynor & Epstein, 2001).

Sedentary Lifestyles   Four out of ten American adults report that they *never* exercise, play sports, or engage in physically active hobbies like gardening or walking the dog. Both men and women tend to become more sedentary with age. When the averages are broken down by gender, more women (43 percent) than men (37 percent) lead sedentary lifestyles (National Center for Health Statistics, 2000b).

body mass index (BMI)
A numerical scale indicating adult height in relation to weight; calculated as (703 × weight in pounds)/(height in inches)².

obese
Condition characterized by excessive body fat and a body mass index equal to or greater than 30.0.

cafeteria diet effect
The tendency to eat more when a wide variety of palatable foods is available.

Figure 11.20   A Complex Page Design
Source: Hockenbury & Hockenbury, 2007, p. 309.

This page has no header or footer with page numbers or section headings.

The involvement of undergraduate students is an important feature of RUI, which provides them with research-rich learning environments. However, the primary purpose of RUI is to support faculty research, thereby maintaining the intellectual vibrancy of faculty members in the classroom and research community.

RUI provides the following types of support:

• **Single-Investigator and Collaborative Faculty Research Projects**—Provides support through NSF research programs in response to proposals submitted by individual faculty members or by groups of collaborating investigators. RUI proposals differ from standard NSF proposals in that they include an RUI Impact Statement describing the expected effects of the proposed research on the research and education environment of the institution.

• **Shared Research Instrumentation and Tools**—Provides support for (1) the purchase or upgrade of instrumentation or equipment necessary to support research that will be conducted by several faculty members and (2) the development of new instrumentation.

• **Research Opportunity Awards (ROA's)**—Enable faculty members at predominantly undergraduate institutions to pursue research as visiting scientists with NSF-supported investigators at other institutions. ROA's are usually funded as supplements to ongoing NSF research grants. ROA's are intended to increase the visitors' research capability and effectiveness; improve research and teaching at their home institution; and enhance the NSF-funded research of the host principal investigator.

For More Information

For further information about the RUI activity, including guidelines for the preparation and submission of proposals, see program announcement NSF 00-144.

Prospective applicants for RUI grants and principal investigators interested in hosting an ROA visiting researcher are urged to contact a program officer in the appropriate discipline.

4.   **Minority Research Planning Grants and Career Advancement Awards**—These awards are part of NSF's overall effort to give members of minority groups that are underrepresented in science and engineering greater access to scientific research support.

• **Minority Research Planning Grants (MRPG's)**—Enable eligible minorities who have not had prior independent Federal research support to develop competitive research projects by supporting preliminary studies and similar activities. These are one-time awards of up to $18K for a maximum of 18 months.

• **Minority Career Advancement Awards (MCAA's)**—Support activities that can expand the research career potential of promising applicants. These awards are

Chunking is poor. The reader cannot easily see where one section begins and ends. There should be greater leading between sections than within sections.

The same typeface and size are used in the two different headings and at the start of the bullet items, violating the principle of repetition.

The effect of the bullets is diminished because the turnovers are not indented.

Figure 11.21   A Poorly Designed Page
Source: National Science Foundation, 2001 <www.nsf.gov/pubs/2001.nsf013/nsf013.pdf>.

INTERACTIVE SAMPLE DOCUMENT

Analyzing a Page Design

The following page is from a government report. The questions in the margin ask you to think about page design (as discussed on pages 263–78). E-mail your responses to yourself and/or your instructor on TechComm Web.

USAID IN BULGARIA: 1990–2007

TRAINING AND EDUCATION

Daniela Dimitrova
Director, Association of
Community Funds (2006 – present)

"The assistance we received from USAID through the training programs and a strong know-how developed the community funds model in Bulgaria. The opportunity to see in person the work of community funds elsewhere was exceptionally important. This led us to believe in our own abilities and inspired us to work even harder."

PARTICIPANT TRAINING – OPENING MINDS TO NEW HORIZONS

Training was a cornerstone of the USAID program in Bulgaria. It helped instill new ideas and build the capacity of individuals and organizations to lead Bulgaria during the transition and into the future. Although most USAID programs provided at least some training directly to target groups, the USAID Participant Training Program (PTP), which began in 1993, formed the main foundation of USAID training efforts. World Learning, the PTP implementer, supported virtually all USAID programs and arranged training activities in the United States and 39 other countries. USAID provided more than $18 million for training, seminars, conferences, and study tours for almost 4000 Bulgarians from 1993 to 2007, and awarded 44 small grants for participants to implement ideas developed during their training.

Initially, PTP exposed Bulgarian policy makers and leaders to U.S. models for reform and introduced new ideas. PTP later emphasized appropriate European training as Bulgaria approached EU accession. In recent years, PTP conducted most of its training activities in Bulgaria as USAID emphasized building local training capacity. PTP provided a lasting legacy of more knowledgeable and skilled professionals and organizations throughout Bulgaria.

Eyes on Four Paws

"We started with nothing but an idea and a lot of goals," says Albena Alexieva, chairperson of the "Eyes on Four Paws" Foundation. The Yellow Lab puppies sleeping peacefully in the room across the hall are evidence of how that idea has become a reality.

In 2001, the Foundation was established with the aim of creating a Bulgarian school for guide dogs for blind people. The school was officially opened in Sofia in 2003 and two trained dogs were handed over to their new owners in Plovdiv and Haskovo for a symbolic one lev (about half a euro).

"Eyes on Four Paws" participated in the first grants competition for social enterprises sponsored by the USAID Community Fund and Social Enterprise Program. They received support for their plans to offer training courses for dog owners as one way to make money for the school. Under a USAID Participant Training Program study tour for fledgling social enterprises, the NGO asked a school for seeing-eye dogs in Prague, Czech Republic, and acquired practical experience in organizing a social enterprise and interacting successfully with businesses.

"The organizational and theoretical knowledge we received through USAID was extremely valuable for the development of our activities," remarks Mihail Medko, coordinator of the social action program at "Eyes on Four Paws." The NGO has since attracted business sponsors such as MTel, one of the largest mobile phone operators in Bulgaria.

Today the school is a busy place, with two dogs preparing to start training after their tour, two in mid-trip and three dogs preparing to begin their new lives as companions to the blind. Seven blind people are on the waiting list to receive a guide dog.

34

Source: U.S. Agency, 2007 <www.usaid.gov/locations/europe_eurasia/countries/bg/17years.pdf>.

1. Describe the use of columns. In what ways do they work well?

2. Describe the text justification. Is it effective?

3. Describe the use of contrast as a design principle on this page. How effective is it?

4. Describe the use of proximity as a design principle on this page. How effective is it?

On TechComm Web

To e-mail your responses to yourself and/or your instructor, click on Interactive Sample Documents for Ch. 11 on <bedfordstmartins.com/techcomm>.

DESIGNING WEB SITES

The preceding discussion of designing printed documents focuses on four components: size, paper, bindings, and accessing tools. Of these four components, only accessing tools are relevant to Web sites. But they are vitally important for an obvious reason: if you can't figure out how to find the information you want on a Web site, you're out of luck. With a printed document, you can at least flip through the pages, hoping that you'll see what you're trying to find.

The following discussion focuses on making it easy for readers to find and understand the information on your Web site. Five principles apply:

- Create informative headers and footers.
- Help readers navigate the site.
- Include extra features readers might need.
- Design for readers with disabilities.
- Design for a multicultural audience.

Create Informative Headers and Footers

Headers and footers will help readers understand and navigate your site, and they will help establish your credibility. You want readers to know that they are visiting the official site of your organization and that it was created by professionals. Figure 11.22 shows a typical Web site header, and Figure 11.23 shows a typical Web site footer.

Notice that a header for a Web site provides much more accessing information than a header for a printed document.

This header lets readers search the site (or the whole Web).

The header presents a row of graphic navigation links that enable readers to purchase products and begin to navigate the site.

Figure 11.22　Web Site Header
Source: Corel, 2008 <www.corel.com/servlet/Satellite/us/en/Content/1150905725000>.

This footer presents the main navigation links as text. Readers with impaired vision who use text-to-speech devices will be able to understand these textual links, but they will not be able to understand the graphic links in the header.

This footer also provides a link to the "terms of use" information, which describes readers' legal rights and responsibilities when they visit the site. Finally, the footer links to the company's privacy policy.

Figure 11.23　Web Site Footer
Source: Corel, 2008 <www.corel.com/servlet/Satellite/us/en/Content/1150905725000>.

Help Readers Navigate the Site

Because readers of a Web site can view only the page that appears on the screen, each page should help them see where they are in the site and get where they want to go. One important way to help readers navigate your site is to create and sustain a consistent visual design on every page. Make the header, footer, background color or pattern, typography (typeface, type size, and color), and placement of the navigational links the same on every page. That way, readers will know where to look for these items.

Guidelines

Making Your Site Easy to Navigate

▶ **Include a site map or index.** A site map, which lists the pages on the site, can be a graphic or textual list of pages, classified according to logical categories. An index is an alphabetized list of pages. Figure 11.24 on page 286 shows a section of the Google site map.

▶ **Use a table of contents at the top of a long page.** If your page extends for more than a couple of screens, include a table of contents—a set of links to the items on that page—so that readers do not have to scroll down to find the topic they want. A table of contents can link to information farther down on the same page or information on separate pages. Figure 11.25 on page 286 shows an excerpt from the table of contents at the top of a frequently asked questions (FAQ) page.

▶ **Help readers get back to the top of a long page.** If a page is long enough to justify a table of contents, include a "*Back to top*" link (a textual link or a button or icon) before the start of each new chunk of information.

▶ **Include a link to the home page on every page.** This link can be a simple "*Back to home page*" textual link, a button, or an icon.

▶ **Include textual navigational links at the bottom of every page.** If you are using buttons or icons for links, include textual versions of those links at the bottom of the page. Readers with impaired vision might be using special software that reads the information on the screen. This software interprets text only, not graphics.

> **On TechComm Web**
>
> For advice on how to design an effective site map, see Jakob Nielsen's "Site Map Usability." Click on Links Library for Ch. 11 on <bedfordstmartins.com/techcomm>.

Include Extra Features Readers Might Need

Because readers with a range of interests and needs will visit your site, consider adding several or all of the following five features:

- *An FAQ.* A list of frequently asked questions helps new readers by providing basic information, explaining how to use the site, and directing them to more-detailed discussions.

- *A search page or engine.* A search page or search engine lets readers enter a keyword or phrase and find all the pages on the site that contain it.

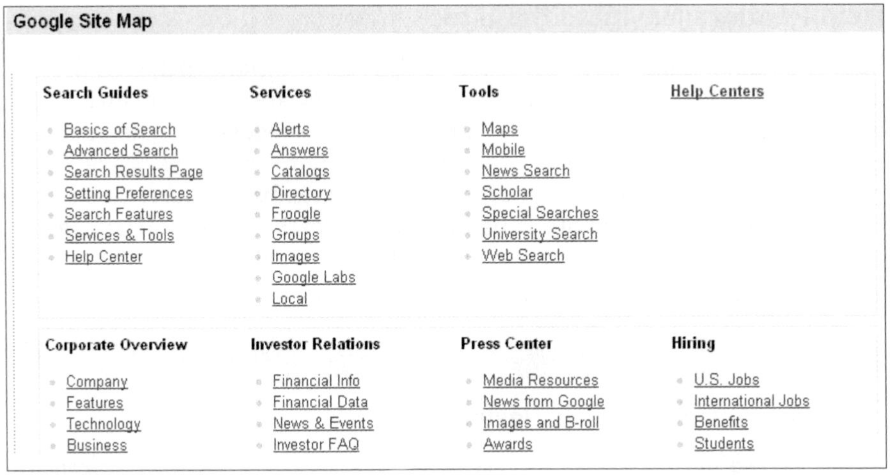

Figure 11.24   Site Map
Source: Google, Inc., 2008 <www.google.com/sitemap.html>.

Readers click on the red text to go to the answer to a question.

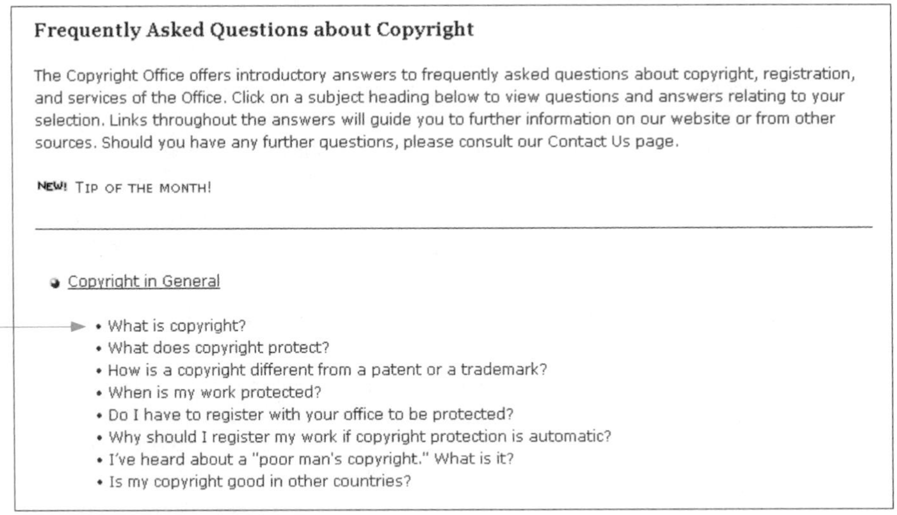

Figure 11.25   Table of Contents
Source: U.S. Copyright Office, 2008 <www.copyright.gov/help/faq>.

- *Resource links.* If one of the purposes of your site is to educate readers, provide links to other sites.

- *A printable version of your site.* A Web site is designed for a screen, not a page. A printable version of your site, with black text on a white background and all the text and graphics consolidated into one big file, saves readers paper and ink.

- *A text-only version of your site.* Many readers with impaired vision rely on text because their specialized software cannot interpret graphics. Consider creating a text-only version of your site. If you do, include a link to it on your home page.

Design for Readers with Disabilities

The Internet has proved to be a terrific technology for people with disabilities because it brings a world of information to their desktops, allowing them to work from home and participate in virtual communities. However, most sites on the Internet are not designed to accommodate people with disabilities. In 1996, a court ruled that the Americans with Disabilities Act covered commercial Web sites, which must be accessible to people with disabilities.

The following discussion highlights several ways to make your site easier to use for people with disabilities. Consider three main types of disabilities as you design your site:

- *Vision impairment.* People who cannot see, or cannot see well, rely on text-to-speech software. Provide either a text-only version of the site or textual equivalents of all your graphics. Use the "alt" (alternate) tag to create a textual label that appears when the reader holds the mouse over the graphic.

  Do not rely on color or graphics alone to communicate information. For example, if you use a red icon to signal a warning, also use the word *warning.* If you use tables to create columns on the screen, label each column clearly using a text label rather than just an image.

  Use 12-point type or larger throughout your site, and provide audio feedback—for example, having a button beep when the reader presses it.

- *Hearing impairment.* If you use video, provide captions and, if the video includes sound, a volume control. Also use visual feedback techniques; for example, make a button flash when the reader presses it.

- *Mobility impairment.* Some people with impaired mobility find it easier to use a keyboard than a mouse. Therefore, build in keyboard shortcuts wherever possible. If readers have to click on an area of the screen using a pointing device, make the area large so that it is easy to see and click.

Design for Multicultural Audiences

Approximately 70 percent of the people using the Internet are nonnative speakers of English, and that percentage is growing as more people from developing nations go online (Internet, 2008). Therefore, it makes sense to plan your site as if many of your readers will not be proficient in English.

> **On TechComm Web**
> For a detailed look at accessibility issues, see the Web Content Accessibility Initiative from the World Wide Web Consortium. Click on Links Library for Ch. 11 on <bedfordstmartins.com/techcomm>.

> **On TechComm Web**
> Also see "Guidelines for Accessible Web Sites: Technology & Users" by Michele Ward, Philip Rubens, and Sherry Southard. Click on Links Library for Ch. 11 on <bedfordstmartins.com/techcomm>.

> ### Ethics Note
>
> **Designing Legal and Honest Web Pages**
>
> You know that the words and images you see on the Internet are covered by copyright, even if you see no copyright symbol. The only exception is information that is in the public domain because it is not covered by copyright (such as information created by federal government sources), because the copyright has expired (the author has been dead for more than 70 years), or because the creator of the information explicitly states that the information is in the public domain and you are free to copy it.
>
> But what about the design of a Web site? Almost all Web designers readily admit to spending a lot of time looking at other sites and pages for inspiration. And they admit to looking at the code to see how the author achieved that design. This is perfectly ethical. So is copying the code for routine elements such as tables. But is it ethical to download the code for a whole page, including the layout and design, then plug in your own data? I don't think so. Your responsibility is to create your own information, then display it with your own design.

▶ **In This Book**
For more about copyright law, see Ch. 2, p. 25.

Planning for a multicultural Web site is similar to planning for a multicultural printed document:

- *Use short sentences and paragraphs, as well as common words.*
- *Avoid idioms, both verbal and visual, that might be confusing.* For instance, don't use sports metaphors, such as *full-court press*, or a graphic of an American-style mailbox to suggest an e-mail link.
- *If a large percentage of your readers speak a language other than English, consider creating a version of your site in that language.* The expense can be considerable, but so can the benefits.

DESIGNING WEB PAGES

Well-designed Web pages are simple, with only a few colors and nothing extraneous. In addition, the text is written simply and chunked effectively, and the links are written so that readers know where they are being directed.

Aim for Simplicity

When you create a Web site, it doesn't cost anything to use all the colors in the rainbow, to add sound effects and animation, or to make text blink on and off. Most of the time, however, these effects just slow the download and annoy readers. If a special effect serves no useful function, avoid it.

Guidelines

Designing a Simple Site

▶ **Use simple backgrounds.** A plain white background or a pale pastel is best. Avoid loud patterns that distract readers from the words and graphics of the text. You don't want readers to notice the background.

▶ **Use conservative color combinations to increase text legibility.** The greater the contrast between the text color and the background color, the more legible the text. The most legible color combination is black text on a white background. Bad idea: black on purple.

▶ **Avoid decorative graphics.** Don't waste space using graphics that convey no useful information. Think twice before you use clip art.

▶ **Use thumbnail graphics.** Instead of a large graphic, which takes up space and requires a long time to download, use a thumbnail so that readers can click on it if they wish to open a larger version.

▶ On TechComm Web

For an introduction to color theory as it applies to the Web, see Dmitry's Design Lab. Click on Links Library for Ch. 11 on <bedfordstmartins.com/ techcomm>.

Make the Text Easy to Read and Understand

Web pages are harder to read than paper documents because screen resolution is much less sharp—usually 72 dots per inch (dpi) versus 1200 dpi on a basic laser printer and 2400 dpi in some books.

Guidelines

Designing Easy-to-Read Text

▶ **Keep the text short.** Poor screen resolution makes reading long stretches of text difficult. In general, pages should contain no more than two or three screens of information.

▶ **Chunk information.** When you write for the screen, chunk information to make it easier to understand. Use frequent headings, brief paragraphs, and lists.

▶ **Make the text as simple as possible.** Use common words and short sentences to make the information as simple as the subject allows.

▶ On TechComm Web

For more about writing for the Web, see John Morkes and Jakob Nielsen's "Concise, SCANNABLE, and Objective: How to Write for the Web." Click on Links Library for Ch. 11 on <bedfordstmartins.com/ techcomm>.

▶ In This Book

For more about chunking, see p. 263.

Create Clear, Informative Links

Well-phrased links are easy to read and understand. By clearly telling readers what kind of information the linked site provides, links help readers decide whether to follow them. The following Guidelines box is based on Sun Microsystems' "Guide to Web Style" (Sun, 1999).

Writing Clear, Informative Links

▶ **Structure your sentences as if there were no links in your text.**

AWKWARD	Click here to go to the Rehabilitation Center page, which links to research centers across the nation.
SMOOTH	The Rehabilitation Center page links to research centers across the nation.

▶ **Indicate what information the linked page contains.** Readers get frustrated if they wait for a file to download and then discover that it doesn't contain the information they expected.

UNINFORMATIVE	See the Rehabilitation Center.
INFORMATIVE	See the Rehabilitation Center's hours of operation.

▶ **Don't change the colors of text links.** Readers are used to two common colors: blue for links that have not yet been clicked and purple for links that have been clicked.

ANALYZING SOME WEB PAGES

The best way to learn about designing Web sites and their pages is to study them. Figures 11.26–11.28 offer examples of good Web page design.

This page is simple and attractive, with a clear purpose, effective organization, and large clear type.

The name of the organization.

The name of the page.

Large, easy-to-read textual links.

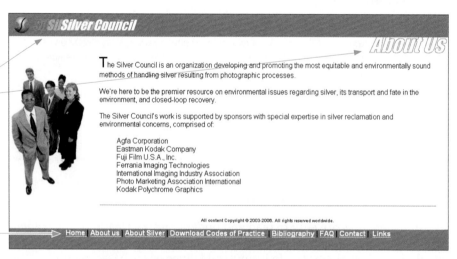

Figure 11.26   The Silver Council "About Us" Page
Source: Silver Council, 2008 <http://www.silvercouncil.org/html/aboutus.htm>.

This home page is simple and easy to use.

The header includes the company logo, sign-in information, and a box for choosing the language displayed on the site.

The main content portion of the page explains what a blog is and how to create a blog.

The footer contains the standard links, as well as textual links to major areas of the site.

Figure 11.27   The Blogger Home Page
Source: Blogger, 2008 <www.blogger.com/start>.

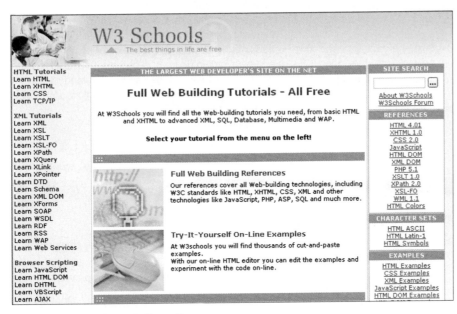

This page is designed to contain a large number of links to tutorials and other reference information. Tutorials are presented in the left-hand column, an explanation of how to use the site is presented in the middle column, and other reference material is presented in the right-hand column.

Figure 11.28   W3 Schools Home Page
Source: W3 Schools, 2008 <www.w3schools.com>.

Writer's Checklist

Did you

- ☐ analyze your audience: their knowledge of the subject, attitudes, and reasons for reading, as well as the kinds of tasks they will be carrying out? (p. 257)
- ☐ determine the purpose or purposes you are trying to achieve? (p. 257)
- ☐ determine your resources in time, money, and equipment? (p. 258)

Designing Documents and Pages

Did you

- ☐ consider the best size for the document? (p. 259)
- ☐ consider the best paper? (p. 259)
- ☐ consider the best binding? (p. 260)
- ☐ think about which accessing tools would be most appropriate, such as icons, color, dividers, tabs, and cross-reference tables? (p. 261)
- ☐ use color, if you have access to it, to highlight certain items, such as warnings? (p. 261)
- ☐ devise a style for headers and footers? (p. 262)
- ☐ devise a style for page numbers? (p. 262)
- ☐ draw thumbnail sketches and page grids that define columns and white space? (p. 265)
- ☐ choose typefaces that are appropriate to your subject? (p. 268)
- ☐ use appropriate styles from the type families? (p. 269)
- ☐ use type sizes that are appropriate for your subject and audience? (p. 270)
- ☐ choose a line length that is suitable for your subject and audience? (p. 271)
- ☐ choose line spacing that is suitable for your line length, subject, and audience? (p. 271)
- ☐ decide whether to use left-justified text or full-justified text? (p. 272)
- ☐ design your title for clarity and emphasis? (p. 275)
- ☐ devise a logical, consistent style for each heading level? (p. 275)
- ☐ use rules, boxes, screens, marginal glosses, and pull quotes where appropriate? (p. 276)

Designing Web Sites and Pages

Did you

- ☐ create informative headers and footers? (p. 284)
- ☐ help readers navigate the site by including a site map, a table of contents, back-to-top links, and textual navigation buttons? (p. 285)
- ☐ include extra features readers might need, such as frequently asked questions, a search page or engine, resource links, a printable version of the site, or a text-only version of the site? (p. 285)
- ☐ design for readers with impaired vision, hearing, or mobility? (p. 287)
- ☐ design for multicultural audiences? (p. 287)
- ☐ aim for simplicity in page design by using simple backgrounds and conservative color combinations and by avoiding decorative graphics? (p. 288)
- ☐ make the text easy to read and understand by keeping it short, chunking the information, and writing simply? (p. 289)
- ☐ create clear, informative links? (p. 289)

Exercises

 **In This Book** For more about memos, see Ch. 14, p. 377.

1. Study the first and second pages of an article in a journal in your field. Describe 10 different design features you find on these two pages. Which features are most effective for the audience and purpose? Which are least effective?

2. **GROUP EXERCISE** Form small groups for this collaborative exercise in analyzing design. Photocopy or scan a page from a book or a magazine. Choose a page that does not contain advertisements. Have each person work independently for the first part of the project:

- Have one person describe the design elements.
- Have one person evaluate the design: which aspects are effective, and which could be improved?
- Have one person create a new design using thumbnail sketches.

Then meet as a group and compare notes. Do all members of the group agree with the first member's description of the design? With the second member's evaluation of the design? Do all members like the third member's redesign? What have your discussions taught you about design? Write a memo to your instructor presenting your findings. Include the photocopied page with your memo.

3. Study the following page from a Micron data sheet (Micron, 2005, p. 26). Describe its major design characteristics: its typography and use of margins and white space. What are the strengths of its design? What are the weaknesses? What design features would you recommend changing or adding to make it more attractive and easier to read? If appropriate, devise headings that

can be added to the page. Present your analysis and recommendations in a memo to your instructor.

4. **INTERNET EXERCISE** Find the sites of three manufacturers within a single industry, such as personal watercraft, cars, computers, or medical equipment. Study the three sites, focusing on one of these aspects of site design:

- use of color
- quality of the writing
- quality of the site map or index

 256Mb, 128Mb, 64Mb, 32Mb
Q-FLASH MEMORY

CLEAR STATUS REGISTER Command

The ISM sets the status register bits SR5, SR4, SR3, and SR1 to "1s." These bits, which indicate various failure conditions, can only be reset by the CLEAR STATUS REGISTER command. Allowing system software to reset these bits can perform several operations (such as cumulatively erasing or locking multiple blocks or writing several bytes in sequence). To determine if an error occurred during the sequence, the status register may be polled. To clear the status register, the CLEAR STATUS REGISTER command (50h) is written. The CLEAR STATUS REGISTER command functions independently of the applied V_{PEN} voltage and is only valid when the ISM is off or the device is suspended.

BLOCK ERASE Command

The BLOCK ERASE command is a two-cycle command that erases one block. First, a block erase setup is written, followed by a block erase confirm. This command sequence requires an appropriate address within the block to be erased. The ISM handles all block preconditioning, erase, and verify. Time tWB after the two-cycle block erase sequence is written, the device automatically outputs status register data when read. The CPU can detect block erase completion by analyzing the output of the STS pin or status register bit SR7. Toggle OE# or CEx to update the status register. Upon block erase completion, status register bit SR5 should be checked to detect any block erase error. When an error is detected, the status register should be cleared before system software attempts corrective actions. The CEL remains in read status register mode until a new command is issued. This two-step setup command sequence ensures that block contents are not accidentally erased. An invalid block erase command sequence results in status register bits SR4 and SR5 being set to "1." Also, reliable block erasure can only occur when V_{CC} is valid and $V_{PEN} = V_{PENH}$. Note that SR3 and SR5 are set to "1" if block erase is attempted while $V_{PEN} \leq V_{PENLK}$. Successful block erase requires that the corresponding block lock bit be cleared. Similarly, SR1 and SR5 are set to "1" if block erase is attempted when the corresponding block lock bit is set.

BLOCK ERASE SUSPEND Command

The BLOCK ERASE SUSPEND command allows block erase interruption in order to read or program data in another block of memory. Writing the BLOCK ERASE SUSPEND command immediately after starting the block erase process requests that the ISM suspend the block erase sequence at an appropriate point in the algorithm. When reading after the BLOCK ERASE SUSPEND command is written, the device outputs status register data. Polling status register bit SR7, followed by SR6, shows when the BLOCK ERASE operation has been suspended. In the default mode, STS also transitions to V_{OH}. ^{t}LES defines the block erase suspend latency. At this point, a READ ARRAY command can be written to read data from blocks other than that which is suspended. During erase suspend to program data in other blocks, a program command sequence can also be issued. During a PROGRAM operation with block erase suspended, status register bit SR7 returns to "0" and STS output (in default mode) transitions to V_{OL}. However, SR6 remains "1" to indicate block erase suspend status. Using the PROGRAM SUSPEND command, a program operation can also be suspended. Resuming a SUSPENDED programming operation by issuing the Program Resume command enables the suspended programming operation to continue. To resume the suspended erase, the user must wait for the programming operation to complete before issuing the Block ERASE RESUME command. While block erase is suspended, the only other valid commands are READ QUERY, READ STATUS REGISTER, CLEAR STATUS REGISTER, CONFIGURE, and BLOCK ERASE RESUME. After a BLOCK ERASE RESUME command to the Flash memory is completed, the ISM continues the block erase process. Status register bits SR6 and SR7 automatically clear and STS (in default mode) returns to V_{OL}. After the ERASE RESUME command is completed, the device automatically outputs status register data when read. V_{PEN} must remain at V_{PENH} (the same V_{PEN} level used for block erase) during block erase suspension. Block erase cannot resume during block erase suspend until PROGRAM operations are complete.

0900Saef80b5a323
MT28F640L3.fm – Rev. M 10/04 EN

26

Micron Technology, Inc., reserves the right to change products or specifications without notice.
©2000 Micron Technology. Inc

- navigation, including the clarity and placement of links to other pages on the site
- accommodation of multicultural readers
- accommodation of people with disabilities
- phrasing of the links

Which of the three sites is most effective? Which is least effective? Why? Compare and contrast the three sites in terms of their effectiveness.

5. **INTERNET EXERCISE** Using a search engine, find a site that serves the needs of people with a physical disability (for example, the Glaucoma Research Foundation, <www.glaucoma.org>). What attempts have the designers made to accommodate readers' needs? How effective do you think those attempts have been?

Case 11: Designing a Report Template

▶ In This Book For more about memos, see Ch. 14, p. 377.

Background

You are part of the information staff for the Animal and Plant Health Inspection Service's Plant Protection and Quarantine (PPQ) program, which is part of the U.S. Department of Agriculture. The organization's goal is to protect the health and value of American agriculture and natural resources. Working with other federal agencies, Congress, the states, agricultural interests, and the general public, the PPQ responds to potential acts of agricultural bioterrorism, invasive species, and diseases of wildlife and livestock. The organization's information staff helps PPQ scientists communicate research findings to both a general audience and expert audiences from agriculture, industry, government, science, and education.

Amid growing concerns of new pest introductions to domestic plant resources, the PPQ is undertaking a safeguarding review. This review's goal is to propose specific recommendations on how to improve the PPQ's ability to protect the nation's plant resources from harmful plant pests. Drawing on the expertise of representatives from government, industry, and academia, the PPQ plans to publish a final report documenting the review's findings and recommendations, as well as several follow-up reports.

"Creating this report will be a little tricky," your supervisor, Charlotte McQuarrie, explains. "This report will include findings and recommendations from four separate committees: Pest Exclusion, Pest Detection and Response, International Pest Information, and Permit. Unless we give the committees some guidance, we are likely to get four different page designs—"

"—and that means we'll spend hours reformatting all the material so the report has a consistent design," you say, interrupting.

"You got it. I think we need to start thinking about the design of the whole report right now. If we can decide on its overall design and page layout, we can give each committee a Word template to follow. Our job will be a lot easier when it comes time to compile all the information into a single report. I'm also planning to use this design for other follow-up reports the PPQ will publish over the next year and a half."

"Do you have any ideas for the design of the report?" you ask.

"Not yet. I want you to come up with a design and develop a template based on that design. I have some unformatted text and some graphics from the Pest Exclusion Committee for you to experiment with. I've added some brief comments using Word's reviewing toolbar to get you started." (See Document 11.1.)

"What do you have in mind?"

"I'd like to be able to e-mail each committee a Word template for the report. This template would reflect the design of the report. For example, if we go with a two-column design, the template would already have a two-column layout. All the writers would need to do is add content. They could use styles that we've defined for headings, body text, lists, captions, and so on. Your first step is to create the report's page design."

Your Assignment

1. Using the techniques discussed in this chapter, create a page design for the body of the report. Write Charlotte a memo in which you justify your design decisions. Attach a copy of your sample page design to your memo.

2. Using Word's Styles and Formatting and document template features, create a report template based on your design for committee writers to use when they draft their reports.

|Pest Exclusion Committee Report|

|<<snip snip>>|

|2.26 Detector Dogs|

|The use of dogs to detect meat and plant products is employed at a number of POEs. Dogs are used to monitor international mail, air passengers, and certain cargo entries. The APHIS-PPQ plans to integrate The Beagle Brigade Program into a number of AQI operations including airport baggage clearance, international mail facilities, cargo inspection, land border surveillance, and smuggling interdiction. It also has plans to explore other areas outside AQI where use of dogs may be helpful and to explore cross-utilization possibilities.|

At this time PPQ's program is constrained by a commitment to use beagles and a specific passive training technique. Customs and California's dog programs use both passive and aggressive search and alert techniques specific to the assigned task and select breeds based on the traits desired for a specific task. As a result, APHIS is self-limited in its ability to expand its use of dog scenting.

|The San Ysidro, CA, border crossing from Mexico with the normal daily volume of vehicular traffic. Note the Customs officer with a detector dog conducting a primary inspection for controlled substances.|

|Recommendations|

Place detector dog teams at all high-risk ports of entry to facilitate passenger and baggage clearance.

Review APHIS's training and breed selection program to maximize use of different screening techniques and breed capabilities.

Negotiate with Customs to cross-train its dogs to screen for agricultural products at smaller ports of entry.

Document 11.1
Unformatted Content for the PPQ's Safeguarding Review Report
Source: Based on National Plant Board, 1999 <www.aphis.usda.gov/ppq/safeguarding/MainReport.PDF>.

Comment: This is the first-level heading for the chapter. You will need to create a design for first- through third-level headings.

Comment: I deleted text here (sections 2.1-2.25) so that I could show you two shorter sections containing the elements we need to include in the page design.

Comment: This is a second-level heading.

Comment: You need to decide how to design the body text. Consider such elements as page grids, white space, columns, typography, and other design features. Don't forget to include accessing aids in your design.

On TechComm Web

For digital versions of case documents, click on Downloadable Case Documents on <bedfordstmartins.com/techcomm>.

Comment: This is a caption for the graphic.

Comment: This is a third-level heading.

2.27 X-Ray Application

X-ray equipment is currently used to screen passenger baggage for pre-departure and at some ports of entry, at international mail facilities, and for cargo containers at various high volume locations and devanning sites along the U.S./Mexico border.

|Truck x-ray, Otay Mesa, CA, used principally by U.S. Customs for drug interdiction. A detailed X-ray of an entire semitruck with cargo requires 10 minutes.|

Customs plans to install additional truck x-ray equipment at additional southern border locations and at northern border crossing locations as funding allows.

The development of tomographic x-ray equipment to facilitate inspection at POEs is currently stalled. Originally under development by the Federal Aviation Agency to facilitate explosion detection, funding by that agency was rescinded when this technology failed to detect sheet explosives at the required levels.

Vivid Technology has developed a dual energy x-ray system that will enable a high speed analysis of baggage for quarantine commodities which uses the atomic number, mass, and density of objects to discriminate targeted materials from non-targeted objects. Implementation of this x-ray technology is planned to begin at JFK's Terminal One as a pilot program and then expand to other international airports.

Other x-ray technology under development in addition to heavy pallet x-ray and improved truck x-ray capability include imaging and relocatable inspection systems (IRIS or VACIS) and a railcar inspection system that uses gamma rays to detect objects as a train moves slowly through the equipment.

Recommendations

Develop or abandon development of tomographic x-ray technology.

Acquire and begin using Vivid Technology's dual energy x-ray system, and any other identified smart x-ray equipment to expedite screening and clearance of cargo, baggage, and mail.

Negotiate with Customs to use its truck x-ray capability to screen cargo containers.

|2.28 Future Possibilities and Research Needed|

|<<snip snip>>|

Comment: Another caption

Comment: This is another second-level heading.

Comment: I deleted the rest of the text in this chapter.

Creating Graphics

The Functions of Graphics 298

Characteristics of an Effective
 Graphic 299

Understanding the Process of
 Creating Graphics 301

Planning Graphics 301

Creating Graphics 304

Revising Graphics 306

Citing Graphics 306

Using Color Effectively 307

Choosing the Appropriate Kind of
 Graphic 309

Illustrating Numerical Information 312

Illustrating Logical Relationships 325

Illustrating Process Descriptions and
 Instructions 325

Illustrating Visual and Spatial
 Characteristics 329

Showing Motion in Graphics 332

Creating Effective Graphics for
 Multicultural Readers 333

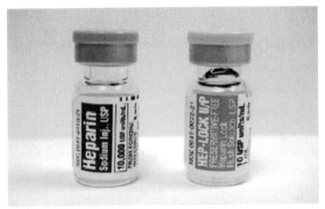

Source: Deutsch, 2007 <www.fda.gov/medWatch/SAFETY/2007/heparin_DHCP_02-06-2007.pdf>.

In the World . . .

Baxter Healthcare, one maker of the drug heparin, received unwelcome publicity in late 2007 when twin infants, children of a movie star and his wife, were administered 1,000 times the intended dosage of the drug. The error was discovered quickly, and the infants survived. The accident was attributed in part to the fact that the labels for the two dosages—10 units/mL and 10,000 units/mL—had a similar blue background. In a letter to physicians earlier in 2007, a Baxter executive wrote,

> Baxter is aware of fatal medication errors that have occurred when two Heparin products with shades of blue labeling were mistaken for each other. Three infant deaths resulted when the higher dosage Heparin Sodium Injection 10,000 units/mL was inadvertently administered instead of the lower dosage of HEP-LOCK U/P 10 units/mL.

This incident suggests the importance of using colors and graphics carefully.

Graphics are the "pictures" in technical communication: drawings, maps, photographs, diagrams, charts, graphs, and tables. Graphics range from realistic, such as photographs, to highly abstract, such as organization charts. In terms of function, graphics range from the decorative, such as clip art that shows people seated at a conference table, to highly informative, such as a schematic diagram of an electronic device.

Graphics are important in technical communication because they do the following:

- catch readers' attention and interest
- help writers communicate information that is difficult to communicate with words
- help writers clarify and emphasize information
- help nonnative speakers of English understand information
- help writers communicate information to multiple audiences with different interests, aptitudes, and reading habits

THE FUNCTIONS OF GRAPHICS

We have known for decades that graphics motivate people to study documents more closely. Some 83 percent of what we learn derives from what we see, whereas only 11 percent derives from what we hear (Gatlin, 1988). Because we are good at acquiring information through sight, a document that includes a visual element beyond words on the page is more effective than one that does not. People studying a text with graphics learn about one-third more than people studying a text without graphics (Levie & Lentz, 1982). And people remember 43 percent more when a document includes graphics (Morrison & Jimmerson, 1989). Readers like graphics. According to one survey, readers of computer documentation consistently want more graphics and fewer words (Brockmann, 1990, p. 203).

Graphics offer benefits that words alone cannot:

- *Graphics are indispensable in demonstrating logical and numerical relationships.* For example, an organization chart effectively represents the lines of authority in the organization. If you want to communicate the number of power plants built in each of the past 10 years, a bar graph works better than a paragraph.
- *Graphics can communicate spatial information more effectively than words alone.* If you want to show the details of a bicycle derailleur, a diagram of the bicycle with a close-up of the derailleur is more effective than a verbal description.
- *Graphics can communicate steps in a process more effectively than words alone.* A troubleshooting guide, a common kind of table, explains what might be causing a problem in a process and how you might fix it. Or a diagram can show clearly how acid rain forms.

- *Graphics can save space.* Consider the following paragraph:

> In the Wilmington area, some 90 percent of the population aged 18 to 34 watches movies on a DVD player. They watch an average of 2.86 movies a week. Among 35- to 49-year-olds, the percentage is 82, and the average number of movies is 2.19. Among the 50- to 64-year-old age group, the percentage is 67, and the number of movies watched averages 2.50. Finally, among those people 65 years old or older, the percentage is 48, and the average number of movies watched weekly is 2.71.

Presented as a paragraph, this information is uneconomical and hard to remember. Presented as a table, however, the information is more concise and more memorable.

Age	Percentage watching movies	Number of movies watched per week
18–34	90	2.86
35–49	82	2.19
50–64	67	2.50
65+	48	2.71

- *Graphics can reduce the cost of documents intended for international readers.* Translation costs can reach 30 to 40 cents per word. Used effectively, graphics can reduce the number of words you have to translate (Corante, 2005).

As you plan and draft your document, look for opportunities to use graphics to clarify, emphasize, summarize, and organize information.

CHARACTERISTICS OF AN EFFECTIVE GRAPHIC

Effective graphics must be clear, understandable, and meaningfully related to the larger discussion. Follow these five principles:

- *A graphic should serve a purpose.* Don't include a graphic unless it will help readers understand or remember information. Avoid content-free clip art, such as drawings of businesspeople shaking hands.
- *A graphic should be simple and uncluttered.* Three-dimensional bar graphs are easy to make, but they are harder to understand than two-dimensional ones, as shown in Figure 12.1 on page 300.
- *A graphic should present a manageable amount of information.* Presenting too much information can confuse readers. Consider audience and purpose: what kinds of graphics are readers familiar with, how much do they already know about the subject, and what do you want the document to do? Because readers learn best if you present information in small chunks, create several simple graphics rather than a single complicated one.
- *A graphic should meet readers' format expectations.* Through experience, readers learn how to read different kinds of graphics. Follow the

Unnecessary 3-D is one example of chartjunk, a term used by Tufte (1983) to describe the ornamentation that clutters up a graphic, distracting readers from the message.

The two-dimensional bar graph is clean and uncluttered, whereas the three-dimensional graph is more difficult to understand because the additional dimension obscures the main data points. The number of uninsured emergency-room visits in February, for example, is very difficult to see in the three-dimensional graph.

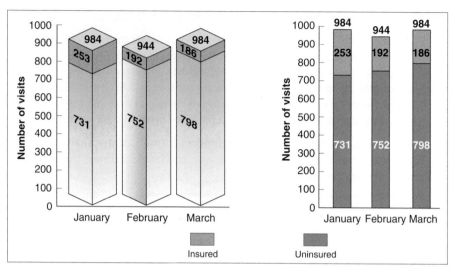

Figure 12.1　Chartjunk and Clear Art

conventions—for instance, use diamonds to represent decision points in a flowchart—unless you have a good reason not to.

- *A graphic should be clearly labeled.* Give every graphic (except a brief, informal one) a unique, clear, informative title. Fully label the columns of a table and the axes and lines of a graph. Don't make readers guess whether you are using meters or yards, or whether you are also including statistics from the previous year.

Ethics Note

Creating Honest Graphics

- If you did not create the graphic or generate the data, cite your source. If you want to publish it, obtain permission. For more on citing graphics, see page 306.

- Include all relevant data. For example, if you have a data point that you cannot explain, do not change the scale to eliminate it.

- Begin the axes in your graphs at zero—or mark them clearly—so that you represent quantities honestly.

- Do not use a table to hide a data point that would be obvious in a graph.

- Show items as they really are. Do not manipulate a photograph of a computer monitor to make the screen look bigger than it is.

- Do not use color or shading to misrepresent an item's importance. A light-shaded bar in a bar graph, for example, appears larger and nearer than a dark-shaded bar of the same size.

Common problem areas are pointed out in the discussions of various kinds of graphics throughout this chapter.

Guidelines

Integrating Graphics and Text

▶ **Place the graphic in an appropriate location.** If readers need the graphic to understand the discussion, put it directly after the relevant point in the discussion, or as soon after it as possible. If the graphic merely supports or elaborates a point, include it as an appendix.

▶ **Introduce the graphic in the text.** Whenever possible, refer to a graphic before it appears (ideally, on the same page). Refer to the graphic by number: "see Figure 7." Do not refer to "the figure above" or "the figure below," because the graphic might be moved during the production process. If the graphic is in an appendix, cross-reference it: "For complete details of the operating characteristics, see Appendix, Part B, page 19."

▶ **Explain the graphic in the text.** State what you want readers to learn from it. Sometimes a simple paraphrase of the title is enough: "Figure 2 compares the costs of the three major types of coal gasification plants." At other times, however, you might need to explain why the graphic is important or how to interpret it. If the graphic is intended to make a point, be explicit:

> As Figure 2 shows, a high-sulfur bituminous coal gasification plant is more expensive than either a low-sulfur bituminous or anthracite plant, but more than half of its cost is cleanup equipment. If these expenses could be eliminated, high-sulfur bituminous would be the least expensive of the three types of plants.

Graphics are often accompanied by captions, explanations ranging from a sentence to several paragraphs.

▶ **Make the graphic clearly visible.** Distinguish the graphic from the surrounding text by adding white space or rules (lines) or by enclosing it in a box.

▶ **Make the graphic accessible.** If the document is more than a few pages long and contains more than four or five graphics, consider including a list of illustrations so that readers can find them easily.

▶ In This Book

For more about white space and rules, see Ch. 11, pp. 265 and 275. For more about lists of illustrations, see Ch. 19, p. 513.

UNDERSTANDING THE PROCESS OF CREATING GRAPHICS

Creating graphics involves planning, creating, revising, and citing.

Planning Graphics

Whether you think first about the text or the graphics, consider the following four aspects of the document as you plan.

- *Audience.* Will readers understand the kinds of graphics you want to use? Will they know the standard icons in your field? Are they motivated to read your document, or do you need to enliven the text—for example, by adding color for emphasis—to hold their attention? General audiences know how to read common graphics, such as the types that appear frequently in newspapers. General readers, for example, could use this bar graph to compare two bottles of wine.

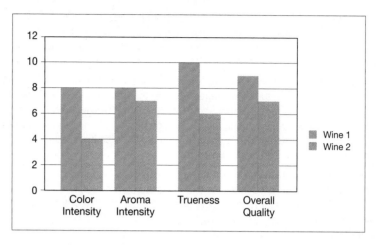

However, they would probably have trouble with the following radar graph:

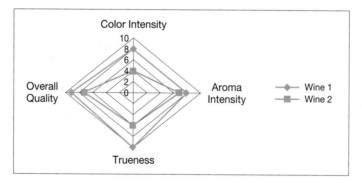

- *Purpose.* What point are you trying to make with the graphic? As Figure 12.2 shows, even a few simple facts can yield a number of different points. Your responsibility is to determine what you want to show and how best to show it. Don't rely on your software to do your thinking; it can't. Imagine what you want your readers to know and do with the information. For example, if you want readers to know the exact dollar amounts spent on athletics by a college, use a table:

Year	Men's Athletics	Women's Athletics
2005	$38,990	$29,305
2006	$42,400	$30,080
2007	$44,567	$44,213

Rail Line	November		December		January	
	Disabled by electrical problems	Total disabled	Disabled by electrical problems	Total disabled	Disabled by electrical problems	Total disabled
Bryn Mawr	19	27	17	28	20	26
Swarthmore	12	16	9	17	13	16
Manayunk	22	34	26	31	24	33

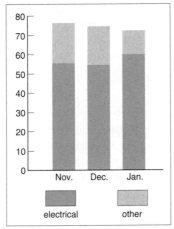

a. Number of railcars disabled,
   November–January

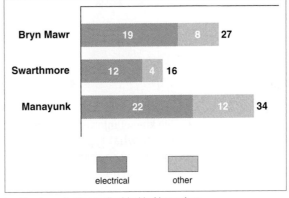

b. Number of railcars disabled in November

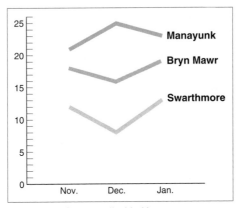

c. Number of railcars disabled by
   electrical problems, November–January

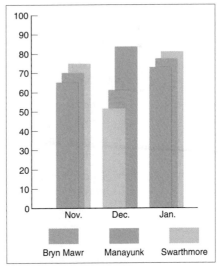

d. Range in percentage of railcars, by line, disabled
   by electrical problems, November–January

Figure 12.2   Different Graphics Emphasizing Different Points

Each of these four graphs emphasizes a different point derived from the data in the table. Graph (a) focuses on the total number of railcars disabled each month, classified by cause; graph (b) focuses on the three rail lines during one month; and so forth. For information on bar graphs, see pages 314 and 316–20; for information on line graphs, see page 323.

If you want readers to know how spending on athletics is changing over time, use a line graph.

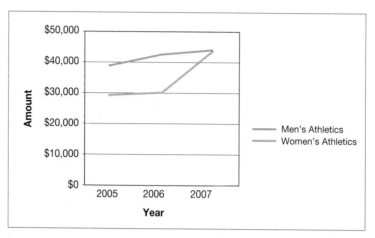

- *The kind of information you want to communicate.* Your subject will help you decide what type of graphic to include. For example, in writing about languages spoken by your state's citizens, you might use tables for the statistical data, maps for the patterns of language use, and graphs for statistical trends over time.

- *Physical conditions.* The physical conditions in which readers will use the document—amount of lighting, amount of surface space available, and so forth—will influence the type of graphic as well as its size and shape, the thickness of lines, the size of type, and the color.

As you plan how you are going to create your graphics, consider four important factors:

- *Time.* Because making a complicated graphic can take a lot of time, you need to establish a schedule.

- *Money.* A high-quality graphic can be expensive. How big is the project budget? How can you use that money effectively?

- *Equipment.* Determine what tools and software you will require, such as spreadsheets for tables and graphs or graphics software for diagrams.

- *Expertise.* How much do you know about creating graphics? Do you have access to the expertise of others?

▶ **In This Book**
For more about planning and budgeting, see Ch. 3, p. 47.

Creating Graphics

Usually, you won't have all the resources you would like. If that's the case, you will have to choose one of the following four approaches:

- *Use existing graphics.* For a student paper that *will not be published*, some instructors allow the use of photocopies or scans of existing graphics;

TECH TIP

How to Insert and Modify Graphics

To highlight, clarify, summarize, and organize information, you can insert and modify graphics by using the **Picture** button and the **Format** tab.

To **insert a graphic** that you have on file—such as a photograph, drawing, chart, or graph—place your cursor where you want to insert the graphic and then select the **Picture** button in the **Illustrations** group on the **Insert** tab.

You can also insert clip art, shapes, and SmartArt.

To **modify an image** that is already in your document, double-click on it and then use the **Format** tab. The **Format** tab allows you to modify the appearance, size, and layout of a picture.

Buttons in the **Arrange** group allow you to position your graphic and control how text wraps around it.

The **Picture Style** dialog box launcher opens the **Format Picture** dialog box, which enables you to modify the appearance of a picture.

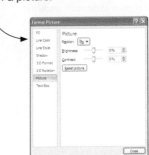

KEYWORDS: format tab, arrange group, picture style, size, insert picture, format picture, modify picture

---

other instructors do not. For a document that *will be published*, whether written by a student or a professional, using an existing graphic is permissible if the graphic is in the public domain, if it is the property of the writer's organization, or if that organization has obtained permission to use it. Be particularly careful about graphics you find on the Web. Many people mistakenly think that anything on the Web can be used without permission. The same copyright laws that apply to printed material apply to Web-based material, whether words or graphics. For more on citing graphics, see page 306.

Aside from the issue of copyright, think carefully before you use existing graphics. The style of the graphic might not match that of the others you want to use, or the graphic might lack some features you want or include others you don't want. If you use an existing graphic, assign it your own number and title.

- *Modify existing graphics.* You can redraw an existing graphic or use a scanner to digitize the graphic and then modify it electronically with graphics software.

- *Create graphics on a computer.* You can create many kinds of graphics using your spreadsheet software and the drawing tools in your word processor. Consult Selected Bibliography, page 735, for a list of books about graphics, design, and Web pages.

▶ In This Book
For more about work made for hire, see Ch. 2, p. 26.

- *Have someone else create the graphics.* Professional-level graphics software can cost hundreds of dollars and require hundreds of hours of practice. Some companies have technical-publications departments with graphics experts, but others subcontract this work. Many print shops and service bureaus have graphics experts on staff or can direct you to them.

Revising Graphics

As with any other aspect of technical communication, you need to build in enough time and budget enough money to revise the graphics. Create a checklist and evaluate each graphic for effectiveness. The Writer's Checklist at the end of this chapter is a good starting point. Show the graphics to people whose backgrounds are similar to your intended readers' and ask them for suggestions. Revise the graphics and solicit more reactions.

Citing Graphics

▶ In This Book
For more about copyright, see Ch. 2, p. 25.

If you wish to publish a graphic that is protected by copyright (even if you have revised it), you need to obtain written permission. Related to the issue of permission is the issue of citing. Of course, you do not have to cite a graphic if you created it yourself from scratch or if your organization owns the copyright.

In all other cases, however, you should include a citation, even if the document is a course assignment and will not be published. Citing graphics, even those you have revised substantially, shows your instructor that you understand professional conventions and your ethical responsibilities.

▶ In This Book
For more about style manuals, see Appendix, Part B.

If you are following a style manual, check to see whether it presents a format for citing graphics. In addition to citing a graphic in the reference list, most style manuals call for a source statement in the caption:

Print Source

Source: Verduijn, 2007, p. 14. Copyright 2007 by Tedopres International B.V. Reprinted with permission.

Online Source

Source: Johnson Space Center Digital Image Collection. Copyright 2007 by NASA. Reprinted with permission.

If your graphic is based on an existing graphic, the source statement should state that your graphic is "based on" or "adapted from" your source:

Source: Adapted from Jónklaas et al., 2008, p. 771. Copyright 2008 by *American Medical Association*. Reprinted with permission.

USING COLOR EFFECTIVELY

Color draws attention to information you want to emphasize, establishes visual patterns to promote understanding, and adds interest. But it is also easy to misuse. The following discussion is based on Jan V. White's excellent text *Color for the Electronic Age* (1990).

In using color in graphics and page design, keep these six principles in mind:

- *Don't overdo it.* Readers can interpret only two or three colors at a time. Use colors for small items, such as portions of graphics and important words. And don't use colors where black and white will work better.

- *Use color to emphasize particular items.* People interpret color before they interpret shape, size, or placement on the page. Color effectively draws readers' attention to a particular item or group of items on a page. In Figure 12.3, for example, color adds emphasis to two different kinds of items.

- *Use color to create patterns.* The principle of repetition—readers learn to recognize patterns—applies in graphics and document design. In creating patterns, also consider shape. For instance, use red for safety comments, but place them in octagons resembling a stop sign. This way, you give readers two visual cues to help them recognize the pattern. Figure 12.4 on page 308 shows a page in a biology textbook that uses color to establish patterns.

Color is also an effective way to emphasize design features such as text boxes, rules, screens, and headers and footers.

On TechComm Web

See Xerox Small Business Resource Center for articles about color theory. Click on Links Library for Ch. 12 on <bedfordstmartins.com/techcomm>.

In This Book

For more about designing your document, see Ch. 11.

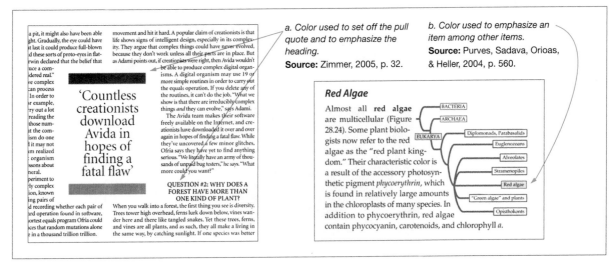

Figure 12.3   Color Used for Emphasis

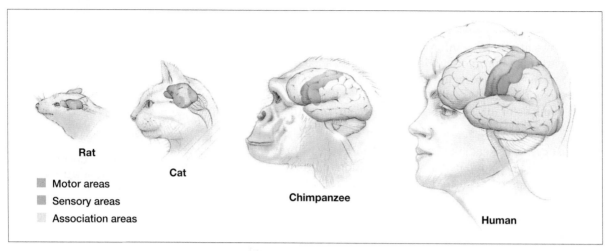

Figure 12.4   Color Used to Establish Patterns
Source: Myers, 2007, p. 79.

Notice that a color washes out if the background color is too similar.

Figure 12.5   The Effect of Background in Creating Contrast

- *Use contrast effectively.* The visibility of a color is a function of the background against which it appears (see Figure 12.5). The strongest contrasts are between black and white and between black and yellow.

  The need for effective contrast also applies to graphics used in presentations, as shown here:

⌖ **In This Book**

For more about presentation graphics, see Ch. 21, p. 584.

In graphic (a), the text is hard to read because of insufficient contrast. In graphic (b), the increased contrast makes the text easier to read.

a. Insufficient contrast   b. Effective contrast

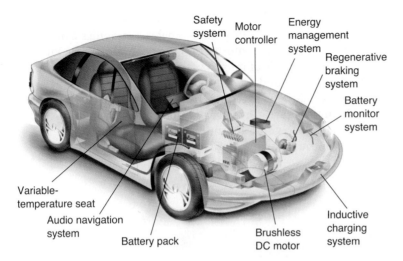

The batteries are red. The warm red contrasts effectively with the cool green of the car body.

Figure 12.6   Colors Have Clear Associations for Readers

- *Take advantage of any symbolic meanings colors may already have.* In American culture, for example, red signals danger, heat, or electricity; yellow signals caution; and orange signals warning. Using these warm colors in ways that depart from their familiar meanings could be confusing. The cooler colors—blues and greens—are more conservative and subtle. (Figure 12.6 illustrates these principles.) Keep in mind, however, that different cultures interpret colors differently.

▶ **In This Book**

For more about cultural patterns, see Ch. 5, p. 96.

- *Be aware that color can obscure or swallow up text.*

Is this text
the same size?

Is this text
the same size?

This line of type appears to reach out to the reader.
This line of type appears to recede into the background.

If you are using print against a colored background, you might need to make the type a little bigger, because color makes text look smaller.

Text printed against a white background looks bigger than the same size text printed against a colored background. White letters counteract this effect.

CHOOSING THE APPROPRIATE KIND OF GRAPHIC

Graphics used in technical documents fall into two categories: tables and figures. Tables are lists of data, usually numbers, arranged in columns. Figures are everything else: graphs, charts, diagrams, photographs, and the like. Typically, tables and figures are numbered separately: the first table in a document is Table 1; the first figure is Figure 1. In documents of more than one chapter (like this book), the graphics are usually numbered within each chapter. That is, Figure 3.2 is the second figure in Chapter 3.

There is no simple system for choosing a graphic, because in many situations several types would work. In general, however, graphics can be categorized according to the kind of information they contain. (Some kinds of graphics can convey several kinds of information. For instance, a table can include both numerical values and procedures.)

The discussion that follows is based on the classification system in William Horton's "Pictures Please—Presenting Information Visually," in *Techniques for Technical Communicators* (Barnum & Carliner, 1993). Figure 12.7 presents an overview of the following discussion.

Figure 12.7 Choosing the Appropriate Kind of Graphic (Based on Horton [1993])

Purpose	*Type of graphic*		*What the graphic does best*
Illustrating numerical information	Table	| Jan Feb Mar Total East | 14 14 10 38 West | 12 8 14 34 South | 9 15 18 42 Total | 35 37 42 114	Shows large amounts of numerical data, especially when there are several variables for a number of items
	Bar graph	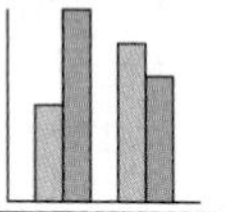	Shows the relative values of two or more items.
	Pictograph	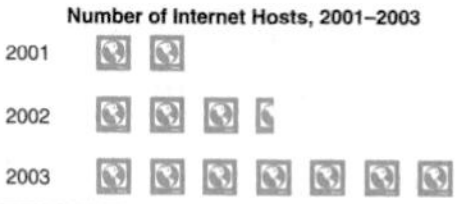	Enlivens statistical information for the general reader.
	Line graph	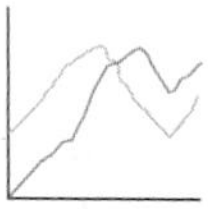	Shows how the quantity of an item changes over time. A line graph can accommodate much more data than a bar graph can.
	Pie chart	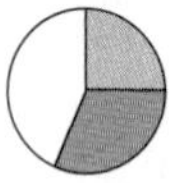	Shows the relative size of the parts of a whole. Pie charts are instantly familiar to most readers.
Illustrating logical relationships	Diagram	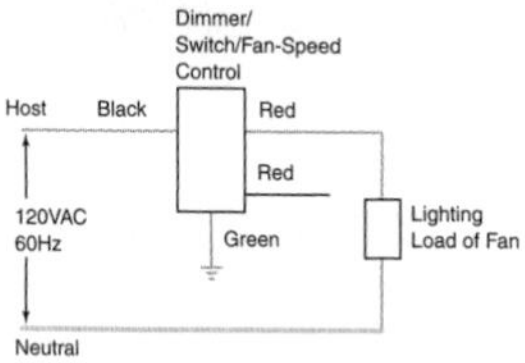	Represents items or properties of items.
	Organization chart	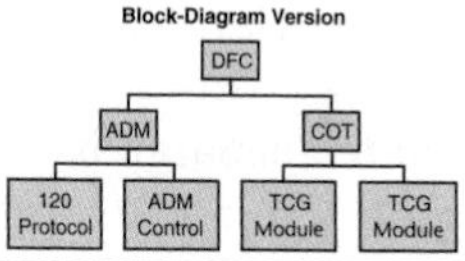	Shows the lines of authority and responsibility in an organization.

Figure 12.7   (continued)

Purpose	Type of graphic		What the graphic does best
Illustrating instructions and process descriptions	Checklist	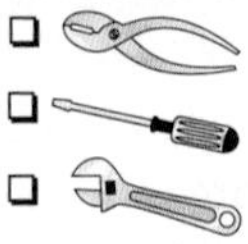	Lists or shows what equipment or materials to gather, or describes an action.
	Table	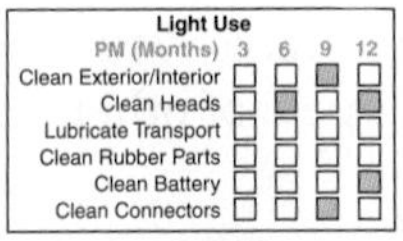	Shows numbers of items or indicates the state (on/off) of an item.
	Flowchart	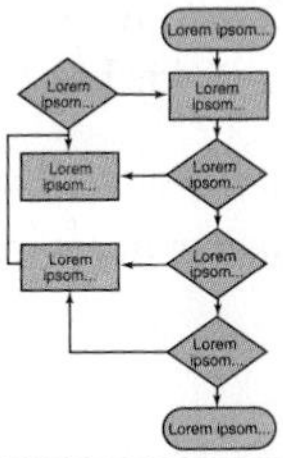	Shows the stages of a procedure or a process.
	Logic tree	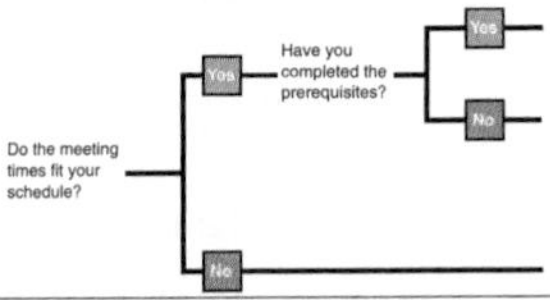	Shows which of two or more paths to follow.
Illustrating visual and spatial characteristics	Drawing	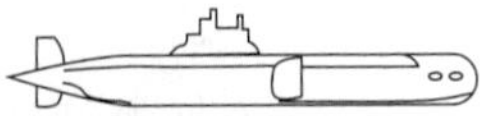	Shows simplified representations of objects.
	Map	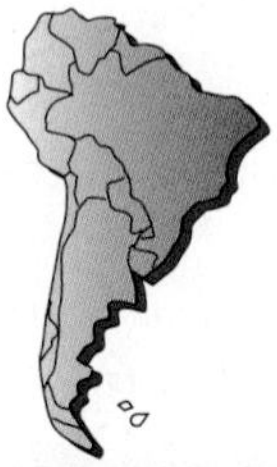	Shows geographic areas.
	Photograph		Shows precisely the external surface of objects.
	Screen shot	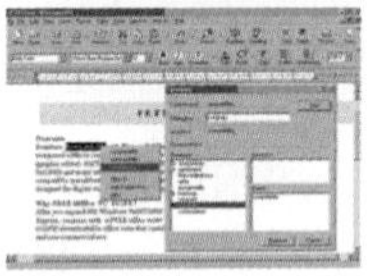	Shows what appears on a computer screen.

Illustrating Numerical Information

The kinds of graphics used most often to display numerical values are tables, bar graphs, pictographs, line graphs, and pie charts.

Tables   Tables convey large amounts of numerical data easily, and they are often the only way to present several variables for a number of items. For example, if you want to show how many people are employed in six industries in 10 states, a table would probably be most effective. Although tables lack the visual appeal of other kinds of graphics, they can handle much more information.

Figure 12.8 illustrates the standard parts of a table. Tables are identified by number ("Table 1") and an informative title that includes the items being compared and the basis (or bases) of comparison:

Table 3. Mallard Population in Rangeley, 2007–2008

Table 4.7. The Growth of the Robotics Industry in Japan and the United States, 2007

Table number
Table title
Column heads
Column subheads
Row
Data cell
Stub
Source statement
Caption

■ TABLE 19-1

Effective Tax Rates

	1979	1985	1990	1995	2000	2003
	Total effective tax rate					
All households	22.2%	20.9%	21.5%	22.6%	23.0%	19.8%
Bottom quintile	8.0%	9.8%	8.9%	6.3%	6.4%	4.8%
Top quintile	27.5%	24.0%	25.1%	27.8%	28.0%	25.0%
	Effective income tax rate					
All households	11.0%	10.2%	10.1%	10.2%	11.8%	8.5%
Bottom quintile	0.0%	0.5%	−1.0%	−4.4%	−4.6%	−5.9%
Top quintile	15.7%	14.0%	14.4%	15.5%	17.5%	13.9%
	Effective payroll tax rate					
All households	6.9%	7.9%	8.4%	8.5%	7.9%	8.4%
Bottom quintile	5.3%	6.6%	7.3%	7.6%	8.2%	8.1%
Top quintile	5.4%	6.5%	6.9%	7.2%	6.3%	7.2%
	Effective corporate tax rate					
All households	3.4%	1.8%	2.2%	2.8%	2.4%	2.0%
Bottom quintile	1.1%	0.6%	0.6%	0.7%	0.5%	0.3%
Top quintile	5.7%	2.8%	3.3%	4.4%	3.7%	3.4%
	Effective excise tax rate					
All households	1.0%	0.9%	0.9%	1.0%	0.9%	0.8%
Bottom quintile	1.6%	2.2%	2.0%	2.4%	2.3%	2.3%
Top quintile	0.7%	0.7%	0.6%	0.7%	0.5%	0.5%

Congressional Budget Office (2005), Table 1A.

The top panel of this table shows the total effective federal tax rate on all households and on the top and bottom quintiles of the income distribution. The other panels show the effective tax rates of various other types of federal taxes.

The data in this table consist of numbers, but tables can also present textual information or a combination of numbers and text.

Tables are usually titled at the top because readers scan them from top to bottom. This table should contain a more complete title: Effective Tax Rates, 1979–2003.

Include a stub head. The stub—the left-hand column—lists the items for which data are displayed. The stub head in this table should be "Households."

Notice that a screen is used behind the column subheads for emphasis.

In most cases, the caption is placed directly after the table title. The writer here places it beneath the table.

Figure 12.8   Parts of a Table
Source: Gruber, 2008, p. 570.

Guidelines

Creating Effective Tables

▶ **Indicate the units of measure.** If all the data are expressed in the same unit, indicate that unit in the title:

> Farm Size in the Midwestern States (in hectares)

If the data in different columns are expressed in different units, indicate the units in the column heads:

| Population (in millions) | Per Capita Income (in thousands of U.S. dollars) |

If all the *data cells* in a column use the same unit, indicate that unit in the column head, not in each data cell:

> Speed (knots)
>
> 15
> 18
> 14

You can express data in both real numbers and percentages. A column head and the first data cell under it might read as follows:

> Number of Students (Percentage)
>
> 53 (83)

▶ **In the stub (the left-hand column) list the items being compared.** Arrange the items in a logical order: big to small, important to unimportant, alphabetical, chronological, geographical, and so forth. If the items fall into several categories, include the names of the categories in the stub:

> *Snowbelt States* . . . .
>   Connecticut . . . .
>   New York . . . .
>   Vermont . . . .
>
> *Sunbelt States* . . . .
>   Arizona . . . .
>   California . . . .
>   New Mexico . . . .

If the items in the stub are not grouped in logical categories, skip a line after every five rows to help readers follow the rows across the table. Or use a screen or a colored background for every other set of five rows. Also useful are dot leaders—a row of dots that links the stub and the next column (as shown above).

▶ **In the other columns, arrange the data clearly and logically.** Use the decimal-tab feature to line up the decimal points:

> 3,147.4
>   365.7
> 46,803.5

▶ **In This Book**

For more about screens, see Ch. 11, p. 277.

In general, don't change units unless the quantities are so dissimilar that readers would have a difficult time understanding them if expressed in the same units.

3.4 hr
12.7 min
4.3 sec

This list would probably be easier for most readers to understand than one in which all quantities were expressed in the same unit.

▶ **Do the math.** If readers will need to know the totals for the columns or the rows, provide them. If readers will need to know percentage changes from one column to the next, present them:

Number of Students (Percentage Change from Previous Year)

2007	2008	2009
619	644 (+4.0)	614 (−4.7)

▶ **Use dot leaders if a column contains a "blank" spot—a place where there are no appropriate data:**

3,147
. . .
46,803

But don't substitute dot leaders for a quantity of zero.

▶ **Don't make the table wider than it needs to be.** Readers should be able to scan across a row easily. As White (1984) points out, there is no reason to make the table as wide as the text column in the document. If a column head is long—more than five or six words—stack the words:

Computers Sold
Without a CD-RW Drive

▶ **Minimize the use of rules.** Grimstead (1987) recommends using rules only when necessary: to separate the title and the heads, the heads and the body, and the body and the notes. When you use rules, make them thin rather than thick.

▶ **Provide footnotes where necessary.** All the information readers need to understand the table should accompany it.

▶ **If you did not generate the information yourself, indicate your source.** See the discussion of citing graphics on page 306.

Bar Graphs   Like tables, bar graphs can communicate numerical values, but they are better at showing the relative values of two or more items. Figure 12.9 on page 316 shows typical horizontal and vertical bar graphs that you can make easily using your spreadsheet. Figure 12.10 on page 316 shows an effective bar graph that uses grid lines.

TECH TIP

How to Use Tab Stops

To control the placement of text on a page or in a table, you can align text by using the **tab stops** in the **horizontal ruler**.

For example, use the **decimal tab** to align numbers in a column:

Incorrectly Aligned	Correctly Aligned
213.76	213.76
3.17	3.17
46.13	46.13

1. Click the **tab indicator** on the horizontal ruler to change the type of tab stop displayed.

The following table describes common tab stops.

Tab stop	Description
	Lines up text to the left
	Lines up text to the right
	Centers text at tab stop
	Aligns numbers on their decimal points

2. When the appropriate tab stop appears, click the horizontal ruler where you want to align the text.

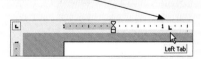

To remove a tab stop, drag it away from the ruler.

3. After you have set a tab stop, place the cursor to the left of the text you want to align and press the **Tab key**.

KEYWORDS: set tab stops, horizontal ruler, indent text or numbers in a table

TECH TIP

How to Create Tables

To create tables, use the **Table** feature.

To **create a table**, place your cursor where you want to create a table and then use the **Table** button on the **Insert** tab.

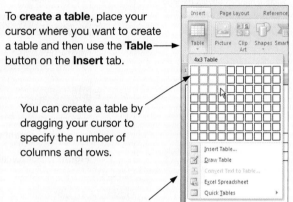

You can create a table by dragging your cursor to specify the number of columns and rows.

You can also insert or create a table by drawing the table grid, converting existing text into a table, importing data from Excel, or selecting a **Quick Tables** template and replacing the data with your own.

You can use the **Insert Table** dialog box to specify the number of columns and rows.

To **modify a table**, double-click on it, then use the **Table Styles** group on the **Design** tab.

KEYWORDS: tables, tables and borders, insert table, insert tab, AutoFit, merge cells, split cells

Horizontal bars are best for showing quantities such as speed and distance. Vertical bars are best for showing quantities such as height, size, and amount. However, these distinctions are not ironclad; as long as the axes are clearly labeled, readers should have no trouble understanding the graph.

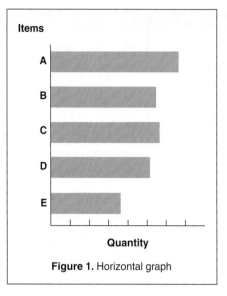

Figure 1. Horizontal graph

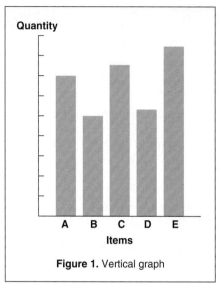

Figure 1. Vertical graph

Figure 12.9   Structures of Horizontal and Vertical Bar Graphs

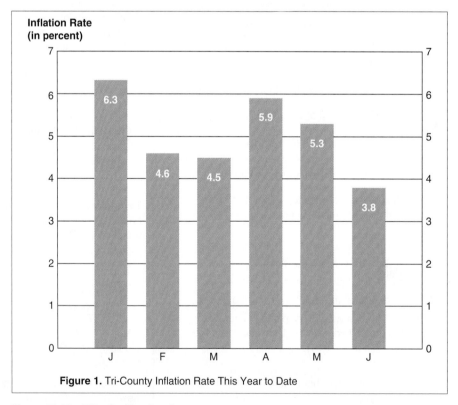

Figure 1. Tri-County Inflation Rate This Year to Date

Figure 12.10   Effective Bar Graph

TECH TIP

How to Create Graphics in Excel

You can create many types of graphics discussed in this chapter using a spreadsheet program such as Microsoft Excel. First you enter the data that the graphic will display; then you select the type of graphic to create.

1. After you have entered your data in a spreadsheet, select the type of graphic by using the drop-down menus in the **Charts** group on the **Insert** tab.

You may also select the **Chart** dialog box launcher in the **Charts** group and then select the type of graphic using the **Insert Chart** dialog box.

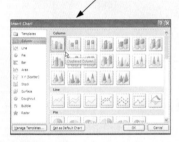

2. After you have created your graphic, you may modify the data range included and add or modify elements such as a title, labels, a legend, and grid lines by using the **Design** and **Layout** tabs.

After creating a graphic, you can use the **Copy** and **Paste** commands to insert your graphic in your document.

▶ **On TechComm Web**

For more help with displaying data graphically, click on Tutorials on <bedfordstmartins.com/techcomm>.

KEYWORDS: chart wizard, chart type, data series, data range, data labels, legends

Guidelines

Creating Effective Bar Graphs

▶ **Make the proportions fair.** Make your vertical axis about 25 percent shorter than your horizontal axis. An excessively long vertical axis exaggerates the differences in quantities; an excessively long horizontal axis minimizes the differences. Make all the bars the same width, and make the space between them about half as wide as a bar. Here are two poorly proportioned graphs.

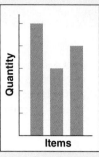

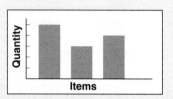

a. Excessively long vertical axis   b. Excessively long horizontal axis

▶ **If possible, begin the quantity scale at zero.** Doing so ensures that the bars accurately represent the quantities. Notice how misleading a graph can be if the scale doesn't begin at zero.

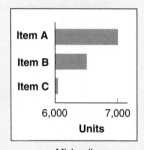

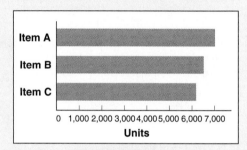

a. Misleading   b. Accurately representative

If it is not practical to start the quantity scale at zero, break the quantity axis clearly at a common point on all the bars.

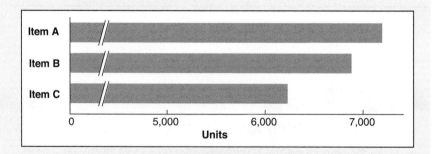

▶ **Use tick marks—marks along the axis—to signal the amounts.** Use grid lines—tick marks that extend through the bars—if the table has several bars, some of which are too far away from the tick marks to allow readers to gauge the quantities easily. (See Figure 12.10 on page 316.)

▶ **Arrange the bars in a logical sequence.** For a vertical bar graph, use chronology if possible. For a horizontal bar graph, arrange the bars in order of descending size, beginning at the top of the graph, unless some other logical sequence seems more appropriate.

▶ **Place the title below the figure.** Unlike tables, which are usually read from top to bottom, figures are usually read from the bottom up.

▶ **Indicate the source of your information if you did not generate it yourself.**

The five variations on the basic bar graph shown in Table 12.1 can help you accommodate different communication needs. You can make all these types using your spreadsheet.

Table 12.1 Variations on the Basic Bar Graph

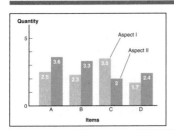

Grouped bar graph. The *grouped* bar graph lets you compare two or three quantities for each item. Grouped bar graphs would be useful, for example, for showing the numbers of full-time and part-time students at several universities. One bar could represent full-time students; the other, part-time students. To distinguish between the bars, use hatching (striping), shading, or color, and either label one set of bars or provide a key.

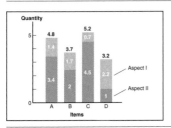

Subdivided bar graph. In the *subdivided* bar graph, Aspect I and Aspect II are stacked like wooden blocks placed on top of one another. Although totals are easy to compare in a subdivided bar graph, individual quantities are not.

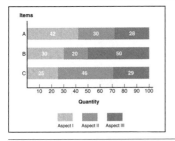

100-percent bar graph. The *100-percent* bar graph, which shows the relative proportions of the elements that make up several items, is useful in portraying, for example, the proportion of full-scholarship, partial-scholarship, and no-scholarship students at a number of colleges.

Table 12.1 (continued)

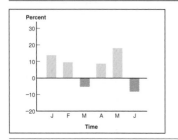

Deviation bar graph. The *deviation* bar graph shows how various quantities deviate from a norm. Deviation bar graphs are often used when the information contains both positive and negative values, such as profits and losses. Bars on the positive side of the norm line represent profits; bars on the negative side, losses.

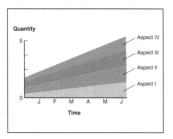

Stratum graph. The *stratum graph*, also called an *area graph*, shows the change in quantities of several items over time. Although stratum graphs are used frequently in business and scientific fields, general readers sometimes have trouble understanding how to read them.

Pictographs   Pictographs—bar graphs in which the bars are replaced by a series of symbols—are used primarily to present statistical information to general readers. The quantity scale is usually replaced by a statement indicating the numerical value of each symbol. Thousands of clip-art symbols and pictures are available for use in pictographs. Figure 12.11 shows an example.

Represent quantities in a pictograph honestly. Figure 12.12 shows an inherent problem: a picture drawn to scale can appear many times larger than it should.

Clip-art pictures and symbols are available online for use in pictographs. Arrange pictographs horizontally rather than vertically.

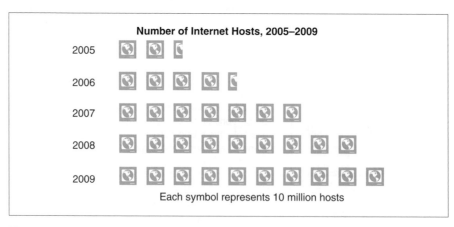

Figure 12.11 Pictograph

TECH TIP

How to Use Drawing Tools

Although you can make many types of graphics using a spreadsheet, some types, such as pictographs, call for drawing tools. Your word processor includes basic drawing tools.

To **create shapes** and **SmartArt**, use the **Illustrations** group.

Use the **Shapes** drop-down menu to select a shape, such as a line, arrow, rectangle, or oval, then drag your cursor to create the shape.

You can also select complex shapes from the **SmartArt** drop-down menu in the **Illustrations** group.

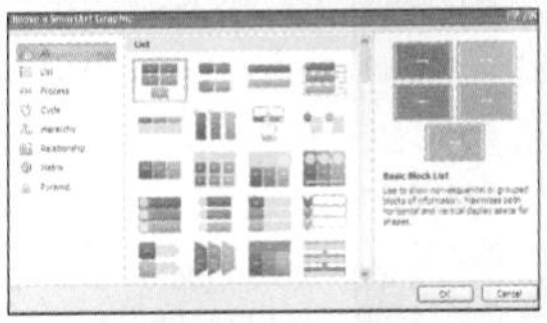

Once you have created a shape, you can position the shape on your document by selecting and dragging it.

To **modify a shape**, double-click on it and use the **Format** tab.

Groups on the **Format** tab allow you to modify the appearance, size, and layout of a shape.

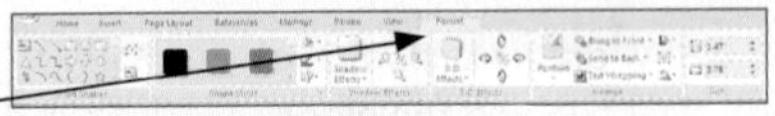

KEYWORDS: shapes, illustrations group, SmartArt, format tab

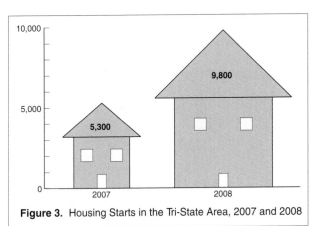

The reader sees the total area of the symbol rather than its height.

Figure 3. Housing Starts in the Tri-State Area, 2007 and 2008

Figure 12.12　Misleading Pictograph

INTERACTIVE SAMPLE DOCUMENT

Balancing Clarity and Drama in Graphics

The following graphic, a bar graph accompanied by a drawing, is included on a Web site addressed to general readers. The questions in the margin ask you to think about the principles of graphics (page 299), color (page 307), and bar graphs (page 317). E-mail your responses to yourself and/or your instructor on TechComm Web.

1. How effectively has the designer used the two colors?

2. How do the drawings of the child and the elderly man help communicate the point?

3. Create a rough sketch of a graph that communicates the text on the right. Should this information be communicated in words or in a graphic? Why?

On TechComm Web

To e-mail your responses to yourself and/or your instructor, click on Interactive Sample Documents for Ch. 12 on <bedfordstmartins.com/techcomm>.

Really young vs. really old

The most rapidly growing group of Americans is aged 80 or above.

The population under age 5

Age 80+

It's projected that by the time the youngest becomes age 65 in 2029, almost 20% of Americans will be elderly—2.5 times the proportion in 1950.

1995

2040

Source: Holmes & Bagby, 2002 <www.understandingusa.com/chaptercc=2&cs=18.html>.

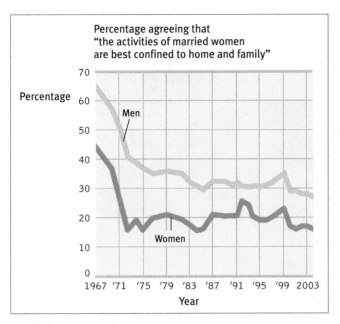

Figure 12.13   Line Graph
Source: Myers, 2007, p. 132.

Using different colors for the lines helps readers distinguish them.

If you can put the labels near the lines themselves, as this writer has done with "Men" and "Women," readers do not have to look elsewhere to see what the lines represent. If you cannot put the labels near the lines, let your software create a legend off to the side that explains what the lines represent.

Line Graphs   Line graphs are used almost exclusively to show changes in quantity over time—for example, the month-by-month production figures for a product. A line graph focuses readers' attention on a change in quantity, whereas a bar graph emphasizes the quantities themselves.

You can plot three or four lines on a line graph. If the lines intersect, use different colors or patterns to distinguish them. If the lines intersect too often, however, the graph will be unclear; in this case, draw separate graphs. Figure 12.13 shows a line graph.

Guidelines

Creating Effective Line Graphs

▶ **If possible, begin the quantity scale at zero.** Doing so is the best way to portray the information honestly. If you cannot begin at zero, clearly indicate a break in the axis.

▶ **Use reasonable proportions for the vertical and horizontal axes.** As with bar graphs, make the vertical axis about 25 percent shorter than the horizontal axis.

▶ **Use grid lines—horizontal, vertical, or both—rather than tick marks when readers need to read the quantities precisely.**

Pie charts are often used to show how proportions of quantities that make up a whole change over time.

Note that the labels are presented within the slices when they will fit and outside the slices when they will not.

Your spreadsheet will automatically maintain consistent colors for the slices from one pie chart to the next in a set of charts like this.

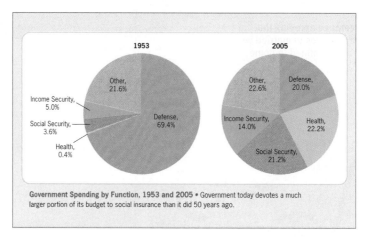

Government Spending by Function, 1953 and 2005 • Government today devotes a much larger portion of its budget to social insurance than it did 50 years ago.

Figure 12.14   Pie Charts
Source: Gruber, 2008, p. 315.

Pie Charts   The pie chart is a simple but limited design used for showing the relative size of the parts of a whole. You can make pie charts with your spreadsheet. Figure 12.14 shows typical examples.

Guidelines

Creating Effective Pie Charts

▶ **Restrict the number of slices to six or seven.** As the slices get smaller, judging their relative sizes becomes more difficult.

▶ **Begin with the largest slice at the top and work clockwise in decreasing order, unless you have a good reason to arrange them otherwise.**

▶ **Include a miscellaneous slice for very small quantities that would make the chart unclear.** Explain its contents in a footnote. This slice, sometimes called "other," follows the other sections.

▶ **Label the slices (horizontally, not radially) inside the slice, if space permits.** Include the percentage that each slice represents and, if appropriate, the raw numbers.

▶ **To emphasize one slice, use a bright, contrasting color or separate the slice from the pie.** Do this, for example, when you introduce a discussion of the item represented by that slice.

▶ **Check to see that your software follows the appropriate guidelines for pie charts.** Some spreadsheets add fancy visual effects that can hurt comprehension. For instance, many spreadsheets portray the pie in three dimensions, as shown here.

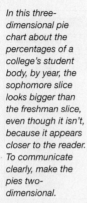

In this three-dimensional pie chart about the percentages of a college's student body, by year, the sophomore slice looks bigger than the freshman slice, even though it isn't, because it appears closer to the reader. To communicate clearly, make the pies two-dimensional.

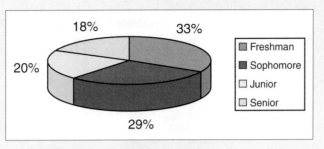

▶ **Don't overdo fill patterns.** Fill patterns are designs, shades, or colors that distinguish one slice from another. In general, use simple, understated patterns, or none at all.

▶ **Check that your percentages add up to 100.** If you are doing the calculations yourself, check your math.

Illustrating Logical Relationships

Graphics can help you present logical relationships among items. For instance, in describing a piece of hardware, you might want to show its major components. The two kinds of graphics that best show logical relationships are diagrams and organization charts.

Diagrams   A diagram is a visual metaphor that uses symbols to represent items or their properties. In technical communication, common kinds of diagrams are blueprints, wiring diagrams, and schematics. Figure 12.15 on page 326 is a diagram.

Organization Charts   A popular form of diagram is the organization chart, in which simple geometric shapes, usually rectangles, suggest logical relationships, as shown in Figure 12.16 on page 326. The drawing program in your word processor can create organization charts.

Illustrating Process Descriptions and Instructions

Graphics often accompany process descriptions and instructions (see Chapter 20). The following discussion looks at some of the graphics used in writing about actions: checklists, tables, flowcharts, and logic trees.

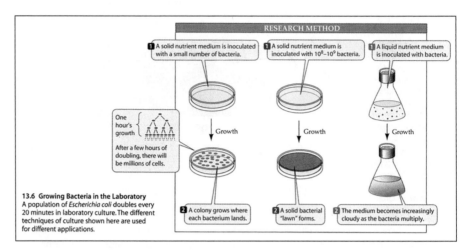

Figure 12.15   Diagram
Source: Purves et al., 2004, p. 264.

An organization chart is often used to show the hierarchy in an organization, with the president of a company, for example, in the box at the top.

Alternatively, as shown here, an organization chart can show the functional divisions of a system, such as the human nervous system.

Note that the two boxes at the bottom should be drawn so that they align clearly under "Autonomic." As drawn here, they appear to align under "Autonomic" and "Somatic."

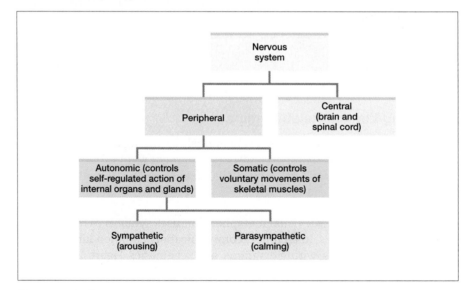

Figure 12.16   Organization Chart
Source: Myers, 2007, p. 61.

Checklists   In explaining how to carry out a task, you often need to show readers what equipment or materials to gather, or describe an action or series of actions to take. A checklist is a list of items, each preceded by a check box. If readers might be unfamiliar with the items you are listing, include drawings of the items, as shown in Figure 12.17. The list function in your word processor can create check boxes.

Often, you need to indicate that readers are to carry out certain tasks at certain intervals. A table is a useful graphic for this kind of information, as illustrated in Figure 12.18.

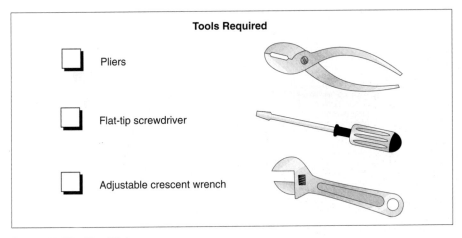

Figure 12.17   Checklist

Regular Maintenance, First 40,000 Miles

	Mileage							
	5,000	*10,000*	*15,000*	*20,000*	*25,000*	*30,000*	*35,000*	*40,000*
change oil, replace filter	✓	✓	✓	✓	✓	✓	✓	✓
rotate tires	✓	✓	✓	✓	✓	✓	✓	✓
replace air filter				✓				✓
replace spark plugs				✓				✓
replace coolant fluid								✓
replace ignition cables								✓
replace timing belt								✓

Figure 12.18   A Table Used to Illustrate a Maintenance Schedule

Flowcharts   A flowchart, as the name suggests, shows the various stages of a process or procedure. Flowcharts are useful, too, for summarizing instructions. In a basic flowchart, stages are represented by labeled geometric shapes. Flowcharts can portray open systems (those that have a "start" and a "finish") or closed systems (those that end where they began). Figure 12.19 on page 328 shows an open-system flowchart and a closed-system flowchart.

Figure 12.20 on page 328 shows a deployment flowchart, which you can make using the drawing tools in your word processor.

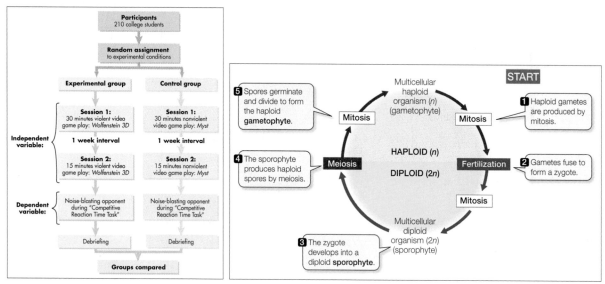

a. Open-system flowchart

b. Closed-system flowchart

Figure 12.19   Flowcharts
Source: (left) Hockenbury & Hockenbury, 2007; (right) Purves, Sadava, Orians & Heller, 2007.

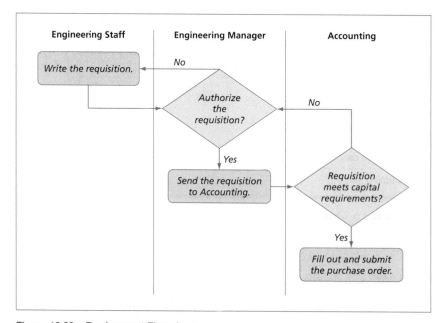

A deployment flowchart shows who is responsible for carrying out which tasks. Here the engineering staff writes the requisition, then sends it to the Engineering Manager.

Figure 12.20   Deployment Flowchart

Logic Trees   Logic trees use a branching metaphor. The logic tree shown in Figure 12.21 helps students think through the process of registering for a course.

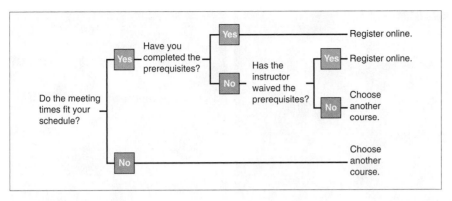

Figure 12.21   Logic Tree

Illustrating Visual and Spatial Characteristics

To illustrate visual and spatial characteristics, use photographs, screen shots, line drawings, and maps.

Photographs   Photographs are unmatched for reproducing visual detail. Sometimes, however, a photograph can provide too much information. In a sales brochure for an automobile, a glossy photograph of the dashboard might be very effective. But in an owner's manual, if you want to show how to use the trip odometer, use a diagram that focuses on that one item.

Sometimes a photograph can provide too little information. The item you want to highlight might be located inside the mechanism or obscured by another component.

Guidelines

Presenting Photographs Effectively

▶ **Eliminate extraneous background clutter that can distract readers.** Crop the photograph or digitize it and delete unnecessary detail. Figure 12.22 on page 330 shows examples of cropped and uncropped photographs.

▶ **Do not electronically manipulate the photograph.** There is nothing unethical about digitizing a photograph, removing blemishes, and cropping it. However, manipulating a photograph—for example, enlarging the size of the monitor that comes with a computer system—is unethical.

▶ **Help readers understand the perspective.** Most objects in magazines and journals are photographed at an angle to show the object's depth as well as its height and width.

▶ **If appropriate, include some common object, such as a coin or a ruler, in the photograph to give readers a sense of scale.**

▶ **If appropriate, label components or important features.**

Cropping a photograph lets you direct the reader's attention to the information you wish to emphasize. The image on the right is a cropped and enlarged version of the photo on the left.

The original version emphasizes the vastness of space; the cropped version emphasizes the shape of the space station.

Figure 12.22   Cropping a Photograph
Source: NASA, 2004 <http://spaceflight.nasa.gov/gallery/images/station/crew9/html/iss009e05034.html>.

Screen Shots   Screen shots—images of what appears on a computer monitor—are often used in software manuals to show readers what the screen looks like at various points during the use of a program. Figure 12.23 is an example of a screen shot.

In this screen shot from a tutorial, the image is grayed out, except for the portion of the screen that the writer wishes to emphasize. Notice that the cursor points to the important portion of the screen.

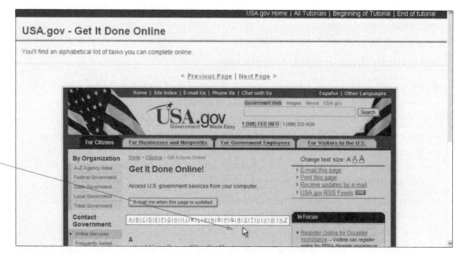

Figure 12.23   Screen Shot
Source: USA.gov, 2008 <www.usa.gov/tutorials/online/done_online_2.html>.

TECH TIP

How to Create Screen Shots

To show readers what appears on a computer monitor, you can create a **screen shot** of an entire screen or just an active window using the **Print Screen** feature of your computer.

To **create a screen shot of the entire screen**, press the **Print Screen** key on your keyboard.

To **create a screen shot of an active window**, click in the window you wish to copy and then simultaneously press the **Alt** and **Print Screen** keys on your keyboard.

An active window has a dark blue border. ——

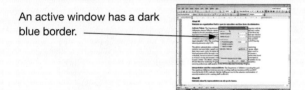

After you have copied a screen or window, open your document, click where you want to insert the shot, and then select **Paste** from the **Home** tab.

You can modify screen shots already placed in your document by using the **Format** tab. For example, you can use the **Crop** tool in the **Size** group to hide unnecessary details.

If you plan to create many screen shots, you should consider using software designed to capture and edit images efficiently on a computer screen. Search the Internet for "screen capture software," such as TechSmith's SnagIt.

KEYWORDS: screen shots, format tab, crop

Line Drawings   Line drawings are simplified visual representations of objects. Line drawings can have three advantages over photographs:

- Line drawings can focus readers' attention on desired information better than a photograph can.

- Line drawings can highlight information that might be obscured by bad lighting or a bad angle in a photograph.

- Line drawings can be easier for readers to understand than photographs are.

Figure 12.24 on page 332 shows the effectiveness of a line drawing.

You have probably seen the three variations on the basic line drawing shown in Figure 12.25 on page 332.

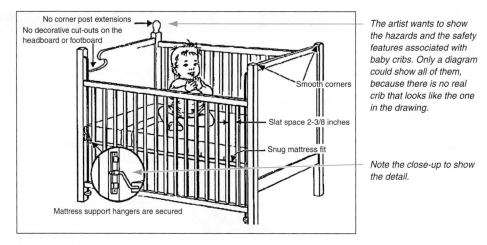

No corner post extensions
No decorative cut-outs on the
headboard or footboard

Smooth corners

Slat space 2-3/8 inches

Snug mattress fit

Mattress support hangers are secured

*The artist wants to show
the hazards and the safety
features associated with
baby cribs. Only a diagram
could show all of them,
because there is no real
crib that looks like the one
in the drawing.*

*Note the close-up to show
the detail.*

Figure 12.24   Line Drawing
Source: U.S. Consumer Product Safety Commission, 1999 <www.cpsc.gov/cpscpub/pubs/usedcrib.pdf>.

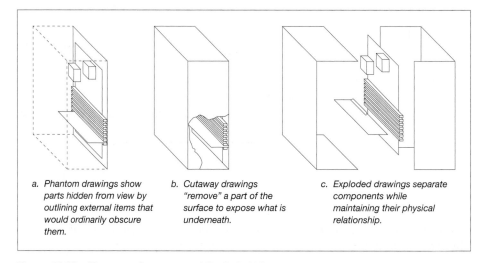

*a. Phantom drawings show
parts hidden from view by
outlining external items that
would ordinarily obscure
them.*

*b. Cutaway drawings
"remove" a part of the
surface to expose what is
underneath.*

*c. Exploded drawings separate
components while
maintaining their physical
relationship.*

Figure 12.25   Phantom, Cutaway, and Exploded Views

Maps   Maps are readily available as clip art that can be modified with a graphics program. Figure 12.26 shows a map derived from clip art.

Showing Motion in Graphics

You will often want to show motion in technical documents. For instance, in an instruction manual for helicopter technicians, you might want to illustrate the process of removing an oil dipstick or tightening a bolt, or you might want to show a warning light flashing. Although document designers

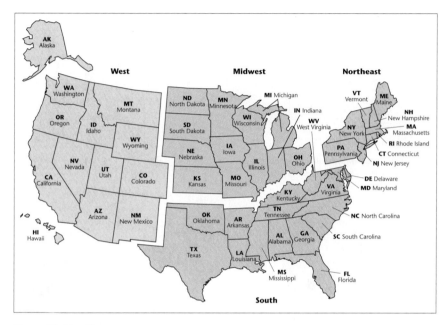

Include a scale and a legend if the map is one that is not thoroughly familiar to your readers. Also, use conventional colors, such as blue for water.

Figure 12.26   Map

frequently use animation or video, printed graphics are still needed to communicate this kind of information.

If the reader is to perform the action, show the action from the reader's point of view, as in Figure 12.27.

Figure 12.28 on page 334 illustrates four additional techniques for showing motion. These techniques are conventional but not universal. If you are addressing readers from another culture, consult a qualified person from that culture to make sure your symbols are clear and inoffensive.

Creating Effective Graphics for Multicultural Readers

Whether you are writing for people within your organization or outside it, consider the needs of readers whose first language is different from your own. Like words, graphics have cultural meanings. If you are unaware of these meanings, you could communicate something very different from what you intend. The following guidelines are based on William Horton's (1993) article "The Almost Universal Language: Graphics for International Documents."

- *Be aware that reading patterns differ.* In some countries, people read from right to left or from top to bottom. In some cultures, direction signifies value: the right-hand side is superior to the left, or the reverse. You need to think about how to sequence graphics that show action, or where you

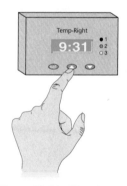

Figure 12.27   Showing Action from the Reader's Perspective

In many cases, you need to show only the person's hands, not the whole body.

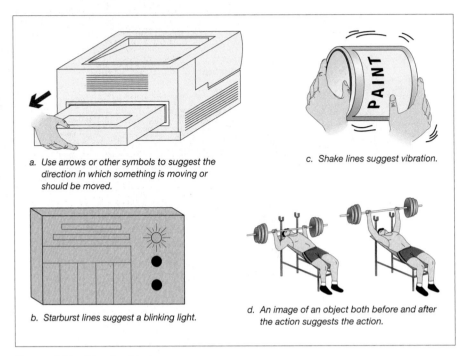

a. *Use arrows or other symbols to suggest the direction in which something is moving or should be moved.*

c. *Shake lines suggest vibration.*

b. *Starburst lines suggest a blinking light.*

d. *An image of an object both before and after the action suggests the action.*

Figure 12.28   Showing Motion

put "before" and "after" graphics. If you want to show a direction, as in an informal flowchart, consider using arrows to indicate how to read the chart.

- *Be aware of varying cultural attitudes toward giving instructions.* Instructions for products made in Japan are highly polite and deferential: "Please attach the cable at this time." Some cultures favor spelling out general principles but leaving readers to supply the details. For people in these cultures, instructions containing a detailed close-up of how to carry out a task might appear insulting.

- *Deemphasize trivial details.* Because common objects, such as plugs on the ends of power cords, come in different shapes around the world, draw them to look generic rather than specific to one country.

- *Avoid culture-specific language, symbols, and references.* Don't use a picture of a mouse to symbolize a computer mouse because the device is not known by that name everywhere. Avoid the casual use of national symbols (such as the maple leaf or national flags) because you might make an error in a detail that would insult readers. Use colors carefully: red means danger to most people from Western cultures, but it is a celebratory color to the Chinese.

- *Portray people very carefully.* Every aspect of a person's appearance, from clothing to hairstyle to features, is culture or race specific. A photograph of a woman in casual Western attire seated at a workstation would be ineffective in an Islamic culture, where only the hands and eyes of women may be shown. Horton (1993) recommends using stick figures or silhouettes that do not suggest any one culture, race, or sex.

- *Be particularly careful in portraying hand gestures.* Many Western hand gestures, such as the "okay" sign, are considered obscene in other cultures, and long red fingernails are inappropriate. Use hands in graphics only when necessary—for example, carrying out a task—and obscure the person's sex and race.

Cultural differences are many and subtle. Learn as much as possible about your readers and about their culture and outlook, and have the graphics reviewed by a native of the culture.

Writer's Checklist

This checklist focuses on the characteristics of an effective graphic.

- ☐ Does the graphic have a purpose? (p. 299)
- ☐ Is the graphic honest? (p. 300)
- ☐ Is the graphic simple and uncluttered? (p. 299)
- ☐ Does the graphic present a manageable amount of information? (p. 299)
- ☐ Does the graphic meet readers' format expectations? (p. 299)
- ☐ Is the graphic clearly labeled? (p. 300)
- ☐ For an existing graphic, do you have the legal right to use it? (p. 304) If so, have you cited it appropriately? (p. 306)

- ☐ Does the graphic appear in a logical location in the document? (p. 301)
- ☐ Is the graphic introduced clearly in the text? (p. 301)
- ☐ Is the graphic explained in the text? (p. 301)
- ☐ Is the graphic clearly visible in the text? (p. 301)
- ☐ Is the graphic easily accessible to your readers? (p. 301)
- ☐ Is the graphic inoffensive to your readers? (p. 301)

Exercises

1. Find out from the admissions department at your college or university the number of students enrolled from the different states or from the different counties in your state. Present this information in four different kinds of graphics:

   a. map

   b. table

   c. bar graph

   d. pie chart

   In three or four paragraphs, explain why each graphic is appropriate for a particular audience and purpose and how each emphasizes different aspects of the information.

2. Design a flowchart for a process you are familiar with, such as applying for a summer job, studying for a test, preparing a paper, or performing some task at work. Your audience is someone who will be carrying out the process.

3. The following table (U.S. Census, 2007, p. 119) provides statistics on injuries. Study the table, then perform the following tasks:

a. Create two different graphics, each of which communicates information about the cost of lost wages and productivity.

b. Create two different graphics, each of which compares wage and productivity losses to the total of other losses due to unintentional injuries.

Table 174. Costs of Unintentional Injuries: 2004

[**574.8 represents** $574,800,000,000. Covers costs of deaths or disabling injuries together with vehicle accidents and fires]

Cost	Amount (bil. dol.)					Percent distribution				
	Total [1]	Motor vehicle	Work	Home	Other	Total [1]	Motor vehicle	Work	Home	Other
Total	574.8	240.6	142.2	129.0	83.4	100.0	100.0	100.0	100.0	100.0
Wage and productivity losses [2]	298.4	86.4	73.3	85.1	57.6	51.9	35.9	51.5	66.0	69.1
Medical expense	98.9	30.0	26.0	27.7	17.0	17.2	12.5	18.3	21.5	20.4
Administrative expenses [3]	111.9	81.0	31.0	6.8	5.7	19.5	33.7	21.8	5.3	6.8
Motor vehicle damage	41.0	41.0	1.6	(NA)	(NA)	7.1	17.0	1.1	(NA)	(NA)
Employer uninsured cost [4]	14.8	2.2	7.9	3.3	1.8	2.6	0.9	5.6	2.6	2.2
Fire loss	9.8	(NA)	2.4	6.1	1.3	1.7	(NA)	1.7	4.7	1.6

NA Not available.   [1] Excludes duplication between work and motor vehicle ($20.4 billion in 2004).   [2] Actual loss of wages and household production, and the present value of future earnings lost.   [3] Home and other costs may include costs of administering medical treatment claims for some motor-vehicle injuries filed through health insurance plans.   [4] Estimate of the uninsured costs incurred by employers, representing the money value of time lost by noninjured workers.

Source: National Safety Council, Itasca, IL, *Accident Facts*, annual through 1998, beginning 1999, *Injury Facts, Annual* (copyright); <http://www.nsc.org/lrs/statstop.htm>.

---

4. For each of the following four graphics, write a paragraph evaluating its effectiveness and describing how you would revise it.

a.

	2006	2007	2008
Civil Engineering	236	231	253
Chemical Engineering	126	134	142
Comparative Literature	97	86	74
Electrical Engineering	317	326	401
English	714	623	592
Fine Arts	112	96	72
Foreign Languages	608	584	566
Materials Engineering	213	227	241
Mechanical Engineering	196	203	201
Other	46	42	51
Philosophy	211	142	151
Religion	86	91	72

b.

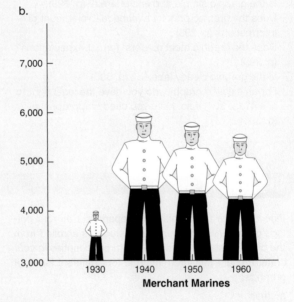

Merchant Marines

c. **Expenses at Hillway Corporation**

d. **Costs of the Components of a PC**

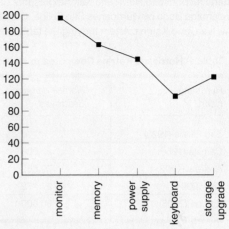

5. The following three graphs illustrate the sales of two products—Series 1 and Series 2—for each quarter of 2008. Which is the most effective in conveying the information? Which is the least effective? What additional information would make the most effective graph better?

a.

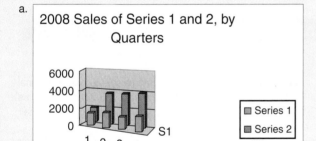

b.

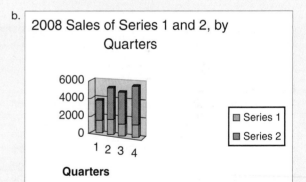

c.

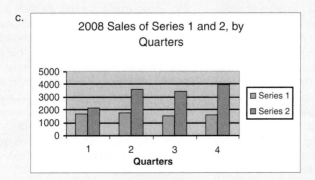

6. The following table from a report (Townsend, 2006) on the federal response to Hurricane Katrina presents data on the damage done by Hurricanes San Felipe, Camille, Andrew, Ivan, and Katrina. After studying the table, write a paragraph in which you explain the data to general readers interested in comparing the damage done by Hurricane Katrina with the damage done by other major hurricanes in U.S. history.

Table 1 Hurricane Katrina Compared to Hurricanes San Felipe, Camille, Andrew, and Ivan

Hurricane (year)	Homes damaged or destroyed	Property damage (in billions of dollars)	Deaths
San Felipe (1928)	*	<1	2,750
Camille (1969)	22,008	6	335
Andrew (1992)	79,663	33	61
Ivan (2004)	27,772	15	57
Katrina (2005)	300,000	96	1,330

*Data not available.

7. **INTERNET EXERCISE** Locate a graphic on the Web that you consider inappropriate for an international audience because it might be offensive or unclear in some cultures. Imagine an intended audience for the graphic, such as people from the Middle East, and write a brief statement explaining the potential problem. Finally, revise the graphic so that it would be appropriate for its intended audience.

Case 12: Evaluating Graphics Made in a Spreadsheet Program

▶ In This Book For more about memos, see Ch. 14, p. 377.

Background

The National Highway Traffic Safety Administration (NHTSA), under the U.S. Department of Transportation, carries out safety programs focusing on improving the safety performance of motor vehicles and motor-vehicle equipment. The NHTSA also conducts research on driver behavior, vehicle use, and highway safety. You work in the documentation group for the Research and Development (R&D) program at the NHTSA. The R&D program provides scientific evidence to support the NHTSA's safety initiatives. You help R&D scientists prepare documents reporting the results of research and crash investigations. Often, the scientists' first opportunity to present their findings is at various professional conferences. The scientists use spreadsheet programs to create the graphics they need for their presentations and conference papers.

Recently, some scientists have retired and been replaced by new hires. Your boss, Elsa Beardsley, has asked you to help some of the new scientists: "I want you to work with Dana Shapiro, Megan Hamilton, and Allison Yamamoto. All three of them are preparing papers for the 20th International Technical Conference on the Enhanced Safety of Vehicles in Nagoya, Japan. Specifically, I'd like you to review their graphics."

You ask Elsa why she thinks they need help with their graphics. "They're all good researchers," she replies. "However, when they report their findings, they don't always choose the most appropriate kind of graphics. They also unnecessarily complicate their graphics by adding a bunch of chartjunk. The spreadsheet application gives them too many choices when it comes to selecting a type of graphic or modifying a graphic, but the program doesn't offer them any help in choosing what kind of chart works best for different kinds of information and readers."

Dana Shapiro and you are good friends, so you decide to stop by her office first. Dana shows you three graphics (Documents 12.1–12.3) that she is planning to use in her conference paper. She also shows you the spreadsheet data she used to create each graphic.

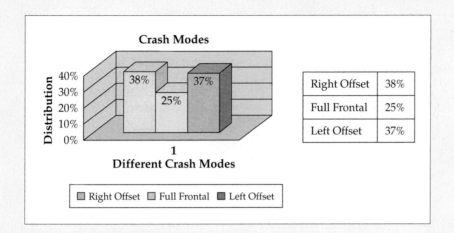

Document 12.1   Vertical Bar Graph

On TechComm Web

For digital versions of case documents, click on Downloadable Case Documents on <bedfordstmartins.com/techcomm>.

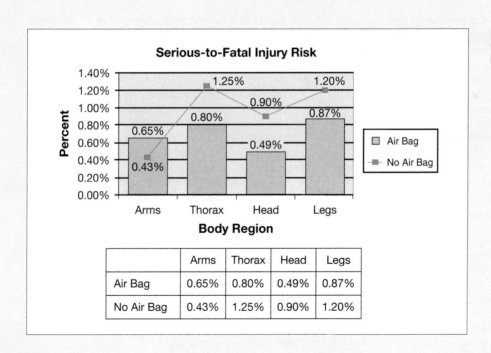

Document 12.2 Combination Bar and Line Graph

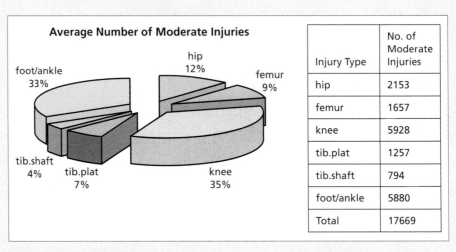

Average Number of Moderate Injuries

Injury Type	No. of Moderate Injuries
hip	2153
femur	1657
knee	5928
tib.plat	1257
tib.shaft	794
foot/ankle	5880
Total	17669

Document 12.3   Pie Chart

Dana tells you that the Conference on the Enhanced Safety of Vehicles brings together about 1,000 representatives from government agencies, industry, and safety-advocacy groups worldwide to discuss research findings and advanced technologies related to vehicle safety. Her paper reports on the development phase of the NHTSA's research program on improved frontal protection. Specifically, her research assesses the crash conditions that result in the highest number of injuries/fatalities to drivers with air bags.

"What are you trying to convey in each figure?" you ask.

"In this first figure," Dana explains, "I want to show the distribution of frontal crashes into three different crash modes. In the second figure, I'm showing how the presence of air bags affects drivers' risk of sustaining serious or fatal injuries in four body regions. I want to show that arm injuries are slightly more likely with air bags than without them, but that lower-extremity injuries—the type that often lead to lifelong disabilities—are lower with air bags. In the last figure, I just want to show the average number of moderate lower-extremity injuries occurring annually to front-seat occupants in air-bag-equipped vehicles in our data set. I want to communicate the scope of the problem. I

want people to know that an average total of 17,669 lower-extremity injuries occur annually in frontal crashes involving air-bag-equipped vehicles."

"What type of injuries are 'tib.plat' and 'tib.shaft'?" you ask.

"They're both types of injuries to the tibia, the lower leg."

"Thanks. I'll take a look at these more closely and get back to you later this week."

You also briefly visit with Megan Hamilton and Allison Yamamoto. You note that their graphics feature the same flaws as Dana's graphics. You decide that brief guidelines for choosing graphics in a spreadsheet program would be useful to the new R&D scientists. Besides, the guidelines might save you from repeating the same information to several scientists.

Your Assignment

1. Using the techniques explained in this chapter, create guidelines to help the R&D program scientists decide which type of chart or graph to create.

2. Revise Dana Shapiro's graphics. Write Dana a brief memo explaining your revisions.

Reviewing, Evaluating, and Testing Documents and Web Sites

Understanding Reviewing,
Evaluating, and Testing 342

Reviewing Documents
and Web Sites 343

Revising 344

Editing 344

Proofreading 346

Conducting Usability Evaluations 346

Conducting Usability Tests 349

The Basic Principles of Usability
Testing 350

Preparing for a Usability Test 350

Conducting a Usability Test 352

Interpreting and Reporting the Data
from a Usability Test 353

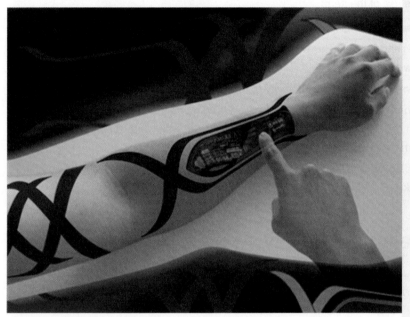

Source: Frog Design, Inc., 2008 <www.frogdesign.com/case-study/dattoos.html>.

In the World . . .

The idea behind the Dattoo (DNA Tattoo), a concept from Frog Design, "is to use the body itself as hardware and interaction platform, through the use of minimally-invasive, recyclable materials." Using the body's electricity to power the device, the wearer would be able to take pictures, make calls, and perform other digital tasks. To determine whether anyone would want to buy a Dattoo, a manufacturer would usability test the design using a prototype. There's no sense in carrying out all the research and development needed to make this product if people think it's creepy, not cool.

This chapter focuses on techniques for improving the usability of documents and Web sites. In technical communication, *usability* refers to how easily a person can use a document, Web site, or software program to carry out a task. More specifically, according to Usability.gov (2008b), *usability* refers to five factors related to a person's use of the item:

- *Ease of learning.* The time it takes a person to learn how to use the item.
- *Efficiency of use.* The time it takes a person to carry out a task after learning how to do it.
- *Memorability.* A person's ability to remember how to carry out a task.
- *Error frequency, severity, and recovery.* The number and severity of errors a person makes in carrying out a task, and the ease with which a person recovers from those errors.
- *Subjective satisfaction.* How much a person likes (or dislikes) carrying out the task.

UNDERSTANDING REVIEWING, EVALUATING, AND TESTING

As a writer, you can improve the usability of documents and Web sites by reviewing, evaluating, and testing them.

- *Reviewing* refers to three techniques—revising, editing, and proofreading—that you can use to study your draft and change it in order to make it easier to use. You have used these techniques in this writing course and in previous courses.
- *Evaluating* refers to having other people help you by reading the draft and communicating with you about its strengths and weaknesses. You have probably had people help you evaluate some of your drafts in the past.
- *Testing* refers to formal techniques of observing people and analyzing their actions as they try to use your draft to carry out tasks. You likely have not used testing before.

Figure 13.1 shows the relationships among reviewing, evaluating, and testing. How do you know whether you should go straight from reviewing to publishing or you need to have the draft evaluated and perhaps tested? Typically, you need to consider three factors:

- *Importance.* If a document or site is important, evaluate and test as much as you can. For instance, an annual report is so important that companies do everything they can to make it perfect. A company's Web site also is crucial, and you should make every effort to perfect your company's site by continuing to evaluate and test it even after it is launched. By contrast,

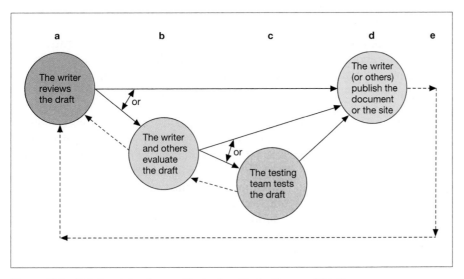

Figure 13.1   Relationships Among Reviewing, Evaluating, and Testing

The solid lines represent the process of moving a draft toward publication. At point (a), the writer reviews the draft. The writer then decides either to publish it as is (d) or to have it evaluated (b). If the draft is evaluated (b), it is next either published (d) or tested (c). After the draft is tested, it is published (d). The broken lines represent instances in which the draft might be sent back for further work. At point (e), the document or Web site has been published. The broken line extending to the right of (e) and then back around to (a) suggests that once the draft is published, the story might not be over. Web sites and documents are routinely rewritten— sometimes partially, sometimes completely—to make them more usable.

a routine memo describing a workaround for a technical problem is not so important. You can just review it yourself, then send it out.

- *Time.* Almost everything in technical communication has a deadline, and almost every deadline comes too quickly. If a document is even moderately important and you have the hours, days, or weeks to evaluate and test it, do so.

- *Money.* It costs money to evaluate and test drafts, including employee time and fees for test participants. If there is no good reason to spend the money, don't.

REVIEWING DOCUMENTS AND WEB SITES

Reviewing a document or Web site entails studying a draft and making it easier to use. Reviewing a document consists of three tasks: revising, editing, and proofreading. In carrying out these tasks, you will likely work from larger issues to smaller issues, first reviewing the document as a whole (for scope, organization, and development) and saving the smaller issues (such as sentence-level concerns) for later. That way, you won't waste time on awkward paragraphs or sentences that you might eventually throw out.

Revising

**In This Book**
For more about audience and purpose, see Ch. 5.

**In This Book**
For more about revising, see Ch. 3, pp. 51–53.

Revising is the process of looking again at your draft to see if your initial assumptions about your audience, purpose, and subject still pertain, then making any necessary changes. These changes can range from minor, such as adding one or two minor topics, to major, such as adding whole new sections and deleting others.

For example, imagine that you are revising a set of instructions to help new sales associates at your company understand how to return unsold merchandise to the supplier for credit. Since you started working on the instructions last month, your company has instituted a new policy: sales associates must write reports to management analyzing the costs and benefits of returning the unsold merchandise versus discounting it heavily and trying to sell it. You need to do some additional research to be sure you understand the new policy, gather or create some examples of employee reports, write new instructions, and integrate them into your draft.

Editing

After revising the draft, you think it is in good shape. It meets the needs of your readers, it fulfills your purpose or purposes, and it covers the subject effectively, presenting the right information. Now it's time for editing: going a little deeper into the draft.

**On TechComm Web**
For more about editing, see Purdue University's Online Writing Lab handouts on revising. Click on Links Library for Ch. 13 on <bedfordstmartins.com/ techcomm>.

Guidelines

Editing the Draft

After you finish your draft, look through it to make sure the writing is clear and effective. Start with the big picture by answering these four questions:

▶ **Is the design effective?** Documents and sites should look professional and attractive, and they should be easy to navigate. Will your readers find it easy to locate the information they need? For more about design, see Chapter 11.

▶ **Does your draft meet your readers' expectations?** If, for instance, the readers of a report expect a transmittal letter, they might be distracted if they don't see one. Check to make sure that your draft both includes the information readers expect and looks the way they expect it to. Be especially careful if your document or site will be used by people from other cultures, who might have different expectations about the draft. For more about writing for multicultural readers, see Chapter 5, page 98.

▶ **Is your draft honest, and does it adhere to appropriate legal standards?** Have you presented your information honestly, without being misleading or omitting information that might counter your argument? Have you adhered to appropriate legal standards of intellectual property, such as copyright law? For more on ethical and legal issues, see Chapter 2.

▶ **Do you come across as reliable, honest, and helpful?** Check to see that your persona is professional: modest, understated, and cooperative. For more about persona, see Chapter 8, page 189.

Next, answer these four questions related to the organization and development of the draft:

▶ **Have you left out anything in turning your outline into a draft?** Check your outline to make sure that all the topics are included in the document itself. Or switch to the outline view in your word processor so that you can focus on the level 1 and 2 headings. Is anything missing? For more about the outline view, see Chapter 3, page 46.

▶ **Is the organization logical?** Your draft is likely to reflect several different organizational patterns. For instance, the overall pattern might be chronological. Within that pattern, sections might be organized from more important to less important. As you look at the headings in the outline view, can you see the patterns you used, and do those patterns seem to work well? For more about organizational patterns, see Chapter 7.

▶ **Is the emphasis appropriate throughout the draft?** If a major point is treated only briefly, mark it for possible expansion. If a minor topic is treated at great length, mark it for possible condensing.

▶ **Are your arguments well developed?** Have you presented your claims clearly and emphatically? Have you done sufficient and appropriate research to gather the right evidence to support your claims effectively? Is your reasoning valid and persuasive? For more about conducting research, see Chapter 6. For more about using evidence effectively, see Chapter 8, page 182.

Finally, answer these four questions related to the verbal and visual elements of the draft:

▶ **Are all the elements presented consistently?** Check to see that items are presented consistently. For example, are all your headings on the same level structured the same way (for instance, as noun phrases or -*ing* gerunds)? Check for grammatical parallelism, particularly in lists but also in traditional sentences. For more about parallel structure, see Chapter 10, page 230.

▶ **Are your paragraphs well developed?** Does each paragraph begin with a clear topic sentence that previews or summarizes the main point? Have you included appropriate and sufficient support to validate your claims? For more about paragraph development, see Chapter 9, page 206.

▶ **Are your sentences clear, emphatic, and correct?** Review the draft to make sure each sentence is easy to understand, is structured to emphasize the appropriate information, and is grammatically correct. For more about writing effective sentences, see Chapter 10.

▶ **Have you used graphics appropriately?** Do you see more opportunities to translate verbal information into graphics to make your communication easier to understand and more emphatic? Have you chosen the proper types of graphics, created them effectively, and linked them to your text? For more about graphics, see Chapter 12.

Editing your draft thoroughly requires a lot of work. Naturally, you hope that once you're done editing, you won't have to go back and retrieve parts of an earlier draft. But experienced writers know that things don't always go that smoothly. Half the time when you throw out a sentence, paragraph, or section that you are absolutely convinced you will never need again, you soon realize that you do need it again. For this reason, it's smart to archive all your drafts. The easiest way to do this is to use a version number at the end of the file name. For example, call the first draft of a lab renovation proposal LabRenPropV1. When it comes time to edit that draft, open the file and immediately rename it LabRenPropV2.

Proofreading

Proofreading is the long, slow process of reading through your draft one last time to make sure you have written what you intended to write. You are looking for small problems caused by carelessness or haste. For instance, have you written *filename* on one page and *file name* on another? Have you been consistent in expressing quantities as numerals or words? Have you been consistent in punctuating entries in your list of works cited? Although your software can help you with some of these chores, it isn't sophisticated enough to do it all. You need time—and willpower.

Look particularly for problems in word endings. For instance, a sentence such as "We studying the records from the last quarter" contains a careless error left over from an earlier draft. Change it to "We studied the records from the last quarter." Also look for missing and repeated words: "We studied the from the last quarter"; "We studied the the records from the last quarter."

How do you reduce your chances of missing these errors? Read the draft slowly, out loud, listening to what you have written and marking things that look wrong. After you fix those problems, go through the draft one more time, one line at a time, looking for more problems. Some instructors suggest reading the document backward—last page first, last line first, right to left—so that you can focus on individual words. If you can stand doing it, do it.

CONDUCTING USABILITY EVALUATIONS

What is a usability evaluation? When you evaluate the usability of a draft, you are asking someone else to study the draft, looking for ways to improve its usability. That person then communicates his or her impressions and suggestions to you, either in writing or through an interview.

You can perform usability evaluations on both existing and prototype documents and Web sites. A *prototype* is a model that is built to simulate the look and feel of an item before it is produced commercially. In technical communication, a prototype is typically an early draft of a document, Web site, or software program. A prototype can range in sophistication from a simple drawing

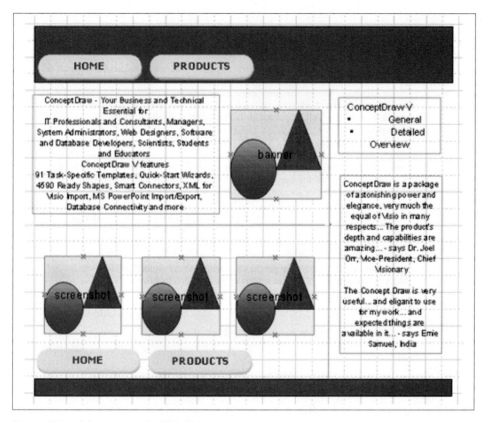

Figure 13.2   A Prototype of a Web Page

This software program lets you draw realistic prototypes of Web sites. That is, you can add buttons and icons that function as hyperlinks, enabling people to navigate the prototype as they would the Web site. This prototype combines words and images to show (approximately) the design and content of the site's home page as it would look on a user's computer screen.

Source: Computer Systems, 2008 <www.conceptdraw.com/en/products/webwave/lessons/lesson2.php>.

of a computer screen with sticky notes representing buttons to a fully functioning system that looks exactly like a commercial product. Figure 13.2 shows a prototype of a home page of a Web site created using specialized software.

Several people are usually involved in the main types of usability evaluations. Figure 13.3 on page 348 explains the roles of the major players in the process.

Although there are many varieties of usability evaluations, four major forms are used most often:

- *Surveying or interviewing users.* An evaluator surveys or interviews users to learn about the strengths and weaknesses of a document or site. These techniques can sometimes reveal problems that can be fixed. For instance, you might learn that your users would like to have a printed list of keyboard

In This Book

For more about interviewing and writing questionnaires, see
Ch. 6, pp. 136 and 138.

- **Writer.** That's you. You wrote the draft that is being evaluated. Although you might not participate actively in the evaluation, you are important to the process.
- **User.** In technical communication, a user is a person who uses a document, Web site, or program, usually as part of his or her job. For example, you are a computer user. Users can be existing or prospective (they might be users in the future). They can be novice, experienced, or expert. They are probably *not* people who work for the company that makes the product. Such people are likely to have specialized knowledge that makes them atypical users.
- **Subject-matter expert (SME).** An SME is someone who knows a lot about a subject related to the document, Web site, or software. For instance, a database engineer is presumably an SME in database software. Because this person probably would be able to identify more—and different—potential problems in a new database program than a typical user would, he or she can be very useful in evaluating a draft.
- **Usability expert.** A usability expert—an SME in ergonomics, human-computer interaction, usability engineering, or cognitive psychology—is the person who designs the usability evaluation. That is, he or she determines which questions about the draft need to be answered and how to answer them most effectively and efficiently. The usability expert also might carry out the evaluation.
- **Evaluator.** An evaluator is the person who carries out the evaluation. He or she is likely to be either an SME in the subject of the draft or a usability expert.

Figure 13.3   Major Participants in a Usability Evaluation

shortcuts to tape to the office wall. More often, however, these techniques provide attitudinal information; that is, they reveal users' attitudes about aspects of using the draft.

- *Observing users.* To understand how people use an existing document or Web site, an evaluator goes to their workplaces and observes them as they work. Observations can reveal, for example, that typical users are unaware of a feature that you assumed they used. This insight can help you see that you need to make that feature easier to find and use. Arrange workplace visits beforehand—and bring food.

- *Interviewing SMEs and usability experts.* The evaluator can ask an expert to study the draft for usability and then interview that person. In the interview, the evaluator can ask general questions about the strengths and weaknesses of the draft or focused questions about particular aspects of the draft. One well-known version of an expert evaluation is called a *cognitive walkthrough*, in which the evaluator asks an expert to carry out a set of tasks, such as signing up for automatic updates from a Web site, on a prototype or existing site. The evaluator watches and notes the expert's actions and comments. When the expert completes the tasks, the evaluator interviews the expert. Another version of an expert evaluation is called a *heuristic evaluation.* A *heuristic* is a guideline or desirable characteristic. For example, every page of a Web site should include an easy-to-find link to the home page. In a heuristic evaluation of a Web site, an expert might

On TechComm Web

For Jakob Nielsen's well-known set of heuristics for Web sites, click on Links Library for Ch. 13 on <bedfordstmartins.com/techcomm>.

assess whether the site includes such a link. After a heuristic evaluation, the evaluator interviews the expert about his or her findings.

- *Conducting focus groups.* A focus group is a group of people who meet to discuss an idea or product. Typically, the people are real or prospective users. Let's say your company sells a software program called Floor-Traxx, which helps people design custom floors. A focus group might consist of FloorTraxx customers and perhaps other people who have indicated an interest in designing custom floors for their homes. The moderator would lead a discussion focusing on what these customers liked or disliked about using the product, whether they are satisfied with the results, and what changes they would recommend in an updated version. The moderator would also seek to learn what information prospective customers would need before deciding to purchase the product.

If your users include people from other cultures, be sure to include members of those cultures in your interviews and focus groups. If possible, use interviewers from the same cultures. Vatrapu and Pérez-Quiñones (2006) have shown that people from other cultures are sometimes reluctant to criticize a draft for fear of embarrassing the interviewer. When the interviewer is from the same culture, however, people are more forthcoming.

After you complete any usability evaluation, you need to gather all the important information you have learned and share it with interested people in your company through a presentation, a Web site, or a collection of documents on the company intranet.

CONDUCTING USABILITY TESTS

Usability testing draws on many of the same principles as usability evaluations. For example, in a test, you start by determining what you want to learn. You choose test participants carefully, and you repeat the test with many participants. You change the draft and retest with still more participants. You record what you have learned.

The big difference between usability testing and usability evaluations is that testing always involves real users (or people who match the characteristics of real users) carrying out real tasks, often takes place in a specialized lab, is recorded using more sophisticated media, and is documented in more formal reports that are distributed to more people.

This section covers four topics:

- the basic principles of usability testing
- preparing for a usability test
- conducting a usability test
- interpreting and reporting the data from a usability test

 On TechComm Web

For an article describing the Online Computer Library Center's usability testing program, click on Links Library for Ch. 13 on <bedfordstmartins.com/ techcomm>.

The Basic Principles of Usability Testing

There are three basic principles of usability testing:

- *Usability testing permeates product development.* Usability testing involves testing the document, site, or software rigorously and often to make sure it works and is easy to use. Prototypes, newly completed products, and products that have been in use for a while are all tested.

- *Usability testing involves studying real users as they use the product.* Unlike most types of usability evaluations, which involve experts, testing involves real users, who can provide important information that experts cannot. Real users make mistakes that experts don't make. One well-known example is the computer software that included this error-recovery message: "Press Any Key to Continue." The manufacturer received hundreds of calls from users who couldn't find the "Any" key.

- *Usability testing involves setting measurable goals and determining whether the product meets them.* The first step in usability testing is determining what the user is supposed to be able to do. For instance, in testing a help system for a word-processing program, the testers might decide that the user should be able to find the section on saving a file and perform that task successfully in less than two minutes.

Preparing for a Usability Test

Usability testing requires careful planning. According to Kantner (1994), planning accounts for one-half to three-quarters of the time devoted to testing. In planning a usability test, you must complete eight main tasks:

- *Understand users' needs.* As discussed in the section on usability evaluations, companies use focus groups to discuss a product or an issue. In addition, they test existing products, have experts review the product, and conduct on-site interviews and observations of real users in the workplace.

- *Determine the purpose of the test.* Testers can test an idea even before the product is designed, to see if people understand it and like it. Or they can test a prototype to see if it is easy to use, or a finished product to see if it needs any last-minute improvements.

- *Staff the test team.* Extensive programs in usability testing involve many specialists, each doing one job. Smaller programs involve only a handful of people, each doing many jobs. For instance, a testing team might include an SME, who can suggest workarounds if necessary; a test administrator, who administers the test; a note taker, who fills out the evaluation forms and records important user comments; and a videographer, who operates the recording equipment.

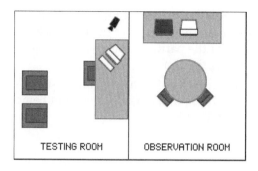

Figure 13.4   A Usability Lab

In the testing room shown here, the man is administering the test to the woman. Note the camera on the computer monitor, which is recording the woman's movements. Behind the large one-way mirror is the observation room, where the other members of the test team sit and monitor the test.

Source: Xperience Consulting, 2008 <www.xperienceconsulting.com/eng/servicios.asp?ap=25#3>.

- *Set up the test environment.* A basic environment includes a room for the test participant and another room for the test observers. Figure 13.4 shows a diagram and a photograph of a usability lab.

- *Develop a test plan.* A *test plan* is a proposal requesting resources; it describes and justifies what the testers plan to do.

- *Select participants.* Testers recruit participants who match the profile of the intended users. Generally, it is best not to use company employees, who might know more about the product than a real user would.

In This Book

For information about proposals, see Ch. 16.

- *Prepare the test materials.* Most tests require legal forms, an orientation script to help the participant understand the purpose of the test, background questionnaires, instructions for the participant to follow, and a log for the testers to record data during the test.

- *Conduct a pilot test.* A pilot test is a usability test for the usability test. A pilot test can uncover problems with the equipment, the document being tested, the test materials, and the test design.

Conducting a Usability Test

The testing team has to plan the test carefully and stay organized. Typically, the team creates a checklist and a schedule for the test day, including every task that every person, including the test participant, is to carry out. Conducting the test includes interacting with the test participant both during the formal test and later, during a debriefing session.

Interacting with the Test Participant   Among the most popular techniques for eliciting information from the test participant is the *think-aloud test*, in which the participant says aloud what he or she is thinking. In the example of FloorTraxx software for designing custom floors presented earlier, you would first create a set of tasks for the participant to carry out:

- Calculate the area of a floor.
- Calculate the number of tiles needed for a project.
- Estimate the amount of adhesive needed for a project.
- Generate the bill of materials needed for a project.
- Calculate the cost of materials and labor for a project.

As the participant carries out each task, he or she "thinks aloud" about the process. Because this process might make the participant feel awkward, the test administrator might demonstrate the process at the beginning of the session by thinking aloud while using one of the features on a cell phone or locating a particular song on a digital music player.

While the participant thinks aloud, a note taker records anything that is confusing and any point at which the participant is not sure about what to do. If the participant gets stuck, the administrator asks a leading question, such as "Where do you think that function might be located?" or "What did you expect to see when you clicked on that link?" Questions should not take the participant's knowledge for granted or embarrass the participant for failing a task. For example, "Why didn't you click on the Calculate button?" assumes that the participant both saw the button and knew how to use it. In addition, questions should not bias the participant. When the administrator asks a question, he or she should try not to reveal the expected answer.

The administrator shouldn't say, "Well, that part of the test was pretty easy, wasn't it?" Regardless of whether the participant thought it was simple or difficult, his or her impulse would be to answer yes. Dumas and Redish (1993, p. 298) recommend using neutral phrasing, such as "How was it performing that procedure?" or "Did you find that procedure easy or difficult?" In responding to questions, the administrator should be indirect. If the participant asks, "Should I press Enter now?" the administrator might respond, "Do *you* think you should?" or "I'd like to see you decide."

To ensure that the test stays on schedule and is completed on time, the test planners should set a time limit for each task. If the participant cannot complete the task in the allotted time, the administrator should move on to the next task.

Debriefing the Test Participant   After the test, the test team usually has questions about the participant's actions. For this reason, the testers debrief, or interview, the participant. The debriefing is critically important, for once the participant walks out the door, it will be difficult and expensive to ask any follow-up questions, and the participant likely will have forgotten the details of the test. Consequently, the debriefing can take as long as the test itself.

While the participant fills out the posttest questionnaire, the test team quickly looks through the data log and notes the most important areas to investigate. Their purpose in debriefing is to obtain as much information as possible about what occurred during the test; their purpose is not to think of ways of redesigning the product to prevent future problems. Rubin (1994, p. 246) suggests beginning the debriefing with a neutral question, such as "So, what did you think?" This kind of question encourages the participant to start off with an important suggestion or impression. During the debriefing, the testers address high-level concerns before getting to the smaller details. They try not to get sidetracked by a minor problem.

Interpreting and Reporting the Data from a Usability Test

After a usability test, testers have a great deal of data, including notes, questionnaires, and videos. Turning that data into useful information involves three steps:

- *Tabulating the information.* Testers gather all the information from the test, including *performance* measures, such as how long it took a participant to complete a task, and *attitude* measures, such as how easy the participant found it to perform the task.

- *Analyzing the information.* Testers analyze the information, concentrating on the most important problems revealed in the test and trying to determine the severity and the frequency of each one.

Ethics Note

Understanding the Ethics of Informed Consent

For legal and ethical reasons, organizations that conduct usability tests—especially tests that involve recording the test participant's behavior—abide by the principle of informed consent. Informed consent means that the organization fully informs the participant of the conditions under which the test will be held, as well as how the results of the test will be used. Only if the participant gives his or her consent in writing will the test occur.

Following are six important elements of informed consent:

- Explain that the test participant can leave at any time or report any discomfort to the testing team, at which point the team will stop the test.

- Explain that a camera will be used and ask for permission before the taping begins.

- Explain the purpose of the videotaping and how the video will be used. If, for example, the video might be used later in advertising, the test participant must be informed of this.

- Explain who will have access to the video and where it might be shown. A participant might object to having the video shown at a professional conference.

- Explain how the test participant's identity will be disguised, if at all, if the video is shown publicly.

- Give the test participant the opportunity to view the video and then change his or her mind about how the video might be used.

On TechComm Web

For more about informed consent, see Wendy Mackey's "Ethics, Lies and Videotape . . . ." Click on Links Library for Ch. 13 on <bedfordstmartins.com/techcomm>.

- *Reporting the information.* Writing a clear, comprehensive report often leads testers to insights they might not have achieved otherwise.

Although usability testing might seem extremely expensive and difficult, testers who are methodical, open-minded, and curious about how people use their documents and Web sites find that it is the least expensive and most effective way to improve document and Web site quality.

INTERACTIVE SAMPLE DOCUMENT
Obtaining Informed Consent

The following videotaping consent form is presented by Usability.gov, the U.S. government's usability site. The questions in the margin ask you to consider the guidelines for informed consent (as presented on page 354). E-mail your responses to yourself and/or your instructor on TechComm Web.

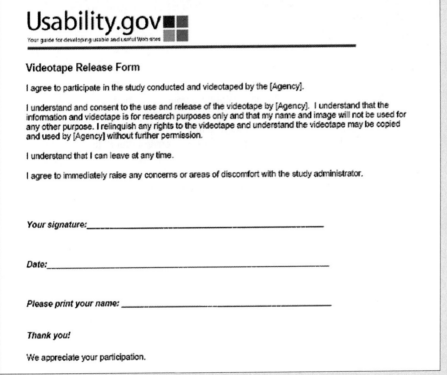

Usability.gov
Your guide for developing usable and useful Web sites

Videotape Release Form

I agree to participate in the study conducted and videotaped by the [Agency].

I understand and consent to the use and release of the videotape by [Agency]. I understand that the information and videotape is for research purposes only and that my name and image will not be used for any other purpose. I relinquish any rights to the videotape and understand the videotape may be copied and used by [Agency] without further permission.

I understand that I can leave at any time.

I agree to immediately raise any concerns or areas of discomfort with the study administrator.

Your signature:_____

Date:_____

Please print your name: _____

Thank you!

We appreciate your participation.

Source: Usability.gov, 2008a <www.usability.gov/templates/docs/release.doc>.

1. Which concepts of an effective consent form, as described in the Ethics Note on page 354, does this form include?

2. Which concepts of an effective consent form does this form *not* include?

3. Is anything in the form potentially unclear?

On TechComm Web

To e-mail your responses to yourself and/or your instructor, click on Interactive Sample Documents for Ch. 13 on <bedfordstmartins.com/techcomm>.

Writer's Checklist

Revising, Editing, and Proofreading

☐ Did you think about how your audience, purpose, and subject might have changed since you planned and drafted your document or Web site? (p. 343)

In editing your draft, did you check to see that

☐ the design is effective? (p. 344)

☐ the draft meets your readers' expectations? (p. 344)

☐ the draft is honest and adheres to appropriate legal standards? (p. 344)

☐ you come across as reliable, honest, and helpful? (p. 345)

☐ you have not omitted anything from your outline? (p. 345)

☐ the organization is logical? (p. 345)

☐ the emphasis is appropriate throughout the draft? (p. 345)

☐ your arguments are well developed? (p. 345)

☐ the elements of the draft are presented consistently? (p. 345)

☐ the paragraphs are well developed? (p. 345)

☐ the sentences are clear, emphatic, and correct? (p. 345)

☐ graphics are used appropriately? (p. 345)

☐ Have you archived drafts using a logical file-naming system? (p. 346)

Did you proofread your draft carefully, looking for small problems such as

☐ inconsistent spelling and punctuation? (p. 346)

☐ incorrect word endings? (p. 346)

☐ repeated or missing words? (p. 346)

Usability Evaluations

☐ Did you, if appropriate, survey or interview users? (p. 347)

☐ Did you, if appropriate, observe users using your existing document or Web site? (p. 348)

☐ Did you, if appropriate, interview SMEs and usability experts using heuristic evaluation? (p. 348)

☐ Did you, if appropriate, conduct focus groups? (p. 349)

Usability Tests

Did you prepare for the usability test by

☐ understanding your users' needs? (p. 350)

☐ determining the purpose of the test? (p. 350)

☐ staffing the test team? (p. 350)

☐ setting up the test environment? (p. 351)

☐ developing a test plan? (p. 351)

☐ selecting participants? (p. 352)

☐ preparing the test materials? (p. 352)

☐ conducting a pilot test? (p. 352)

Did you conduct the usability test effectively by

☐ interacting appropriately with each participant? (p. 352)

☐ debriefing the participant? (p. 353)

Did you interpret and report the test data by

☐ tabulating the information? (p. 353)

☐ analyzing the information? (p. 353)

☐ reporting the information? (p. 354)

☐ Did you obtain informed consent from each test participant? (p. 355)

Exercises

▶ **In This Book** For more about memos, see Ch. 14, p. 377.

1. Edit and proofread the following passage. Be prepared to share your work with the class.

Here are a list of the questions you shouldn't be asked by a perspective employer: What is or was your spouse's name or job? Has a Workers Compensation claim been filed on your behalf? Were you ever injured on the job. Do you have any physical empairments that prevents you from performing the job for which your applying? Have you ever been arrested? If yes, what for? What is your hair/eye color? Your height/weight? Have you ever been hospitalized? If so, why. Have you ever been treated by a psyhiatrist or psychologist? If so, for what condition? Is there any health-related reasons you may not be able to preform the job for which you're applying? How many days were you absent from work because of illness? Are you now taking any drugs? Have you ever had a problem with for drug adiction or alcoholism?

2. Contact local manufacturing companies and computer hardware and software companies to see whether they perform usability tests. If so, interview a person who performs these tests at one of the organizations. Write a 1,000-word memo to your instructor describing how the process of conducting usability tests at this organization differs from the process described in this chapter.

3. If a local company conducts usability tests, find out whether you can be a test participant. After the test,

write a 1,000-word memo to your instructor describing the experience, focusing on what you learned about usability tests.

4. **GROUP EXERCISE** Form a group of four or five students and conduct an informal usability test for assembling or using one of the following products:

   a. a piece of computer hardware, such as a printer

   b. a piece of software (or a portion of a piece of software)

   c. a document that accompanies a piece of software (or a portion of one)

   d. a piece of equipment used in your major field of study

   e. a product such as an MP3 player or a Bluetooth headset

Submit a brief usability report to your instructor.

Case 13: Reviewing and Testing Documents

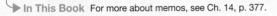 In This Book For more about memos, see Ch. 14, p. 377.

Background

Word Weaver is a product being created by Education Word Games, Inc., which specializes in making games for use in the classroom. Complementing the company's already successful word-search game maker, Word Weaver enables users to create custom crossword puzzles easily, using their own words. Word Weaver will be primarily marketed to educators, newsletter editors, and businesses. The company is looking for some help reviewing and testing its documentation. It posted a help-wanted announcement in your school's student union, and you responded. You are now meeting with Lisa Carlson, Chief Operating Officer of the company.

"Word Weaver 1.0 launches in less than two months, and we need to finish the getting-started documentation," Lisa explains. "We also need to get some feedback on the effectiveness of some of the last-minute additions to the user interface of the software."

"How would teachers use Word Weaver in the class-room?" you ask.

"Teachers use crosswords as fun learning tools. For example, during a unit on Greek mythology, an English

teacher might create a custom crossword puzzle using the names of gods, demigods, and heroes from the Greek pantheon. Students could then use the puzzle as an interactive way to check their knowledge of Greek lore."

"How else would people use the crossword builder?"

"Editors include crossword puzzles in newsletters as a way to add some pizzazz to their publications and to get people to read them. Businesses use custom crosswords to reinforce training and as marketing gimmicks. Puzzle lovers might use the software to create themed puzzles to put in holiday letters and cards."

"What do you need me to do?"

"We would like to give the beta version of Word Weaver to a few people and get their impressions of the product before the finished version is ready for wide release."

"What's the beta version?"

"That's our prerelease version of the software. The company would like to know the usefulness of the getting-started instructions." (See Document 13.1.)

Lisa explains that the software developers also added to the user interface a new Publish Puzzle dialog box with several buttons and that she would like to know if the icons

Welcome to Word Weaver 1.0!!!

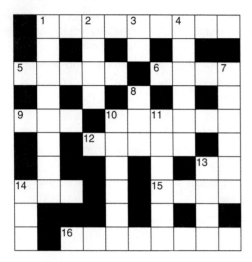

Restrictions: Purchasers may not use, copy, modify, translate, or transfer the Word Weaver software. Purchaser may use the software on a single computer only, unless a enough licenses have been purchased for network deployment. Purchaser may not remove or modify any copyright indicators. All other rights not specifically granted in this license are reserved by Education Word Games, Inc.

The biggest problem we get asked about is how to unlock Word Weaver. You need to enter your licensing number <u>exactly</u> as well as your name (the name you gave us when you purchased the software). If you don't enter it exactly, the software will not unlock. If this is the problem, go back and make sure the number entered matches the licensing number sent when the product was paid for. Next, check that the name you enter matches exactly the name you gave us

Let's Get Started!

Word Weaver allows users to create a custom crossword puzzle using their own words and only their words. Let's create a new puzzle! Start Word Weaver 1.0. After starting the program, in the FILE pull-down menu, select NEW PUZZLE. The Puzzle Builder window will now appear with the cursor flashing in the Title text field. Enter a title for the puzzle. The title will appear at the top of the crossword puzzle.

Users will notice that the Puzzle Window has two columns. The first column is labeled **Puzzle Words** and the second column is labeled **Clues**. Enter the words to be included in the puzzle. If users wish to enter a multiple word entry (e.g., San Francisco), enter the phrases with no spaces between words (e.g., sanfrancisco)—capitalization doesn't matter for **Puzzle Words**. Now, take a few minutes to enter many words you wish to appear in the puzzle.

After users enter a puzzle word, they need to enter a clue for the word in the **Clues** column: e.g., City near the Golden Gate Bridge. If users can't think of a good clue, try a thesaurus for synonyms for one-word puzzle words (e.g., puzzle word = creepy; clue = scary) or Google the puzzle word and see what information can be learned. Users are bound to find something to use as a clue.

When users have entered all the puzzle words and clues they wish, we recommend they select the SPELLING CHECKER button from the interface to check for any embarrassing spelling errors that your students will definitely catch. Users can choose to ignore, replace, or add words to Word Weaver's Dictionary. Your last step is to select the PUZZLE CREATE button to create your puzzle!! Once created and SAVED (remember to do this—always save your file *first* as a Word Weaver .wwf file), users can use the **Publish Puzzle** dialog box to publish the puzzle to the Internet, as a JPEG image, as a PDF, or email the puzzle to a friend as an attachment to an email message.

You have now completed the your own crossword puzzle!! Congratulations!! You may want to take time to learn about some of the other features of the program by reading the online help.

Document 13.1   Getting-Started Documentation for Word Weaver 1.0

used on the buttons are intuitive to users. She hands you a sheet of paper listing the new buttons and what each button does (Document 13.2).

"I'd like your advice on how to revise the getting-started instructions and how we should find out if the documenta-tion is helpful to users," Lisa says. "I'd also be interested in how you recommend we find out if people will understand the new buttons based just on the icons we're using. These icons represent actions users might want to take when using the software."

New puzzle buttons for the Publish Puzzle dialog box

Button	Function
	Save as Web page (.html)
	Save as JPEG file (.jpg)
	Save as PDF (.pdf)
	Save as Word Weaver file (.wwf)
	E-mail puzzle to a friend
	Print

Document 13.2   New User Interface Buttons with Icons

Your Assignment

1. Before you get any feedback on the instructions and icons, Lisa asks that you serve as another reviewer of the getting-started documentation. Based on what you have learned about reviewing documents, revise, edit, and proofread the instructions.

2. Who should Lisa contact to get feedback regarding the effectiveness of the getting-started instructions, and what is the best way to elicit such feedback? Write Lisa an e-mail in which you identify the type(s) of people she should contact, then write a set of questions you think would help her gather the feedback she is seeking.

3. Think about what steps you need to take to test the effectiveness of the new interface buttons. Write Lisa an e-mail in which you briefly outline how she could test the buttons.

On TechComm Web

For digital versions of case documents, click on Download-able Case Documents on <bedfordstmartins.com/techcomm>.

PART 4 Learning Important Applications

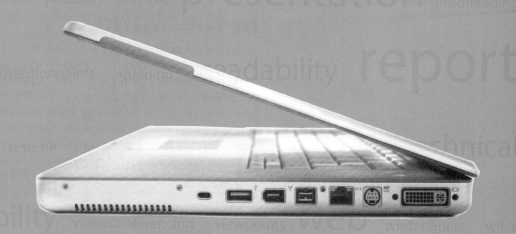

14

Writing Letters, Memos, and E-mails

Understanding the Process of Writing
Letters, Memos, and E-mails 363

Selecting a Type
of Correspondence 364

Presenting Yourself Effectively in
Correspondence 364

Use the Appropriate Level
of Formality 365

Communicate Correctly 365

Project the "You Attitude" 366

Avoid Correspondence Clichés 366

Communicate Honestly 366

Writing Letters 368

Understand the Elements
of a Letter 368

Learn the Format of a Letter 368

Understand Common Types
of Letters 371

Writing Memos 377

Writing E-mails 379

Writing Business Correspondence to
Intercultural Readers 382

Source: Missty/Flickr, 2007 <www.flickr.com/photos/missty/1337034307>.

In the World . . .

Is this the last person who will ever use e-mail? According to *Wired* (Russell, 2007), teenagers much prefer communicating through social-networking sites to writing e-mail. Only 14 percent of teenagers use e-mail every day to communicate with their friends. What will happen when teenagers enter the working world, where billions of e-mails are sent every day? Will the business world change them, or will they change it? One thing is certain: electronic correspondence, whether it takes the form of e-mail, instant messaging, or some form that hasn't yet been invented, will account for a bigger and bigger slice of the business-correspondence pie.

To communicate with others in the workplace, you will use a number of different media. You will talk face-to-face with others, you will use the phone, and you will use text messaging and instant messaging. This chapter discusses the three major formats used for producing workplace correspondence: letters, memos, and e-mails.

UNDERSTANDING THE PROCESS OF WRITING LETTERS, MEMOS, AND E-MAILS

The process of writing letters, memos, and e-mails is essentially like that of writing any other kind of workplace document. Figure 14.1 presents an overview of this process.

Figure 14.1 The Process of Writing Letters, Memos, and E-mails

Analyze Your Audience
Consider your readers' characteristics and attitudes and how they will use the document. Remember that the tone, content, and format of letters, memos, and e-mails differ from culture to culture.

Analyze Your Purpose
What do you want to accomplish in the document? After they read it, what do you want your readers to know, believe, or do?

Gather Information About Your Subject
Use appropriate techniques of primary and secondary research. For more information, see Chapter 6.

Choose a Type of Document
Letters are best for formal situations. Memos are less formal than letters. E-mails are the least formal, but they still require a moderately formal tone and correctness.

Draft the Document
Clearly state your purpose, use headings to help your readers, summarize your message, provide adequate background, organize the discussion, and highlight action items.

Format the Document
Use a conventional format but adapt it to meet the special needs of your audience, purpose, and subject.

Figure 14.1
(continued)

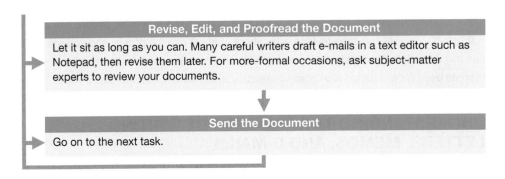

> **Revise, Edit, and Proofread the Document**
>
> Let it sit as long as you can. Many careful writers draft e-mails in a text editor such as Notepad, then revise them later. For more-formal occasions, ask subject-matter experts to review your documents.

> **Send the Document**
>
> Go on to the next task.

SELECTING A TYPE OF CORRESPONDENCE

When you need to correspond with others in the workplace, your first task is to decide on the appropriate format. Here are the major characteristics of each type:

- *Letters.* Because letters still use centuries-old conventions such as the salutation and complimentary close, they are the most formal of the three types and are therefore most appropriate for communicating with people outside your organization or, in some formal situations, with people in your organization.
- *Memos.* This type of correspondence is moderately formal and therefore appropriate for people in your organization.
- *E-mail.* This type is best for quick, relatively informal communication with one or many recipients. Recipients can store and forward an e-mail easily, as well as capture the text and reuse it in other documents. In addition, the writer can attach other files to an e-mail.

PRESENTING YOURSELF EFFECTIVELY IN CORRESPONDENCE

When you write business correspondence, follow these five suggestions for presenting yourself as a professional:

- Use the appropriate level of formality.
- Communicate correctly.
- Project the "you attitude."
- Avoid correspondence clichés.
- Communicate honestly.

Use the Appropriate Level of Formality

Even though the three types of business correspondence differ in their levels of formality, make sure your writing is at least moderately formal because the writing represents you and your organization.

People are most tempted to use informal writing in e-mails. Resist the temptation. Remember that e-mails, like memos and letters, are legally the property of the organization for which you work, and they are almost always archived digitally, even after recipients have deleted them from their computers. Remember, too, that your e-mails might be read by the company president, or they might appear in a newspaper or court of law. Therefore, use a moderately formal tone to avoid potential embarrassment.

TOO INFORMAL	Our meeting with United went south right away when they threw a hissy fit, saying that we blew off the deadline for the progress report.
MODERATELY FORMAL	In our meeting, the United representative expressed concern that we had missed the deadline for the progress report.

In memos and letters, strive for the same moderately formal tone, but don't try to sound like a dictionary.

TOO FORMAL	It was indubitably the case that our team was successful in presenting a proposal that was characterized by quality of the highest order. My appreciation for your industriousness is herewith extended.
MODERATELY FORMAL	I think we put together an excellent proposal. Thank you very much for your hard work.

Communicate Correctly

One issue closely related to formality is correctness. As discussed in Chapter 1, correct writing is writing that is free of grammar, punctuation, style, usage, and spelling errors. The most problems with correctness arise when people use e-mail.

Some writers mistakenly think that because e-mail is a quick, informal medium, they need not worry about correctness. They are wrong. You have to plan your e-mails just as you plan any other written communication. And you have to revise, edit, and proofread them as well. Sending an e-mail that contains errors of correctness is unprofessional because it suggests a lack of respect for your reader—and for yourself. It also causes your reader to think that you are careless about your job.

▶ In This Book

For more about editing and proofreading, see Ch. 13, pp. 344 and 346.

Project the "You Attitude"

Correspondence must convey a courteous, positive tone. The key to accomplishing this task is using the "you attitude"—that is, looking at the situation from the reader's point of view and adjusting the content, structure, and tone to meet his or her needs. For example, if you are writing to a supplier who has failed to deliver some merchandise on the agreed-upon date, the "you attitude" dictates that you not discuss problems you are having with other suppliers—those problems don't concern your reader. Instead, concentrate on explaining clearly and politely that the reader has violated your agreement and that not having the merchandise is costing you money. Then propose ways to expedite the shipment.

Following are two examples of thoughtless sentences, each followed by an improved version that shows the "you attitude."

ACCUSING	You must have dropped the engine. The housing is badly cracked.
BETTER	The badly cracked housing suggests that your engine must have fallen onto a hard surface from some height.
SARCASTIC	You'll need two months to deliver these parts? Who do you think you are, the post office?
BETTER	Surely, you would find a two-month delay for the delivery of parts unacceptable in your business. That's how I feel, too.

A calm, respectful tone makes the best impression and increases the chances that you will achieve your goal.

Avoid Correspondence Clichés

In This Book
For more about choosing the right words and phrases, see Ch. 10, p. 233.

Over the centuries, a set of words and phrases has come to be associated with business correspondence; one common example is *as per your request*. These phrases sound stilted and insincere. Don't use them.

Figure 14.2 is a list of common clichés and their more natural equivalents. Figure 14.3 shows two versions of the same letter: one written in clichés, the other in plain language.

Communicate Honestly

You should communicate honestly when you write any kind of document, and business correspondence is no exception. Communicating honestly shows respect for your reader and for yourself.

Letter clichés	Natural equivalents
attached please find	attached is
enclosed please find	enclosed is
pursuant to our agreement	as we agreed
referring to your ("Referring to your letter of March 19, the shipment of pianos . . .")	"As you wrote in your letter of March 19, the . . ." (or subordinate the reference at the end of your sentence)
wish to advise ("We wish to advise that . . .")	(The phrase doesn't say anything. Just say what you want to say.)
the writer ("The writer believes that . . .")	"I believe . . ."

Figure 14.2 Letter Clichés and Natural Equivalents

Letter containing clichés	Letter in natural language
Dear Mr. Smith:	Dear Mr. Smith:

Figure 14.3 Sample Letters with and Without Clichés

The letter on the right side avoids clichés and shows an understanding of the "you attitude." Instead of focusing on the violation of the warranty, it presents the conclusion as good news: the snowmobile is not ruined, and it can be repaired and returned in less than a week for a small charge.

Letter containing clichés

Dear Mr. Smith:

Referring to your letter regarding the problem encountered with your new Trailrider Snowmobile, our Customer Service Department has just submitted its report.

It is their conclusion that the malfunction is caused by water being present in the fuel line. It is our conclusion that you must have purchased some bad gasoline. We trust you are cognizant of the fact that while we guarantee our snowmobiles for a period of not less than one year against defects in workmanship and materials, responsibility cannot be assumed for inadequate care. We wish to advise, for the reason mentioned hereinabove, that we cannot grant your request to repair the snowmobile free of charge.

Permit me to say, however, that the writer would be pleased to see that the fuel line is flushed at cost, $30. Your Trailrider would then give you many years of trouble-free service.

Enclosed please find an authorization card. Should we receive it, we shall perform the above-mentioned repair and deliver your snowmobile forthwith.

Sincerely yours,

Letter in natural language

Dear Mr. Smith:

Thank you for writing to us about the problem with your new Trailrider Snowmobile.

Our Customer Service Department has found water in the fuel line. Apparently some of the gasoline was bad. While we guarantee our snowmobiles for one year against defects in workmanship and materials, we cannot assume responsibility for problems caused by bad gasoline. We cannot, therefore, grant your request to repair the snowmobile free of charge.

However, no serious harm was done to the snowmobile. We would be happy to flush the fuel line at cost, $30. Your Trailrider would then give you many years of trouble-free service. If you will authorize us to do this work, we will have your snowmobile back to you within four working days. Just fill out the enclosed authorization card and drop it in the mail.

Sincerely yours,

> ### Ethics Note
>
> #### Writing Honest Business Correspondence
>
> Why is dishonesty a big problem in business correspondence? Maybe it has something to do with the fact that the topics discussed in e-mails, memos, and letters often relate to the writer's professionalism and the quality of his or her work. For instance, when a salesperson working for a supplier writes to a customer explaining why the product did not arrive on time, he is tempted to make it seem as if his company—and he personally—is blameless. Similarly, when a manager has to announce a new policy that employees will dislike, she might be tempted to distance herself from the policy.
>
> The most professional thing a writer can do is tell the truth. If you mislead a reader in explaining why the shipment didn't arrive on time, the reader will likely double-check the facts, conclude that you are trying to avoid responsibility, and end your business relationship. If you try to convince a reader that you had nothing to do with a new, unpopular policy, he or she will probably know if you are being misleading, and you will lose your most important credential: your credibility.

WRITING LETTERS

 On TechComm Web

For more about letter writing, search for "business letters" at Purdue University's Online Writing Lab. Click on Links Library for Ch. 14 on <bedfordstmartins.com/techcomm>.

Letters are still a basic means of communication between organizations, with millions written each day. To write effective letters, you need to understand the elements of a letter, learn its format, and understand the typical kinds of letters sent in the business world.

Understand the Elements of a Letter

Most letters include a heading, inside address, salutation, body, complimentary close, signature, and reference initials. Some letters also include one or more of the following: attention line, subject line, enclosure line, and copy line. Figure 14.4 shows the elements of a letter.

Learn the Format of a Letter

Two typical formats are used for letters: modified block and full block. Figure 14.5 on page 371 illustrates these formats.

DAVIS TREE CARE

1300 Lancaster Avenue
Berwyn, PA 19092
www.davisfortrees.com

May 12, 2009

Fairlawn Industrial Park
1910 Ridgeway Drive
Rollins, MO 84639

Attention: Director of Maintenance

Subject: Fall pruning

Dear Director of Maintenance:

Do you know how much your trees are worth? That's right—your trees. As a maintenance director, you know how much of an investment your organization has in its physical plant. And the landscaping is a big part of your total investment.

Most people don't know that even the hardiest trees need periodic care. Like shrubs, trees should be fertilized and pruned. And they should be protected against the many kinds of diseases and pests that are common in this area.

At Davis Tree Care, we have the skills and experience to keep your trees healthy and beautiful. Our diagnostic staff is made up of graduates of major agricultural and forestry universities, and all of our crews attend special workshops to keep current with the latest information on tree maintenance. Add to this our proven record of 43 years of continuous service in the Berwyn area, and you have a company you can trust.

Heading. *Most organizations use letterhead stationery with their heading printed at the top. This preprinted information and the date the letter is sent make up the heading. If you are using blank paper rather than letterhead, your address (without your name) and the date form the heading. Use letterhead for the first page and do not number it. Use blank paper for the second and all subsequent pages.*

Inside Address. *If you are writing to an individual who has a professional title— such as Professor, Dr., or, for public officials, Honorable—use it. If not, use Mr. or Ms. (unless you know the recipient prefers Mrs. or Miss). If the reader's position fits on the same line as the name, add it after a comma; otherwise, drop it to the line below. Spell the name of the organization the way the organization itself does: for example, International Business Machines calls itself IBM. Include the complete mailing address: street number and name, city, state, and zip code.*

Attention Line. *Sometimes you will be unable to address a letter to a particular person because you don't know (and cannot easily find out) the name of the individual who holds that position in the company.*

Subject Line. *Use either a project number (for example, "Subject: Project 31402") or a brief phrase defining the subject (for example, "Subject: Price quotation for the R13 submersible pump").*

Salutation. *If you decide not to use an attention line or a subject line, put the salutation, or greeting, two lines below the inside address. The traditional salutation is* Dear, *followed by the reader's courtesy title and last name, followed by a colon (not a comma):*
    Dear Ms. Hawkins:

Figure 14.4   Elements of a Letter

Header *for second page.*

Letter to Fairlawn Industrial Park
Page 2
May 12, 2009

May we stop by to give you an analysis of your trees—absolutely
without cost or obligation? A few minutes with one of our diagnos-
ticians could prove to be one of the wisest moves you've ever
made. Just give us a call at 555-9187, and we'll be happy to arrange
an appointment at your convenience.

Sincerely yours,

Jasmine Brown

Jasmine Brown
President

Enclosure: Davis Tree Care brochure

c: Darrell Davis, Vice President

Body. *In most cases, the body contains at
least three paragraphs: an introductory
paragraph, a concluding paragraph, and one
or more body paragraphs.*

Complimentary Close. *The conventional phrases*
Sincerely, Sincerely yours, Yours sincerely, Yours very
truly, *and* Very truly yours *are interchangeable.*

Signature. *Type your full name on the fourth
line below the complimentary close. Sign the
letter, in ink, above the typewritten name.
Most organizations prefer that you include
your position under your typed name.*

Copy Line. *If you want the primary
recipient to know that other people
are receiving a copy of the letter,
include a copy line. Use the symbol
c (for "copy") followed by the names
of the other recipients (listed either
alphabetically or according to
organizational rank). If appropriate,
use the symbol cc (for "courtesy
copy") followed by the names of
recipients who are less directly
affected by the letter.*

Enclosure Line. *If the envelope contains
documents other than the letter, include an
enclosure line that indicates the number of
enclosures. For more than one enclosure, add
the number: "Enclosures (2)." In determining
the number of enclosures, count only separate
items, not pages. A 3-page memo and a 10-page
report constitute only two enclosures. Some
writers like to identify the enclosures:*

> *Enclosure: 2008 Placement Bulletin*
> *Enclosures (2): "This Year at Ammex"*
> *2008 Annual Report*

Figure 14.4 (continued)

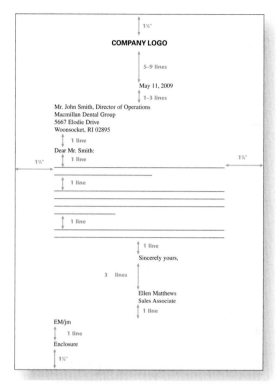

a. Modified block format

b. Full block format—everything aligned along the left margin

Figure 14.5 Typical Letter Formats
The dimensions and spacing shown for the modified block format also apply to the full block format.

Understand Common Types of Letters

Organizations send out many different kinds of letters. This section focuses on four types of letters written frequently in the workplace: inquiry, response to an inquiry, claim, and adjustment.

Inquiry Letter   Figure 14.6 on page 372 shows an inquiry letter, in which you ask questions.

Response to an Inquiry   Figure 14.7 on page 373 shows a response to the inquiry letter in Figure 14.6.

Claim Letter   Figure 14.8 on page 374 is an example of a claim letter that the writer faxed to the reader.

In This Book

Two other types of letters are discussed in this book: the transmittal letter (see Ch. 19, p. 511) and the job-application letter (see Ch. 15, p. 415).

You write an inquiry letter to acquire information. Explain who you are and why you are writing. Make your questions precise and clear, and therefore easy to answer. Explain what you plan to do with the information and how you can compensate the reader for answering your questions.

This writer's task is to motivate the reader to provide some information. That information is not likely to lead to a sale because the writer is a graduate student doing research, not a potential customer.

Notice the flattery in the first sentence.

The writer presents specific questions in a list format, making the questions easy to read and understand.

In the final paragraph, the writer politely indicates his schedule and requests the reader's response. Note that he offers to send the reader a copy of his report.

If the reader provides information, the writer should send a thank-you letter.

14 Hawthorne Ave.
Belleview, TX 75234
November 2, 2009

Dr. Andrea Shakir
Director of Technical Services
Orion Corporation
721 West Douglas Avenue
Maryville, TN 31409

Dear Dr. Shakir:

I am writing to you because of Orion's reputation as a leader in the manufacture of adjustable x-ray tables. I am a graduate student in biomedical engineering at the University of Texas, and I am working on an analysis of diagnostic equipment for a seminar paper. Would you be able to answer a few questions about your Microspot 311?

1. Can the Microspot 311 be used with lead oxide cassettes, or does it accept only lead-free cassettes?
2. Are standard generators compatible with the Microspot 311?
3. What would you say is the greatest advantage, for the operator, of using the Microspot 311? For the patient?

My project is due on January 15. I would greatly appreciate your assistance in answering these questions. Of course, I would be happy to send you a copy of my report when it is completed.

Yours very truly,

Albert K. Stern

Albert K. Stern

Figure 14.6 Inquiry Letter

ORION

721 WEST DOUGLAS AVE.
MARYVILLE, TN 31409

(615) 619-8132
www.orioninstruments.com

November 7, 2009

Mr. Albert K. Stern
14 Hawthorne Ave.
Belleview, TX 75234

Dear Mr. Stern:

I would be pleased to answer your questions about the Microspot 311. We think it is the best
unit of its type on the market today.

1. The 311 can handle lead oxide or lead-free cassettes.
2. At the moment, the 311 is fully compatible only with our Duramatic generator. However,
    special wiring kits are available to make the 311 compatible with our earlier generator
    models—the Olympus and the Saturn. We are currently working on other wiring kits.
3. For the operator, the 311 increases the effectiveness of the radiological procedure while
    at the same time cutting down the amount of film used. For the patient, it reduces the
    number of repeat exposures and therefore reduces the total dose.

I am enclosing a copy of our brochure on the Microspot 311. If you would like additional
information, please visit our Web site at www.orioninstruments.com/products/microspot311.
I would be happy to receive a copy of your analysis when it is complete. Good luck!

Sincerely yours,

Andrea Shakir, M.D.
Director of Technical Services

Enclosure

c: Robert Anderson, Executive Vice President

In responding to an inquiry letter, answer the questions if you can. If you cannot, either because you don't know the answers or because you cannot divulge proprietary information, explain the reasons and offer to assist with other requests.

The writer responds graciously.

The writer answers the three questions posed in the inquiry letter.

The writer encloses other information to give the reader a fuller understanding of the product.

The writer uses the enclosure notation to signal that she is attaching an item to the letter.

The writer indicates that she is forwarding a copy to her supervisor.

Figure 14.7   Response to an Inquiry

A claim letter is a polite, reasonable complaint. If you purchase a defective or falsely advertised product or receive inadequate service, you write a claim letter. If the letter is convincing, your chances of receiving an equitable settlement are good because most organizations realize that unhappy customers are bad for business. In addition, claim letters help companies identify weak points in their product or service.

The writer indicates clearly in the first paragraph that he is writing about an unsatisfactory product. Note that he identifies the product by model name.

The writer presents the background, filling in specific details about the problem. Notice how he supports his earlier claim that the problem embarrassed him professionally.

The writer states that he thinks the reader will agree that there was a problem with the equipment.

Then the writer suggests that the reader's colleague did not respond satisfactorily.

The writer proposes a solution: that the reader take appropriate action. The writer's clear, specific account of the problem and his professional tone increase his chances of receiving the solution he proposes.

RC | **ROBBINS CONSTRUCTION, INC.**

255 Robbins Place, Centerville, MO 65101 | (417) 555-1850 | www.robbinsconstruction.com

August 18, 2009

Mr. David Larsyn
Larsyn Supply Company
311 Elmerine Avenue
Anderson, MO 63501

Dear Mr. Larsyn:

As steady customers of yours for over 15 years, we came to you first when we needed a quiet pile driver for a job near a residential area. On your recommendation, we bought your Vista 500 Quiet Driver, at $14,900. We have since found, much to our embarrassment, that it is not substantially quieter than a regular pile driver.

We received the contract to do the bridge repair here in Centerville after promising to keep the noise to under 90 dB during the day. The Vista 500 (see enclosed copy of bill of sale for particulars) is rated at 85 dB, maximum. We began our work and, although one of our workers said the driver didn't seem sufficiently quiet to him, assured the people living near the job site that we were well within the agreed sound limit. One of them, an acoustical engineer, marched out the next day and demonstrated that we were putting out 104 dB. Obviously, something is wrong with the pile driver.

I think you will agree that we have a problem. We were able to secure other equipment, at considerable inconvenience, to finish the job on schedule. When I telephoned your company that humiliating day, however, a Mr. Meredith informed me that I should have done an acoustical reading on the driver before I accepted delivery.

I would like you to send out a technician—as soon as possible—either to repair the driver so that it performs according to specifications or to take it back for a full refund.

Yours truly,

Jack Robbins

Jack Robbins, President

Enclosure

Figure 14.8   Claim Letter

Larsyn Supply Company

311 Elmerine Avenue
Anderson, MO 63501
(417) 555-2484
www.larsynsupply.com

August 22, 2009

Mr. Jack Robbins, President
Robbins Construction, Inc.
255 Robbins Place
Centerville, MO 65101

Dear Mr. Robbins:

I was very unhappy to read your letter of August 18 telling me about the failure of the Vista 500. I regretted most the treatment you received from one of my employees when you called us.

Harry Rivers, our best technician, has already been in touch with you to arrange a convenient time to come out to Centerville to talk with you about the driver. We will of course repair it, replace it, or refund the price. Just let us know your wish.

I realize that I cannot undo the damage that was done on the day that a piece of our equipment failed. To make up for some of the extra trouble and expense you incurred, let me offer you a 10 percent discount on your next purchase or service order with us, up to a $1,000 total discount.

You have indeed been a good customer for many years, and I would hate to have this unfortunate incident spoil that relationship. Won't you give us another chance? Just bring in this letter when you visit us next, and we'll give you that 10 percent discount.

Sincerely,

Dave Larsyn, President

An adjustment letter, a response to a claim letter, tells the customer how you plan to handle the situation. Your purpose is to show that your organization is fair and reasonable and that you value the customer's business.

If you can grant the request, the letter is easy to write. Express your regret, state the adjustment you are going to make, and end on a positive note by encouraging the customer to continue doing business with you.

The writer wisely expresses regret about the two problems cited in the claim letter.

The writer describes the actions he has already taken and formally states that he will do whatever the reader wishes.

The writer expresses empathy in making the offer of adjustment. Doing so helps to create a bond: you and I are both professionals who rely on our good reputations.

This polite conclusion appeals to the reader's sense of fairness and good business practice.

On TechComm Web

For excellent advice on adjustment letters, see Business Communication: Managing Information and Relationships. Click on Links Library for Ch. 14 on <bedfordstmartins.com/techcomm>.

Figure 14.9 **"Good News" Adjustment Letter**

Adjustment Letter   Figures 14.9 and 14.10 (page 376) show "good news" and "bad news" adjustment letters. The first is a reply to the claim letter shown in Figure 14.8.

If you are writing a "bad news" adjustment letter, salvage as much goodwill as you can by showing that you have acted reasonably. In denying a request, explain your side of the matter, thus educating the customer about how the problem occurred and how to prevent it in the future.

The writer does not begin by stating that he is denying the reader's request. Instead, he begins politely by trying to form a bond with the reader. In trying to meet the customer on neutral ground, be careful about admitting that the customer is right. If you say "We are sorry that the engine you purchased from us is defective," it will bolster the customer's claim if the dispute ends up in court.

The writer summarizes the facts of the incident, as he sees them.

The writer explains that he is unable to fulfill the reader's request. Notice that the writer never explicitly denies the request. It is more effective to explain why granting the request is not appropriate. Also notice that the writer does not explicitly say that the reader failed to make a backup copy of the plan and therefore the problem is her fault.

The writer shifts from the bad news to the good news. The writer explains that he has already responded appropriately to the reader's request.

The writer ends with a polite conclusion. A common technique is to offer the reader a special discount on another, similar product.

Quality Storage Media

2077 Highland, Burley, ID 84765
208 · 555 · 1613
www.qualstorage.com

February 3, 2009

Ms. Dale Devlin
1903 Highland Avenue
Glenn Mills, NE 69032

Dear Ms. Devlin:

Thank you for writing us about the portable disc you purchased on January 11, 2009. I know from personal experience how frustrating it is when a disc fails.

According to your letter, you used the disc to store the business plan for your new consulting business. When you attempted to copy that file to your hard drive, the portable disc failed, and the business plan was lost. You have no other copy of that file. You are asking us to reimburse you $1,500 for the cost of re-creating that business plan from notes and rough drafts.

As you know, our discs carry a lifetime guarantee covering parts and workmanship. We will gladly replace the defective portable disc. However, the guarantee states that the manufacturer and the retailer will not assume any incidental liability. Thus we are responsible only for the retail value of the blank disc, not for the cost of duplicating the work that went into making the files stored on the disc.

However, your file might still be recoverable. A reputable data-recovery firm might be able to restore the data from the file at a very reasonable cost. To prevent such problems in the future, we always recommend that you back up all valuable files periodically.

We have already sent out your new portable disc by overnight delivery. It should arrive within the next two days.

Please contact us if we can be of any further assistance.

Sincerely yours,

Paul R. Blackwood, Manager
Customer Relations

Figure 14.10   "Bad News" Adjustment Letter

WRITING MEMOS

Even in the age of e-mail, memos are likely to survive, because sometimes writers want a slightly more formal document. Like letters, memos have a characteristic format, which consists of the elements shown in Figure 14.11.

Print the second and all subsequent pages of a memo on plain paper rather than on letterhead. Include three items in the upper right-hand or left-hand corner of each page: the name of the recipient, the date of the memo, and the page number. See Figure 14.4 on page 369 for header information.

AMRO	MEMO
To:	B. Pabst
From:	J. Alonso **J. A.**
Subject:	MIXER RECOMMENDATION FOR PHILLIPS
Date:	12 June 2009

Write out the month instead of using the all-numeral format (6/12/09); multicultural readers might use a different notation for dates and could be confused.

INTEROFFICE

To:	C. Cleveland	c:	B. Aaron
From:	H. Rainbow **H. R.**		K. Lau
Subject:	Shipment Date of Blueprints to Collier		J. Manuputra W. Williams
Date:	2 October 2009		

List the names of persons receiving photocopies of the memo, either alphabetically or in descending order of organizational rank.

**NORTHERN PETROLEUM COMPANY
INTERNAL CORRESPONDENCE**

Date:	January 3, 2009
To:	William Weeks, Director of Operations
From:	Helen Cho, Chemical Engineering Dept. **H. C.**
Subject:	Trip Report — Conference on Improved Procedures for Chemical Analysis Laboratory

Most writers put their initials or signature next to the typed name (or at the end of the memo) to show that they have reviewed the memo and accept responsibility for it.

Figure 14.11 Identifying Information in a Memo

Some organizations prefer the full names of the writer and reader; others want only the first initials and last names. Some prefer job titles; others do not. If your organization does not object, include your job title and your reader's. The memo will then be informative for someone who refers to it after either of you has moved on to a new position, as well as for others in the organization who might not know you.

The subject line is specific: the reader can tell at a glance that the memo reports on a trip to Computer Dynamics, Inc. If the subject line read only "Computer Dynamics, Inc.," the reader would not know what the writer is going to discuss about that company.

The memo begins with a clear statement of purpose, as discussed in Ch. 5, p. 103.

Note that the writer has provided a summary, even though the memo is less than a page. The summary gives the writer an opportunity to convey his main request: he would like to meet with the reader.

The main section of the memo is the discussion, which conveys the detailed version of the writer's message. Often the discussion begins with the background: the facts that readers will need to know to understand the memo. In this case, the background consists of a two-paragraph discussion of the two models in the company's 500 series. Presumably, the reader already knows why the writer went on the trip.

Note that the writer ends this discussion with a conclusion, or statement of the meaning of the facts. In this case, the writer's conclusion is that the company should consider only the external drive.

A recommendation is the writer's statement of what he would like the reader to do next. In this case, the writer would like to sit down with the reader to discuss how to proceed.

Dynacol Corporation

INTEROFFICE COMMUNICATION

To:　　G. Granby, R&D
From:　P. Rabin, Technical Services　**P.R.**
Subject:　Trip Report—Computer Dynamics, Inc.
Date:　September 22, 2009

The purpose of this memo is to present my impressions of the Computer Dynamics technical seminar of September 19. The goal of the seminar was to introduce their new PQ-500 line of high-capacity storage drives.

Summary
In general, I was impressed with the technical capabilities and interface of the drives. Of the two models in the 500 series, I think we ought to consider the external drives, not the internal ones. I'd like to talk to you about this issue when you have a chance.

Discussion
Computer Dynamics offers two models in its 500 series: an internal drive and an external drive. Both models have the same capacity (10 G of storage), and they both work the same way: they extend the storage capacity of a server by integrating an optical disk library into the file system. The concept is that they move files between the server's faster, but limited-capacity, storage devices (hard disks) and its slower, high-capacity storage devices (magneto-optical disks). This process, which they call data migration and demigration, is transparent to the user.

For the system administrator, integrating either of the models would require no more than one hour. The external model would be truly portable; the user would not need to install any drivers, as long as his or her device is docked on our network. The system administrator would push the necessary drivers onto all the networked devices without the user having to do anything.

Although the internal drive is convenient—it is already configured for the computer—I think we should consider only the external drive. Because so many of our employees do teleconferencing, the advantage of portability outweighs the disadvantage of inconvenience. The tech rep from Computer Dynamics walked me through the process of configuring both models. A second advantage of the external drive is that it can be salvaged easily when we take a computer out of service.

Recommendation
I'd like to talk to you, when you get a chance, about negotiating with Computer Dynamics for a quantity discount. I think we should ask McKinley and Rossiter to participate in the discussion. Give me a call (x3442) and we'll talk.

Figure 14.12　Sample Memo

Figure 14.12 is a sample memo: a trip report, or record of a business trip written after the employee returned to the office. The reader is less interested in an hour-by-hour narrative of what happened than in a carefully written discussion of what was important. Although both writer and reader in this example appear to be relatively equal in rank, the writer

Guidelines

Organizing a Memo

When you write a memo, organize it so that it is easy to follow. Consider these five important organizational elements.

▶ **A specific subject line.** "Breast Cancer Walk" is too general. "Breast Cancer Walk Rescheduled for May 14" is better.

▶ **A clear statement of purpose.** As discussed in Chapter 5, page 104, the purpose statement is built around an infinitive verb that clearly states what you want readers to know, believe, or do.

▶ **A brief summary.** Even if a memo fits on one page, consider including a summary. For readers who want to read the whole memo, the summary is an advance organizer. For readers in a hurry, reading the summary substitutes for reading the whole memo.

▶ **Informative headings.** Headings make a memo easier to read by enabling readers to skip sections they don't need and to know at a glance what each section is about. Headings make a memo easier to write because they prompt the writer to provide the kind of information readers need.

▶ **A prominent recommendation.** Many memos end with one or more recommendations. Sometimes, these recommendations take the form of action steps: bulleted or numbered lists of what the writer will do or would like others to do. Here is an example:

> **Action Items**
> I would appreciate it if you would work on the following tasks and have your results ready for the meeting on Monday, June 9.
> - Henderson: Recalculate the flow rate.
> - Smith: Set up a meeting with the regional EPA representative for sometime during the week of May 13.
> - Falvey: Ask Amitra in Houston for his advice.

---

goes to the trouble of organizing the memo to make it easy to read and refer to later.

WRITING E-MAILS

Before you write an e-mail in the workplace, find out your organization's e-mail policies. Most companies have written policies that discuss circumstances under which you may and may not use e-mail, principles you should use in writing e-mails, and monitoring of employee e-mails. Figure 14.13 on page 380 shows the basic elements of an e-mail.

When you write e-mails in the workplace, you should adhere to netiquette guidelines. *Netiquette* refers to etiquette on a network.

"CC" stands for courtesy copy. All of your recipients will know that you are sending a copy to this person or group.

"BC" or "Bcc" stands for blind copy or blind courtesy copy. None of your readers will know that you are sending a copy to this person or group.

You can create a "group" for people whom you e-mail frequently.

Like a memo, an e-mail should have a specific subject line.

By naming her readers at the start, the writer is showing respect for them.

The first paragraph of the e-mail clarifies the writer's purpose.

The second paragraph describes the idea. You want to be sure your readers understand the context.

Notice that paragraphs are relatively brief and that the writer skips a line between paragraphs.

The writer explains what she would like her readers to do, and she states a deadline.

The writer ends politely.

The writer has created a signature, which includes her contact information. This signature is attached automatically to her e-mails.

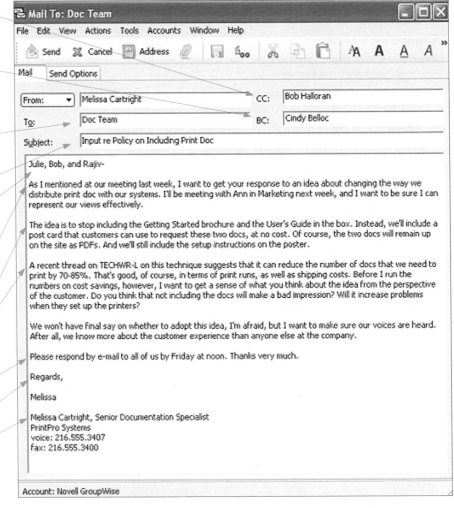

Figure 14.13 Elements of an E-mail

Guidelines

Following Netiquette

▶ **Stick to business.** Don't send jokes or other nonbusiness messages.

▶ **Don't waste bandwidth.** Keep the message brief. When you reply to another e-mail, don't quote long passages from it. Instead, establish the context of the original e-mail by paraphrasing it briefly or by including a short quotation from it. When you quote, delete the routing information from the top as well as the signature block from the bottom. And make sure to send the e-mail only to people who need to read it.

▶ **Use appropriate formality.** As discussed on page 365, avoid informal writing.

▶ **Write correctly.** As discussed on page 365, you should revise, edit, and proofread your e-mails before sending them.

▶ **Don't flame.** To *flame* is to scorch a reader with scathing criticism, usually in response to something that person wrote in a previous message. When you are angry, keep your hands away from the keyboard.

▶ **Make your message easy on the eyes.** Use uppercase and lowercase letters, and skip a line between paragraphs. Use uppercase letters (sparingly) for emphasis. Keep the line length under 65 characters so that lines do not get broken up if the recipient's monitor has a smaller screen.

▶ **Don't forward a message to another person or to an online discussion forum without the writer's permission.** Doing so is unethical and illegal; the e-mail is the intellectual property of the writer.

▶ **Don't send a message unless you have something to say.** If you can add something new, do so, but don't send a message just to be part of the conversation.

> **On TechComm Web**
>
> See Albion.com's discussion of netiquette. Click on Links Library for Ch. 14 on <bedfordstmartins.com/techcomm>.

Figure 14.14a shows an e-mail that violates netiquette guidelines. The writer is a technical professional working for a microchip manufacturer. Figure 14.14b on page 382 shows a revised version of this e-mail message.

| To: Supers and Leads | *The writer does not clearly state his purpose in the subject line and the first paragraph.* |
| Subject: | |

LATELY, WE HAVE BEEN MISSING LASER REPAIR FILES FOR OUR 16MEG WAFERS. AFTER BRIEF INVESTIGATION, I HAVE FOUND THE MAIN REASON FOR THE MISSING DATA.

OCCASIONALLY, SOME OF YOU HAVE WRONGLY PROBED THE WAFERS UNDER THE CORRELATE STEP AND THE DATA IS THEN COPIED INTO THE NONPROD STEP USING THE QTR PROGRAM. THIS IS REALLY STUPID. WHEN DATE IS COPIED THIS WAY THE REPAIR DATA IS NOT COPIED. IT REMAINS UNDER THE CORRELATE STEP.

TO AVOID THIS PROBLEM, FIRST PROBE THE WAFERS THE RIGHT WAY. IF A WAFER MUST BE PROBED UNDER A DIFFERENT STEP, THE WAFER IN THE CHANGE FILE MUST BE RENAMED TO THE ** FORMAT.

EDITING THE WAFER DATA FILE SHOULD BE USED ONLY AS A LAST RESORT, IF THIS BECOMES A COMMON PROBLEM, WE COULD HAVE MORE PROBLEMS WITH INVALID DATA THAT THERE ARE NOW.

SUPERS AND LEADS: PLEASE PASS THIS INFORMATION ALONG TO THOSE WHO NEED TO KNOW.

ROGER VANDENHEUVAL

Using all uppercase letters gives the impression that the writer is yelling at the readers.

The writer has not proofread.

With long lines and no spaces between paragraphs, this e-mail is difficult to read.

a. E-mail that violates netiquette guidelines

Figure 14.14   Netiquette

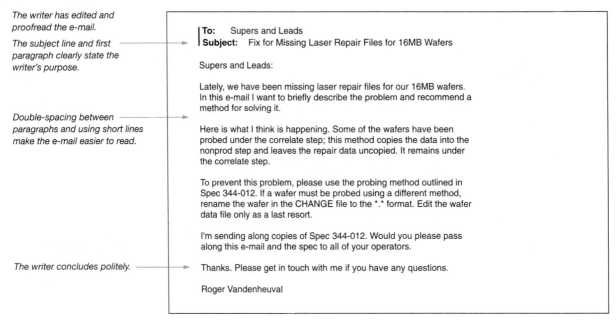

The writer has edited and proofread the e-mail.

The subject line and first paragraph clearly state the writer's purpose.

Double-spacing between paragraphs and using short lines make the e-mail easier to read.

The writer concludes politely.

To: Supers and Leads
Subject: Fix for Missing Laser Repair Files for 16MB Wafers

Supers and Leads:

Lately, we have been missing laser repair files for our 16MB wafers. In this e-mail I want to briefly describe the problem and recommend a method for solving it.

Here is what I think is happening. Some of the wafers have been probed under the correlate step; this method copies the data into the nonprod step and leaves the repair data uncopied. It remains under the correlate step.

To prevent this problem, please use the probing method outlined in Spec 344-012. If a wafer must be probed using a different method, rename the wafer in the CHANGE file to the *.* format. Edit the wafer data file only as a last resort.

I'm sending along copies of Spec 344-012. Would you please pass along this e-mail and the spec to all of your operators.

Thanks. Please get in touch with me if you have any questions.

Roger Vandenheuval

b. E-mail that adheres to netiquette guidelines

Figure 14.14   (continued)

WRITING BUSINESS CORRESPONDENCE TO INTERCULTURAL READERS

The three forms of business correspondence discussed in this chapter are used in all countries around the world. The ways they are used, however, can differ significantly from the ways they are used in the United States. These differences fall into three categories:

- *Cultural practices.* As discussed in Chapter 5, cultures differ in a number of ways, such as the focus on individuals or groups, the distance between power ranks, and attitudes toward uncertainty. Typically, a culture's attitudes are reflected in its business communication. For instance, people in the United States are surprised when they send a fax to a Japanese company but don't receive a reply for a week. The reason? Japanese culture is highly group oriented, and in most companies, employees sit down once a week to sort through their incoming faxes and delegate people to respond to them (Brannen and Wilen, 1993). In addition, in cultures in which people in top positions are treated with great respect by their subordinates, the reader might be addressed as "Most Esteemed Mr. Director."

In This Book
For more about cultural variables, see Ch. 5, p. 95.

- *Language use and tone.* In the United States, writers tend to use contractions, the first names of their readers, and other informal language. In many other countries, this informality is potentially offensive. Also potentially offensive is U.S. directness. An American might write, for

INTERACTIVE SAMPLE DOCUMENT
Following Netiquette in an E-mail Message

This message was written in response to a question e-mailed to several colleagues by a technical communicator seeking advice on how to write meeting minutes effectively. A response to an e-mail message should adhere to the principles of effective e-mails and proper netiquette. The questions in the margin ask you to think about these principles (explained on pages 380–82). E-mail your responses to yourself and/or your instructor on TechComm Web.

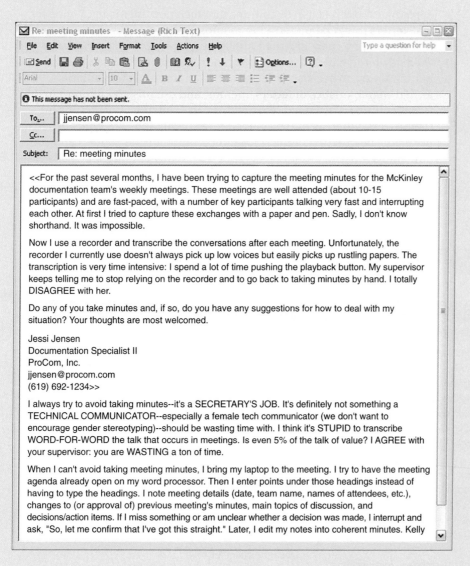

1. How effectively has the writer conserved bandwidth?

2. How effectively has the writer stated her purpose?

3. How effectively has the writer projected a "you attitude" (explained on page 366)?

4. How effectively has the writer made her message easy to read?

On TechComm Web

To e-mail responses to yourself and/or your instructor, click on Interactive Sample Documents for Ch. 14 on <bedfordstmartins.com/techcomm>.

example, "Fourteen percent of the products we received from you failed to meet the specifications." A Korean would more likely write, "We were pleased to note that 86 percent of the products we received met the specifications." The Korean writer either would not refer to the other 14 percent (assuming that the reader would get the point and replace the defective products quickly) or would write, "We would appreciate replacement of the remaining products." Many other aspects of business correspondence differ from culture to culture, such as preferred length, specificity, and the use of seasonal references in the correspondence.

- *Application choice and use.* In cultures in which documents tend to be formal, letters might be preferred to memos, or face-to-face meetings to phone calls or e-mail. In Asia, for instance, a person is more likely to walk down the hall to deliver a brief message in person than to send a written message because doing so shows more respect. In addition, the formal characteristics of letters, memos, and e-mails are different in different cultures. The French, for instance, use indented paragraphs in their letters, whereas in the United States paragraphs are typically left-justified. The ordering of the information in the inside address and complimentary close of letters varies widely. In many countries, e-mails are structured like memos, with the "to," "from," "subject," and "date" information added at the top of the e-mail, even though this information is already present in the routing information.

Try to study letters, memos, and e-mails written by people from the culture you will be addressing. Also try to have important letters, memos, and e-mails reviewed by a person from that culture before you send them.

Writer's Checklist

Letter Format

- ☐ Is the first page typed on letterhead stationery? (p. 369)
- ☐ Is the date included? (p. 369)
- ☐ Is the inside address complete and correct? (p. 369)
- ☐ Is the appropriate courtesy title used? (p. 369)
- ☐ If appropriate, is an attention line included? (p. 369)
- ☐ If appropriate, is a subject line included? (p. 369)
- ☐ Is the salutation appropriate? (p. 369)
- ☐ Is the complimentary close typed with only the first word capitalized? (p. 370)
- ☐ Is the signature legible, and is the writer's name typed beneath the signature? (p. 370)
- ☐ If appropriate, is an enclosure line included? (p. 370)
- ☐ If appropriate, is a copy and/or courtesy-copy line included? (p. 370)
- ☐ Is the letter typed in one of the standard formats? (p. 370)

Types of Letters

Does the inquiry letter

- ☐ explain why you chose the reader to receive the inquiry? (p. 372)
- ☐ explain why you are requesting the information and to what use you will put it? (p. 372)
- ☐ specify by what date you need the information? (p. 372)
- ☐ list the questions clearly and, if appropriate, provide room for the reader's responses? (p. 372)
- ☐ offer, if appropriate, the product of your research? (p. 372)

- ☐ Does the response to an inquiry letter answer the reader's questions or explain why they cannot be answered? (p. 373)

Does the claim letter

- ☐ identify specifically the unsatisfactory product or service? (p. 374)

☐ explain the problem(s) clearly? (p. 374)
☐ propose an adjustment? (p. 374)
☐ conclude courteously? (p. 374)

Does the "good news" adjustment letter
☐ express your regret? (p. 375)
☐ explain the adjustment you will make? (p. 375)
☐ conclude on a positive note? (p. 375)

Does the "bad news" adjustment letter
☐ meet the reader on neutral ground, expressing regret but not apologizing? (p. 376)
☐ explain why the company is not at fault? (p. 376)
☐ clearly deny the reader's request? (p. 376)
☐ attempt to create goodwill? (p. 376)

Memos
☐ Does the identifying information adhere to your organization's standards? (p. 377)
☐ Did you clearly state your purpose at the start of the memo? (p. 378)
☐ Did you use headings to help your readers? (p. 378)

☐ If appropriate, did you summarize your message? (p. 378)
☐ Did you provide appropriate background for the discussion? (p. 378)
☐ Did you organize the discussion clearly? (p. 378)
☐ Did you highlight items requiring action? (p. 378)

E-mails
☐ Did you refrain from discussing nonbusiness subjects? (p. 380)
☐ Did you keep the e-mail as brief as possible and send it only to appropriate people? (p. 380)
☐ Did you use appropriate formality? (p. 381)
☐ Did you write correctly? (p. 381)
☐ Did you avoid flaming? (p. 381)
☐ Did you check with the writer before forwarding his or her message? (p. 381)
☐ Did you write a specific, accurate subject line? (p. 381)
☐ Did you use uppercase and lowercase letters? (p. 381)
☐ Did you skip a line between paragraphs? (p. 381)
☐ Did you set the line length under 65 characters? (p. 381)

Exercises

1. A beverage container you recently purchased for $8.95 has a serious leak. The grape drink you put in it ruined a $35 white tablecloth. Inventing any reasonable details, write a claim letter to the manufacturer of the container.

2. As the recipient of the claim letter described in Exercise 1, write an adjustment letter granting the customer's request.

3. You are the manager of a private swimming club. A member has written saying that she lost a contact lens (value $75) in your pool and she wants you to pay for a replacement. The contract that all members sign explicitly states that the management is not responsible for the loss of personal possessions. Write an adjustment letter denying the request. Invent any reasonable details.

4. As manager of an electronics retail store, you guarantee that you will not be undersold. If a customer who buys something from you can prove within one month that another retailer sells the same equipment at a lower price, you will refund the difference. A customer has written to you and enclosed an ad from another store showing that it is selling the router he purchased for $26.50 less than he paid at your store. The advertised price at the other store was a one-week sale that began five weeks after the date of his purchase. He wants a $26.50 refund. Inventing any reasonable details, write an adjustment letter denying his request. You are willing, however, to offer him a 2GB USB drive worth $9.95 if he would like to come pick it up.

5. **GROUP EXERCISE** Form small groups for this exercise on claim and adjustment letters. Have each member of your group study the following two letters. Meet and discuss your reactions to the letters. How effectively does the writer of the claim letter present his case? How effective is the adjustment letter? Does its writer succeed in showing that the company's procedures for ensuring hygiene are effective? Does its writer succeed in projecting a professional tone? Write a memo to your instructor discussing the two letters. Attach a revision of the adjustment letter to the memo.

Seth Reeves
19 Lowry's Lane
Morgan, TN 30610

April 13, 2009

Sea-Tasty Tuna
Route 113
Lynchburg, TN 30563

Gentlemen:

I've been buying your tuna fish for years, and up to now it's been OK.

But this morning I opened a can to make myself a sandwich. What do you think was staring me in the face? A fly. That's right, a housefly. That's him you see taped to the bottom of this letter.

What are you going to do about this?

Yours very truly,

SEA-TASTY TUNA
Route 113
Lynchburg, TN 30563
www.seatastytuna.com

April 21, 2009

Mr. Seth Reeves
19 Lowry's Lane
Morgan, TN 30610

Dear Mr. Reeves:

We were very sorry to learn that you found a fly in your tuna fish.

Here at Sea-Tasty we are very careful about the hygiene of our plant. The tuna are scrubbed thoroughly as soon as we receive them. After they are processed, they are inspected visually at three different points. Before we pack them, we rinse and sterilize the cans to ensure that no foreign material is sealed in them.

Because of these stringent controls, we really don't see how you could have found a fly in the can. Nevertheless, we are enclosing coupons good for two cans of Sea-Tasty tuna.

We hope this letter restores your confidence in us.

Truly yours,

6. Louise and Paul work for the same manufacturing company. Louise, a senior engineer, is chairing a committee to investigate ways to improve the hiring process at the company. Paul, a technical editor, also serves on the committee. The excerpts quoted in Louise's e-mail are from an e-mail written by Paul to all members of the committee in response to Louise's request that members describe their approach to evaluating job-application materials. How would you revise Louise's e-mail to make it more effective?

> To: Paul
>
> From: Louise
>
> Sometimes I just have to wonder what you're thinking, Paul.
>
> >Of course, it's not possible to expect perfect
> >resumes. But I have to screen them, and last
> >year I had to read over 200. I'm not looking for
> >perfection, but as soon as I spot an error I make
> >a mental note of it and, when I hit a second and
> >then a third error I can't really concentrate on the
> >writer's credentials.
>
> Listen, Paul, you might be a sharp editor, but the rest of us have a different responsibility: to make the products and move them out as soon as possible. We don't have the luxury of studying documents to see if we can find errors. I suggest you concentrate on what you were hired to do, without imposing your "standards" on the rest of us.
>
> >From my point of view, an error can include a
> >misused trademark.
>
> Misusing a "tradmark," Paul? Is that Error Number 1?

7. **INTERNET EXERCISE** Because students use e-mail to communicate with other group members when they write collaboratively, your college or university would like to create a one-page handout on how to use e-mail responsibly. Using a search engine, find three or four netiquette guides on the Internet that focus on using e-mail. Study these guides and write a one-page student guide to using e-mail to communicate with other students. Somewhere in the guide, be sure to list the sites you studied, so that students can visit them for further information about netiquette.

Case 14: Projecting the "You Attitude" When Corresponding with Customers and Colleagues

Background

You work for the Customer Service Department at United Tools, a successful manufacturer and marketer of tools and equipment for professional tool users in the United States. Product lines include hand and power tools for vehicle-service, industrial, agricultural, electrical, and construction applications. Recently, United Tools received a letter from a hardware store that carries its products (Document 14.1). You try to speak to your supervisor, Russ Ong, about the situation. Unfortunately, Russ has just learned about a shipping error that loaded all tool orders from West Coast retailers on a truck heading to New York. While rushing off to a meeting, Russ tells you, "Anytime a weekend warrior gets hurt using one of our tools, the tool is always assumed to be the problem. People need to learn to use tools for what they're designed for. Pipe wrenches are for gripping

and turning a pipe. They are not designed to be used as crowbars, hammers, or pliers. I don't have time for this."

You decide to investigate the situation. A colleague in Marketing sends you an e-mail message (Document 14.2) providing some background on the pipe wrench in question, the UT904.

You decide to investigate the situation further. One of the company engineers replies to your request for information on the UT904 (Document 14.3).

At lunch you explain the situation to Maureen Perez, a colleague in the Customer Service Department: "I think I may have uncovered a problem with our UT9 pipe wrenches. But I don't think Russ, Marketing, or R&D believes a problem exists."

"Be careful how you handle this," Maureen cautions. "Remember what happened to Bev when she accused Richard—in a widely circulated e-mail message—of

---

Handee Hardware, Inc.
Millersville, AL 61304
www.handeehardware.com

December 4, 2009
United Tools
20 Central Avenue
Dover, TX 76104

Gentlemen:

I have a problem I'd like to discuss with you. I've been carrying your line of hand tools for many years.

Your 9" pipe wrench has always been a big seller. But there seems to be something wrong with its design. I have had two complaints in the last few months about the handle snapping off when pressure is exerted on it. In one case, the user cut his hand seriously enough to require stitches.

Frankly, I'm hesitant to sell any more of the 9" pipe wrenches but still have more than two dozen in inventory.

Have you had any other complaints about this product?

Sincerely yours,

Chel Thomas

Chel Thomas

Document 14.1 Claim Letter from Handee Hardware

 **On TechComm Web**

For digital versions of case documents, click on Downloadable Case Documents on <bedfordstmartins.com/techcomm>.

designing an unsafe brake-line flaring tool. Switched to the night shift, one negative performance evaluation, and three weeks later Bev was gone."

Your Assignment

1. Write a memo or letter to an appropriate officer in the company alerting him or her to the situation you have uncovered and presenting appropriate recommendations. (For a discussion of ethical and legal considerations, see Chapter 2.)

2. Assume that your supervisor has authorized you to draft a letter offering an appropriate adjustment to the retailers and the retail customers who wrote claim letters to your company. Draft the letter.

Document 14.2   E-mail from Marketing Department

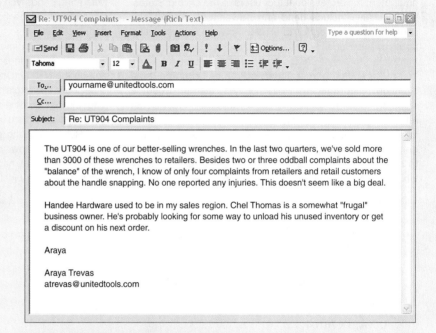

To...: yourname@unitedtools.com

Subject: Re: UT904 Complaints

The UT904 is one of our better-selling wrenches. In the last two quarters, we've sold more than 3000 of these wrenches to retailers. Besides two or three oddball complaints about the "balance" of the wrench, I know of only four complaints from retailers and retail customers about the handle snapping. No one reported any injuries. This doesn't seem like a big deal.

Handee Hardware used to be in my sales region. Chel Thomas is a somewhat "frugal" business owner. He's probably looking for some way to unload his unused inventory or get a discount on his next order.

Araya

Araya Trevas
atrevas@unitedtools.com

Document 14.3   E-mail from Research and Development Department

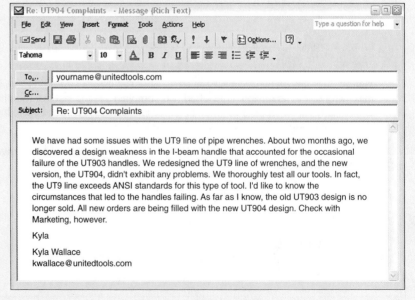

To...: yourname@unitedtools.com

Subject: Re: UT904 Complaints

We have had some issues with the UT9 line of pipe wrenches. About two months ago, we discovered a design weakness in the I-beam handle that accounted for the occasional failure of the UT903 handles. We redesigned the UT9 line of wrenches, and the new version, the UT904, didn't exhibit any problems. We thoroughly test all our tools. In fact, the UT9 line exceeds ANSI standards for this type of tool. I'd like to know the circumstances that led to the handles failing. As far as I know, the old UT903 design is no longer sold. All new orders are being filled with the new UT904 design. Check with Marketing, however.

Kyla

Kyla Wallace
kwallace@unitedtools.com

Preparing Job-Application Materials

Understanding the Process of Preparing Job-Application Materials 390

Planning the Job Search 390

Understanding Seven Ways to Look for a Position 393

Understanding the Risks and Benefits of Social-Networking Sites and the Job Search 394

Writing Paper Résumés 395

Appearance of the Résumé 395

Content of the Résumé 396

Elements of the Chronological Résumé 399

Elements of the Skills Résumé 407

Writing Electronic Résumés 407

Content of the Electronic Résumé 412

Format of the Electronic Résumé 413

Writing Job-Application Letters 415

The Concepts of Selectivity and Development 415

Elements of the Job-Application Letter 417

Preparing for a Job Interview 422

Writing Follow-up Letters After an Interview 424

Felicia E. Chong
My Professional Portfolio

Home
Resume
Education
Employment History
Coursework
Honors and Awards
Skills
Internship
Volunteer Activities
References
Contact Information

Search

GO
⊙ Full Site
○ This Section

Search Tips

Introduction

Hello! Welcome to my professional portfolio! This site has been composed to offer you an ability to look at my Resume, Educational Folio, and Work Folio.

I am currently teaching Graphics Communications and Photography classes at Patrick Henry High School in North Minneapolis, MN.

I consider myself a self-motivated, flexible and highly responsible professional and technical communicator who has the following qualities:

- Possess outstanding written and verbal communication skills
- Learn and apply new skills quickly
- Exhibit superior organizational and multi-tasking skills by completing projects within time and budget constraints
- Demonstrate dynamic leadership qualities/team player
- Excel at computer skills—well-versed in Microsoft Word, Excel, PowerPoint, Publisher and FrontPage, Macromedia Dreamweaver (HTML and CSS) and Adobe Photoshop
- Speak and write fluently in Chinese (Mandarin)

Note: This site is best viewed using Internet Explorer.

Last updated on June 23, 2007.

Printer-friendly Version

Home | Resume | Education | Employment History | Coursework | Honors and Awards | Skills | Internship | Volunteer Activities | References | Contact Information

Copyright © 2007 Felicia E. Chong

Electronic Portfolio Technology Provided By

Minnesota STATE COLLEGES & UNIVERSITIES eFolio e

Source: Chong, 2007 <www.feliciachong.efoliomn.com>.

In the World . . .

Felicia Chong's professional portfolio appears on eFolio Minnesota, a Web site showcasing that state's residents. Some students present their portfolios on sites maintained by their college or university's career center; others maintain their own Web sites or use social-networking sites. The Internet is rapidly changing almost every aspect of how employers advertise openings and how applicants look for work. Two things that haven't changed are that employers still want employees who are honest, professional, and articulate, and that applicants still have to show those qualities by preparing a set of job-application materials.

Almost certainly, you will not work for one employer, or even a few employers, for your whole career. According to the U.S. Department of Labor (2006), the typical American worker holds more than 10 different jobs while he or she is between the ages of 18 and 38. Obviously, these jobs don't last long. Even when American workers begin a job between the ages of 33 and 38, nearly 40 percent of them will no longer be with that company at the end of one year. And 70 percent of them will no longer be with that company in five years. Every time you change your job, you will need to change your résumé and your other job-application materials.

For most of you, the first nonacademic test of your technical-communication skills comes when you prepare job-application materials. And it's an important test. A survey of 120 major U.S. corporations concluded that writing ability is related to workplace success: "People who cannot write and communicate clearly will not be hired, and if already working, are unlikely to last long enough to be considered for promotion" (College Entrance, 2004).

UNDERSTANDING THE PROCESS OF PREPARING JOB-APPLICATION MATERIALS

Preparing job-application materials requires weeks and months, not days, and there is no way to cut corners. Figure 15.1 presents an overview of the process.

PLANNING THE JOB SEARCH

In planning a job search, you have four main tasks:

- *Do a self-inventory.* Before you can start thinking of where you want to work, you need to answer some questions about yourself:
  - *What are your strengths and weaknesses?* Are your skills primarily technical? Do you work best with others or on your own?
  - *What subjects do you like?* Think about what you have liked or disliked about your jobs and college courses.
  - *What kind of organization would you like to work for?* Profit or nonprofit? Government or private industry? Small or large?
  - *What are your geographical preferences?* If you are free to relocate, where would you like to live? How do you feel about commuting?
- *Learn about the employers.* Don't base your job search exclusively on information in an ad. Learn about the organization through other means as well:
  - *Attend job fairs.* Your college and your community probably hold job fairs, where employers provide information about their organizations. Sometimes, a single organization will hold a job fair to find qualified candidates for a wide variety of jobs.

Figure 15.1   An Overview of the Process of Preparing Job-Application Materials

Plan the Job Search

Do a self-inventory, learn as much as you can about potential employers, and begin to plan your materials.

Decide How to Look for a Position

Use as many resources as you can, including the college-placement office on campus, published ads, and company Web sites.

Learn as Much as You Can About the Organizations to Which You Will Apply

Use appropriate techniques of primary and secondary research. See Chapter 6.

Draft the Résumé and Application Letter

Decide whether to write a chronological or a skills résumé. Include the traditional sections—identifying information, objectives, education, employment history, personal information, and references—and other appropriate sections, such as military service, language skills, or computer skills. For a skills résumé, include a skills section. Decide whether to write a scannable résumé.

Write the letter to elaborate on several key points from the résumé. Include the traditional introductory and concluding paragraphs, as well as at least one paragraph about your job experience and one about your education.

Revise, Edit, and Proofread the Résumé and Letter

You want these documents to be perfect. Try to have several people help you review them. See the Writer's Checklist on page 426.

Prepare for Job Interviews

Study job interviews, research the organizations you applied to, think about what you can offer these organizations, study lists of common interview questions, compile a list of questions to ask, and rehearse the interview.

Write Appropriate Follow-up Letters

With any luck, you'll get to write a letter of appreciation after an interview and then a letter accepting a job offer.

▶ On TechComm Web

To find the *Occupational Outlook Handbook,* click on Links Library for Ch. 15 on <bedfordstmartins.com/techcomm>.

— *Find out about trends in your field.* Read the *Occupational Outlook Handbook,* published by the U.S. Department of Labor, for information about your field and related fields. Talk with professors and with the staff at your job-placement office.

— *Research the companies that interest you.* Visit their Web sites. Scan the index of *The Wall Street Journal* for articles about them. Study their annual reports on their Web sites.

- *Prepare a résumé and job-application letter.* You know you will write these documents and go on interviews. Start planning early by obtaining materials from the career-placement office. Talk with friends who have gone through the process successfully; study their application materials. Read books and visit Web sites about different aspects of the job search.

▶ On TechComm Web

For more about online portfolios, see "Developing Your Online Portfolio" by Kevin M. Barry and Jill C. Wesolowski. Click on Links Library for Ch. 15 on <bedfordstmartins.com/techcomm>.

- *Prepare a portfolio.* A portfolio is a collection of your best work. You'll want to give a prospective employer a copy of the portfolio to showcase your skills. For technical communicators, the portfolio will include a variety of documents created in courses and in previous positions. For technical professionals, it might include proposals, reports, computer simulations, Web sites, and presentation graphics. A portfolio can be presented in a loose-leaf notebook, with each item preceded by a descriptive and evaluative statement. Often, it is digital, presented on a CD or Web site.

  Items typically presented in an electronic portfolio include a résumé; letters of recommendation; transcripts and professional certifications; and reports, papers, Web sites, slides of oral presentations, and other kinds of documents the applicant has written or created as a student or an employee.

  Because the portfolio is electronic, it can include all kinds of media, from simple word-processed documents to HTML files, video, audio, and animation. And it's relatively easy to update an electronic portfolio: just add the new items as you create them. One important point comes across clearly in a carefully prepared electronic portfolio: you know how to create a Web site.

If you wish to apply for a position in another country, keep in mind that the conventions of the process vary—sometimes quite a bit. You will need to adapt your résumé and letter to the expectations of the country in which you would like to work. Consult one of the following sources for advice on drafting résumés when applying for international positions:

- Goinglobal.com <www.goinglobal.com/topic/resumes.asp>.
- Krannich, R. L., & Enelow, W. S. (2002). *Best résumés and CVs for international jobs.* Manassas Park, VA: Impact Publications.
- Monster Work Abroad <http://international.monster.com>.
- Segal, N., & Kocher, E. (2003). *International jobs: Where they are and how to get them.* (6th ed.). Jackson, TN: Basic Books.
- Thompson, M. A. (2002). *The global résumé and CV guide.* Hoboken, NJ: John Wiley & Sons.

UNDERSTANDING SEVEN WAYS TO LOOK FOR A POSITION

Once you have done your planning, you can start to look for a position. There are seven major ways to find a job.

- *Through a college or university placement office.* Placement offices bring companies and students together. Student résumés are made available to representatives of business, government, and industry, who arrange on-campus interviews. The students who do best in the campus interviews are then invited to visit the organization for a tour and another interview.

- *Through a professional placement bureau.* A professional placement bureau offers essentially the same service as a college placement office but charges a fee to either the employer or the new employee. Placement bureaus cater primarily to more-advanced professionals who are changing jobs.

- *Through a published job ad.* Organizations publish ads in public-relations catalogs (such as *College Placement Annual*), technical journals, magazines, and newspapers. Be sure to check the online versions of journals in your field, as well as large metropolitan newspapers. And do not overlook bulletin-board sites such as CraigsList. In responding to an ad, you most likely will send a résumé and a job-application letter.

- *Through an organization's Web site.* Most organizations list their job offerings on their Web sites and explain how to apply.

- *Through a job board on the Internet.* Job boards are sites sponsored by federal agencies, Internet service providers, and private organizations. Some sites merely list positions, to which you respond by regular mail or e-mail; others let you submit your résumé electronically, so that employers can get in touch with you. Use a search engine to search for "employment," "careers," and "jobs." Or combine one of these terms with the name of your field, as in "careers and forestry." Among the biggest job boards are the following:

  — AfterCollege
  — CareerBuilder
  — CareerMag
  — CareerOneStop (sponsored by the U.S. Department of Labor)
  — Indeed (a metasearch engine for job seekers)
  — Monster

    Many of these sites contain articles about searching for jobs electronically, including how to research companies, how to write electronic résumés, and how to prepare for interviews.

In This Book

For more about job-application letters, see p. 415. For more about electronic résumés, see p. 407.

On TechComm Web

To find these sites and additional job-related resources on the Web, click on Links Library for Ch. 15 on <bedfordstmartins.com/techcomm>.

One caution about using job boards: once you post something to an Internet site, you probably have lost control of it. Here are four questions to ask before you post to a job board:

— Who has access to your résumé? You might want to remove your home address and phone number from it if everyone can view it.
— How will you know if an employer requests your résumé? Will you be notified by the job board?
— Can your current employer see your résumé? If your employer knows you are looking for a new job, your current position could be jeopardized.
— Can you update your résumé at no cost? Some job boards charge you each time you update it.

- *Through an unsolicited letter to an organization.* Instead of waiting for an ad or a notice on a Web site, consider sending an unsolicited application. The disadvantage is obvious: there might not be an opening. Yet many professionals favor this technique, because there are fewer competitors for those jobs that do exist, and organizations do not advertise all available positions. Sometimes, an impressive unsolicited application can even prompt an organization to create a position.

  Before you write an unsolicited application, learn as much as you can about the organization: current and anticipated major projects, hiring plans, and so forth. The business librarian at your college or university will be able to point out additional sources of information, such as the Dun and Bradstreet guides, the *F&S Index of Corporations*, and indexed newspapers such as *The New York Times*, *The Washington Post*, and *The Wall Street Journal*. You should also study the organization's Web site.

- *Through connections.* A relative or an acquaintance can exert influence, or at least point out a new position. Other good contacts include past employers and professors. Also consider becoming active in the student chapter of your field's professional organization, through which you can meet professionals in your area.

UNDERSTANDING THE RISKS AND BENEFITS OF SOCIAL-NETWORKING SITES AND THE JOB SEARCH

Long before you plan to begin a job search, you should carefully consider how you currently appear online. Employers regularly search the Internet while screening job applicants. They are sure to visit social-networking sites such as MySpace and Facebook (ExecuNet, 2006). Employers also search for blog and online-forum postings written by job applicants. Pictures of you at a raucous party, a blog critical of your current boss, or an unflattering YouTube video can jeopardize your job search or even your current employment.

You should closely monitor the content and images posted on your own sites and periodically search the Internet for your name to see what prospective employers are likely to find. When searching for a job, use your accounts on social-networking sites to make a good first impression. Assume that prospective employers will visit your personal sites. Use their visits as an opportunity to market yourself by displaying text and images that demonstrate your best qualities.

Expand your networking activities online by using sites to connect with people who share your professional interests and to hear about job openings. Create a profile tailored to the type of job you seek, project a professional persona, follow through with what you say you will do, and help others make career connections (networking works in both directions). Used appropriately, social-networking sites are another tool to help you land a job.

▶ **On TechComm Web**

For advice on how to use networking sites to your advantage, see Alison Doyle's "Your Professional Brand." Click on Links Library for Ch. 15 on <bedfordstmartins.com/techcomm>.

WRITING PAPER RÉSUMÉS

This section discusses the fundamentals of preparing paper résumés. The next section discusses electronic résumés.

Many students wonder whether they should write their résumés themselves or use a résumé-preparation agency. It is best to write your own résumé, for three reasons:

- *You know yourself better than anyone else does.* No matter how professional the work of a résumé-preparation agency, you can do a better job communicating important information about yourself.

- *Employment officers know the style of the local agencies.* Readers who realize that you did not write your own résumé might wonder whether you are hiding any deficiencies.

- *If you write your own résumé, you will be more likely to adapt it to different situations.* You are unlikely to return to a résumé-preparation agency and pay an additional fee to make a minor revision.

The résumé communicates in two ways: through its appearance and through its content.

Appearance of the Résumé

Your résumé has to look professional. When employers look at a résumé, they see the documents they will be reading if they hire you. Résumés should appear neat and professional and have the following characteristics:

- *Generous margins.* Leave a one-inch margin on all four sides.
- *Clear type.* Use a good-quality laser printer.
- *Balance.* Arrange the information so that the page has a balanced appearance.

- *Clear organization.* Use adequate white space. The line spacing between items should be greater than the line spacing within an item. That is, there should be more space between your education section and your employment section than between items within either of those sections. You should be able to see the different sections clearly if you stand and look down at the résumé on the floor by your feet.

Indent appropriately. When you arrange items in a vertical list, indent *turnovers*, the second and subsequent lines of any item, a few spaces. The following list, from the computer-skills section of a résumé, could be confusing:

Computer Experience

Systems: PC, Macintosh, UNIX, Andover AC-256, Prime 360
Software: Dreamweaver, XMetal, Flash, DBase V, PlanPerfect, Micrografx Designer, Adobe FrameMaker, Microsoft Office
Languages: C#, C++, Java, HTML, XHTML

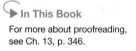
In This Book
For more about page design, see Ch. 11, p. 263.

When the second line of the long entry is indented, the arrangement is much easier to understand:

Computer Experience

Systems: PC, Macintosh, UNIX, Andover AC-256, Prime 360
Software: Dreamweaver, XMetal, Flash, DBase V, PlanPerfect, Micrografx Designer, Adobe FrameMaker, Microsoft Office
Languages: C#, C++, Java, HTML, XHTML

Figure 15.2 shows how an unattractive résumé creates a negative impression, whereas an attractive one creates a positive impression.

Content of the Résumé

Although experts advocate different approaches to résumé writing, they all agree that résumés must be informative and attractive.

- *The résumé must provide clear, specific information, without generalizations or self-congratulation.* Your résumé is a sales document, but you are both the salesperson and the product. You cannot gracefully say "I am a terrific job candidate." Instead, you have to provide the details that will lead readers to conclude that you are a terrific job candidate.

In This Book
For more about proofreading, see Ch. 13, p. 346.

- *The résumé must be free of errors.* Writing errors cast doubt on the accuracy of the information in the résumé. Ask for assistance after you have written your draft, and proofread the finished product at least twice. Then have someone else proofread it, too.

A résumé should be long enough to include all pertinent information but not so long that it bores or irritates readers. If you have less than 10 years' experience or are applying for an entry-level position, most readers will expect

James K. Wislo	1628 Rossi Street Boise, ID 83706 (208) 555 2697 jameswislo@mail.boisestate.edu
Objective	Entry-level position as a general assistant
Education	Boise State University, Boise, ID BS in Biomechanical Engineering Current GPA: 3.1 Expected date of graduation: August 2011 *Related course work* Basic Mechanics I Skeletal Development and Evolution Biomechanics of Movement Technical Communication
Employment	1/2007–present (20 hours per week): Custodial and maintenance *Boise State University, recreation center, Boise, ID* Install and maintain soap dispenser machines. Treat all floors (wooden and linoleum) with appropriate chemicals. Pressure-wash showers and sauna using TENNANT 750 machine. Report damaged equipment in the building. Report any shortage or lack of cleaning detergent and equipment. Organize daily and weekly cleaning schedule. 10/2006–1/2007: Food server *Aramark Food Service, Boise, ID* Serve food across counter. Prepare all condiments to be served. Clean kitchen and eating area after regular open hours. Act as a liaison between students and chef: report on likes and dislikes of students.
Honors	National Dean's list 2006–2007 Awarded $4,500 GEM scholarship from Boise State University
Activities	Member, Boise State University international student organization Certified CPR Instructor, American Red Cross
References	Available upon request

a. Unattractively designed résumé

Figure 15.2   Unattractive and Attractive Résumés

The unattractive résumé, with its inadequate margins, poor balance, and poor line spacing, is a chore to read. The attractive résumé is much easier to read and makes a much better impression on readers.

Figure 15.2   (continued)

James K. Wislo

1628 Rossi Street
Boise, ID 83706

(208) 555-2697
jameswislo@mailboisestate.edu

Objective

Entry-level position as a general assistant

Education

Boise State University, Boise, ID
BS in Biomechanical Engineering
Current GPA: 3.1
Expected date of graduation: August 2011

Related course work
  Skeletal Development and Evolution
  Biomechanics of Movement
  Basic Mechanics I
  Technical Communication

Employment

1/2007–present (20 hours per week): Custodial and maintenance
Boise State University, recreation center, Boise, ID
- Install and maintain soap dispenser machines.
- Treat all floors (wooden and linoleum) with appropriate chemicals.
- Pressure-wash showers and sauna using TENNANT 750 machine.
- Report damaged equipment in the building.
- Report any shortage or lack of cleaning detergent and equipment.
- Organize daily and weekly cleaning schedule.

10/2006–1/2007: Food server
Aramark Food Service, Boise, ID
- Serve food across counter.
- Prepare all condiments to be served.
- Clean kitchen and eating area after regular open hours.
- Act as a liaison between students and chef: report on likes and dislikes of students.

Honors

- National Dean's List 2006–2007
- Awarded $4,500 GEM scholarship from Boise State University

Activities

- Member, Boise State University international student organization
- Certified CPR Instructor, American Red Cross

References

Available upon request

b. Attractively designed résumé

> ### Ethics Note
>
> **Writing Honest Job-Application Materials**
>
> Many résumés contain lies or exaggerations. Job applicants say they attended colleges they didn't and were awarded degrees they weren't, give themselves inflated job titles, say they were laid off when they were really fired for poor performance, and inflate their accomplishments. Companies take this problem seriously. One survey (JobWeb.com, 2004) found that of the top 10 qualities employers look for in job applicants, number one is communication skills (both written and oral), and number two is honesty and integrity. According to Maxwell (2006), 79 percent of employers routinely check applicants' credentials. Employers hire agencies that verify each candidate's education and employment history, check for a criminal record, and check with the appropriate department of motor vehicles. If the company finds any discrepancies, which Maxwell (2006) says happens almost half the time, it does not offer the candidate a position. If the person is already working for the company, he or she is fired (Wait & Dizard, 2003).

a one- or perhaps two-page résumé. If you have more than 10 years' experience or the job is more advanced than an entry-level position, readers will expect a two-page résumé (Isaacs, 2004). If the information comes to just over a page, either eliminate or condense some of the material to make it fit onto one page or modify the layout so that it fills a substantial part of the second page.

Two common résumé styles are chronological and skills. In a *chronological résumé*, you use time as the organizing pattern for each section, including education and experience, and discuss your responsibilities for each job you have held. In a *skills résumé*, you merely list your previous jobs but include a skills section in which you describe your talents and achievements.

Recent graduates usually use the chronological résumé because in most cases they lack the record of skills and accomplishments needed for a skills résumé. However, if you have a lot of professional work experience, consider the skills style.

Elements of the Chronological Résumé

Most chronological résumés have six basic elements: identifying information, objectives or summary of qualifications, education, employment history, interests and activities, and references.

Identifying Information Include your full name, address, phone number, and e-mail address. Use your complete address, including the zip code. If your address during the academic year differs from your home address, list both and identify them clearly. An employer might call during an academic holiday to arrange an interview.

Objectives or Summary of Qualifications   After the identifying information, add a statement of objectives or a summary of qualifications.

A *statement of objectives*, used most often by candidates new to the field, is a brief phrase or sentence—for example, "Objective: Entry-level position as a hospital dietitian" or "Summer internship in manufacturing processes." In drafting your statement, follow these three suggestions:

- *State only the goals or duties explicitly mentioned or clearly implied in the job advertisement.* If you unintentionally suggest that your goals are substantially different from the job responsibilities, the reader might infer that you would not be happy working there and not consider you further.

- *Focus on the reader's needs, not on your goals.* Instead of stating that you are looking for a position with "opportunities for advancement" or that "offers a high salary," find out what the company needs: for example, "Position in Software Engineering specializing in database-applications development that enables me to use my four years of experience developing large-enterprise database solutions based on a normalized relational design."

- *Be specific.* You accomplish little by writing "Position offering opportunities in the field of health science, where I can use my communication and analytical skills." Specify what kind of position you want—nurse, physician, hospital administrator, pharmaceutical researcher.

Job candidates with more experience tend to write a summary of their qualifications. This statement is usually a brief paragraph that highlights three or four important skills or accomplishments. For example:

Summary of Qualifications

Six years' experience creating testing documentation to qualify production programs that run on Automated Test and Handling Equipment. Four years' experience running QA tests on software, hardware, and semiconductor products. Bilingual English and Italian. Secret-security clearance.

Education   If you are a student or a recent graduate, place the education section next. If you have substantial professional experience, place the employment experience section before the education section.

Include at least the following information in the education section:

- *The degree.* After the degree abbreviation (such as BS, BA, AA, or MS), list your academic major (and, if you have one, your minor)—for example, "BS in Materials Engineering, minor in General Business."

- *The institution.* Identify the institution by its full name: "Louisiana State University," not "LSU."

- *The location of the institution.* Include the city and state.

- *The date of graduation.* If your degree has not yet been granted, add "Anticipated date of graduation" or a similar phrase.

- *Information about other schools you attended.* List any other institutions you attended beyond high school, even those from which you did not earn a degree. The descriptions of other institutions should include the same information as the main listing. Arrange entries in reverse chronological order: that is, list first the school you attended most recently.

Guidelines

Elaborating on Your Education

The following guidelines can help you develop the education section of your résumé.

▶ **List your grade-point average.** If your average is significantly above the median for the graduating class, list it. Or list your average in your major courses, or in all your courses for the past two years. Calculate it however you wish, but be honest and clear.

▶ **Compile a list of courses.** Include courses that will interest an employer, such as advanced courses in your major or communications courses, such as technical communication, public speaking, and organizational communication. For example, a list of business courses on an engineer's résumé shows special knowledge and skills. But don't bother listing required courses (everyone else in your major took the same courses). Include the substantive titles of listed courses; employers won't know what "Chemistry 450" is. Call it by its official title: "Chemistry 450. Organic Chemistry."

▶ **Describe a special accomplishment.** For a special senior design or research project, present the title and objective of the project, any special or advanced techniques or equipment you used, and, if you know them, the major results: "A Study of Shape Memory Alloys in Fabricating Actuators for Underwater Biomimetic Applications—a senior design project to simulate the swimming styles and anatomy of fish." A project discussion makes you seem more like a professional: someone who designs and carries out projects.

▶ **List honors and awards you received.** Scholarships, internships, and academic awards suggest exceptional ability. If you have received a number of such honors or some that were not exclusively academic, you might list them separately (in a section called "Honors" or "Awards") rather than in the education section. Decide where this information will make the best impression.

The education section is the easiest part of the résumé to adapt in applying for different positions. For example, a student majoring in electrical engineering who is applying for a position requiring strong communication skills can list communications courses in one version of the résumé and advanced electrical engineering courses in another version. As you compose the education section, emphasize those aspects of your background that meet the requirements for a particular job.

Employment History   Present at least the basic information about each job you have held: the dates of employment, the organization's name and location, and your position or title. Then add carefully selected details. Readers want to know what you did and accomplished. Provide at least a two- to three-line description for each position. For particularly important or relevant jobs, write more, focusing on one or more of the following factors:

- *Skills.* What technical skills did you use on the job?
- *Equipment.* What equipment did you operate or oversee? In particular, mention computer equipment or software with which you are familiar.
- *Money.* How much money were you responsible for? Even if you considered your data-entry position fairly easy, the fact that the organization grossed, say, $2 million a year shows that the position involved real responsibility.
- *Documents.* What important documents did you write or assist in writing, such as brochures, reports, manuals, proposals, or Web sites?
- *Personnel.* How many people did you supervise?
- *Clients.* What kinds of, and how many, clients did you do business with in representing your organization?

Whenever possible, emphasize *results.* If you reorganized the shifts of the weekend employees you supervised, state the results:

> Reorganized the weekend shift, resulting in a cost savings of more than $3,000 per year.

> Wrote and produced (with Adobe FrameMaker) a 56-page parts catalog that is still used by the company and that increased our phone inquiries by more than 25 percent.

When you describe positions, functions, or responsibilities, use the active voice ("supervised three workers") rather than the passive voice ("three workers were supervised by me"). The active voice highlights action. Note that writers often omit the *I* at the start of sentences: "Prepared bids" rather than "I prepared bids." Whichever style you use, be consistent. Figure 15.3 lists some strong verbs to use in describing your experience.

▶ **In This Book**
For more about using strong verbs, see Ch. 10, p. 229.

administered	coordinated	evaluated	maintained	provided
advised	corresponded	examined	managed	purchased
analyzed	created	expanded	monitored	recorded
assembled	delivered	hired	obtained	reported
built	developed	identified	operated	researched
collected	devised	implemented	organized	solved
completed	directed	improved	performed	supervised
conducted	discovered	increased	prepared	trained
constructed	edited	instituted	produced	wrote

Figure 15.3   Strong Action Verbs Used in Résumés

Here is a sample listing of employment history:

June–September 2008: Student Dietitian
Millersville General Hospital, Millersville, TX
Gathered dietary histories and assisted in preparing menus for a 300-bed hospital.
Received "excellent" on all seven items in evaluation by head dietitian.

In just a few lines, you can show that you sought and accepted responsibility and that you acted professionally. Do not write "I accepted responsibility"; instead, present facts that will lead readers to that conclusion.

Naturally, not all jobs entail professional skills and responsibilities. Many students find summer work as laborers, sales clerks, and so forth. If you have not held a professional position, list the jobs you have held, even if they were unrelated to your career plans. If the job title is self-explanatory, such as waitperson or service-station attendant, don't elaborate. If you can write that you contributed to your tuition or expenses, such as by earning 50 percent of your annual expenses through a job, employers will be impressed by your self-reliance.

One further suggestion: if you have held a number of nonprofessional as well as several professional positions, group the nonprofessional ones:

Other Employment: cashier (summer 2004), salesperson (part-time, 2005), clerk (summer 2006)

This strategy prevents the nonprofessional positions from drawing readers' attention away from the more-important positions.

List jobs in reverse chronological order to highlight your most recent employment.

Two circumstances that occur frequently call for some subtlety:

- *You have some gaps in your employment history.* If you were not employed for several months or years because you were raising children, attending school, recovering from an accident, or for other reasons, consider using a skills résumé, which focuses more on your skills and less on your job history. Also, you can explain the gaps in the cover letter. For instance, you could write "I spent 2004 and part of 2006 caring for my elderly parent, but during that time I was able to do some substitute teaching and study at home to prepare for my A+ and Network+ certification, which I earned in late 2005." Do not lie or mislead about your dates of employment.

- *You have had several positions with the same employer.* If you want to show that you have had several positions with the same employer, you can present one description that encompasses all the positions or present a separate description for each position.

Presenting One Description

Blue Cross of Iowa, Ames, Iowa (January 2000–present)

- *Internal Auditor II (2004–present)*
- *Member Service Representative/Claims Examiner II (2002–2004)*
- *Claims Examiner II (2000–2002)*

As Claims Examiner II, processed national account inquiries and claims in accordance with. . . . After promotion to Member Service Representative/Claims Examiner II position, planned policies and procedures. . . . As Internal Auditor II, audit claims, enrollment, and inquiries; run data-set population and sample reports. . . .

This format enables you to mention your promotions and to create a clear narrative that emphasizes your progress within the company.

Presenting Separate Descriptions

Blue Cross of Iowa, Ames, Iowa (January 2000–present)

- *Internal Auditor II (2004–present)*

  Audit claims, enrollment, and inquiries . . .
- *Member Service Representative/Claims Examiner II (2002–2004)*

  Planned policies and procedures . . .
- *Claims Examiner II (2000–2002)*

  Processed national account inquiries and claims . . .

This format, which enables you to create a more detailed description of each position, is effective if you are trying to show that each position is distinct and you wish to describe the more recent positions more fully.

Interests and Activities   Résumés do not include information such as the writer's height, weight, date of birth, and marital status. Federal legislation prohibits organizations from requiring this information. In addition, most people feel that such information is irrelevant to a person's ability.

However, the "interests and activities" section of the résumé is the appropriate place for several kinds of information:

- participation in community-service organizations (such as Big Brothers/Big Sisters) or volunteer work in a hospital
- hobbies related to your career (for example, electronics for an engineer)
- sports, especially those that might be socially useful in your professional career, such as tennis, racquetball, and golf
- university-sanctioned activities, such as membership on a team, work on the college newspaper, or election to a responsible position in an academic organization or residence hall

Do not include activities that might create a negative impression, such as gambling or performing in a rock band. And always omit such mundane activities as meeting people and reading; everybody does these things.

References Potential employers will want to learn more about you from your professors and previous employers. People who are willing to speak or write on your behalf are called *references*.

Choose your references carefully. Solicit references only from those who know your work best and for whom you have done your best work—for instance, a previous employer with whom you worked closely or a professor from whom you received A's. Don't solicit references from prominent professors who do not know your work well; they will be unable to write informative letters.

Do not simply assume that someone is willing to serve as a reference for you. Give the person an opportunity to decline gracefully. Sometimes he or she has not been as impressed with your work as you think. If you simply ask the person to serve as a reference, he or she might accept and then write a lukewarm letter. It is better to say "Would you be able to write an enthusiastic letter for me?" or "Do you feel you know me well enough to write a strong recommendation?" If the person shows any hesitation or reluctance, withdraw the request. It may be a little embarrassing, but it is better than receiving a weak recommendation.

Once you have secured your references' permission to list them, create a references page. This page should begin with your name and contact information, just as for your résumé. Some job applicants add a sentence or two describing their relationship with each reference: "Dr. Willerton was my adviser and my instructor for two courses, one in technical editing and one in document design." Figure 15.4 on page 406 shows a references page.

Other Elements The sections discussed so far appear on almost everyone's résumé. Other sections are either discretionary or appropriate for only some job seekers.

- *Computer skills.* Classify your skills in categories such as hardware, software, languages, and operating systems. List any professional certifications you have earned.

- *Military experience.* If you are a veteran, describe your military service as if it were a job, citing dates, locations, positions, ranks, and tasks. List positive job-performance evaluations.

- *Language ability.* A working knowledge of another language can be very valuable, particularly if the potential employer has international interests and you could be useful in translation or foreign service. List your proficiency, using terms such as *beginner*, *intermediate*, and *advanced*. Some applicants distinguish among reading, writing, and speaking abilities.

- *Willingness to relocate.* If you are willing to relocate, say so. Many organizations will find you a more attractive candidate.

Less-advanced job applicants are more likely than more-advanced job applicants to list personal references.

Samantha Breveux	5986 Center Street Boise, ID 83703 208.555.8693 sbreveux@gmail.com

Professional References

Dr. Dale Cletis
Professor of English
Boise State University
Boise, ID 83725
208.555.2637
dcletis@boisestate.edu

Dr. Cletis was my instructor in three literature courses, as well as my adviser.

Dr. Miriam Finkelstein
Professor of Economics
Boise State University
Boise, ID 83725
208.555.9375
mfinkel@boisestate.edu

Dr. Finkelstein encouraged me to study for a minor in economics, which I did. She was my instructor in two courses.

Dr. Charles Tristan
Professor of English
Boise State University
Boise, ID 83725
208.555.1355
ctristan@boisestate.edu

Dr. Tristan, my instructor in two courses, encouraged me to study abroad. I spent my junior year in Paris.

Personal References

Mr. Heiko Yamamoto
Yamamoto Paving
1450 Industrial Drive
Eagle, ID 83467
208.555.2387
heiko@yamamotopaving.com

For three summers, beginning after my high-school graduation, I worked in Mr. Yamamoto's office as a bookkeeper.

Mr. Paul Engels
Yellow House Literary Cabin
1877 Capitol Boulevard
Boise, ID 83703
208.555.3827
pengels@yellowhouse.org

I volunteered my services writing and distributing press releases and advertising for the Yellow House Literary Cabin.

Martha Cummings, R.N.
St. Luke's Regional Medical Center
322 Bannock Street
Boise, ID 83604
208.555.3489
mcummings@stlukesrmc.org

For many years, my family has trained service dogs for hospital visitations. I worked with Ms. Cummings during high school and my first two years in college in helping other service-dog trainers.

Figure 15.4   References Page

Elements of the Skills Résumé

A skills résumé differs from a chronological one in that it includes a separate section, usually called "Skills" or "Skills and Abilities," that emphasizes job skills and knowledge. In a skills résumé, the employment section becomes a brief list of information about your employment history: company, dates of employment, and position. Here is an example of the skills section.

Skills and Abilities

Management

> Served as weekend manager of six employees in the retail clothing business. Also trained three summer interns at a health-maintenance organization.

Writing and Editing

> Wrote status reports, edited performance appraisals, participated in assembling and producing an environmental-impact statement using desktop publishing.

Teaching and Tutoring

> Tutored in the University Writing Center. Taught a two-week course in electronics for teenagers. Coach youth basketball.

In a skills section, you choose the headings, the arrangement, and the level of detail. Your goal, of course, is to highlight those skills the employer is seeking.

Figures 15.5, 15.6, and 15.7 on pages 408–11 show three examples of effective résumés.

WRITING ELECTRONIC RÉSUMÉS

Although paper résumés continue to be popular, especially after a company has decided to interview you, electronic résumés are more popular, especially for organizations that receive many applications and especially for a candidate's first contact with the organization. In fact, more than 80 percent of U.S. employers now prefer applicants to submit their initial job applications electronically (Hansen, 2008b). For this reason, you will need an electronic résumé in addition to your traditional paper résumé.

Most companies use computerized applicant-tracking systems to evaluate the dozens, hundreds, or even thousands of job applications they receive every day. Companies store the information from these applications in databases, which they search electronically for desired keywords to generate a pool of applicants for specific positions. An electronic résumé can take several forms:

- A *formatted résumé attached to an e-mail message.* You attach the word-processing file to an e-mail message. Or you save your résumé as a Portable Document Format (PDF) file and attach it. (A PDF file retains the

The writer uses design to emphasize his name and provides his contact information, including his e-mail address.

The writer could modify his objective to name the company to which he is applying.

The writer chooses to emphasize his advanced engineering courses. For another position, he might emphasize other courses.

The writer wisely creates a category that calls attention to his academic awards and his membership in his field's major professional organization.

The writer lists his references on a separate page and includes this page in his application materials only if an employer requests it. For each reference, the writer provides complete contact information and a statement describing his relationship to the person, as shown in Fig. 15.4 on p. 406.

CARLOS RODRIGUEZ
3109 Vista Street   Philadelphia, PA 19136   (215) 555-3880   crodrig@dragon.du.edu

Objective
Entry-level position in signal processing

Education
BS in Electrical Engineering
Drexel University, Philadelphia, PA
Anticipated 6/2009
Grade-Point Average: 3.67 (on a scale of 4.0)
Senior Design Project: "Enhanced Path-Planning Software for Robotics"

Advanced Engineering Courses

Digital Signal Processing	Computer Hardware
Introduction to Operating Systems I, II	Systems Design
Digital Filters	Computer Logic Circuits I, II

Employment
6/2006–1/2007 Electrical Engineering Intern II
RCA Advanced Technology Laboratory, Moorestown, NJ
Designed ultra-large-scale integrated circuits using VERILOG and VHDL hardware description languages. Assisted senior engineer in CMOS IC layout, modeling, parasitic capacitance extraction, and PSPICE simulation operations.

6/2005–1/2006 Electrical Engineering Intern I
RCA Advanced Technology Laboratory, Moorestown, NJ
Verified and documented several integrated circuit designs. Used CAD software and hardware to simulate, check, and evaluate these designs. Gained experience with Mathcad.

Honors and Organizations
Eta Kappa Nu (Electrical Engineering Honor Society)
Tau Beta Pi (General Engineering Honor Society)
IEEE

References
Available upon request

⌐▷ **In This Book**
Many of the job boards listed on page 393 include samples of résumés.

Figure 15.5   Chronological Résumé of a Traditional Student

CARLOS RODRIGUEZ
3109 Vista Street   Philadelphia, PA 19136   (215) 555-3880   crodrig@dragon.du.edu

References

Ms. Anita Feller Engineering Consultant 700 Church Road Cherry Hill, NJ 08002 (609) 555-7836 anitafeller@live.com	Ms. Feller helped me plan several events for a local IEEE chapter.
Mr. Fred Borelli Unit Manager RCA Advanced Technology Laboratory Route 38 Moorestown, NJ 08057 (609) 555-2435 fborelli@rca.com	Mr. Borelli was my intern supervisor when I worked at RCA.
Mr. Sam Shamir Comptroller RCA Advanced Technology Laboratory Route 38 Moorestown, NJ 08057 (609) 555-7849 sshamir@rca.com	Mr. Shamir worked closely with me on several projects when I worked at RCA.
Ms. Pat Spector Professional Engineer Think Solutions, Inc. 312 Orchard Place Philadelphia, PA 19136 (215) 555-1972 pspector@think.com	Ms. Spector provided guidance on my senior design project.

Figure 15.5   (continued)

The writer uses a table format for her résumé. Notice that all her headings are contained within the left-hand column.

The writer indicates that she is interested in an internship, not a continuing position.

The writer's list of courses includes several outside her technical subject area to emphasize the skills she has demonstrated in her career.

All of the writer's positions show an interest in working with people.

The volunteer position says something about the writer's character.

Before attending college, the writer worked as an office manager. Notice how the description of her position suggests that she is a skilled and responsible worker.

The writer believes that the skills required in raising children are relevant in the workplace. Others might think that because a résumé describes job credentials, this information should be omitted.

Alice P. Linder   1781 Weber Road
Warminster, PA 18974
(215) 555-3999
linderap423@aol.com

Objective   An internship in molecular research that uses my computer skills

Education   Harmon College, West Yardley, PA
BS in Bioscience and Biotechnology
Expected Graduation Date: 6/2009

Related Course Work

General Chemistry I, II, III	Biology I, II, III
Organic Chemistry I, II	Statistical Methods for Research
Physics I, II	Technical Communication
Calculus I, II	

Employment Experience   6/2006–present (20 hours per week): Laboratory Assistant Grade 3
GlaxoSmithKline, Upper Merion, PA
Analyze molecular data on E&S PS300, Macintosh, and IBM PCs. Write programs in C# and wrote a user's guide for an instructional computing package. Train and consult with scientists and deliver in-house briefings.

8/2003–present: Volunteer, Physical Therapy Unit
Children's Hospital of Philadelphia, Philadelphia, PA
Assist therapists and guide patients with their therapy. Use play therapy to enhance strengthening progress.

6/1995–1/1999: Office Manager
Anchor Products, Inc., Ambler, PA
Managed 12-person office in $1.2 million company. Also performed general bookkeeping and payroll.

Honors   Awarded three $5,000 tuition scholarships (2005–2007) from the Gould Foundation.

Additional Information   Member, Harmon Biology Club, Yearbook Staff
Raising three school-age children
Tuition 100% self-financed

References   Available upon request

Figure 15.6   Chronological Résumé of a Nontraditional Student

Alice P. Linder

1781 Weber Road
Warminster, PA 18974

(215) 555-3999
linderap423@aol.com

This is another version of the résumé in Fig. 15.6.

Objective

An internship in molecular research that uses my computer skills

Skills and Abilities

Laboratory Skills
- Analyze molecular data on E&S PS300, Macintosh, and IBM PCs. Write programs in C#.
- Have taken 12 credits in biology and chemistry labs.

In a skills résumé, you present the skills section at the start. This organization lets you emphasize your professional attributes. Notice that the writer uses specific details—names of software, number of credits, types of documents, kinds of activities—to make her case.

Communication Skills
- Wrote a user's guide for an instructional computing package.
- Train and consult with scientists and deliver in-house briefings.

Management Skills
- Managed 12-person office in $1.2 million company.

Education

Harmon College, West Yardley, PA
BS in Bioscience and Biotechnology
Expected Graduation Date: 6/2009

Related Course Work

General Chemistry I, II, III	Biology I, II, III
Organic Chemistry I, II	Statistical Methods for Research
Physics I, II	Technical Communication
Calculus I, II	

Employment Experience

6/2006–present (20 hours per week)
GlaxoSmithKline, Upper Merion, PA
Laboratory Assistant Grade 3

The employment section now contains a list of positions rather than descriptions of what the writer did in each position.

8/2003–present
Children's Hospital of Philadelphia, Philadelphia, PA
Volunteer, Physical Therapy Unit

6/1995–1/1999
Anchor Products, Inc., Ambler, PA
Office Manager

Honors

Awarded three $5,000 tuition scholarships (2005–2007) from the Gould Foundation.

Additional Information

Member, Harmon Biology Club, Yearbook Staff
Raising three school-age children
Tuition 100% self-financed

References

Available upon request

Figure 15.7   Skills Résumé of a Nontraditional Student

formatting of your résumé and prevents others from modifying it.) Or you can save your file in Rich Text Format (RTF) with the file extension .rtf. An RTF file retains some formatting and makes the information compatible across platforms (Apple, IBM, and UNIX) and word-processing programs (Word, WordPerfect, and others). Attaching an RTF file is a good choice when you do not know which file format the employer prefers. Follow the instructions the company offers on which file type to use and how to submit your materials. If the job ad requests, for example, "a plain-text document sent in the body of the message," do not attach a file.

- A *text résumé.* Also referred to as a *plain-text résumé* or *ASCII résumé*, a text résumé uses the limited ASCII character set and is saved as a .txt file, which can be entered directly into the organization's keyword-searchable database. You can also paste text résumés piece by piece into Web-based forms, which often do not allow you to paste your complete résumé all at once.

- A *scannable résumé (one that will be scanned into an organization's database).* There are several popular database programs for this purpose, such as ResTrac and Resumix. Because most employers now prefer electronic submissions, scannable résumés are less common. However, if you submit a printed résumé to a company, you should consider how well the document will scan electronically.

- A *Web-based résumé.* You can put your résumé on your own Web site and hope that employers will come to you, or you can post it to a job board on the Web. As with any information you post on the Internet, you should carefully consider what you include in your Web-based résumé.

Ways of creating and sending résumés will undoubtedly change as the technology changes. For now, the traditional printed résumé is only one of several ways to present your credentials, and you should keep abreast of new techniques for applying for positions. Which form should your résumé take? Whichever form the organization prefers. If you learn of a position from an ad on an organization's Web site, the notice will tell you how to apply.

Content of the Electronic Résumé

Most of the earlier discussion of the content of a printed résumé also applies to an electronic résumé. The résumé must be honest and free of errors, and it must provide clear, specific information.

If the résumé is to be entered into a database instead of read by a person, include industry-specific jargon: all the keywords an employment officer might use in searching for qualified candidates. If an employment officer is looking for someone with experience writing Web pages, be sure you include the terms "Web page," "Internet," "HTML," "Java," "CSS," and any other relevant keywords. If your current position requires an understanding of programming languages, list the languages you know. Also use keywords that refer to your communication skills, such as "public speaking," "oral communication," and "communication skills." In short, whereas a traditional printed résumé focuses on *verbs*—tasks you have done—an electronic résumé focuses on *nouns*.

One hiring consultant (Hansen, 2008a) has put it this way: "The bottom line is that if you apply for a job with a company that searches databases for keywords, and your résumé doesn't have the keywords the company seeks for the person who fills that job, you are pretty much dead in the water."

Format of the Electronic Résumé

Because electronic résumés must be easy to read and scan, they require a very simple design. Consequently, they are not as attractive as paper-based résumés, and they are longer, because they use only a single narrow column of text.

> **On TechComm Web**
>
> For more about formatting electronic résumés, see The Riley Guide: Résumés, Cover Letters. Click on Links Library for Ch. 15 on <bedfordstmartins.com/techcomm>.

Guidelines

Preparing a Text Résumé

▶ **Use ASCII text only.** ASCII text includes letters, numbers, and basic punctuation marks. Avoid boldface, italics, underlining, and special characters such as "smart" quotation marks or math symbols. Also avoid horizontal or vertical lines and graphics. To be sure you are using only ASCII characters, save your file as "plain text." Then open it up using your software's text editor, such as Notepad, and check to be sure it contains only ASCII characters. Non-ASCII characters will appear as garbage text.

▶ **Left-align the information.** Do not try to duplicate the formatting of a traditional paper résumé. You can't. Instead, left-align each new item. Here is a sample listing from the employment-experience section:

> 6/06–present
> (20 hours per week)
> GlaxoSmithKline
> Upper Merion, PA
> Analyst I
>
> Analyze molecular data on E & S PS300, Macintosh, and IBM PCs. Write programs in C++ and wrote a user's guide for an instructional computing package. Train and consult with scientists and deliver in-house briefings.

▶ **Send yourself a test version of the résumé.** When you finish writing and formatting the résumé, send yourself a copy, then open it in your text editor and see if it looks professional.

INTERACTIVE SAMPLE DOCUMENT
Preparing a Text Résumé

The following résumé was written by a graduating college senior who wanted to work for a wildland firefighting agency such as the U.S. Bureau of Land Management or U.S. Forest Service. The writer plans to save the résumé as a .txt file and enter it directly into these agencies' employment databases. The questions in the margins ask you to think about electronic résumés (as discussed on pages 407–13). E-mail your responses to yourself and/or your instructor on TechComm Web.

1. How effectively has the writer formatted this résumé?

2. What elements are likely to be problematic when the writer saves this résumé as a .txt file?

3. What is the function of the industry-specific jargon in this résumé?

4. Why does the writer place the education section below the sections on career history and fire and aviation qualifications?

On TechComm Web

To e-mail your responses to yourself and/or your instructor, click on Interactive Sample Documents for Ch. 15 on <bedfordstmartins.com/techcomm>.

BURTON L. KREBS

34456 West Jewell St.   208-555-9627
Boise, ID 83704   burtonkrebs@mail.com

Objective
Lead crew position on rappel crew.

Career History
- Senior Firefighter, Moyer Rappel Crew, 05/08-present
- Senior Firefighter, Boise Helitack, 05/07-10/07
- Hotshot Crew Member, Boise Interagency Hotshot Crew, 07/06-09/06
- Helirappel Crew Member, Moyer Rappel Crew, 06/02-09/05

Fire and Aviation Qualifications
Crew Boss (T)
Helicopter Manager
Helicopter Rappeller
Helirappel Spotter
Helispot Manager
Type 2 Helibase Manager (T)
Incident Commander Type 4 (T)

Education
Bachelor of Arts in Communication Training and Development, Boise State University, Boise, Idaho, GPA 3.57, May 2009

Skills
- Excellent oral and written communication skills
- Proficient in Word, Excel, and PowerPoint
- Knowledgeable of helicopter contract administration
- Perform daily and cumulative flight invoice cost summaries

Awards
"Outstanding Performance" Recognition, U.S. Bureau of Land Management, 2007
"Outstanding Performance" Recognition, U.S. Forest Service, 2004, 2005, 2006

If you are mailing a paper résumé that will be scanned, follow the seven additional guidelines outlined below. Figure 15.8 on page 416 is an example of a scannable résumé.

Guidelines

Preparing a Scannable Résumé

▶ **Use a good-quality laser printer.** The better the resolution, the better the scanner will work.

▶ **Use white paper.** Even a slight tint to the paper can increase the chances that the scanner will misinterpret a character.

▶ **Do not fold the résumé.** The fold line can confuse the scanner.

▶ **Use a simple sans-serif typeface.** Scanners can easily interpret large, open typefaces such as Arial.

▶ **Use a single-column format.** Double-column text will scan inaccurately. Left-align everything.

▶ **Use wide margins.** Instead of an 80-character width, set your software for 65. This way, regardless of the equipment the reader is using, the lines will break as you intend them to.

▶ **Use the space bar instead of the Tab key.** Tabs will be displayed according to the settings on the reader's equipment, not the settings on your equipment. Therefore, use the space bar to move text horizontally.

WRITING JOB-APPLICATION LETTERS

Most job applications call for a résumé and a letter. The letter is crucial because it is likely the first thing your reader will see. If the letter is ineffective, the reader will not bother to read the résumé. Make your letter appeal as directly and specifically as possible to a particular person.

The Concepts of Selectivity and Development

The keys to a good letter are selectivity and development. *Select* two or three points of special interest to the potential employer and *develop* them into paragraphs. Emphasize results, such as improved productivity or quality or decreased costs. If one of your previous part-time positions called for skills the potential employer is looking for, write a substantial paragraph about that position, even though the résumé devotes only a few lines to it.

For most candidates, a job-application letter should fill the better part of a page. For more-experienced candidates, it might fill up to two pages.

In This Book

For more about formatting letters, see Ch. 14, p. 368.

Figure 15.8 Scannable Résumé

This is an electronic version of the résumé in Fig. 15.7. Notice that the writer uses ASCII text and left justification.

Throughout, the writer includes keywords such as C#, IBM, PC, Macintosh, bioscience, biotechnology, molecular research, laboratory assistant, management, volunteer, and physical therapy.

Alice P. Linder
1781 Weber Road
Warminster, PA 18974
(215) 555-3999
linderap423@aol.com

Objective: An internship in molecular research that uses my computer skills

Skills and Abilities:
Laboratory Skills. Analyze molecular data on E&S PS300, Macintosh, and IBM PCs. Write programs in C#. Have taken 12 credits in biology and chemistry labs.

Communication Skills. Wrote a user's guide for an instructional computing package. Train and consult with scientists and deliver in-house briefings.

Management Skills. Managed 12-person office in $1.2 million company.

Education:
Harmon College, West Yardley, PA
BS in Bioscience and Biotechnology
Expected Graduation Date: June 2009

Related Course Work:
General Chemistry I, II, III
Organic Chemistry I, II
Physics I, II
Calculus I, II
Biology I, II, III
Statistical Methods for Research
Technical Communication

Employment Experience:
June 2006-present (20 hours per week)
GlaxoSmithKline, Upper Merion, PA
Laboratory Assistant Grade 3

August 2003-present
Children's Hospital of Philadelphia, Philadelphia, PA
Volunteer, Physical Therapy Unit

June 1995-January 1999
Anchor Products, Inc., Ambler, PA
Office Manager

Honors:
Awarded three $5,000 tuition scholarships (2005-2007) from the Gould Foundation.

Additional Information:
Member, Harmon Biology Club, Yearbook Staff
Raising three school-age children
Tuition 100% self-financed

References:
Available upon request

Regardless, if you write at length on a minor point, you become boring and appear to have poor judgment. Employers seek candidates who can say a lot in a small space.

Elements of the Job-Application Letter

The inside address—the name, title, organization, and address of the recipient—is important because you want to be sure your materials get to the right person. And you don't want to offend that person with a misspelling or an incorrect title. If you are uncertain about any of the information—the recipient's name, for example, might have an unusual spelling—verify it by researching the organization on the Internet or by phoning.

When you do not know who should receive the letter, phone the company to find out who manages the department. If you are unsure of the appropriate department or division to write to, address the letter to a high-level executive, such as the president. The letter will get to the right person. Also, because the application includes both a letter and a résumé, use an enclosure notation.

The four-paragraph example that will be discussed here is only a basic model, consisting of an introductory paragraph, two body paragraphs, and a concluding paragraph. At a minimum, your letter should include these four paragraphs, but there is no reason it cannot have five or six.

Plan the letter carefully. Draft it and then revise it. Let it sit for a while, revise it again, and then edit and proofread it. Spend as much time on it as you can.

> **In This Book**
> For more about developing paragraphs, see Ch. 9, p. 206.

The Introductory Paragraph   The introductory paragraph has four specific functions.

- It *identifies your source of information*. For an unsolicited application, all you can do is ask if a position is available. For a solicited application, however, state your source of information.

- It *identifies the position you are interested in*. Often, the organization you are applying to is advertising several positions. If you omit the title of the position you are interested in, your reader might not know which one you are seeking.

- It *states that you wish to be considered for the position*. Although the context makes your wish obvious, you should mention it, because the letter would be awkward without it.

- It *forecasts the rest of the letter*. Choose a few phrases that forecast the body of the letter so that the letter flows smoothly. For example, if you use the phrase "retail experience" in the opening paragraph, you are preparing your reader for the discussion of your retail experience later in the letter.

These four points need not appear in any particular order, nor does each need to be covered in a single sentence. The following sample paragraphs demonstrate different ways of providing the necessary information:

Response to a Job Ad

I am writing in response to your notice in the May 13 online version of *The New York Times*. I would like to be considered for the position in system programming. I hope you find that my studies in computer science at Eastern University, along with my programming experience at Airborne Instruments, qualify me for the position.

Unsolicited

My academic training in hotel management and my experience with Sheraton International have given me a solid background in the hotel industry. Would you please consider me for any management trainee position that might be available?

Unsolicited Personal Contact

Mr. Howard Alcott of your Research and Development Department suggested that I write to you. He thinks that my organic chemistry degree and my practical experience with Brown Laboratories might be of value to XYZ Corporation. Do you have an entry-level position in organic chemistry for which I might be considered?

The Education Paragraph   For most students, the education paragraph should come before the employment paragraph, because the education paragraph will be stronger. However, if your employment experience is stronger, present it first.

In writing your education paragraph, take your cue from the job ad (if you are responding to one). What aspect of your education most directly fits the job requirements? If the ad stresses versatility, you might structure your paragraph around the range and diversity of your courses. Also, you might discuss course work in a subject related to your major, such as business or communication skills. Extracurricular activities are often very valuable; if you were an officer in a student organization, you could discuss the activities and programs you coordinated. Perhaps the most popular strategy for developing the education paragraph is to discuss skills and knowledge gained from advanced course work in your major field.

Example 1

At Eastern University, I have taken a wide range of science courses, but my most advanced work has been in chemistry. In one laboratory course, I developed a new aseptic brewing technique that lowered the risk of infection by more than 40 percent. This new technique was the subject of an article in the *Eastern Science Digest*. Representatives from three national breweries have visited our laboratory to discuss the technique with me.

Note that the writer identifies the date of the ad, the name of the publication, and the name of the position. Then she forecasts the main points she will make in the body of the letter.

The writer politely requests that the reader consider his application.

Notice the tone in all three of these samples: quiet self-confidence. Don't oversell yourself ("I am the candidate you have been hoping for") or undersell yourself ("I don't know that much about computers, but I am willing to learn").

Note that the writer develops one idea, presenting enough information about it to interest the reader. Paragraphs that merely list a number of courses that the writer has taken are ineffective: everyone takes courses.

Example 2

To broaden my education at Southern University, I took eight business courses in addition to my requirements for a degree in civil engineering. Because your ad mentions that the position will require substantial client contact, I believe that my work in marketing, in particular, would be of special value. In an advanced marketing seminar, I used FrameMaker to produce a 20-page sales brochure describing the various kinds of building structures for sale by Oppenheimer Properties to industrial customers in our section of the city. That brochure is now being used at Oppenheimer, where I am an intern.

> The writer elaborates on a field other than his major. Note how he develops an idea based on a detail in the job ad. This strategy shows that he studied the ad carefully and wrote a custom letter. This initiative makes him the sort of candidate most hiring officials would like to interview.

Example 3

The most rewarding part of my education at Western University occurred outside the classroom. My entry in a fashion-design competition sponsored by the university won second place. More important, through the competition I met the chief psychologist at Western Regional Hospital, who invited me to design clothing for people with disabilities. I have since completed six different outfits, which are now being tested at the hospital. I hope to be able to pursue this interest once I start work.

> The writer develops an effective paragraph about a small aspect of her credentials. She sounds like a focused, intelligent person who wants to do some good.

An additional point: if you haven't already specified your major and your college or university in the introductory paragraph, be sure to do so here.

The Employment Paragraph   Like the education paragraph, the employment paragraph should begin with a topic sentence and develop a single idea. That idea might be that you have a broad background or that one job in particular has given you special skills that make you especially well suited for the available job.

Example 1

For the past three summers and part-time during the academic year, I have worked for Redego, Inc., a firm that specializes in designing and planning industrial complexes. I began as an assistant in the drafting room. By the second summer, I was accompanying a civil engineer on field inspections. Most recently, I have used Auto-CAD to assist an engineer in designing and drafting the main structural supports for a 15-acre, $30 million chemical facility.

> The writer makes the point that he is being promoted within the company because of his good work. Notice his reference to the specialized software and the size of the project.

Example 2

Although I have worked every summer since I was 15, my most recent position, as a technical editor, was the most rewarding. I was chosen by Digital Systems, Inc., from among 30 candidates because of my dual background in computer science and writing. My job was to coordinate the editing of computer manuals. Our copy editors, most of whom were not trained in computer science, needed someone to help verify the technical accuracy of their revisions. When I was unable to answer their questions, I was responsible for interviewing our systems analysts to find the correct answers and to make sure the computer novice could follow them. This position gave me a good understanding of the process by which operating manuals are created.

> The writer starts by suggesting that he is hardworking. Notice that he doesn't say it explicitly; rather, he provides evidence to lead the reader to that conclusion.
>
> Another theme in this paragraph is that the writer knows how to work with people effectively. Again, he doesn't say it; he implies it.

Example 3

I have worked in merchandising for three years as a part-time and summer salesperson in men's fashions and accessories. I have had experience running inventory-control software and helped one company switch from a manual to an online system. Most recently, I assisted in clearing $200,000 in out-of-date men's fashions. I coordinated a campaign to sell half of the merchandise at cost and was able to convince the manufacturer's representative to accept the other half for full credit. For this project, I received a certificate of appreciation from the company president.

In this paragraph, the writer suggests that she has technical and interpersonal skills and that her company thought she did an excellent job on a project she coordinated.

The theme of all these samples is that an effective paragraph has a sharp focus and specific evidence and that it clearly suggests the writer's qualifications.

Although you will discuss your education and experience in separate paragraphs, try to link these two halves of your background. If an academic course led to an interest that you were able to pursue in a job, make that point in the transition from one paragraph to the other. Similarly, if a job experience helped shape your academic career, tell the reader about it.

The Concluding Paragraph   The purpose of the concluding paragraph is to motivate the reader to invite you for an interview. In the preceding paragraphs, you provided the information that you hope has convinced the reader to give you another look. In the last paragraph, you want to make it easy for him or her to do so. The concluding paragraph contains three main elements:

- A *reference to your résumé*. If you have not yet referred to it, do so now.
- A *polite but confident request for an interview*. Use the phrase *at your convenience*. Don't make the request sound as if you're asking for a personal favor.
- *Your phone number and e-mail address*. State the time of day you can be reached.

Adding an e-mail address gives the employer one more way to get in touch with you.

Example 1

The enclosed résumé provides more information about my education and experience. Could we meet at your convenience to discuss the skills and experience I could bring to Pentamax? You can leave a message for me anytime at (303) 555-5957 or cfilli@claus.cmu.edu.

All job-application letters end with a paragraph that urges the reader to contact the writer and provides the contact information that makes it easy for the reader to do so.

Example 2

More information about my education and experience is included on the enclosed résumé, but I would appreciate the opportunity to meet with you at your convenience to discuss my application. You can reach me after noon on Tuesdays and Thursdays at (212) 555-4527 or leave a message anytime.

The examples of effective job-application letters in Figures 15.9 and 15.10 on pages 421–22 correspond to the résumés in Figures 15.5 and 15.6.

3109 Vista Street
Philadelphia, PA 19136

January 20, 2009

Mr. Stephen Spencer, Director of Personnel
Department 411
Boeing Naval Systems
103 Industrial Drive
Wilmington, DE 20093

Dear Mr. Spencer:

I am writing in response to your advertisement in the January 16 *Philadelphia Inquirer*. Would you please consider me for the position in Signal Processing? I believe that my academic training in electrical engineering at Drexel University, along with my experience with the RCA Advanced Technology Laboratory, would qualify me for the position.

My education at Drexel has given me a strong background in computer hardware and system design. I have concentrated on digital and computer applications, developing and designing computer and signal-processing hardware in two graduate-level engineering courses. For my senior design project, I am working with four other undergraduates in using OO programming techniques to enhance the path-planning software for an infrared night-vision robotics application.

While working at the RCA Advanced Technology Laboratory, I was able to apply my computer experience to the field of DSP. I designed ultra-large-scale integrated circuits using VERILOG and VHDL hardware description languages. In addition, I assisted a senior engineer in CMOS IC layout, modeling, parasitic capacitance extraction, and PSPICE simulation operations.

The enclosed résumé provides an overview of my education and experience. Could I meet with you at your convenience to discuss my qualifications for this position? Please write to me at the above address or leave a message anytime at (215) 555-3880. My e-mail address is crodrig@dragon.du.edu.

Yours truly,

Carlos Rodriguez

Carlos Rodriguez

Enclosure (1)

Figure 15.9
Job-Application Letter

Notice that the writer's own name does not appear at the top of his letter.

In the inside address, he uses the reader's courtesy title, "Mr."

The writer points out that he has taken two graduate courses. Notice that he discusses his senior design project, which makes him look more like an engineer solving a problem than a student taking a course.

Notice the use of "In addition" to begin the third sentence. This phrase breaks up the "I" openings of several sentences.

An enclosure notation refers to his résumé.

In This Book

Many of the job boards listed on page 393 include samples of application letters.

**Figure 15.10
Job-Application Letter**

1781 Weber Road
Warminster, PA 18974

January 17, 2009

Ms. Hannah Gail
Fox Run Medical Center
399 N. Abbey Road
Warminster, PA 18974

Dear Ms. Gail:

Last April I contacted your office regarding the possibility of an internship as a laboratory assistant at your center. Your assistant, Mary McGuire, told me then that you might consider such a position this year. With the experience I have gained since last year, I believe I would be a valuable addition to your center in many ways.

At Harmon College, I have earned a 3.7 GPA in 36 credits in chemistry and biology; all but two of these courses had laboratory components. One skill stressed at Harmon is the ability to communicate effectively, both in writing and orally. Our science courses have extensive writing and speaking requirements; my portfolio includes seven research papers and lab reports of more than 20 pages each, and I have delivered four oral presentations, one of 45 minutes, to classes.

At GlaxoSmithKline, where I currently work part-time, I analyze molecular data on an E & S PS300, a Macintosh, and an IBM PC. I have tried to remain current with the latest advances; my manager at GlaxoSmithKline has allowed me to attend two different two-day in-house seminars on computerized data analysis using SAS. My experience as the manager of a 12-person office for four years helped me acquire interpersonal skills that would benefit Fox Run.

More information about my education and experience is included on the enclosed résumé, but I would appreciate the opportunity to meet with you at your convenience to discuss my application. If you would like any additional information about me or Harmon's internship program, please write to me at the above address, call me at (215) 555-3999, or e-mail me at linderap423@aol.com.

Very truly yours,

Alice P. Linder

Alice P. Linder

Enclosure

The writer gracefully suggests that she would be an even better candidate this year than last year.

The writer is making two points: she is experienced in the lab, and she is an experienced communicator.

By mentioning her portfolio, she is suggesting that she would be happy to show the reader her documents. This statement is an example of understated self-confidence.

PREPARING FOR A JOB INTERVIEW

If your job-application letter is successful, you will be invited to a job interview, where both you and the organization can start to see whether you would be a good fit there.

Guidelines

Preparing for a Job Interview

For every hour you spend in a job interview, you need to do many hours of preparation.

▶ **Study job interviews.** The dozens of books and Web sites devoted to job interviews cover everything from how to do your initial research to common interview questions and how to dress. Although you can't prepare for everything that will happen, you can prepare for a lot of things.

▶ **Study the organization to which you applied.** If you inadvertently show that you haven't done your homework, the interviewer might conclude that you're always unprepared. Learn what products or services the organization provides, how well it has done in recent years, what its plans are, and so forth. Start with the organization's own Web site, then proceed to other online and print resources. Search for the organization's name on the Internet.

▶ **Think about what you can offer the organization.** Your goal during the interview is to show how you can help the organization accomplish its goals. Think about how your academic career, your work experience, and your personal characteristics and experiences have prepared you to solve problems and carry out projects to help the organization succeed. Make notes about projects you carried out in courses, experiences on the job, and experiences in your personal life that can serve as persuasive evidence to support claims about your qualifications.

▶ **Study lists of common interview questions.** Interviewers study these lists; you should, too. You're probably familiar with some of the favorites:
 — Can you tell me about yourself?
 — Where do you see yourself in five years?
 — Why did you apply to our company?
 — What do you see as your greatest strengths and weaknesses?
 — Tell me about an incident that taught you something important about yourself.
 — What was your best course in college? Why?

▶ **Compile a list of questions you wish to ask.** Near the end of the interview, the interviewer will probably ask if you have any questions. The interviewer expects you to have compiled a brief list of questions about working for the organization. Do not focus on salary, vacation days, or sick leave. Instead, ask about ways you can continue to develop as a professional, improving your ability to contribute to the organization.

▶ **Rehearse the interview.** It's one thing to think about how you might answer an interview question. It's another to have to answer it. Rehearse the interview by asking friends or colleagues to play the role of the interviewer, making up questions you haven't thought about. Then ask these people for constructive criticism.

On TechComm Web

For links to Web sites about employment, click on Links Library for Ch. 15 on <bedfordstmartins.com/ techcomm>.

In This Book

For more about research techniques, see Ch. 6.

In This Book

For more about communicating persuasively, see Ch. 8.

◣ **In This Book**
For a list of Internet job boards, see p. 393.

Job boards on the Internet can help you prepare for a job interview. They discuss questions such as the following:

- When should you arrive for the interview?
- What should you wear?
- How do interviewers interpret your body language?
- What questions are you likely to be asked?
- How long should your answers be?
- How do you know when the interviewer wishes to end the interview?
- How can you get the interviewer's contact information to write a follow-up letter?

WRITING FOLLOW-UP LETTERS AFTER AN INTERVIEW

◣ **In This Book**
Many of the job boards listed on p. 393 include samples of follow-up letters for different situations that occur during the job search.

After an interview, you should write a letter of appreciation. If you are offered the job, you also may have to write a letter accepting or rejecting the position.

- *Letter of appreciation after an interview.* Thank the representative for taking the time to see you, and emphasize your particular qualifications. You can also restate your interest in the position. A follow-up letter can do more good with less effort than any other step in the job-application process because so few candidates take the time to write one.

> Dear Mr. Weaver:
>
> Thank you for taking the time yesterday to show me your facilities and to introduce me to your colleagues.
>
> Your advances in piping design were particularly impressive. As a person with hands-on experience in piping design, I can appreciate the advantages your design will have.
>
> The vitality of your projects and the good fellowship among your employees further confirm my initial belief that Cynergo would be a fine place to work.
>
> Sincerely yours,
>
> *Harriet Bommarito*
>
> Harriet Bommarito

- *Letter accepting a job offer.* This one is easy: express appreciation, show enthusiasm, and repeat the major terms of your employment.

Dear Mr. Weaver:

Thank you very much for the offer to join your staff. I accept.

I look forward to joining your design team on Monday, July 19. The salary, as you indicated in your letter, is $48,250.

As you recommended, I will get in touch with Mr. Matthews in Personnel to get a start on the paperwork.

I appreciate the trust you have placed in me, and I assure you that I will do what I can to be a productive team member at Cynergo.

Sincerely yours,

Mark Greenberg

- *Letter rejecting a job offer.* If you decide not to accept a job offer, express your appreciation and, if appropriate, explain why you are declining the offer. Remember, you might want to work for this company sometime in the future.

Dear Mr. Weaver:

I appreciate very much the offer to join your staff.

Although I am certain that I would benefit greatly from working at Cynergo, I have decided to take a job with a firm in Baltimore, where I have been accepted at Johns Hopkins to pursue my master's degree at night.

Again, thank you for your generous offer.

Sincerely yours,

Cynthia O'Malley

Cynthia O'Malley

- *Letter acknowledging a rejection.* Why write back after you have been rejected for a job? To maintain good relations. You might get a phone call the next week explaining that the person who accepted the job has had to change her plans and offering you the position.

Dear Mr. Weaver:

I was disappointed to learn that I will not have a chance to join your staff, because I feel that I could make a substantial contribution. However, I realize that job decisions are complex, involving many candidates and many factors.

Thank you very much for the courtesy you have shown me.

Sincerely yours,

Paul Goicochea

Paul Goicochea

Writer's Checklist

Printed Résumé

- [ ] Does the résumé have a professional appearance, with generous margins, a symmetrical layout, adequate white space, and effective indentation? (p. 395)
- [ ] Does the résumé meet the needs of its readers? (p. 396)
- [ ] Is the résumé honest? (p. 396)
- [ ] Is the résumé free of errors? (p. 396)
- [ ] Does the identifying information contain your name, address(es), phone number(s), and e-mail address(es)? (p. 399)
- [ ] Does the résumé include a clear statement of your job objectives or a summary of your credentials? (p. 400)
- [ ] Does the education section include your degree, your institution and its location, and your (anticipated) date of graduation, as well as any other information that will help a reader appreciate your qualifications? (p. 400)
- [ ] Does the employment section include, for each job, the dates of employment, the organization's name and location, and (if you are writing a chronological résumé) your position or title, as well as a description of your duties and accomplishments? (p. 402)
- [ ] Does the "interests-and-activities" section include relevant hobbies or activities, including extracurricular interests? (p. 404) Have you omitted any personal information that might reflect poorly on you? (p. 405)
- [ ] Does the references section include the names, job titles, organizations, mailing addresses, and phone numbers of three or four references? (p. 405) If you are not listing this information, does the strength of the rest of the résumé offset the omission? (p. 405)
- [ ] Does the résumé include any other appropriate sections, such as computer skills and abilities, military service, language skills, or honors? (p. 405)

Electronic Résumé

In addition to the items mentioned in the checklist for the printed résumé, did you

- [ ] use plain text? (p. 415)
- [ ] use a simple sans-serif typeface? (p. 415)
- [ ] use a single-column format? (p. 415)
- [ ] use wide margins? (p. 415)
- [ ] use the space bar instead of the Tab key? (p. 415)

Job-Application Letter

- [ ] Does the letter meet your reader's needs? (p. 415)
- [ ] Is the letter honest? (p. 396)
- [ ] Does the letter look professional? (p. 417)
- [ ] Does the introductory paragraph identify your source of information and the position you are applying for, state that you wish to be considered, and forecast the rest of the letter? (p. 417)
- [ ] Does the education paragraph respond to your reader's needs with a unified idea introduced by a topic sentence? (p. 418)
- [ ] Does the employment paragraph respond to your reader's needs with a unified idea introduced by a topic sentence? (p. 419)
- [ ] Does the concluding paragraph include a reference to your résumé, a request for an interview, your phone number, and your e-mail address? (p. 420)
- [ ] Does the letter include an enclosure notation? (p. 421)

Preparing for a Job Interview

Did you

- [ ] study job interviews? (p. 423)
- [ ] study the organization to which you applied? (p. 423)
- [ ] think about what you can offer the organization? (p. 423)
- [ ] study lists of common interview questions? (p. 423)
- [ ] compile a list of questions you wish to ask? (p. 423)
- [ ] rehearse the interview? (p. 423)

Follow-up Letters

- [ ] Does your letter of appreciation for a job interview thank the interviewer and briefly restate your qualifications? (p. 424)
- [ ] Does your letter accepting a job offer show enthusiasm and repeat the major terms of your employment? (p. 424)
- [ ] Does your letter rejecting a job offer express your appreciation and, if appropriate, explain why you are declining the offer? (p. 425)
- [ ] Does your letter acknowledging a rejection have a positive tone that will help you maintain good relations? (p. 425)

Exercises

In This Book For more about memos, see Ch. 14, p. 377.

1. **INTERNET EXERCISE** Using a job board on the Web, list and briefly describe five positions in your field in your state. What skills, experience, and background does each position require? What is the salary range for each?

2. **INTERNET EXERCISE** Locate and provide the URLs of three job boards that provide interactive forms for creating a résumé automatically. In a brief memo to your instructor, describe the strengths and weaknesses of each. Which job board appears to be the easiest to use? Why?

3. The following résumé was submitted in response to an ad describing these duties: "CAM Technician to work with other technicians and manage some GIS and mapping projects. Also perform updating of the GIS database. Experience required." In a brief memo to your instructor, describe how effective the résumé is. What are some of its problems?

Kenneth Bradley

530 Maplegrove   Bozeman, Mont. 59715 (406)-484-2916

Objective	Entry level position as a CAM Technician. I am also interested in staying with the company until after graduation, possibly moving into a position as a Mechanical Engineer.
Education	Enrolled at Montana State University August 2007- Present
Employment	Fred Meyer 65520 Chinden Garden City, MT (208)-323-7030

Janitor- 7/06-6/07
Responsible for cleaning entire store, as well as equipment maintenance and floor maintenance and repair.

Assistant Janitorial Manager- 6/07-9/07
Responsible for cleaning entire store, equipment maintenance, floor maintenance and repair, scheduling, and managing personnel

Head of Freight- 9/07-Present

In charge of braking down all new freight, stocking shelves, cleaning the stock room, and managing personnel

Montana State University
Bozeman, MT
Teachers Aide ME 120- 1/06-5/06
Teachers Aide ME 120
In charge of keeping students in line and answering any questions related to drafting.

References   Timothy Rayburn
Janitorial Manager
(406)-555-8571

Eduardo Perez
Coworker
(406)-555-2032

4. The following application letter responds to an ad describing these duties: "CAM Technician to work with other technicians and manage some GIS and mapping projects. Also perform updating of the GIS database. Experience required." In a brief memo to your instructor, describe how effective the letter is and how it could be improved.

530 Maplegrove
Bozeman, Mont. 59715
November 11, 2009

Mr. Bruce Hedley
Adecco Technical
Bozeman, Mont. 59715

Dear Mr. Hedley,

I am writing you in response to your ad on Monsterjobs.com. Would you please consider me for the position of CAM technician? I believe that my academic schooling at Montana State University, along with my work experience would make me an excellent candidate for the position.

While at Montana State University, I took one class in particular that applies well to this job. It was a CAD drafting class, which I received a 97% in. The next semester I was a Teachers Aid for that same class, where I was responsible for answering questions about drafting from my peers. This gave me a much stronger grasp on all aspects of CAD work than I could have ever gotten from simply taking the class.

My employment at Fred Meyer is also a notable experience. While there is no technical aspects of either positions I have held, I believe that my experience there will shed light on my work ethic and interpersonal skills. I started out as a graveyard shift janitor, with no previous experience. All of my coworkers were at least thirty years older than me, and had a minimum of five years of janitorial experience. However after working there for only one year I was promoted to assistant manager. Three months after I received this position, I was informed that Fred Meyer was going to contract out the janitorial work and that all of us would be losing our jobs. I decided that I wanted to stay within the company, and I was able to receive a position as head of freight.

The enclosed resumé provides an overview of my education and work experience. I would appreciate an opportunity to meet with you at your convience to disscuss my qualifications for this position. Please write me at the above address or leave a message anytime. If you would like to contact me by e-mail, my e-mail address is kbradley@montanastate.edu.

Yours truly,

Ken Bradley

5. How effective is the following letter of appreciation? How could it be improved? Present your findings in a brief memo to your instructor.

914 Imperial Boulevard
Durham, NC 27708

November 13, 2009

Mr. Ronald O'Shea
Safeway Electronics, Inc.
Holland, MI 49423

Dear Mr. O'Shea:

Thanks very much for showing me around your plant. I hope I was able to convince you that I'm the best person for the job.

Sincerely yours,

Robert Harad

6. INTERNET EXERCISE In a newspaper or journal or on the Internet, find a job ad for a position in your field for which you might be qualified. Write a résumé and a job-application letter in response to the ad; include the job ad or a photocopy. You will be evaluated not only on the content and appearance of the materials but also on how well you have targeted them to the job ad.

Case 15: Identifying Transferable Skills for a Career Changer

Background

"I'm thinking about changing careers," your friend Mercedes tells you. After 10 years of teaching mathematics, she wants a job in industry. "I'm looking for something that's a little more challenging. I can't stand the thought of teaching beginning algebra for another year, not to mention another 20 years. Besides, I don't see much opportunity for career advancement as a teacher. Because I'm not interested in switching to administration, the best I can hope for is to become the chair of the mathematics department someday. A job in industry would offer me new challenges, and I might have more opportunities for advancement."

"What career are you thinking of?" you ask.

"I've done a little research, and I'm thinking of using my math skills as an actuary."

"What's an actuary?"

"Actuaries work in the insurance field, using their background in mathematics to calculate insurance premiums, set reserve funds, and estimate the costs of implementing new benefits. In last Sunday's newspaper, I found a job advertisement for an actuarial analyst." (See Document 15.1.)

"Do you qualify for this job?"

"I think I do. But I'm not sure how to describe ten years of teaching mathematics so that the skills I've acquired seem relevant to the position."

"I remember when my friend Terry left the army and made the transition from military to civilian life. Because there are not many job openings for an artillery officer in business, Terry had to focus on transferable skills. Terry

Document 15.1 Job Advertisement for an Actuarial Analyst

> ### Actuarial Analyst
>
> Collects and analyzes data for pricing, reserving, underwriting, and forecasting at Gold Star Insurance. Requires BA or BS degree in Mathematics, Statistics, Computer Science, Economics, or related area. College math, including calculus, statistics, and/or numerical analysis. Proficient in using spreadsheet and statistical software. Ability to analyze complex issues about pricing, experience monitoring, reserving, and forecasting. Projects will include management reporting, health data trend studies, financial analysis and planning, supervising special projects, and some travel. Detail-oriented and able to clearly communicate highly technical issues orally and in writing.
>
> Send a letter of application and a résumé to Ms. Roberta Klein, Director of Actuarial Services, Gold Star Insurance, PO Box 2233, St. Louis, MO 63136.

On TechComm Web

For digital versions of case documents, click on Downloadable Case Documents on <bedfordstmartins.com/techcomm>.

Mercedes Viana

927 Emerald Street   208-555-1510
Boise, ID 83704   mviana@hotmail.com

Education

MA   **Mathematics Education**, *State University of New York at Albany, December 1999*. GPA 3.96.
   Courses include: Chaos and Complexity, Vector Analysis.

BA   **Mathematics**, Minor in Economics, *State University of New York at Albany, Academic Excellence in Mathematics Award, May 1998*.
   Overall GPA 3.66, Major GPA 3.78.
   Courses include: Production and Operations Management for Engineers, Engineering Project Management, Introduction to Engineering Analysis, Human Resource Management, Writing and Critical Thinking.

Teaching Experience

Boise State University, Adjunct Faculty, Mathematics, Boise, ID, 2004–Present.
   Researched, designed, and taught courses including College Algebra, Pre-Calculus, Finite Mathematics, and Introduction to Mathematical Thought. Selected texts and created online and print materials. Developed innovative methods to present technical material to nonexperts. Student evaluations consistently listed my strengths as the following: organization, preparedness, and clarity of presentation.

Boise City Schools, Mathematics Teacher, Boise, ID, 2005–Present.
   Developed project plan for academic year, adjusting approach based on student progress data. Provided instruction and written and oral feedback, maintained progress records, and supervised activities of over 120 students daily. Generated written reports on student progress with curriculum recommendations and presented this material to administration and parents. Participated in school, district, and regional team meetings to address educational mandates. Communicated with parents, teachers, and administration daily via e-mail, phone, and written correspondence. Supervised three cheerleader squads of 20 students. Directed two coaches, practice and event scheduling, and fund-raising opportunities.

Rockingham County Schools, Mathematics Teacher, Bridgewater, VA, 2002–2004.
   Guided over 90 students to above-state-average results on Virginia Standards of Learning (SOL) examinations in Algebra and Geometry. Worked with multidisciplinary team to create material addressing SOL objectives. Supervisor evaluations highlighted strengths including "works very hard to make sure each student understands the problem being worked."

Pulaski Technical College, Instructor, N. Little Rock, AR, 2001–2002.
   Designed material to address the needs of approximately 80 diverse adult learners. Provided group instruction, arranged and led small-group tutoring sessions, and created assessment tools. Also taught Advanced Placement Calculus at local high school to accelerated sophomores.

used the experience she acquired in the army, along with college course work, volunteer activities, and hobbies, to apply for a management position she was interested in. You can do something similar. You need to identify which of your qualifications and experiences are relevant to the actuarial analyst position."

"You seem to know what you're talking about. Would you be willing to help me apply for this position?"

"Sure. Send me your current résumé (Document 15.2), and I'll see what I can do. In the meantime, I'll e-mail you a few resources on the Internet that describe the concept of transferable skills."

Document 15.2
(continued)

Pulaski County School District, Mathematics Teacher, Little Rock, AR, 2000–2001.
Taught mathematics with an emphasis on integrating technology. Wrote reports to district administration on innovative plans to include multicultural material in the traditional math classroom. Supervisor evaluations highlighted strengths including "constantly on the growing edge of learning, . . . personable, possesses a pleasing and positive attitude, . . . relates well with people."

SUNY Albany, School of Education, Computer Consultant, NY, 1998–1999.
Assisted math and science faculty with advanced computer skills such as programming, computer networking, and use of statistical programs.

Technical Skills

- MS Office Software: Word, Excel, PowerPoint.
- Desktop Publishing Software: FrameMaker, Photoshop, Adobe Acrobat.
- Web-Authoring Software: FrontPage, Blackboard (Web-Based Training).
- Mathematics and Database Software: SAS, Maple V, Access.
- Computer-Aided Drafting: Pro-Engineer.
- Programming Languages: C#, C++, Java, Fortran.

Honors

- *Kappa Delta Pi*, National Educational Honors Society, 1999.
- *Phi Theta Kappa*, National Honor Society, 1996.
- Science Award, Mathematics Award, and Academic Award, Cazenovia College, 1996.
- Dean's List, Cazenovia College, Rensselaer Polytechnic Institute, and SUNY at Albany, 1995–1998.

Professional Development

- International Society for Technology in Education Certified, 2005.
- Graduate Course Work in Computer Science, James Madison University, 2003–2004.
- Society for Technical Communicators National Annual Conference, Chicago, IL, 2004.
- National Teacher Training Institute in Mathematics, Science, and Technology, Harrisonburg, VA, 2004.
- Teachers Teaching with Technology Statistics Institute, Hot Springs, AR, 2001.

References

Available upon request.

Your Assignment

1. Using an Internet search engine such as Google, locate three or four Internet resources describing transferable skills for career changers. Write Mercedes a brief e-mail message in which you list the resources you located and provide a one-paragraph summary of each resource.

2. Revise Mercedes's current résumé (Document 15.2) so that it emphasizes transferable skills relevant to the actuarial analyst position (Document 15.1).

3. Draft a job-application letter that Mercedes could use to respond to the actuarial analyst ad.

Writing Proposals

Source: U.S. Air Force, 2007 <www.916arw.afrc.af.mil/shared/media/photodb/photos/060407-F-1600L-001.jpg>.

In the World . . .

Shot from inside an airborne tanker, this photo shows a military jet being refueled. The U.S. Air Force is studying proposals from several manufacturers for a $40 billion project to build 179 tankers. Like almost all organizations large and small, the military buys almost everything it uses—from food and water to uniforms, equipment, weapons systems, and security—from suppliers that compete for contracts by writing proposals.

Understanding the Process of Writing Proposals 432

The Logistics of Proposals 433

External and Internal Proposals 433

Solicited and Unsolicited Proposals 434

The "Deliverables" of Proposals 435

Research Proposals 436

Goods and Services Proposals 436

Persuasion and Proposals 437

Understanding Readers' Needs 437

Describing What You Plan to Do 438

Demonstrating Your Professionalism 439

Writing a Proposal 440

The Structure of the Proposal 441

Summary 441

Introduction 441

Proposed Program 442

Qualifications and Experience 443

Budget 443

Appendices 444

Sample Internal Proposal 447

A proposal is an offer to carry out research or to provide a product or service. For instance, a physical therapist might write a proposal to her supervisor for funding to attend a convention to learn about current rehabilitation practices. A director of a homeless shelter might write a proposal for funding to expand the services offered by the shelter. Whether the project is small or big, within your own company or outside it, it is likely to call for a proposal.

UNDERSTANDING THE PROCESS OF WRITING PROPOSALS

Writing a proposal calls for the same process of planning, drafting, revising, editing, and proofreading that you use for other kinds of documents. Figure 16.1 presents an overview of this process.

Figure 16.1 An Overview of the Process of Writing Proposals

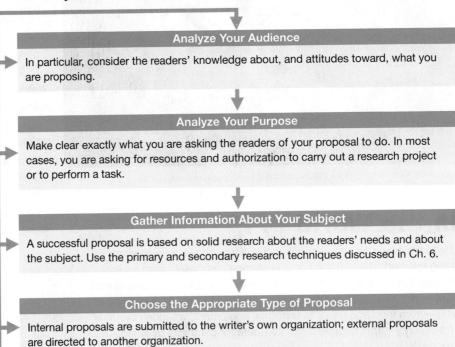

Analyze Your Audience

In particular, consider the readers' knowledge about, and attitudes toward, what you are proposing.

Analyze Your Purpose

Make clear exactly what you are asking the readers of your proposal to do. In most cases, you are asking for resources and authorization to carry out a research project or to perform a task.

Gather Information About Your Subject

A successful proposal is based on solid research about the readers' needs and about the subject. Use the primary and secondary research techniques discussed in Ch. 6.

Choose the Appropriate Type of Proposal

Internal proposals are submitted to the writer's own organization; external proposals are directed to another organization.

Draft the Proposal

Follow the instructions in any request for proposals (RFP) or information for bid (IFB) from the prospective customer. If there is none, include an **introduction**, which shows specifically that you understand your readers' problem or opportunity; a **proposed program**, which describes what you will do if the proposal is accepted; a **qualifications and experience** section, including evidence of other successful projects; a **budget**; and **appendices**, such as a task schedule and a description of evaluation techniques.

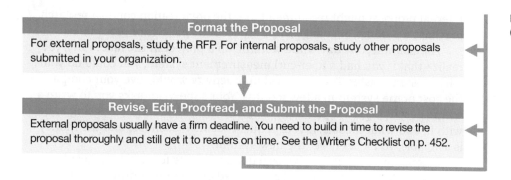

Figure 16.1
(continued)

| Format the Proposal |
| For external proposals, study the RFP. For internal proposals, study other proposals submitted in your organization. |

| Revise, Edit, Proofread, and Submit the Proposal |
| External proposals usually have a firm deadline. You need to build in time to revise the proposal thoroughly and still get it to readers on time. See the Writer's Checklist on p. 452. |

THE LOGISTICS OF PROPOSALS

Proposals can be classified as either external or internal; external proposals are either solicited or unsolicited. Figure 16.2 shows the relationship among these four terms.

External and Internal Proposals

Proposals are either external (if submitted to another organization) or internal (if submitted to the writer's own organization).

External Proposals   No organization produces all the products or provides all the services it needs. Web sites need to be designed, written, and maintained; inventory databases need to be created; facilities need to be constructed. Sometimes, projects require unusual expertise, such as sophisticated market analyses. Because many companies supply these products and services, most organizations require that a prospective supplier compete for the business by submitting a proposal, a document arguing that it deserves the business.

Internal Proposals   An internal proposal is an argument, submitted within an organization, for carrying out an activity that will benefit the organization. An

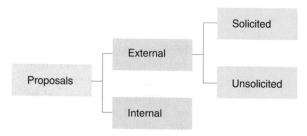

Figure 16.2   The Logistics of Proposals

internal proposal might recommend that the organization conduct research, purchase a product, or change some aspect of its policies or procedures.

For example, one day while working on a project in the laboratory, you realize that if you had a fiber-curl measurement system, you could do your job better and faster. The increased productivity would save your company the cost of the system in a few months. Your supervisor asks you to write a memo describing what you want, why you want it, what you're going to do with it, and what it costs. If your request seems reasonable and the money is available, you'll likely get the new system.

Often, the scope of the proposal determines its format. A request for a small amount of money might be conveyed orally or in writing, by e-mail or in a brief memo. A request for a large amount, however, is usually presented in a formal document such as a report.

Solicited and Unsolicited Proposals

External proposals are either solicited or unsolicited. A *solicited proposal* is submitted in response to a request from a prospective customer. An *unsolicited proposal* is submitted by a supplier who believes that the prospective customer has a need for goods or services.

Solicited Proposals   When an organization wants to purchase a product or service, it publishes one of two basic kinds of statements:

- An *information for bid* (IFB) is used for standard products. When a state agency needs desktop computers, for instance, it informs computer manufacturers of the configuration it needs. All other things being equal, the supplier that offers the lowest bid wins the contract.

- A *request for proposals* (RFP) is used for more-customized products or services. For example, if the Air Force needs an "identification friend or foe" device, the RFP it publishes might be a long and detailed set of technical specifications. The supplier that can design, produce, and deliver the device most closely resembling the specifications—at a reasonable price—will probably win the contract.

On TechComm Web

For links to FedBizOpps, click on Links Library for Ch. 16 on <bedfordstmartins.com/ techcomm>.

Most organizations issue RFPs and IFBs in print and online. Government RFPs and IFBs are published on the FedBizOpps Web site. Figure 16.3 shows a sample IFB.

Unsolicited Proposals   An unsolicited proposal is like a solicited proposal except that it does not refer to an RFP. Even though the potential customer never formally requested the proposal, in most cases the supplier was invited to submit the proposal after people from the two organizations met and discussed the project. Because proposals are expensive to write, suppliers are reluctant to submit them without assurance that they will be considered carefully. Thus, the word *unsolicited* is only partially accurate.

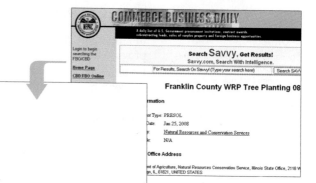

Franklin County WRP Tree Planting 08

General Information
Document Type: PRESOL
Posted Date: Jan 25, 2008
Category: <u>Natural Resources and Conservation Services</u>
Set Aside: N/A

Contracting Office Address
Department of Agriculture, Natural Resources Conservation Service, Illinois State Office, 2118 West Park Court, Champaign, IL, 61821, UNITED STATES

Description
Franklin County WRP Tree Planting Project located in Franklin County, Illinois. Project consists of furnishing all equipment, labor, supplies, materials and incidentals necessary to plant mixed upland and bottomland sites on one WRP easement located in Franklin County, Illinois as follows: Site #1: 551.2 acres; Site #2: 501.5 acres; and Site #3: 701.8 acres. Sites shall each require a mowing and shall be planted with 435 bare-root seedlings per acre. The Government anticipates making up to three separate contract awards. A site showing for all projects will be held Wednesday, February 13th, 2008, at 1:00 p.m. local time at the Benton NRCS Field Office located at 711 N. DuQuoin Street, Benton, IL. After a brief meeting concerning the bidding process and contract requirements, the group will be given a general tour of the planting sites....

Original Point of Contact
POC Bernita Clark, Contract Specialist, Phone 217-353-6615, Fax 217-353-6677

Place of Performance
Address:
North of West Frankfort, Illinois in Franklin County, IL
62812, UNITED STATES

Figure 16.3   Excerpt from an IFB
Source: CBD/FBO Online, 2008 <http://cbdweb.com/index.php/search/show/21764263>.

THE "DELIVERABLES" OF PROPOSALS

A *deliverable* is what the supplier will deliver at the end of the project. Deliverables can be classified into two major categories: research or goods and services.

On TechComm Web

For sample proposals and writing checklists, see Writing Guidelines for Engineering and Science Students. Click on Links Library for Ch. 16 on <bedfordstmartins.com/techcomm>.

In This Book

For more about progress reports, see Ch. 17, p. 464. For more about completion reports, see Ch. 19.

Research Proposals

In a research proposal, you are promising to perform research and then provide a report about it. For example, a biologist for a state bureau of land management writes a proposal to the National Science Foundation requesting resources to build a window-lined tunnel in the forest to study tree and plant roots and the growth of fungi. The biologist also wishes to investigate the relationship between plant growth and the activity of insects and worms. The deliverable will be a report submitted to the National Science Foundation and perhaps an article published in a professional journal.

A research proposal often leads to two other applications: progress reports and completion reports.

After the proposal has been approved and the researchers have begun work, they often submit one or more *progress reports*, which tell the sponsor of the project how the work is proceeding. Is it following the plan of work outlined in the proposal? Is it going according to schedule? Is it staying within budget?

At the end of the project, researchers prepare a *completion report*, often called a *final report*, *project report*, *recommendation report*, or simply *report*. A completion report tells the whole story of the research project, beginning with the problem or opportunity that motivated it, the methods used in carrying it out, and the results, conclusions, and recommendations.

People carry out research projects to satisfy their curiosity and to advance professionally. Organizations often require that their professional employees carry out research and publish in appropriate reports, journals, or books. Government researchers and university professors, for instance, are expected to remain active in their fields. Writing proposals is one way to get the resources—time and money for travel, equipment, and assistants—to carry out the research.

Goods and Services Proposals

A goods and services proposal is an offer to supply a tangible product (a fleet of automobiles), a service (building maintenance), or some combination of the two (the construction of a building).

A vast network of goods and services contracts spans the working world. The U.S. government, the world's biggest customer, spent $104 billion in 2007 buying military equipment from organizations that submitted proposals (U.S. Department of Commerce, 2007, p. 328). But goods and services contracts are by no means limited to government contractors. One auto manufacturer buys engines from another; a company that makes spark plugs buys steel from another company.

Another kind of goods and services proposal requests funding to support a local organization. For example, a homeless shelter might receive some of its funding from a city or county but also rely on grants from private philanthropies. Typically, an organization such as a shelter would apply for a grant to fund increased demand for its services due to a natural disaster or an economic slowdown in the community. Or it might apply for a grant to fund a pilot program to offer job training at the shelter. Most large corporations have philanthropic programs offering grants to help local colleges and universities, arts organizations, and social service groups.

PERSUASION AND PROPOSALS

A proposal is an argument. You must convince readers that the future benefits will outweigh the immediate and projected costs. Basically, you must persuade readers of three things:

- that you understand their needs
- that you have already determined what you plan to do and that you are able to do it
- that you are a professional and are committed to fulfilling your promises

▶ **In This Book**

For more about persuasion, see Ch. 8.

Understanding Readers' Needs

The most crucial element of the proposal is the definition of the problem or opportunity to which the proposed project responds. Although this point seems obvious, people who evaluate proposals agree that the most common weakness they see is an inadequate or inaccurate understanding of the problem or opportunity.

▶ **In This Book**

For more about analyzing your audience, see Ch. 5.

Readers' Needs in an Internal Proposal   Writing an internal proposal is both simpler and more complicated than writing an external one. It is simpler because you have more access to internal readers than you do to external readers and you can get more information more easily. However, it is more complicated because you might find it hard to understand the situation in your organization. Some colleagues might not be willing to tell you that your proposal is a long shot or that your ideas might threaten someone in the organization. Before you write an internal proposal, discuss your ideas with as many potential readers as you can to learn what the organization really thinks of them.

Readers' Needs in an External Proposal   Most readers will reject a proposal as soon as they realize that it doesn't address their needs. When you receive an RFP, study it thoroughly. If you don't understand something in it, contact the organization requesting the proposal. Someone there will be happy to clarify it, because a poor proposal wastes everyone's time.

When you write an unsolicited proposal, analyze your audience carefully. How can you define the problem or opportunity so that your readers will understand it? Keep in mind readers' needs and, if possible, their backgrounds.

Concentrate on how the problem has decreased productivity or quality or how your ideas would create new opportunities. When you submit an unsolicited proposal, your task in many cases is to convince readers that a need exists. Even when you have reached an understanding with some of your customer's representatives, your proposal will still have to persuade other officials in the company.

When you are preparing a proposal to be submitted to an organization in another culture, keep in mind the following six suggestions (Newman, 2006):

- *Understand that what makes an argument persuasive can differ from one culture to another.* Paying attention to the welfare of the company or the community may be more persuasive than a low bottom-line price. An American company was surprised to learn that the Venezuelan readers of its proposal had selected a French company instead of it because the French company "had been making personal visits for years, bringing their families, and engaging in social activities long before there was any question of a contract" (Thrush, 2000).

- *Budget enough time for translating.* If your proposal has to be translated into another language, build in plenty of time. Translating long technical documents is a lengthy process, because even though some of the work can be done by computer software, the machine translation needs to be reviewed by native speakers of the target language.

- *Use simple graphics, with captions.* To reduce the chances of misunderstanding, use a lot of simple graphics, such as pie charts and bar graphs. Be sure to include captions so that readers can understand the graphics easily without having to look through the text to see what each graphic means.

- *Write short sentences, using common vocabulary.* Short sentences are easier to understand than long sentences. Choose words that have few meanings. For example, use the word *right* only as the opposite of *left*; use *correct* as the opposite of *wrong*.

- *Use local conventions regarding punctuation, spelling, and mechanics.* Be aware that these conventions differ from place to place, even in the English-speaking world. For instance, the Australian state of New South Wales uses a different dictionary for spelling than all the other Australian states.

- *Ask if the prospective customer will do a read-through.* A *read-through* is the process of reading a draft of the proposal to determine whether it might lead to any misunderstandings due to language or cultural differences. Why would a prospective customer do this? Because it's in everyone's interest if the proposal responds clearly to the customer's needs.

▶ **In This Book**
For more about graphics, see Ch. 12.

Describing What You Plan to Do

Once you have shown that you understand what needs to be done and why, describe what you plan to do. Convince readers that you can respond effectively to the situation you have just described. Discuss procedures and equipment you would use. If appropriate, justify your choices. For example, if you say that you want to do ultrasonic testing on a structure, explain why, unless the reason is obvious.

Present a complete picture of what you would do from the first day of the project to the last. You need more than enthusiasm and good faith; you need a detailed plan showing that you have already started to do the work. Although no proposal can anticipate every question about what you plan to do, the more planning you have done before you submit the proposal, the greater the chances that you will be able to do the work successfully if the proposal is approved.

Demonstrating Your Professionalism

Once you have shown that you understand readers' needs and can offer a well-conceived plan, demonstrate that you are the kind of person (or that yours is the kind of organization) that is committed to delivering what you promise. Convince readers that you have the pride, ingenuity, and perseverance to solve the problems that are likely to occur. In short, show that you are a professional.

Guidelines

Demonstrating Your Professionalism in a Proposal

Demonstrate your ability to carry out a project by providing four kinds of information:

▶ **Credentials and work history.** Show that you know how to do this project because you have done similar ones. Who are the people in your organization with the qualifications to carry out the project? What equipment and facilities do you have that will enable you to do the work? What management structure will you use to coordinate the activities and keep the project running smoothly?

▶ **Work schedule.** Sometimes called a *task schedule*, a work schedule is a graph or chart that shows when the various phases of the project will be carried out. The work schedule reveals more about your attitudes toward your work than about what you will be doing on any given day. A detailed work schedule shows that you have tried to foresee problems that might threaten the project.

▶ **Quality-control measures.** Describe how you would evaluate the effectiveness and efficiency of your work. Quality-control procedures might consist of technical evaluations carried out periodically by the project staff, on-site evaluations by recognized authorities or by the prospective customer, or progress reports.

▶ **Budget.** Most proposals conclude with a detailed budget, a statement of how much the project will cost. Including a budget is another way of showing that you have done your homework on a project.

Ethics Note

Writing Honest Proposals

When an organization approves a proposal, it needs to trust that the people who will carry out the project will do it professionally. Over the centuries, however, dishonest proposal writers have perfected a number of ways to trick prospective customers into thinking that a project will go smoothly:

- saying that certain qualified people will participate in the project, even though they will not
- saying that the project will be finished by a certain date, even though it will not
- saying that the deliverable will have certain characteristics, even though it will not
- saying that the project will be completed under budget, even though it will not

There are three reasons to be honest in writing a proposal:

- to avoid serious legal trouble stemming from breach-of-contract suits
- to avoid acquiring a bad reputation, thus ruining your business
- to do the right thing

WRITING A PROPOSAL

On TechComm Web

For proposal-writing advice, see Joseph Levine's "Guide for Writing a Funding Proposal." Click on Links Library for Ch. 16 on <bedfordstmartins.com/techcomm>.

Although writing a proposal requires the same writing process that you use for most other kinds of technical documents, a proposal can be so large that two aspects of the writing process—resource planning and collaboration—are even more important than they are in smaller documents.

As discussed in Chapter 5, planning a project requires a lot of work. You need to see whether your organization can devote resources to writing the proposal and then to carrying out the project if the proposal is approved. Sometimes, an organization writes a proposal, wins the contract, and then loses money because it lacks the resources to do the project and must subcontract major portions of it. The resources you need fall into three basic categories:

- *Personnel.* Will you have the technical personnel, managers, and support people?
- *Facilities.* Will you have the facilities, or can you lease them? Can you profitably subcontract tasks to companies that have the right facilities?
- *Equipment.* Do you have the right equipment? If not, can you buy it or lease it, or can you subcontract the work? Some contracts provide for the purchase of equipment, but others don't.

Don't write the proposal unless you are confident that you can carry out the project if you get the go-ahead.

Collaboration is critical in large proposals, because no one person has the time and expertise to do all the work. Writing major proposals requires the expertise of technical personnel, writers, editors, graphic artists, managers, lawyers, and document-production specialists. Usually, a project manager coordinates the process.

Proposal writers almost always reuse existing information, including *boilerplate*, such as descriptions of other projects the company has done, histories and descriptions of the company, and résumés of the important personnel who will work on the project. This reuse of information is legal and ethical—as long as it is the intellectual property of the company.

In This Book
For more about collaboration, see Ch. 4.

In This Book
For more about boilerplate, see Ch. 2, p. 28.

THE STRUCTURE OF THE PROPOSAL

Proposal structures vary greatly from one organization to another. A long, complex proposal might have 10 or more sections, including introduction, problem, objectives, solution, methods and resources, and management. If the authorizing agency provides an IFB, RFP, or set of guidelines, follow it closely. If you have no guidelines, or if you are writing an unsolicited proposal, use the structure shown here as a starting point. Then modify it according to your subject, your purpose, and the needs of your audience. An example of a proposal is presented on pages 447–50.

On TechComm Web
To view the proposal guidelines of the Society for Human Resource Management, click on Links Library for Ch. 16 on <bedfordstmartins.com/techcomm>.

Summary

For a proposal of more than a few pages, provide a summary. Many organizations impose a length limit, such as 250 words, and ask the writer to present the summary, single-spaced, on the title page. The summary is crucial, because it might be the only item that readers study in their initial review of the proposal.

The summary covers the major elements of the proposal but devotes only a few sentences to each. Define the problem in a sentence or two. Next, describe the proposed program and provide a brief statement of your qualifications and experience. Some organizations wish to see the completion date and the final budget figure in the summary; others prefer that this information be presented separately on the title page along with other identifying information about the supplier and the proposed project.

In This Book
For more about summaries, see Ch. 19, p. 515.

Introduction

The purpose of the introduction is to help readers understand the context, scope, and organization of the proposal.

Guidelines

Introducing a Proposal

The introduction to a proposal should answer the following seven questions:

▶ **What is the problem or opportunity?** Describe the problem or opportunity in specific monetary terms, because the proposal itself will include a budget, and you want to convince your readers that spending money on what you propose is smart. Don't say that a design problem is slowing down production; say that it is costing $4,500 a day in lost productivity.

▶ **What is the purpose of the proposal?** The purpose of the proposal is to describe a problem or opportunity and propose activities that will culminate in a deliverable. Be specific in explaining what you want to do.

▶ **What is the background of the problem or opportunity?** Although you probably will not be telling readers anything they don't already know, show them that you understand the problem or opportunity: the circumstances that led to its discovery, the relationships or events that will affect the problem and its solution, and so on.

▶ **What are your sources of information?** Review the relevant literature, ranging from internal reports and memos to published articles or even books, so that readers will understand the context of your work.

▶ **What is the scope of the proposal?** If appropriate, indicate what you are—and are not—proposing to do.

▶ **What is the organization of the proposal?** Explain the organizational pattern you will use.

▶ **What are the key terms you will use in the proposal?** If you will use any specialized or unusual terms, define them in the introduction.

Proposed Program

In the proposed program, sometimes called the *plan of work*, explain what you want to do. Be specific. You won't persuade anyone by saying that you plan to "gather the data and analyze it." How will you gather and analyze the data? Justify your claims. Every word you say—or don't say—will give readers evidence on which to base their decision.

If your project concerns a subject written about in the professional literature, show your familiarity with the scholarship by referring to pertinent studies. However, don't just string together a bunch of citations. For example, don't write "Carruthers (2006), Harding (2007), and Vega (2006) have all researched the relationship between global warming and groundwater contamination." Rather, use the recent literature to sketch the necessary background and provide the justification for your proposed program. For instance:

> Carruthers (2006), Harding (2007), and Vega (2006) have demonstrated the relationship between global warming and groundwater contamination. None of these studies, however, included an analysis of the long-term contamination of the aquifer. The current study will consist of. . . .

On TechComm Web

For a sample literature review, see Writing Guidelines for Engineering and Science Students. Click on Links Library for Ch. 16 on <bedfordstmartins.com/techcomm>.

You might include only a few references to recent research. However, if your topic is complex, you might devote several paragraphs or even several pages to recent scholarship.

In This Book
For more about researching a subject, see Ch. 6.

Whether your project calls for primary research, secondary research, or both, the proposal will be unpersuasive if you haven't already done a substantial amount of the research. For instance, say you are writing a proposal to do research on industrial-grade lawn mowers. You are not being persuasive if you write that you are going to visit Wal-Mart, Lowe's, and Home Depot to see what kinds of lawn mowers they carry. This statement is unpersuasive for two reasons:

- You need to justify why you are going to visit those three retailers rather than others. Anticipate your readers' questions: Why did you choose those retailers? Why didn't you choose more-specialized dealers?

- You should already have visited the appropriate stores and completed any other preliminary research. If you haven't done your homework, readers have no assurance that you will in fact do it or that it will pay off for them. If your supervisor authorizes the project and then learns that none of the lawn mowers on the market meets your organization's needs, you will have to go back and submit a different proposal—an embarrassing move.

Unless you can show in your proposed program that you have done the research—and that the research indicates that the project is likely to succeed—readers have no motivation to authorize the project.

Qualifications and Experience

After you have described how you would carry out the project, show that you can do it. The more elaborate the proposal, the more substantial the discussion of your qualifications and experience has to be. For a small project, include a few paragraphs describing your technical credentials and those of your co-workers. For larger projects, include the résumés of the project leader, often called the *principal investigator*, and the other important participants.

External proposals should discuss the qualifications of the supplier's organization, describing similar projects the supplier has completed successfully. For example, a company bidding on a contract to build a large suspension bridge should describe other suspension bridges it has built. It also should focus on the equipment and facilities the company already has and on the management structure that will ensure that the project will go smoothly.

Budget

Good ideas aren't good unless they're affordable. The budget section of a proposal specifies how much the proposed program will cost.

Budgets vary greatly in scope and format. For simple internal proposals, add the budget request to the statement of the proposed program: "This study will take two days, at a total cost of about $400" or "The variable-speed recorder currently costs $225, with a 10 percent discount on orders of five or more." For more-complicated internal proposals and for all external proposals, include a more explicit and complete budget.

Most budgets are divided into two parts: direct costs and indirect costs.

- *Direct costs* include expenses such as salaries and fringe benefits of program personnel, travel costs, and necessary equipment, materials, and supplies.

- *Indirect costs* cover the intangible expenses that are sometimes called *overhead*: general secretarial and clerical expenses not devoted exclusively to any one project, as well as operating expenses such as utilities and maintenance. Indirect costs are usually expressed as a percentage— ranging from less than 20 percent to more than 100 percent—of the direct costs.

Appendices

Many types of appendices might accompany a proposal. Most organizations have boilerplate descriptions of themselves and of other projects they have completed. These descriptions might be included as appendices. Another popular kind of appendix is the supporting letter: a testimonial to the supplier's skill and integrity written by a reputable and well-known person in the field. Two other kinds of appendices deserve special mention: the task schedule and the description of evaluation techniques.

Task Schedule   The task schedule is almost always drawn in one of three graphical formats: table, bar chart, or network diagram.

Tables   The simplest but least informative way to present a task schedule is in a table, as shown in Figure 16.4. As with all graphics, provide a textual reference that introduces and, if necessary, explains the table.

Although displaying information in a table is better than writing it out in sentences, readers still cannot "see" the information. They have to read it to figure out how long each activity will last, and they cannot tell whether any of the activities are interdependent. They have no way of determining what would happen to the overall project schedule if one of the activities was delayed.

Figure 16.4 Task Schedule as a Table

TASK SCHEDULE

Activity	Start date	Finish date
Design the security system	4 Oct. 08	19 Oct. 08
Research available systems	4 Oct. 08	3 Jan. 09
Etc.		

Tasks	Time			
	Month 1	Month 2	Month 3	Month 4
Task A	⬚⬚⬚⬚⬚⬚			
Task B	⬚⬚⬚			
Task C		⬚⬚⬚⬚⬚⬚⬚		
Task D			⬚⬚⬚⬚⬚⬚⬚⬚⬚	

← Time →

Figure 16.5   Task Schedule as a Bar Chart
Source: SmartDraw.com, 2004 <www.smartdraw.com/tutorials/gantt/tutorial1.htm#what>.

Bar Charts   Bar charts, also called *Gantt charts* after the early-twentieth-century civil engineer who first used them, are more informative than tables. The basic bar chart shown in Figure 16.5 allows readers to see how long each task will take and when different tasks occur simultaneously. Like tables, however, bar charts do not indicate the interdependency of tasks.

Network Diagrams   Network diagrams show the interdependence among various activities, clearly indicating which ones must be completed before others can begin. Even the relatively simple network diagram shown in Figure 16.6 can be difficult to read. You would probably not use this type of diagram in a document intended for general readers.

Description of Evaluation Techniques   Although *evaluation* can mean different things to different people, an *evaluation technique* typically refers to any procedure used to determine whether the proposed program is both effective and efficient. Evaluation techniques can range from simple progress reports to sophisticated statistical analyses. Some proposals call for evaluation by an outside agent, such as a consultant, a testing laboratory, or a university. Other proposals describe evaluation techniques that the supplier itself will perform, such as cost-benefit analyses.

The issue of evaluation is complicated by the fact that some people think in terms of *quantitative evaluations*—tests of measurable quantities, such as production increases—whereas others think in terms of *qualitative*

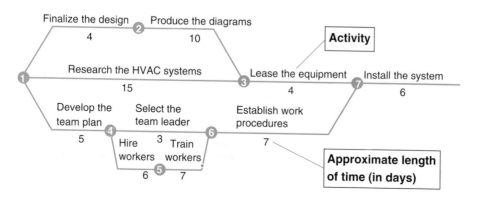

Figure 16.6   Task Schedule as a Network Diagram

A network diagram provides more useful information than either a table or a bar chart.

TECH TIP

How to Create a Gantt Chart

If you want to show how activities occur over time, you can create a simple **Gantt chart** using the **Table** feature in Word.

1. Create a **table** with enough cells to include your tasks and dates.

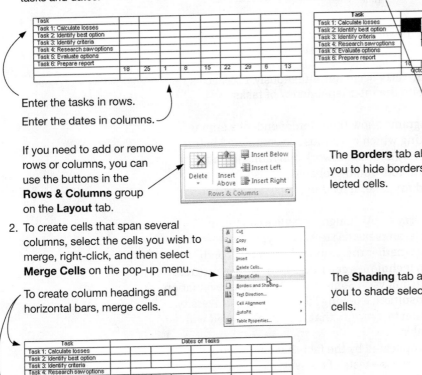

Enter the tasks in rows.

Enter the dates in columns.

If you need to add or remove rows or columns, you can use the buttons in the **Rows & Columns** group on the **Layout** tab.

2. To create cells that span several columns, select the cells you wish to merge, right-click, and then select **Merge Cells** on the pop-up menu.

To create column headings and horizontal bars, merge cells.

3. To differentiate completed tasks (black bars) from tasks yet to be completed (gray bars) or to hide borders, select the cells you wish to modify and then choose the **Page Borders** button in the **Page Background** group on the **Page Layout** tab. The **Borders and Shading** dialog box will appear.

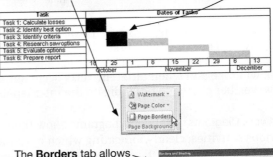

The **Borders** tab allows you to hide borders of selected cells.

The **Shading** tab allows you to shade selected cells.

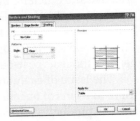

KEYWORDS: table, cells, merge cells, borders, shading

evaluations—tests of whether a proposed program is improving, say, the workmanship of a product. And some people include both qualitative and quantitative testing when they refer to evaluation. An additional complication is that projects can be tested while they are being carried out (*formative evaluations*) as well as after they have been completed (*summative evaluations*).

When an RFP calls for "evaluation," experienced proposal writers contact the prospective customer to determine precisely what the word means.

SAMPLE INTERNAL PROPOSAL

The following example of an internal proposal (Pritiken & Turner, 2008) has been formatted as a memo rather than as a formal proposal. (See Chapter 17, pages 467–71, for the progress report written after this project was under way and Chapter 19, pages 519–34, for the recommendation report.)

Total Gym Fitness

2206 Leadville Ave.
Boise, ID 83706

(208) 555-9635
totalgym@msn.com

Memo

Date: November 3, 2008
To: Jill Bookwalter, Owner and Manager
From: Jessie Pritiken, Senior Fitness Trainer
Megan Turner, Fitness Trainer
Subject: Proposal for Feasibility Study on Music Options at Total Gym Fitness

Purpose
The purpose of our proposal is to request authorization and funding to study whether offering MP3 players for our members' use would increase customer satisfaction regarding our music options and improve the gym attendance of some of our members.

Summary
Total Gym Fitness has been in the Boise area for more than twenty years, and we have a reputation for offering a high-quality gym experience and being responsive to customer requests. We pride ourselves on our ability to meet the fitness needs of all our members by keeping a close watch on emerging fitness trends and by incorporating the latest health and fitness research into our gym programs.

As you know, we frequently get complaints regarding the music we play at our facility. In fact, our 2007 Annual Member Satisfaction Survey revealed that the majority of our members are clearly dissatisfied with the music we play (see Figure 1). In addition, several members indicated that the music annoyed them so much that they cut short their workouts. Rather than motivating our members, it seems the music we play prevents some of them from getting a good workout.

Because of the growing concern over our music and our interest in motivating exercisers, we propose to begin researching options for offering members the use of MP3 players with custom playlists designed for various exercise routines. We would begin by determining if we could meet our members' music needs with our current speaker system. If not, we would calculate the cost of offering MP3 players for member checkout and assessing how many members would be interested in this service. If sufficient member interest existed, we would then establish criteria for evaluating MP3 players, research available MP3 options, and evaluate these options according to our criteria.

To perform this research and present a report on our findings, we estimate that we would require 20 hours over the next two months, for a total cost of $320. The MP3 team would consist of fitness trainers Jessie Pritiken and Megan Turner. If you were to accept this proposal, we would begin our research immediately, submitting to you a progress report on November 24, 2008, and a completion report on December 22, 2008. The completion report would include the details of our research and a recommendation for addressing our members' music needs.

An effective subject line indicates the purpose ("Proposal") and the subject of the memo ("Feasibility Study on Music Options at Total Gym Fitness").

Memos of more than one page should begin with a clear statement of purpose and a summary.

The background of the problem. Don't assume that your readers know what you are discussing.

The problem at the heart of the project.

The proposal. Note that the writers have already planned what they will do if the proposal is accepted. But note that the writers use the conditional tense ("would") because they cannot assume that their proposal will be authorized.

A summary of the schedule, the budget, and the writers' credentials. Because the reader will likely want to read this entire proposal, the summary functions as an advance organizer.

The introduction begins with a clear statement of the two aspects of the problem: dissatisfaction with music at the facility and its effect on some members' motivation to exercise.

The pie chart helps the writers show that the majority of members responding to the survey were dissatisfied with the music at the gym. Note that the writers have sequenced the slices from highest percentage to lowest, the typical sequence in pie charts. Even if the two "disagree" slices were not in percentage order—if, for example, "strongly agree" had been 27 percent—the writers probably would have decided to violate the more-to-less sequence in order to keep the two slices together.

In describing how music affects the motivation of members to use the facility, the writers show that they have already begun to research the problem. The more work a writer has done in advance, the less risk the reader is taking in approving their proposal.

The introduction concludes with an advance organizer for the rest of the proposal.

Introduction

We are seeking approval for a project to study whether offering MP3 players to members would improve member satisfaction as well as improve some members' attendance at the gym. This proposal is based on member dissatisfaction with the music we play over the speakers as well as the negative effect our music has on some members' motivation to exercise.

As Figure 1 shows, the majority of members who responded to our 2007 Annual Member Satisfaction Survey were not satisfied with the music we play at our facility. We are very proud of our track record when it comes to member satisfaction in all areas, and we feel that our commitment to member satisfaction is what sets us apart from our competitors. However, as our 2007 survey revealed, we can improve the music options available to our members.

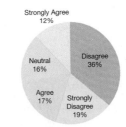

Figure 1.   Level of Member Agreement with 2007 Survey Statement "I am satisfied with the music played at the facility"

Dissatisfaction with the music we play also affects the motivation of our members to use our facility. As the comments from our annual survey revealed, the music we play has caused some members to cut their workouts short or stop coming to the gym on certain days or at certain times. One member wrote on the survey, "The music was so annoying last Wednesday morning that I just got off the Precor and went home." Another member wrote, "I heard that same Miley Cyrus song five times during my workout. I almost puked." This is disappointing because research has shown that listening to music while exercising can add variety to exercise routines and can also "increase the duration of exercise due to its motivating effect" (Mercola, 2004). Listening to music also helps people stay focused on their workouts (Emerick, 2006). More important, research suggests that listening to music may "boost weight loss and help [people] stick to a fitness plan" (Hitti, 2005). By offering members MP3 players with playlists representing a range of music styles, we could use music to motivate our members to exercise more, not less.

We propose to study options for improving our members' satisfaction with the music available at our facility. Our research will help our manager and owner determine whether we should take no action, change the music we play currently, or offer members a choice of music by making MP3 players available.

The following sections of this memo include the proposed tasks, the schedule, our experience, the proposed budget for the research, and the references cited.

Proposed Tasks

With your approval, we will perform the following tasks to determine the best solution to addressing our members' dissatisfaction with the music played at our facility.

1. *Investigate the extent of the problem by determining if we can use our current speaker system to meet our members' music preferences.*
   We will use data from the 2007 Annual Member Satisfaction Survey to determine if our current system of playing music throughout our facility can be used to address members' concerns. Using this data, we will determine if there is a consensus among members regarding their music preferences while exercising and whether our current speaker system can accommodate their preferences.

2. *Identify our options for addressing the music problem.*
   We will consider the cost of offering members MP3 players to use while they exercise. In addition, we will distribute a questionnaire to members asking them whether they would be interested in this service. We have already searched the Web sites of electronics retailers such as Overstock.com, Circuit City, and Best Buy. These resources suggest that there are several durable MP3 players for less than $100 each that might meet our needs. We will need to determine whether our members will be best served by our continuing to offer music only over our speaker system or whether we should also invest in several MP3 players for member use. We will also need to investigate the intellectual-property issues surrounding the use of MP3 players in a commercial business.

3. *Identify the main criteria by which we will compare the MP3 players.*
   To help us determine the necessary and desirable criteria, we have already identified two articles that discuss using MP3 players at gyms (Waehner, 2007; Morris, 2005) and important features to consider when selecting an MP3 player (PCMag.com and MP3.com). As part of the questionnaire we distribute to members, we will ask which features are important to them in an MP3 player for use in a gym.

4. *Research available MP3 options.*
   To create a list of MP3 players to evaluate, we will conduct online research and informally ask members which MP3 players they use in the gym. Similarly, we will visit local electronics retailers to try out MP3 players and talk to people who have been selling and using MP3 players for several years.

5. *Evaluate MP3 options based on the criteria identified.*
   Using a point system and a scoring key that we will create for each criterion, we will compare MP3 player options and calculate a numeric score for each MP3 player under consideration.

6. *Prepare a recommendation report.*
   We will prepare a recommendation report that explains the music problem, our research methods, and our findings. We will include information about our current music option, how we established our criteria, and how we selected which MP3 players to study. We will include the evaluations of the selected players that helped define our final recommendation. We will submit the recommendation report by December 22, 2008.

By presenting the project as a set of tasks, the writers show that they are well organized. This organization by tasks will be used in the progress report (see Ch. 17, pp. 467–71) and the recommendation report (see Ch. 19, pp. 519–34).

The writers will start with primary research to determine the extent of the problem. If the problem at the gym is not serious, there is no reason to proceed with the secondary research.

The writers will define and describe their options. Note that one option is to do nothing. If most gym members are not interested in the MP3 option, there will be no reason to proceed.

The proposal sounds credible because the writers have already begun their secondary research.

In a feasibility study, it is smart to determine your criteria first, before you study the options. This way, you appear to be an unbiased investigator.

After describing their criteria, the writers describe techniques they will use to identify their specific options.

The writers will evaluate each option against each criterion. This method will help them keep the analysis as objective as possible.

Preparing the recommendation report is part of the project. The completion report is the deliverable for this project.

Organizing the project by tasks makes it easy for the writers to present a Gantt chart and will help them stay on track if the proposal is approved.

Note that the tasks are presented with parallel grammar, which helps make the writers seem careful and professional.

The Tech Tip on p. 446 explains how to create a Gantt chart.

The writers summarize their credentials. Strong credentials help reinforce the idea that they are professionals.

The simple budget makes it easy for readers to understand the cost of carrying out the research. Note that the total line is presented in boldface for emphasis.

Note that the writers list only those sources cited in the proposal and that every source cited appears in the references list.

Memo to Jill Bookwalter   November 3, 2008   Page 4

Schedule

Following is a schedule of the tasks we will complete for this project.

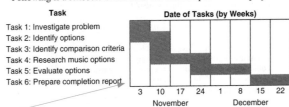

Figure 2.   Schedule of Project Tasks

Experience

We bring 16 years of combined experience as fitness trainers to the project:

- Jessie Pritiken, Senior Fitness Trainer, has nine years' experience as an NASM (National Academy of Sports Medicine) certified personal trainer. She has a degree in Corporate and Commercial Fitness from Radford University.
- Megan Turner, Fitness Trainer, has seven years' experience as an ACSM (American College of Sports Medicine) certified personal trainer as well as a current ACE (American Council on Exercise) group fitness instructor certification. She has a bachelor's degree in Sports Medicine from Pepperdine University.

Budget

Following is an itemized budget for our proposed research.

Name	Hours	Hourly Rate	Cost
Jessie Pritiken	10	$17	$170
Megan Turner	10	$15	$150
		Total:	**$320**

References

Emerick, J. (2006). Music aids in exercise motivation. Retrieved November 10, 2008, from http://media.www.fsunews.com/media/storage/paper920/news/2006/08/31/ArtsAndEntertainment/Music.Aids.In.Exercise.Motivation-2353196.shtml

Hitti, M. (2005). iPod may jam off the pounds. Retrieved November 11, 2008, from http://www.medicinenet.com/script/main/art.asp?articlekey=56334

Mercola, J. (2004). Listening to music while exercising boosts brain power. Retrieved November 10, 2008, from http://articles.mercola.com/sites/articles/archive/2004/04/10/music-exercise.aspx

Morris, J. (2005). Best MP3 players for the gym. Retrieved November 9, 2008, from http://reviews.cnet.com/4520-10166_7-5759920-1.html

Waehner, P. (2007). Top 5 music players & accessories for gym-goers. Retrieved November 9, 2008, from http://exercise.about.com/od/videosmusicsoftware/tp/musicplayers.htm

INTERACTIVE SAMPLE DOCUMENT
Writing a Project Description

The following project description (Ohio Office, 2003) is excerpted from a sample grant proposal seeking funding to begin a project to help police officers stay healthy. The questions in the margin ask you to think about how to describe the project in a proposal. E-mail your responses to yourself and/or your instructor on TechComm Web.

PROJECT DESCRIPTION

The proposed project is comprised of several different, but related activities:

A. Physical Evaluation of the Officers

The first component of this project is the physical examination of all Summerville P.D. sworn employees. Of special interest for purposes of the project are resting pulse rate, target pulse rate, blood pressure, and percentage of body fat of the program participants. Dr. Feinberg will perform the physical examinations of all participating officers. The measurement of body fat will be conducted at the University of Summerville's Health Center under the direction of Dr. Farron Updike.

B. Renovation of Basement

Another phase of this project involves the renovation of the basement of police headquarters. The space is currently being used for storing Christmas decorations for City Hall.

The main storage room will be converted into a gym. This room will accommodate the Universal weight machine, the stationary bike, the treadmill and the rowing machine. Renovation will consist of first transferring all the Christmas decorations to the basement of the new City Hall. Once that is accomplished, it will be necessary to paint the walls, install indoor/outdoor carpeting and set up the equipment.

A second, smaller room will be converted into a locker room. Renovation will include painting the floors and the installation of lockers and benches.

To complete the fitness center, a third basement room will be equipped as a shower room. A local plumber will tap into existing plumbing to install several showerheads.

C. Purchase of Fitness Equipment

The Department of Public Safety has identified five vendors of exercise equipment in the greater Summerville area. Each of these vendors submitted bids for the following equipment:

- Universal Weight Machine
- Atlas Stationary Bike
- Yale Rowing Machine
- Speedster Treadmill

D. Training of Officers

Participating officers must be trained in the safe, responsible use of the exercise equipment. Dr. Updike of the University of Summerville will hold periodic training sessions at the Department's facility.

---

1. The writer has used a lettering system to describe the four main tasks that he will undertake if he receives funding. What are the advantages of a lettering system?

2. How effective is the description of Task A? What factors contribute to the description's effectiveness or lack of effectiveness?

3. The descriptions of the tasks do not include cost estimates. Where would those estimates be presented in the proposal? Why would they be presented there?

4. How effective is the description of Task D? What additional information would improve its effectiveness?

 On TechComm Web

To e-mail your responses to yourself and/or your instructor, click on Interactive Sample Documents for Ch. 16 on <bedfordstmartins.com/techcomm>.

Writer's Checklist

The following checklist covers the basic elements of a proposal. Guidelines established by the recipient of the proposal should take precedence over these general suggestions.

Does the summary provide an overview of

- ☐ the problem or the opportunity? (p. 441)
- ☐ the proposed program? (p. 441)
- ☐ your qualifications and experience? (p. 441)

Does the introduction indicate

- ☐ the problem or opportunity? (p. 442)
- ☐ the purpose of the proposal? (p. 442)
- ☐ the background of the problem or opportunity? (p. 442)
- ☐ your knowledge of the professional literature? (p. 442)
- ☐ the scope of the proposal? (p. 442)
- ☐ the organization of the proposal? (p. 442)
- ☐ the key terms that will be used in the proposal? (p. 442)

- ☐ Does the description of the proposed program provide a clear, specific plan of action and justify the tasks you propose performing? (p. 442)

Does the description of qualifications and experience clearly outline

- ☐ your relevant skills and past work? (p. 443)
- ☐ the skills and background of the other participants? (p. 443)
- ☐ your department's (or organization's) relevant equipment, facilities, and experience? (p. 443)

Is the budget

- ☐ complete? (p. 444)
- ☐ correct? (p. 444)
- ☐ accompanied by an in-text reference? (p. 444)

- ☐ Do the appendices include the relevant supporting materials, such as a task schedule, a description of evaluation techniques, and evidence of other successful projects? (p. 444)

Exercises

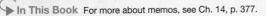 **In This Book** For more about memos, see Ch. 14, p. 377.

1. **INTERNET EXERCISE** Study the National Science Foundation's Grant Proposal Guide (click on Links Library for Chapter 16 on <bedfordstmartins.com/techcomm>). What are the important ways in which this guide differs from the advice provided in this chapter? What accounts for these differences? Present your findings in a 500-word memo to your instructor.

2. **INTERNET/GROUP EXERCISE** Form groups according to major. Using the FedBizOpps Web site, find a request for proposals (RFP) for a project related to your academic field (click on Links Library for Chapter 16 on <bedfordstmartins.com/techcomm>). Study the RFP. What can you learn about the needs of the organization that issued it? How effectively does the RFP describe what the issuing organization expects to see in the proposal? Is the RFP relatively general or specific? What sorts of evaluation techniques does the RFP call for? In your response, include a list of questions that you would ask the issuing organization if you were considering responding to the RFP. Present your results in a memo to your instructor.

3. Write a proposal for a research project that will constitute a major assignment in this course. Your instructor will tell you whether the proposal is to be written individually or collaboratively. Start by defining a technical subject that interests you. (This subject could be one that you are involved in at work or in another course.) Using abstract services and other bibliographic tools, compile a bibliography of articles and books on the subject. (See Chapter 6 for a discussion of finding information.) Create a reasonable real-world context. Here are three common scenarios from the business world:

- Our company uses Technology X to perform Task A. Should we instead be using Technology Y to perform Task A? For instance, our company uses traditional surveying tools in its contracting business. Should we be using GPS surveying tools instead?

- Our company has decided to purchase a tool to perform Task A. Which make and model of the tool should we purchase, and from which supplier should we buy or lease it? For instance, our company has decided to purchase 10 multimedia computers. Which brand and model should we buy, and from whom should we buy them?

- Our company does not currently perform Function X. Is it feasible to perform Function X? For instance, we do not currently offer day care for our employees. Should we? What are the advantages and disadvantages of doing so? What forms can day care take? How is it paid for?

Following are some additional ideas for topics:

- the need to provide legal file-sharing access to students
- the value of using the Internet to form ties with another technical-communication class on another campus
- the need for expanded opportunities for internships in your major
- the need to create an advisory board of people from industry to provide expertise about your major
- the need to raise money to keep the college's computer labs up-to-date
- the need to evaluate your major to ensure that it is responsive to students' needs

- the advisability of starting a campus branch of a professional organization in your field
- the need to improve parking facilities on campus
- the need to create or improve organizations for minorities or women on campus

These topics can be approached from different perspectives. For instance, the first one—providing file-sharing access to students—could be approached in several ways:

- Our college currently purchases journals but does not provide legal file-sharing access for students. Should we consider reducing the library's journal budget to subsidize legal file-sharing access?
- Our college has decided to provide legal file-sharing access for students. How should it do so? What vendors provide such services? What are the strengths and weaknesses of each vendor?
- Our college does not offer legal file-sharing access for students. Should we make it a goal to do so? What are the advantages and disadvantages of doing so?

Case 16: Selecting a Funding Source

▶ In This Book For more about memos, see Ch. 14, p. 377.

Background

A seaside community, the city of Port Hueneme, California, is located in a fertile coastal plain. Year-round temperatures moderated by the ocean help the region produce as many as six fresh fruit and vegetable crops a year. You have just started work as a technical-communication intern at the Port Hueneme Discovery Center, an interactive science center. Focusing on the region's natural resources, the center's mission is to provide educational opportunities that inspire lifelong learning and interest in science, math, and technology. Your role is to help the center write proposals to fund upcoming exhibits and educational programs.

"Near the end of her internship, Heather Blanchard, our last intern, started to research funding sources for our upcoming exhibit on saltwater intrusion," explains John Orr, the center's Exhibits and Education Director. "Saltwater

intrusion is probably the most common and widespread contamination in aquifers, our source of groundwater wells and springs. When fresh water is withdrawn from the ground at a faster rate than it can be replenished, salt water from the ocean intrudes into the freshwater aquifer, resulting in our water supplies becoming contaminated with salt water."

"I assume that saltwater intrusion could wreak havoc on our agricultural crops?" you ask.

"It already has. Although our water district has built water-diversion structures, spreading grounds, and distribution facilities to augment the natural recharge of our aquifers, the region still needs to combat seawater intrusion. We want to educate our visitors about saltwater intrusion. Unfortunately, Heather's internship ended before she could recommend a funding source. I'd like you to pick up where she left off."

"What work has already been accomplished?"

"Heather wrote a brief outline of our project to help focus her search for funding. After not having much success locating sources of state or federal dollars, she decided to take advantage of our 501(c)(3) status and concentrate on private funding sources, especially those interested in environmental education." (See Document 16.1.)

"What does 501(c)(3) indicate?" you ask.

**Document 16.1
Proposed Saltwater
Intrusion Exhibit**

Proposed Saltwater Intrusion Exhibit

Background
The overpumping of water in Ventura County, especially the Oxnard Plain, has caused the water levels in underground aquifers to drop well below sea level. As a result, seawater has intruded into underground basins and contaminated the groundwater used for everything from farming to drinking water.

Goals
1. To help Discovery Center visitors realize the nature and importance of groundwater to Ventura County, the state of California, and the nation
2. To help Discovery Center visitors understand the saltwater intrusion problem in Ventura County as well as possible solutions

Approaches
1. Provide Discovery Center visitors the opportunity to use a hand pump to draw drinkable water to the surface. Such an activity shows where drinkable water comes from and introduces the concept of an aquifer.
2. Use large samples of local bedrock with water seeping through to demonstrate how water percolates down through seemingly solid layers of rock and gravel.
3. Use transparent tubes filled with rock, sand, soil, gravel, and water in such a way that visitors can appreciate how aquifers can store and supply groundwater.
4. Construct a small-scale representation of a coastal plain with an adjacent body of salt water. Visitors can pump water from the coastal plain's aquifer and watch as salt water invades the groundwater supply.
5. Install four graphic panels describing the effect of saltwater intrusion and strategies for combating it.
6. Include bedrock drill samples taken around the Oxnard Plain so visitors can both see and touch the bedrock directly below their feet.

Cost
We estimate that the exhibit described above, exclusive of the drilling of the well, will cost approximately $40,000. We estimate drilling the well will cost $16,000.

On TechComm Web

For digital versions of case documents, click on Downloadable Case Documents on <bedfordstmartins.com/techcomm>.

"A 501(c)(3) designation by the Internal Revenue Service indicates that an organization is both tax-exempt and non-profit. Such a designation helps the Discovery Center apply for funding from many private funding sources. Heather consulted *Environmental Grantmaking Foundations* and created profiles of four possible funding sources. I'd like you to take a look at the profiles and recommend which, if any, of the potential funders is a good match." (See Document 16.2.)

Document 16.2   Profiles of Four Potential Funding Sources

Name: Phantom Creek Trust

Contact information: c/o Kathleen Gainter & Associates, P.O. Box 93312, Seattle, WA 98101-3312.

History and philosophy: Established in 1962 by George Moomey, founder of Crown Fisheries in Seattle, Washington. The foundation has one primary goal: to protect and restore the natural environment of the Pacific Coast, especially in the Pacific Northwest.

Interests: Funding priorities include projects that educate the public, support quality environmental education, foster sustainable agricultural policies and practices, protect aquatic resources, and protect environmentally sensitive areas.

Issues funded: Climate and atmosphere, biodiversity, endangered lands, agriculture, water, oceans and coasts, energy.

Activities funded: Direct action, education, media projects.

Funding analysis:

	FY 2007	FY 2008
Environmental grants authorized	$5,297,101	$5,843,390
Number	108	129
Award range	$3,000–$205,000	$2,500–$1,000,000
Median award	$55,000	$55,000

Sample grants: Kooskooskie Commons ($20,000), bring together local farming, environmental, and business organizations to focus on restoration of salmon habitat and stream flows in the Walla Walla River; *Ecological Awareness Resources* ($62,000), planning and implementation of an ecosystem-wide K–12 environmental educational plan for the Seattle, Washington, area.

Emphases: Educational institutions, nonprofit organizations, advocacy, Pacific Northwest, environmental education, special projects.

Restrictions: No individuals.

Name: Faria Family Foundation

Contact information: Joe Faria, Program Director, 7634 PCH, Ventura, CA 93001.

History and philosophy: Established in 1967 by Joe Faria, a prosperous citrus farmer, this organization is committed to conserving California's freshwater supplies through voluntary actions, fostering sustainable use of our natural resource base, and conservation education targeting young people, educators, community leaders, and private landowners.

Interests: Support for water resources, environmental education excellence, and education on all levels.

Issues funded: Biodiversity, endangered lands, agriculture, water, oceans and coasts, energy, toxic substances.

Activities funded: Education.

Document 16.2
(continued)

Funding analysis:

	FY 2007	FY 2008
Environmental grants authorized	$2,730,000	$3,532,000
Number	43	52
Award range	$20,000–$80,000	$20,205–$80,000
Median award	$60,000	$60,000

Sample grants: *The Tides Foundation* ($61,000), develop and test a water-quality and pollution prevention–training package for students engaged in community-based service learning; *River Watch Network* ($55,000), assist communities in educating themselves about the connections between environmental contamination and public health and to develop water-quality monitoring tools.

Emphases: Educational institutions, nonprofit organizations, demonstration programs, education, innovative programs, training, special projects.

Restrictions: No individuals, no land acquisition, lobbying, litigation, basic research, annual campaigns, mortgage reduction, operating costs.

Name: Lorenzo Foundation

Contact information: Martha Gimigan, Director, 504 Pacific Avenue, San Francisco, CA 94133.

History and philosophy: Established in 1972, the Lorenzo Foundation is a private philanthropy interested primarily in the advancement and preservation of the governance of society by partici-pation in the democratic process, with protection of basic rights as provided by the Constitution and Bill of Rights.

Interests: Supports government accountability projects with respect to the environment, espe-cially public education and mobilization seeking to ensure that environmental laws and regulations are enforced.

Issues funded: Climate and atmosphere, biodiversity, endangered lands, water, toxic substances.

Activities funded: Advocacy, education, litigation, media projects.

Funding analysis:

	FY 2007	FY 2008
Environmental grants authorized	$393,180	$751,000
Number	11	27
Award range	$5,000–$65,000	$5,000–$120,000
Median award	$25,000	$20,000

Sample grants: *Los Padres Biodiversity* Project ($25,000), public education to help ensure U.S. Forest Service compliance with existing environmental laws and regulations; *Military Toxics Project* ($70,000), monitoring, education, and citizen organizing to investigate health effects of U.S. Department of Defense activities along Pacific Coast.

Emphases: Nonprofit organizations, special projects, action-oriented projects.

Restrictions: Not reported.

Name: National Organization for Environmental Education & Training

Contact information: Eugene Robertson, President, 50 Olive Street, Suite 128, Phoenix, AZ 85064.

History and philosophy: Established in 1998 by a dot-com venture capitalist and an active philanthropist who left most of his estate to the organization.

Interests: Watershed protection, conservation of natural resources, environmental education.

Issues funded: Endangered lands, water, agriculture, oceans and coasts.

Activities funded: Direct action, education, media projects, research.

Funding analysis:

	FY 2007	FY 2008
Environmental grants authorized	$6,225,000	$8,449,397
Number	7	11
Award range	$100,000–$5,000,000	$100,000–$5,000,000
Median award	$150,000	$300,000

Sample grants: Upper Sespe Riverkeeper ($200,000), expansion of watershed education programs; *National Fish and Wildlife Foundation* ($450,000), Coastal Plain Stewards Project to help private farmers manage land for wildlife as well as agriculture.

Emphases: Educational institutions, museums, nonprofit organizations, public agencies.

Restrictions: No individuals, no support for loans or operating costs.

Your Assignment

1. John Orr wishes to submit a proposal to one of the four funding sources profiled by Heather Blanchard (Document 16.2). Write a memo to John explaining which funding source would be most appropriate and why. If you feel that none of the profiled organizations is a good funding source for the saltwater intrusion exhibit, write John a memo in which you explain your decision and recommend an alternative funding source.

2. Major funding sources often ask potential funding recipients to submit a brief *letter of inquiry* before submitting a full proposal. Outlining a program and its funding needs, this letter helps a funding source determine whether it would be interested in the project and would like to receive a full proposal. Using strategies discussed in this chapter, as well as information you have learned about your recommended funding source, write a letter of inquiry.

Writing Informational Reports

Understanding the Process of Writing
Informational Reports 459

Writing Directives 461

Writing Field Reports 463

Writing Progress and Status
Reports 464

Organizing Progress and Status
Reports 465

Concluding Progress and Status
Reports 466

Sample Progress Report 466

Writing Incident Reports 472

Writing Meeting Minutes 473

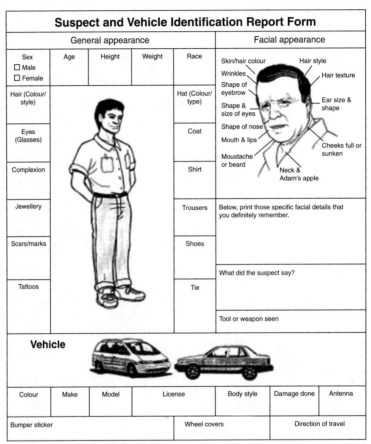

Suspect and Vehicle Identification Report Form						
General appearance					Facial appearance	
Sex ☐ Male ☐ Female	Age	Height	Weight	Race	Skin/hair colour · Hair style · Wrinkles · Hair texture · Shape of eyebrow · Ear size & shape · Shape & size of eyes · Shape of nose · Mouth & lips · Cheeks full or sunken · Moustache or beard · Neck & Adam's apple	
Hair (Colour/ style)				Hat (Colour/ type)		
Eyes (Glasses)				Coat		
Complexion				Shirt		
Jewellery				Trousers	Below, print those specific facial details that you definitely remember.	
Scars/marks				Shoes		
Tattoos				Tie	What did the suspect say?	
					Tool or weapon seen	
Vehicle						
Colour	Make	Model	License		Body style	Damage done	Antenna
Bumper sticker			Wheel covers		Direction of travel	

Source: Saskatchewan Labour, 2007 <http://fpse1.labour.gov.sk.ca/safety/violence/policy/printpage.htm>.

In the World . . .

In the Canadian province of Saskatchewan, companies are required to have employees fill out various incident forms after an accident or crime occurs in the workplace. The page shown here is an example of the form that the province recommends companies use in case of assault. Incident reports often are presented as forms, which prompt the writer to record the information that authorities will need to investigate an incident. This is just one type of informational report.

A fundamental skill used in technical communication is the ability to report information clearly, specifically, and accurately. This chapter focuses on informational reports. Whether they are presented as memos, e-mails, reports, or Web pages, *informational reports* share one goal: to describe something that happened. Sometimes, informational reports also analyze the situation. An *analysis* is an explanation of why or how something happened. For instance, in an incident report about an accident on the job, the writer might speculate about why and how the accident occurred.

Informational reports include the following five kinds of communication:

- A supervisor writes a *directive* explaining the company's new policy on recycling and describing informational sessions that the company will offer to help employees understand how to implement the policy.

- An insurance adjuster writes a *field report* presenting the results of his inspection of a building after a storm caused extensive damage.

- A research team writes a *progress report* explaining what the team has accomplished in the first half of a project, speculating on whether it will finish the project on time and on budget, and describing how the team has responded to unexpected problems.

- A worker at a manufacturing company writes an *incident report* after a toxic-chemical spill.

- A recording secretary writes a set of *meeting minutes* that will become the official record of what occurred during a meeting of the management team of a government agency.

This chapter discusses informational reports, in which the main purpose is to provide information to an audience. Chapter 18 discusses lab reports, a kind of informational report that is used extensively in college and university courses, as well as in the workplace. Chapter 19 discusses recommendation reports, in which the main purpose is to provide information and recommend what readers should do next.

UNDERSTANDING THE PROCESS OF WRITING INFORMATIONAL REPORTS

Writing informational reports involves the same writing process used in most other kinds of technical communication. Figure 17.1 on page 460 outlines this process.

Figure 17.1   An Overview of the Process of Writing Informational Reports

Analyze Your Audience

In some cases, it is easy to identify your audience and purpose. For instance, meeting minutes are addressed to all the members of the committee or department. In other cases, determining your audience is not as easy. For example, you might be reporting on an accident on the job. To whom should you address the report: Your direct supervisor? Your direct supervisor and others? Once you have identified your audience, analyze their knowledge of the subject, their attitudes toward it, and how they will use the information. See Ch. 5 for more information on audience.

Analyze Your Purpose

What is your purpose: To describe what happened? To recommend some course of action? In this situation, you need to analyze your purpose just as carefully as you would for any other kind of document. See Ch. 5 for more information on purpose.

Research the Subject and Compile Your Information

Sometimes, assembling information is as simple as printing a file. Other times, it requires sophisticated information-gathering techniques using primary and secondary research. See Ch. 6 for more about research methods.

Choose an Appropriate Format

The most common formats for informational reports are e-mails and memos. In some organizations, covers, title pages, and other elements usually associated with more-formal reports are used for all reports. Therefore, the choice of format is often determined by your organization, as well as by your audience and purpose.

Draft the Report

For routine reports, you can sometimes use sections of previous reports. In a status report, for instance, you can copy the description of your current project from the previous report and then update it as necessary. This reuse of information is ethical. Some informational reports are drafted on-site. For instance, an engineer might use a hand-held computer to "draft" an informational report as she walks around a site.

Revise, Edit, and Proofread the Report

Informal does not mean careless.

If your informational report will be addressed to people from other cultures, consider the following three questions:

- *How might your readers react to your report?* According to Walsham (2001, p. 30), a software company in India working with an American company chose not to use monthly progress reports because it did not want to conform to American business practices.

- *Will your readers be comfortable with your choice of application?* For example, in a culture in which it is appropriate to use a highly formal style, you might decide to use a letter rather than a memo for communicating the results of an inspection you completed.

- *Do you need to adjust your writing style?* Should you include a glossary or add parenthetical definitions? Use shorter sentences? Use more headings? Use more graphics?

▶ **In This Book**

For more about analyzing an audience from another culture, see Ch. 5, p. 90.

WRITING DIRECTIVES

In a *directive*, you explain a policy or a procedure you want your readers to follow. Even though you have the authority to require your readers to follow the new policy, you want to explain why the new policy is desirable or at least necessary. As discussed in Chapter 8, you are most persuasive when you present clear, compelling evidence (in the form of commonsense arguments, numerical data, and examples); when you consider opposing arguments effectively; and when you present yourself as cooperative, moderate, fair-minded, and modest. If appropriate, include arguments that appeal to your readers' broader goals of security, recognition, and personal and professional growth. Figure 17.2 is an example of a directive.

Quimby Interoffice

Date: March 19, 2009
To: All supervisors and sales personnel
From: D. Bartown, Engineering
Subject: Avoiding Customer Exposure to Sensitive Information Outside Conference Room B

Recently I have learned that customers meeting in Conference Room B have been allowed to use the secretary's phone directly outside the room. This practice presents a problem: the proposals that the secretary is working on are in full view of the customers. Proprietary information such as pricing can be jeopardized unintentionally.

In the future, would you please escort any customers or non-Quimby personnel needing to use a phone to the one outside the Estimating Department? Thanks very much.

The writer begins with a clear explanation of the problem the directive addresses. Presenting the reasons for the new policy shows respect for the readers and therefore makes the directive more persuasive.

The writer's polite but informal tone throughout the memo is likely to motivate readers to cooperate. Notice the use of "please" and "thanks" in the second paragraph.

Figure 17.2   A Directive

INTERACTIVE SAMPLE DOCUMENT
Writing a Persuasive Directive

The following directive was sent to the members of a Montana government department. The questions in the margin ask you to think about the process of writing persuasive directives (as discussed on page 461). E-mail your responses to yourself and/or your instructor on TechComm Web.

1. How would you describe the tone used by the writer? Provide an example to support your claim.

2. The writer presents examples of what he calls violations of the state travel policy. Do these examples provide solid evidence that violations of the policy have in fact occurred?

3. How effectively has the writer encouraged his staff to abide by the travel policy? How might he improve the persuasiveness of the directive?

▶ On TechComm Web

To e-mail your responses to yourself and/or your instructor, click on Interactive Sample Documents for Ch. 17 on <bedfordstmartins.com/ techcomm>.

To: Members, Budget Allocation Office
From: Harold J. Jefferson, Director
Subject: Travel Policy
Date: January 23, 2009

It has come to my attention that certain members of this office are not abiding by the travel policies approved by the state. Let me offer a few examples.

The Montana Revised Code includes this statement in its introduction:

> Persons who travel on State business are encouraged to incur the lowest practical and reasonable expense while still traveling in an efficient and timely manner. Those traveling on State business are expected to avoid impropriety, or the appearance of impropriety, in any travel expense. They must conduct State business with integrity, in compliance with applicable laws, and in a manner that excludes consideration of personal advantage.

Yet I have learned from official sources that on four occasions in the last fiscal year, employees of this office have acted in flagrant violation of this policy. Two occasions involved choosing a flight that left at a more convenient time in the morning but that cost almost $160 more. One involved selecting a cab, rather than a shuttle bus, for a trip from the airport to downtown (a $24 difference), and one involved using room service when the motel has a café (a $14 difference).

Another provision of the travel policy that has been violated on more than one occasion is the following:

> Travel expenses are not paid in advance except for airfare charged to the State air travel card, for online (Internet) air or train ticket purchases, and for conference registrations.

Two employees have on more than three occasions each received reimbursements for air and/or train reservations made using their personal credit cards. As you know, using personal credit cards leaves the State without official documentation of the expense and gives the traveler bonus miles and/or cash back that properly belongs to the State.

These are just two of the kinds of irregularities that have been brought to my attention. I do not need to tell you that these violations constitute serious breaches of public ethics. If they recur, they will be dealt with harshly. I sincerely hope that I do not have to address this issue again.

WRITING FIELD REPORTS

A common kind of informational report describes inspections, maintenance, and site studies. This type of report, often known as a *field report*, explains the problem, methods, results, and conclusions, but it deemphasizes the methods and can include recommendations. The report in Figure 17.3 illustrates possible variations on this standard report structure.

Figure 17.3
A Field Report

Because the writer and the reader work for different companies, the letter is the appropriate format for this brief informational report.

LOBATE CONSTRUCTION
3311 Industrial Parkway
Speonk, NY 13508

Quality Construction Since 1957

April 11, 2009

Ms. Christine Amalli, Head
Civil Engineering
New York Power
Smithtown, NY 13507

Dear Ms. Amalli:

We are pleased to report the results of our visual inspection of the Chemopump after Run #9, a 30-day trial on Kentucky #10 coal.

The word visual *describes the methods.*

The inspection was designed to determine if the new Chemopump is compatible with Kentucky #10, the lowest-grade coal that you anticipate using. In preparation for the 30-day test run, the following three modifications were made by your technicians:

The writer states the purpose of the inspection.

- New front-bearing housing buffer plates of tungsten carbide were installed.
- The pump-casting volute liner was coated with tungsten carbide.
- New bearings were installed.

Our summary is as follows. A number of small problems with the pump were observed, but nothing serious and nothing surprising. Normal break-in accounts for the wear. The pump accepted the Kentucky #10 well.

This writer has chosen to incorporate the words summary *and* conclusion *in the body of the letter rather than use headings as a method of organization.*

The following four minor problems were observed:

- The outer lip of the front-end bell was chipped along two-thirds of its circumference.
- Opposite the pump discharge, the volute liner received a slight wear groove along one-third of its circumference.
- The impeller was not free-rotating.
- The holes in the front-end bell were filled with insulating mud.

The following three components showed no wear:

- 5½" impeller
- suction neck liner
- discharge neck liner

Our conclusion is that the problems can be attributed to normal break-in for a new Chemopump. The Kentucky #10 coal does not appear to have caused any extraordinary problems. In general, the new Chemopump seems to be operating well.

Figure 17.3   (continued)

Informational reports sometimes include recommendations. ———▶

The writer concludes politely. ———▶

---

page 2

We would recommend, however, that the pump be modified as follows:

1. Replace the front-end bell with a tungsten carbide-coated front-end bell.
2. Replace the bearings on the impeller.
3. Install insulation plugs in the holes in the front-end bell.

Further, we recommend that the pump be reinspected after another 30-day run on Kentucky #10.

If you have any questions or would like to authorize these modifications, please call me at 555-1241. As always, we appreciate the trust you have placed in us.

Sincerely,

Marvin Littridge
Director of Testing and Evaluation

Guidelines

Responding to Readers' Questions in a Field Report

Be sure to answer the following six questions:

▶ What is the purpose of the report?

▶ What are the main points covered in the report?

▶ What were the problems leading to the decision to perform the procedure?

▶ What methods were used?

▶ What were the results?

▶ What do the results mean?

If appropriate, also discuss what you think should be done next.

WRITING PROGRESS AND STATUS REPORTS

A *progress report* describes an ongoing project. A *status report*, sometimes called an *activity report*, describes the entire range of operations of a department or division. For example, the director of marketing for a manufacturing company might submit a monthly status report.

A progress report is an intermediate communication between the proposal (the argument that a project be undertaken) and the completion report (the comprehensive record of a completed project). Progress reports let you check in with your audience.

Regardless of how well the project is proceeding, explain clearly and fully what has happened and how it will affect the overall project. Your tone

⬥ In This Book

For more about proposals, see Ch. 16. For more about completion reports, see Ch. 19.

Ethics Note

Reporting Your Progress Honestly

Withholding bad news is unethical because it can mislead readers. As sponsors or supervisors of a project, readers have a right to know how it is going. If you find yourself faced with any of the following three common problems, consider responding in these ways:

- *The deliverable—the document or product you will submit at the end of the project—won't be what you thought it would be.* Without being defensive, describe the events that led to the situation and explain how the deliverable will differ from what you described in the proposal.

- *You won't meet your schedule.* Explain why you are going to be late and state when the project will be completed.

- *You won't meet the budget.* Explain why you need more money and state how much more you will need.

should be objective, neither defensive nor casual. Unless ineptitude or negligence caused a particular problem, you're not to blame. Regardless of the news you are delivering—good, bad, or mixed—your job is the same: to provide a clear and complete account of your activities and to forecast the next stage of the project.

When things go wrong, you might be tempted to cover up problems and hope that you can solve them before the next progress report. This course of action is unwise and unethical. Chances are, problems will multiply, and you will have a harder time explaining why you didn't alert your readers earlier.

Organizing Progress and Status Reports

The *time pattern* and the *task pattern*, two organizational patterns frequently used in progress or status reports, are illustrated in Figure 17.4. A status

In the time pattern, you describe all the work that you have completed in the present reporting period and then sketch in the work that remains. Some writers include a section on present work, which enables them to focus on a long or complex task still in progress.	**The time pattern**
	
	Discussion
	    A. Past Work
	    B. Future Work
		The task pattern
		
		Discussion
		    A. Task 1
		        1. Past work
		        2. Future work
		    B. Task 2
		        1. Past work
		        2. Future work
			The task pattern allows you to describe, in order, what has been accomplished on each task. Often a task-oriented structure incorporates the chronological structure.

Figure 17.4   Organizational Patterns in Progress and Status Reports

report is usually organized according to task. By its nature, a status report covers a specified time period.

Concluding Progress and Status Reports

In the conclusion of a progress or status report, evaluate how the project is proceeding. In the broadest sense, there are two possible messages: things are going well, or things are not going as well as anticipated.

Guidelines

Projecting an Appropriate Tone in a Progress or Status Report

▶ **If the news is good, convey your optimism but avoid overstatement.**

OVERSTATED	We are sure the device will do all that we ask of it and more.
REALISTIC	We expect that the device will perform well and that it might offer some unanticipated advantages.

Beware of promising early completion. Such optimistic forecasts rarely prove accurate, and it is always embarrassing to have to report a failure to meet the optimistic deadline.

▶ **Don't panic if the preliminary results are not as promising as you had planned or if the project is behind schedule.** Even the best-prepared proposal writers cannot anticipate all problems. As long as the original proposal was well planned and contained no wildly inaccurate computations, don't feel responsible. Just do your best to explain unanticipated problems and the status of the project. If your news is bad, at least give readers as much time as possible to deal with it effectively.

On TechComm Web

To see two sample progress reports, one for a study about counting American Sign Language as a foreign language and one for a study about selecting a table saw for a woodworking company, click on Links Library for Ch. 17 on <bedfordstmartins.com/techcomm>.

Find other samples of progress reports at Writing Guidelines for Engineering and Science Students. Click on Links Library for Ch. 17 on <bedfordstmartins.com/techcomm>.

If appropriate, use appendices for supporting materials, such as computations, printouts, schematics, diagrams, tables, or a revised task schedule. Be sure to cross-reference these appendices in the body of the report, so that readers can find them easily.

Sample Progress Report

The following progress report (Pritiken & Turner, 2008) was written for the project proposed in Chapter 16, pages 447–50. The recommendation report for this study appears in Chapter 19, pages 519–34.

Total Gym Fitness

2206 Leadville Ave.
Boise, ID 83706

(208) 555-9635
totalgym@msn.com

Memo

Date: November 24, 2008
To: Jill Bookwalter, Owner and Manager
From: Jessie Pritiken, Senior Fitness Trainer
Megan Turner, Fitness Trainer
Subject: Progress Report for Feasibility Study on Music Options at Total Gym Fitness

The subject line and the purpose statement identify the purpose of the document: to report on progress.

Purpose

This is a progress report on our feasibility study on music options for Total Gym Fitness.

Summary

We have been researching whether continuing to use the current music system, changing our music format, or offering MP3 players would improve our members' satisfaction with the music we play at our facility. We have investigated the extent of our music problem and identified our options for addressing this problem. We are now researching MP3 player options.

The summary briefly explains the purpose of the project and answers the question "How is the project going, and will it be completed on schedule and on budget?"

Our study is currently on budget and on schedule, and we expect to submit a completion report by the December 22 deadline noted in the proposal.

Introduction

On November 6, we received approval of our proposal to study options for improving our members' music options at Total Gym Fitness. This proposal was based on growing member dissatisfaction with the music we play. The results of this research will be presented in a completion report to be delivered on December 22.

Total Gym Fitness has a reputation for offering a high-quality gym experience and being responsive to customer requests. Unfortunately, we frequently get complaints regarding the music we play at our facility. Our most recent Annual Member Satisfaction Survey revealed that the majority of our members are clearly dissatisfied with the music we play. In addition, several members indicated that the music annoyed them so much that they cut short their workouts. Rather than motivating our members, the music seems to prevent some of them from getting a good workout. The facility manager asked us to study the problem and see whether we could propose a solution that will cost no more than $2,000 for initial capital outlay.

Most of the information in the introduction is taken directly from the proposal. This reuse of text is ethical. There is one new item in the introduction: a limit of $2,000 for capital outlay. Research projects are dynamic, not static. Expect the context to evolve as you work on a project.

Results of Research

First we discuss the completed work: Tasks 1–3. Then we discuss our future work: Tasks 4–6.

The writers begin by describing the organization of the results section. For a progress report, a chronological organization makes good sense.

The writers organize their discussion by task, as they did in the proposal.

These data will be presented again in the recommendation report.

Notice that the writers skillfully integrate their secondary research into their discussion. By doing so, they enhance their credibility.

This cross-reference to the questionnaire helps readers find the information quickly.

The writers have devised a logical approach: classifying the criteria into two categories, necessary and desirable. If an MP3 player does not meet the necessary criteria, it will not be considered further.

Again, the writers add a cross-reference to the questionnaire.

Memo to Jill Bookwalter   November 24, 2008   Page 2

Completed Work

Task 1. Investigate the extent of the problem by determining if we can use our current speaker system to meet our members' music preferences.

Based on the annual survey data from 2007, about 55 percent of responding members are not satisfied with the music we play. There appears to be no clear consensus regarding the type of music people prefer to listen to while exercising. Our data indicate that 88 percent of responding members are satisfied with the volume of the music. We also reviewed all the Member Suggestion cards submitted from January 2008 through November 2008. During that time, 98 suggestions were submitted, 30 percent of which offered negative comments on the music we play at our facility.

Task 2. Identify our options for addressing the music problem.

We considered three options:

- *Continuing to use the current music system and music format.* We immediately ruled out this option because it would not address our members' concerns and we are likely to lose members to our competitors unless we make a change.
- *Changing our music format.* We ruled out this option because it would not address the majority of our members' concerns. Although four music formats are clearly preferred over other formats, choosing any one of these formats would ignore the music preferences of the majority of our members. We determined that playing a different music format in each area of the gym was impractical.
- *Offering members MP3 players to use while they exercise.* Our research suggested that members are interested in having MP3 players available for checkout. Moreover, a quick look at online articles confirmed what we already knew: music motivates people to exercise more (Mercola, 2004), music helps people focus on their workouts (Emerick, 2006), and music helps people meet their fitness goals (Hitti, 2005). We determined that no intellectual-property issues will prevent us from offering our members the use of MP3 players; we will simply need to comply with the music vendors' stipulations when we load the music on the players. We therefore decided to concentrate our research on finding the best available MP3 player on the market for our needs.

Task 3. Identify the main criteria by which we will compare the MP3 players.

We consulted online advice on the best music players for use in the gym and distributed a questionnaire to 200 randomly selected members of our gym (see Appendix, page 4). Based on our research, we determined our *necessary* criteria: to be considered an option and for us to further evaluate it, an MP3 player will have to meet our necessary durability and cost criteria.

Next we determined four *desirable* criteria against which we will evaluate the different options:

- *Playlist feature.* Data from our member questionnaire (see page 4) suggests that the majority of our members are interested in being able to select from different playlists. Consequently, we need an MP3 player that will allow a member to select a specific playlist during his or her workout.
- *Quality.* A high-quality MP3 player will save the gym money and meet our members' expectations for high-quality gym equipment.

- *Ease of use.* Data from our questionnaire (see page 4) suggest that only about half of our members are comfortable using MP3 player controls. Consequently, we want an easy-to-use MP3 player. For this criterion, we will visit local retail shops and ask one of our longtime members to test each player being considered. We will ask the member to rate each player's ease of use on a 10-point scale (1 = very hard to use; 10 = very easy to use).
- *Physical size.* Our members would overwhelmingly prefer a compact (45 percent) or wallet-size (50 percent) MP3 player to a wide-screen one (5 percent). (See page 5, question 6.)

The primary research, based on the questionnaire distributed to gym members, also enhances the writers' credibility by showing that they went to the trouble of finding out what their members want in an MP3 player.

Future Work

We are now at work on Task 4: researching available MP3 options.

The writers explain what they need to do to complete the project.

Task 4. Research available MP3 options.
   We conducted online research on PCMag.com, MP3.com, and CNET.com. We are informally asking members this week which MP3 player they use at the gym. Later this week, we will visit experts at two local retail outlets to create a list of possible MP3 player options.

Task 5. Evaluate MP3 options based on the criteria identified.
   We will compare available styles, brands, and models against our criteria. For each criterion, we will use a scoring key to aid us in assigning point values.

Task 6. Prepare a completion report.
   We will prepare a completion report that explains the music problem, our research methods, and our findings. We will include detailed information about our current music option, how we established our criteria, and how we selected which MP3 players to study. We will include the evaluations of the selected players that helped define our recommendation. We will submit the completion report by December 22, 2008.

Updated Schedule

   The black bars represent completed tasks; the gray bars represent tasks yet to be completed.

Task

Task 1: Investigate problem
Task 2: Identify options
Task 3: Identify comparison criteria
Task 4: Research MP3 options
Task 5: Evaluate MP3 options
Task 6: Prepare completion report

Date of Tasks (by Weeks)

3   10   17   24   1   8   15   22

November   December

The Gantt chart shows the progress toward completing each of the project tasks. See the Tech Tip in Ch. 16, p. 446, for advice on how to create Gantt charts.

The conclusion summarizes the status of the project.

Conclusion

Our team has successfully completed Tasks 1–3 and begun Task 4. We are on schedule to complete Tasks 4–6 by the December 22 deadline. We have investigated our facility's music problem, identified our options for addressing this problem, and determined necessary and desirable criteria for selecting an MP3 player. We are currently assembling a list of MP3 player options. Next, we will evaluate these options using our criteria. We will include our recommendation for addressing the facility's music problem in the December 22 completion report.

The writers end with a polite offer to provide additional information.

Please contact Jessie Pritiken (extension 4211) if you have questions or comments or would like to discuss this project further.

References

Emerick, J. (2006). Music aids in exercise motivation. Retrieved November 10, 2008, from http://media.www.fsunews.com/media/storage/paper920/news/2006/08/31/ArtsAndEntertainment/Music.Aids.In.Exercise.Motivation-2353196.shtml

Hitti, M. (2005). iPod may jam off the pounds. Retrieved November 11, 2008, from http://www.medicinenet.com/script/main/art.asp?articlekey=56334

Mercola, J. (2004). Listening to music while exercising boosts brain power. Retrieved November 10, 2008, from http://articles.mercola.com/sites/articles/archive/2004/04/10/music-exercise.aspx

Appendix: Member Questionnaire

This is a copy of the questionnaire we asked 200 randomly selected members to complete. We received 120 completed questionnaires. In return for their participation, respondents were given a Total Gym Fitness T-shirt. Their responses are included with each question.

Total Gym Fitness Questionnaire

Presenting the questionnaire—complete with the data it generated—enhances the writers' credibility.

Directions: We are considering making available for checkout MP3 players with custom playlists. We would like your feedback on this idea and your help deciding which features we should consider when evaluating our MP3 player options, if we choose to offer this service. For each question, please circle only one option.

Each question is designed so that it yields quantitative data. Presenting the data makes it simple for readers to understand the members' preferences.

1. If MP3 players with custom playlists were offered for checkout at no cost to you, how likely would you be to use this service?
   A. Very likely **35%**   B. Likely **20%**   C. Not sure **15%**   D. Unlikely **20%**
   E. Very unlikely **10%**

2. If you used this service, how likely would you be to bring your own ear buds or purchase an inexpensive pair available in our pro shop?
   A. Very likely **45%**   B. Likely **25%**   C. Not sure **15%**   D. Unlikely **5%**
   E. Very unlikely **10%**

3. If you have ever used a portable music player (e.g., Walkman, MP3 player) while exercising, how do you prefer to carry the player?
    A. Armband **60%**   B. Waist **20%**   C. Pocket **10%**   D. Hold it **5%**
    E. Other **5%**

4. If several playlists tailored for different types of workouts (e.g., weight training, stretching, yoga, cardio) were available on the MP3 player, how likely would you be to use specific playlists?
    A. Very likely **30%**   B. Likely **45%**   C. Not sure **15%**   D. Unlikely **5%**
    E. Very unlikely **5%**

5. In a typical session, how long do you exercise?
    A. Less than 30 minutes   **10%**
    B. 31 to 45 minutes   **20%**
    C. 46 to 60 minutes   **45%**
    D. 61 to 90 minutes   **15%**
    E. Longer than 90 minutes   **10%**

6. When exercising, how large do you prefer your MP3 player to be?
    A. Compact **45%**   B. Wallet size **50%**   C. Wide screen **5%**

7. How comfortable are you with using common MP3 player user interfaces (e.g., controls for song selection, volume)?
    A. Very comfortable   **30%**
    B. Somewhat comfortable   **20%**
    C. Not sure   **20%**
    D. Somewhat uncomfortable   **15%**
    E. Very uncomfortable   **15%**

WRITING INCIDENT REPORTS

An incident report describes events such as workplace accidents, health or safety emergencies, and equipment problems. (Specialized kinds of incident reports go by other names, such as *accident reports* or *trouble reports*.) The purpose of an incident report is to explain what happened, why it

U.S. Chemical Safety and Hazard Investigation Board

INVESTIGATION REPORT

NTSB Identification: DFW08IA074A

Scheduled 14 CFR Part 121: Air Carrier operation of SOUTHWEST AIRLINES CO

Incident occurred Saturday, March 01, 2008 in Dallas, TX

Aircraft: Boeing 737-7H4, registration: N741SA

Injuries: 244 Uninjured.

The report begins with the identifying information for the report and for the aircraft. Note that this is a preliminary report.

This is preliminary information, subject to change, and may contain errors. Any errors in this report will be corrected when the final report has been completed.

On March 1, 2008, at 1013 central standard time, a Boeing B-737-7H4, N741SA, that was being operated by Southwest Airlines Company under provisions of 14 Code of Federal Regulations (CFR) Part 121 scheduled passenger service as Southwest Airlines Flight 411, collided during taxi with a stationary Boeing 737-3H4, N652SW,

The body of the report begins with an objective description of the two aircraft and what happened to them.

that was being operated by Southwest Airlines Company under provisions of 14 Code of Federal Regulations (CFR) Part 121 scheduled passenger service as Southwest Airlines Flight 15 during ground operations at Dallas Love Field (DAL), Dallas, Texas. There were no injuries to the two airline transport pilots, three flight attendants, and the 102 passengers onboard Flight 411, or to the two airline transport pilots, three flight attendants, and the 132 passengers onboard Flight 15. Both airplanes were damaged. Day instrument meteorological conditions prevailed and an instrument flight rules (IFR) flight plan had been filed for Flight 411 on the flight from the Birmingham International Airport, Birmingham, Alabama and an instrument flight rules (IFR) flight plan had been filed for Flight 15 with the intended destination of William P. Hobby Airport (HOU), Houston, Texas.

Note that the writer states the source of all the information he reports.

Preliminary information provided by the DAL Air Traffic Control Tower and statements from the crew members revealed Flight 15 had completed a pushback from gate 15 and was waiting for a clearance to taxi for takeoff, and Flight 411 had a clearance to taxi to gate 2. While taxiing past Flight 15, the left winglet of Flight 411 sustained damage when it struck and damaged the left horizontal stabilizer of Flight 15.

Examination of both airplanes by two NTSB investigators and a Federal Aviation Administration (FAA) inspector revealed that Flight 15 exhibited minor damage to the left horizontal stabilizer, and Flight 411 sustained minor damage to the left winglet.

At 0953 hours central standard time, the weather observation facility at Dallas, Texas, reported wind from 140 degrees at 6 knots, visibility 3 statute miles in haze, overcast clouds at 500 feet, temperature 59 degrees Fahrenheit, dew point 57 degrees Fahrenheit, and a barometric pressure of 30.27 inches of Mercury.

Figure 17.5 An Accident Report
Source: National Transportation Safety Board, 2008 <www.ntsb.gov/ntsb/brief.asp?ev_id =20080307X00283&key=1>.

happened, and what the organization did (or is going to do) to follow up on the incident.

Figure 17.5 is the incident report filed by the National Transportation Safety Board (NTSB) after the collision of two airplanes on a runway in Dallas, Texas.

WRITING MEETING MINUTES

Minutes, an organization's official record of a meeting, are distributed to all those who belong to the committee or any other unit represented at the meeting. Sometimes, minutes are written by administrative assistants; other times, they are written by technical professionals.

In writing minutes, be clear, comprehensive, objective, and diplomatic. Do not interpret what happened; simply report it. Because meetings rarely follow the agenda perfectly, you might find it challenging to provide an accurate record of the meeting. If necessary, interrupt the discussion to request clarification.

Do not record emotional exchanges between participants. Because minutes are the official record of the meeting, you want them to reflect positively on the participants and the organization.

Figure 17.6 on page 474, an example of an effective set of minutes, was written using a Microsoft Word template. Many organizations today use such a template, which has three advantages:

- Because it is a word-processing template, the note taker can enter information on his or her laptop during the meeting, reducing the time it takes to publish the minutes.

- Because the template is a form, it prompts the note taker to fill in the appropriate information, thus reducing the chances that he or she will overlook something important.

- Because the template is a table, readers quickly become accustomed to reading it and thereby learn where to look to find the important information they seek.

In This Book

For more about conducting meetings, see Ch. 4, p. 61.

The first section of this template calls for information about the logistics of the meeting. You can modify the template to make it appropriate for your organization.

Weekly Planning Committee Meeting

MINUTES   FEBRUARY 14, 2009   3:40 P.M.   CONFERENCE ROOM

MEETING CALLED BY	Principal Robert Barson
TYPE OF MEETING	regular weekly
NOTE TAKER	Zenda Hill
ATTENDEES	William Sipe, Patty Leahy, George Zaerr, Herbert Simon, Robert Barson, Zenda Hill. Absent: Heather Evett

The second section of this template is devoted to the agenda items for the meeting.

Agenda topics

2 MINUTES   APPROVAL OF MINUTES   ZENDA HILL

DISCUSSION	The minutes of the February 7, 2009, meeting were read.		
ACTION ITEMS		**PERSON RESPONSIBLE**	**DEADLINE**
One correction was made: In paragraph 2, "800 hours" was replaced with "80 hours." The minutes were then unanimously approved.		Zenda Hill	N/A

Note that for each agenda item, the note taker is prompted to state how long the discussion took, the subject of the discussion, and the name of the person leading the discussion.

30 MINUTES   AUTHORIZATION FOR ANTIDRUG PRESENTATION BY ALAN WINSTON   PRINCIPAL BARSON

| DISCUSSION | Principal Barson reported on his discussion with Peggy Giles of the School District, who offered positive comments about Winston's presentations at other schools in the district last year.

Mr. Zaerr expressed concern about the effect of the visit on the teaching schedule. Principal Barson acknowledged that the visit would disrupt one whole day but said that the chairs unanimously approved of the visit. Student participation would be voluntary, and the chairs offered to give review sessions to those students who elected not to attend.

Ms. Hill asked if there was any new business. There was none. | | |
|---|---|---|---|
| **ACTION ITEMS** | | **PERSON RESPONSIBLE** | **DEADLINE** |
| Ms. Hill called for a vote on the motion. The motion carried 5–0, with one abstention. | | Ms. Hill will arrange the Winston visit. | February 23, 2009 |
| There being no new business, Ms. Hill moved that the committee adjourn. Motion passed. The committee adjourned at 4:05 p.m. | | N/A | N/A |

For each agenda item, the note taker records the main points of the discussion and the action items. Because the template calls for the action item (such as a vote or a task to be done), the name of the person responsible for doing the task, and the deadline for the task, there should be no confusion about who is to do what task and when it is due.

Figure 17.6   A Set of Meeting Minutes

Writer's Checklist

☐ Did you choose an appropriate application for the informational report? (p. 459)

Does the directive
☐ clearly and politely explain your message? (p. 461)
☐ explain your reasoning, if appropriate? (p. 461)

Does the field report
☐ clearly explain the important information? (p. 464)
☐ use, if appropriate, a problem-methods-results-conclusion-recommendations organization? (p. 464)

Does the progress or status report
☐ clearly announce that it is a progress or status report? (p. 464)
☐ use an appropriate organization? (p. 465)

☐ clearly and honestly report on the subject and forecast the problems and possibilities of the future work? (p. 466)
☐ append supporting materials that substantiate the discussion? (p. 466)

Does the incident report
☐ explain what happened? (p. 472)
☐ explain why it happened? (p. 472)
☐ explain what the organization did about it or will do about it? (p. 473)

Do the minutes
☐ provide the necessary housekeeping details about the meeting? (p. 473)
☐ explain the events of the meeting accurately? (p. 473)
☐ reflect positively on the participants and the organization? (p. 473)

Exercises

▷ **In This Book** For more about memos, see Ch. 14, p. 377.

1. As the manager of Lewis, Lewis, and Wollensky Law, LPC, you have received some complaints from clients that the tattoos on the arms and chests of some employees create negative impressions. Write a directive in the form of a memo defining a new policy: employees are required to wear clothing that covers tattoos on their arms and chests.

2. Write a progress report about the research project you are working on in response to Exercise 3 on page 452 in Chapter 16. If the proposal was a collaborative effort, collaborate with the same group members on the progress report.

3. **INTERNET/GROUP EXERCISE** You are one of three members of the Administrative Council of your college's student association. Recently, the three of you have

concluded that your weekly meetings have become chaotic, largely because you do not use parliamentary procedure (rules for conducting meetings so that they are efficient and fair) and because controversial issues have arisen that have attracted numerous students (the meetings are open to all students). You have decided that it is time to consider adopting parliamentary procedure. Look on the Web for models based on parliamentary procedure. Is there one that you can adopt? Could you combine elements of several models to create an effective model for your group? Find or put together a brief set of procedures, being sure to cite your sources. In a memo to your instructor, discuss the advantages and disadvantages of the model you propose and submit it along with the procedures.

Case 17: Revising an Injury Report Form

▶ **In This Book** For more about memos, see Ch. 14, p. 377.

Background

"Did you know that over 50 percent of the serious injuries to female athletes happen to cheerleaders?" asks Joan Jacqua, the Clubs and Activities Coordinator for Acorn Valley Academy, a private, coeducational high school.

"I had no idea that cheerleading was so risky," Principal John Robinson responds.

"Cheerleading is no longer just pom-poms, megaphones, and high kicks. Cheerleading is gymnastics with stunts and tricks. Last year, more than 25,000 cheerleaders were treated in emergency rooms for injuries to the ankle, shoulder, head, and neck. I just came from a meeting with Robin Dungan, our new cheerleading coach. She told me some of these statistics, and frankly, they scared me. She asked if we have a written emergency plan for what to do if a cheerleader is injured at practice or while cheering at an event."

"Do we?"

"Yes, we have detailed emergency plans for each of our clubs and athletic teams. These plans describe specific roles for each staff member or volunteer in case of emergency. However, according to Robin, we don't have a very good injury report form (Document 17.1). Robin looked at our current form and said that it doesn't encourage a standardized approach to documenting all the necessary information about an injury. She thinks that our injury form, even if completely filled out, won't meet the needs of everyone who reads or uses these reports."

"What do you think?" Principal Robinson asks.

"After looking at the form, I agree with Robin. These injury reports need to satisfy a diverse audience. The adage 'If you didn't write it down, you didn't do it' seems to apply here," Joan says.

"Asking advisers to 'give a full account' seems too broad an instruction," Principal Robinson notes. "It would be helpful if the form prompted advisers to document specific information and details. In addition, the form needs to work not only for cheerleading but also for our athletic teams and clubs, such as theater, chess, and science."

"I agree. I think this form should be revised."

"I'd like to have a revised injury report form ready for when parents and students attend our clubs and activities orientation at the start of next year. We might want to discuss the form at the orientation, or we might just want to go over the form at the first coaches and advisers meeting. I'm not sure. Would you ask one of our school volunteers with a background in technical communication to look into this situation and make some recommendations?"

Later that afternoon, Joan picks up the phone and dials your number.

Your Assignment

1. Write Joan a memo in which you describe the purpose of the injury report form, identify the audiences for the injury report, and describe each of the audience's needs.

2. Based on your analysis of the report's purpose and audience, redesign the academy's report form (Document 17.1). Attach a memo to Joan justifying your design choices and recommending who, if anyone, should review this form before it is finalized.

3. Write Joan a brief memo in which you recommend whether the injury report should be discussed at the student-parent orientation on Clubs and Activities Night. If you feel that it should be discussed with students and parents, justify your recommendation and explain which elements of the form should be addressed. If you feel that the form should not be discussed at the orientation, justify your recommendation and discuss how the form should be introduced to advisers and coaches.

Acorn Valley Academy
Injury Report

Directions: Please type or write in block capitals using black ink.
Routing: Originator to Clubs and Activities Coordinator to Principal

Section I: Injured Student

Student's Name: _____

Address: _____

Phone:_____

Parent Day Phone #1: _____

Parent Day Phone #2: _____

Section II: Injury Details (to be completed by club or activity adviser)
In the space below, give a full account of the injury.

_____

_____

_____

_____

_____

_____

_____

_____

_____

_____

Section III: Adviser's Contact Information

Adviser's Name: _____

Department: _____

Extension:_____

E-mail:_____

Section IV: Signature

Signature: _____

Date: _____

Document 17.1   Acorn Valley Academy's Injury Report Form

⬤ **On TechComm Web**

For digital versions of case documents, click on Downloadable Case Documents on <bedfordstmartins.com/techcomm>.

18

Writing Lab Reports

Persuasion and Lab Reports 479

Understanding the Process of Writing
Lab Reports 480

Understanding the Structure of the
Lab Report 481

Title 481

Abstract 482

Introduction 482

Materials and Methods 483

Results 484

Discussion 485

Conclusion 486

Acknowledgments 486

References 486

Appendices 488

Understanding the Role of Science
and Engineering Articles 489

Sample Lab Report 491

Source: National Oceanic, 2006 <http://coastalscience.noaa.gov/news/feature/12012006.html>.

In the World . . .

If you have taken lab courses, you are already familiar with some of the goals and techniques of research. For the fruits of that research to be applied and help people, the scientist or engineer has to record it, usually in the form of a lab report. Then he or she elaborates on the research in an article and disseminates it through established media, such as journals or professional Web sites. This photo shows two scientists dropping an automated underwater vehicle from their research vessel as part of their study of a harmful algal bloom. Eventually, they will present their findings in a journal article and then apply them in the field to try to counter the problem. A lab report functions as an important step in the process of understanding a scientific problem and solving it in the real world.

Scientists and engineers spend a significant portion of their professional lives writing, because communicating ideas in writing is central to the process of creating and publicizing knowledge. Lab reports are one important way they communicate the results of their work. Adding new knowledge to a field is the collective effort of many people, each contributing small pieces of information and building on the work of others. Although scientists and engineers might work alone or in small groups in a lab, if they want to contribute to their fields, they must convince readers that their findings are valid. For this reason, the ability to write clearly and persuasively is both necessary and valued in the sciences and engineering.

PERSUASION AND LAB REPORTS

Early in your course work, you will likely be required to write lab reports presenting routine findings. That is, you will be asked to replicate studies and test hypotheses that have already been replicated and tested. The reason your instructor will ask you to do such labs is to introduce you to the scientific method and teach you important lab skills that you will need later when you conduct original research.

A written lab report is the primary evidence on which your audience will judge your credibility and skills as a researcher. Sloppy writing, poor design, and a lack of attention to the conventions of written English will suggest that you might also be a sloppy researcher, thus casting doubt on your report. If you fail to convince your audience of the value of your work, you might lose funding to continue.

At first glance, a lab report might appear to be an unadorned presentation of methods, data, and formulas. It isn't. It is a carefully crafted argument meant to persuade an audience to accept your findings and conclusions. You need to justify virtually everything you did in the lab or the field. Here are some questions that you need to answer to be persuasive:

- Why is this topic important?
- What have others already learned about the subject?
- What remains to be learned about the subject?
- Why are you using this methodology, as opposed to other methodologies, in carrying out the work?
- Why do you draw these inferences, as opposed to others, from the data you generated?
- What should be done next? Why?

These questions do not have only one correct answer. You have to make the case that you have done your work professionally and used good judgment—from the reading you did, to the research in the field or the lab, to the writing of the report. In other words, you have to be persuasive. In each section of your lab report, you must persuade your readers that you are a competent researcher who is familiar with your subject area and that you are presenting information that is both interesting and significant.

Because of the way people read lab reports, each section of the report must be persuasive. Although the report is organized as a single cohesive argument, most readers probably will not read it in a linear fashion, from start to finish. In fact, many readers will not read the whole report. They might begin with the title and abstract. If these two elements suggest that the report might be relevant and useful, they might skip to the end and read the conclusions. If the conclusions are persuasive, they might next read the introduction. If the introduction makes it clear that you are familiar with the field and know what you are doing, readers might read the other sections of the report.

If English is not your first language, you should allow extra time to revise, edit, and proofread your lab reports. You might also consider asking a native speaker of English to review them and point out areas where you could be clearer.

UNDERSTANDING THE PROCESS OF WRITING LAB REPORTS

Many scientists and engineers record their laboratory work in notebooks with numbered pages or using specialized software. These notebooks contain enough information for other researchers or colleagues to understand what a researcher did, why he or she did it, and what he or she discovered. Your instructor might ask you to keep a lab notebook.

Although lab notebooks can be useful in legal disputes over who was the first to conduct an experiment or make a discovery, their main purpose is to serve as researchers' personal records. When researchers are ready to communicate their findings, they turn to the information in their notebooks to write their lab reports. If you understand what information goes where in a lab report, you can plan ahead during your research.

The sections of a lab report need not be written in sequence. Some sections can be written early in the writing process, whereas others must wait until you finish your analysis of the data. For example, although the title and abstract are often the first items to be read, they are usually the last items to be written. Likewise, it's easier to write the introduction after you have written your methods, results, and discussion. Only then will you have a clear idea of how you wish to introduce your argument.

UNDERSTANDING THE STRUCTURE OF THE LAB REPORT

Most lab reports have eight basic elements: title, abstract, introduction, materials and methods, results, discussion, conclusion, and references. Some lab reports have additional elements, such as acknowledgments and appendices. Although each researcher or instructor might prefer a slightly different format and style to organize and present information, most lab reports follow a common structure reflecting the scientific method that has been valued by scientists and engineers for centuries. This structure is followed in most lab reports in which you test a hypothesis or attempt to answer a question. It might also be used in lab reports in which you merely follow a procedure and report your results.

If you are a student, be sure to follow your instructor's guidelines for the structure of the report. For example, some instructors prefer that you combine the results and discussion sections. In studies involving multiple procedures and generating large amounts of data, your instructor might prefer that you present one group of data and analyze it before you introduce the next group of data.

The following discussion focuses on writing lab reports for undergraduate science and engineering courses.

Title

The title should be informative enough to enable readers to decide whether the report interests them. When scientists and engineers use abstracting and indexing services, an informative title helps them locate the most relevant research for their needs and saves them time.

Write your title with your readers in mind. Use only words and abbreviations that are familiar to them. The keywords in your title should be the terms usually used by readers searching for information in your subject area. Keep in mind that because effective titles are specific, they also tend to be long.

WEAK	Babbler Behavior
IMPROVED	Endocrine Correlates of Social and Reproductive Behaviors in a Group-Living Australian Passerine, the White-Browed Babbler
WEAK	New Technologies for Power Plants
IMPROVED	Evaluating New Instrumentation and Control Technologies for Safety-Related Applications in Nuclear Power Plants

Abstract

The abstract summarizes the entire report, mirroring its structure: introduction, methods, results, discussion, and conclusion. However, because of space limitations, each section is addressed in only a sentence or two. Because your abstract might be distributed more widely than your entire report, it should contain enough information so that your readers can quickly decide whether to read the whole report or not. Abstract readers are most interested in what questions motivated your study (introduction), what answers you discovered (results), and what implications your findings have (conclusions). A well-written abstract can also meet readers' need to stay up-to-date on research findings without spending a lot of time doing so.

Most readers prefer *informative abstracts*, which present the major findings. Less popular are *descriptive abstracts*, which simply state the topics covered without presenting the important results or conclusions.

▶ In This Book

For more about informative and descriptive abstracts, see Ch. 19, p. 511.

Introduction

The introduction is the section of the report in which you begin to establish that your work is relevant and significant. Here, you place your work in the broader context of your field by describing what hypothesis or question your study attempted to answer and why this question is important. Your introduction should include a concise review of previous research relevant to your study and describe how your study extends the knowledge in your field or addresses a weakness in previous studies. By placing your study in the context of current research in your field, you establish the significance of your study. Provide just enough detail to help readers understand how your study contributes new information to the field and to communicate the purpose of your study.

If you think readers will need specialized knowledge or theoretical background to understand your study, define important terms and present theoretical concepts in this section. Use your understanding of your audience to help you determine how much theoretical background to include. Often, instructors will ask you to write for an audience of classmates who are familiar with the general subject area but not familiar with the specific lab you are reporting.

Your introduction should also briefly describe your methods: what you did to find an answer to your research question. Although your methods section will provide a detailed account of your approach, the introduction should persuade readers that your methods were appropriate given what has been done in previous studies.

If you include formulas in the introduction, adhere to the conventions presented in the Guidelines box.

▶ In This Book

For more about definitions, see Ch. 20, p. 540.

Guidelines

Writing Equations

Follow these four suggestions when you write equations:

▶ **Use an equation editor or write equations by hand.** Some word processors include an equation editor, which enables you to insert type associated with equations, such as mathematical symbols, Greek letters, integrals, and fractions. Unless your word processor includes an equation editor or you have access to a separate equation editor, do not try to approximate an equation with standard text and punctuation. Many instructors allow students to add handwritten equations to lab reports after they have been printed. Check with your instructor.

▶ **Place each equation on a separate line.** Because equations often involve raised or lowered text as well as odd-shaped symbols, equations included in the body of your text will often create awkward line spacing, making the text difficult to read. Start each equation on a new line, with plenty of white space surrounding it.

▶ **Number each equation.** Label each equation with a number in ascending order. Refer to the equation by number in your text: "The line represents the theoretical curve based on equation 1."

▶ **If appropriate, omit routine equations.** If your instructor's guidelines permit it, omit basic equations with which your readers are familiar, especially in advanced lab reports. Starting at too basic a level will make your report too long and interrupt your reader's train of thought.

Materials and Methods

Your purpose in writing the materials and methods section (also called *equipment and methods*) is to convince your readers that your approach was appropriate for the question you hoped to answer and that you conducted your experiment carefully. Your methods should be detailed enough that another researcher could perform the same experiment using the same materials and methods. This ability, called *replicability*, is one of the foundations of the scientific method.

Most researchers begin this section with a description or list of materials. Include any human subjects, organisms, chemicals, tools, and measuring devices. Your description of materials might also include sketches, diagrams, schematics, or photographs or drawings of equipment and how you set up that equipment.

Next, describe your procedures. Include relevant conditions such as temperatures, observation dates and times, instrument settings and calibration, and site locations for field studies. Also indicate whether you encountered any difficulties with standard procedures and how you modified your approach to address these difficulties. Finally, if you had to make subjective decisions in collecting data, explain your choices. Although your readers might want to repeat your experiment, some instructors prefer that you avoid numbered, step-by-step instructions, presenting instead an organized description of what you did in sufficient detail that readers can understand your process. Organize this section chronologically, in the order in which you conducted your experiment. Include only those procedures that led to results that you present in the report.

When providing details, assume that your readers are unfamiliar with the particulars of your experiment but know enough about lab procedures to evaluate your efforts. Your credibility rests on your ability to explain clearly what you did and why.

▶ **In This Book**

For more about active and passive voice, see Ch. 10, p. 234.

Although writing in the active voice ("I collected three soil samples") is generally more concise, clearer, and more interesting than writing in the passive voice ("Three soil samples were collected"), the sciences and engineering have a long tradition of using the latter. The passive voice emphasizes the material studied and the actions taken while deemphasizing the role of the researcher. However, more and more publications in the sciences and engineering are using the active voice. Check with your instructor to learn which style he or she prefers.

Results

Think of the results section as an opportunity to present the evidence you will use to support the claims you will make in your discussion. How persuasive this evidence is depends on how successfully you present it to your readers.

▶ **In This Book**

For more about organizing patterns, see Ch. 7, p. 152.

Your research will likely produce raw data in the form of numbers. In the results section, your task is to summarize the data relevant to the question or hypothesis you discussed in your introduction. Omit irrelevant data, but explain why you are doing so. When summarizing your data, help your readers understand your findings by emphasizing major trends, magnitude of values, associations, patterns of statistical significance, and exceptions. Typically, results are presented in the same order in which they are described in the methods section, but you can change the order if you have a good reason to do so. For instance, you might use the more-important-to-less-important organizing pattern by beginning with the one set of data that most clearly supports or negates your hypothesis.

▶ **In This Book**

For more about explaining the significance of graphics, see Ch. 12, p. 298.

Be sure your data are complete and organized. For each major trend or pattern, begin with a statement of your findings and then support your statement with data. Depending on the type of data, you may present your supporting evidence with a combination of text and graphics (such as tables, graphs, and diagrams). If you include graphics, refer to them in the text with a statement explaining their significance.

Ethics Note

Presenting Data Honestly

The hallmark of good science is the honest and complete presentation of results, even if some of those results undercut the hypothesis. It is unethical to omit data that do not support your hypothesis. For instance, your hypothesis might be that as temperature increases, the growth rate of the organism you are studying increases. However, some of your data show that above a certain temperature, the growth rate remains steady. You have replicated the procedure several times and gotten the same results, but you can't explain it. What do you do? You present the data and offer your best explanation, but you also state clearly that you can't explain the data. In other words, you tell the truth.

Likewise, it is unethical to choose a type of graphic that obscures negative findings or design a graphic so that data points are omitted. For example, you use a spreadsheet to record your data about temperature and growth rate. To present these data in a graphic, such as a line graph, you must select the cells you want to be represented in the graph. It is easy to omit cells that include negative or inexplicable findings. However, doing so would be dishonest and therefore unethical—an obvious violation of the norms of scientific practice. Inconsistent data or contradictory results often lead researchers to examine their approach and assumptions more carefully, which can lead to breakthroughs in the understanding of a field.

Remember that inconsistent data or contradictory results do not necessarily mean that you performed the lab unprofessionally. They simply mean that reality is complicated. Readers will accept that. But they won't accept a misleading or dishonest lab report.

WEAK	Results of bacteria sampling are shown in Table 1.
IMPROVED	As Table 1 shows, bacterial growth increased as groundwater temperature increased.

In the results section, avoid interpreting or explaining your data. Likewise, avoid speculating about problematic or atypical data. Save those explanations for the next section, the discussion.

Discussion

Sometimes called *analysis*, the discussion section is where you interpret your results: that is, you answer the question or support (or argue against) the hypothesis you discussed in your introduction.

In organizing the discussion section, start by presenting the most important findings, which might include major trends, magnitude of values, associations, patterns of statistical significance, and exceptions. Focus on offering explanations for your findings. Support your argument with data from your results, and do not hesitate to discuss problematic data or "failed" experiments. Sometimes, a negative result or a failure to find a significant difference helps researchers create new knowledge in your field. If your results do not support your hypothesis, argue for rejecting the hypothesis. If appropriate, support your argument with references to other researchers' work, describing the degree to which your results match the results of previous studies. If your findings do not match the results of previous studies, suggest possible explanations for the differences.

Conclusion

Summarize the main points covered by your report in a concise paragraph or two. Begin by reviewing the purpose of your lab and the hypothesis (or hypotheses) you tested. Next, summarize the most important implications of your findings. The conclusion is your final opportunity to persuade your audience of the significance of your work. Do not introduce any new information or analysis in this section.

Acknowledgments

Sometimes scientists and engineers are assisted by colleagues during a study or while preparing the lab report. If this is the case, you should identify and thank these people in an acknowledgments section. If your study was supported by funding, you should list the source of financial support in this section as well. Figure 18.1 shows a concise acknowledgments section. Typically, scientists and engineers ask permission of the people they wish to thank before including them in the acknowledgments.

Use *we* if the report was written by more than one author. Use *I* if you are the sole author.

References

List all the references you cited in your report. Do not list any sources that you consulted but did not cite. Most of your citations will appear in the

---

Acknowledgments

We wish to express our appreciation to the Robert Wood Johnson Foundation for their generous support of this study. We also thank Dr. Mark Greenberg, Dr. David Jones, and Dr. Eileen Whitney for their valuable comments about an early draft of this report.

Figure 18.1   Acknowledgments

INTERACTIVE SAMPLE DOCUMENT
Evaluating Lab Reports

The grading sheet included here is used by an engineering professor to evaluate the lab reports written by students in his Principles of Environmental Engineering lab course. One of the labs in that course requires students to evaluate the efficiencies of several wastewater-treatment strategies and then determine whether the strategies can meet or exceed proposed discharge-effluent limits. The questions in the margin ask you to consider the grading sheet based on the discussion of lab reports in this chapter. E-mail your responses to yourself and/or your instructor on TechComm Web.

SOLIDS REPORT GRADING SHEET

Total: /100		Student Names:
Points Earned	**Points Possible**	**Report Section**
	2	Cover (1) and title page (1)
	10	Abstract, including the following:
		Problem statement (3)
		Methods used (2)
		Results (2)
		Conclusions/Recommendations (3)
	6	Indices (generated by the software), including the following:
		Table of Contents (2)
		List of Figures (2)
		List of Tables (2)
	12	Summary includes the following:
		Evaluation of results (6)
		Answers to questions that management would be concerned with (6)
	10	Introduction includes the following:
		Background information (2)
		Problem/purpose statement (2)
		Plan/procedures for testing; outline for selection/solution (2)
		Description of rest of report (2)
		Definition of terms/limitations/assumptions (2)
	5	Procedures correctly name the tests and reference the procedures.
	10	Results summarize final results in paragraph form and include tables or graphs as appropriate. Results reference raw data and all example calculations.

1. In what ways does this grading sheet follow the basic format of a lab report discussed in this chapter? In what ways does it not follow the basic format?

2. In what ways do you agree or disagree with the relative importance placed on report elements in this grading sheet?

3. If the instructor distributed this grading sheet at the start of a lab assignment, how might students in the lab use it to help them write their lab reports?

Points Earned	Points Possible	Report Section
	10	Discussion correctly interprets results and discusses their meanings; correctly discusses acceptable/typical/reasonable ranges and explains unexpected results.
	5	References (complete and correctly using CSE style)
	10	Appendices
	10	Sample calculations presented accurately (5 each)
	10	Writing skill and format:
		Correct spelling and grammar (4)
		Consistency of headings, capitalization, bolding, italicization, table and graph appearance, etc. (2)
		Correct numbering and titling of tables (2)
		Correct numbering, titling, and design of graphs (axes labeled correctly, clear legends) (2)
	100	**TOTAL POINTS**

On TechComm Web

To e-mail your responses to yourself and/or your instructor, click on Interactive Sample Documents for Ch. 18 on **<bedfordstmartins.com/ techcomm>**.

introduction, materials and methods, and discussion sections. However, check the other sections as well to make sure you include all of the sources cited. Most scientists and engineers follow a particular documentation system for their discipline (see Appendix, Part B). Check with your instructor for his or her preferences.

Appendices

An appendix, which appears after the references, is the appropriate place for ancillary information that is not needed to understand the body of your lab report. For example, an appendix might include long tables of measurements, specialized data, logs, analyses, or calculations.

Following the basic structure of a lab report discussed here will help your readers manage the large quantities of information produced in science and engineering. The title and abstract will help them decide whether your report is relevant. The introduction and conclusion will provide the context for and most important results of your study. If readers are persuaded to read further, the methods, results, and discussion will provide the detailed information they seek.

UNDERSTANDING THE ROLE OF SCIENCE AND ENGINEERING ARTICLES

Once science and engineering students enter the working world, they will have many opportunities to write about their fields. Rather than writing for an audience of teachers, they will be writing for an audience of supervisors, professional boards, government officials, clients, other scientists or engineers, and potential funding sources. Their reports might be read only by people in their organizations, or they might have a global audience.

Both researchers and practitioners sometimes develop lab reports into articles for publication in professional journals. Some companies offer employees a monetary bonus for publishing articles in journals. These articles help companies gain recognition as leaders in innovation and help researchers demonstrate their ability to contribute new ideas to the field.

Articles in science and engineering are often organized like lab reports. However, rather than following an instructor's preferences, a researcher in the workplace follows the *author guidelines* of the particular journal to which he or she will submit the article. Figure 18.2 on page 490 is an example of author guidelines.

When a scientist or engineer submits an article for publication, the author's argument and supporting evidence are carefully evaluated by other professionals in his or her field. This type of evaluation is called a *peer review*. Peer reviewers make suggestions for revision and, ultimately, recommend whether the editor of the journal should accept the article for publication or reject it. The review process can involve extensive revisions, multiple drafts, and sometimes disagreements. After the peer reviewers agree that the article represents a persuasive scientific argument and offers significant new insights, the article is scheduled for editing and eventual publication in the journal. The entire process, from initial submission to publication, can take several months to more than a year.

This page provides prospective authors with information about how to prepare a manuscript for submission to IEEE journals. IEEE (which originally stood for Institute of Electrical and Electronics Engineers, Inc.) is the world's leading professional association for the advancement of technology. With 375,000 members, including 80,000 student members, IEEE publishes almost 150 journals and magazines.

The instructions explain how to number various parts of a manuscript; how to format articles; what to include in an abstract; and how to document references.

IEEE publications require a specific documentation style and format. Examples of common types of references are shown here.

The more closely an article follows the author guidelines, the more likely it is to be accepted for publication and the more quickly it will be available to readers.

---

in the subjects being treated. The papers are of long-range interest and broad significance. Applications and technological issues, as well as theory, are emphasized. The topics include all aspects of electrical and computer engineering and science. From time to time, papers on managerial, historical, economic, and ethical aspects of technology are published. Papers are authored by recognized authorities and reviewed by experts. They include extensive introductions written at a level suitable for the nonspecialist, with ample references for those who wish to probe further. Several issues a year are devoted to a single subject of special importance.

Prospective authors, before preparing a full-length manuscript, are urged to submit a proposal containing a description of the topic and its importance to PROCEEDINGS readers, a detailed outline of the proposed paper and its type of coverage, and a brief biography showing the authors' qualifications for writing the paper. A proposal can be reviewed most efficiently if it is sent electronically to the Managing Editor at j.calder@ieee.org. If the proposal receives a favorable review, the author will be encouraged to prepare the paper for publication consideration through the normal review process.

PROCEEDINGS OF THE IEEE
445 Hoes Lane
P.O. Box 1331
Piscataway, NJ 08855-1331 USA
Fax: +1 732 562 5456

IV. GENERAL MANUSCRIPT PREPARATION

A. Consecutive Numbering of Parts

All manuscript pages, footnotes, equations, and references should be labeled in consecutive numerical order. Illustrations and tables should be cited in text in numerical order. See Section IV-G of this guide.

B. Manuscript Formats

See copies of the publications for examples of proper paper formats and requirements for the types of papers accepted for each publication (i.e., Full Papers, Letters, Short Papers, etc.).

Full length papers generally consist of the title, byline, author affiliation, footnote (including any financial support acknowledgment), index terms, abstract, nomenclature if present, introduction, body, conclusions, reference list, list of figures and table captions, and original figures and tables for reproduction. A paper may also include appendixes, a glossary of symbols, and an acknowledgment of nonfinancial support.

C. Abstract

The abstract should be limited to 50–200 words and should concisely state what was done, how it was done, principal results, and their significance. The abstract will appear later in various abstracts journals and should contain the most critical information of the paper.

D. References

A numbered list of references must be provided at the end of the paper. The list should be arranged in the order of citation in text, not in alphabetical order. List only one reference per reference number.

In text, each reference number should be enclosed by square brackets. Citations of references may be given simply as "in [1] ...", rather than as "in reference [1] ...". Similarly, it is not necessary to mention the authors of a reference unless the mention is relevant to the text. It is almost never useful to give dates of references in text. These will usually be deleted by Staff Editors if included.

Footnotes or other words and phrases that are not part of the reference format do not belong on the reference list. Phrases such as "For example," should not introduce references in the list, but should instead be given in parentheses in text, followed by the reference number, i.e., "For example, see [5]."

Sample correct formats for various types of references are as follows.

Books:
[1] G. O. Young, "Synthetic structure of industrial plastics," in *Plastics,* 2nd ed., vol. 3, J. Peters, Ed. New York: McGraw-Hill, 1964, pp. 15–64.
[2] W.-K. Chen, *Linear Networks and Systems.* Belmont, CA: Wadsworth, 1993, pp. 123–135.

Periodicals:
[3] J. U. Duncombe, "Infrared navigation—Part I: An assessment of feasibility," *IEEE Trans. Electron Devices,* vol. ED-11, pp. 34–39, Jan. 1959.
[4] E. P. Wigner, "Theory of traveling-wave optical laser," *Phys. Rev.,* vol. 134, pp. A635–A646, Dec. 1965.
[5] E. H. Miller, "A note on reflector arrays," *IEEE Trans. Antennas Propagat.,* to be published.

Articles from Conference Proceedings (published):
[6] D. B. Payne and J. R. Stern, "Wavelength-switched passively coupled single-mode optical network," in *Proc. IOOC-ECOC,* 1985, pp. 585–590.

Papers Presented at Conferences (unpublished):
[7] D. Ebehard and E. Voges, "Digital single sideband detection for interferometric sensors," presented at the 2nd Int. Conf. Optical Fiber Sensors, Stuttgart, Germany, Jan. 2-5, 1984.

Standards/Patents:
[8] G. Brandli and M. Dick, "Alternating current fed power supply," U.S. Patent 4 084 217, Nov. 4, 1978.

Technical Reports:
[9] E. E. Reber, R. L. Mitchell, and C. J. Carter, "Oxygen absorption in the Earth's atmosphere," Aerospace Corp., Los Angeles, CA, Tech. Rep. TR-0200 (4230-46)-3, Nov. 1968.

4

Figure 18.2   Excerpt from IEEE Author Guidelines
Source: IEEE, 2007 <www.ieee.org/portal/cms_docs_iportals/iportals/publications/authors/transjnl/auinfo07.pdf>.

SAMPLE LAB REPORT

The following lab report (adapted from Thomford, 2008) was written for an undergraduate human-physiology lab experiment.

Bile Salts Enhance Lipase Digestion of Fats

Keywords in the title reflect the major focus of the lab.

Abstract

Bile salts, which are secreted by the gall bladder into the small intestine, play an important role in the digestion of dietary fats by pancreatic lipase. The digestion of milk fat by pancreatic lipase in the presence and absence of bile salts was tested to demonstrate whether bile salts help pancreatic lipase digest fat more efficiently. Based on pH measurements at four time intervals, the production of fatty acids occurred most quickly in the test group containing bile salts and pancreatic lipase. In the test group containing only bile salts, no fat digestion occurred. Bile salts enhanced the rate of lipase-fat digestion but did not digest fats alone. This lab shows that bile salts act only to emulsify fats, enabling pancreatic lipase to digest fats more efficiently.

The abstract concisely communicates the purpose of the lab, the approach, the results, and the significance of the findings. Some instructors require an abstract, and some do not.

1

Introduction

The pancreas secretes various enzymes into the small intestine. One of these enzymes, pancreatic lipase, digests dietary fats into products such as glycerol and fatty acids (Mader, 2007). However, fat is insoluble in water-based *chyme* (the liquefied food processed by the stomach), and in the intestines the fats cling together, providing little surface area for attachment of the enzymes. This prolongs the time it takes the lipase to digest the fat.

In order to speed up the fat digestion process, bile salts, secreted by the gall bladder into the small intestine, act as a detergent that breaks up the fat droplets in the watery chyme, thus increasing the surface area for enzymatic digestion by lipase (Martini & Timmons, 2005). In other words, bile is an emulsifying agent. Emulsification of fats is achieved upon exposure to bile salts, which allows pancreatic lipase to digest the fat more efficiently. To demonstrate that bile salts enhance the digestion of fats, the digestion of milk fat by pancreatic lipase in the presence and absence of bile salts was tested.

Headings reflect common elements in a lab report and help communicate the organization of the report.

Because the discussion moves from general to specific, readers are introduced to background concepts necessary to understand the rest of the report.

Statements are supported by references to research relevant to the lab.

The purpose of the lab is clearly stated.

2

Materials and Methods

Methods are detailed enough so that another researcher could perform the same experiment using the same methods.

Three groups of test tubes were set up; three replicates were set up in each group in order to provide an adequate sample size. To each group of three test tubes, the following were added:

Group 1: 3.0 ml of whole milk + 5.0 ml of water + 3 grains of bile salts
Group 2: 3.0 ml of whole milk + 5.0 ml of pancreatin solution (*see below for concentration*)
Group 3: 3.0 ml of whole milk + 5.0 ml of pancreatin solution + 3 grains of bile salts

Methods include relevant procedures, such as the type of pH paper used, incubation temperature, and testing intervals. Note that the entire materials and methods section is written in the past tense.

Dehydrated pancreatin, derived from pig pancreas, was reconstituted in water (@ 1g/100ml) immediately before use. This solution contained the pancreatic lipase enzyme that was used to digest the milk fats. Dried grains of bile salts, derived from the pig gall bladder, were dissolved directly in each test tube.

To determine the increase in fatty acid end-products during the digestion of fats, the pH of the incubated solutions (as fatty acid concentration increases, pH decreases) was tested. The pH of each test tube was determined at time zero (beginning of the experiment) using "short range" pH paper (reads pH 6–10). The test tubes were incubated at 37°C for 1 hour. During that hour, the pH was tested every 20 minutes.

3

Results

The pH did not decrease during the 60-minute incubation period in the negative control group 1, which contained only milk and bile salts (Table 1). In groups 2 and 3, the pH did decrease as the digestion of fats progressed, and fatty acids built up in the test tubes. After 20 minutes, the pH decreased in group 2 from 8.5 to 7.5, while there was a greater change in tube 3 (from pH 8.5 to 7.0). At 40 minutes incubation, the pH of the solutions in both groups 2 and 3 had dropped to 6.5 and did not decrease further at 60 minutes.

Table 1. Mean* pH of whole milk during incubation with bile salts and/or pancreatin

Time (minutes)	Group 1 (+ B.S.[1])	Group 2 (+ pancreatin)	Group 3 (+ B.S. + pancreatin)
0	8.3	8.5	8.5
20	8.4	7.5	7.0
40	8.3	6.5	6.5
60	8.3	6.5	6.5

*Mean pH of three sample tubes per group
[1]Bile salts

The data for all three groups are visually plotted in Figure 1.

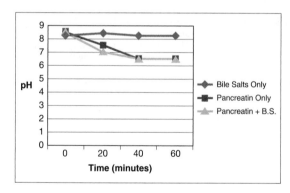

Figure 1.   Mean pH of whole milk during incubation with bile salts and/or pancreatin

Data are presented not only in a table but also in the text. Both the table and figure are referenced in the text. Note that the results are not interpreted in this section of the lab report.

Note that the entire results section is written in the past tense.

The table and figure are labeled with informative titles. Each graphic clearly presents a manageable amount of information.

4

The discussion explains
the purpose of the lab: to
demonstrate that bile salts
enhance the digestion of fats.

The discussion also explains
why the experiment yielded the
results that it did. Relevant
research findings are referenced
to support the writer's
explanations.

The final paragraph discusses
the ambiguity of some of the
results and suggests further
experiments to address new
questions raised by the current
experiment.

Discussion

The negative control tube containing only bile salts and milk did not exhibit a pH change. Therefore, it was concluded that bile salts alone did not digest milk fats. Digestion of milk fats occurred in tubes 2 and 3, based on the observation of fatty acid by-product accumulation, as measured by a decrease in pH. However, the production of fatty acids occurred faster in group 3, as evidenced by the data at 20 minutes. This finding suggests that something present in the solution of group 3 aided in the digestion of the fats. Since the concentration of pancreatin was identical in groups 2 and 3, the addition of bile salts must have contributed to the digestion of the fats by breaking up those fat droplets into smaller particles, which increased the availability of substrate in group 3. The action of bile salts enhanced the rate of the lipase-fat digestion. The data from group 1, as a negative control, demonstrates that bile salts do not digest fats; therefore, bile salts must act only to emulsify the fats, thus enabling pancreatic lipase to act more efficiently. This conclusion is also supported by work done by Patton and Carey (1979) and reported by Bowen (2007).

It was also determined that either the enzymatic activity of pancreatic lipase is inhibited below pH 6.5, or the fat substrates were depleted by 40 minutes in tubes 2 and 3, since there was no change in pH between 40 and 60 minutes. Further experimentation will reveal which of these two possibilities occurred. Fox (2008) reported that the optimal activity of pancreatic lipase occurs at a pH of 8. Therefore, it is most likely that the lack of change in pH between 40 and 60 minutes in tubes 2 and 3 was due to the fact that the accumulation of fatty acid end-products produced an excessively acidic environment (pH 6.5 at 40 minutes), thereby inhibiting further enzyme activity. This may suggest that pancreatic lipase is denatured in weakly acidic conditions between pH 7.0 and 6.5. However, if this is not the case, an alternative conclusion may be that depletion of substrate occurred during the experimental period. This experiment should be re-run using cream or vegetable oil, both of which contain significantly more fat than whole milk.

5

References

Bowen, R. (2007, August 8). Absorption of lipids. Retrieved February 21, 2008, from http://www.vivo.colostate.edu/hbooks/pathphys/digestion/smallgut/absorb_lipids.html

Fox, S. (2008). *A laboratory guide to human physiology, concepts and clinical applications.* New York: McGraw-Hill Science/Engineering/Math.

Mader, S. (2007). *Human biology* (10th ed.). New York: McGraw-Hill Science/Engineering/Math.

Martini, F., & Timmons, M. (2005). *Human anatomy* (5th ed.). San Francisco: Benjamin Cummings.

Patton, J., & Carey, M. (1979). Watching fat digestion. *Science 204*, 145–148.

The references contain all the works cited in the body of the report. References are a mix of up-to-date sources and older but still relevant research. References follow American Psychological Association (APA) format.

Writer's Checklist

Does the title

- [ ] convey the major focus of your study? (p. 481)
- [ ] use words and abbreviations familiar to your readers? (p. 481)
- [ ] use keywords that readers would likely use to search for research in your subject area? (p. 481)

Does the abstract

- [ ] state the problem or question addressed by your study? (p. 482)
- [ ] summarize your approach? (p. 482)
- [ ] summarize key results and conclusions? (p. 482)
- [ ] briefly discuss the implications of your study? (p. 482)
- [ ] make sense to readers who have not read your entire report? (p. 482)

Does the introduction

- [ ] concisely review research relevant to your study? (p. 482)
- [ ] explain how your study contributes to the field? (p. 482)
- [ ] state the purpose of your study? (p. 482)
- [ ] briefly describe your approach? (p. 482)

Does the materials and methods section

- [ ] describe the materials and (if appropriate) equipment used? (p. 483)
- [ ] describe your procedures with enough detail for readers to understand what you did? (p. 483)
- [ ] address any problems encountered and your solutions? (p. 483)
- [ ] include a description and rationale for any subjective measurements? (p. 483)
- [ ] present information in a logical order? (p. 484)

Does the results section

- [ ] summarize all the data relevant to addressing the question or hypothesis you discussed in your introduction? (p. 484)
- [ ] exclude data not applicable to your argument? (p. 484)
- [ ] emphasize important trends and patterns? (p. 484)
- [ ] use text and graphics to present data concisely? (p. 484)

- [ ] introduce and explain (if appropriate) each graphic in your text? (p. 484)
- [ ] avoid interpreting, analyzing, and speculating about data? (p. 484)

Does the discussion section

- [ ] address the question or hypothesis discussed in your introduction? (p. 485)
- [ ] address the major trends, magnitude of values, associations, patterns of statistical significance, and exceptions in your study? (p. 485)
- [ ] present plausible explanations for your results? (p. 485)
- [ ] support your argument with data from your results? (p. 485)
- [ ] comment on (if appropriate) problematic or "negative" results? (p. 485)
- [ ] compare and comment on relevant work of other researchers? (p. 485)

Does the conclusion section

- [ ] briefly review the purpose of the lab? (p. 486)
- [ ] summarize implications of the study? (p. 486)
- [ ] avoid introducing new information? (p. 486)

Does the acknowledgments section

- [ ] thank the people who helped you conduct the lab or write the lab report? (p. 486)
- [ ] identify any sources of financial support for the study? (p. 486)
- [ ] identify only those people and organizations that have specifically given permission to be listed? (p. 486)

Does the references section

- [ ] identify each source cited in your lab report? (p. 486)
- [ ] contain complete and accurate information for each citation? (p. 486)
- [ ] follow your instructor's preferred format for references? (p. 486)

Do the appendices

- [ ] contain information too bulky for the body of your report? (p. 488)

Exercises

▶ **In This Book** For more about memos, see Ch. 14, p. 377.

1. **INTERNET EXERCISE** Using an Internet search engine, locate three or four sample lab reports. In a brief memo to your instructor, compare and contrast the basic elements of the reports. Do they follow a similar format? If so, explain how they are similar. If the reports differ in format, why do you think the authors chose to present information in the manner they did?

2. Locate a word-processing program with an equation editor or download a free equation editor from the Internet. Practice creating four to six equations you might use in your field. If you do not regularly use equations, locate a few equations in science or math textbooks and copy these equations. In a brief memo to your instructor, evaluate the ease of use of the editor.

3. The following abstract (Kress and Gifford, 1984) accompanied a research report published in a water-resources journal. In a brief memo to your instructor, describe how effective the abstract is. What are some of its strengths and weaknesses?

    > Cowpies molded to a standard configuration and size were subjected to simulated rainfall, and the fecal coliform counts were determined using the most probable number (MPN) method of enumeration. The standard cowpie deposits were exposed to simulated rainfall once at ages 2 through 200 days. The effects of rainfall intensity and recurrent rainfall were also tested. Naturally occurring fecal deposits were also tested to compare their results with those from the standard cowpies.
    >
    > A log-log regression was found to describe the decline in peak fecal coliform release with fecal deposit age. The 100-day-old fecal deposits produced peak counts of 4,200 fecal coliform per 100 milliliters of water. This quantity of release is minimal compared to the release from fresher fecal material.
    >
    > Rainfall intensity had little effect on peak fecal coliform release from fecal deposits that were 2 or 10 days old. At age 20 days, the effect of rainfall intensity was significant; the highest intensity gave the lowest peak counts, and the lowest intensity gave the highest peak counts. The effect of rainfall intensity appears to be related to the dryness of the fecal deposits.
    >
    > Peak fecal coliform counts were significantly lowered when the fecal deposits were rained on more than once. This decline was thought to be produced by the loss of bacteria from the fecal deposits during the previous wettings.
    >
    > Standard cowpies produced a peak release regression that was not significantly different from the regression for the natural fecal deposits. Apparently, grossly manipulating the fecal deposits did not significantly change the release patterns.

4. **INTERNET/GROUP EXERCISE** Form groups so that each group has different majors represented. Have each group member locate author guidelines for a journal in his or her field. Often, author guidelines can be found on the Web site for a journal or in the back of journal issues. As a group, compare the guidelines. In what ways are the guidelines similar? In what ways are they different? Present your results in a memo to your instructor.

Case 18: Describing the Purpose of Lab Report Sections

▶ **In This Book** For more about memos, see Ch. 14, p. 377.

Background

Maelee Kwan is enrolled in Civil Engineering (CE) 320: Principles of Environmental Engineering, as well as CE 321, the lab for CE 320. The lab focuses on environmental-engineering problems, with an emphasis on the analysis and presentation of lab findings. Maelee has just completed the first lab on wastewater-treatment strategies and is struggling to write her lab report, which is due in two weeks. "It just seems like I'm repeating the same information in several sections of my report," Maelee tells you.

As a peer writing consultant assigned to CE 320/321, you have seen a number of students this week. Several others have sent you e-mails. Most have said that they aren't clear about the purpose of each section in a lab report.

"Have you downloaded and read the assignment sheet that lists your instructor's expectations for this lab?" you ask.

"All he's given us is a grading sheet that lists the types of content that must be included in the final lab report," Maelee says, showing you the sheet (see the Interactive Sample Document on pages 487–88).

After reviewing the grading sheet, you ask, "Who is the audience for this lab report?"

"We are supposed to be employees of a company that has been hired to evaluate a preliminary design of an im-proved wastewater-treatment system. We're writing our lab reports to present our findings to our company executives. It just seems like I'm writing the exact same information in the abstract, summary, and discussion. I'm not even sure why I need to include a summary if I already have an abstract. What's the difference?" Maelee hands you rough drafts of what she has written so far for these three sections (Documents 18.1–18.3).

Document 18.1   Draft of Lab Report Abstract

Abstract

Geo-Hydro Corporation has decided to build a new novelty manufacturing plant located in Lander, Wyoming. The company has decided to build a water-treatment facility of its own in order to provide its own drinking water to be used in the new plant. We have been asked to study and analyze four possible sources of water they could use, to avoid using the municipal water supply. All four sources were tested for alkalinity, acidity, and hardness to determine which one is the most suitable for the company's needs. The results showed that the Wild River water would be the best choice for the company's use, even though it had some turbidity issues. The solution for this issue was to make a jar test to create an optimum water pH-alum coagulant combination to use in a settling column test to try to achieve the desired levels of turbidity for drinking water. Since the settling test was not enough to achieve this, the filtration test results that followed showed that such a technique can remove the remaining solids in the water that would be required to pass the required standards. We recommended Geo-Hydro Corporation use the Wild River as their water source.

Document 18.2   Draft of Lab Report Executive Summary

Summary

Geo-Hydro Corporation has decided to build a new manufacturing plant located in Lander, Wyoming. The plant will include its own water-treatment facility in order to provide its own drinking water to be used in the new plant. Our company was retained to determine the best sources of water for this water-treatment facility. The four sources of water tested were Wild River, Shoshone Aquifer, High Mountain Spring, and Foothills Spring. After doing some of the preliminary tests to determine alkalinity, acidity, and hardness, we concluded that the Wild River was the best source that could be used since its natural pH is 7.92 and the hardness is below 60 mg/L $CaCO_3$, which means it is just below the limit of being a hard water; therefore, there are not a lot of changes required to any of the char-acteristics of this water source. However, the water is 11.6 NTU and, thus, requires a certain level of water treatment to achieve a level acceptable for drinking water. For this we determined that 20 mg of alum were required to flocculate the suspended particles and remove turbidity. At the same time, to optimize the particle removal of this alum dosage, the ideal pH should be 7.12. These values are used on the settling test and filtering tests. First, we did a settling test to try to remove 85% of the solid particles in the water at a side water depth of 6 feet. Since the settling was only able to remove 75% of the turbidity in the water, comprising basically larger particles in the water, we used filtration to remove the residual turbidity, eliminating more than 93% of the particles in the water if we use a loading rate of 2 gpm/ft^2. This yields a final turbidity acceptable for drinking water standards. Therefore, with some treatment for turbidity, the Wild River water can be used in the manufacturing plant.

Document 18.3 Draft of Lab Report Discussion

Discussion

Requested by Geo-Hydro Corporation, four water samples from four local sources were drawn and tested in order to determine the best water source for the company's proposed wooden novelty manufacturing facility in Dearth, Wyoming. From the alkalinity, acidity, and hardness tests, the Wild River was determined to be the best water source for the company's new facility since it has relatively moderate alkalinity and acidity, and low hardness compared to other water sources. Also, from the jar test, the pH was determined to be 7.15, which is close to 7; therefore, no treatment is required to adjust the three issues above. However, treatment is required to resolve the turbidity of the water. A jar test was conducted to determine the coagulate dose to use for the settling column. From the settling analysis, the detention time for 85% solids removal was determined to be 53 minutes. However, the settling process alone cannot remove all the contaminants. Therefore, a filtration column with loading rate gpm/ft^2 can be introduced after settling in order to achieve a higher percentage of solid removal, in which the settling column removes the large particles and the filter column removes the small particles. The combination of the two methods can achieve the 85% removal requirement. With the use of both methods above, the Wild River water can be treated to levels suitable for drinking. Based on the results from the laboratory, water from Wild River with the water treatment option is recommended for use with Geo-Hydro's new manufacturing facility.

 **On TechComm Web**

For digital versions of case documents, click on Downloadable Case Documents on **<bedfordstmartins.com/techcomm>**.

"I can see how you might be confused," you say. "Including a summary in a lab report is not very common. Science and engineering articles in scholarly journals, for example, do not contain summaries. However, this assignment might be intended to prepare you to write lab reports for engineering firms that conduct research for other companies. Readers of these lab reports want to know how your findings can improve operations at their companies. In these cases, a summary is an appropriate section to include. You're not the first person in the course to ask me about this. Let me get in touch with your instructor, and I'll get back to you by this weekend."

Your Assignment

1. Using an Internet search engine, locate three or four Internet resources describing how to write executive summaries. Write Maelee a brief e-mail message in which you address her concerns about repeating information. Also offer her some advice, based on her drafts, about how to write an effective abstract, summary, and discussion.

2. Create a one- to two-page handout for students enrolled in CE 320/321 describing the purpose of each of these three sections of the lab report requested by their instructor.

19

Writing Recommendation Reports

Using a Problem-Solving Model for Preparing Recommendation Reports 502

Identify the Problem or Opportunity 502

Establish Criteria for Responding to the Problem or Opportunity 503

Determine the Options 504

Study Each Option According to the Criteria 505

Draw Conclusions About Each Option 506

Formulate Recommendations Based on the Conclusions 506

Writing Recommendation Reports 507

Writing the Body of the Report 508

Writing the Front Matter 511

Writing the Back Matter 516

Sample Recommendation Report 518

Source: Trampe, 2008 <www.trampe.no/english/photogallery.php>.

In the World . . .

The college city of Trondheim, Norway, where 90 percent of the students use bicycles to get around, has a huge hill. Bicyclist Jarle Wanvik invented a device called a bicycle lift to help people get up the hill. You put your right foot on a metal plate that sticks out of a track. Up you go at two meters per second. In 1992, Wanvik proposed his idea to the city's Public Roads Administration as a way to increase bicycle usage and decrease automobile traffic. The Public Roads Administration tested a prototype of the device and wrote a recommendation report urging the city to fund the project. Since 1993, when it was installed, some 250,000 people have used it, without a single injury.

C hapter 17 discussed informational reports: those in which the writer's main purpose is to present information. This chapter discusses recommendation reports. A *recommendation report* presents information but goes one step further by offering suggestions about what readers ought to do next.

Here are some examples of the kinds of questions a recommendation report addresses:

- *What should we do about Problem X?* What should we do about the large number of calls to Technical Support?

- *Should we do Function X?* Although we cannot afford to reimburse tuition for all college courses our employees wish to take, can we reimburse them for classes directly related to their work?

- *Should we use Technology A or Technology B to do Function X?* Should we buy several high-output copiers or a larger number of low-output copiers?

- *We currently use Method A to do Function X. Should we be using Method B?* We sort our bar-coded mail by hand. Should we buy an automatic sorter?

Each of these questions can lead to a wide variety of recommendations, ranging from "Do nothing" to "Study this some more" to "Take the following actions immediately."

A recommendation report can be the final link in a chain of documents that begins with a proposal and continues with one or more progress reports. This last, formal report is often called a *final report*, *project report*, *recommendation report*, *completion report*, or simply *report*. The sample report beginning on page 519 is the recommendation report in the series about buying MP3 players for a gym begun in Chapter 16, page 447, and Chapter 17, page 467.

A recommendation report can also be a freestanding document, one that was not preceded by a proposal or by progress reports. For instance, you might be asked to recommend whether your company should use comp pay: compensating employees who work overtime with time off rather than with overtime pay. This task would call for you to research the subject and write a single recommendation report.

Most recommendation reports discuss questions of feasibility. *Feasibility* is a measure of the practicality of a course of action. For instance, a company might conduct a *feasibility study* of whether it should acquire a competing company. In this case, the two courses of action are to acquire the competing company or not to acquire it. Or a company might do a study to determine which make and model of truck to buy for its fleet.

A feasibility report is a report that answers three kinds of questions:

- *Questions of possibility.* We would like to build a new rail line to link our warehouse and our retail outlet, but if we cannot raise the money, the project is not

▶**In This Book**

For more about proposals and progress reports, see Ch. 16 and Ch. 17, p. 464.

possible. Even if we have the money, do we have government authorization? If we do, are the soil conditions appropriate for the rail link?

- *Questions of economic wisdom.* Even if we can afford to build the rail link, should we do so? If we use all our resources on this project, which other projects will have to be postponed or canceled? Is there a less expensive or a less financially risky way to achieve the same goals?

- *Questions of perception.* If your company's workers have recently accepted a temporary wage freeze, they might view the rail link as inappropriate. The truckers' union might see it as a threat to truckers' job security. Some members of the public might also be interested parties, because any large-scale construction might affect the environment.

USING A PROBLEM-SOLVING MODEL FOR PREPARING RECOMMENDATION REPORTS

The writing process for a recommendation report is similar to that for any technical communication:

- *Planning.* Analyze your audience, determine your purpose, and visualize the deliverable: the report you will submit. Conduct appropriate secondary and primary research.

- *Drafting.* Write a draft of the report.

- *Revising.* Think again about your audience and purpose, then make appropriate changes to your draft.

- *Editing.* Improve the writing in the report, starting with the largest issues of development and emphasis and working down to the sections, paragraphs, sentences, and individual words.

- *Proofreading.* Go through the draft slowly, making sure you have written what you wanted to write. Get help from others.

▶ **In This Book**
For more about the writing process, see Ch. 3 and Ch. 13, p. 342.

In addition to this model of the writing process, you need to understand a problem-solving model for conducting the analysis that will enable you to write the recommendation report. Figure 19.1 shows this problem-solving model. The following discussion explains this model in more detail.

Identify the Problem or Opportunity

What is not working, or not working as well as it might? What situation presents an opportunity for us to decrease costs or improve the quality of our product or service? Without a clear statement of your problem or opportunity, you cannot plan your research.

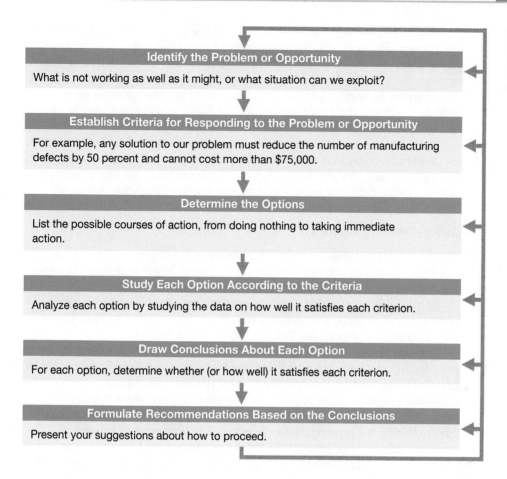

Figure 19.1
A Problem-Solving
Model for
Recommendation
Reports

Identify the Problem or Opportunity

What is not working as well as it might, or what situation can we exploit?

Establish Criteria for Responding to the Problem or Opportunity

For example, any solution to our problem must reduce the number of manufacturing defects by 50 percent and cannot cost more than $75,000.

Determine the Options

List the possible courses of action, from doing nothing to taking immediate action.

Study Each Option According to the Criteria

Analyze each option by studying the data on how well it satisfies each criterion.

Draw Conclusions About Each Option

For each option, determine whether (or how well) it satisfies each criterion.

Formulate Recommendations Based on the Conclusions

Present your suggestions about how to proceed.

For example, your company's employees who smoke are absent and ill more often than those who don't smoke. Your supervisor has asked you to investigate whether the company should offer a free smoking-cessation program. The company can offer the program only if the company's insurance carrier will pay for it. The first thing you need to do is talk with the insurance agent. If the insurance carrier will pay for the program, you can proceed with your investigation. If the agent says no, you have to determine whether another insurance carrier offers better coverage or whether there is some other way to encourage employees to stop smoking.

Establish Criteria for Responding to the Problem or Opportunity

Criteria are standards against which you measure your options. Criteria can take two forms: *necessary* and *desirable*. For example, if you want to buy a photocopier for your business, necessary criteria might be that each copy cost less than two cents to produce and that the photocopier be able to handle oversize documents. If the photocopier doesn't fulfill those two criteria, you will not consider it further. By contrast, desirable criteria might include that the photocopier do double-sided copying and stapling. Desirable criteria let you make distinctions among a variety of similar objects, objectives, actions, or effects. If a photocopier does not fulfill a desirable criterion, you will still consider it, although it will be less attractive.

Until you can establish your criteria, you don't know what your options are. Sometimes, you inherit your criteria: your supervisor tells you how much money you can spend, for instance, and that figure becomes one of your necessary criteria. Other times, you derive your criteria from your research.

▶ **In This Book**

For more about establishing criteria, see Ch. 7, p. 160.

Determine the Options

After you establish your criteria, you determine your options. *Options* are potential courses of action you can take in responding to a problem or opportunity. Determining your options might be simple or complicated.

Sometimes, your options are presented to you. For instance, your supervisor asks you to study two vendors for accounting services and recommend one of them. The options are Vendor A or Vendor B. Simple.

In other cases, you have to consider a series of options. For example, your department's photocopier is old and breaking down. Your first decision is whether to repair it or replace it. Once you have answered that question, you might have to make more decisions. If you are going to replace it, what features should you look for in a new one? Each time you make a decision, you have to answer more questions until, eventually, you arrive at a recommendation. For a complicated scenario like this, you might find it helpful to use logic boxes or flowcharts to sketch the logic of your options, as shown in Figure 19.2.

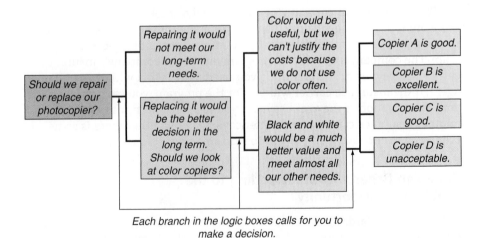

Each branch in the logic boxes calls for you to make a decision.

Figure 19.2   Using Logic Boxes to Plot a Series of Options

As you research your topic, your understanding of your options will likely change. At this point, however, it is useful to understand the basic logic of your options or series of options.

Study Each Option According to the Criteria

Once you have identified your options (or series of options), study each one according to the criteria. For the photocopier project, secondary research would include studying articles about photocopiers in technical journals and specification sheets from the different manufacturers. Primary research might include observing product demonstrations, as well as interviewing representatives from different manufacturers and managers who have purchased different brands.

▶ **In This Book**

For more about research techniques, see Ch. 6.

To make the analysis of the options as objective as possible, professionals sometimes create a *matrix*, a method for systematically evaluating each option according to each criterion. A matrix is a table (or a spreadsheet), as shown in Figure 19.3. Here, the writer is nearly at the end of his series of options: he is evaluating four similar photocopiers according to four criteria.

Does using a matrix ensure an objective analysis? No. Bias can creep in at three stages:

- *Determining which criteria to examine.* In Figure 19.3, the Xerox Model 4500 (option 2) did very poorly on criterion 4. If criterion 4 were removed from the analysis, or if many other criteria were added, the Xerox might score much higher.

- *Deciding the range of values for each criterion.* There is no one "correct" way to determine the range of values for each criterion. If one of your criteria

Option	Criterion 1: Pages per Minute	Criterion 2: Ability to Duplex	Criterion 3: Extra Paper Bins	Criterion 4: Color Printing	Total Points
Option 1: Ricoh Model 311	9	8	7	9	**33**
Option 2: Xerox Model 4500	8	9	7	2	**26**
Option 3: Savin Model 12X	10	8	8	9	**35**
Option 4: Sharp Model S350	7	8	8	9	**32**

Figure 19.3   A Matrix

To use a matrix, you assign a value (0–10 is a common range) for each criterion for each option. Then you add up the values for each option and compare the totals. In this case, option 3 scores the highest, with 35 points; option 2 scores the lowest, with 26 points.

To help your readers understand how you derived your values, you need to explain the scoring system in the report.

was whether the copier could staple, how would you decide to score a machine that does stapling and a machine that does not? If you gave 10 points to a machine that does stapling and 0 points to a machine that does not, you would probably eliminate the nonstapling machine. However, if stapling was relatively unimportant, it might be more reasonable to assign a value of 8 points to nonstapling machines. To help readers understand your thinking, include a brief statement explaining your reasoning for each criterion. For example, for the duplexing criterion in Figure 19.3, explain that you gave a copier 9 points if it could print duplex and 8 points if it could not, because printing duplex was a relatively unimportant criterion. However, for the color criterion, you gave a copier 9 points if it could print in color and 2 points if it could not, because color printing was very important.

- *Assigning values to criteria.* If one of your criteria was ease of operation, you might give one machine a 9, whereas someone else might give it a 3, because he or she is not as familiar with photocopiers as you are. Other criteria might be equally difficult to assess objectively. For example, what value would you give to the cost criterion if one machine cost $12,500 per year to operate and another cost $14,300?

▶**In This Book**

The sample recommendation report in this chapter includes a decision matrix on p. 531.

Evaluating options according to criteria is always subjective. Still, the main advantage of a matrix is that it helps you do a methodical analysis. For your readers, a matrix makes your analysis easier to follow because it clearly presents your methods and results.

Draw Conclusions About Each Option

Whether you use a matrix or a less-formal means of recording your evaluations, the next step is to draw conclusions about the options you studied—by interpreting your results and writing evaluative statements about the options.

For the study of photocopiers, your conclusion might be that the Savin model is the best copier: it meets all your necessary criteria and the greatest number of desirable criteria, or it scores highest on your matrix. Depending on your readers' preferences, present your conclusions in one of three ways.

- *Rank all the options.* The Savin copier is the best option, the Ricoh copier is second best, and so forth.
- *Classify all the options as either acceptable or unacceptable.*
- *Present a compound conclusion.* The Savin offers the most technical capabilities; the Ricoh is the best value.

Formulate Recommendations Based on the Conclusions

If you conclude that Option A is better than Option B and you see no obvious problems with Option A, recommend Option A. But if the problem has changed or your company's priorities or resources have changed, you might decide to recommend a course of action that is inconsistent with the conclusions you derived. Your responsibility is to use your judgment and recommend the best course of action.

WRITING RECOMMENDATION REPORTS

The following discussion presents a basic structure for a recommendation report. Remember that every document you write should reflect its audience, purpose, and subject. Therefore, you are likely to need to modify, add to, or delete some of the elements discussed here.

The easiest way to draft a report is to think of it as consisting of three sections: the front matter, the body, and the back matter. Table 19.1 on page 508 shows the purposes of and typical elements in the three sections.

You will probably draft the body before the front matter and the back matter. This sequence is easiest because you think through what you want to say in the body, then draft the front matter and back matter based on it.

If you are writing your recommendation report for readers from another culture, keep in mind that conventions differ from one culture to another. In the United States, reports are commonly organized from general to specific. That is, the most general information (the abstract and the executive summary) appears early in the report. In many cultures, however, reports are organized from specific to general. Detailed discussions of methods and results precede discussions of the important findings.

Similarly, elements of the front and back matter are rooted in culture. For instance, in some cultures—or in some organizations—writers do not create executive summaries, or their executive summaries differ in length or organization from those discussed here. According to Honold (1999), German

Table 19.1 Elements of a Typical Report

Section of the report	Purposes of the section	Typical elements in the section
Front matter	• to orient the reader to the subject • to provide summaries for technical and managerial readers • to help readers navigate the report • to help readers decide whether to read the document	• letter of transmittal (p. 511) • cover (p. 511) • title page (p. 511) • abstract (p. 511) • table of contents (p. 512) • list of illustrations (p. 513) • executive summary (p. 515)
Body	• to provide the most comprehensive account of the project, from the problem or opportunity that motivated it, to the methods and the most important findings	• introduction (p. 508) • methods (p. 509) • results (p. 509) • conclusions (p. 510) • recommendations (p. 510)
Back matter	• to present supplementary information, such as more-detailed explanations than are provided in the body • to enable readers to consult the secondary sources the writers used	• glossary (p. 516) • list of symbols (p. 516) • references (p. 518) • appendices (p. 518)

users of high-tech products rely on the table of contents in a manual because they like to understand the scope and organization of the manual. Therefore, writers of manuals for German readers should include comprehensive, detailed tables of contents.

Study samples of writing produced by people from the culture you are addressing to see how they organize their reports and use front and back matter.

Writing the Body of the Report

The elements that make up the body of a report are discussed here in the order in which they usually appear. However, you should draft the elements in whatever order you prefer. The sample recommendation report beginning on page 519 shows these elements.

Introduction   The introduction helps readers understand the technical discussion that follows. Start by analyzing who the readers are, then consider these questions:

- *What is the subject of the report?* If the report follows a proposal and a progress report, you can probably copy this information from one of these documents and modify it as necessary. Reusing this information is efficient and ethical.

- *What is the purpose of the report?* The purpose of the report is not the purpose of the project. The purpose of the report is to present information and offer recommendations.

- *What is the background of the report?* Include this information, even if you have presented it before; some of your readers might not have read your previous documents or might have forgotten them.

- *What are your sources of information?* Briefly describe your primary and secondary research, to prepare your readers for a more detailed discussion of your sources in subsequent sections of the report.

- *What is the scope of the report?* Indicate the topics you are including, as well as those you are not.

- *What are the most significant findings?* Summarize the most significant findings of the project.

- *What are your recommendations?* In a short report containing a few simple recommendations, include those recommendations in the introduction. In a lengthy report containing many complex recommendations, briefly summarize them in the introduction, then refer readers to the more detailed discussion in the recommendations section.

- *What is the organization of the report?* Indicate your organizational pattern so that readers can understand where you are going and why.

- *What key terms are you using in the report?* The introduction is an appropriate place to define new terms. If you need to define many terms, place the definitions in a glossary and refer readers to it in the introduction.

In This Book

For more about purpose statements, see Ch. 5, p. 105.

Methods   The methods section answers the question "What did you do?" In drafting the methods section, consider your readers' knowledge of the field, their perception of you, and the uniqueness of the project, as well as their reasons for reading the report and their attitudes toward the project. Provide enough information to help readers understand what you did and why you did it that way. If others will be using the report to duplicate your methods, include sufficient detail.

Results   Whereas the methods section answers the question "What did you do?" the results section answers the question "What did you see?"

Results are the data you have discovered or compiled. Present the results objectively, without comment. Save the interpretation of the results—your conclusions—for later. If you combine results and conclusions, your readers might not be able to follow your reasoning or to tell whether the evidence justifies your conclusions.

Your audience's needs will help you decide how to structure the results. How much they know about the subject, what they plan to do with the report, what they expect your recommendation(s) to be—these and many other factors will affect how you present the results. For instance, suppose that your company is considering installing a VoIP phone system that will allow you to transmit telephone calls over the Internet. In the introduction, you explain the disadvantages of the company's current phone system. In the methods section, you describe how you established the criteria you applied to the available phone systems, as well as your research procedures. In the results section, you provide the details of each phone system you are considering, as well as the results of your evaluation of each system.

Conclusions   Conclusions answer the question "What does it mean?" They are the implications of the results. To draw conclusions, you need to think carefully about your results, weighing whether they point clearly to a single meaning.

In This Book
For more about evaluating evidence, see Ch. 6, pp. 128–32.

Recommendations   Recommendations answer the question "What should we do?" As discussed earlier in this chapter, recommendations do not always flow directly from conclusions. Always consider recommending that the organization take no action, or no action at this time.

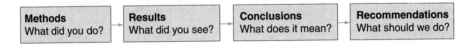

| **Methods** What did you do? | **Results** What did you see? | **Conclusions** What does it mean? | **Recommendations** What should we do? |

Guidelines

Writing Recommendations

As you draft your recommendations, consider the following four factors:

▶ **Content.** Be clear and specific. If the project has been unsuccessful, don't simply recommend that your readers "try some other alternatives." What alternatives do you recommend and why?

▶ **Tone.** When you recommend a new course of action, be careful not to offend whoever formulated the earlier course. Do not write that following your recommendations will "correct the mistakes" that have been made. Instead, your recommendations should "offer great promise for success." A restrained, understated tone is more persuasive because it shows that you are interested only in the good of your company, not personal rivalries.

▶ **Form.** If the report leads to only one recommendation, use traditional paragraphs. If the report leads to more than one recommendation, consider a numbered list.

▶ **Location.** Consider including a summary of the recommendations—or, if they are brief, the full list—after the executive summary or in the introduction as well as at the end of the body of the report.

Writing the Front Matter

Front matter is common in reports, proposals, and manuals. As discussed in Table 19.1 on page 508, front matter helps readers understand the whole report and find the information they seek.

Most organizations have established formats for front matter. Study the style guide used in your company or, if there isn't one, examples from the files to see how other writers have assembled their reports.

Letter of Transmittal   The letter of transmittal, which can take the form of a letter or a memo, introduces the primary reader to the purpose and content of the report. It is attached to the report, bound in with it, or simply placed on top of it. Even though the letter likely contains no information that is not included elsewhere in the report, it is important because it is the first thing the reader sees. It establishes a courteous and professional tone. Letters of transmittal are customary even when the writer and the reader both work for the same organization. See page 519 in the sample recommendation report for an example of a transmittal letter.

▶ **In This Book**
For more about formatting a letter, see Ch. 14, p. 368.

Cover   The cover protects the report from normal wear and tear and from harsher environmental conditions such as water or grease. The cover usually contains the title of the report, the name and position of the writer, the date of submission, and the name or logo of the writer's company. Sometimes, the cover also includes a security notice or a statement of proprietary information.

▶ **In This Book**
For information about materials used in covers and types of bindings, see Ch. 11, p. 260.

Title Page   A title page states at least the title of the report, the names of the authors, and the date of submission. A more complex title page might also include a project number, a list of additional personnel who contributed to the report, and a distribution list. See page 520 in the sample recommendation report for an example of a title page.

Abstract   An abstract is a brief technical summary of the report, usually no more than 200 words. It addresses readers who are familiar with the technical subject and who need to decide whether they want to read the full report. In an abstract, you can use technical terminology and refer to advanced concepts in the field. Abstracts are sometimes published by abstract services, which are useful resources for researchers.

▶ **In This Book**
For more about abstract services, see Ch. 6, p. 123.

Abstracts often contain a list of half a dozen or so keywords, which are entered into electronic databases. As the writer, one of your tasks is to think of the various keywords that will lead people to the information in your report.

There are two types of abstracts: descriptive and informative. A *descriptive abstract*—sometimes called a *topical, indicative,* or *table-of-contents*

This abstract is descriptive rather than informative because it does not explain the criteria or describe the system.

ABSTRACT

"Design of a Radio-Based System for Distribution Automation"

by Brian D. Crowe

At this time, power utilities' major techniques of monitoring their distribution systems are after-the-fact indicators such as interruption reports, meter readings, and trouble alarms. These techniques are inadequate because they are expensive and they fail to provide the utility with an accurate picture of the dynamics of the distribution system. This report describes a project to design a radio-based system for a pilot project. This report describes the criteria we used to design the system, then describes the hardware and software of the system.

Keywords: distribution automation, distribution systems, load, meters, radio-based systems, utilities

Figure 19.4   Descriptive Abstract
Source: Crowe, 1985.

abstract—describes the kinds of information contained in the report. It does not include the major findings (important results, conclusions, or recommendations). It simply lists the topics covered, giving equal emphasis to each. Figure 19.4 is a descriptive abstract from a report by a utility company about its pilot program for measuring how much electricity its customers are using. A descriptive abstract is used most often when space is at a premium. Some government proposals, for example, call for a descriptive abstract to be placed at the bottom of the title page.

An *informative abstract* presents the major findings. If you don't know which kind of abstract the reader wants, write an informative one.

The distinction between descriptive and informative abstracts is not absolute. Sometimes, you have to combine elements of both in a single abstract. For instance, if there are 15 recommendations—far too many to list—you might simply note that the report includes numerous recommendations.

See page 521 in the sample recommendation report for an example of an informative abstract.

Table of Contents   The table of contents, the most important guide to navigating the report, has two main functions: to help readers find the information they want and to help them understand the scope and organization of the report.

A table of contents uses the same headings as the report itself. Therefore, to create an effective table of contents, you must first make sure that the headings are clear and that you have provided enough of them. If the table of contents shows no entry for five or six pages, you probably need to partition the report into additional subsections. In fact, some tables of contents have one entry, or even several, for every report page.

The following table of contents, which relies exclusively on generic headings (those that describe an entire class of items), is too general to be useful.

Table of Contents

Introduction 1
Materials 3
Methods . . . . .4 ◄— *This methods section, which goes from page 4 to page 18, should have sub-entries to break up the text and to help readers find the information they seek.*
Results 19
Recommendations 23
References 26
Appendices 28

For more-informative headings, combine the generic and the specific:

Recommendations: Five Ways to Improve Information-Retrieval Materials Used in the Calcification Study

Results of the Commuting-Time Analysis

Then build more subheadings into the report itself. For instance, in the "Recommendations" example above, you could create a subheading for each of the five recommendations. Once you establish a clear system of headings within the report, use the same text attributes—capitalization, boldface, italics, and outline style (traditional or decimal)—in the table of contents.

When adding page numbers to your report, remember two points:

- The table of contents does not contain an entry for itself.
- Front matter is numbered using lowercase Roman numerals (i, ii, and so forth), often centered at the bottom of the page. The title page of a report is not numbered, although it represents page i. The abstract is usually numbered page ii. The table of contents is usually not numbered, although it represents page iii. The body of the report is numbered with Arabic numerals (1, 2, and so on), typically in the upper outside corner of the page.

See page 522 in the sample recommendation report for an example of a table of contents.

List of Illustrations   A list of illustrations is a table of contents for your figures and tables. List the figures first, then the tables. (If the report contains only figures, call it a *list of figures*. If it contains only tables, call it a *list of tables*.) You may begin the list of illustrations on the same page as the table of

In This Book
For more about text attributes such as typefaces, case, and size, see Ch. 11, p. 268.

In This Book
For more about pagination, see Ch. 9, p. 215.

TECH TIP

How to Format Headers, Footers, and Page Numbers

In writing a report, you might want to use different headers, footers, and page-numbering schemes and styles in different sections of the report. To do this, you will create different sections in your Word file. Within each section, you can modify the headers, footers, and page numbers by using the **Header & Footer** group.

To **insert**, **remove**, or **edit the format** of headers, footers, and page numbers, use the drop-down menus in the **Header & Footer** group on the **Insert** tab.

The **Header & Footer** drop-down menus allow you to insert headers and footers with **built-in styles**.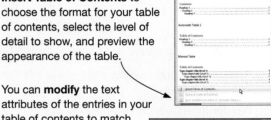

You may also add and modify header and footer text, insert page numbers and dates, and choose the format of page numbers by double-clicking on the header or footer in **Print Layout View** and using the groups on the **Design** tab.

The **Options** group, for example, allows you to specify dif-ferent headers and footers for odd and even pages, as well as for the first page.

The **Page Number** drop-down menu allows you to change the format of page numbers.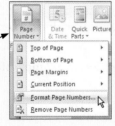

KEYWORDS: header & footer group, options group, header, footer, print layout view, design tab, page number, format page numbers

TECH TIP

How to Create a Table of Contents

To make a table of contents automatically in Word, you must use the **Styles** feature to format the headings in your report.

Place your cursor where you want to create your table of contents.

Use the **Table of Contents** drop-down menu to insert a table of contents with a **built-in style**.

You may also select **Insert Table of Contents** to choose the format for your table of contents, select the level of detail to show, and preview the appearance of the table.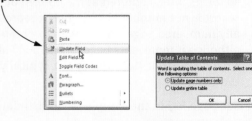

You can **modify** the text attributes of the entries in your table of contents to match the text attributes of the corresponding elements in your report.

If you later change your report and its pagination, you can update the page numbers or the entire table of contents by right-clicking in the table of contents and then select-ing **Update Field**.

KEYWORDS: table of contents, table of contents group, update field, update table of contents

LIST OF ILLUSTRATIONS

Figures

Figure 1.1   U.S. R&D Spending on Biotechnology 11
Figure 1.2   ESCA R&D Spending v. Biotech R&D Spending...14
Figure 2.1   Annual Sales 16
Figure 3.1   Hypothetical New-Product Decision Tree 21
Figure 3.2   Annual Sales 23

Tables

Table 1.1   Industry Costs of the Final Rule (2000 Dollars)..12
Table 1.2   Industry Costs of the Final Rule (2005 Dollars)..12
Table 2.1   Government Costs of the Final Rule (2000 Dollars) 17
Table 2.2   Government Costs of the Final Rule (2005 Dollars) 18
Table 3.1   Applications Not Subject to ESCA..23
Table 3.2   Examples of Microbial Applications Under ESCA 26

Figure 19.5   List of Illustrations

contents, or you may begin the list on a separate page and list it in the table of contents. Figure 19.5 shows a list of illustrations.

Executive Summary   The executive summary (sometimes called the *epitome, executive overview, management summary,* or *management overview*) is a brief condensation of the report addressed to managers. Most managers need only a broad understanding of the projects that the organization undertakes and how they fit together to create a coherent whole.

An executive summary for a report under 20 pages is typically one page (double-spaced). For longer reports, the maximum length is often calculated as a percentage of the report, such as 5 percent.

The executive summary presents information to managers in two parts:

- *Background.* This section explains the problem or opportunity: what was not working, or not working effectively or efficiently; or what potential modification of a procedure or product had to be analyzed.

- *Major findings and implications.* This section might include a brief description—only one or two sentences—of the methods, followed by a full paragraph about the conclusions and recommendations.

An executive summary differs from an informative abstract. An abstract focuses on the technical subject (such as whether the new radio-based system monitors energy usage effectively); an executive summary concentrates on whether the system can improve operations *at a particular company.*

See page 523 in the sample recommendation report for an example of an executive summary.

Guidelines

Writing an Executive Summary

Follow these five suggestions in writing executive summaries:

▶ **Use specific evidence in describing the background.** For most managers, the best evidence includes costs and savings. Instead of writing that the equipment you are now using to cut metal foil is ineffective, write that the equipment jams once every 72 hours on average, costing $400 in materials and $2,000 in productivity. Then add up these figures for a monthly or an annual total.

▶ **Be specific in describing the research.** For instance, research suggests that if your company had a computerized energy-management system, you could cut your energy costs by 20 to 25 percent. If your energy costs last year were $300,000, you could save $60,000 to $75,000.

▶ **Describe the methods briefly.** If you think your readers are interested, include a brief description—no more than a sentence or two.

▶ **Describe the findings according to your readers' needs.** If your readers want to know your results, provide them. If your readers are unable to understand the technical data or are uninterested, go directly to the conclusions and recommendations.

▶ **Ask an outside reader to review your draft.** Give it to someone who has had no connection to the project. That person should be able to read your summary and understand what the project means to the organization.

Writing the Back Matter

The back matter can include any or all of the following items: glossary, list of symbols, references, and appendices.

Glossary and List of Symbols   A glossary, an alphabetical list of definitions, is particularly useful if some of your readers are unfamiliar with the technical vocabulary in your report. Instead of slowing down your discussion by defining technical terms as they appear, you can use boldface, or some similar method of highlighting words, to indicate that the term is defined in the glossary. The first time a boldfaced term appears, explain this system in a footnote. For example, the body of the report might say, "Thus the **positron*** acts as the . . ." while a note at the bottom of the page explains:

*This and all subsequent terms in boldface are defined in the Glossary, page 26.

Although the glossary is usually placed near the end of the report, before the appendices, it can also be placed immediately after the table of contents if the glossary is brief (less than a page) and if it defines essential terms. Figure 19.6 on page 518 shows an excerpt from a glossary.

INTERACTIVE SAMPLE DOCUMENT
Analyzing an Executive Summary

The following executive summary comes from a corporate report on purchasing BlackBerry devices for employees. The questions in the margin ask you to think about the discussion of executive summaries (beginning on page 515). E-mail your responses to yourself and/or your instructor on TechComm Web.

Executive Summary

On May 11, we received approval to study whether BlackBerry devices could help our 20 engineers receive e-mail, monitor their schedules, take notes, and store files they need in the field. In our study, we addressed these problems experienced by many of our engineers:

- They have missed deadlines and meetings and lost client information.
- They have been unable to access important files from the field.
- They have complained about the weight of the binders and other materials—sometimes weighing more than 40 pounds—that they have to carry.
- They have to spend time keyboarding notes that they took in the field.

In 2007, missed meetings and other schedule problems cost the company more than $400,000 in lost business. In addition, our insurance carrier settled a claim for $50,000 from an engineer who experienced back and shoulder problems due to the weight of his pack.

We researched the capabilities of BlackBerry devices, then established these criteria for our analysis:

- The device must weigh less than four ounces.
- It must be compatible with Windows back to 98.
- It must have a full keyboard.
- It must have a built-in GPS.
- It must have a 2.0MP camera.
- It must have at least 64MB of flash memory.
- It must have Bluetooth capability.
- It must cost $400 or less.

On the basis of our analysis, we recommend that the company purchase five BlackBerry Curve 8310 devices, for a total cost of $2,000. These devices best meet all our technical and cost criteria. We further recommend that after a six-month trial period, the company decide whether to purchase an additional 15 devices for the other engineers.

---

1. How clearly does the writer explain the background? Identify the problem or opportunity described in this executive summary.

2. Does the writer discuss the methods? If so, identify the discussion.

3. Identify the findings: the results, conclusions, and recommendations. How clearly has the writer explained the benefits to the company?

 **On TechComm Web**

To e-mail your responses to yourself and/or your instructor, click on Interactive Sample Documents for Ch. 19 on **<bedfordstmartins.com/techcomm>**.

A list of symbols is formatted like a glossary, but it defines symbols and abbreviations rather than terms. It, too, may be placed before the appendices or after the table of contents. Figure 19.7 on page 518 shows a list of symbols.

Glossary

Applicant: A state agency, local government, or eligible private nonprofit organization that submits a request to the Grantee for disaster assistance under the state's grant.

Case Management: A systems approach to providing equitable and fast service to applicants for disaster assistance. Organized around the needs of the applicant, the system consists of a single point of coordination, a team of on-site specialists, and a centralized, automated filing system.

Cost Estimating Format (CEF): A method for estimating the total cost of repair for large, permanent projects by use of construction industry standards. The format uses a base cost estimate and design and construction contingency factors, applied as a percentage of the base cost.

Declaration: The President's decision that a major disaster qualifies for federal assistance under the Stafford Act.

Hazard Mitigation: Any cost-effective measure that will reduce the potential for damage to a facility from a disaster event.

Figure 19.6   Glossary

List of Symbols

β	beta
CRT	cathode-ray tube
γ	gamma
Hz	hertz
rcvr	receiver
SNR	signal-to-noise ratio
uhf	ultra high frequency
vhf	very high frequency

Figure 19.7   List of Symbols

References   Many reports contain a list of references (sometimes called a *bibliography* or *list of works cited*) as part of the back matter. References and the accompanying textual citations throughout the report are called *documentation*. Documentation acknowledges your debt to your sources, establishes your credibility as a writer, and helps readers locate and review your sources. See Appendix, Part B, for a discussion of documentation.

Appendices   An appendix is any section that follows the body of the report (and the glossary, list of symbols, or list of references or bibliography). Appendices (or *appendixes*) convey information that is too bulky for the body or that will interest only a few readers. Appendices might include maps, large technical diagrams or charts, computations, computer printouts, test data, and texts of supporting documents.

Appendices, usually labeled with letters rather than numbers (Appendix A, Appendix B, and so on), are listed in the table of contents and are referred to at the appropriate points in the body of the report. Therefore, they are accessible to any reader who wants to consult them.

SAMPLE RECOMMENDATION REPORT

The following example (Pritiken & Turner, 2008) is the recommendation report on the MP3 project proposed in Chapter 16, page 447. The progress report for this project appears in Chapter 17, page 467.

Total Gym Fitness

2206 Leadville Ave.
Boise, ID 83706

(208) 555-9635
totalgym@msn.com

Memo

Date: December 22, 2008
To: Jill Bookwalter, Owner and Manager
From: Jessie Pritiken, Senior Fitness Trainer
Megan Turner, Fitness Trainer
Subject: Completion Report for Feasibility Study on Music Options for Total Gym Fitness

We have attached our completion report for our feasibility study on music options at our facility. We completed the tasks described in our proposal of November 3, 2008: investigating our members' dissatisfaction with the music we play and researching options for meeting our members' music needs as they exercise.

First, we investigated the extent of the problem by examining the data from our 2007 Annual Member Satisfaction Survey. More than half our members are not satisfied with the music we play. Then we identified our options for addressing this problem. We found that there does not seem to be a clear consensus regarding the type of music people prefer, and playing a different type of music in each area of our facility would be impractical. Therefore, we decided to focus on the purchase of MP3 players for our members' use. Next, we established MP3 player selection criteria and researched available MP3 players according to our criteria.

Based on the information we gathered and reviewed, we recommend buying 15 SanDisk Sansa c240 MP3 players, 15 Tune Belt MP3 Armband Carriers, and five Napster to Go accounts from Napster. We recommend that the gym try a pilot program in which we offer this MP3 service to our members for two months, at a total cost of $1,985, and then revisit the issue and decide whether to continue, revise, or discontinue the program.

We appreciate the opportunity to research options for improving operations at Total Gym Fitness. We look forward to working on other projects in the future. If you have any questions or comments, please contact Jessie Pritiken at extension 4211.

Transmittal "letters" can be presented as memos.

The writers include their titles and that of their primary reader. This way, future readers will be able to tell the positions of the reader and writers.

The subject line indicates the subject (the feasibility study on music options) and the purpose of the report (completion report).

The purpose of the study. Notice that the writers link the completion report to the proposal, giving them an opportunity to state the problem that led to the study.

The methods the writers used to carry out the research. Note that the writers clarify the logic they used: how they decided to study the topic.

The major recommendation.

A polite offer to provide more information.

A good title indicates the subject and purpose of the document. One way to indicate the purpose is to use a generic term—such as analysis, recommendation, summary, or instructions—in a phrase following a colon. For more about titles, see Ch. 9, p. 200.

The names and positions of the principal reader and the writers of the document.

The date the document was submitted.

The name or logo of the writers' organization.

Feasibility Study on Music Options:
A Completion Report

Prepared for: Jill Bookwalter, Owner and Manager

Prepared by: Jessie Pritiken, Senior Fitness Trainer
                  Megan Turner, Fitness Trainer

December 22, 2008

Total Gym Fitness

2206 Leadville Ave.
Boise, ID 83706

(208) 555-9635
totalgym@msn.com

Abstract

"Feasibility Study on Music Options: A Completion Report"

Prepared by: Jessie Pritiken, Senior Fitness Trainer
Megan Turner, Fitness Trainer

In November 2008, Jill Bookwalter, owner and manager of Total Gym Fitness, commissioned a study of how to improve gym members' satisfaction with the music played at the facility. Dissatisfaction with the music played on the overhead speakers has caused members to avoid the gym at certain times and on certain days or to stop their workouts and leave. Because of our members' concern about our music and our interest in not only retaining our members but also helping them reach their fitness goals, we proposed researching options for meeting our members' music needs while exercising. Jill authorized $2,000 for the project, including $1,680 for the MP3 players and accessories and $320 for research labor. First, we researched options for continuing to use the current music system and music format or changing our music format. We concluded that offering members MP3 players to use while they exercise would best meet their needs. We then researched MP3 players. Based on our online research, a questionnaire completed by 120 members, an informal survey of our members, visits to retail outlets, and an evaluation of seven MP3 players, we recommend the SanDisk Sansa c240 as the best choice for the gym. Offering exceptional value and user-friendly features, the Sansa features flash memory, a rechargeable battery, and a compact design. In addition, it supports several audio formats (MP3, WMA, WAV, WMA DRM). By offering MP3 players to our members, Total Gym Fitness can effectively address a major source of member dissatisfaction and introduce an innovative strategy to motivate our members to exercise.

Keywords: fitness, exercise, gym, music, motivation, MP3, SanDisk, Sansa

The title of the report is often enclosed in quotation marks because the abstract might be placed outside the report, in which case the report is a separate document.

Abstracts are often formatted as a single paragraph.

The purpose of the study.

The methods.

The major recommendation.

Note that the writers provide technical information about the MP3 player they are recommending.

A keywords list ensures that if the report is searched electronically, it will register "hits" for each of the terms listed.

Note that the typeface and design of the headings in the table of contents match the typeface and design of the headings in the report itself.

In this table of contents, the two levels of headings are distinguished by type size, type style (roman versus italic), and indentation.

Table of Contents

Executive Summary 1

Introduction 2

Research Methods 3

Results 5

    1. Investigating the Extent of the Problem 5

    2. Identifying Our Best Music Option 6

    3. Determining Our Necessary and Desirable Criteria 7

    4. Selecting MP3 Player Options 8

    5. Evaluating Each MP3 Player Against Our Criteria .9

Conclusions 10

Recommendation 11

References 12

Appendix: Member Questionnaire 13

List of Illustrations

Figures

A list of illustrations (figures and tables) enables the reader to refer to them quickly.

Figure 1. Level of Member Agreement with 2007 Survey Statement 5

Figure 2. Music Format Preference of Members in 2007 6

Tables

Table 1. MP3 Player Necessary Criteria Evaluation 9

Table 2. MP3 Player Decision Matrix 9

Table 3. Cost of MP3 Player Pilot Program 11

1

Executive Summary

We have a reputation at Total Gym Fitness for offering a high-quality gym experience and being responsive to customer requests. We pride ourselves on our ability to meet the fitness needs of all our members by keeping a close watch on emerging fitness trends and by incorporating the latest health and fitness research in our gym programs.

Unfortunately, the majority of our members are clearly dissatisfied with the music we play at our facility. Some members are not renewing their memberships and are taking their business to other facilities. Rather than motivating our members, it seems the music we play prevents some of them from getting a good workout. We are very proud of our focus on member satisfaction in all areas of our facility, and we feel that our commitment to member satisfaction is what sets us apart from our competitors. Yet we are currently driving away our members to our competitors and, consequently, losing money.

We researched options for changing our music format and concluded that offering members MP3 players to use would enable us to meet most of their music needs. By consulting online resources, distributing a questionnaire to 200 members, informally asking our members their preferences for MP3 players while exercising, and visiting retail outlets, we identified several qualified MP3 players that would solve our problem.

After analyzing the data we collected, we recommend the SanDisk Sansa c240 MP3 player for its durability, playlist feature, quality of construction, ease of use, and compact size. The Sansa c240 is the second-most-popular MP3 player on the U.S. market, behind the much more expensive Apple iPod. Based on feedback from our members, most of them would welcome the opportunity to check out an MP3 player to use during their workouts; the custom playlists would help them select music that would motivate them to reach their fitness goals. The total cost for a two-month pilot program would be $1,985, just below our $2,000 budget. Offering MP3 players would address a major concern of our members, add an innovative tool to our already strong fitness program offerings, and distinguish Total Gym Fitness from our competitors.

The executive summary describes the project with a focus on the managerial aspects, particularly the recommendation. Note the writers' emphasis on the problem at Total Gym Fitness and references to customer service and losing business to competitors.

Mentioning member dissatisfaction gets the reader's attention. The writers then describe the symptoms of the problem in customer-service terms. Notice the reference to the financial impact of dissatisfied members.

The writers summarize their methods briefly.

The discussion of the technology is brief. Most managers are not interested in the technical details.

Managers want the bottom line: how much will it cost to implement your recommendation, and what impact will it have on business?

2

Introduction

In some organizations, all first-level headings begin a new page.

On November 6, 2008, we received approval of our proposal to research music options for Total Gym Fitness. This report presents the findings of our study. We researched members' dissatisfaction with the music we play at our facility and considered the impact of such dissatisfaction on their willingness to renew their memberships. We researched our options and concluded that it would be best to conduct a two-month pilot program in which we offered members MP3 players with custom playlists. We then researched available features and associated costs of available MP3 players.

The background and purpose of the report.

An overview of the methods.

The problem we studied is that, based on data from our 2007 Annual Member Satisfaction Survey, the majority of our members are dissatisfied with the music we play. Moreover, their comments revealed that some of our members avoid the gym on certain days or at certain times based on the music we play, and others cut short their workouts. This is troubling not only because we are driving our members away to our competitors but also because we are missing a great opportunity to use music to help our members reach their fitness goals.

A more detailed statement of the background and problem.

Considering this problem, we researched options for changing our music format and concluded that offering members MP3 players to use while they exercise would be the best option for meeting their fitness needs. By consulting online resources, distributing a questionnaire to 200 members, informally asking our members their preferences for MP3 players while exercising, and visiting retail outlets, we identified several qualified MP3 players that would solve our problem.

A more detailed statement of the methods.

We concluded that the SanDisk Sansa c240 MP3 player, at a cost of $75 per player, would be the best fit for our facility. Its durability, cost, playlist feature, quality of construction, and ease of use put it ahead of the competition. Featuring flash memory, a rechargeable battery, and a compact design (1.3 × 3.1 × 0.6 inches), the Sansa c240 supports a variety of audio formats (MP3, WMA, WAV, WMA DRM). We therefore recommend that we purchase 15 SanDisk Sansa c240 MP3 players for our gym, as well as 15 Tune Belt MP3 Armband Carriers and five subscriptions to Napster to Go. We recommend that we try a pilot program in which we offer this MP3 service to our members for two months.

The introduction can present the major findings of the report.

Notice the writers' use of the phrases "We concluded" at the beginning of the paragraph and "We therefore recommend" near the end. Repeating key terms in this way helps readers understand the logic of a report and concentrate on the technical information it contains.

In the following sections, we provide additional details about our research methods, the results we obtained, the conclusions we drew from those results, and our recommendation.

An advance organizer for the rest of the report.

3

Research Methods

To better understand our members' music concerns and consider our options, we performed the following research:

1. We investigated the extent of the problem by determining if we could use our current speaker system to meet our members' music preferences. We used data from the 2007 Annual Member Satisfaction Survey to determine if our current system of playing music throughout our facility could be used to address our members' concerns. Using these data, we sought to determine whether there is a consensus among members regarding their music preferences while exercising.

2. We identified our options for addressing this problem:
    *   *Continuing to use the current music system and music format.* We considered our members' responses on the 2007 Annual Member Satisfaction Survey, as well as relevant comments from members made on Member Suggestion cards in 2008.
    *   *Changing our music format.* We considered our members' music preferences as well as our ability to offer different music formats in different parts of the gym. For example, we might play up-tempo rock music in the free-weight area and classical music in the stretching area.
    *   *Offering members MP3 players to use while they exercise.* Because of the popularity of MP3 players, there are many on the market, and they continue to improve in quality. We distributed a questionnaire to gym members asking them whether they would be interested in this service and which features would be important to them in an MP3 player for use in the gym. We also conducted secondary research on music, electronics, and fitness Web sites to learn whether offering MP3 players for checkout would be a feasible option. We determined whether there would be any intellectual-property issues that might prevent us from creating playlists of songs purchased online and then letting members use the MP3 players in a commercial gym.

3. We identified the main criteria against which we would evaluate the different MP3 players. We started by identifying two necessary criteria:
    *   *Durability.* Exercise often involves strenuous physical activity, repetitive impact, and exposure to moisture. We would need an MP3 player that could withstand the day-to-day rigors of a busy gym. Because of the harsh conditions in which the MP3 players would be used, we decided to consider only those players that were sturdy enough for use in a gym. Therefore, our primary technical question was whether the MP3 player was durable enough to withstand the varied workouts of our members.
    *   *Cost.* We needed to work within a budget of $2,000 for the whole project, including the research.

    Next, we identified four desirable criteria to help us make distinctions among MP3 players. To learn what criteria are important to consider when evaluating an MP3 player, we consulted online resources and distributed a questionnaire (see Appendix, page 13) to a random sample of 200 members, 120 of whom responded. Here are the desirable criteria, from most important to least important:

The writers use the same task organization as in the proposal and progress report.

Because the project is now completed, they have dropped the word task *from their numbered system.*

Notice how the writers describe their primary-research methods. In many organizational reports, writers rely on company records for information.

The writers begin their analysis by determining what their major options were.

The writers' research is woven into the discussion throughout.

If an MP3 player did not meet the two necessary criteria, the writers would not consider it further.

In most projects, writers need to work within a budget. For this reason, cost is often a necessary criterion.

The logic of the research strategy makes sense: use the necessary criteria to narrow down the list of options, then use the desirable criteria to rank all the remaining options.

4

- *Playlist feature.* To meet our members' music preferences, we would need to offer several different playlists on each MP3 player. Consequently, we would need an MP3 player that would enable us to create playlists and allow a member to select a specific playlist during his or her workout.
- *Quality.* An MP3 player made of high-quality material would save the gym money by reducing the need to purchase replacements.
- *Ease of use.* Only about half of our members are comfortable with MP3 player controls, so we would not want to buy an MP3 player that they would find hard to use.
- *Physical size.* Few members would want to wear a heavy, bulky MP3 player while exercising. We would need a lightweight player that could easily fit into an armband carrier.

4. We researched available MP3 player options. To create a list of MP3 players to evaluate, we conducted online research and informally asked members which MP3 player they use at the gym. Our visits to local electronics retailers enabled us to try out MP3 players and talk to people who have been selling and using them for several years.

5. We compared available styles, brands, and models against our criteria. For each criterion, we agreed on a scoring key to aid us in assigning point values. To help us evaluate the MP3 players, we asked a member to try each of them.

6. Finally, we analyzed our data and formulated a recommendation.

The writers assembled a list of options: MP3 players that met the necessary and desirable criteria. Note how they discuss their research methods.

The writers then compared each option against each criterion to see which option best fulfilled the company's needs.

The writers drew conclusions and formulated a recommendation.

5

Results

In this section, we present the results of our research. We cover the extent of our members' dissatisfaction with our current music, options for addressing their concerns, criteria for selecting an MP3 player, and a comparison of qualified MP3 players. The following results correspond to the first five tasks described in the Research Methods section.

The writers present an advance organizer for the results section.

1. *Investigating the Extent of the Problem*

People have a choice of where to exercise in the Boise area, and our members tell us they joined Total Gym Fitness because of our reputation for offering the latest fitness equipment and classes. Our members also tell us that they renew their memberships because of our great customer service. Consequently, when we learned from our 2007 Annual Member Satisfaction Survey that our members are dissatisfied with the music we play at our facility (see Figure 1), we took their concerns very seriously.

The writers present their data on member dissatisfaction with music at the gym.

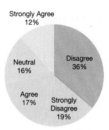

Figure 1.   Level of Member Agreement with 2007 Survey Statement "I am satisfied with the music played at the facility"

Because 55 percent of responding members said that they are not satisfied with the music we play, we examined the survey data more closely to see how we might improve our music. At first we thought that we might address our music problem by simply changing the type of music we play or adjusting the volume. However, there does not seem to be a clear consensus regarding the type of music people prefer to listen to while exercising (see Figure 2, page 6). Although most members prefer country, classic rock, Top 40, and alternative music formats, 20 percent of them prefer other formats. In addition, data from the annual survey indicated that 88 percent of our members are satisfied with the volume of the music.

The writers explain that the music problem can't be easily addressed.

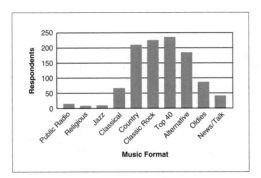

Figure 2.   Music Format Preference of Members in 2007

Finally, we reviewed all the Member Suggestion cards submitted from January 2008 through November 2008. During this time, 98 suggestions were submitted, of which 30 percent offered a negative comment on the music we play. For example, one member commented, "Thank you. Thank you. Thank you for not playing that awful rock music. If you can just play something less monotonous, I'll be in bliss for the next two months until my membership expires and I can join another gym." Such a comment sums up our music problem: many of our members are annoyed by the music we play. Unless we address their concerns, we might lose their business.

The writers explain the business consequences of the problem.

2.   *Identifying Our Best Music Option*
We studied three options:
- *Continuing to use the current music system and music format.* We immediately ruled out this option because it would not address our members' concerns, and we are likely to lose members to other gyms unless we make a change.
- *Changing our music format.* We ruled out this option because it would not address the majority of our members' concerns. Although four music formats are clearly preferred over other formats (see Figure 2), choosing any one of these formats ignores the music preferences of the majority of our members. Because members use different areas during their workouts, and because it is difficult to predict a member's music preference based on where he or she is exercising, we ruled out playing a different music format in each area of the gym. Likewise, because we do not have barriers (e.g., walls) separating many exercise areas, the different music formats would overlap in some areas of the facility and likely just give our members headaches.

The writers ruled out the first two options because neither would effectively address members' concerns.

7

- *Offering members MP3 players to use while they exercise.* Based on data from our annual member survey, it was clear that we can't meet all our members' music needs with an overhead speaker system. However, data from our member questionnaire suggests that members are interested in having MP3 players for checkout. Offering members an opportunity to use an MP3 player with several playlists would address the music problem and offer us a new strategy to keep our members motivated. A member could check out an MP3 player. Moreover, a quick look at online articles confirmed what we already knew as fitness trainers: music motivates people to exercise more (Mercola, 2004), music helps people focus on their workouts (Emerick, 2006), and music helps people meet their fitness goals (Hitti, 2005).

  References to the writers' primary research enhance their credibility.

After reading the conditions of use on several MP3 file vendors' sites, such as iTunes (iTunes, 2008) and Napster (Napster, 2006), we concluded that there appear to be no restrictions on the use of their files in a commercial business. The only restrictions are on the number of players to which you can download a purchased file. For example, Apple allows downloading to seven players, Napster to three. We spoke on the phone with a Napster customer-service representative, Sebastian Dykstra (personal communication, November 11, 2008), to confirm our understanding of the terms of use for Napster songs. No intellectual-property issues would prevent us from offering our members the use of MP3 players. We therefore decided to concentrate our research on finding the best available MP3 player on the market for our needs.

3. Determining Our Necessary and Desirable Criteria

To learn what criteria are important to consider when evaluating an MP3 player for gym use, we consulted online advice on the best music players for a gym and distributed a questionnaire to 200 randomly selected members of our gym.

Based on our research, we determined that for an MP3 player to be considered for further evaluation, it had to meet our necessary durability and cost criteria:

- *Durability.* We valued durability highly. The MP3 player would need to be able to withstand the punishment our members inflict as they exercise. Our primary technical question was this: is the MP3 player durable enough to withstand the varied workouts of our members? We found that whether an MP3 player has moving parts (i.e., a hard drive) has the greatest impact on whether it can hold up to repeated strenuous workouts (Waehner, 2007; Morris, 2005). Consequently, we wanted an MP3 player with flash memory (no moving parts).

  The writers explain how their secondary research helped them understand what makes an MP3 player durable.

- *Cost.* We needed to work within a budget of $2,000. Our primary costs would be purchasing the MP3 players, the armband carriers, and the songs for each player. We wanted to make 15 MP3 players available to members. To keep within our budget, each MP3 player would need to cost less than $100. The remaining money would be spent on armband carriers ($10 each) and five subscriptions to Napster to Go for unlimited music downloads ($12.95 a month per subscription). Keeping the cost of each MP3 player below $100 would also make it less of a budget drain to replace one if it were accidentally broken. Based on responses to our questionnaire, we decided that some costs would be passed on to members who use this service. For example, because of health reasons, we would ask members to bring their own ear buds or purchase inexpensive ear buds available in our pro shop.

8

The writers present their findings based on their desirable criteria.

Cross-referencing the appendix improves the accessibility of the report.

Next, we determined four desirable criteria against which we would evaluate the different options.

- *Playlist feature.* To meet our members' music preferences, we would need to offer several different playlists on each MP3 player. Data from our member questionnaire (see Appendix, page 13) suggest that 75 percent of our members are interested in being able to select from different playlists. Consequently, we wanted an MP3 player that would enable us to create playlists and allow each member to select a specific playlist during his or her workout.
- *Quality.* An MP3 player made of high-quality material would save the gym money by reducing the need to purchase replacements. In addition, our members have come to expect high-quality gym equipment.
- *Ease of use.* We wanted to buy an MP3 player that our members would find easy to use. According to our member questionnaire (see Appendix, page 13), only about half of our members are comfortable using MP3 player controls. It is difficult to evaluate an MP3 player's ease of use just by looking at pictures. To investigate this criterion, we visited local retail shops and asked one of our longtime members, Andrea Luther, to test each player being considered. Because Andrea enjoys listening to music while exercising but does not own an MP3 player, we thought she would effectively serve as a representative user. We asked her to rate each player's ease of use on a 10-point scale (1 = very hard to use; 10 = very easy to use).
- *Physical size.* Our members overwhelmingly would prefer a compact (45 percent) or wallet-size (50 percent) MP3 player (see Appendix, page 13). We also wanted the MP3 player to easily fit in the Tune Belt MP3 Armband Carrier. Recommended by several gym members, this inexpensive ($10) armband carrier offers convenient access to the player; provides protection from bumps and perspiration; and easily adjusts with one hand up to 20 inches circumference (Armband, 2008).

The writers skillfully document their process of compiling a list of MP3 players to investigate further.

4. Selecting MP3 Player Options

We conducted online research (PCMag.com, MP3.com, and CNET.com), informally asked members which MP3 player they use at the gym, and visited experts at our two local retail outlets (Best Buy and Circuit City) to create a list of possible MP3 player options. In each instance, we explained our gym's needs and asked the salespeople to recommend three or four MP3 players that might meet our needs. Based on the information gathered, we chose the seven most commonly recommended models to investigate further:

- Apple iPod Classic (80 GB)
- Apple iPod Nano (third generation, 4 GB)
- Apple iPod Shuffle (second generation, 1 GB)
- iRiver Clix (2 GB)
- Creative Zen (4 GB)
- Creative Zen V Plus (4 GB)
- SanDisk Sansa c240 (1 GB)

9

5. *Evaluating Each MP3 Player Against Our Criteria*

We started by investigating whether our seven recommended models met our necessary criteria for durability and cost (see Table 1). Next, we evaluated each model that met our necessary criteria by using our four desirable criteria. To make our evaluation of remaining options as objective as possible, we created a decision matrix (see Table 2). Included in our matrix is an explanation of how we scored each MP3 player on each criterion.

Table 1. MP3 Player Necessary Criteria Evaluation

Player	Memory Device	Meets Durability Criterion?[1]	Cost	Meets Cost Criterion?[2]	Consider Further?
Apple iPod Classic	Disk Drive	No	$220	No	No
Apple iPod Nano	Flash	Yes	$149	No	No
Apple iPod Shuffle	Flash	Yes	$80	Yes	Yes
iRiver Clix	Flash	Yes	$125	No	No
Creative Zen	Flash	Yes	$90	Yes	Yes
Creative Zen V Plus	Flash	Yes	$95	Yes	Yes
SanDisk Sansa c240	Flash	Yes	$75	Yes	Yes

[1]To meet our necessary *durability* criterion, the player must have flash memory.
[2]To meet our necessary *cost* criterion, the player must retail for less than $100.

The writers explain the logic behind their evaluation system. Without an explanation, this decision matrix would be of little value.

Table 2. MP3 Player Decision Matrix

Player	Playlist Score[1]	Quality Score[2]	Ease-of-Use Score[3]	Physical Size Score[4]	Total Score
Apple iPod Shuffle	0	14	10	10	34
Creative Zen	20	15	7	10	52
Creative Zen V Plus	20	13	6	10	49
SanDisk Sansa c240	20	14	9	10	53

[1]Player scored 0 points for no screen and 20 points for a screen that enables the user to navigate easily among artists, albums, or playlists.
[2]Player scored points (0–20) equal to the sum of the CNET Editors' Rating rounded to the nearest whole number and the CNET Average User Rating rounded to the nearest whole number.
[3]Player scored points equal to the tester's ease-of-use rating on a 10-point scale.
[4]Player scored 10 points if it could fit securely in the Tune Belt MP3 Armband Carrier.

The writers explain their scoring system. This explanation is necessary because the total score for each option will determine the writers' conclusions and recommendation.

10

Conclusions

The function of a conclusion is to explain what the data mean. Here the writers explain why they think the SanDisk Sansa c240 is the best choice for their gym. Notice that a conclusion is not the same as a recommendation.

All seven models—Apple iPod Classic, Apple iPod Nano, Apple iPod Shuffle, iRiver Clix, Creative Zen, Creative Zen V Plus, and SanDisk Sansa c240—are high-quality MP3 players, but the Sansa c240 fared best in our assessment of each player's durability, cost, playlist feature, quality, ease of use, and physical size.

The Sansa c240 is the second-most-popular device on the U.S. market (behind the Apple iPod). The Sansa c240 offers exceptional value and user-friendly features. Featuring flash memory, a rechargeable battery, and a compact design (1.3 × 3.1 × 0.6 inches), the Sansa c240 supports a variety of audio formats (MP3, WMA, WAV, WMA DRM). Although it is the least expensive player that we tested, it received a "very good" Average User Rating on CNET.com. Overall, the Sansa c240 is a durable, inexpensive, easy-to-use, compact MP3 player with the features and quality that will meet our members' music needs.

Although iTunes would allow us to download a single song to seven MP3 players, the unlimited music downloads offered by Napster to Go will give us greater flexibility in creating playlists that will be of interest to our members. This flexibility offsets the need to have a separate subscription for every three MP3 players we want to use.

11

Recommendation

This recommendation states explicitly what the writers think the reader should do next.

We recommend buying 15 SanDisk Sansa c240 MP3 players for our gym. We also recommend the purchase of 15 Tune Belt MP3 Armband Carriers, using the remaining money to purchase five subscriptions to Napster to Go, which would give us access to unlimited songs for $12.95 per month (per subscription). We recommend trying a pilot program in which we offer this MP3 service to our members for two months (see Table 3), at the end of which time we will have an idea of how popular the service is. At that point, we will revisit the issue and decide whether to continue our subscriptions to Napster to Go or switch to another one of Napster's several plans.

The recommendation largely repeats information presented in other places in the report. In technical communication, repetition can reinforce important information and increase your chances of reaching readers who read only selected portions of long documents.

This table concisely presents the cost of the pilot program.

Table 3. Cost of MP3 Player Pilot Program[1]

Expense	Cost[2]
15 Sansa c240 MP3 players	$1,210
15 Tune Belt MP3 Armband Carriers	$175
5 Napster to Go subscriptions	$130
Staff time to create playlists	$150
Staff time already spent on study	$320
Total:	$1,985

[1]Pilot program will last two months.
[2]Cost includes applicable taxes and shipping charges.

We conclude that offering an MP3 player service to our members is most likely to address their dissatisfaction with the music at our gym and to help motivate them to reach their fitness goals.

12

References

Armband carrier for MP3 players & more. (2008). Retrieved November 10, 2008, from
http://www.tunebelt.com/domino/tunebelt/tunebelt.nsf/ab3

CNET MP3 player finder. (2008). Retrieved November 10, 2008, from
http://reviews.cnet.com/4247-6490_7-10-0.html

Emerick, J. (2006). Music aids in exercise motivation. Retrieved November 10, 2008,
from http://media.www.fsunews.com/media/storage/paper920/news/2006/08/31/
ArtsAndEntertainment/Music.Aids.In.Exercise.Motivation-2353196.shtml

Hitti, M. (2005). iPod may jam off the pounds. Retrieved November 11, 2008, from
http://www.medicinenet.com/script/main/art.asp?articlekey=56334

iTunes store terms and conditions. (2008). Retrieved November 9, 2008, from
http://www.apple.com/legal/itunes/ww/

Mercola, J. (2004). Listening to music while exercising boosts brain power. Retrieved
November 10, 2008, from http://articles.mercola.com/sites/articles/archive/2004/04/10/
music-exercise.aspx

Morris, J. (2005). Best MP3 players for the gym. Retrieved November 9, 2008, from
http://reviews.cnet.com/4520-10166_7-5759920-1.html

Napster subscription service and music store terms and conditions. (2006). Retrieved
November 11, 2008, from http://home.napster.com/info/terms.html

Waehner, P. (2007). Top 5 music players & accessories for gym-goers. Retrieved
November 9, 2008, from http://exercise.about.com/od/videosmusicsoftware/tp/
musicplayers.htm

This list of references is written according to the APA documentation style, which is discussed in Appendix, Part B.

13

Appendix: Member Questionnaire

This is a copy of the questionnaire we asked 200 randomly selected members to complete. We received 120 completed questionnaires. In return for their participation, respondents were given a Total Gym Fitness T-shirt. Their responses are included with each question.

Total Gym Fitness Questionnaire

Directions: We are considering making available for checkout MP3 players with custom playlists. We would like your feedback on this idea and your help deciding which features we should consider when evaluating our MP3 player options, if we choose to offer this service. For each question, please circle only one option.

1. If MP3 players with custom playlists were offered for checkout at no cost to you, how likely would you be to use this service?
   A. Very likely **35%**   B. Likely **20%**   C. Not sure **15%**
   D. Unlikely **20%**   E. Very unlikely **10%**

2. If you used this service, how likely would you be to bring your own ear buds or purchase an inexpensive pair available in our pro shop?
   A. Very likely **45%**   B. Likely **25%**   C. Not sure **15%**
   D. Unlikely **5%**   E. Very unlikely **10%**

3. If you have ever used a portable music player (e.g., Walkman, MP3 player) while exercising, how do you prefer to carry the player?
   A. Armband **60%**   B. Waist **20%**   C. Pocket **10%**
   D. Hold it **5%**   E. Other **5%**

4. If several playlists tailored for different types of workouts (e.g., weight training, stretching, yoga, cardio) were available on the MP3 player, how likely would you be to use specific playlists?
   A. Very likely **30%**   B. Likely **45%**   C. Not sure **15%**
   D. Unlikely **5%**   E. Very unlikely **5%**

5. In a typical session, how long do you exercise?
   A. Less than 30 minutes   **10%**   D. 60 to 90 minutes   **15%**
   B. 30 to 45 minutes   **20%**   E. Longer than 90 minutes   **10%**
   C. 45 to 60 minutes   **45%**

6. When exercising, how large do you prefer your MP3 player to be?
   A. Compact **45%**   B. Wallet size **50%**   C. Wide screen **5%**

7. How comfortable are you with using common MP3 player user interfaces (e.g., controls for song selection, volume)?
   A. Very comfortable   **30%**   D. Somewhat uncomfortable   **15%**
   B. Somewhat comfortable   **20%**   E. Very uncomfortable   **15%**
   C. Not sure   **20%**

Writer's Checklist

In planning your recommendation report, did you

- ☐ analyze your audience? (p. 503)
- ☐ analyze your purpose? (p. 503)
- ☐ identify the questions that need to be answered? (p. 503)
- ☐ carry out appropriate research? (p. 503)
- ☐ draw valid conclusions about the results (if appropriate)? (p. 506)
- ☐ formulate recommendations based on the conclusions (if appropriate)? (p. 506)

Does the transmittal letter

- ☐ clearly state the title and, if necessary, the subject and purpose of the report? (p. 511)
- ☐ clearly state who authorized or commissioned the report? (p. 511)
- ☐ briefly state the methods you used? (p. 511)
- ☐ summarize your major results, conclusions, and recommendations? (p. 511)
- ☐ acknowledge any assistance you received? (p. 511)
- ☐ courteously offer further assistance? (p. 511)

Does the cover include

- ☐ the title of the report? (p. 511)
- ☐ your name and position? (p. 511)
- ☐ the date of submission? (p. 511)
- ☐ the company name or logo? (p. 511)

Does the title page

- ☐ include a title that clearly states the subject and purpose of the report? (p. 511)
- ☐ list the names and positions of both you and your principal reader(s)? (p. 511)
- ☐ include the date of submission of the report and any other identifying information? (p. 511)

Does the abstract

- ☐ list the report title, your name, and any other identifying information? (p. 511)
- ☐ clearly define the problem or opportunity that led to the project? (p. 511)
- ☐ briefly describe (if appropriate) the research methods? (p. 511)
- ☐ summarize the major results, conclusions, and recommendations? (p. 511)

Does the table of contents

- ☐ clearly identify the executive summary? (p. 513)
- ☐ contain a sufficiently detailed breakdown of the major sections of the body of the report? (p. 513)
- ☐ reproduce the headings as they appear in the report? (p. 513)
- ☐ include page numbers? (p. 513)

- ☐ Does the list of illustrations (or list of tables or list of figures) include all the graphics found in the body of the report? (p. 513)

Does the executive summary

- ☐ clearly state the problem or opportunity that led to the project? (p. 515)
- ☐ explain the major results, conclusions, recommendations, and managerial implications of your report? (p. 515)
- ☐ avoid technical vocabulary and concepts that a managerial audience is not likely to know? (p. 516)

Does the introduction

- ☐ explain the subject of the report? (p. 508)
- ☐ explain the purpose of the report? (p. 509)
- ☐ explain the background of the report? (p. 509)
- ☐ describe your sources of information? (p. 509)
- ☐ indicate the scope of the report? (p. 509)
- ☐ briefly summarize the most significant findings of the project? (p. 509)
- ☐ briefly summarize your recommendations? (p. 509)
- ☐ explain the organization of the report? (p. 509)
- ☐ define key terms used in the report? (p. 509)

- ☐ Does the methods section describe your methods in sufficient detail? (p. 509)
- ☐ Have you justified your methods where necessary, explaining, for instance, why you chose one method over another? (p. 509)

Are the results presented

- ☐ clearly? (p. 509)
- ☐ objectively? (p. 509)
- ☐ without interpretation? (p. 509)

Are the conclusions

- ☐ presented clearly? (p. 510)
- ☐ drawn logically from the results? (p. 510)

Are the recommendations

- ☐ clear? (p. 510)
- ☐ objective? (p. 510)
- ☐ polite? (p. 510)
- ☐ in an appropriate form (list or paragraph)? (p. 510)
- ☐ in an appropriate location? (p. 510)

☐ Does the glossary include definitions of all the technical terms your readers might not know? (p. 516)

☐ Does the list of symbols include all the symbols and abbreviations your readers might not know? (p. 516)

☐ Does the list of references include all your sources and adhere to an appropriate documentation system? (p. 518)

☐ Do the appendices include the supporting materials that are too bulky to present in the report body or are of interest to only a small number of your readers? (p. 518)

Exercises

▶ **In This Book** For more about memos, see Ch. 14, p. 377.

1. An important element in carrying out a feasibility study is determining the criteria by which to judge each option. For each of the following topics, list five necessary criteria and five desirable criteria you might apply in assessing the options.

   a. buying a cell phone

   b. selecting a major

   c. choosing a company to work for

   d. buying a car

   e. choosing a place to live while you attend college

2. **INTERNET EXERCISE** In Links Library for Chapter 6 on <bedfordstmartins.com/techcomm>, find a site that links to government agencies and departments. Find a recommendation report on a subject that interests you. In what ways does the structure of the report differ from the structure described in this chapter? In other words, does it lack some of the elements described in this chapter, or does it have additional elements? Are the elements arranged in the same order in which they are described in this chapter? In what ways do the differences reflect the audience, purpose, and subject of the report?

3. **GROUP EXERCISE** Write the recommendation report for the research project you proposed in response to Exercise 3 on page 452 in Chapter 16. Your instructor will tell you whether the report is to be written individually or collaboratively, but work with a partner in reviewing and revising your report. You and your partner will work together closely at the end of the project as you revise your reports, but keep in mind that a partner can be very helpful during the planning phase, too, as you choose a topic, refine it, and plan your research.

4. **INTERNET EXERCISE** Secure a recommendation report for a project subsidized by a city or federal agency, a private organization, or a university committee or task force. (Be sure to check your university's Web site; universities routinely publish strategic planning reports and other sorts of self-study reports. Also check <www.nas.edu>, which is the site for the National Academy of Sciences, the National Academy of Engineering, the Institute of Medicine, and the National Research Council, all of which publish reports on the Web.) In a memo to your instructor, analyze the report. Overall, how effective is the report? How could the writers have improved the report? If possible, submit a copy of the report along with your memo.

Case 19: Analyzing Options and Drawing Conclusions

In This Book For more about memos, see Ch. 14, p. 377.

Background

Pioneer Construction, based in Syracuse, New York, offers a range of construction services, including feasibility studies, negotiated design construction, traditional-plan and spec-bid construction, and construction management. With more than 100 full-time employees and sales reaching $38 million annually, Pioneer builds everything from shopping centers and warehouses to restaurants and churches. In addition to heavy-duty construction equipment and vehicles, Pioneer maintains a fleet of 10 pickup trucks. Pioneer's construction supervisors use these trucks to travel to construction sites, haul tools and equipment, and transport clients.

Currently, Pioneer is using an aging fleet of trucks. Bought before many of the safety and comfort features standard in new pickups were available, these trucks do not reflect the focus on safety and quality that the company wishes to convey to clients, nor do they allow the construction supervisors to carry out their duties efficiently. At a recent meeting, a construction supervisor lamented, "My truck spends more time out of service than in service." This remark prompted dozens of other comments critical of the company's trucks. These comments only reinforced what the company president, Mattias van Noordennen, already knew: it was time to replace the company's pickup trucks.

"What type of truck should we buy?" Mattias asked.

"Ram 2500 Quad Cab," one supervisor suggested.

"I like the GMC Sierra 2500's tight turning radius," another suggested.

Someone else added, "The ground clearance of the Chevrolet Silverado 2500HD is impressive."

A fourth supervisor began, "I agree. The Silverado's 3,125-pound payload capacity—"

"Wait a second," Mattias interrupted. "Do we know if we need that heavy a capacity for our pickups? I think we should first determine what we *need* our new trucks to be able to do. Then we can decide what we'd *like* them to be able to do. I know that your job duties vary, but I am confident that each of you can describe typical ways in which you use your pickup at work." Mattias then outlined how he would like to proceed: each construction supervisor will send him an e-mail message in which the supervisor briefly summarizes how he or she typically uses his or her truck.

After the meeting, Mattias stopped by your office. He asked you and your colleagues in the documentation department to help him develop evaluation criteria. "Because of your team's experience in responding to evaluation criteria in our clients' RFPs, as well as in developing criteria for our company's IFBs, I thought you could help us come up with evaluation criteria to use when we select a replacement truck for our pickup fleet. Take a look at the construction supervisors' comments and figure out what they are looking for in a pickup truck. Our budget will limit the cost of each truck to no more than $35,000." (See Document 19.1.)

Your Assignment

1. Based on the information provided by the construction supervisors and your own research on heavy-duty pickups, write Mattias a memo in which you recommend the *necessary* and *desirable* criteria the company should use to select a replacement vehicle for the pickup fleet.

2. Create a decision matrix for company officials to use to evaluate each vehicle option systematically according to each desirable criterion you have established. Include a scoring key that lists the range of values for each criterion and explains how to use the guide to score the vehicle options objectively.

3. Based on data from your decision matrix, write the conclusions and recommendations sections of a feasibility report on replacing the pickup fleet at Pioneer.

**Document 19.1
Construction Supervisors'
Comments**

On TechComm Web

For digital versions of case documents, click on Downloadable
Case Documents on
<bedfordstmartins.com/
techcomm>.

Chris Wetzler

I practically live in my truck, so comfort and safety are important to me. I need a truck that is comfortable enough for daily use and rugged enough for off-road use. I probably spend 60% of my time on paved roads and the rest on dirt or snow. Although many of us don't often fill the truck's bed to full capacity, when I do, I need at least 6 feet 6 inches to comfortably haul materials—a short bed won't do. This stuff isn't very heavy (half a ton at most).

Geordie Olsson

I carry a lot of tools with me, both in the cab and in the bed. I also tow up to 10,000 lbs. a couple of times a month. I use the front seat of my truck as a desk. I'm frequently on dirt roads requiring high clearance. In the winter, 4WD has helped me get to sites that I couldn't reach with 2WD. When visiting sites, I use the cab to carry blueprints and other large items that are too fragile or sensitive to leave exposed to the elements.

Libby Sabanosh

Towing equipment every day, I lug a healthy 7,000 to 9,000 pounds to work sites. A truck with lots of muscle would be great. It seems that it's never just me in the truck. I usually take a few folks from the office to a site. I also taxi people back to the office. At times, I need to carry one-ton loads in the bed. The items are not bulky but can be almost seven feet in length.

Hank de Vre

I frequently take two or three clients to a site. I'm a little embarrassed to ask all of them to squeeze into the front seat with me. The backseat is just not big enough for adults to ride comfortably. I also notice the look on their faces when they discover that my truck is missing its seat belts in back. I tow up to 9,500 lbs. and loads up to 2,000 lbs. in the bed.

Sara Fedarko

I haul building supplies or other cargo of significant length and weight: up to seven feet and 2,500 pounds. Although I usually travel by myself, a couple of times a month I drive with passengers. I frequently use 4WD at muddy sites, especially in the winter. Electronic traction control would be nice. Thankfully, I've never needed air bags, but I'd appreciate front and side air bags.

Writing Definitions, Descriptions, and Instructions

20

Writing Definitions 540

Analyzing the Writing Situation for Definitions 541

Determining the Kind of Definition to Write 541

Deciding Where to Place the Definition 547

Writing Descriptions 549

Analyzing the Writing Situation for Descriptions 549

Indicating the Nature and Scope of the Description 550

Introducing the Description Clearly 550

Providing Appropriate Detail 552

Concluding the Description 553

A Look at Sample Descriptions 554

Writing Instructions 558

Designing a Set of Instructions 558

Planning for Safety 560

Drafting Effective Instructions 562

Revising, Editing, and Proofreading Instructions 566

A Look at Sample Instructions 566

Writing Manuals 572

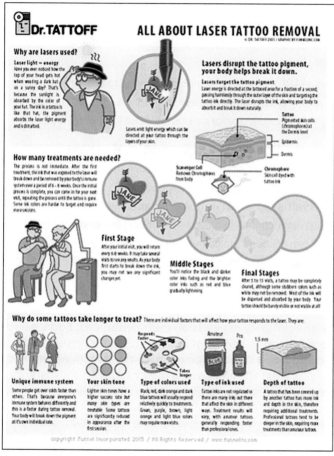

Source: Funnel, Inc., 2005 <www.funnelinc.com/funl_tattoff_detail.html>.

In the World . . .

Graphics are fundamentally important in writing descriptions and instructions, because they can clarify complex concepts, show actions that occur over time, and help bridge language barriers. Even though you cannot easily read the text in this description of the process of removing tattoos, the graphics help you understand the concepts.

W e need to start with three definitions:

- A *definition* is typically a brief explanation of an item or concept using words and (sometimes) graphics. You could write a definition of *file format* or of *regenerative braking.*

- A *description* is typically a longer explanation, usually accompanied by graphics, of an item, concept, or process. You could write a description of a *windmill*, of *global warming*, or of *shale-oil extraction.*

- A set of *instructions* is a kind of process description intended to enable a person to carry out a task. It is almost always accompanied by graphics. You could write a set of instructions for laying a brick patio or for making a playlist for your MP3 player.

Regardless of your field, you will write definitions, descriptions, and instructions frequently in the workplace. A NASA physicist speaking to a congressional hearing about plans to build a *solar-sail-powered spacecraft* might define it, then describe it and its capabilities. If the spacecraft is approved and goes into production, technical communicators will write various instructional documents describing its construction, use, and maintenance. Whether you are communicating with other technical professionals, with managers, or with the public, you need to be able to define and describe your topic.

WRITING DEFINITIONS

The world of business and industry depends on clear definitions. Suppose you learn at a job interview that the employer pays tuition and expenses for employees' job-related education. You'll need to study the employee-benefits manual to understand just what the company will pay for. Who, for instance, is an *employee*? Is it anyone who works for the company, or is it someone who has worked for the company full-time (40 hours per week) for at least six uninterrupted months? What is *tuition*? Does it include incidental laboratory or student fees? What is *job-related education*? Does a course about time management qualify under the company's definition? What, in fact, constitutes *education*?

Definitions are common in communicating policies and standards "for the record." Definitions also have many uses outside legal or contractual contexts. Two such uses occur frequently:

- *Definitions clarify a description of a new development or a new technology in a technical field.* For instance, a zoologist who has discovered a new animal species names and defines it.

- *Definitions help specialists communicate with less-knowledgeable readers.* A manual explaining how to tune up a car includes definitions of parts and tools.

Definitions, then, are crucial in many kinds of technical communication, from brief letters and memos to technical reports, manuals, and journal articles. All readers, from the general reader to the expert, need effective definitions to carry out their jobs.

Analyzing the Writing Situation for Definitions

The first step in writing effective definitions is to analyze the writing situation: the audience and the purpose of the document.

▷ In This Book
For more about audience and purpose, see Ch. 5.

Unless you know who your readers will be and how much they know about the subject, you cannot determine which terms to define or what kind of definition to write. Physicists wouldn't need a definition of *entropy*, but lawyers might. Builders know what a Molly bolt is, but many insurance agents don't.

When you write to people whose first language is not English, definitions are particularly important. Consider the following suggestions:

- *Add a glossary: a list of definitions.* For more about glossaries, see Chapter 19, page 516.

- *Use Simplified English and easily recognizable terms in definitions.* For more about Simplified English, see Chapter 10, page 245.

- *Pay close attention to key terms.* Be sure to carefully define terms that are essential for understanding the document. If, for instance, your document is about angioplasty, you will want to be especially careful when defining it.

- *Use visuals to help readers understand a term or concept.* Graphics are particularly helpful to readers of different languages, and they reduce the cost of translating text from one language to another.

Think, too, about your purpose. For readers who need only a basic understanding of a concept—say, *time-sharing vacation resorts*—a brief, informal definition is usually sufficient. However, readers who need to understand an object, process, or concept thoroughly and be able to carry out related tasks need a more formal and elaborate definition. For example, the definition of a "Class 2 Alert" written for operators at a nuclear power plant must be comprehensive, specific, and precise.

Determining the Kind of Definition to Write

Definitions can be short or long, informal or formal; it depends on your audience and your purpose. There are three basic types of definitions: parenthetical, sentence, and extended.

Writing Parenthetical Definitions   A *parenthetical definition* is a brief clarification within an existing sentence. Sometimes, a parenthetical definition is simply a word or phrase that is enclosed in parentheses or commas or introduced by a colon or dash. In the following examples, the term being defined is shown in italics, and the definition is underscored:

The computers were infected by a *Trojan horse* (<u>a destructive program that appears to be benign</u>).

Before the metal is plated, it is immersed in the *pickle*: <u>an acid bath that removes scales and oxides from the surface</u>.

Parenthetical definitions are not meant to be comprehensive; rather, they serve as quick and convenient ways of introducing terms. But make sure your definition is clear. You have gained nothing if readers don't understand it:

Next, check for blight on the *epicotyl*, <u>the stem portion above the cotyledons.</u>

Readers who need a definition of *epicotyl* are unlikely to know the meaning of *cotyledons*.

Writing Sentence Definitions   A *sentence definition*—a one-sentence clarification—is more formal than a parenthetical definition. A sentence definition usually follows a standard pattern: the item to be defined is placed in a category of similar items and then distinguished from them.

Item	=	*Category*	+	*Distinguishing characteristics*
Crippleware	is	shareware		in which some features of the program are disabled until the user buys a license to use the program.
Hypnoanalysis	is	a psychoanalytical technique		in which hypnosis is used to elicit information from a patient's unconscious mind.

In many cases, a sentence definition also includes a graphic. For example, a definition of an electron microscope would probably include photographs, diagrams, or drawings.

Writers often use sentence definitions to present a working definition for a particular document: "In this report, *electron microscope* refers to any microscope that uses electrons rather than visible light to produce magnified images." Such definitions are sometimes called *stipulative definitions*, because the writer is stipulating how the term will be used in the document.

Guidelines

Writing Effective Sentence Definitions

The following four suggestions can help you write effective sentence definitions:

▶ **Be specific in stating the category and the distinguishing characteristics.** If you write "A Bunsen burner is a burner that consists of a vertical metal tube connected to a gas source," the imprecise category—"a burner"—ruins the definition: many types of large-scale burners use vertical metal tubes connected to gas sources.

▶ **Don't describe a specific item if you are defining a general class of items.** If you wish to define *catamaran*, don't describe a particular catamaran. The catamaran you see on the beach in front of you might be made by Hobie and have a white hull and blue sails, but those characteristics are not essential to catamarans in general.

▶ **Avoid writing circular definitions—that is, definitions that merely repeat the key words or the distinguishing characteristics of the item being defined in the category.** The definition "A required course is a course that is required" is useless: required of whom, by whom? However, in defining electron microscopes, you can repeat *microscope* because *microscope* is not the difficult part of the item. The purpose of defining *electron microscope* is to clarify *electron* as it applies to a particular type of microscope.

▶ **Be sure the category contains a noun or a noun phrase rather than a phrase beginning with *when*, *what*, or *where*.**

INCORRECT	A brazier is what is used to . . .
CORRECT	A brazier is a metal pan used to . . .
INCORRECT	Hypnoanalysis is when hypnosis is used to . . .
CORRECT	Hypnoanalysis is a psychoanalytical technique in which . . .

Writing Extended Definitions   An *extended definition* is a detailed explanation—usually one or more paragraphs—of an object, process, or idea. Often, an extended definition begins with a sentence definition, which is then elaborated. For instance, the sentence definition "An electrophorus is a laboratory instrument used to generate static electricity" tells you the basic function of the device, but it doesn't explain how it works, what it is used for, and its strengths and limitations. An extended definition would address these and other topics.

There is no one way to "extend" a definition. Your analysis of the audience and purpose of your communication will help you decide which method to use. In fact, an extended definition sometimes employs several of the eight techniques discussed here.

Graphics   Perhaps the most common way to present an extended definition in technical communication is to use a graphic, then explain it. Graphics are useful in defining not only physical objects but also concepts and ideas.

In This Book
For more about graphics, see Ch. 12.

A definition of *temperature inversion*, for instance, might include a diagram showing the forces that create temperature inversion.

The following passage from an extended definition of *additive color* shows how graphics can complement words in an extended definition.

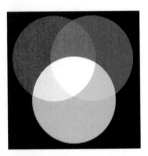

The graphic effectively and economically clarifies the concept of additive color.

Additive color is the type of color that results from mixing colored light, as opposed to mixing pigments such as dyes or paints. When any two colored lights are mixed, they produce a third color that is lighter than either of the two original colors, as shown in this diagram. And when green, red, and blue lights are mixed together in equal parts, they form white light.

We are all familiar with the concept of additive color from watching TV monitors. A TV monitor projects three beams of electrons—one each for red, blue, and green—onto a fluorescent screen. Depending on the combinations of the three colors, we see different colors on the screen.

Examples   Examples are particularly useful in making an abstract term easier to understand. The following paragraph is an extended definition of *hazing activities* (Fraternity, 2003).

No chapter, colony, student or alumnus shall conduct nor condone hazing activities. Hazing activities are defined as: "Any action taken or situation created, intentionally, whether on or off fraternity premises, to produce mental or physical discomfort, embarrassment, harassment, or ridicule. Such activities may include but are not limited to the following: use of alcohol; paddling in any form; creation of excessive fatigue; physical and psychological shocks; quests, treasure hunts, scavenger hunts, road trips or any other such activities carried on outside or inside of the confines of the chapter house; wearing of public apparel which is conspicuous and not normally in good taste; engaging in public stunts and buffoonery; morally degrading or humiliating games and activities; and any other activities which are not consistent with academic achievement, fraternal law, ritual or policy or the regulations and policies of the educational institution or applicable state law."

This extended definition is effective because the writer has presented a clear sentence definition followed by numerous examples.

Partition   Partitioning is the process of dividing a thing or an idea into smaller parts so that readers can understand it more easily. The following example (Brain, 2005) uses partition to define *computer infection*.

▶ **In This Book**

For more about partitioning, see Ch. 7, p. 162.

Types of Infection

When you listen to the news, you hear about many different forms of electronic infection. The most common are:

- **Viruses**—A virus is a small piece of software that piggybacks on real programs. For example, a virus might attach itself to a program such as a spreadsheet program. Each time the spreadsheet program runs, the virus runs, too, and it has the chance to reproduce (by attaching to other programs) or wreak havoc.

- **E-mail viruses**—An e-mail virus moves around in e-mail messages, and usually replicates itself by automatically mailing itself to dozens of people in the victim's e-mail address book.

- **Worms**—A worm is a small piece of software that uses computer networks and security holes to replicate itself. A copy of the worm scans the network for another machine that has a specific security hole. It copies itself to the new machine using the security hole, and then starts replicating from there, as well.

- **Trojan horses**—A Trojan horse is simply a computer program. The program claims to do one thing (it may claim to be a game) but instead does damage when you run it (it may erase your hard disk). Trojan horses have no way to replicate automatically.

Principle of Operation   Describing the principle of operation—the way something works—is an effective way to develop an extended definition, especially for an object or a process. The following excerpt from an extended definition of *adaptive cruise control* (U.S. Department of Transportation, 2007) is based on the mechanism's principle of operation.

Without target vehicle

With target vehicle

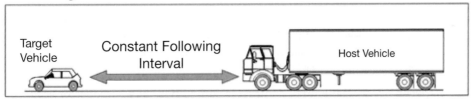

The system maintains the host vehicle's following interval by adjusting its speed. If the target vehicle speeds up, increasing the following interval between the two vehicles, the system informs the engine control module to accelerate and increase the vehicle's speed until either the set following interval or the cruise control preset speed are reached. However, if the gap between the target and the host vehicles is decreasing, the system informs the engine control module to reduce the vehicle's speed. The engine control module then issues a command to dethrottle the engine (e.g., by reducing fuel), apply the engine brake, and, when available, downshift the automated transmission.

Comparison and Contrast   Using comparison and contrast, a writer discusses the similarities or differences between the item being defined and an item with which readers are more familiar. The following definition of VoIP (Voice over Internet Protocol) contrasts this new form of phone service to the form we all know.

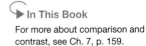

In This Book

For more about comparison and contrast, see Ch. 7, p. 159.

Voice over Internet Protocol is a form of phone service that lets you connect to the Internet through your cable or DSL modem. VoIP service uses a device called a telephony adapter, which attaches to the broadband modem, transforming phone pulses into IP packets sent over the Internet.

VoIP is considerably cheaper than traditional phone service: for as little as $20 per month, users get unlimited local and domestic long-distance service. For international calls, VoIP service is only about three cents per minute, about a third the rate of traditional phone service. In addition, any calls from one person to another person with the same VoIP service provider are free.

However, sound quality on VoIP cannot match that of a traditional land-based phone. On a good day, the sound is fine on VoIP, but frequent users comment on clipping and dropouts that can last up to a second. In addition, sometimes the sound has the distant, tinny quality of some of today's cell phones.

In this excerpt, the second and third paragraphs briefly compare VoIP and traditional phone service. Notice that this passage is organized according to the part-by-part comparison-and-contrast pattern. For more about this organizational pattern, see Ch. 7, p. 160.

Analogy   An *analogy* is a specialized kind of comparison. In a traditional comparison, the writer compares one item to another, similar item: an electron microscope to a common microscope, for example. In an analogy, however, the item being defined is compared to an item that is in some ways completely different but that shares some essential characteristic. For instance, the central processing unit of a computer is often compared to a brain. Obviously, these two items are very different, except that the relationship of the central processing unit to the computer is similar to that of the brain to the body.

The following example from a definition of *decellularization* (Falco, 2008) shows an effective use of an analogy.

Researchers at the University of Minnesota were able to create a beating [rat] heart using the outer structure of one heart and injecting heart cells from another rat. Their findings are reported in the journal *Nature Medicine*. Rather than building a heart from scratch, which has often been mentioned as a possible use for stem cells, this procedure takes a heart and breaks it down to the outermost shell. It's similar to taking a house and gutting it, then rebuilding everything inside. In the human version, the patient's own cells would be used.

The writer of this passage uses the analogy of gutting a house to clarify the meaning of decellularization.

Negation   A special kind of contrast is sometimes called *negation* or *negative statement*. Negation clarifies a term by distinguishing it from a different term with which readers might confuse it. The following example uses negation to distinguish the term *ambulatory* from *ambulance*.

An ambulatory patient is not a patient who must be moved by ambulance. On the contrary, an ambulatory patient is one who can walk without assistance from another person.

Negation is rarely the only technique used in an extended definition; in fact, it is used most often in a sentence or two at the start. Once you have explained what the item is not, you still have to explain what it is.

Etymology   *Etymology*, the derivation of a word, is often a useful and interesting way to develop a definition. The following example uses the etymology of *spam*—unsolicited junk e-mail—to define it.

For many decades, Hormel Foods has manufactured a luncheon meat called Spam, which stands for "Shoulder Pork and hAM"/"SPiced hAM." Then, in the 1970s, the English comedy team Monty Python's Flying Circus broadcast a skit about a restaurant that served Spam with every dish. In describing each dish, the waitress repeats the word *Spam* over and over, and several Vikings standing in the corner chant the word repeatedly. In the mid-1990s, two businessmen hired a programmer to write a program that would send unsolicited ads to thousands of electronic newsgroups. Just as Monty Python's chanting Vikings drowned out other conversation in the restaurant, the ads began drowning out regular communication online. As a result, people started calling unsolicited junk e-mail *spam*.

Etymology is a popular way to begin definitions of *acronyms*, which are abbreviations pronounced as words:

RAID, which stands for redundant array of independent (or inexpensive) disks, refers to a computer storage system that can withstand a single (or, in some cases, even double) disk failure.

Etymology, like negation, is rarely used alone in technical communication, but it is an effective way to introduce an extended definition.

A Sample Extended Definition   Figure 20.1 on page 548 is an example of an extended definition addressed to a general audience.

Deciding Where to Place the Definition

If you are writing a sentence definition or an extended definition, you need to decide where to put it. A definition is typically placed in one of these six locations:

- *In the text.* The text is an appropriate place for sentence definitions that many or most of your readers will need and for extended definitions of important terms.

- *In a marginal gloss.* Sentence definitions placed in the margin are easy to see, and they don't interrupt readers who don't need them.

- *In a hyperlink.* In a hypertext document such as a Web page, definitions can be put in a separate file, enabling readers to click on (or mouse over) highlighted or underlined words to view the definitions.

- *In a footnote.* A footnote is a logical place for an occasional sentence definition or extended definition. Readers who don't need it will ignore it. However, footnotes can slow readers down by interrupting the flow of the discussion. If you think you will need more than one footnote for a definition on every two to three pages, consider including a glossary.

- *In a glossary.* A glossary—an alphabetized list of definitions—can accommodate sentence definitions and extended definitions of fewer than three or four paragraphs in one convenient location. A glossary can be

In This Book

For more about glossaries and appendices, see Ch. 19, pp. 516 and 518.

The first paragraph of this extended definition of the greenhouse effect begins with a general description and ends with a sentence that explains the etymology of the term.

The body of this extended definition is a discussion of the factors that have increased the greenhouse effect.

Questions are effective in topic sentences, particularly in discussions aimed at general readers.

This diagram aids the reader by visually summarizing the principle of operation of the greenhouse effect.

THE GREENHOUSE EFFECT

Energy from the sun drives the earth's weather and climate, and heats the earth's surface; in turn, the earth radiates energy back into space. Atmospheric greenhouse gases (water vapor, carbon dioxide, and other gases) trap some of the outgoing energy, retaining heat somewhat like the glass panels of a greenhouse.

Without this natural "greenhouse effect," temperatures would be much lower than they are now, and life as known today would not be possible. Instead, thanks to greenhouse gases, the earth's average temperature is a more hospitable 60°F. However, problems may arise when the atmospheric concentration of greenhouse gases increases.

Since the beginning of the industrial revolution, atmospheric concentrations of carbon dioxide have increased nearly 30%, methane concentrations have more than doubled, and nitrous oxide concentrations have risen by about 15%. These increases have enhanced the heat-trapping capability of the earth's atmosphere. Sulfate aerosols, a common air pollutant, cool the atmosphere by reflecting light back into space; however, sulfates are short-lived in the atmosphere and vary regionally.

Why are greenhouse gas concentrations increasing? Scientists generally believe that the combustion of fossil fuels and other human activities are the primary reason for the increased concentration of carbon dioxide. Plant respiration and the decomposition of organic matter release more than 10 times the CO_2 released by human activities; but these releases have generally been in balance during the centuries leading up to the industrial revolution with carbon dioxide absorbed by terrestrial vegetation and the oceans.

What has changed in the last few hundred years is the additional release of carbon dioxide by human activities. Fossil fuels burned to run cars and trucks, heat homes and businesses, and power factories are responsible for about 98% of U.S. carbon dioxide emissions, 24% of methane emissions, and 18% of nitrous oxide emissions. Increased agriculture, deforestation, landfills, industrial production, and mining also contribute a significant share of emissions. In 1997, the United States emitted about one-fifth of total global greenhouse gases.

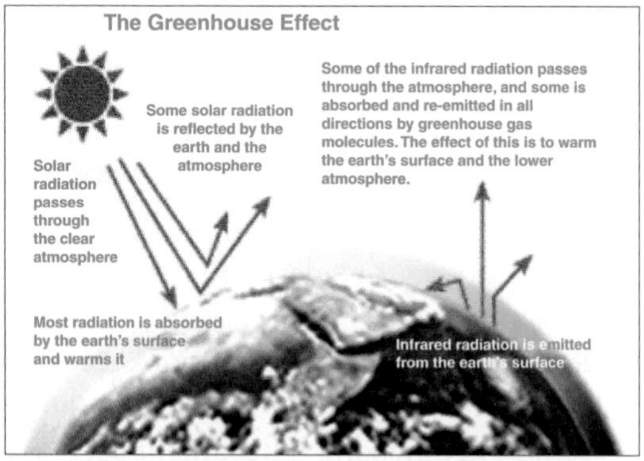

Estimating future emissions is difficult, because it depends on demographic, economic, technological, policy, and institutional developments. Several emissions scenarios have been developed based on differing projections of these underlying factors. For example, by 2100, in the absence of emissions control policies, carbon dioxide concentrations are projected to be 30–150% higher than today's levels.

The Greenhouse Effect

Some solar radiation is reflected by the earth and the atmosphere

Solar radiation passes through the clear atmosphere

Most radiation is absorbed by the earth's surface and warms it

Some of the infrared radiation passes through the atmosphere, and some is absorbed and re-emitted in all directions by greenhouse gas molecules. The effect of this is to warm the earth's surface and the lower atmosphere.

Infrared radiation is emitted from the earth's surface

Figure 20.1   An Extended Definition
Source: U.S. Environmental Protection Agency, 2001 <www.epa.gov/globalwarming/climate/index/html>.

placed at the beginning of a document (for example, after the executive summary in a report) or at the end, preceding the appendices.

- *In an appendix.* An appendix is appropriate for an extended definition of one page or longer, which would be cumbersome in a glossary or footnote.

WRITING DESCRIPTIONS

Technical communication often requires descriptions: verbal and visual representations of objects, mechanisms, and processes.

- *Objects.* An object is anything ranging from a physical site such as a volcano to a synthetic artifact such as a hammer. A tomato plant is an object, as is an automobile tire or a book.
- *Mechanisms.* A mechanism is a synthetic object consisting of a number of identifiable parts that work together. A DVD player is a mechanism, as is a voltmeter, a lawn mower, or a submarine.
- *Processes.* A process is an activity that takes place over time: species evolve; steel is made; plants perform photosynthesis. *Descriptions of processes*, which explain how something happens, differ from *instructions*, which explain how to do something. Readers of a process description want to *understand* the process; readers of instructions want a step-by-step guide to help them *perform* it.

Descriptions of objects, mechanisms, and processes appear in virtually every kind of technical communication. For example, an employee who wants to persuade management to buy some equipment includes a mechanism description of the equipment in the proposal to buy it. A company manufacturing a consumer product provides a description and a graphic on its Web site to attract buyers. A developer who wants to build a housing project includes in his proposal to municipal authorities descriptions of the geographical area and of the process he will use in developing that area.

Typically, a description is part of a larger document. For example, a maintenance manual for an air-conditioning system might begin with a description of the system to help readers understand first how it operates and then how to fix or maintain it.

Analyzing the Writing Situation for Descriptions

Before you begin to write a description, consider carefully how the audience and the purpose of the document will affect what you write.

What does the audience already know about the general subject? For example, if you want to describe how the next generation of industrial robots will affect car manufacturing, you first have to know whether your readers understand the current process and whether they understand robotics.

Your sense of your audience will determine not only how technical your vocabulary should be but also how long your sentences and paragraphs should be. Another audience-related factor is your use of graphics. Less-knowledgeable readers need simple graphics; they might have trouble understanding sophisticated schematics or decision charts. As you consider your audience, think about whether any of your readers are from other cultures and might therefore expect different topics, organization, or writing style in the description.

Consider, too, your purpose. What are you trying to accomplish with this description? If you want your readers to understand how a personal computer works, write a *general description* that applies to several varieties of computers. If you want your readers to understand how a specific computer works, write a *particular description*. A general description of personal computers might classify them by size, then go on to describe palmtops, laptops, and desktops in general terms. A particular description, however, will describe only one model of personal computer, such as a Millennia 2500. Your purpose will determine every aspect of the description, including its length, the amount of detail, and the number and type of graphics.

There is no single structure or format used for descriptions. Because descriptions are written for different audiences and different purposes, they can take many shapes and forms. However, the following four suggestions will guide you in most situations:

- Indicate the nature and scope of the description.
- Introduce the description clearly.
- Provide appropriate detail.
- Conclude the description.

Indicating the Nature and Scope of the Description

▶ **In This Book**
For more about titles and headings, see Ch. 9, pp. 200 and 201.

If the description is to be a separate document, give it a title. If the description is to be part of a longer document, give it a section heading. In either case, clearly state the subject and indicate whether the description is general or particular. For instance, a general description of an object might be titled "Description of a Minivan," and a particular description might be called "Description of the 2009 Honda Odyssey." A general description of a process might be titled "Description of the Process of Designing a New Production Car," and a particular description might be called "Description of the Process of Designing the Chevrolet Malibu."

Introducing the Description Clearly

Provide information that readers need in order to understand the detailed information that follows. Most introductions to descriptions are general: you want to give readers a broad understanding of the object, mechanism, or process. You might also provide a graphic that introduces readers to the overall concept. For example, in describing a process, you might include a flowchart summarizing the steps in the body of the description; in describing an object, such as a bicycle, you might include a photograph or a drawing showing the major components you will describe in detail in the body.

Table 20.1 shows some of the basic kinds of questions you might want to answer in introducing object, mechanism, and process descriptions. If the answer is obvious, simply move on to the next question.

Figure 20.2 on page 552 shows the introductory graphic accompanying a description of a headlamp.

Table 20.1 Questions to Answer in Introducing a Description

For object and mechanism descriptions	*For process descriptions*
• *What is the item?* You might start with a sentence definition.	• *What is the process?* You might start with a sentence definition.
• *What is the function of the item?* If the function is not implicit in the sentence definition, state it: "Electron microscopes magnify objects that are smaller than the wavelengths of visible light."	• *What is the function of the process?* Unless the function is obvious, state it: "The central purpose of performing a census is to obtain current population figures, which government agencies use to revise legislative districts and determine revenue sharing."
• *What does the item look like?* Include a photograph or drawing if possible. (See Chapter 12 for more about incorporating graphics with text.) If not, use an analogy or comparison: "The USB drive is a plastic- or metal-covered device, about the size of a pack of gum, with a removable cap that covers the type-A USB connection." Mention the material, texture, color, and the like, if relevant. Sometimes, an object is best described with both graphics and words.	• *Where and when does the process take place?* "Each year the stream is stocked with hatchery fish in the first week of March." Omit these facts only if your readers already know them.
	• *Who or what performs the process?* If there is any doubt about who or what performs the process, state it.
• *How does the item work?* In a few sentences, define the operating principle. Sometimes, objects do not "work"; they merely exist. For instance, a ship model has no operating principle.	• *How does the process work?* "The four-treatment lawn-spray plan is based on the theory that the most effective way to promote a healthy lawn is to apply different treatments at crucial times during the growing season. The first two treatments—in spring and early summer—consist of. . . ."
• *What are the principal parts of the item?* Limit your description to the principal parts. A description of a bicycle, for instance, would not mention the dozens of nuts and bolts that hold the mechanism together; it would focus on the chain, gears, pedals, wheels, and frame.	• *What are the principal steps of the process?* Name the steps in the order in which you will describe them. The principal steps in changing an automobile tire, for instance, include jacking up the car, replacing the old tire with the new one, and lowering the car back to the ground. Changing a tire also includes secondary steps, such as placing chocks against the tires to prevent the car from moving once it is jacked up. Explain or refer to these secondary steps at the appropriate points in the description.

Figure 20.2 Graphic with Enlarged Detailed Graphics

In this description of a headlamp, the introductory graphic includes five graphics showing different portions or views of the headlamp or additional components. Notice the use of the numbered boxes to help readers link the individual boxes to the main photograph of the headlamp.
Source: Petzl, 2005.

Providing Appropriate Detail

In the body of a description—the part-by-part or step-by-step section—treat each major part or step as a separate item. In describing an object or a mechanism, define each part and then, if applicable, describe its function, operating principle, and appearance. In discussing the appearance, include shape, dimensions, material, and physical details such as texture and color (if essential). Some descriptions might call for other qualities, such as weight or hardness. If a part has important subparts, describe them in the same way.

In describing a process, treat each major step as if it were a separate process. Do not repeat your answer to the question about who or what performs the action unless a new agent performs it, but do answer the other important questions: what the step is; what its function is; and when, where, and how it occurs. If the step has important substeps, explain them, too.

A description resembles a map with a series of detailed insets. A description of a computer system includes a keyboard as one of its parts, and the description of the keyboard includes the numeric keypad as one of its parts. And the description of the numeric keypad includes the arrow keys as one of its parts. The level of detail depends on the complexity of the item and the readers' needs. The same principle applies in describing processes: a step might have substeps. For each substep, you need to describe who or what performs it (if it is not obvious), and you need to describe what the substep is, what its function is, and when, where, and how it occurs.

Guidelines

Providing Appropriate Detail in Descriptions

Use the following techniques to flesh out your descriptions.

For mechanism and object descriptions	*For process descriptions*
• **Choose an appropriate organizing principle.** Two organizational principles are common: — Functional: how the item works or is used. In a radio, the sound begins at the receiver, travels into the	• **Structure the step-by-step description chronologically.** If the process is a closed system—such as the cycle of evaporation and condensation—and thus has no first step, begin with any principal step.

For mechanism and object descriptions	*For process descriptions*
amplifier, and then flows out through the speakers. — Spatial: based on the physical structure of the item: from top to bottom, east to west, outside to inside, and so forth. Descriptions can be organized in various ways. For instance, the description of a house could be organized functionally (the different electrical and mechanical systems) or spatially (top to bottom, inside to outside, east to west, and so on). A complex description can use a combination of patterns at different levels in the description. • **Use graphics.** Present a graphic for each major part. Use photographs to show external surfaces, drawings to emphasize particular items on the surface, and cutaways and exploded diagrams to show details beneath the surface. Other kinds of graphics, such as graphs and charts, are often useful supplements (see Chapter 12).	• **Explain causal relationships among steps.** Don't present the steps as if they have nothing to do with one another. In many cases, one step causes another. In the operation of a four-stroke gasoline engine, for instance, each step creates the conditions for the next step. • **Use the present tense.** Discuss steps in the present tense unless you are writing about a process that occurred in the historical past. For example, use the past tense in describing how the Snake River aquifer was formed: "The molten material condensed. . . ." However, use the present tense in describing how steel is made: "The molten material is then poured into. . . ." The present tense helps readers understand that, in general, steel is made this way. • **Use graphics.** Whenever possible, use graphics to clarify each point. Consider additional flowcharts or other kinds of graphics, such as photographs, drawings, and graphs. For example, in a description of how a four-stroke gasoline engine operates, use diagrams to illustrate the position of the valves and the activity occurring during each step.

Concluding the Description

A typical description has a brief conclusion that summarizes it and prevents readers from overemphasizing the part or step discussed last.

A common technique for concluding descriptions of mechanisms and of some objects is to state briefly how the parts function together. At the end of a description of how the Apple iPhone touch screen works, for example, the conclusion might include the following paragraph:

> When you touch the screen, electrical impulses travel from the screen to the iPhone processor, which analyzes the characteristics of your touch. These characteristics include the size, shape, and location of the touch, as well as whether you touched the screen in several places at once or moved your fingers. The processor then begins to process these data by removing any background noise and mapping and calculating the touch area or areas. Using its gesture-interpreting software, which combines these data with what it already knows about which function (such as the music player) you were using, the processor then sends commands to the music-player software and to the iPhone screen. How long does this process take? A nanosecond.

Like an object or mechanism description, a process description usually has a brief conclusion: a short paragraph summarizing the principal steps. Here, for example, is the concluding section of a description of how a four-stroke gasoline engine operates:

> In the intake stroke, the piston moves down, drawing the air-fuel mixture into the cylinder from the carburetor. As the piston moves up, it compresses this mixture in the compression stroke, creating the conditions necessary for combustion. In the power stroke, a spark from the spark plug ignites the mixture, which burns rapidly, forcing the piston down. In the exhaust stroke, the piston moves up, expelling the burned gases.

For descriptions of more than a few pages, a discussion of the implications of the process might be appropriate. For instance, a description of the Big Bang might conclude with a discussion of how the theory has been supported and challenged by recent astronomical discoveries and theories.

A Look at Sample Descriptions

A look at some sample descriptions will give you an idea of how different writers adapt basic approaches for particular audiences and purposes.

Figure 20.3 shows the extent to which a process description can be based on graphics. Figure 20.4 is an excerpt from a mechanism description.

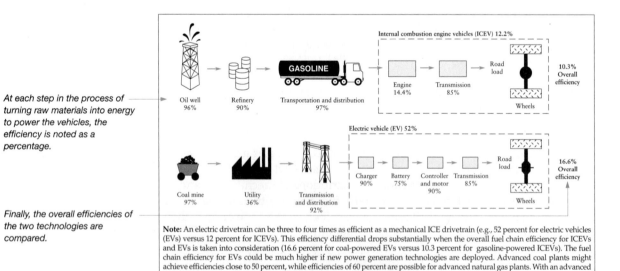

At each step in the process of turning raw materials into energy to power the vehicles, the efficiency is noted as a percentage.

Finally, the overall efficiencies of the two technologies are compared.

Note: An electric drivetrain can be three to four times as efficient as a mechanical ICE drivetrain (e.g., 52 percent for electric vehicles (EVs) versus 12 percent for ICEVs). This efficiency differential drops substantially when the overall fuel chain efficiency for ICEVs and EVs is taken into consideration (16.6 percent for coal-powered EVs versus 10.3 percent for gasoline-powered ICEVs). The fuel chain efficiency for EVs could be much higher if new power generation technologies are deployed. Advanced coal plants might achieve efficiencies close to 50 percent, while efficiencies of 60 percent are possible for advanced natural gas plants. With an advanced natural gas plant the overall fuel chain efficiency for EVs could rise to 27 percent.

Source: John Brogan and S. Venkateswaran, "Diverse Choices for Hybrid and Electric Motor Vehicles," in *Proceedings of the International Conference on Urban EVs* (Stockholm, Sweden: Organization for Economic Cooperation and Development, May 1992).

Figure 20.3 A Process Description Based on Graphics

Notice how effectively graphics show the relative efficiencies of an internal combustion engine vehicle (top row) and an electric vehicle (bottom row). The graphics clarify the process and make it interesting.

Source: U.S. Congress, Office of Technology Assessment, 1995.

**Figure 20.4   Excerpt from
a Mechanism Description**
Source: Quamut, 2008
<www.quamut.com/quamut/
buying_a_hybrid_car/page/
how_hybrid_cars_work.html>.

Hybrid Cars: Gasoline and Electric

The propulsion system of a typical hybrid car is similar to that of a conventional car—the major difference is that hybrid cars use an **electric motor** in addition to a **gas-powered engine** to provide the transmission with the power it needs to turn the wheels. The electric motor is itself powered by **batteries**, whose flow of electricity is controlled by a **power electronics box**.

This excerpt from a mechanism description begins with a brief comparison of hybrid cars and conventional cars.

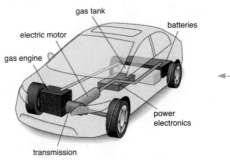

gas tank

batteries

electric motor

gas engine

power electronics

transmission

the power train of a typical hybrid vehicle

The typical mechanism description begins with a graphic that highlights the components that will be discussed in the description.

The Electric Motor

In all hybrid cars, an electric motor is used to supplement the gas-powered engine. It can do so in a variety of ways:

- **The electric motor powers the transmission:** The transmission turns the car's wheels, so whatever powers the transmission makes the car go. In some hybrid cars, the electric motor powers the transmission on its own when the car is at low speeds. At these speeds, the gas-powered engine contributes no power and uses no gas.
- **The electric motor assists the engine:** When the electric motor isn't powering the car by itself, it adds **torque**, which assists the engine in turning the transmission. Hybrid cars have smaller engines than gasoline-only cars, since the motor works alongside the engine to power the transmission. The combined operation of the smaller engine and the electric motor means that hybrid cars need less gasoline than conventional cars to spin their wheels with the same amount of power.
- **The electric motor turns off and restarts the engine:** Conventional cars use gasoline when they idle, since the engine continues to run when the car is stopped. Hybrid cars don't use gasoline when they idle. The motor on a hybrid car acts as a starter that turns the engine on when it's needed and off when it's not needed (for example, when stopped at a red light). The motor also keeps the air conditioning and other electronics on whenever the car is operating.
- **The electric motor recharges the batteries:** The electric motor can also generate its own power by recharging its batteries during normal vehicle operation.

These four main functions of the electric motor help make hybrid cars run just as efficiently as conventional cars while using less gas. But not *all* hybrid car models have electric motors that perform all four functions. The more of these four functions a hybrid car's motor does perform, the more fuel-efficient the car is.

The section describing the electric motor focuses on the four jobs it performs in a hybrid car. Notice that the audience and purpose of this description determine the kind of information it contains. Because the description seeks to answer the question "How does a hybrid work?" the discussion of the electric motor focuses on its function, not on the materials it is made of or on its technical specifications.

Figure 20.5 is an excerpt from a set of specifications. Figure 20.6 is an effective process definition.

Figure 20.5 Excerpt from a Set of Specifications
Source: AB Volvo, 2007 <www.volvo.com/ constructionequipment/na/ en-us/products/ skidsteerloaders/MC60B>.

Specifications are a special kind of description. A typical set of specifications consists of a graphic and statistics about the device and its performance characteristics. Specifications help readers understand the capabilities of an item. They are written about devices as small as transistors and as large as aircraft carriers.

| Specifications | Features & Benefits | Build & Price | Compare Volvo | Cost of ownership | |

MC60B Specifications

MC60B	Specifications
Rated operating capacity (SAE)	1,400 lb (635 kg)
SAE Gross (DIN ISO3046)	49.5 HP (36.9 kW)
SAE Net (SAE1349 DIN ISO3046)	45.3 HP (33.7 kW)
Flow at rated RPM - Mechanical	17.1 gal/min (64.8 Lit/min)
Flow at rated RPM - Pilot	20.0 gal/min (75.6 Lit/min)
Maximum travel speed, Mechanical	6.9 mph (11 kph)
Maximum travel speed, Pilot	6.4 mph (10.3 kph)
Operating weight	5,624 lb (2,552 kg)
Height to loader hinge pin	113.7 in (2,888 mm)
Overall length - with dirt bucket	130.2 in (3,306 mm)
Bucket width	68 in (1,727 mm)
Height to top of cab/ROPS	78.3 in (1,990 mm)
Ground clearance	8.2 in (208 mm)

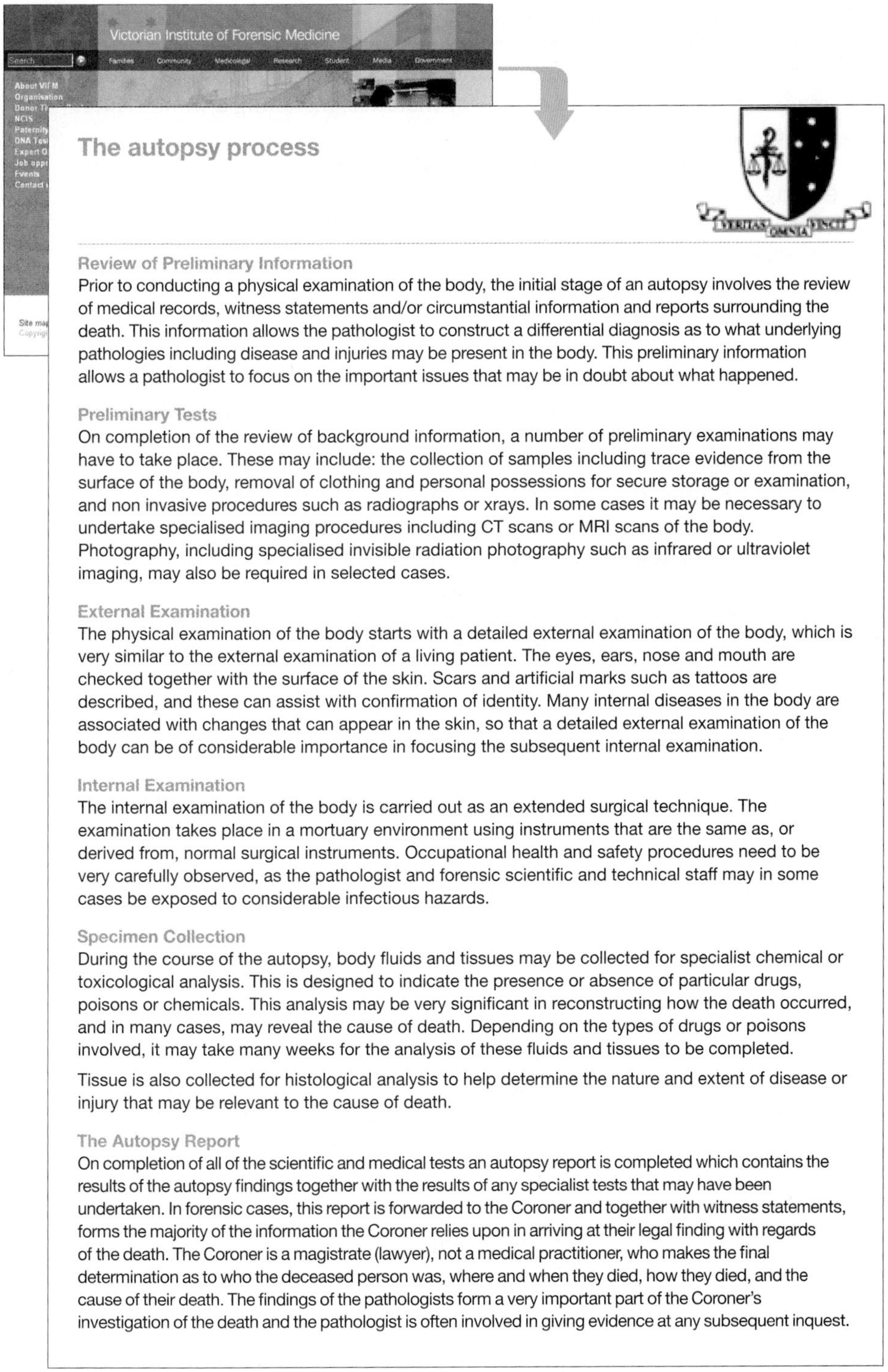

Figure 20.6   An Effective Process Description
Source: Victorian Institute, 2005 <www.vifm.org/fp _autopsyprocess.phtml>.

The autopsy process

Review of Preliminary Information

Prior to conducting a physical examination of the body, the initial stage of an autopsy involves the review of medical records, witness statements and/or circumstantial information and reports surrounding the death. This information allows the pathologist to construct a differential diagnosis as to what underlying pathologies including disease and injuries may be present in the body. This preliminary information allows a pathologist to focus on the important issues that may be in doubt about what happened.

Preliminary Tests

On completion of the review of background information, a number of preliminary examinations may have to take place. These may include: the collection of samples including trace evidence from the surface of the body, removal of clothing and personal possessions for secure storage or examination, and non invasive procedures such as radiographs or xrays. In some cases it may be necessary to undertake specialised imaging procedures including CT scans or MRI scans of the body. Photography, including specialised invisible radiation photography such as infrared or ultraviolet imaging, may also be required in selected cases.

External Examination

The physical examination of the body starts with a detailed external examination of the body, which is very similar to the external examination of a living patient. The eyes, ears, nose and mouth are checked together with the surface of the skin. Scars and artificial marks such as tattoos are described, and these can assist with confirmation of identity. Many internal diseases in the body are associated with changes that can appear in the skin, so that a detailed external examination of the body can be of considerable importance in focusing the subsequent internal examination.

Internal Examination

The internal examination of the body is carried out as an extended surgical technique. The examination takes place in a mortuary environment using instruments that are the same as, or derived from, normal surgical instruments. Occupational health and safety procedures need to be very carefully observed, as the pathologist and forensic scientific and technical staff may in some cases be exposed to considerable infectious hazards.

Specimen Collection

During the course of the autopsy, body fluids and tissues may be collected for specialist chemical or toxicological analysis. This is designed to indicate the presence or absence of particular drugs, poisons or chemicals. This analysis may be very significant in reconstructing how the death occurred, and in many cases, may reveal the cause of death. Depending on the types of drugs or poisons involved, it may take many weeks for the analysis of these fluids and tissues to be completed.

Tissue is also collected for histological analysis to help determine the nature and extent of disease or injury that may be relevant to the cause of death.

The Autopsy Report

On completion of all of the scientific and medical tests an autopsy report is completed which contains the results of the autopsy findings together with the results of any specialist tests that may have been undertaken. In forensic cases, this report is forwarded to the Coroner and together with witness statements, forms the majority of the information the Coroner relies upon in arriving at their legal finding with regards of the death. The Coroner is a magistrate (lawyer), not a medical practitioner, who makes the final determination as to who the deceased person was, where and when they died, how they died, and the cause of their death. The findings of the pathologists form a very important part of the Coroner's investigation of the death and the pathologist is often involved in giving evidence at any subsequent inquest.

Perhaps because visitors to this Web site do not need a definition of autopsy, *the writer begins with the first step.*

Notice that the second step is linked to the first step: the first step has to take place before the second step can be carried out. When you write any description, don't forget to explain logical relationships between steps.

Notice that most of this description is written in the passive voice. The writer is emphasizing the activities, not the person performing them. For more about passive voice, see Ch. 10, p. 234.

Note that most of the headings are noun phrases ("Internal Examination") rather than verb phrases ("Performing an Internal Examination"). In Australia, where this document was composed, more-formal noun phrases are used more than in the United States.

Note that this description contains no graphics. Although it would be possible to create a flowchart showing the steps, the writer apparently concluded that this treatment of the subject would not benefit from graphics.

WRITING INSTRUCTIONS

This section discusses instructions, which are process descriptions written to help readers perform a specific task—for instance, installing a water heater in a house.

When you write instructions, you use the same planning, drafting, revising, editing, and proofreading process that you use with other kinds of technical documents. In addition, you might perform one other task—usability testing—to ensure that the instructions are accurate and easy to follow.

Designing a Set of Instructions

As you plan to write a set of instructions, think about how readers will be using it. Analyzing your audience and purpose and gathering and organizing your information will help you decide whether you should write a one-page set of instructions or a longer document that needs to be bound. You might realize that the information would work better as a Web-based document that allows readers to link to the information they need. Or you might decide to write several versions of the information: a brief paper-based set of instructions and a longer, Web-based document with links that users will access from the company intranet.

As always in technical communication, imagining how readers will use what you write will help you plan your document. For example, having decided that your audience, purpose, and subject call for a paper-based set of instructions of perhaps 1,000 words and a dozen drawings and photographs, you can start to design the document. You will need to consider your resources, especially your budget: long documents cost more than short ones; color costs more than black and white; heavy paper costs more than light paper; secure bindings cost more than staples.

Designing a set of instructions is much like designing any other kind of technical document. As discussed in Chapter 11, you want to create a document that is attractive and easy to use. When you design a set of instructions, you need to consider a number of issues related to both document design and page design:

- *What are your readers' expectations?* For instructions that accompany a simple, inexpensive product such as a light switch, readers will expect instructions written on the back of the package or, at most, printed in black and white on a small sheet of paper folded inside the package. For instructions that accompany an expensive consumer product such as a high-definition TV, readers will expect a more sophisticated full-color document printed on high-quality paper.

- *Do you need to create more than one set of instructions for different audiences?* If you are writing about complex devices such as electronic thermostats, you might decide to create one set of instructions for electricians (who

▶ **In This Book**

For a discussion of usability testing, see Ch. 13, p. 349.

▶ **In This Book**

For more about planning, see Ch. 3.

▶ **On TechComm Web**

For examples of instructions, see Writing Guidelines for Engineering and Science Students. Click on Links Library for Ch. 20 on <bedfordstmartins.com/techcomm>.

will install and maintain the device) and one set for homeowners (who will operate the device). You might decide to create a paper-based document that can also be read easily on the Internet.

- *What languages should you use?* In most countries, including the United States, several or many languages are spoken. You might decide to include instructions in two or more languages. Doing so will help you communicate better with more people, and it can help you avoid legal problems. In liability cases, U.S. courts sometimes find that if a company knows that many of its customers speak only Spanish, for example, the instructions should appear in Spanish as well as in English. You have two choices: simultaneous or sequential. In a *simultaneous design*, you might create a multicolumn page. One column presents the graphics; another presents the text in English; another presents the text in Spanish. Obviously, this won't work if you have more than two or three languages, but it is efficient because you can present each graphic only once. In a *sequential design*, you present all the information in English (say, on pages 1–8), then all the information in Spanish (on pages 9–16). The sequential design is easier for readers to use because they are not distracted by text in other languages, but you will have to present all the graphics several times, which will make the instructions longer.

- *Will readers be anxious about the information?* If readers will find the information intimidating, make the design unintimidating. For instance, if you are writing to general readers about how to set up a wireless network for home computers, create open pages with a lot of white space and graphics. Use large type and narrow text columns so that each page contains a relatively small amount of information.

- *Will the environment in which the instructions are read affect the document design?* If people will be using the instructions outdoors, you will need to use a coated paper that can tolerate a little water. If people will be reading the instructions while sitting in a small, enclosed area, you might select a small paper size and a binding that enables readers to fold the pages over to save space. If people have a lot of room, you might decide to create poster-size instructions that can be taped to the wall and that are easy to read from across the room.

Guidelines

Designing Clear, Attractive Pages

To design pages that are clear and attractive, follow these two guidelines:

▶ **Create an open, airy design.** Do not squeeze too much information onto the page. Build in space for wide margins and effective line spacing, use large type, and chunk the information effectively.

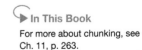

In This Book
For more about chunking, see Ch. 11, p. 263.

▶ **Clearly relate the graphics to the text.** In the step-by-step portions of a set of instructions, you will want to present graphics to accompany every step or almost every step. Create a design that makes it clear which graphics go with each text passage. One easy way to do this is to use a table, with the graphics in one column and the text in the other. A horizontal rule or extra line spacing separates the text and graphics for one step from the text and graphics for the next step.

Figure 20.7 illustrates these points.

a. Cluttered design

This page is cluttered, containing far too much information. The page is not chunked effectively. As a result, the reader's eyes don't know where to focus. Would you look forward to using these instructions to assemble this cabinet?
Source: Slide-Lok, 2005

b. Attractive design

This page is well designed, containing an appropriate amount of information presented in a simple two-column format. Notice the effective use of white space and the horizontal rules separating the steps.
Source: Anthro, 2005 <www.anthro.com/ assemblyinstructions/300-5237-00.pdf>.

Figure 20.7   Cluttered and Attractive Page Designs in a Set of Instructions

Planning for Safety

If the subject you are writing about involves safety risks, your most important responsibility is to do everything you can to ensure your readers' safety.

Protecting Your Readers' Safety

To a large extent, the best way to keep your readers safe is to be honest and write clearly. If readers will encounter safety risks, explain what those risks are and how to minimize them. Doing so is a question of rights. Readers have a right to the best information they can get.

Protecting readers' safety is also a question of law. People who get hurt can sue the company that made the product or provided the service. As discussed in Chapter 2, this field of law is called *liability law*. Your company is likely to have legal professionals on staff or on retainer whose job is to ensure that the company is not responsible for putting people at unnecessary risk.

When you write safety information, be clear and concise. Avoid complicated sentences.

COMPLICATED	It is required that safety glasses be worn when inside this laboratory.
SIMPLE	You must wear safety glasses in this laboratory.
SIMPLE	Wear safety glasses in this laboratory.

Sometimes a phrase works better than a sentence: "Safety Glasses Required."

Because a typical set of instructions or manual can contain dozens of comments—both safety and nonsafety—experts have devised *signal words* to indicate the seriousness of the advice. Unfortunately, signal words are not used consistently. For instance, the American National Standards Institute (ANSI) and the U.S. military's MILSPEC publish definitions that differ significantly, and many private companies have their own definitions. Figure 20.8 on page 562 presents the four most popular signal words. The first three signal words are accompanied by symbols showing the color combinations endorsed by ANSI in its standard Z535.4.

Whether the safety information is printed in a document or on machinery or equipment, it should be prominent and easy to read. Many organizations use visual symbols to represent levels of danger, but these symbols are not standardized.

Organizations that create products that are used only in the United States use safety information that conforms with standards published by ANSI and with the federal Occupational Safety and Health Administration (OSHA). Organizations that create products that are also used outside the United States use safety information that conforms with standards published by the International Organization for Standardization (ISO). Figure 20.9 on page 562 shows a safety label that incorporates ANSI and ISO standards.

On TechComm Web

For advice on communicating safety information on Web pages, see Lisa A. Tallman's "Designing for the Web: Special Considerations for Safety Information." Click on Links Library for Ch. 20 on <bedfordstmartins.com/techcomm>.

Signal Word	Explanation	Example
Danger **⚠ DANGER**	*Danger* is used to alert readers about an immediate and serious hazard that will likely be fatal. Notice that writers often use all-uppercase letters for danger statements.	DANGER: EXTREMELY HIGH VOLTAGE. STAND BACK.
Warning **⚠WARNING**	*Warning* is used to alert readers about the potential for serious injury or death or serious damage to equipment. Notice that writers often use all-uppercase letters for warning statements.	WARNING: TO PREVENT SERIOUS INJURY TO YOUR ARMS AND HANDS, YOU MUST MAKE SURE THE ARM RESTRAINTS ARE IN PLACE BEFORE OPERATING THIS MACHINE.
Caution **⚠ CAUTION**	*Caution* is used to alert readers about the potential for anything from moderate injury to serious equipment damage or destruction.	Caution: Do not use nonrechargeable batteries in this charging unit; they could damage the charging unit.
Note	*Note* is used for a tip or suggestion to help readers carry out the procedure successfully.	Note: Two kinds of washers are provided—regular washers and locking washers. Be sure to use the locking washers here.

Figure 20.8   Signal Words

Figure 20.9   A Typical Safety Label
Source: HCS, LLC, 2004
<www.safetylabel.com/search/index
.php?pn=H6010-CDDHPL>.

The yellow triangle is consistent with the ISO approach. Because ISO creates standards for international use, its safety labels use icons, not words, to represent safety dangers.

The Danger *signal word and the text are consistent with the ANSI approach. The information is presented in English.*

Part of planning for safety is asking what is the best location for the safety information. This question has no easy answer, because you cannot control how your audience will read your document. Be conservative: put safety information wherever you think readers are likely to see it, and don't be afraid to repeat yourself. A reasonable amount of repetition—such as including the same safety comment at the top of each page—is effective. But don't repeat the same piece of advice in each of 20 steps, because readers will stop paying attention to it. If your company's format for instructions calls for a safety section near the beginning of the document, place the information there and repeat it just before the appropriate step in the step-by-step section.

Figure 20.10 shows one industry association's guidelines for placing safety information on palletizers.

Drafting Effective Instructions

Instructions can be brief (a small sheet of paper) or extensive (up to 20 pages or more). Brief instructions might be produced by a writer, a graphic artist,

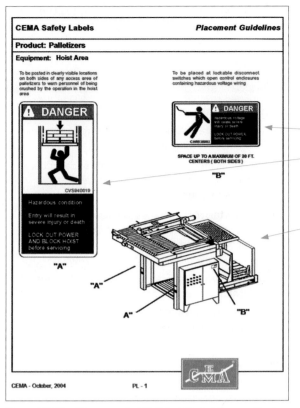

This page shows the two safety labels that the industry association recommends for use on palletizers.

The diagram of the palletizer shows where the organization recommends placing the safety labels.

Figure 20.10   Placement of Safety Information on Equipment
Source: CEMA, 2004 <www.cemanet.org/safety/p11.pdf>.

and a subject-matter expert. Longer instructions might call for additional people, such as marketing and legal personnel.

Regardless of the size of the project, most instructions are organized like process descriptions. The main difference is that the conclusion of a set of instructions is not a summary but an explanation of how to make sure readers have followed the instructions correctly. Most sets of instructions contain four elements: a title, a general introduction, step-by-step instructions, and a conclusion.

Drafting Titles   A good title for instructions is simple and clear. Two forms are common:

- *How-to.* This is the simplest: "How to Install the J112 Shock Absorber."
- *Gerund.* The gerund form is the *-ing* form of the verb: "Installing the J112 Shock Absorber."

One form to avoid is the noun string, which is awkward and hard for readers to understand: "J112 Shock Absorber Installation Instructions."

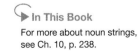

▶ **In This Book**

For more about noun strings, see Ch. 10, p. 238.

Drafting General Introductions   The general introduction provides the preliminary information that readers will need to follow the instructions safely and easily.

Guidelines

Drafting Introductions for Instructions

Every set of instructions is unique and therefore calls for a different introduction. Where appropriate, consider answering the following six questions:

▶ **Who should carry out this task?** Sometimes you need to identify or describe the person or persons who are to carry out a task. Aircraft maintenance, for example, may be performed only by those certified to do it.

▶ **Why should the reader carry out this task?** Sometimes the reason is obvious: you don't need to explain why a backyard barbecue grill should be assembled. But you do need to explain the rationale for many tasks, such as changing radiator antifreeze in a car.

▶ **When should the reader carry out this task?** Some tasks, such as rotating tires or planting crops, need to be performed at particular times or at particular intervals.

▶ **What safety measures or other concerns should the reader understand?** In addition to the safety measures that apply to the whole task, mention any tips that will make the job easier:

  NOTE: For ease of assembly, leave all nuts loose. Give only three or four complete turns on bolt threads.

▶ **What items will the reader need?** List necessary tools, materials, and equipment so that the reader will not have to interrupt his or her work to hunt for something. If you think the reader might not be able to identify these items easily, include drawings next to the names.

▶ **How long will the task take?** Consider stating how long the task will take readers with no experience, some experience, and a lot of experience.

Drafting Step-by-Step Instructions   The heart of a set of instructions is the step-by-step information.

Guidelines

Drafting Steps in Instructions

▶ **Number the instructions.** For long, complex instructions, use two-level numbering, such as a decimal system.

  1
    1.1
    1.2

On TechComm Web

For examples of instructions, see Knowledge Hound. Click on Links Library for Ch. 20 on <bedfordstmartins.com/ techcomm>.

2
   2.1
   2.2

etc.

If you need to present a long set of steps, such as 50, group them logically into, say, six sets of eight or nine steps, and begin each set with a clear heading.

▶ **Present the right amount of information in each step.** Each step should define a single task that readers can carry out easily, without having to refer to the instructions.

TOO MUCH INFORMATION	1. Mix one part cement with one part water, using the trowel. When the mixture is a thick consistency without any lumps bigger than a marble, place a strip of the mixture about 1″ high and 1″ wide along the face of the brick.
TOO LITTLE INFORMATION	1. Pick up the trowel.
RIGHT AMOUNT OF INFORMATION	1. Mix one part cement with one part water, using the trowel, until the mixture is a thick consistency without any lumps bigger than a marble.
	2. Place a strip of the mixture about 1″ high and 1″ wide along the face of the brick.

▶ **Use the imperative mood.** For example, "Attach the red wire. . . ." The imperative is more direct and economical than the indicative mood ("You should attach the red wire . . ." or "The operator should attach the red wire . . ."). Avoid the passive voice ("The red wire is attached . . ."), because it can be ambiguous: is the red wire already attached?

▶ **Do not confuse steps and feedback statements.** A *step* is an action that readers are to perform. A *feedback statement* describes an event that occurs in response to a step. For instance, a step might read "Insert the disk in the drive." That step's feedback statement might read, "The system will now update your user information." Do not make a feedback statement a numbered step. Present it as part of the step to which it refers. Some writers give all feedback statements their own design.

▶ **Include graphics.** When appropriate, add a photograph or a drawing to show readers what to do. Some activities—such as adding two drops of a reagent to a mixture—do not need an illustration, but they might be clarified by charts or tables.

▶ **Do not omit articles (*a, an, the*) to save space.** Omitting articles can make the instructions unclear and hard to read. In the sentence "Locate midpoint and draw line," for example, readers cannot tell if "draw line" is a noun (as in "locate the draw line") or a verb and its object (as in "draw the line").

In This Book

For more about the imperative mood and passive voice, see Ch. 10, pp. 233 and 234.

Drafting Conclusions   Instructions often conclude by stating that the reader has now completed the task or by describing what the reader should do next. For example:

> Now that you have replaced the glass and applied the glazing compound, let it sit for at least five days so that the glazing can cure. Then prime and paint the window.

Some conclusions end with *maintenance tips* or a *troubleshooting guide*. A troubleshooting guide, usually presented as a table, identifies common problems and explains how to solve them.

Revising, Editing, and Proofreading Instructions

You want to revise, edit, and proofread all the documents you write to make sure they are honest, clear, accurate, comprehensive, accessible, concise, professional in appearance, and correct. When you write instructions, you should be extra careful, for two reasons.

First, your readers will rely on your instructions to carry out the task. If they can't complete it—or they do complete it but the device doesn't work correctly—they'll be unhappy. Nobody likes to spend a few hours assembling a garage-door opener, then find half a dozen parts left over. Second, your readers will rely on you to help them complete the task safely. To prevent injuries—and liability actions—build time into the budget to revise, edit, and proofread your instructions carefully. Finally, if you can, usability test the instructions.

▶ In This Book
For a discussion of usability testing, see Ch. 13, p. 349.

A Look at Sample Instructions

Figure 20.11 is an excerpt from a set of instructions. Figure 20.12 on page 568 is a list of tools and materials from a set of instructions. Figure 20.13 on page 569 is an excerpt from the safety information in a set of instructions. Figure 20.14 on page 570 is an excerpt from the conclusion to a set of instructions. Figure 20.15 on page 570 is an excerpt from the troubleshooting guide in the instructions for a lawn mower.

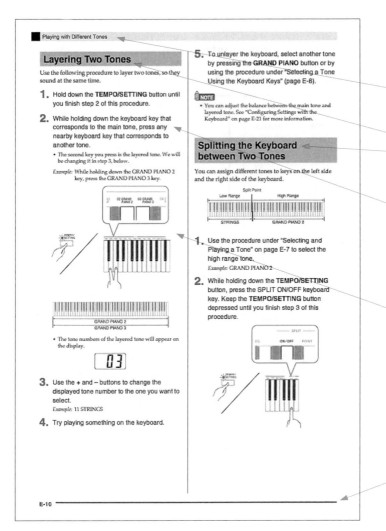

Figure 20.11   Excerpt from a Set of Instructions

Source: Casio, 2008 <http://ftp.casio.co.jp/pub/world_manual/emi/en/px_800/01_e.pdf>.

This is a page from the user's manual for a Casio digital piano. The two-column design enables the company to present a lot of information without making the page too crowded.

The header indicates the section of the manual: "Playing with Different Tones."

The two tasks are presented as gerunds (-ing phrases): "layering" and "splitting." Gerunds are appropriate for instructions because they suggest action.

The steps are numbered clearly and presented in the imperative mood: "do this." Note that step 2 has bulleted feedback statements. Step 5 has a note, presented with its own icon and design.

The diagrams clarify the verbal descriptions. Note that they are not meant to be representational. For instance, the hands pressing the buttons are way too small compared to the buttons, but they effectively convey the intended idea.

The footer includes the page number. The instructions use a dual-numbering system: this page is page 10 of section E.

Figure 20.12   List of Tools and Materials
Source: General Electric, 2003.

Drawings of tools, materials, and parts are more effective than lists.

Installation Instructions

PREPARE TO INSTALL THE RANGE

FOR YOUR SAFETY:

All rough-in and spacing dimensions must be met for safe use of your range. Electricity to the range can be disconnected at the outlet without moving the range if the outlet is in the preferred location (remove lower drawer).

To reduce the risk of burns or fire when reaching over hot surface elements, cabinet storage space above the cooktop should be avoided. If cabinet storage space is to be provided above the cooktop, the risk can be reduced by installing a range hood that sticks out at least 5" beyond the front of the cabinets. Cabinets installed above a cooktop must be no deeper than 13."

Be sure your appliance is properly installed and grounded by a qualified technician.

Make sure the cabinets and wall coverings around the range can withstand the temperatures (up to 200°F.) generated by the range.

MATERIALS YOU MAY NEED

Tin Snips   Lag Bolts   Anchor Sleeves

(For Anti-Tip Bracket Mounted on Concrete Floors Only)

(UL Approved 40 AMP)
4-Wire Cord **OR** 3-Wire Cord
4' Long   4' Long

Squeeze Connector
(For Conduit Installations Only)

PARTS INCLUDED

Anti-Tip Bracket Kit

1   REMOVE SHIPPING MATERIALS

Remove packaging materials. Failure to remove packaging materials could result in damage to the appliance.

TOOLS YOU WILL NEED

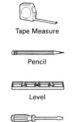

Drill with 1/8" Bit   Safety Glasses

Adjustable Wrench   Tape Measure

Pliers   Pencil

1/4" Nut Driver   Level

Phillips Screwdriver   Flat-blade Screwdriver

IMPORTANT SAFETY INFORMATION
READ THE FOLLOWING WARNINGS BEFORE YOU OR YOUR CHILD PLAY VIDEO GAMES

WARNING - Seizures

- Some people (about 1 in 4000) may have seizures or blackouts triggered by light flashes or patterns, such as while watching TV or playing video games, even if they have never had a seizure in the past.
- Anyone who has had a seizure, loss of awareness, or other symptom linked to an epileptic condition should consult a doctor before playing a video game.
- Parents should watch when their children play video games. Stop playing and consult a doctor if you or your child has any of the following symptoms:

Convulsions	Eye or muscle twitching
Loss of awareness	Altered vision
Involuntary movements	Disorientation

- To reduce the likelihood of a seizure when playing video games:
  1. Sit or stand as far from the screen as possible.
  2. Play video games on the smallest available television screen.
  3. Do not play if you are tired or need sleep.
  4. Play in a well-lit room.
  5. Take a 10 to 15 minute break every hour.

This excerpt from a longer set of safety information describes dangers inherent in playing video games. The more serious the safety risk, the longer and more detailed the safety information.

This sentence should use mandatory language: "You must read the following warnings...."

Although this excerpt uses appropriate signal words, it should also use icons to emphasize the importance of the information.

Figure 20.13   Excerpt from Safety Information
Source: Nintendo, 2005 <www.nintendo.com/customer/manuals/precautions_gcn_english.jsp>.

There's more information about using iPhone, in onscreen help and on the web.

The following table describes where to get more iPhone-related software and service information.

To learn about	Do this
Using iPhone safety	Go to www.apple.com/support/manuals/iphone for the latest *Important Product Information Guide,* including any updates to the safety and regulatory information.
iPhone Service and support, tips, forums, and Apple software downloads	Go to www.apple.com/support/iphone.
Service and support for your carrier	Contact your carrier or go to your carrier's website.
The latest information about iPhone	Go to www.apple.com/iphone.
Using iTunes	Open iTunes and choose Help > iTunes Help. For an online iTunes tutorial (available in some areas only), go to www.apple.com/support/itunes.
Using iPhoto on Mac OS X	Open iPhoto and choose Help > iPhoto Help.
Using Address Book on Mac OS X	Open Address Book and choose Help > Address Book Help.
Using iCal on Mac OS X	Open iCal and choose Help > iCal Help.

Figure 20.14 Excerpt from the Conclusion of a Set of Instructions
Source: Apple, Inc., 2008 <http://manuals.info.apple.com/en/iPhone_User_Guide.pdf>.

Problem	Cause	Correction
The mower does not start.	1. The mower is out of gas. 2. The gas is stale. 3. The spark plug wire is disconnected from the spark plug.	1. Fill the gas tank. 2. Drain the tank and refill it with fresh gas. 3. Connect the wire to the plug.
The mower loses power.	1. The grass is too high. 2. The air cleaner is dirty. 3. There is a buildup of grass, leaves, or trash in the underside of the mower housing.	1. Set the mower to a "higher cut" position. See page 10. 2. Replace the air cleaner. See page 11. 3. Disconnect the spark plug wire, attach it to the retainer post, and clean the underside of the mower housing. See page 8.

Figure 20.15 Excerpt from a Troubleshooting Guide

INTERACTIVE SAMPLE DOCUMENT
Presenting Clear Instructions

The following page is from a set of instructions contained in a user's manual. The questions in the margin ask you to think about the discussion of instructions (on page 558). E-mail your responses to yourself and/or your instructor on TechComm Web.

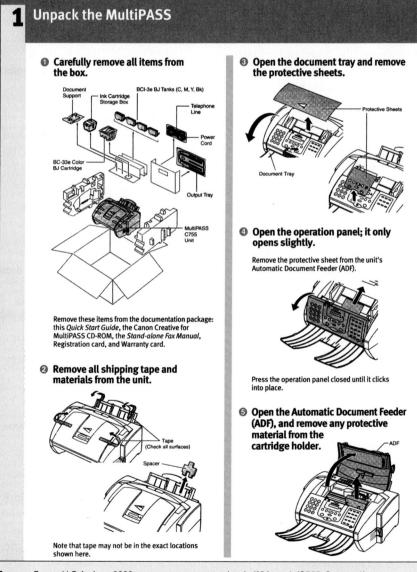

1. How has the designer tried to ensure that readers will follow the steps in the correct order?

2. Is the amount of information presented in each step appropriate?

3. What kind of information is presented in the imperative mood? What kind of information is not?

4. How effectively are graphics used to support the textual information on this page?

▶ **On TechComm Web**

To e-mail your responses to yourself and/or your instructor, click on Interactive Sample Documents for Ch. 20 on <bedfordstmartins.com/ techcomm>.

Source: Canon U.S.A., Inc., 2002 <www.usa.canon.com/cpr/pdf/Manuals/C755_Setup.pdf>.

WRITING MANUALS

There is no absolute distinction between a set of instructions and a manual. Typically, the two share a main purpose: to explain how to carry out a task safely, effectively, and efficiently. A set of instructions is typically shorter (usually 1 to 20 pages) and more limited in its subject. For example, a set of instructions might discuss how to use an extension ladder, whereas a manual might discuss how to use a laptop computer. Obviously, using a laptop includes many more topics than using a ladder.

Manuals are not more important simply because they tend to be longer and more involved than instructions. Both kinds of documents can include safety information. The ladder instructions need to explain how to avoid power lines and how to avoid falling off the ladder. The laptop manual needs to explain how to avoid electrocution when you open the case.

A manual, therefore, includes much of the same sort of information found in a set of instructions. In addition, however, it is likely to include some sections not found in a set of instructions. For instance, it typically has a title page. The main difference between the two is that a manual has more-elaborate front matter and back matter:

- *More-elaborate front matter.* The introduction, sometimes called the *preface*, often contains an *overview of the contents*, frequently in the form of a table, which explains the main contents of each section and chapter. It also contains a *conventions* section, which explains the typography of the manual. For instance, *italics* are used for the titles of books, **boldface** for keyboard keys, and so forth. It also might include a *where to get help* section, referring readers to other sources of information, such as the company's Web site and a customer-support phone center. And it might contain a section listing the *trademarks* of the company's own products and those of other companies.

- *More-elaborate back matter.* Manuals typically include a set of *specifications* for the device or system, a list of relevant government *safety regulations* and *industry standards* that the device or system supports, *tips on maintenance and servicing* the device, a *copyright page* listing bibliographic information about the manual, and an *index*. Many manuals also include *glossaries*.

Organizations work hard to make their instructions and manuals appropriate for their multicultural readers. Because important instructions and manuals might be read by readers from several or even dozens of cultures, you need to answer three important questions as you plan the documents:

- *In what language should the information be written?* You can either translate the document into each group of readers' native language or try to make the English easy to understand. Although translation is sometimes the best or only alternative, companies often use Simplified English or some other form of English with a limited grammar and vocabulary. On many organizations' Web sites, you will find manuals available as PDF documents in various languages.

▶ **In This Book**
For more about typography, see Ch. 11, p. 268.

▶ **In This Book**
For more about trademarks, see Ch. 2, p. 26.

▶ **In This Book**
For more about glossaries, see Ch. 19, p. 516.

▶ **In This Book**
For more about Simplified English, see Ch. 10, p. 245.

- *Do the graphics or text need to be modified?* As discussed in Chapter 5, communicators need to be aware of cultural differences. For example, although a printer manual translated for an Italian audience presented nude models with strategically placed rectangles showing the various colors the machine could reproduce, it carefully avoided explicit advice about how to use the printer, because Italian readers prefer suggestions (Delio, 2002).

- *What is the readers' technological infrastructure?* If your readers don't have Internet access, there is no point in making a Web version of the information. If your readers pay by the minute for Internet access, you will want to create Web-based information that downloads quickly.

 **On TechComm Web**

Read Michelle Delio's article about cultural factors and manuals in *Wired News*. Click on Links Library for Ch. 20 on <bedfordstmartins.com/techcomm>.

Writer's Checklist

Parenthetical, Sentence, and Extended Definitions
☐ Are all necessary terms defined? (p. 541)

Are the parenthetical definitions
☐ appropriate for the audience? (p. 541)
☐ clear? (p. 542)
☐ smoothly integrated into the sentences? (p. 542)

Does each sentence definition
☐ contain a sufficiently specific category and distinguishing characteristics? (p. 543)
☐ avoid describing one particular item when a general class of items is intended? (p. 543)
☐ avoid circular definition? (p. 543)
☐ contain a noun or noun phrase in the category? (p. 543)

☐ Are the extended definitions developed logically and clearly? (p. 543)
☐ Is each definition placed in the location most useful to readers? (p. 547)

Descriptions of Objects and Mechanisms
☐ Did you clearly indicate the nature and scope of the description? (p. 550)

In introducing the description, did you answer, if appropriate, the following questions:
☐ What is the item? (p. 551)
☐ What does it do? (p. 551)
☐ What is its function? (p. 551)
☐ What does it look like? (p. 551)
☐ What is its principle of operation? (p. 551)
☐ What are its principal parts? (p. 551)

☐ Did you include a graphic identifying all the principal parts? (p. 552)

In providing detailed information, did you
☐ answer, for each of the major components, the questions listed in the second item in this section? (p. 552)
☐ choose an appropriate organizing principle? (p. 552)
☐ include graphics for each of the components? (p. 553)

In concluding the description, did you
☐ summarize the major points in the part-by-part description? (p. 553)
☐ include (where appropriate) a description of the item performing its function or an attempt to motivate readers to take action? (p. 553)

Process Descriptions
☐ Did you clearly indicate the nature and scope of the description? (p. 549)

In introducing the description, did you answer, if appropriate, the following questions:
☐ What is the process? (p. 551)
☐ What is its function? (p. 551)
☐ Where and when does the process take place? (p. 551)
☐ Who or what performs it? (p. 551)
☐ How does the process work? (p. 551)
☐ What are its principal steps? (p. 551)

☐ Did you include a graphic identifying all the principal steps? (p. 552)

In providing detailed information, did you
☐ answer, for each of the major steps, the questions for introducing a description in Table 20.1? (p. 551)
☐ discuss the steps in chronological order or other logical sequence? (p. 552)

- ☐ make clear the causal relationships among the steps? (p. 553)
- ☐ include graphics for the principal steps? (p. 553)

In concluding the description, did you

- ☐ summarize the major points in the step-by-step description? (p. 553)
- ☐ discuss, if appropriate, the importance or implications of the process? (p. 553)
- ☐ attempt, if appropriate, to motivate readers to take action? (p. 553)

Instructions

- ☐ Do the instructions have a clear title? (p. 563)

Does the introduction to the set of instructions

- ☐ state the purpose of the task? (p. 564)

- ☐ describe safety measures or other concerns that readers should understand? (p. 564)
- ☐ list necessary tools and materials? (p. 564)

Are the step-by-step instructions

- ☐ numbered? (p. 564)
- ☐ expressed in the imperative mood? (p. 565)
- ☐ simple and direct? (p. 565)

☐ Are appropriate graphics included? (p. 565)

Does the conclusion

- ☐ include any necessary follow-up advice? (p. 566)
- ☐ include, if appropriate, a troubleshooting guide? (p. 566)

☐ Are the instructions designed effectively, with adequate white space? (p. 565)

☐ Is there a clear relationship between graphics and the accompanying text? (p. 565)

Exercises

▶ **In This Book** For more about memos, see Ch. 14, p. 377.

1. Add a parenthetical definition for each italicized term in the following sentences:

   a. Reluctantly, he decided to *drop* the physics course.

   b. Last week, the computer was *down*.

   c. The department is using *shareware* in its drafting course.

2. Write a sentence definition for each of the following terms:

   a. catalyst

   b. job interview

   c. Web site

3. Revise any of the following sentence definitions that need revision:

   a. A thermometer measures temperature.

   b. The spark plugs are the things that ignite the air-gas mixture in a cylinder.

   c. Parallel parking is where you park next to the curb.

   d. A strike is when the employees stop working.

   e. Multitasking is when you do two things at once while you're on the computer.

4. Write a 500- to 1,000-word extended definition of one of the following terms or of a term used in your field of study. If you do secondary research, cite your sources clearly and accurately. In addition, check that the graphics are appropriate for your audience and purpose. In a brief note at the start, indicate your audience and purpose.

   a. flextime

   b. binding arbitration

   c. robotics

   d. an academic major (Don't focus on any particular major; instead, define what a major is.)

   e. bioengineering

5. Write a 500- to 1,000-word description of one of the following items or of a piece of equipment used in your field. Include appropriate graphics. In a note preceding the description, specify your audience and indicate the type of description (general or particular) you are writing.

   a. dead-bolt lock

   b. photocopy machine

   c. ammeter

   d. automobile jack

   e. camera phone

6. Write a 500- to 1,000-word description of one of the following processes or a similar process with which you are familiar. Include appropriate graphics. In a note preceding the description, specify your audience and indicate the type of description (general or particular) you are writing. If you use secondary sources, cite them properly (see Appendix, Part B, for documentation systems).

a. how a nuclear power plant works

b. how a food co-op works

c. how a suspension bridge is constructed

d. how we see

e. how a baseball player becomes a free agent

7. INTERNET EXERCISE Study a set of instructions from Knowledge Hound <www.knowledgehound.com>. Write a memo to your instructor evaluating the quality of the instructions. Attach a printout of representative pages from the instructions.

8. You work in the customer-relations department of a company that makes plumbing supplies. The head of product development has just handed you the draft of installation instructions for a sliding tub door (see below). She has asked you to comment on their effectiveness. Write a memo to her, evaluating the instructions and suggesting improvements.

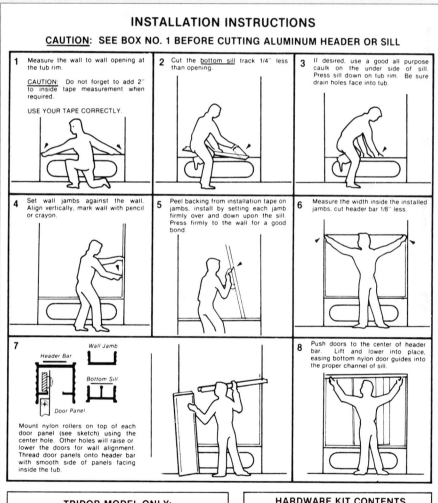

INSTALLATION INSTRUCTIONS

CAUTION: SEE BOX NO. 1 BEFORE CUTTING ALUMINUM HEADER OR SILL

1 Measure the wall to wall opening at the tub rim.

CAUTION: Do not forget to add 2" to inside tape measurement when required.

USE YOUR TAPE CORRECTLY.

2 Cut the bottom sill track 1/4" less than opening.

3 If desired, use a good all purpose caulk on the under side of sill. Press sill down on tub rim. Be sure drain holes face into tub.

4 Set wall jambs against the wall. Align vertically, mark wall with pencil or crayon.

5 Peel backing from installation tape on jambs, install by setting each jamb firmly over and down upon the sill. Press firmly to the wall for a good bond.

6 Measure the width inside the installed jambs, cut header bar 1/8" less.

7 Header Bar   Wall Jamb   Bottom Sill   Door Panel

Mount nylon rollers on top of each door panel (see sketch) using the center hole. Other holes will raise or lower the doors for wall alignment. Thread door panels onto header bar with smooth side of panels facing inside the tub.

8 Push doors to the center of header bar. Lift and lower into place, easing bottom nylon door guides into the proper channel of sill.

TRIDOR MODEL ONLY:

To reverse direction of panels, raise panels out of bottom track and slide catches past each other thereby reversing direction so that shower head does not throw water between the panels.

HARDWARE KIT CONTENTS
TUDOR MODEL
4 nylon bearings
4 ball bearing screws # 8-32 × 3/8"
TRIDOR MODEL
6 nylon bearings
6 ball bearing screws # 8-32 × 3/8"

9. Write a brief manual for a process familiar to you. Consider writing a procedures manual for a school activity or a part-time job, such as your work as the business manager of the school newspaper or as a tutor in the Writing Center.

10. **GROUP EXERCISE** Write instructions for one of the following activities or for a process used in your field. Include appropriate graphics. In a brief note preceding the instructions, indicate your audience and purpose. Exchange these materials with a partner. Observe your partner and take notes as he or she attempts to carry out the instructions. Then revise your instructions and share them with your partner; discuss whether the revised instructions are easier to understand and apply; if so, how? Submit your instructions to your instructor.

   a. how to change a bicycle tire

   b. how to convert a WAV file to an MP3 file

   c. how to find an online discussion group and subscribe to it

   d. how to locate, download, and install a file from CNET's Shareware.com (<www.shareware.com>), CNET's Download.com (<www.download.com>), or a similar site

---

Case 20: Writing Instructions for Installing a Programmable Thermostat

In This Book For more about memos, see Ch. 14, p. 377.

Background

You are the new technical-communication intern at Owyhee Engineers, a diversified manufacturer of control technologies for buildings, homes, and industry. The company is developing a programmable thermostat, the Energy Control 37 (EC37), for use in homes. Your documentation group is responsible for writing the installation and operation instructions for the EC37. Your supervisor, Warren Fu, asked you to interview Alexis Jaeger, a product engineer, about the thermostat. After the interview, you report back to Warren.

"In short, a programmable thermostat automatically sets back the temperature in your home based upon a predetermined schedule," you summarize. "The chief advantage of a programmable thermostat is that you no longer need to adjust the setting before leaving the house or before bedtime. In fact, by automatically adjusting the temperature to a lower energy setting while you are sleeping or out of the house, you can reduce energy use by 17 to 25 percent. That translates into more money in your pocket.

"I took notes when Alexis explained the installation procedure, and she gave me some possible graphics for the instructions." (See Documents 20.1 and 20.2.)

"I'd like you to start by writing the installation instructions and choosing the graphics to accompany them," Warren says. "Before you start writing, spend some time thinking about our customers. Most are do-it-yourself homeowners and not professional contractors."

"What else can you tell me about our customers?"

"A lot of homeowners are afraid of doing the installation themselves. They imagine all the things that can go wrong, especially when they picture a tangled mass of electrical wiring lurking behind their walls. They decide it's too much to handle. They return our thermostats and ask for a refund.

They need to understand that the seemingly complicated installation is really just a series of small steps. If they take their time and follow the directions, they can do it."

"Thanks," you respond. "This information will help me plan the instructions."

Your Assignment

1. Using principles discussed in this chapter, revise the information in Document 20.1. Design the installation instructions so that they are professional in appearance and easy to read. Add any necessary information that is missing, especially safety information.

2. Review the proposed graphics for the instructions (Document 20.2) and decide which, if any, of the graphics are appropriate, given the instructions' audience and purpose. In a memo to Warren, recommend which graphic to use and where the graphic should be placed. If none of the graphics seems appropriate to you, or if you think additional graphics are needed, describe the kind of information that should be provided and where it should be placed. For example, if you think the instructions would benefit from a line graph comparing the monthly heating and cooling costs in homes with a programmable thermostat versus homes without a programmable thermostat, write the following: "Insert at the top of the page a line graph showing monthly energy costs to heat and cool a house with a programmable thermostat versus a comparable house without a programmable thermostat. Show a 12-month period and use different colors to distinguish the two lines." The more specific your statement, the easier it will be for Warren to understand how to revise the instructions.

Document 20.1   Notes for Installing a Programmable Thermostat

▶ **On TechComm Web**

For digital versions of case documents, click on Downloadable Case Documents on <bedfordstmartins.com/techcomm>.

Installation Notes

Need #1 Phillips (small) screwdriver, drill, 3/16" bit

Homeowner has two options: (1) Install new thermostat in place of the old one, unless the current thermostat is located in a place with unusual heating conditions (e.g., near stove, direct sunlight, fireplace, hot-water pipes) or unusual cooling conditions (e.g., draft from stairwell, door, or window); in a damp area such as a bathroom (this leads to corrosion); or in a place with poor air circulation (e.g., corner, alcove, behind door). (2) Pick a new location. If picking a new location, locate unit on an inside wall about 5 feet above the floor in an often-used room. However, wait to install until all work such as painting has been completed.

To avoid shock and damage to furnace, AC, and thermostat, power should be turned off at circuit breaker, fuse box, or appliance before installation begins. Remove the old thermostat's cover: some covers snap on and pull off; others have locking screws on the side that must be loosened.

Wires must be labeled before they are removed. Use the labels that come packaged with the EC37. Letters (G, Y, W, RH, B, O, RC) will be printed near the terminals on the old unit. Label each wire as it is removed from the old unit's terminal, making sure wires don't fall back into hole in the wall. Then remove the old unit by loosening all the screws that attach it to the wall. Discard.

Prepare to install the EC37 by stripping insulation (about 3/8") from the wires coming out of the wall. This will clean off any corrosion. In addition, fill wall opening with non-flammable insulation. This will prevent drafts from affecting the unit. Separate the EC37's body from the baseplate by pressing latch at bottom on the unit. New holes for the screws used to attach the baseplate to the wall might need to be drilled if mounting unit to soft material such as plasterboard. If so, drill 3/16" holes for each screw, and use the plastic anchors included in the package. Hold the base against the wall with the wires coming through the opening in the baseplate and attach to wall with the two screws included.

Attach the wires to the matching terminals (e.g., wire labeled G to terminal labeled G). Wires should not touch each other or other parts of the terminal. Make sure wires are trapped between black spacer and brass terminal. Tighten wires securely. Snap the unit's body onto the baseplate.

Warning of Electrical Shock Hazard #1

Warning of Electrical Shock Hazard #2

Warning of Electrical Shock Hazard #3

Thermostat Placement

Wire-Terminal Attachment Showing Black Spacer

Base of EC37 Showing Wires Attached to Terminals

Stripping Insulation from Wire #1

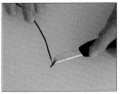

Stripping Insulation from Wire #2

Document 20.2   Possible Graphics for the Installation Instructions

Understanding the Role of Oral Presentations 579

Understanding the Process of Preparing and Delivering an Oral Presentation 580

Preparing a Presentation 580

Analyzing the Speaking Situation 580

Organizing and Developing the Presentation 582

Preparing Presentation Graphics 584

Choosing Effective Language 594

Rehearsing the Presentation 596

Delivering a Presentation 597

Calming Your Nerves 597

Using Your Voice Effectively 598

Using Your Body Effectively 599

Answering Questions After a Presentation 600

Sample Evaluation Form 601

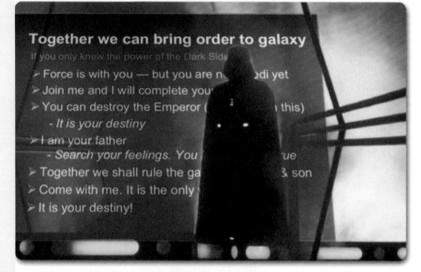

Source: Reynolds, 2006 <http://presentationzen.blogs.com/presentationzen/2006/01/contrasts_in_pr.html>.

In the World . . .

The highly regarded graphics scholar Edward Tufte (2003) created quite a stir a few years ago by declaring that PowerPoint is evil. Others followed suit, one claiming that PowerPoint makes you stupid, another that it makes you dumb. It is true that there are a lot of bad PowerPoint presentations delivered every day, but it is silly to say that PowerPoint is evil. We all need to take a deep breath. PowerPoint isn't evil or good. It's software.

You might not have had much experience in public speaking, and perhaps your few attempts have been difficult. That is understandable. Many people fear speaking in public; one famous study even concluded that people fear public speaking more than death.

But if you approach it logically, an oral presentation is simply another application you need to master in your role as a technical professional or technical communicator. Once you learn that the people in the room are there to hear what you have to say—not to stare at you or evaluate your clothing or catch you making a grammar mistake—you can calm down and deliver your information effectively. After giving a few presentations and realizing that the process can be mastered, you will be able to take advantage of the many opportunities that come your way to project your professionalism while communicating effectively.

There are four basic types of presentations:

- *Impromptu presentations.* You deliver the presentation without advance notice. For instance, your supervisor calls on you during a meeting to speak for a few minutes about a project you are working on.

- *Extemporaneous presentations.* You planned and rehearsed the presentation, and you might refer to notes or an outline, but you create the sentences as you speak. At its best, an extemporaneous presentation is clear and sounds spontaneous.

- *Scripted presentations.* You read a text that was written out completely in advance (by you or someone else). You sacrifice naturalness for increased clarity and precision.

- *Memorized presentations.* You speak without notes or a script. Memorized presentations are not appropriate for most technical subjects because most people cannot memorize presentations of more than a few minutes.

This chapter discusses extemporaneous and scripted presentations.

UNDERSTANDING THE ROLE OF ORAL PRESENTATIONS

An oral presentation has one big advantage over a written one: it permits a dialogue between the speaker and the audience. Listeners can make comments or simply ask questions. And the speaker and listeners can talk before and after the presentation. Oral presentations are common in technical communication. You can expect to give oral presentations to four types of audiences:

- *Clients and customers.* You present your product's features and its advantages over the competition. After the sale, you might provide oral operating instructions and maintenance tips to users.

- *Colleagues in your organization.* You might instruct fellow workers on a subject you know well. After you return from an important conference or an out-of-town project, your supervisors want a briefing—an oral report. If you have an idea for improving operations at your organization, you write an informal proposal and then present it orally to a small group of managers. Your presentation helps them determine whether to study the idea.
- *Fellow professionals at technical conferences.* You might speak about your own research project or about a team project. You might be addressing other professionals in your field or professionals in other fields.
- *The public.* You might deliver oral presentations to civic organizations and government bodies.

UNDERSTANDING THE PROCESS OF PREPARING AND DELIVERING AN ORAL PRESENTATION

Figure 21.1 presents an overview of the process of preparing and delivering an oral presentation. The rest of this chapter discusses this process, beginning with how to prepare a presentation.

PREPARING A PRESENTATION

When you see an excellent 20-minute presentation, you are seeing only the last 20 minutes of a process that took many hours. Experts recommend devoting 20 to 60 minutes for each minute of the presentation (Smith, 1991). At an average of 40 minutes of preparation time, you would need more than 13 hours to prepare a 20-minute presentation. Obviously, there are many variables, including your knowledge of the subject and your experience creating graphics and giving presentations on that subject. But the point is that good presentations don't just happen.

Preparing an oral presentation requires five steps:

- analyzing the speaking situation
- organizing and developing the presentation
- preparing presentation graphics
- choosing effective language
- rehearsing the presentation

Analyzing the Speaking Situation

First analyze your audience and purpose, then determine how much information you can deliver in the allotted time.

Analyze the Speaking Situation

How much does your audience know about the subject? What are your listeners' goals? What is your purpose—to inform or persuade, or both? Budget your time for the presentation.

Organize and Develop the Presentation

Use or adapt one or several of the organizational patterns described in Chapter 7. Gather the information you will need.

Prepare the Presentation Graphics

Effective graphics are visible, legible, simple, clear, and correct. Choose the appropriate technology based on the speaking situation and the available resources.

Choose Effective Language

Use language to signal advance organizers, summaries, and transitions. Choose memorable language by involving the audience, referring to people, and using interesting facts, figures, and quotations.

Rehearse the Presentation

Rehearse at least three times to make sure you are comfortable with the information. Use the Speaker's Checklist on page 603.

Deliver the Presentation

First, calm your nerves. In the presentation, use your voice effectively. Maintain eye contact and use natural gestures. Don't block the audience's view of the screen. At the end, politely solicit questions and answer them effectively.

Analyzing Your Audience and Purpose   In planning an oral presentation, consider audience and purpose, just as you would in writing a document.

- *Audience.* What does the audience know about your subject? Your answer will help you determine the level of technical vocabulary and concepts you will use, as well as the types of graphics. Why are audience members listening to your presentation? Are they likely to be hostile, enthusiastic, or neutral? A presentation on the virtues of free trade, for instance, will be received one way by conservative economists and another way by U.S.

steelworkers. Are they nonnative speakers of English? If so, prepare to slow down the pace of the delivery and use simple vocabulary.

- *Purpose.* Are you attempting to inform, or to inform and persuade? If you are explaining how windmill farms work, you might describe the process. If you are explaining why your windmills are an economical way to generate power, you might compare their results with those of other power sources.

Your analysis of your audience and purpose will affect the content and form of your presentation. For example, you might have to emphasize some aspects of your subject and ignore others altogether. Or you might have to arrange topics to accommodate an audience's needs.

Table 21.1 Time Allotment for a 20-Minute Presentation

Task	Time (minutes)
• Introduction	2
• Body	
– First Major Point	4
– Second Major Point	4
– Third Major Point	4
• Conclusion	2
• Questions	4

Budgeting Your Time   At most professional meetings, each speaker is given a maximum time, such as 20 minutes. If the question-and-answer period is part of your allotted time, plan accordingly. Even for an informal presentation, you will probably have to work within an unstated time limit that you must determine from the speaking situation. If you take more than your time, eventually your listeners will resent you or simply stop paying attention.

For a 20-minute presentation, the time allotment shown in Table 21.1 is typical. For a scripted presentation, most speakers need a little more than a minute to deliver a double-spaced page of text effectively.

Organizing and Developing the Presentation

The speaking situation will help you decide how to organize and develop the information you will present.

In This Book
For more about organizational patterns, see Ch. 7.

Start by considering the organizational patterns used typically in technical communication. One of them might fit the speaking situation. For instance, if you are a quality-assurance engineer working for a computer-chip manufacturer and addressing your technical colleagues on why one of the company's products is experiencing a failure rate higher than normal, think in terms of cause and effect: the high failure rate is the effect, but what is the cause? Or think in terms of problem-methods-solution. The high failure rate is the problem; the research you conducted to determine its cause is the method; your recommended action is the solution. Of course, you can combine and adapt several organizational patterns.

While you devise an effective organizational pattern for your presentation, note the kinds of information you will need for each section of the presentation. Some of this information will be data; some of it will be graphics that you can use in your slides; some might be objects that you want to pass around the audience.

This is also a good time to plan the introduction and the conclusion of your presentation.

Planning the Introduction　Like an introduction to a written document, an introduction to an oral presentation helps your audience understand what you are going to say, why you are going to say it, and how you are going to say it.

Guidelines

Introducing a Presentation

In introducing a presentation, consider these five suggestions.

▶ **Introduce yourself.** Unless you are speaking to the colleagues you work with every day, begin with an introduction, such as "Good morning, my name is Omar Castillo, and I'm the Director of Facilities here at United." If you are using slides, put your name and position on the title slide.

▶ **State the title of your presentation.** Like all titles, titles of presentations should explain the audience and purpose, such as "Replacing the HVAC System in Building 3: Findings from the Feasibility Study." Also include the title on your title slide.

▶ **Explain the purpose of your presentation.** This explanation can be brief: "My purpose today is to present the results of the feasibility study carried out by the Facilities Group. As you may recall, last quarter we were charged with determining whether it would be wise to replace the HVAC system in Building 3."

▶ **State your main point.** An explicit statement can help your audience understand the rest of the presentation: "Our main finding is that the HVAC system should be replaced as soon as possible. Replacing it would cost approximately $120,000. The payback period would be 2.5 years. We recommend that we start soliciting bids now, for an installation date in the third week of November."

▶ **Provide an advance organizer.** Listeners need advance organizers: specific statements of where you are going: "First, I'd like to describe our present system, highlighting the recent problems we have experienced. Next, I'd like to. . . . Then I'd like to. . . . Finally, I'd like to conclude and invite your questions."

Planning the Conclusion　Like all conclusions, a conclusion to an oral presentation reinforces what you have said and looks to the future.

Guidelines

Concluding a Presentation

In concluding a presentation, consider these four suggestions.

▶ **Announce that you are concluding.** For example, "At this point, I'd like to conclude my talk." This statement helps the audience focus on your conclusions.

▶ **Summarize the main points.** Because listeners cannot rewind what you have said, you should briefly summarize your main points. If you are using slides, you should list each of your main points in one short phrase.

> ▶ **Look to the future.** If appropriate, speak briefly about what you think (or hope) will happen next: "If the president accepts our recommendation, you can expect the renovation to begin in late November. After a few hectic weeks, we'll have the ability to control our environment much more precisely than we can now."

> ▶ **Invite questions politely.** You want to invite questions because they will help you clarify what you said or communicate information that you did not include in the formal presentation.

Preparing Presentation Graphics

Graphics clarify or highlight important ideas or facts. Statistical data, in particular, lend themselves to graphical presentation, as do abstract relationships and descriptions of equipment or processes. Research reported by Smith (1991) indicates that presentations that include graphics are judged more professional, persuasive, and credible than those that do not. In addition, Smith notes, audiences remember the information better:

	Retention after	
	3 hours	3 days
Without graphics	70%	10%
With graphics	85%	65%

One other advantage of using presentation graphics is that the audience is not always looking at you. Giving the audience another visual focus can reduce your nervousness.

If your audience includes people from different cultures and native languages, use graphics to reinforce your points. Try to devise ways to present information using graphics—flowcharts, diagrams, and so forth—to help your listeners understand you. Putting more textual information in graphics will allow listeners to read the accompanying text while they listen to you explain your points.

Characteristics of an Effective Graphic   An effective presentation graphic has five characteristics:

▶ **In This Book**
For more about creating graphics, see Ch. 12.

- It *presents a clear, well-supported claim.* In a presentation slide, the best way to present a claim and support it is to put the claim in the heading section of the slide and the support in the body of the slide. Michael Alley (2007) recommends the structure shown in Figure 21.2.

- It *is easy to see.* The most common problem with presentation graphics is that they are too small. Don't transfer information from an 8.5 × 11-inch page to a slide or transparency. In general, text has to be in 24-point type or larger to be visible on the screen. Figure 21.3 on page 586 shows that transferring text from a page to a slide makes for a poor slide.

Here you present the claim (in the form of a complete clause) that you will support with the graphics and words below and with the words you speak.

Here you present the support for your claim. The support will consist of graphics, such as photographs, diagrams, and tables. Where appropriate, you should add brief clarifying comments in words. Some slides will include only one large graphic. Others will include several graphics.

a. The structure of a typical slide

Fragments quickly outpace the blast wave and become the primary hazard to personnel

This slide is structured like a paragraph. The words are the topic sentence; the photograph is the support.

b. A slide with a claim and a single large graphic

Figure 21.2   Michael Alley's Claim-and-Support Structure for Presentation Graphics
Source: Rochester, 2004 <www.writing.eng.vt.edu/samples/arl2.pdf>.

In this slide, the heading functions as an advance organizer, introducing the three main sections of the talk.

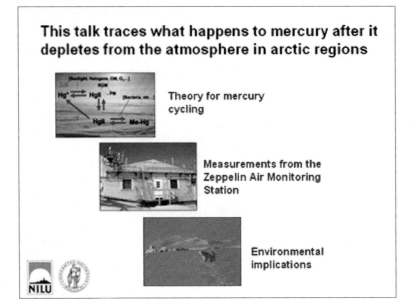

This talk traces what happens to mercury after it depletes from the atmosphere in arctic regions

Theory for mercury cycling

Measurements from the Zeppelin Air Monitoring Station

Environmental implications

c. A slide with a claim, several graphics, and textual annotations

Figure 21.2 (continued)

Source: Aspmo, Berg, & Wibetoe, 2004 <www.writing.eng.vt.edu/slides.html/slide_template.ppt>.

This slide contains far too much text. A common guideline is to put no more than seven words on a line, and no more than seven lines on a slide. Otherwise, the text becomes too small to read easily.

There's another problem with this slide. What is the presenter supposed to do or say while this slide is visible? The presenter cannot read the text, because many people in the audience will find it offensive to have someone read to them.

If you have lengthy text—such as long quotations or a list of sources—distribute a handout at the end of your presentation. During the presentation itself, reduce the text to brief phrases.

The "Workbook" Approach

In explaining the U.S. approach to privacy the "Workbook" describes privacy protection not as ethical practice but as good business:

"In the United States, the importance of protecting the privacy of individuals' personal information is a priority for the federal government and consumers. Consumers repeatedly cite fears that their personal information will be misused as a reason for not doing business online. In this way, moves to bolster online privacy protect consumer interests and fuel the broader growth of online communications, innovation, and business. Self-regulatory initiatives are an effective approach to putting meaningful privacy protections in place. In certain highly sensitive areas, however, legislative solutions are appropriate. These sensitive areas include financial and medical records, genetic information, Social Security numbers, and information involving children." [8]

Figure 21.3 **Text Copied from a Page to a Slide**

- *It is easy to read.* Use clear, legible lines for drawings and diagrams; black on white works best. Use legible typefaces for text; a boldface sans-serif typeface such as Arial or Helvetica is effective because it reproduces clearly on a screen. Avoid shadowed and outlined letters.

- *It is simple.* Text and drawings must be simple. Each graphic should present only one idea. Your listeners have not seen the graphic before and will not be able to linger over it.

- *It is correct.* Everyone makes mistakes of grammar, punctuation, or spelling, but mistakes are particularly embarrassing when they are 10 inches tall on a screen.

When you use presentation software to create a set of graphics for a presentation, avoid the templates, many of which violate basic design principles. Instead, create a simple design using the Slide Master feature (see the Tech Tip on page 588).

Presentation software contains many fancy animation effects. For example, you can set the software so that when a new slide appears, it is accompanied by the sound of applause or of breaking glass, and the headline spins around like a pinwheel. Do not use animation effects that are unrelated to your subject. They will undercut your professionalism and soon (extremely soon) become tiresome.

However, one animation effect, sometimes called *appear and dim*, is useful. When you create a bulleted list, you can set the software to make the next bullet item appear when you click the mouse. When you do so, the previous bullet item dims (see the Tech Tip on page 589). This feature focuses the audience's attention on the bullet item you are discussing.

One more point: you cannot use copyrighted material—images, text, music, video, or other material—in your presentation without written permission to do so.

Graphics and the Speaking Situation   To plan your graphics, analyze four aspects of the speaking situation:

- *Length of the presentation.* How many graphics should you have? Smith (1991) suggests showing a different graphic approximately every 30 seconds. This figure is only a guideline; base your decision on your subject and audience. Still, the general point is valid: it is far better to have a series of simple graphics than to have one complicated one that stays on the screen for five minutes.

- *Audience aptitude and experience.* What kinds of graphics can your audience understand easily? You don't want to present scatter graphs, for example, if your listeners do not know how to interpret them.

- *Size and layout of the room.* Graphics to be used in a small meeting room differ from those to be used in a 500-seat auditorium. Think first about the size of the images, then about the layout of the room. For instance,

In This Book

For more about typefaces, see Ch. 11, p. 268. For more about using color in graphics, see Ch. 12, p. 307.

On TechComm Web

See Dave Zielinski's essay on how copyright law applies to presentations. Click on Links Library for Ch. 21 on <bedfordstmartins.com/techcomm>.

TECH TIP

How to Create a Master Page Design in PowerPoint

To create a page design of your own, you can use the **Slide Master** feature to consistently apply design elements to your slides.

1. Use the **Office** button to open a **blank presentation**.

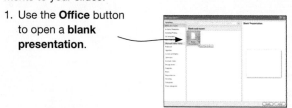

2. Select **Slide Master** from the **Presentation Views** group on the **View** tab.

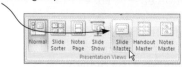

By highlighting elements on the master page and then using the commands on the **Slide Master** tab, you can add a background, choose a color scheme, and choose type styles and sizes.

To add graphical elements (such as a horizontal rule), use the **Illustrations** group on the **Insert** tab.

To modify the format, size, or position of placeholders for header and footer information, right-click on the header or footer box on the slide, then make a selection from the pop-up menu.

To make changes to the type of information displayed in placeholders, select the **Header & Footer** button in the **Text** group on the **Insert** tab, then use the **Header and Footer** dialog box.

3. To save your page design so that you can use it for other presentations, select **Save As** from the **Office** button, then select **PowerPoint Template** from the drop-down menu.

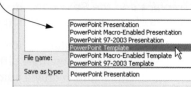

KEYWORDS: slide master, presentation views, background, slide design, placeholder, header and footer, PowerPoint template, my templates

TECH TIP

How to Set List Items to Appear and Dim During a Presentation

To help your audience focus on the point you are discussing, you can apply the **custom animation** feature of PowerPoint to the **Master Page** so that list items appear and dim.

1. To apply a **custom animation**, in the **Slide Master** view select the **Title and Content Layout** slide, highlight the list on the slide, and then select the **Custom Animation** button in the **Animations** group.

Click to edit Master title style

• Click to edit Master text styles
  – Second level
    • Third level
      – Fourth level
        » Fifth level

2. In the **Custom Animation** pane, select **Add Effect**. Then select the **Entrance** category and the **Appear** effect.

3. In the **Animation Order** list, click on the drop-down menu and select **Effect Options**.

4. On the **Effect** tab in the **Appear** dialog box, click on the **After Animation** drop-down menu and select a dim color.

KEYWORDS: custom animation, slide master, effect options, entrance effects, blinds

---

will a window create glare that you will have to consider as you plan the type or placement of the graphics?

- *Equipment.* Find out what kind of equipment will be available in the presentation room. Ask about backups in case of equipment failure. If possible, bring your own equipment. That way, you know it works, and you know how to use it. Some speakers bring graphics in two media just in case; that is, they have slides, but they also have transparencies of the same graphics.

Using Graphics to Signal the Organization of the Presentation   Used effectively, graphics can help you communicate how your presentation is organized. For example, you can use the transition from one graphic to the next to indicate the transition from one point to the next. Figure 21.4 on pages 590–91 shows the slides for a presentation that accompanied the report in Chapter 19, page 519, on selecting an MP3 player for a gym.

Feasibility Study on Music Options:
A Completion Report

Prepared by:
Jessie Pritiken, Senior Fitness Trainer
Megan Turner, Fitness Trainer

Slide 1—the title slide—shows the title of the presentation and the name and affiliation of each speaker.

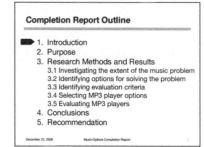

Slide 2 presents an overview, which outlines the presentation. The arrow identifies the point the speaker is addressing.

At the bottom of each slide in the body of the presentation is a footer with the date, the title of the presentation, and the number of the slide.

Notice that the title of Slide 3 uses the numbering system introduced in the previous slide. This cue helps the audience understand the structure of the presentation. Following the colon is an independent clause that presents the claim that will be supported in this slide.

This slide shows a simple pie chart. Although the speakers could have used words in a bulleted list, graphics are more visually interesting and easier to understand.

The photograph makes the point vividly: all that expensive equipment and nobody using it.

Slide 5, not included here, is identical to Slide 2, except for the placement of the blue arrow. The speakers use this slide—and Slides 7, 19, and 21—to help orient listeners.

The slide number at the bottom of each slide enables audience members to ask questions by referring to the number.

To make this slide, the speakers used a public-domain image of the musical notes, then added the words in text boxes.

The formatting that appears throughout the slide set—the background color, the horizontal rule, and the footer—was created in the Slide Master view.

To make this first slide, the speakers inserted an image of a loudspeaker, then reversed the image. In addition, they added the photograph of a man covering his ears. If the images in your presentation are your own intellectual property, you can legally present your slide show anywhere. If the images are not your own intellectual property, you can legally present the show in a college class, because the images are covered by the fair-use provisions of U.S. copyright law. However, if you wish to present your slide show in a business environment, you would need to get formal written permission from the copyright holders of all the images.

To illustrate their point, the speakers used the software's drawing tools to create the universal "no" symbol and placed it over the loudspeaker image used in Slide 9. This symbol is also used in Slides 6 and 17.

Figure 21.4   Selected Slides for a Brief Presentation

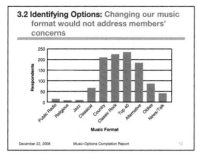

3.2 Identifying Options: Changing our music format would not address members' concerns

The speakers use a simple bar graph to support their point that because gym members like different kinds of music, no one music format will satisfy them all.

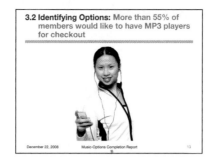

3.2 Identifying Options: More than 55% of members would like to have MP3 players for checkout

3.3 Identifying Evaluation Criteria: We require a durable MP3 player costing less than $100

The speakers combine three images and a symbol in a text box to illustrate their point.

Note that color is used sparingly for emphasis.

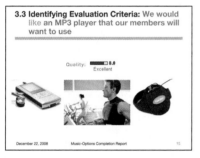

3.3 Identifying Evaluation Criteria: We would like an MP3 player that our members will want to use

When you wish to cite sources of images, you have three choices: add a source statement at the bottom of each slide, make a sources slide that you show at the end of the presentation, or make a paper copy of the sources to distribute.

3.4 Selecting Options: We studied the 7 most-recommended models

- Apple iPod Classic (80 GB)
- Apple iPod Nano (third generation, 4 GB)
- Apple iPod Shuffle (second generation, 1 GB)
- iRiver Clix (2 GB)
- Creative Zen (4 GB)
- Creative Zen V Plus (4 GB)
- San Disk Sansac 240 (1 GB)

Use bulleted lists sparingly to present verbal information. Although they can be helpful, they lack drama.

Use appear and dim *(see the Tech Tip on p. 589)* to highlight each bullet point when you click the mouse.

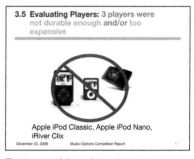

3.5 Evaluating Players: 3 players were not durable enough and/or too expensive

Apple iPod Classic, Apple iPod Nano, iRiver Clix

The images of these three players are protected under U.S. copyright law.

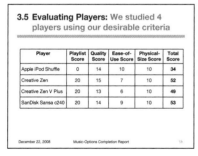

3.5 Evaluating Players: We studied 4 players using our desirable criteria

Player	Playlist Score	Quality Score	Ease-of-Use Score	Physical-Size Score	Total Score
Apple iPod Shuffle	0	14	10	10	34
Creative Zen	20	15	7	10	52
Creative Zen V Plus	20	13	6	10	49
SanDisk Sansa c240	20	14	9	10	53

The speakers use a decision matrix to show the logic of their evaluation of the options based on the desired characteristics.

When you use tables, keep them simple. If you have a lot of rows and columns, present the data on several slides.

4. Conclusions: The Sansa c240 is durable, inexpensive, easy to use, and compact; Napster to Go is the best music source

To illustrate their conclusions, the speakers use images of the recommended player and music service connected by a plus sign.

As discussed in Ch. 19, conclusions are interpretations based on results.

5. Recommendation: Implement a pilot program for 2 months

2-month MP3 program: $1,985

Happy members: priceless

As discussed in Ch. 19, recommendations are statements about what you think should be done next.

Some speakers like to make a final slide labeled "Questions?" to signal the end of the presentation. You can also display contact information (such as your e-mail address) to encourage audience members to get in touch with you.

Figure 21.4   (continued)

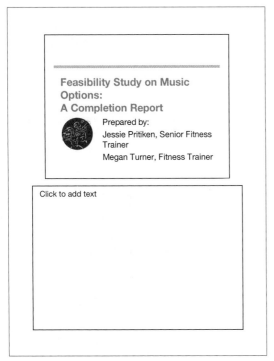

To create speaking notes for each slide, use your presentation software to type the notes in the box under the picture of the slide, then print the notes pages.

You can print the slides on your notes pages in color or black and white.

The problem with using speaking notes is that you cannot read your notes and maintain eye contact at the same time.

Figure 21.5   Speaking Notes

The software is set to display six slides on the page.

Figure 21.6   Handout

Presentation software allows you to create two other kinds of documents—*speaking notes* and *handouts*—that can enhance presentations. Figure 21.5 shows a page of speaking notes. Figure 21.6 shows a handout.

Typical Media Used to Present Graphics   Table 21.2 describes the typical media used to present graphics.

If you are using presentation-graphics software, keep in mind that many of the templates provided with the software are unnecessarily ornate, full of fancy shading, designs, and colors. Choose a simple template, then modify it for your situation. You want the audience to focus on the information, not on the complex design of the graphics.

Table 21.2 Typical Media Used to Present Graphics

Medium	Advantages	Disadvantages
Computer presentations: images are projected from a computer to a screen.	• Very professional appearance. • You can produce any combination of static or dynamic images, from simple graphs to sophisticated, three-dimensional animations, as well as sound and video. • You can launch an Internet browser and display Web sites.	• The equipment is expensive and not available everywhere. • Preparing the graphics can be time-consuming. • Presentations prepared using one piece of software might not run on all systems.
Slide projector: projects previously prepared slides onto a screen.	• Very professional appearance. • Versatile—can handle photographs or artwork, color or black and white. • With a second projector, you can eliminate the pause between slides. • During the presentation, you can easily advance and reverse the slides. • Graphics software lets you create small paper copies of your slides to distribute to the audience after the presentation.	• Slide projectors are no longer being manufactured, but they will likely exist in organizations for at least another decade. • Slides can be expensive to produce. • The room has to be kept relatively dark during the slide presentation.
Overhead projector: projects transparencies onto a screen.	• Transparencies are inexpensive and easy to create. • You can draw transparencies "live." • You can create overlays by placing one transparency over another. • Lights can remain on during the presentation.	• Not as professional-looking as slides. • Each transparency must be loaded separately by hand.
Chalkboard or other hard writing surface.	• Almost universally available. • You have complete control—can add, delete, or modify the graphic easily.	• Complicated or extensive graphics are difficult to create. • Ineffective in large rooms. • Very informal appearance.
Objects: models or samples of material that can be held up or passed around the audience.	• Interesting for the audience. • Provides a close look at the object.	• Audience members might not be listening while they are looking at the object. • It can take a long while to pass an object around a large room. • The object might not survive intact.
Handouts: photocopies of written material given to each audience member.	• Much material can fit on the page. • Audience members can write on their copies and keep them.	• Audience members might read the handout rather than listen to the speaker.

In addition, set the software so that you use the mouse to advance from one graphic to the next. If you set it so that it advances automatically at a specified interval, such as 60 seconds, you will have to speed up or slow down your presentation to keep up with the graphics.

INTERACTIVE SAMPLE DOCUMENT
Integrating Graphics and Text on a Presentation Slide

The following slide is part of a presentation about the Human Genome Project. The questions in the margin ask you to think about the discussion of preparing presentation graphics (on pages 584–93). E-mail your responses to yourself and/or your instructor on TechComm Web.

1. How effective is the Human Genome Project logo in the upper left-hand corner of the slide?

2. How well does the graphic of DNA support the accompanying text on chromosome facts?

3. Overall, how effective is the presentation graphic?

 On TechComm Web

To e-mail your responses to yourself and/or your instructor, click on Interactive Sample Documents for Ch. 21 on <bedfordstmartins.com/techcomm>.

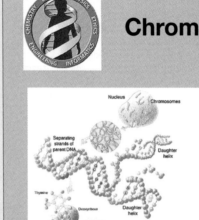

Chromosome Facts

DNA Details

- number of chromosomes: 22 pairs + 1 pair sex-determining chromosomes = 46
  - one chromosome of each pair donated from each parent's egg or sperm
  - sex chromosomes: X,Y for males: X,X for females
  - largest chromosome: #1 = ~263 million base pairs (bp)
  - smallest chromosome: Y = ~59 million bp

Choosing Effective Language

Delivering an oral presentation is more challenging than writing a document, for two reasons:

- Listeners can't go back to listen again to something they didn't understand.
- Because you are speaking live, you must maintain your listeners' attention, even if they are hungry or tired, or if the room is too hot.

Using language effectively helps you meet these two challenges.

If many people in your audience are not native speakers of your language, hire interpreters (people who can translate your words as you speak) and translators (people who can translate your written material in advance). Doing so will enhance the effectiveness of your presentation for nonnative audience members.

Using Language to Signal Advance Organizers, Summaries, and Transitions
Even if you use graphics effectively, listeners cannot "see" the organization of a presentation as well as readers can. For this reason, use language to alert your listeners to advance organizers, summaries, and transitions.

- *Advance organizers.* Use an advance organizer (a statement that tells the listener what you are about to say) in the introduction. In addition, use advance organizers when you introduce main ideas in the body of the presentation.

- *Summaries.* The major summary is in the conclusion, but you might also summarize at strategic points in the body of the presentation. For instance, after a three- to four-minute discussion of a major point, you might summarize it in one sentence before going on to the next major point. Here is a sample summary from a conclusion:

  > Let me conclude by summarizing my three main points about the implications of the new RCRA regulations on the long-range waste-management strategy for Radnor Township. The first point: . . . The second point: . . . The third point: . . . I hope this presentation will give you some ideas as you think about the challenges of implementing the RCRA.

- *Transitions.* As you move from one point to the next, signal the transition clearly. Summarize the previous point, then announce that you are moving to the next point:

  > It is clear, then, that the federal government has issued regulations without indicating how it expects county governments to comply with them. I'd like to turn now to my second main point: . . .

Using Memorable Language   Effective presentations require memorable language.

Guidelines

Using Memorable Language in Oral Presentations

Draw on these three techniques to help make a lasting impression on your audience.

▶ **Involve the audience.** People are more interested in their own concerns than in yours. Talk to the audience about their problems and their solutions. In the introduction, establish a link between your topic and the audience's interests. For instance, a presentation to a city council about waste management might begin like this:

> Picture yourself on the Radnor Township Council two years from now. After exhaustive hearings, proposals, and feasibility studies, you still don't have a waste-management plan that meets federal regulations. What you do have is

a mounting debt: the township is being fined $1,000 per day until you implement an acceptable plan.

▶ **Refer to people, not to abstractions.** People remember specifics; they forget abstractions. To make a point memorable, describe it in human terms:

What could you do with that $365,000 every year? In each computer lab in each school in the township, you could replace each PC every three years instead of every four years. Or you could expand your school-lunch program to feed every needy child in the township. Or you could extend your after-school programs to cover an additional 3,000 students.

▶ **Use interesting facts, figures, and quotations.** Search the Internet for interesting information about your subject. For instance, you might find a brief quotation from an authoritative figure in the field or a famous person not generally associated with the field (for example, Theodore Roosevelt on waste management and the environment).

A note about humor: only a few hundred people in the United States make a good living being funny. With that in mind, don't plan to tell a joke. If something happens during the presentation that provides an opening for a witty remark and you are good at making witty remarks, fine. But don't *prepare* to be funny.

Rehearsing the Presentation

Even the most gifted speakers need to rehearse. It is a good idea to set aside enough time to rehearse your speech thoroughly.

Rehearsing an Extemporaneous Presentation   Rehearse your extemporaneous presentation at least three times.

- *First rehearsal.* Don't worry about posture or voice projection. Just compose your presentation aloud with your presentation slides. Your goal is to see if the speech makes sense—if you can explain all the points and create effective transitions. If you have trouble, stop and try to figure out the problem. If you need more information, get it. If you need a better transition, create one. You are likely to learn that you need to revise the order of your slides. Pick up where you left off and continue the rehearsal, stopping again where necessary to revise.

- *Second rehearsal.* This time, the presentation should flow more easily. Make any necessary changes to the slides. When you have complete control over the organization and flow, check to see if you are within the time limit.

- *Third rehearsal.* After a satisfactory second rehearsal, try the presentation under more realistic circumstances—if possible, in front of other people. The listeners might offer questions or constructive advice about your speaking style. If no one is available, tape-record or videotape the presentation and then evaluate your delivery. If you can visit the site of the presentation to rehearse there, you will find giving the actual speech a little easier.

Rehearse again until you are satisfied with your presentation; don't try to memorize it.

Rehearsing a Scripted Presentation   Rehearsing a scripted presentation is a combination of revising and editing the text and rehearsing it. As you revise, read the script aloud to hear how it sounds. Once you think the presentation says what you want it to say, try reading it into an audio or video recorder. Revise it until you are satisfied, then rehearse it in front of other people. Do not memorize the presentation. There is no need to; you will have your script in front of you on the podium.

DELIVERING A PRESENTATION

When giving your presentation, you will need to concentrate on what you have to say. However, you will also have three other concerns: calming your nerves, using your voice effectively, and using your body effectively.

Calming Your Nerves

Most professional actors admit to being nervous before a performance, so it is no wonder that most technical speakers are nervous. You might well fear that you will forget everything or that no one will be able to hear you. These fears are common. But keep in mind three facts about nervousness:

- *You are much more aware of your nervousness than the audience is.* They are farther away from your trembling hands.
- *Nervousness gives you energy and enthusiasm.* Without energy and enthusiasm, your presentation will be flat. If you seem bored and listless, your audience will become bored and listless.
- *After a few minutes, your nervousness will pass.* You will be able to relax and concentrate on the subject.

This advice is unlikely to make you feel much better if you are distracted by nerves as you wait to give your presentation. Experienced speakers offer three tips for coping with nervousness:

- *Realize that you are prepared.* If you have done your homework, prepared the presentation carefully, and rehearsed it several times, you'll be fine.
- *Realize that the audience is there to hear you, not to judge you.* Your listeners want to hear what you have to say. You are the expert; there's no need to be nervous.
- *Realize that the audience is made up of individuals who happen to be sitting in the same room with you.* You'll feel better if you realize that they also get nervous before making presentations.

Guidelines

Releasing Nervous Energy

Experienced speakers suggest the following strategies for dealing with nervousness before a presentation.

▶ **Walk around.** A brisk walk of a minute or two can calm you by dissipating some of your nervous energy.

▶ **Go off by yourself for a few minutes.** Getting away can help you compose your thoughts and realize that you can handle the nervousness.

▶ **Talk with someone for a few minutes.** For some speakers, distraction works best. Find someone to talk to.

▶ **Take several deep breaths, exhaling slowly.** Doing so will help you control your nerves.

When it is time to begin, don't jump up to the lectern and start speaking quickly. Walk up slowly and arrange your text, outline, or note cards before you. If water is available, take a sip. Look out at the audience for a few seconds before you begin. Say "Good morning" (or "Good afternoon" or "Good evening"), and refer to the officers and dignitaries present. If you have not been introduced, introduce yourself. In less-formal contexts, just begin your presentation.

So that the audience will listen to you and have confidence in what you say, use your voice and your body to project an attitude of restrained self-confidence. Show interest in your topic and knowledge about your subject.

Using Your Voice Effectively

Inexperienced speakers often have problems with five aspects of vocalizing.

- *Volume.* Because acoustics vary greatly from room to room, you won't know how well your voice will carry until you begin speaking. In some rooms, speakers can use a conversational volume. In other rooms, greater voice projection is required. These circumstances aside, more people speak too softly than too loudly. After your first few sentences, ask if the people in the back of the room can hear you. When people speak into a microphone, they tend to speak too loudly. Glance at your audience to see if you are having volume problems. The body language of audience members will be clear.

- *Speed.* Nervousness makes people speak quickly. Even if you think you are speaking at the right rate, you might be going a little too fast for some listeners. Although you know your subject well, your listeners are trying to understand new information. For particularly difficult points, slow down for emphasis. After finishing one major point, pause before introducing the next one.

- *Pitch.* In an effort to control their voices, many speakers end up flattening their pitch. The resulting monotone is boring and, for some listeners, distracting. Try to let the pitch of your voice go up or down as it would in a normal conversation.

- *Articulation.* Nervousness can accentuate sloppy pronunciation. If you want to say *environment*, don't say *envirament*. A related problem involves technical words and phrases, especially the important ones. When a speaker uses a phrase over and over, it tends to get clipped and becomes difficult to understand. Unless you articulate carefully, *Scanlon Plan* will end up as *Scanluhplah*.

- *Nonfluencies.* Avoid such meaningless fillers as *you know, like, okay, right, uh,* and *um.* These phrases do not hide the fact that you aren't saying anything. A thoughtful pause is better than an annoying verbal tic.

Using Your Body Effectively

Besides listening to you, the audience will be looking at you. Effective speakers use body language to help listeners follow the presentation.

Guidelines

Facing an Audience

As you give a presentation, keep in mind four guidelines about physical movement.

▶ **Maintain eye contact.** Eye contact helps you see how the audience is receiving the presentation. You will see, for instance, if listeners in the back are having trouble hearing you. For small groups, look at each listener randomly. For larger groups, look at each segment of the audience frequently during your speech. Do not stare at the screen, the floor, or out the window.

▶ **Use natural gestures.** When people talk, they often gesture with their hands. Most of the time, gestures make the presentation look natural and improve listeners' comprehension. You can supplement your natural gestures by using your arms and hands to signal pauses and to emphasize important points. When referring to graphics, walk toward the screen and point to direct the audience's attention. Avoid physical mannerisms—gestures that serve no useful purpose, such as jiggling the coins in your pocket or pacing back and forth. Like verbal mannerisms, physical mannerisms are often unconscious. Constructive criticism from friends can help you pinpoint them.

▶ **Don't block the audience's view of the screen.** Stand off to the side of the screen. Use a pointer to indicate key words or images on the screen.

▶ **Control the audience's attention.** People will listen to and look at anything that is interesting. If you distribute handouts at the start of the presentation, some people will start to read them and stop listening to you. If you leave an image on the screen after you finish talking about it, some people will keep looking at it instead of listening to you. When you want the audience to look at you and listen to you, remove the graphics or make the screen blank.

If your audience includes people from different cultures, be aware that gestures can have cultural meanings. As discussed in Chapter 12, hand gestures (such as the thumbs-up or the "okay" gesture) have different—and sometimes insulting—meanings in other cultures. Therefore, it's a good idea to limit the use of these gestures. You can't go wrong with an arms-out, palms-up gesture, which projects openness and inclusiveness.

ANSWERING QUESTIONS AFTER A PRESENTATION

When you finish a presentation, thank the audience simply and directly: "Thank you for your attention." Then invite questions. Don't abruptly say "Any questions?" This phrasing suggests that you don't really want any questions. Instead, say something like this: "If you have any questions, I'd be happy to try to answer them now." If invited politely, people will be much more likely to ask. In that way, you will be more likely to communicate your information effectively.

When you respond to questions, you might encounter any of these four situations:

- *You're unsure whether everyone heard the question.* Ask if people have heard it. If they haven't, repeat or paraphrase it, perhaps as an introduction to your response: "Your question is about the efficiency of these three techniques. . . ." Some speakers always repeat the question, which also gives them an extra moment to prepare an answer.

- *You don't understand the question.* Ask for clarification. After responding, ask if you have answered the question adequately.

- *You have already answered the question during the presentation.* Restate the answer politely. Begin your answer with a phrase such as the following: "I'm sorry I didn't make that point clear in my talk. I wanted to explain how. . . ." Never insult the person by pointing out that you already answered the question.

- *A belligerent member of the audience rejects your response and insists on restating his or her original point.* Politely offer to discuss the matter further after the presentation. This way, the person won't bore or annoy the rest of the audience.

Ethics Note

Answering Questions Honestly

If an audience member asks a question to which you do not know the answer, admit it. Simply say "I don't know" or "I'm not sure, but I think the answer is. . . ." Smart people know that they don't know everything. If you have some ideas about how to find out the answer—by checking a certain reference source, for example—share them. If the question is obviously important to the person who asked it, you might offer to meet with him or her to discuss ways for you to give a more complete response, perhaps by e-mail.

If it is appropriate to stay after the presentation to talk individually with members of the audience, offer to do so. Remember to thank them for their courtesy in listening to you.

SAMPLE EVALUATION FORM

Figure 21.7 is a form that can help you focus your thoughts as you watch and listen to a presentation.

Figure 21.7 Sample Evaluation Form

On TechComm Web

To download this form in an electronic format, see Forms for Technical Communication on <bedfordstmartins.com/techcomm>.

Oral Presentation Evaluation Form

Speaker(s)_____   Topic_____

The left-hand column lists statements about different aspects of the presentation. In the middle column, rate the speaker(s) on each aspect of the presentation by writing a number from 1 to 6, with 1 signifying that you strongly disagree with the statement and 6 signifying that you strongly agree with the statement. In the right-hand column, write any comments you wish the speaker(s) to see.

Aspect of the Presentation	Rating (1 = strongly disagree; 6 = strongly agree)	Comments
Organization and Development		
1. In the introduction, the speaker related the topic to the audience's concerns.		
2. In the introduction, the speaker explained the main points he or she wanted to make in the presentation.		
3. In the introduction, the speaker explained the organization of the presentation.		
4. I found it easy to understand the organization of the presentation.		
5. The speaker used appropriate and sufficient evidence to clarify the subject.		
6. In the conclusion, the speaker summarized the main points effectively.		
7. In the conclusion, the speaker invited questions politely.		
8. In the conclusion, the speaker answered questions effectively.		
9. The speaker used the allotted time effectively.		

Figure 21.7 (continued)

Aspect of the Presentation	Rating (1 = strongly disagree; 6 = strongly agree)	Comments
Verbal and Physical Presence		
10. The speaker used interesting, clear language to get the points across.		
11. The speaker used clear and distinct enunciation.		
12. The speaker seemed relaxed and poised.		
13. The speaker exhibited no distracting vocal mannerisms.		
14. The speaker exhibited no distracting physical mannerisms.		
15. The speaker made eye contact effectively.		
16. The speaker was enthusiastic.		
Use of Graphics		
17. The speaker used graphics effectively to reinforce and explain the main points.		
18. The speaker used appropriate kinds of graphics.		
19. The speaker used graphics effectively to highlight the organization of the presentation.		
20. The graphics were easy to see.		
21. The graphics were easy to understand.		
22. The graphics looked correct and professional.		
23. The graphics helped me understand the organization of the presentation.		
For Group Presentations		
24. The group seemed well rehearsed.		
25. The graphics were edited so that they looked consistent from one group member to the next.		
26. The transitions from one group member to the next were smooth.		
27. Each group member seemed to have done an equal amount of work in preparing and delivering the presentation.		

On the other side of this sheet, answer the following two questions.
28. What did you particularly like about this presentation?
29. What would you have done differently if you had been the speaker?

Speaker's Checklist

☐ Did you analyze the speaking situation—the audience and purpose of the presentation? (p. 581)

☐ Did you determine how much information you can communicate in your allotted time? (p. 582)

☐ Did you organize and develop the presentation? (p. 582)

Does each presentation graphic have these five characteristics?

☐ It presents a clear, well-supported claim. (p. 584)

☐ It is easy to see. (p. 584)

☐ It is easy to read. (p. 587)

☐ It is simple. (p. 587)

☐ It is correct. (p. 587)

☐ In planning your graphics, did you consider your audience's aptitude and experience, the size and layout of the room, and the equipment available? (p. 587)

☐ Did you plan your graphics to help the audience understand the organization of your presentation? (p. 589)

☐ Did you make sure that the presentation room will have the necessary equipment for the graphics? (p. 589)

☐ Did you choose appropriate media for your graphics? (p. 592)

☐ Did you choose language to signal advance organizers, summaries, and transitions? (p. 595)

☐ Did you choose language that is vivid and memorable? (p. 595)

☐ Did you rehearse your presentation several times with a tape recorder, videocamera, or live audience? (p. 596)

Exercises

1. Learn some of the basic functions of a presentation program. For instance, modify a template, create your own original design, add footer information to a master slide, insert a graphic on a slide, and set the animation feature to make each bullet item appear only after a mouse click.

2. Using presentation software, create a design to be used for the master slide of a computer presentation. Then, for the same information, create a design to be used in a transparency made on a black-and-white photocopier.

3. Prepare a five-minute presentation, including graphics, on one of the topics listed here. Your audience consists of your instructor and the other students in your class, and your purpose is to introduce them to an aspect of your academic field.

   a. Define a key term or concept in your field.

   b. Describe how a particular piece of equipment is used in your field.

   c. Describe how to carry out a procedure common in your field.

   The instructor and the other students will evaluate your presentation by filling out the form in Figure 21.7.

4. **GROUP EXERCISE** Prepare a five-minute presentation based on either your proposal for a research report or your completion report. Your audience consists of your instructor and the other students in your class, and your purpose is to introduce them to your topic. The instructor and the other students will evaluate your presentation by filling out the form in Figure 21.7. If your instructor wishes, this assignment can be done collaboratively.

Case 21: Choosing Effective Slide Layouts

Background

Once or twice a month, you and your longtime friend Sang Jun Lee meet for lunch to catch up on what is new in your professional and personal lives. As a crime-scene examiner for a county crime lab, Sang collects, examines, and investigates physical evidence at crime scenes that may help locate and convict criminals. During one lunch date, Sang tells you about an article he recently read about the "evils" of PowerPoint. "The author argued that PowerPoint emphasizes format over content," Sang says. "The software encourages speakers to reduce everything to a bulleted list or an incoherent graphic."

"I've heard that before," you reply. "In one of my courses, we read a few articles on PowerPoint. Most of the articles had titles like 'PowerPoint-Induced Sleep,' 'Power-Point Pitfalls,' 'The Pentagon Declares War on Electronic Slide Shows,' and 'Friends Don't Let Friends Use Power-Point.' The authors made the same points as the article you just read. The templates are ugly, and they dumb down presentations and convey information poorly."

"That article made me a little nervous," Sang says. "I'm scheduled to talk to students enrolled in an introduction to crime-scene investigation course next week. The professor asked me to give a brief overview of fingerprinting. I've started to put together a PowerPoint presentation, but now I'm worried that I might be going about it all wrong. Would you be able to help me?"

"Sure. I'll do some Internet research and see if I can find some advice on creating useful slides."

"What I really need help with is how to present my information. I use the default title-and-text slide for almost all my slides. I know the software includes many other slide layouts—two-column text, content over text, text over content—but I'm not sure when to use them."

"E-mail me a few of your slides, and I'll take a look." (See Document 21.1.)

Your Assignment

1. Use the Internet to research guidelines for preparing effective presentation graphics using presentation software. Focus your research on guidelines related to slide *layout* (the way information is arranged and presented on a slide), not slide *design* (the use of color schemes). Write Sang an e-mail reporting your findings.

2. Using strategies discussed in this chapter, revise Sang's sample slides (Document 21.1). Include a brief letter to Sang explaining your revisions.

Document 21.1 Slides and Speaking Notes for Part of a Presentation

---

Some Fingerprint Background

- 2,000 BC—Ancient Babylonians used fingerprints on clay tablets during business transactions.
- 1858—Sir William Herschel required laborers in India to sign contracts with fingerprints.
- 1892—Sir Francis Galton created the foundation of modern fingerprinting science by arguing that fingerprints are unique.
- 1902—Fingerprinting used in the United States.
- 1924—Congress establishes the Identification Division of the FBI.
- 2005—Integrated Automated Fingerprint Identification System (IAFIS) maintained by FBI compares a single fingerprint with a database of 47 million fingerprints.

Go over brief history of fingerprints.

 On TechComm Web

For digital versions of case documents, click on Downloadable Case Documents on <bedfordstmartins.com/techcomm>.

Cyanoacrylate-Fuming Method

- Known as the Super-Glue Method.
- Used by most state and local police in United States.
- A chemical technique used to make latent fingerprints visible.

First used by the Japanese National Police Agency's Criminal Identification Division in 1978. Introduced to the US by the United States Army Criminal Investigation and Bureau of Alcohol, Tobacco, and Firearms Laboratories.

There are three different types of fingerprints: *visible, impression,* and *latent.* Crime scene examiners need permanent, portable copies of fingerprints. *Visible* and *impression* fingerprints can be photographed without too much effort. *Latent* prints must first be made visible before photographing them.

There are three general techniques for making latent fingerprints visible: physical techniques, chemical techniques, and instrumental techniques. Cyanoacrylate fuming is a chemical technique.

Cyanoacrylate fuming works by chemically reacting with the chemicals found in a latent print. Organic compounds exuded through the pores in the fingertips are left when a person's hand touches something. In the case of cyanoacrylate fuming, the super glue reacts with the traces of fatty acids, proteins, and amino acids in the latent fingerprints. Combined with the moisture in the air, the result is a visible, sticky white material that forms along the ridges of the fingerprint, forming an image that can be photographed.

1

2

Different Patterns of Fingerprints

- In a loop, the ridges enter from either side, curve, and exit the same side they entered.
- In a whorl, the ridges are usually circular.
- In an arch, the ridges enter from one side, make a rise in the center, and exit on the opposite side.

Every person's hand (as well as feet) feature minute ridges and valleys. In the fingers and thumbs, these ridges form patterns of loops, whorls, and arches. Explain to class each of these patterns.

3

Document 21.1   (continued)

Identifications

- Scotland Yard requires 16 points
- Australia requires 16 points
- Germany requires 12 points
- Netherlands requires 10 points
- Bulgaria requires 8 points
- South Africa requires 7 points
- United States has no set standard

U.S. courts assume as fact the argument that no two fingers can have identical characteristics. Fingerprint identification is determined not by shape or pattern but by the study of a print's ridge characteristics. Courts require forensic technicians to find a minimum number of "Galton points"—matching characteristics on a fingerprint. Thus, a fingerprint specialist must make a point-by-point comparison to match a fingerprint found at the scene of a crime to a suspect.

However, just how many points are necessary to establish a "match" varies from state to state and country to country. Go over examples of different number of points required. In the United States, for example, the FBI moved away from match requirements based on a minimum number of Galton points half a century ago. Worldwide, labs are doing away with point systems and are, instead, relying upon the opinion of the forensic examiner.

The Future of Fingerprinting

Most commonly used biometric identification methods:
- Fingerprint scan: 58%
- Facial scan: 13.4%
- Hand scan: 12%
- Iris scan: 8.3%
- Voice scan: 5.1%
- Signature scan: 2.4%
- Keystroke scan: .3%

Does not total 100% due to rounding

In addition to criminal investigations, fingerprints play a key role in biometric-security technology. Biometric technology examines a measurable, physical characteristic or personal behavioral trait used to recognize the identity or verify the claimed identity of a person. For example, hand geometry, retinal scan, iris scan, fingerprint patterns, facial characteristics, DNA sequence characteristics, voice prints, and handwritten signature.

Among all the biometric techniques, fingerprint-based identification (e.g., fingerprint scanning) is expected to continue as the biometric technology of choice in the near future. Other biometric technologies will continue to see limited use.

5

Connecting with the Public

Persuasion and Connecting with the
Public 609

Presenting Information
to the Public 610

Newsletters 610

Brochures 613

White Papers 616

Podcasts 618

Collaborating with the Public 620

Discussion Boards 620

Blogs 622

Wikis 624

Source: Johnson, 2008 <www.idratherbewriting.com/2008/05/06/podcast-pushing-your-company
-into-the-wikis-blogs-and-social-networks-of-web-20-interview-with-alan-porter-of-webworks>.

In the World . . .

This screen from Tom Johnson's blog, I'd Rather Be Writing, suggests
the extent to which the interactive capabilities of the Internet are affecting the ways people conduct their work lives. In his blog, Johnson, a
technical communicator in Utah, presents information about many
aspects of his field. Some of this information is presented through articles he has written. Some is provided in podcasts he has made, such
as the one shown on this screen. Why does he do all this work for free?
He answers that question on his "About Me" page: "Whatever job I
worked at, I always pursued some technical accompaniment to make
it interesting." In other words, he has the energy, he likes to provide
helpful information about his field, and he likes to learn from people
who post comments on his blog. Staying current will certainly help
him on the job, and as he establishes a reputation for being smart
and hardworking, he might receive a job offer every once in a while.
Johnson uses his blog and podcasts to connect with people in ways
that didn't exist a decade ago.

When people communicate in the workplace, they typically share information with others inside their organizations. Sometimes, however, they communicate with people on the outside. This chapter involves communicating with the public or, to be more precise, publics: investors, prospective employees, state and local officials, prospective donors, community members, current and prospective customers, and colleagues in industry, to name just a few. It discusses seven common applications that people in organizations use to connect with the public. Some are best for presenting information. Others focus on fostering collaboration between writers and readers.

Why is it important for organizations to connect with their publics? One reason is that American culture values *accountability*. The public expects organizations of all kinds to communicate honestly and clearly and to take responsibility for their actions. The public wants to know, for instance, how a carmaker such as Ford is responding to the challenges of global warming. Here are just a few of the questions that the general public and interest groups ask Ford:

- What are you doing to improve the gas mileage and decrease the toxic emissions of your vehicles?
- What are you doing to improve the safety of your vehicles?
- What are you doing to reduce the carbon footprint of your manufacturing facilities and your supply chain?
- What are you doing to increase employment opportunities for women and minorities?
- What are you doing to improve the socioeconomic conditions in the communities in which you have facilities?

Notice that some of these questions directly relate to technical aspects of Ford's core products, but others relate more to Ford's role as a corporate citizen. Twenty or thirty years ago, Ford thought of itself simply as a maker of cars and trucks. Today, however, the people at Ford see themselves as members of many different communities, from the community of carmakers to the community of Dearborn, Michigan, and many other locations.

Just as organizations now see themselves as members of many communities, so do individuals working for organizations. A person who works for Ford is likely to see herself as a Ford employee but also as a member of one or two community organizations and a political group, as well as a supporter of her daughter's school. As a member of these organizations, this Ford worker might contribute to various outreach and communication efforts by participating in fund-raising events, volunteering her time to help maintain a computer lab at her child's school, writing articles for newsletters, and perhaps maintaining a blog.

Although people have always been able to communicate with the public, computers and the Internet have made it much easier and cheaper to do so. With a personal computer and basic office software, you can write and design brochures, newsletters, flyers, and many other kinds of documents to help you present information to the community. And if you have Internet access, you can easily participate in discussion boards, host wikis, maintain blogs, and create podcasts. This chapter discusses seven such applications, focusing first on those that are best at presenting information and then on those that are best at fostering collaboration with an audience.

PERSUASION AND CONNECTING WITH THE PUBLIC

People and organizations connect with the public for many reasons, ranging from a high-minded desire to present information to help people, to a thinly disguised effort to sell a product or service—and everything in between. Often, a person or organization has several motivations at once. For example, the technical communicator Tom Johnson, who writes the blog shown on page 607, primarily wants to inform people about technical communication. If the blog helps establish him as a credible expert, enabling him to raise his fees if he does any consulting or prompting an organization to offer him a job, all the better. When a large oil company such as ExxonMobil buys expensive ads that describe how much money it spends on research and development of alternative fuels, it wants the public to see it as a responsible corporate citizen, not a predatory big-oil conglomerate. These ads are meant to educate the public and government about how the company is acting responsibly. If the ads also make the public a little less unhappy about the price of gas and discourage the government from imposing windfall-profits taxes on ExxonMobil, all the better. In other words, every one of the applications discussed in this chapter can be created in response to a variety of motivations and serve a number of purposes.

The one characteristic that all the applications share is that if they are to succeed, they must be persuasive. As discussed in Chapter 8, a persuasive message must appeal to one or several of an audience's broader goals: security, recognition, and personal and professional growth. A brochure from the American Cancer Society that explains how to recognize the warning signs of cancer obviously appeals to a reader's goal of security. A blog that explains how to use wikis to improve communication in a company appeals to a reader's desire to grow professionally.

In addition, if the application is to succeed, it must present a persuasive argument. Regardless of whether the organization's motivation is simply to present information or to market a product or service, the communication must contain a clear and compelling claim based on appropriate evidence and rest on valid reasoning and sound logic. For instance, a company offers a service to prevent hackers from invading an organization's database and stealing the personal information of that organization's customers. The company might publish on its Web site a white paper, a document that explains the nature and extent of the threat and describes how its service can help reduce that threat. It's a marketing message, but it won't attract any interest unless it's persuasive. It must be attractive and well written; it must present appropriate evidence that the threat is real and serious; and it must provide compelling evidence that the company's service will work. That evidence might consist of *commonsense arguments* (such as the idea that because hackers look for easy opportunities to invade a company, any sort of obstacles the company erects will reduce the threat); *numerical data* (statistics showing how organizations that purchase the company's service have not been hit by hackers); *examples* (case studies of companies that are satisfied customers); and *expert testimony* (awards and commendations from data-security professional organizations).

PRESENTING INFORMATION TO THE PUBLIC

▶ **In This Book**

For more about collaboration, see Ch. 4.

The four applications discussed in this section—newsletters, brochures, white papers, and podcasts—differ from one another in many ways. For instance, newsletters have been used for hundreds of years, whereas podcasts have been around for only a few. Brochures and newsletters are often created by teams of people working collaboratively: one person might serve as the editor and project manager; someone else might do the layout and graphics; others might do some of the writing. By contrast, podcasts are often produced by one person. Three of the applications can be printed on paper or distributed electronically, whereas podcasts must be downloaded and used electronically.

The common characteristic of these four applications, however, is that they are essentially one-way applications. That is, they are best at presenting information to an audience of readers, listeners, or viewers. Of course, these readers, listeners, or viewers can get back to the person or organization that presented the information by writing an e-mail, phoning, or sending a letter. And these applications typically invite the audience to do so by listing contact information. But a physician who places brochures about his services in a display rack is primarily interested in presenting information to the person who picks up the brochure. The physician hopes that person will follow up by contacting him or her or by passing the brochure along to a friend or family member. But the brochure is meant primarily to communicate a message to an audience.

Newsletters

A newsletter, an organization's newspaper, can help the organization foster a sense of community within its members, both internal and external, such as customers, employees, investors, and the general public. Following are typical news items in a newsletter:

- descriptions of new activities undertaken by the organization
- major investments by the organization in new equipment or facilities
- announcements for upcoming events and summaries of previous events, such as presentations, performances, or lectures given by organization members
- notices of available jobs in the organization
- profiles of new members, officers, or administrators
- important changes in relevant laws or regulations

Many computer programs include templates for newsletters, which often look like miniature newspapers.

Guidelines

Designing an Effective Newsletter

Whether you use a template or create your own design, include these 10 elements to enhance the usefulness and professional appearance of your newsletter.

▶ **Banner or masthead.** Use a distinctive design at the top of the first page to give the newsletter a strong identity. Use the organization's logo. Indicate the date and, if appropriate, the volume and number of the issue.

▶ **Table of contents.** Provide page numbers for each of the main items.

▶ **Headline(s).** Begin the main story on the front page. Many newsletters begin two or even three stories on the front page.

▶ **Bylines.** When several writers contribute newsletter content, clearly identify each author.

▶ **Jump lines.** If a story continues on another page, direct readers there with a jump line, such as "continued on p. 3."

▶ **Continuation headings.** Use descriptive headings to identify stories that began on a previous page.

▶ **Photographs.** Use photos to help convey information quickly and make the story more memorable.

▶ **Pull quotes.** Use quotations or points of information to draw attention to something especially interesting.

▶ **Publisher.** Clearly identify your organization as the publisher.

▶ **Postal information.** Leave sufficient space for your return address, an address label, and postage. See if your organization has a bulk-mail provider; bulk mail can save a lot of money if you send out thousands of copies.

▷ **In This Book**
For more about tables of contents, see Ch. 19, p. 512.

▷ **In This Book**
For more about pull quotes, see Ch. 11, p. 277.

Make sure you have a system to distribute your newsletter. You might post copies on a Web site or place stacks of newsletters in accessible locations, but the most effective technique is to distribute your newsletter to individual readers.

Figure 22.1 on page 612 shows the front page of a newsletter.

The bold masthead clearly identifies the newsletter's name and topic, as well as the volume, issue number, and date.

The headline summarizes the main point of the front-page story.

The photograph clearly shows members of the international research team discussed in the lead article.

The jump line at the bottom of the story directs readers to the page where the story continues.

The design for the front page has three columns: two for text and one for the table of contents and publisher. The two-column design for the main story ensures an easy-to-read line length.

The two-color design (black and blue ink) is more expensive than a one-color design but less expensive than using full color.

CAM AT THE NIH

FOCUS ON COMPLEMENTARY AND ALTERNATIVE MEDICINE

VOLUME XIV, NUMBER 4   FALL 2007

International Team Studies South African Plant for HIV/AIDS

A group of contributors to the Sutherlandia study met in September 2007 in Pietermaritzburg, KwaZulu-Natal, South Africa. Left to right: Douglas Wilson, James Syce, Kevin Rudeen, Laurie Bongani, Tilly Pillay, Makhosi Mvoni, Thulani Hlongwa, Baba Shange, Baba Thabethe, Elliot Makhathini, Bill Folk, Makhosi Xaba, Deborah Hayes, and Makhosi Dlamini. The photo's setting is a shop for supplies for traditional *inyanga* healing.

INSIDE

3   Meet a NACCAM Member: Carlo Calabrese, N.D., M.P.H.

4   Low-Back Pain: NACCAM Symposium

6   News for Researchers

7   First Transagency Fellowship in Cancer CAM

11 Creative Ideas for Curriculum Development

NATIONAL INSTITUTES OF HEALTH

U.S. DEPARTMENT OF HEALTH AND HUMAN SERVICES

"It's just overwhelming. It feels like anything you do is a drop in a huge, huge bucket. But, you drop a drop, and it causes a ripple, and that causes a lot of change. Sometimes you have to be a drop, because that's all you've got."

So Kathleen Goggin, Ph.D., describes part of what draws her to co-lead a groundbreaking study of an African traditional medicine. A plant called Sutherlandia is being examined for its potential to help patients with HIV infection. The study is being cosponsored by NCCAM and NIH's Office of AIDS Research, Office of Dietary Supplements, and Fogarty International Center.

According to the joint United Nations program on HIV/AIDS, or UNAIDS, about 33.2 million people worldwide have HIV infection. AIDS is among the leading causes of death worldwide.

South Africa is one of the countries that have been hardest hit by HIV/AIDS. While changes in South Africa have been taking place (including a new national strategic plan for AIDS) to help prevent transmission of the virus and to treat those who are infected, the challenges are large in scale. UNAIDS states that in South Africa by the end of 2005:

- About 5½ million people (or one in nine) were living with HIV infection. Almost one-quarter million of them were children under 15 years old.
- More than 360,000 people were taking antiretroviral therapy (ART).
- For every person in South Africa who begins taking ART, three more become infected with HIV.

Could a Plant Be Helpful?

Working to create a ripple in the pandemic's bucket are an international team of Western-trained clinicians and researchers from both the United States and South Africa (see box on pg. 2) as well as South African traditional healers. The plant they are studying, Sutherlandia, is a member of the pea family, uniquely native to South Africa, and wild-growing in places there. Its scientific name is *Lessertia frutescens*; some of its popular names are *Insisa*, *Unwele*, *Phetola*, and cancer bush.

Walk into any South African traditional medicine market, and there it is—

(continued on pg. 3)

Figure 22.1   Front Page of a Newsletter

Source: National Institutes of Health, 2007 <http://nccam.nih.gov/news/newsletter/pdf/2007fall.pdf>.

INTERACTIVE SAMPLE DOCUMENT
Evaluating the Design of a Newsletter

The newsletter shown here is distributed to all storm spotters registered with the National Weather Service in Wichita, Kansas. The questions in the margin ask you to think about newsletter design. E-mail your responses to yourself and/or your instructor on TechComm Web.

1. How effectively does the masthead provide a distinctive identity for the newsletter?

2. How effective is the photograph in conveying the main idea of the story? Could the use of the photo be improved?

3. How effective is the alignment of text on this page?

4. Does the story conclude on the first page or continue on to the second? How do you know?

On TechComm Web

To e-mail your responses to yourself and/or your instructor, click on Interactive Sample Documents for Ch. 22 on <bedfordstmartins.com/techcomm>.

Source: National Weather Service, 2007 <www.crh.noaa.gov/images/ict/newsletter/pdf/Fall2007.pdf>.

Brochures

A brochure is a brief document used to provide information or to promote something. Here are some examples of the kinds of information that might be communicated in a brochure:

- products produced by a small manufacturer of roofing materials
- services offered by a new sports-medicine clinic
- benefits of joining a particular professional organization or community group
- techniques for choosing healthy foods and reducing calories

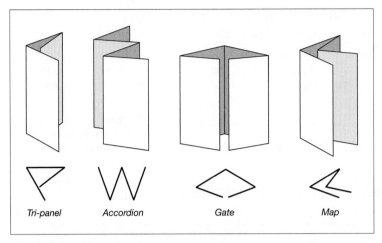

Figure 22.2   Typical Fold Designs for Brochures

Although some brochures consist of more than one page, the typical brochure is made from a single page that is folded as part of the printing process. The folds create panels you can use to group information in logical categories. A brochure for a manufacturer of roofing materials, for instance, might have one panel devoted to composite shingles, another to slate, and another to tile. Or it might have one panel devoted to descriptions of products, one to the warranty, and one to customer service. Most brochures have a three-panel design, although some have four panels. Standard letter-size paper (8.5 × 11 inches) is most common, but legal-size paper (8.5 × 14 inches) provides extra space for content. Figure 22.2 shows typical fold designs for brochures.

Like all applications, brochures must be designed to meet the needs of the audience and fulfill the purpose of the communication. A brochure that is reproduced on a black-and-white photocopier would be appropriate for

Guidelines

Creating a Brochure

Follow these four suggestions when creating a brochure.

▶ **Decide where and how your brochure will be reproduced.** If you will produce your own copies, create a design that your equipment can reproduce effectively. If you will have a print shop produce it, make sure the print shop has compatible software.

▶ **Design your information to fit on the panels appropriately.** Be sure each panel contains a coherent set of information. Avoid designs that separate chunks of information awkwardly.

▶ **Use the front panel to attract attention.** Because the front panel is like the cover of a book, use it to clearly identify the subject, audience, and purpose of the brochure.

▶ **Avoid design clichés.** Inexperienced designers often center everything on every panel, creating a safe but boring design. Try to think of ways to use design elements such as color, rules, boxes, and screens to tie the panels together.

▶**In This Book**

For more about design, see Ch. 11.

answering a set of frequently asked questions (FAQs) about an office or volunteer group, but it would not attract high-end customers for expensive technology or members of an exclusive organization. Similarly, a full-color brochure on glossy paper might seem inappropriately extravagant for a nonprofit organization that relies on donations. Figure 22.3 is an example of an effective brochure.

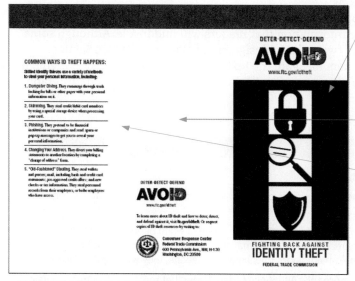

a. The "outside" of a three-panel brochure

This is the cover of the brochure. Notice that each of the three key terms—deter, detect, and defend—is keyed to an appropriate graphical symbol. Notice, too, that the designer has cleverly used the id in avoid to make the design interesting.

If this brochure is to be mailed, the blank area on the middle panel will contain the reader's mailing address.

This panel will be folded inside and therefore will not be immediately visible. Notice that it uses a simple design—red for emphasis and horizontal rules to separate the items—to communicate the five typical methods used to steal a person's identity.

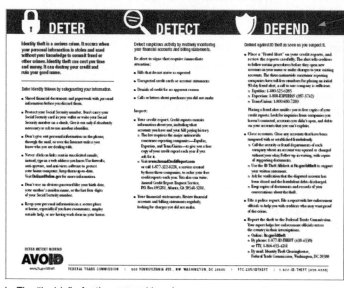

b. The "inside" of a three-panel brochure

The icons at the top of each panel repeat those on the cover.

Each of the three key terms is discussed in its own panel. Note the use of bulleted lists to communicate information clearly and concisely.

The red in the header and footer of the three panels unifies the information by framing it.

The design of this brochure from the Federal Trade Commission is simple and effective. The striking design on the cover summarizes the content of the brochure. Because this brochure uses only black and red, a print shop needs only two colors of ink to produce it, reducing production costs.

Figure 22.3   An Effective Brochure
Source: Federal Trade Commission, 2008 <www.ftc.gov/bcp/edu/pubs/consumer/idtheft/idt01.pdf>.

White Papers

A white paper enables a company to communicate a longer message than can fit in a brochure. A typical white paper is 8 to 12 pages long. It describes a solution to a technological or business challenge in an industry. Its readers are technical experts who implement technology or managers who make purchasing decisions.

Many white papers look like reports. An executive summary on the first page forecasts the information that readers will find inside. Although some white papers use a two-column design, many use one column. Section headings help readers navigate the text. Pull quotes can be used to highlight interesting pieces of information. White papers often include charts, graphs, and photographs.

▶**In This Book**
For more about executive summaries, see Ch. 19, p. 515. For more about design, see Ch. 11. For more about graphics, see Ch. 12.

Guidelines

Writing a White Paper

The following seven suggestions can help you write a white paper that will connect with your readers.

▶ **Communicate useful information.** Readers use white papers to learn something new. If you give readers useful information about industry trends and how your company will help them adapt to changing situations, they will respond favorably.

▶ **Use a subtle approach.** Although readers know that most white papers contain marketing information, they will be alienated by the hard-sell techniques they normally see in ads. Avoid sweeping claims about your company.

▶ **Cite your sources.** Showing that your claims are based on evidence adds credibility. For more on documenting your sources, see Appendix, Part B.

▶ **Make the white paper easy to skim and navigate.** White papers include headings to break up long blocks of text and make it easy for readers to find the information they seek. For more about writing headings, see Chapter 9, page 201, and Chapter 11, page 275.

▶ **Help readers who don't know all the jargon.** Although some readers are not experts in your field, they might have influence over a purchasing decision. Provide parenthetical definitions of acronyms and initialisms, and include a glossary for a highly technical paper. For more on definitions, see Chapter 20, page 540. For more on glossaries, see Chapter 19, page 516.

▶ **Make sure the white paper prints well in black and white.** Although many white papers are now distributed and read on-screen, some readers prefer to print paper copies. Because most printers and copiers produce black-and-white documents, ensure that your white paper will be attractive and readable in black and white.

▶ **End with a call to action.** If your white paper is meant to help your sales force, it should conclude with telephone numbers, e-mail addresses, and URLs that will allow prospective customers to contact you.

Figure 22.4 shows the first page of a white paper. The purposes of this white paper are to forecast industry trends and to market a product. It ends with an explicit marketing message that begins with a lengthy bulleted list, excerpted here:

> One Touch Global provides the following unique advantages:
>
> - **Consulting:** One Touch Global will work within your existing processes to understand what you are doing and who is involved with the lifecycle of documents, keeping your organizational objectives in mind.
>
> - **Systems integration:** One Touch Global helps businesses handle the entire lifecycle of documents via needs analysis, strategic planning, implementation, training, and ongoing support.
>
> - **Remote and on-site service:** Both on-site and remote servicing are available to enable troubleshooting in as little as 15 minutes.

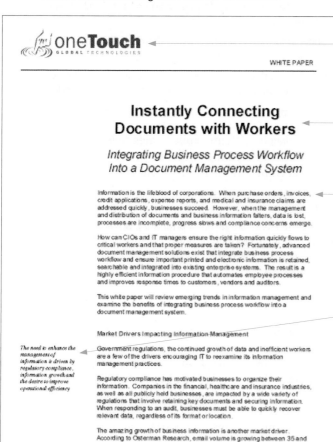

The color logo clearly identifies the company presenting the white paper. The rest of the design, in black and white, conveys a tone of seriousness and credibility.

The title is prominently displayed.

The summary provides an overview to help readers know quickly whether the document will meet their needs.

The note in the margin summarizes an important idea from the text and can help readers who skim.

Figure 22.4   First Page of a White Paper
Source: One Touch, 2006
<www.stelzner.com/PDF/OneTouch.pdf>.

If the white paper had *begun* with an explicit sales message such as this, many readers would have abandoned it. For this reason, the white paper begins with a discussion of trends in the industry, including this statement from the first page:

> How can CIOs and IT managers ensure the right information quickly flows to critical workers and that proper measures are taken? Fortunately, advanced document management solutions exist that integrate business process workflow and ensure important printed and electronic information is retained, searchable, and integrated into existing enterprise systems.

Podcasts

Podcasting, a word that combines *iPod* and *broadcasting*, is a Web-based technology that allows people to present information electronically. A *podcast* is an audio or video file that is downloaded from a Web site and then played on a computer or MP3 player. Some people see podcasting as a hobby that allows them to talk about their favorite subjects. Others create podcasts in their professional lives to connect with customers and reach out to new audiences. Some professors put lectures on podcasts, and many industry professionals create podcasts to inform colleagues and customers about industry trends. For professionals in all fields—from computer science, engineering, and business to the arts and health care—podcasts offer an easy way to learn new information from experts in the field.

Figure 22.5   A Podcast Directory

This directory, Podcast.net, lists 497 podcasts on the subject of computer operating systems. You can link to RSS feeds, and you can add your own podcast to the directory.
Source: Podcast Networks, 2008 <www.podcast.net/cat/48>.

It is easy to find podcasts with your Web browser or a software program called an *aggregator*. Apple's iTunes service also hosts many podcasts. Podcasters can syndicate their programs by setting up an RSS feed. (RSS stands for *rich site summary* or *really simple syndication*.) Aggregators and certain Web browsers check all the RSS feeds you subscribe to and help you download the latest content.

Figure 22.5 shows a podcast directory.

The process of creating a podcast is fairly simple. If your computer has a microphone and some sound-editing software (free versions are available on the Internet), you can create a podcast. Follow these four steps:

1. *Prepare for the podcast.* Develop a script. Use an outline if you know your subject well and are comfortable speaking extemporaneously. Get permission in advance if your podcast includes copyrighted material.

2. *Record the podcast.* Ensure that you will not be interrupted.

3. *Edit the podcast.* Remove any errors or extended silence (also called *dead air*). If you add music at the beginning or end, make sure it is in the public domain or it is your own (or your organization's) intellectual property. For more information on intellectual property, see Chapter 2, page 25.

4. *Publish the podcast.* Upload it to the Web, mention it in your blog, and set up the RSS feed for aggregators, if you haven't already. Because podcast files can be quite large (20 to 30 MB or more), check with your Web host to be sure it can support large files.

COLLABORATING WITH THE PUBLIC

The three applications discussed in this section—discussion boards, blogs, and wikis—are electronic tools used to connect with the public. What distinguishes these three applications from the four discussed in the previous section is that they are designed to foster collaboration between writers and readers.

This collaboration is made simple through specific features of each application. For instance, on a discussion board, a reader replies to a post by clicking on the Reply button and writing a message, which is then sent to all readers of the discussion board. On a blog, each entry is followed by a Comment button, which makes it simple for a reader to send a response that will appear beneath the entry. On a wiki, an Edit button invites authorized readers to submit revisions. In short, all three electronic tools make it easy for writers to solicit and present readers' views.

More important than the buttons you push, however, is that interactivity is an integral part of the application. Although each application has a somewhat different function, all three are designed to invite two-way communication. A discussion board exists to create a conversation among many people about a topic that is important to the community. A blog exists to offer one person (or sometimes several people) a forum for presenting ideas to the community, to which interested members can respond. A wiki exists to enable members of a community to create or revise documents collaboratively. The following discussions focus on how each application is used to encourage collaboration in the workplace.

As you read about these applications, remember that when you use them in the workplace, it's important to act like a professional. People inside and outside your organization are likely to read what you write. Represent yourself and your organization positively. Find out whether your organization has guidelines for appropriate online behavior, and if it does, follow them.

Discussion Boards

A discussion board, sometimes called a *bulletin board* or an *electronic forum*, enables people to have asynchronous discussions about a particular topic. You might use a discussion board to learn what people think about a consumer product you are researching. Or if you are having a problem with a product you own, you might use a discussion board to learn whether others are having a similar problem and how they have tried to fix it.

Often, companies host discussion boards devoted to their own products. For example, Microsoft hosts a number of boards, on which people post questions, answers, and gripes about the company's products. Why would Microsoft devote some of its resources to listening to people complain about its products? Well, if you were Microsoft, would you rather know what customers like and dislike about your products or not have a clue as to what they think? Discussion boards can provide a company with valuable information about its products. In addition, they can help the company maintain a good relationship with its customers by creating a virtual community of people, all of whom want the company to improve its products and customer service.

When people participate in discussion boards, disagreements arise. Avoid the temptation to respond to one disparaging comment with another, especially if you are posting as a member of an organization and not a private citizen.

Guidelines

Participating in Discussion Boards

The following six guidelines will help you post to discussion boards responsibly.

▶ **Share your knowledge.** Because discussion boards thrive when members share what they know, participate by posting when you can contribute.

▶ **Do your homework before posting a question.** Before you ask a question, search the archives and check other sources to see if an answer is already available.

▶ **Support your claims with evidence.** Provide specific data to back up your statements. Give all pertinent background information when asking a question. See Chapter 8 for more about communicating persuasively.

▶ **Stay on topic.** Follow the posted guidelines and make sure your posts are relevant to the topic.

▶ **Avoid personal attacks.** Avoid *flame wars*, angry exchanges on discussion boards. No one benefits from them, and other forum participants tire of them quickly.

▶ **Disclose potential conflicts of interest.** If your connection with a person, a company, or a competitor could affect your writing or how readers interpret it, say so.

Figure 22.6 shows a screen from a discussion board.

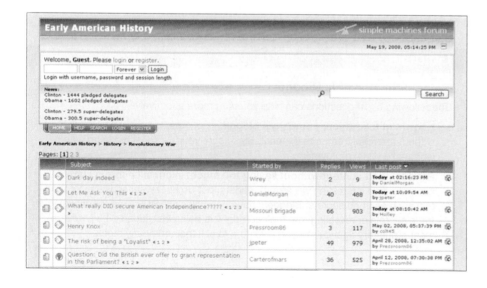

Figure 22.6 A Discussion Board

This discussion board on early American history has a section on the Revolutionary War. Some of the entries (such as the first one, "Dark day indeed") generate only a few replies. Others (such as "Let Me Ask You This") generate dozens of replies in only a few hours.
Source: Early American History, 2008 <http://earlyamericanhistory.net/board/index.php?board=3.0>.

Blogs

Weblogs, more commonly known as blogs, enable people to post their thoughts and opinions on the Web. Many people use blogs in their personal lives to stay in touch with family and friends, write about hobbies or interests, or provide social commentary. Others write blogs about their professional interests by commenting on news stories that affect their industries, discussing new products coming on the market, and keeping track of new trends.

With the number of blogs exceeding 100 million, the practice is redefining the way organizations connect with their publics. Most large companies host blogs by many of their executives, as well as by typical workers. Reporters and columnists working for major newspapers such as *The New York Times*, engineers, physicians, athletes—people and organizations in every field—are blogging in order to present information about their workplaces and to learn from the public. Organizations encourage blogging because it can make them seem less impersonal, thereby helping them build relationships.

For some people, blogging is such an important part of their workplace lives that they are expected to devote a large part of each day to it. They use their blogs to communicate about their organizations' operations and plans and to test new ideas. For these people, blogging is a form of research and development and also a form of marketing. For others, blogging is less central to what they do. Their organizations host their blogs, but they are expected to blog on their own time.

When employees write blogs, they sometimes make comments critical of their organizations. Some companies have responded by trying to prohibit negative comments or to punish bloggers by revoking their right to blog or even firing them. However, many organizations view such negative comments as early warning signs of trouble that they can address before the problem escalates.

Figure 22.7 shows a blog.

► **In This Book**

For more about an employee's obligations to an employer, see Ch. 2, p. 23.

Guidelines

Being a Responsible Blogger

The following six suggestions can help you blog more effectively.

► **Know and follow your company's blogging policies.** Do not start a work blog without approval from management. Make sure your personal blogging won't jeopardize your employment.

► **Provide good content without saying too much.** Information that is current, accurate, and interesting will attract readers, but do not reveal sensitive information such as trade secrets. Bloggers have been disciplined or fired for divulging trade secrets or revealing that their company is being investigated by a government regulatory agency, leading investors to sell their company stock.

⬇

▶ **Use an authentic voice.** Readers want to read blogs written by "real people." If you spin the facts or pretend that everything is perfect, you will lose first your credibility and then your readers.

▶ **Avoid conflicts of interest.** If your relationship with a person, company, or competitor could affect what you write or how readers interpret it, disclose the relationship. Some companies try to bribe bloggers. For instance, several software manufacturers have been caught giving bloggers free software—and the hardware on which to run it.

▶ **Manage your time carefully.** Blogging often takes more time than you expect. Take time to write effectively, but don't let blogging interfere with your other duties.

▶ **Follow up on negative comments.** Briefly acknowledge any negative comments made on a work-related blog, then make sure the right people see them. Don't let problems fall through the cracks.

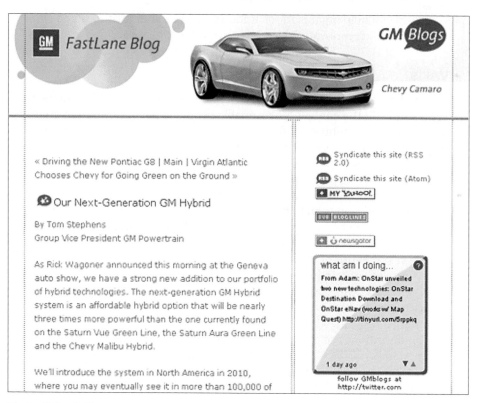

Figure 22.7   A Blog

This blog, written by various top executives at General Motors, enables the company to comment on recent developments and give readers a sense of the planning that goes on at company headquarters.

Source: General Motors, 2008 <http://fastlane.gmblogs.com/archives/2008/03/our_nextgenerat_1.html>.

An integral part of blogging is that readers can respond to a blog entry. For instance, in response to the news in the FastLane Blog in Figure 22.7, one reader commented:

> Any ideas on how much more this hybrid will weigh over its pure gas counterparts? Also, when are we going to get diesel hybrids? It makes a lot of sense, but no one has picked up on it yet. And the heck with your fuel cell vehicles. You only test them in certain areas. Come test in Kansas. That will really put a vehicle through the ropes. Extreme cold and heat. It can be 76 degrees one day and 28 the next.

Another reader wrote:

> I think I would be paying very close attention to what VW is getting ready to release in Europe, which is a diesel/hybrid version of the Golf that will supposedly get around 83MPG. If that be the case, then this presents an excellent case of how existing technology such as diesel engines, which already have good fuel economy, can serve as appropriate complements to a hybrid drive train.

Blogs can help organizations understand customer attitudes and sometimes even elicit innovative ideas.

Wikis

A *wiki* (the Hawaiian word for *fast*) is a type of Web site in which readers can create and edit the content. Wikis enable people to post information quickly and easily. People who work from different locations use wikis as a convenient way of storing and sharing information. Whereas blogs and discussion boards enable users to reply to previous posts, wikis allow users to create new pages, edit existing pages, add tags to identify content, and upload new files. Perhaps the most useful characteristic of wikis is that when a file is revised, the existing version is archived so that it is easy to view and to recover.

Certainly, the best-known public wiki is Wikipedia, the online encyclopedia. Wikipedia has won praise for the collaborative spirit it embodies and for the vast breadth of the topics it covers. However, critics point out that many articles contain inaccuracies and that some groups of users can band together and prevent others from participating (Orlowski, 2005). Used within an organization, however, a wiki is more likely to be supported by a strong community of users with a shared sense of purpose.

Organizations are thinking of more and more ways to use wikis productively. Alan Porter, Vice President of Operations at WebWorks, a software company, describes WebWorks as a "wiki-driven company" (Johnson, 2008). The company uses one wiki for internal communication, a second for customers to use in communicating with the company about joint projects, a third for customers to post questions and help the company revise its product documentation, and a fourth to communicate with people who will be attending conferences the company is supporting.

Figure 22.8 shows a wiki.

Guidelines

Using and Participating in Wikis Effectively

These six suggestions can help you get the most from a wiki.

▶ **Know your audience.** Find out what your audience needs from your wiki, then develop a plan to provide it.

▶ **Keep your wiki up-to-date.** Current information is valuable. Check the wiki periodically to correct outdated and inaccurate information and to generate ideas for new content.

▶ **Integrate the wiki with other documentation.** A familiar look and feel will encourage participation from users, and it will help your organization maintain its image.

▶ **Integrate the wiki within your community.** Wikis work best when supported by a community of users who share interests and goals. Get management support to make the wiki a part of your organization's culture.

▶ **Make organization a high priority.** Create category pages to organize content. Contact authors of uncategorized pages to suggest possible locations for them.

▶ **Help reluctant users get involved.** Offer training to explain what a wiki is and how it works. Reviewers and editors are important to ensure success, and serving in those roles may help users develop into more active participants.

Figure 22.8 A Wiki
Source: Angel.com, 2008 <www.socialtext.net/ivrwiki/index.cgi?can_a_call_be_transferred_from_one_agent_to_another>.

This is a screen from a wiki hosted by a company called Angel.com.

The wiki is called IVR Wiki because all of its content refers to the company's interactive voice response (IVR) documentation.

An authorized participant can click on the Edit button to edit this text.

There have already been seven edits to this text. A participant can click on this link to see the edits. Archiving the edits is useful because the company might want to retrieve an earlier version of the text, just as you might want to retrieve an earlier version of a document you are writing.

Writer's Checklist

Does your newsletter

- ☐ have a distinctive masthead? (p. 611)
- ☐ provide a table of contents on the first page? (p. 611)
- ☐ present the most noteworthy story on the first page? (p. 611)
- ☐ include bylines naming the authors? (p. 611)
- ☐ use jump lines and continuation headings when needed? (p. 611)
- ☐ use photographs to add interest? (p. 611)
- ☐ use pull quotes to add interest? (p. 611)
- ☐ clearly identify the publisher? (p. 611)
- ☐ leave sufficient space for postal information? (p. 611)

Does your brochure

- ☐ present information that fits on the panels appropriately? (p. 614)
- ☐ use the front panel to attract attention? (p. 614)
- ☐ avoid design clichés? (p. 614)

Does your white paper

- ☐ communicate useful information? (p. 616)
- ☐ reflect a subtle approach? (p. 616)
- ☐ include citations of all your sources? (p. 616)
- ☐ include headings that make it easy to skim? (p. 616)
- ☐ provide help for readers unfamiliar with the jargon? (p. 616)
- ☐ print well in black and white? (p. 616)
- ☐ end with a call to action? (p. 616)

Does your podcast

- ☐ respect laws protecting intellectual property? (p. 618)
- ☐ have an RSS feed to which listeners can subscribe? (p. 619)
- ☐ reside on a server capable of hosting it successfully? (p. 619)

In each post to a discussion board, do you

- ☐ share your knowledge with the group? (p. 621)
- ☐ show that you have already checked relevant archives for answers to your questions? (p. 621)
- ☐ use evidence to support your claims? (p. 621)
- ☐ stay on topic? (p. 621)
- ☐ avoid personal attacks? (p. 621)
- ☐ disclose potential conflicts of interest? (p. 621)

In your blog, do you

- ☐ adhere to company policies? (p. 622)
- ☐ provide good content without saying too much? (p. 622)
- ☐ use an authentic voice? (p. 623)
- ☐ avoid conflicts of interest? (p. 623)

Does your wiki

- ☐ show that you understand the specific needs of your audience? (p. 625)
- ☐ include up-to-date information? (p. 625)
- ☐ integrate well with other documentation? (p. 625)
- ☐ have a helpful organizational scheme? (p. 625)

Exercises

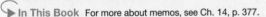 **In This Book** For more about memos, see Ch. 14, p. 377.

1. Find three blogs on a topic that interests you, such as a hobby or your academic major. Review one recent post on each blog, as well as the "About Me" information on the blog. Analyze the persona of each blogger and the nature of the blog: Does the blog provide useful information? Do readers respond with comments? Would you take the time to visit the blog again? Be prepared to share your ideas with the class.

2. Find a white paper on a subject related to your academic major. Find a passage in the white paper that communicates useful information about a trend in the industry. Then find a passage that presents a more direct marketing pitch for the organization that produced the white paper. How effectively does the white paper combine the useful information about the industry with the marketing message? Be prepared to share your ideas with the class.

3. Find three podcasts on a topic that interests you, such as a hobby or your academic major. Make note of who produced each podcast and where you found it. Pick

the podcast you think will provide you with the best information and listen to it. Write a memo summarizing the process you went through to find these podcasts and what you learned from the podcast you listened to.

4. **GROUP EXERCISE** Form a group of three to five people. Assume that your assignment is to create a newsletter about the skills you have learned in your technical-communication class. Have each person write one article, following this process:

   - Select a specific skill to write about.
   - Develop an outline of the main points you want to cover in your article about that skill.
   - Write a headline that will catch readers' attention.
   - Take or find a photograph to illustrate the article.
   - Write the article.

Work together as a group to revise, edit, and proofread the articles and assemble them into a newsletter.

5. **INTERNET EXERCISE** Find a discussion board sponsored by a professional organization in your field. Review the posts in the forum for the past two to four weeks. How would you classify them in terms of their subjects: Are they related to theoretical subjects? To practical subjects, such as tools, equipment, and procedures used in the field? To working conditions for people in that profession? Present your findings in a memo to your instructor.

6. Find a brochure and evaluate how well it meets the guidelines presented in this chapter for an effective brochure. How effectively does it address the needs of its audience and fulfill the writers' purpose? Present your evaluation in a memo to your instructor. Attach a copy of the brochure.

Case 22: Responding to Anti-Employer Blog Posts

In This Book For more about memos, see Ch. 14, p. 377.

Background

After graduating from college a few weeks ago, you started a job at X-Trex, a small company specializing in XML-development, data-management, and Web-services tools. One day you arrive a few minutes late to a staff meeting and find a colleague trying to calm your boss, Alayna Montoya.

"Someone is cybersmearing X-Trex in a blog," Alayna says, "and it can't come at a worse time."

With the release of a major software product just a few weeks away, X-Trex is on the verge of becoming a major player in the software-tools industry and a leader in XML-development tools. If the product succeeds, some long-time X-Trex employees might become very wealthy. Everyone is a little on edge as the release date nears.

"This blog can seriously hurt our bottom line," Alayna says. "It's one thing for a blogger to present product information or offer a critical review of our product. It's another thing for someone to disclose confidential information and reveal to the world that our company is under investigation by federal regulators. It's going to drive down our stock price, really scare our shareholders, and hurt employee morale."

"What exactly did the blogger write?" you ask.

Alayna passes out copies of the blog entry (Document 22.1) and says, "What's worse, the blogger is an X-Trex employee!" The conversation continues, but you tune it out and concentrate on the blog entry.

Alayna says she is going to try to figure out who the blogger is. She turns to you and says, "Maybe you could look into employee blogs and get me some information on legal and ethical issues." She also asks you to contact Human Resources to see if X-Trex has a policy covering employee blogs and, if not, to get back to them with some ideas for creating an effective set of guidelines.

Later that day, you receive a reply from Human Resources describing the electronic-communication policy at X-Trex (Document 22.2). As you suspected, the policy, which was last updated in 2001, does not address newer forms of electronic communication such as blogs. You now turn to investigating blogging guidelines for employees, as Alayna requested.

Today I saw a new post at Bella Zerbe's blog, which I take as a response to my recent musings about X-Trex's new XML editor set to release in a few weeks, where I pointed out several humongous problems with the software, like e.g. the security problem. Don't believe what CEO (aka Chief-Executive-Truth-Stretcher) Alayna is saying. That security problem won't be solved by the scheduled release date. Bet on it: this product won't be on store shelves for a good nine months or a year. Those who read the whole blog undoubtedly noticed that my overall opinion of X-Trex plummeted when I learned that we are under investigation by the Feds for some shady practice (can you spell "collusion"?) the suits are covering up. Oops, did I just write that? Guess it doesn't matter to me. I just work there. I won't see a dime: I was hired a year too late to be part of the soon-to-be-rich crowd. IPO? More like SOL.

Document 22.1   Excerpt from an Anti-Employer Blog Post

From: "Kelly Wegrzyn" <kwegrzyn@x-trex.com>
To: <yourname@x-trex.com>
Subject: Electronic-Communication Policy

I looked up our electronic-communication policy in the X-Trex Employee Handbook. (You should have received a copy when you completed all your hiring paperwork. If you didn't get a copy, just let me know, and I'll get you one or send you a PDF of the handbook.) I've included below the relevant section from our handbook. Because I don't see any mention of blogs specifically in the policy, our handbook probably needs to be revised.

Electronic-Communication Policy

X-Trex has established the following policy that governs the use of electronic-communication systems in the workplace and on the Internet, including the use of general Web sites and personal Web sites. X-Trex reserves the right to amend these policies. An employee's use of X-Trex electronic-communication systems constitutes the employee's agreement to abide by the policies governing the communication systems as set forth below, or as modified at any time in the future.

X-Trex employees are required to use X-Trex electronic-communication media in an ethical, professional, legal, and informed way, conforming to network etiquette, laws, and common courtesy. Misuse of Internet access or computers by X-Trex staff might result in suspension of privileges or other disciplinary action, including, but not limited to, termination of employment.

X-Trex reserves the right to monitor employee use of the Internet and/or e-mail at any time. Employees must abide by security policies, procedures, and guidelines, and are to refrain from practices that might jeopardize the company's computers, data, network, systems security, employee morale, or general work atmosphere.

Document 22.2   E-mail from Human Resources Describing Current Electronic-Communication Policy

Your Assignment

1. Using an Internet search engine, locate three or four Internet resources describing some of the dangers, problems, and legal and ethical issues that employees might encounter when they blog. Write Alayna a 500-word memo in which you describe these issues.

2. Using an Internet search engine, locate three or four Internet resources describing blogging guidelines for employees. Write a memo to Human Resources in which you explain the main goals of blogging guidelines. Attach an annotated list of three sets of effective guidelines.

 On TechComm Web

For digital versions of case documents, click on Downloadable Case Documents on <bedfordstmartins.com/techcomm>.

Appendix:
Reference Handbook

Part A. Skimming Your Sources and Taking Notes   630

Paraphrasing   631
Quoting   633
Summarizing   634

Part B. Documenting Your Sources   637

- APA Style   640
- IEEE Style   657
- MLA Style   665

Part C. Editing and Proofreading Your Documents   683

Grammatical Sentences   684
Punctuation   691
Mechanics   702
Proofreading Symbols and Their Meanings   709

Part D. Guidelines for Multilingual Writers (ESL)   710

Cultural and Stylistic Communication Issues   710
Sentence-Level Issues   712

629

Part A: Skimming Your Sources and Taking Notes

To record the information that will eventually go into your document, you need to skim your potential sources and take notes. Don't try to read every potential source. A careful reading of a work that looks promising might prove disappointing. You might also get halfway through a book and realize that you must start writing immediately to submit your document on time.

Guidelines

Skimming Books and Articles

To skim effectively, read the following parts of books and articles.

In a book, skim:

- *the preface and introduction:* to understand the writer's approach and methods
- *the acknowledgments section:* to learn about help the author received from other experts in the field, or about the author's use of primary research or other resources
- *the table of contents:* to understand the book's scope and organization
- *the notes at the ends of chapters or at the end of the book:* to understand the nature and extent of the author's research
- *the index:* to determine the extent of the coverage of the information you need
- *a few paragraphs from different portions of the text:* to gauge the quality and relevance of the information

In an article, skim:

- *the abstract:* to get an overview of the article's content
- *the introduction:* to understand the article's purpose, main ideas, and organization
- *the notes and references:* to understand the nature and extent of the author's research
- *the headings and several of the paragraphs:* to understand the article's organization and the quality and relevance of the information

Skimming will not always tell you whether a book or article is going to be useful, but it can tell you if a work is *not* going to be useful—because it doesn't cover your subject, for example, or because it is too superficial or too advanced. Eliminating the sources you don't need will give you more time to spend on the ones you do.

Note taking is often the first step in writing the document. The best way to take notes is electronically. If you can download files from the Internet, download bibliographic references from a CD-ROM database, and take notes on a laptop computer, you will save a lot of time and prevent many errors. If you do not have access to these electronic tools, get a pack of note cards.

Most note taking involves three kinds of activities: paraphrasing, quoting, and summarizing. Knowing how to paraphrase, quote, and summarize is important for two reasons:

- To a large extent, the work you do at this point will determine the quality of your finished product. You want to record the information accurately and clearly. Mistakes made at this point can be hard to catch later, and they can ruin your document.

- You want to use your sources responsibly. You don't want to plagiarize unintentionally.

▶ **In This Book**

For a discussion of plagiarism, see Appendix, Part B, p. 637.

Guidelines

Recording Bibliographic Information

Record the bibliographic information for each source from which you take notes.

Information to record for a book	*Information to record for an article*
<ul><li>author</li><li>title</li><li>publisher</li><li>place of publication</li><li>year of publication</li><li>call number</li></ul>	<ul><li>author</li><li>title of the article</li><li>title of the periodical</li><li>volume</li><li>number</li><li>date of publication</li><li>pages on which the article appears</li><li>call number of the periodical</li></ul>

PARAPHRASING

A paraphrase is a restatement, in your own words, of someone else's words. If you simply copy someone else's words—even a mere two or three in a row—you must use quotation marks.

In taking notes, what kind of material should you paraphrase? Any information that you think might be useful: background data, descriptions of mechanisms or processes, test results, and so forth.

Figure A.1 on page 632 shows a paraphrased passage based on the following discussion. The author is explaining the concept of performance-centered design.

Original Passage

In performance-centered design, the emphasis is on providing support for the structure of the work as well as the information needed to accomplish it. One of the best examples is TurboTax®, which meets all the three main criteria of effective performance-centered design:

- **People can do their work with no training on how to use the system.** People trying to do their income taxes have no interest in taking any kind of training.

They want to get their taxes filled out correctly and quickly, getting all the deductions they are entitled to. These packages, over the years, have moved the interface from a forms-based one, where the user had to know what forms were needed, to an interview-based one that fills out the forms automatically as you answer questions. The design of the interface assumes no particular computer expertise.

- **The system provides the right information at the right time to accomplish the work.** At each step in the process, the system asks only those questions that are relevant based on previous answers. The taxpayer is free to ask for more detail or may proceed through a dialog that asks more-detailed questions if the taxpayer doesn't know the answer to the higher-level question. If a taxpayer is married filing jointly, the system presents only those questions for that filing status.

- **Both tasks and systems change as the user understands the system.** When I first used TurboTax 6 years ago I found myself going to the forms themselves. Doing my taxes generally took about 2 days. Each year I found my need to go to the forms to be less and less. Last year, it took me about 2 hours to do my taxes, and I looked at the forms only when I printed out the final copy.

This paraphrase is inappropriate because the three bulleted points are taken word for word from the original. The fact that the student omitted the explanations from the original is irrelevant. These are direct quotes, not paraphrases.

Lovgren, "Achieving Performance-Centered Design"
<www.reisman-consulting.com/pages/a-Perform.html>

example of performance-centered design:
TurboTax® meets three main criteria:

- People can do their work with no training on how to use the system.
- The system provides the right information at the right time to accomplish the work.
- Both tasks and systems change as the user understands the system.

a. Inappropriate paraphrase

This paraphrase is appropriate because the words are different from those used in the original.

When you turn your notes into a document, you are likely to reword your paraphrases. Be sure you don't accidentally use wording from the original source. As you revise your document, check a copy of the original source document to be sure you haven't unintentionally reverted to the wording from the source.

Lovgren, "Achieving Performance-Centered Design"
<www.reisman-consulting.com/pages/a-Perform.html>

example of performance-centered design:
TurboTax® meets three main criteria:

- You don't have to learn how to use the system.
- The system knows how to respond at the appropriate time to what the user is doing.
- As the user gets smarter about using the system, the system gets smarter, making it faster to complete the task.

b. Appropriate paraphrase

Figure A.1   Inappropriate and Appropriate Paraphrased Notes
Source: Adapted from Lovgren, 2000 <www.reisman-consulting.com/pages/a-Perform.html>.

Guidelines

Paraphrasing Accurately

▶ **Study the original until you understand it thoroughly.**

▶ **Rewrite the relevant portions of the original.** Use complete sentences, fragments, or lists, but don't compress the material so much that you'll have trouble understanding it later.

▶ **Title the information so that you'll be able to identify its subject at a glance.** The title should include the general subject and the author's attitude or approach to it, such as "Criticism of open-sea pollution-control devices."

▶ **Include the author's last name, a short title of the article or book, and the page number of the original.** You will need this information later in citing your source.

QUOTING

Sometimes you will want to quote a source, either to preserve the author's particularly well-expressed or emphatic phrasing or to lend authority to your discussion. Avoid quoting passages of more than two or three sentences, or your document will look like a mere compilation. Your job is to integrate an author's words and ideas into your own thinking, not merely to introduce a series of quotations.

Although you probably won't be quoting long passages in your document, recording a complete quotation in your notes will help you recall its meaning and context more accurately when you are ready to integrate it into your own work.

The simplest form of quotation is an author's exact statement:

As Jones states, "Solar energy won't make much of a difference for at least a decade."

To add an explanatory word or phrase to a quotation, use brackets:

As Nelson states, "It [the oil glut] will disappear before we understand it."

Use ellipses (three spaced dots) to show that you are omitting part of an author's statement:

ORIGINAL STATEMENT	"The generator, which we purchased in May, has turned out to be one of our wisest investments."
ELLIPTICAL QUOTATION	"The generator . . . has turned out to be one of our wisest investments."

According to the documentation style recommended by the Modern Language Association (MLA), if the author's original statement has ellipses, you should add brackets around the ellipses that you introduce:

▶ **In This Book**

For more about formatting quotations, see "Quotation Marks," "Ellipses," and "Brackets" in Appendix, Part C. For a discussion of how to document quotations, see Appendix, Part B.

ORIGINAL STATEMENT	"I think reuse adoption offers…the promise to improve business in a number of ways."
ELLIPTICAL QUOTATION	"I think reuse adoption offers…the promise to improve business […]."

SUMMARIZING

Summarizing is the process of rewriting a passage in your own words to make it shorter while still retaining its essential message. Writers summarize to help them learn a body of information or create a draft of one or more of the summaries that will go into the document.

Most long technical documents contain several kinds of summaries:

- a letter of transmittal (see page 511) that provides an overview of the document
- an abstract (see page 511), a brief technical summary
- an executive summary (see page 515), a brief nontechnical summary directed to the manager
- a conclusion (see page 510) that draws together a complicated discussion

The guidelines and examples in this section explain how to summarize the printed information you uncover in your research.

Guidelines

Summarizing

The following advice focuses on extracting the essence of a passage by summarizing it.

- ▶ **Read the passage carefully several times.**

- ▶ **Underline key ideas.** Look for them in the titles, headings, topic sentences, transitional paragraphs, and concluding paragraphs.

- ▶ **Combine key ideas.** Study what you have underlined. Paraphrase the underlined ideas. Don't worry about your grammar, punctuation, or style at this point.

- ▶ **Check your draft against the original for accuracy and emphasis.** Check that you record statistics and names correctly and that your version of a complicated concept faithfully represents the original. Check that you get the proportions right; if the original devotes 20 percent of its space to a particular point, your draft should not devote 5 percent or 50 percent to that point.

- ▶ **Record the bibliographic information carefully.** Even though a summary might contain all your own words, you still must cite it, because the main ideas are someone else's. If you don't have the bibliographic information in an electronic form, put it on note cards.

Figure A.2 is a narrative history of television technology addressed to the general reader. Figure A.3 on page 636 is a summary that includes the key terms. This summary is 10 percent of the length of the original.

Figure A.2
Original Passage
Source: Based on McComb, 1991.

A BRIEF HISTORY OF TELEVISION

Although it seems as if television has been around for a long time, it's a relatively new science, younger than rocketry, internal medicine, and nuclear physics. In fact, some of the people that helped develop the first commercial TV sets and erect the first TV broadcast antennas are still living today.

The Early Years
The first electronic transmission of a picture was believed to have been made by a Scotsman, John Logie Baird, in the cold month of February 1924. His subject was a Maltese Cross, transmitted through the air by the magic of television (also called "Televisor" or "Radiovision" in those days) the entire distance of ten feet.

To say that Baird's contraption was crude is an understatement. His Televisor was made from a cardboard scanning disk, some darning needles, a few discarded electric motors, piano wire, glue, and other assorted odds and ends. The picture reproduced by the original Baird Televisor was extremely difficult to see—a shadow, at best.

Until about 1928, other amateur radiovision enthusiasts toyed around with Baird's basic design, whiling away long hours in the basement transmitting Maltese Crosses, model airplanes, flags, and anything else that would stay still long enough under the intense light required to produce an image. (As an interesting aside, the lighting for Baird's 1924 Maltese Cross transmission required 2,000 volts of power, produced by a roomful of batteries. So much heat was generated by the lighting equipment that Baird eventually burned his laboratory down.)

Baird's electromechanical approach to television led the way to future developments in transmitting and receiving pictures. The nature of the Baird Televisor, however, limited the clarity and stability of images. Most of the sets made and sold in those days required the viewer to peer through a glass lens to watch the screen, which was seldom over seven by ten inches in size. What's more, the majority of screens had an annoying orange glow that often marred reception and irritated the eyes.

Modern Television Technology
In the early 1930s, Vladimir Zworykin developed a device known as the iconoscope camera. About the same time, Philo T. Farnsworth was putting the finishing touches on the image dissector tube, a gizmo that proved to be the forerunner of the modern cathode ray tube or CRT—the everyday picture tube. These two devices paved the way for the TV sets we know and cherish today.

The first commercially available modern-day cathode ray tube televisions were available in about 1936. Tens of thousands of these sets were sold throughout the United States and Great Britain, even though there were no regular television broadcasts until 1939, when RCA started what was to become the first American television network, NBC. Incidentally, the first true network transmission was in early 1940, between NBC's sister stations WNBT in New York City (now WNBC-TV) and WRGB in Schenectady.

Postwar Growth

World War II greatly hampered the development of television, and during 1941–1945, no television sets were commercially produced (engineers were too busy perfecting radar, which, interestingly enough, contributed significantly to the development of conventional TV). But after the war, the television industry boomed. Television sets were selling like hotcakes, even though they cost an average of $650 (based on average wage earnings, that's equivalent to about $4,000 today).

Progress took a giant step in 1948 and 1949 when the four American networks, NBC, CBS, ABC, and Dumont, introduced quality, "class-act" programming, which at the time included *Kraft Television Theatre, Howdy Doody,* and *The Texaco Star Theatre* with Milton Berle. These famous stars of the stage and radio made people want to own a television set.

Color and Beyond

Since the late 1940s, television technology has continued to improve and mature. Color came on December 17, 1953, when the FCC approved RCA's all-electronic system, thus ending a bitter, four-year bout between CBS and RCA over color transmission standards. Television images beamed via space satellite caught the public's fancy in July of 1962, when Telstar 1 relayed images of AT&T chairman Frederick R. Kappell from the U.S. to Great Britain. Pay-TV came and went several times in the 1950s, 1960s, and 1970s; modern-day professional commercial videotape machines were demonstrated in 1956 by Ampex; and home video recorders had appeared on retail shelves by early 1976.

Figure A.2 (continued)

Summary: A Brief History of Television

In 1924, Baird made the first electronic transmission of a picture. The primitive equipment produced only a shadow. Although Baird's design was modified by others in the 1920s, the viewer had to look through a glass lens at a small screen that gave off an orange glow.

Zworykin's iconoscopic camera and Farnsworth's image dissector tube — similar to the modern CRT — led in 1936 to the development of modern TV. Regular broadcasts began in 1939 on the first network, NBC. Research stopped during WWII, but after that, sales grew, even though sets cost approximately $650, the equivalent of $4,000 today.

Color broadcasts began in 1953; satellite broadcasting began in 1962; and home VCRs were introduced in 1976.

Key terms: television, history of television, NBC, color television, satellite broadcasting, videocassette recorders, Baird, Zworykin, Farnsworth.

Figure A.3   Summary of the Original Passage

Part B: Documenting Your Sources

Documentation identifies the sources of the ideas and the quotations in your document. Integrated throughout your document, documentation consists of citations in the text and a reference list (or list of works cited) at the back of your document. Documentation serves three basic functions:

- *To help you acknowledge your debt to your sources.* Complete and accurate documentation is a professional obligation, a matter of ethics. Failure to document a source, whether intentional or unintentional, is plagiarism. At most colleges and universities, plagiarism means automatic failure of the course and, in some instances, suspension or expulsion. In many companies, it is grounds for immediate dismissal.

- *To help you establish credibility.* Effective documentation helps you place your document within the general context of continuing research and define it as a responsible contribution to knowledge in the field. Knowing how to use existing research is one mark of a professional.

- *To help your readers find your source in case they want to read more about a particular subject.*

Three kinds of material should always be documented:

- *Any quotation from a written source or an interview, even if it is only a few words.*

- *A paraphrased idea, concept, or opinion gathered from your reading.* There is one exception. An idea or concept so well-known that it has become general knowledge, such as Einstein's theory of relativity, needs no citation. If you are unsure about whether an item is general knowledge, document it, just to be safe.

- *Any graphic from a written or an electronic source.* Cite the source for a graphic next to the graphic or in the reference list. For an online source, be sure to include a retrieval statement in the bibliographic entry. If you are publishing your work, you must also request permission to use any graphic protected by copyright.

Just as organizations have their own preferences for formatting and punctuation, many organizations also have their own documentation styles. The documentation systems included in this section of the appendix are based on the following style manuals:

- *Publication manual of the American Psychological Association* (5th ed.). (2001). Washington, DC: APA; *APA Style Guide to Electronic References* [PDF]. (2007). Washington, DC: APA. This system, referred to as APA style, is used widely in the social sciences.

- *IEEE standards style manual* [PDF]. (2007). New York: IEEE. This manual is primarily designed to assist in documenting new standards, but it is

On TechComm Web

For more help with documenting sources, click on Re:Writing on <bedfordstmartins.com/techcomm>.

In This Book

For more about quoting and paraphrasing sources, see Appendix, Part A.

In This Book

For more about using graphics from other sources, see Ch. 12, p. 306.

often used for the production of technical documents and standards in areas ranging from computer engineering, biomedical technology, and telecommunications to electric power, aerospace, and consumer electronics.

- Modern Language Association. (2008). *MLA style manual and guide to scholarly publishing* (3rd ed.). New York: MLA. This system, referred to as MLA style, is used widely in the humanities.

Other organizations may use one of the following published style guides.

GENERAL

Chicago manual of style (15th ed.). (2003). Chicago: University of Chicago Press. See also http://www.press.uchicago.edu/Misc/Chicago/cmosfaq/cmosfaq.html

BUSINESS

American Management Association. (1996). *The AMA style guide for business writing.* New York: AMACOM. See also http://www.amanet.org

CHEMISTRY

American Chemical Society. (1997). *ACS style guide: A manual for authors and editors* (2nd ed.). Washington, DC: Author. See also http://www.acs.org

GEOLOGY

Adkins-Heljeson, M., Bates, R. L., & Buchanan, R. (Eds.). (1995). *Geowriting: A guide to writing, editing, and printing in earth science* (5th rev. ed.). Alexandria, VA: American Geological Institute. See also http://www.agiweb.org

GOVERNMENT DOCUMENTS

U.S. Government Printing Office. (2000). *Style manual* (29th ed.). Washington, DC: Author. See also http://www.gpo.gov

JOURNALISM

Christian, D., Jacobsen, S., & Minthorn, J. (Eds.). (2008). *Associated Press stylebook 2008.* New York: Associated Press. See also http://www.ap.org

LAW

Columbia Law Review, Harvard Law Review, University of Pennsylvania Law Review, and Yale Law Journal. (2005). *The bluebook: A uniform system of citation* (18th ed.). Cambridge: Harvard Law Review Association. See also http://www.legalbluebook.com

MATHEMATICS

Higham, N. J. (1998). *Handbook of writing for the mathematical sciences* (2nd ed.). Philadelphia: Society for Industrial and Applied Mathematics. See also http://www.siam.org

MEDICINE

American Medical Association. (1998). *American Medical Association manual of style* (9th ed.). Baltimore: Williams. See also http://www.ama-assn.org

NATURAL SCIENCES

Scientific style and format: The CSE manual for authors, editors, and publishers (7th ed.). New York: Cambridge University Press. See also http://www.councilscienceeditors.org/publications/style.cfm

PHYSICS

American Institute of Physics, Publication Board. (1990). *Style manual for guidance in the preparation of papers* (4th ed.). New York: Author. See also http://www.aip.org

POLITICAL SCIENCE

American Political Science Association. (2006). *Style manual for political science* (rev. ed.). Washington, DC: Author. See also http://www.apsanet.org

SCIENCE AND TECHNICAL WRITING

National Information Standards Organization. (2005). *Scientific and technical reports—Preparation, presentation and preservation.* Bethesda, MD: Author. See also http://www.niso.org

Rubens, P. (Ed.). (2000). *Science and technical writing: A manual of style* (2nd ed.). New York: Routledge.

SOCIAL WORK

National Association of Social Workers. (1995). *Writing for the NASW Press: Information for authors* (rev. ed.). Washington, DC: National Association of Social Workers Press. See also http://www.naswpress.org

SOCIOLOGY

American Sociological Association. (1997). *American Sociological Association style guide* (2nd ed.). Washington, DC: Author. See also http://www.asanet.org

Check with your instructor to see which documentation system to use in the documents you write for class. For documents prepared in the workplace, find out your organization's style and abide by it.

APA STYLE

On TechComm Web

For more information, see the APA Web site. Click on Links Library for the Appendix on <bedfordstmartins.com/techcomm>.

APA style consists of two elements: the citation in the text and the list of references at the end of the document.

APA Style for Textual Citations

1. Summarized or Paraphrased Material   641
2. Quoted Material or Specific Fact   641
3. Source with Multiple Authors   642
4. Source Issued by an Organization   642
5. Source with an Unknown Author   642
6. Multiple Authors with Same Last Name   643
7. Multiple Sources in One Citation   643
8. Personal Communication   643
9. Electronic Document   643

APA Style for Reference List Entries

BOOKS

10. Book by One Author   645
11. Book by Multiple Authors   645
12. Multiple Books by Same Author   645
13. Book Issued by an Organization   645
14. Book by an Unknown Author   647
15. Edited Book   647
16. Chapter or Section in an Edited Book   647
17. Book in Edition Other Than First   647
18. Multivolume Work   647
19. Translated Book   647
20. Non-English Book   647
21. Entry in a Reference Work   647

PERIODICALS

22. Journal Article   647
23. Magazine Article   649
24. Newspaper Article   649
25. Newsletter Article   649

ELECTRONIC SOURCES

26. Nonperiodical Web Document   649

Journal Articles

27. Article with DOI Assigned   651
28. Article with No DOI Assigned   651
29. Preprint Version of Article   651

Electronic Books

30. Entire Book   651

Dissertations and Theses

31. Dissertation Retrieved from Database   651

Reference Materials

32. Online Encyclopedia   653
33. Online Dictionary   653
34. Wiki   653

Raw Data

35. Data Set   653
36. Graphic Representation of Data   653
37. Qualitative Data   653

Gray Literature

38. Technical or Research Report   653
39. Presentation Slides   654

APA Style for Reference List Entries

General-Interest Media and Alternative Presses

40. Newspaper Article   654
41. Audio Podcast   654
42. Online Magazine Content Not Found in Print Version   654
43. Message Posted to a Newsgroup, Online Forum, or Discussion Group   654
44. Weblog Post   654
45. E-mail Message or Real-Time Communication   654
46. Online Posting   655

OTHER SOURCES

47. Technical or Research Report   655
48. Government Document   655
49. Brochure or Pamphlet   655
50. Article from Conference Proceedings   655
51. Lecture or Speech   655
52. Audio Recording   656
53. Motion Picture   656
54. Television Program   656
55. Published Interview   656
56. Personal Interview   656
57. Personal Correspondence   656
58. Unpublished Data   657

APA Textual Citations

In APA style, a textual citation typically includes the name of the source's author and the date of its publication. Textual citations vary depending on the type of information cited, the number of authors, and the context of the citation. The following models illustrate a variety of common textual citations; for additional examples, consult the *Publication Manual of the American Psychological Association*.

1. Summarized or Paraphrased Material   For material or ideas that you have summarized or paraphrased, include the author's name and publication date in parentheses immediately following the borrowed information.

> This phenomenon was identified more than 50 years ago (Wilkinson, 1948).

If your sentence already includes the source's name, do not repeat it in the parenthetical notation.

> Wilkinson (1948) identified this phenomenon more than 50 years ago.

2. Quoted Material or Specific Fact   If the reference is to a specific fact, idea, or quotation, add the page number(s) of the source to your citation.

> This phenomenon was identified more than 50 years ago (Wilkinson, 1948, p. 36).
>
> Wilkinson (1948) identified this phenomenon more than 50 years ago (p. 36).

3. Source with Multiple Authors　For a source written by two authors, cite both names. Use an ampersand (&) in the parenthetical citation itself, but use the word *and* in regular text.

> (Lee & Warner, 2008)
>
> Lee and Warner (2008) argued . . .

For a source written by three, four, or five authors, include all the names the first time you cite the reference; after that, include only the last name of the first author followed by *et al.*

First Reference

> Cashman, Walls, and Thomas (2008) argued . . .

Subsequent References

> Cashman et al. (2008) found . . .

For a source written by six or more authors, use only the first author's name followed by *et al.*

> (Marken et al., 2007)
>
> Marken et al. (2007) reported . . .

4. Source Issued by an Organization　If the author is an organization rather than a person, use the name of the organization.

> There is currently ongoing discussion of the scope and practice of nursing informatics (American Nurses Association, 2008).
>
> In a recent publication, the American Nurses Association (2008) discusses the scope and practice of nursing informatics.

If the organization name has a common abbreviation, you may include it in the first citation and use it in any subsequent citations.

First Reference

> (International Business Machines [IBM], 2008)

Subsequent References

> (IBM, 2008)

5. Source with an Unknown Author　If the source does not identify an author, use a shortened version of the title in your parenthetical citation.

> Hawking made the discovery that under precise conditions, thermal radiation could exit black holes ("World Scientists," 2007).

If the author is identified as anonymous—a rare occurrence—treat *Anonymous* as a real name.

> (Anonymous, 2007)

6. Multiple Authors with Same Last Name   Use first initials if two or more sources have authors with the same last name.

> B. Porter (2007) created a more stable platform for database transfers, while A. L. Porter (2007) focused primarily on latitudinal peer-to-peer outcome interference.

7. Multiple Sources in One Citation   When you refer to two or more sources in one citation, present the sources in alphabetical order, separated by a semicolon.

> This phenomenon has been well documented (Houlding, 2003; Jessen, 2008).

8. Personal Communication   Include the words *personal communication* and the date of the communication when citing personal interviews, phone calls, letters, memos, and e-mails.

> D. E. Walls (personal communication, April 3, 2008) provided the prior history of his . . .

9. Electronic Document   Cite the author and date of the source as you would for other kinds of documents. If the author is unknown, give a shortened version of the title in your parenthetical citation. If the date is unknown, use *n.d.* (for *no date*).

> Interpersonal relationships are complicated by differing goals (Hoffman, n.d.).

If the document is posted as a PDF file, include a page number in the citation. If a page number is not available but the source contains paragraph numbers, give the paragraph number.

> (Tong, 2001, ¶ 4)
>
> (Tong, 2001, para. 4)

If no paragraph or page number is available and the source has headings, cite the appropriate heading and paragraph.

> The CDC (2007) warns that babies born to women who smoke during pregnancy are 30% more likely to be born prematurely (The Reality section, para. 3).

The APA Reference List

A reference list provides the information your readers will need in order to find each source you have cited in the text. It should not include sources you

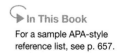

In This Book

For a sample APA-style reference list, see p. 657.

read but did not use. Following are some guidelines for an APA-style reference list.

- *Arranging Entries.* The entries are arranged alphabetically by author's last name. Two or more works by the same author are arranged by date, earliest to latest. Two or more works by the same author in the same year should be listed alphabetically by title and should also include a lowercase letter after the date: Smith 2004a, Smith 2004b, and so on. Works by an organization are alphabetized by the first significant word in the name of the organization.

- *Book Titles.* Titles of books should be italicized. The first word of the book's title and subtitle are capitalized, but all other words (except proper nouns) should be lowercase.

- *Publication Information.* Give the publisher's full name or consult your style guide for the preferred abbreviation. Include both the publisher's city and state or country unless the city is well-known (such as New York, Boston, or London).

- *Periodical Titles.* Titles of periodicals should be italicized, and all major words should be capitalized.

- *Article Titles.* Titles of articles should not be italicized or placed in quotation marks. The first word of the article's title and subtitle are capitalized, but all other words (except proper nouns) should be lowercase.

- *Electronic Sources.* Include as much information as you can about electronic sources, such as author, date of publication, identifying numbers, and retrieval information. Include the digital object identifier (DOI) when one exists. If there is the likelihood that the content could change, be sure to record the date you retrieved the information, because electronic information changes frequently.

- *Indenting.* Use a hanging indent, with the second and subsequent lines of each entry indented 5 to 7 spaces:

Khalturina, D. A., & Korotaev, A. V. (2008, May/June). Alcohol and narcotics as factors of the demographic crisis. *Sociological Research, 47*(3), 18–31.

Paragraph indents, in which the first line of each entry is indented 5 to 7 spaces, may be preferred by your instructor:

Khalturina, D. A., & Korotaev, A. V. (2008, May/June). Alcohol and narcotics as factors of the demographic crisis. *Sociological Research, 47*(3), 18–31.

- *Spacing.* Double-space the entire reference list. Do not add extra spacing between entries.

- *Page Numbers.* When citing a range of page numbers for articles, always give the complete numbers (for example, 121–124, *not* 121–24 or 121–4). If an article continues on subsequent pages interrupted by other articles or advertisements, use a comma to separate the page numbers. Use the abbreviation *p.* or *pp.* only with articles in newspapers, chapters in edited books, and articles from proceedings published as a book.

- *Dates.* Follow this format: year, month, day, with a comma after only the year (2008, October 31).

Following are models of reference list entries for a variety of sources. For further examples of APA-style citations, consult the *Publication Manual of the American Psychological Association* and the *APA Style Guide to Electronic References*.

BOOKS

10. Book by One Author   Begin with the author's last name, followed by the first initial or initials. If the author has a first and a middle initial, include a space between the initials. Place the year of publication in parentheses, then give the title of the book, followed by the location and name of the publisher.

> Harwood, J. (2007). *Understanding communication and aging: Developing knowledge and awareness.* Los Angeles: Sage Publications.

11. Book by Multiple Authors   To cite two or more authors, use the ampersand (&) instead of *and* between their names. Use a comma to separate the authors' names.

> Lee, G. O. M., & Warner, M. (2008). *The political economy of the SARS epidemic: The impact on human resources in East Asia.* London: Routledge.

To cite more than six authors, list only the first six, followed by *et al.*

12. Multiple Books by Same Author   List the entries by the author's name and then by date, with the earliest date first.

> Newman, M. A. (1986). *Health as expanding consciousness.* St. Louis: Mosby.
>
> Newman, M. A. (2008). *Transforming presence: The difference that nursing makes.* Philadelphia: F. A. Davis.

If you use multiple works by the same author written in the same year, list the books alphabetically by title and include *a*, *b*, and so forth after the year—both in your reference list and in your parenthetical citations.

> Agger, B. (2007a). *Fast families, virtual children: A critical sociology of families and schooling.* Boulder, CO: Paradigm.
>
> Agger, B. (2007b). *Public sociology: From social facts to literary acts.* Lanham, MD: Rowman & Littlefield.

13. Book Issued by an Organization   Use the full name of the organization in place of an author's name. If the organization is also the publisher, use the word *Author* in place of the publisher's name.

> American Nurses Association. (2008). *Nursing informatics: Scope and standards of practice.* Silver Spring, MD: Author.

APA: CITING A BOOK BY ONE AUTHOR

When citing a book, use the information from the title page and the copyright page (on the reverse side of the title page), not from the book's cover or a library catalog.

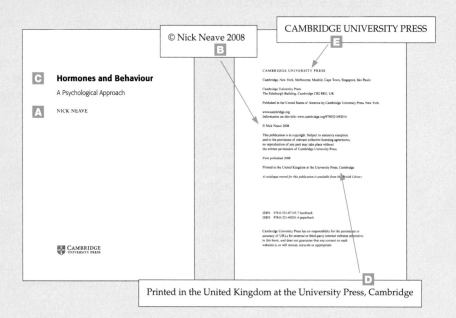

Record the following information:

A **The author.** Give the last name first, followed by a comma and initials for first and middle names. Separate initials with a space (Tufte, E. R.). Separate the names of multiple authors with a comma or commas; use an ampersand (&) before the final author's name.

B **The date of publication.** Put the most recent copyright year in parentheses and end with a period (outside the parentheses).

C **The title.** Give the full title; include the subtitle (if any), preceded by a colon. Italicize the title and subtitle, capitalizing only the first word of the title,

the first word of the subtitle, and any proper nouns. End with a period.

D **The city of publication.** If more than one city is given, use the first one listed. For a city that may be unfamiliar to your readers or confused with another city, add an abbreviation of the state, the province (if Canada; London, Ontario), or the country (Portland, England). Insert a colon.

E **The publisher.** Give the publisher's name. Omit words such as *Inc.* and *Co.* Include and do not abbreviate terms such as *University* and *Press*. End with a period.

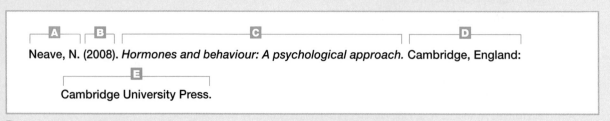

Neave, N. (2008). *Hormones and behaviour: A psychological approach.* Cambridge, England: Cambridge University Press.

▶ **In This Book** For more APA-style models for citing other types of books, see pp. 645 and 647.

14. Book by an Unknown Author   If the author of the book is unknown, begin with the title in italics.

> *PDR psychotropic prescribing guide.* (2005). Montvale, NJ: Thompson.

15. Edited Book   Place the abbreviation *Ed.* or *Eds.* in parentheses after the name(s), followed by a period.

> Zedillo, E. (Ed.). (2008). *Global warming: Looking beyond Kyoto.* New Haven, CT: Center for the Study of Globalization, Yale University.

16. Chapter or Section in an Edited Book

> Smith, T., & Wick, J. (2008). Controversial treatments. In K. Chawarska, A. Kline, & F. R. Volkmar (Eds.), *Autism spectrum disorders in infants and toddlers* (pp. 274–299). New York: Guilford Press.

17. Book in Edition Other Than First   Include the edition number in parentheses following the title.

> Fadem, B. (2009). *High-yield behavioral science* (3rd ed.). Philadelphia: Lippincott Williams & Wilkins.

18. Multivolume Work   Include the number of volumes after the title.

> Dale, D. C., & Federman, D. D. (Eds.). (2007). *ACP medicine: A publication of the American College of Physicians* (Vols. 1–2). New York: WebMD.

19. Translated Book   Name the translator after the title.

> Laïdi, Z. (2007). *The great disruption* (C. Turner, Trans.). Cambridge, England: Polity.

20. Non-English Book   Give the original title, then the English translation in brackets.

> Thomas, J. P. (2008). *Plume et le scalpel: La médecine au prisme de la littérature* [The pen and the scalpel: Medicine through the prism of literature]. Paris: Presses universitaires de France.

21. Entry in a Reference Work   Begin with the title of the entry if it has no author.

> Bakker, R. (2008). Environmental modifications: Home. In *The encyclopedia of elder care: The comprehensive resource on geriatric and social care* (2nd ed., pp. 267–269). New York: Springer.

PERIODICALS

22. Journal Article   Follow the author's name and date with the article title; then give the journal title. If the journal issue is identified by a word such as

Periodicals include journals, magazines, and newspapers. This page gives an example of a citation for a print journal article.

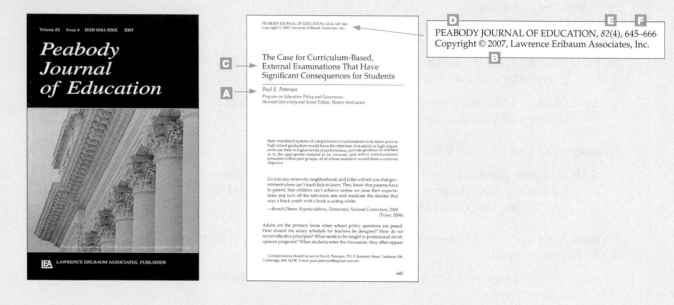

Record the following information:

A **The author.** Give the last name first, followed by a comma and initials for first and middle names. Separate initials with a space (Tufte, E. R.). Separate the names of multiple authors with a comma or commas; use an ampersand (&) before the final author's name.

B **The date of publication.** Put the year in parentheses and end with a period (outside the parentheses). For magazines and newspapers, include the month and, if relevant, the day (2006, May 23).

C **The article title.** Give the full title; include the subtitle (if any), preceded by a colon. Do not underline or italicize the title or put it in quotation marks. Capitalize only the first word of the title, the first word of the subtitle, and any proper nouns. End with a period.

D **The periodical title.** Italicize the periodical title and capitalize all major words. Insert a comma.

E **The volume number and issue number.** For journals, include the volume number (italicized), followed immediately by the issue number in parentheses (not italicized). Insert a comma.

F **Inclusive page numbers.** Give all the numbers in full (316–337, *not* 316–37). For newspapers, include the abbreviation *p.* for *page* (or *pp.* for *pages*) and the section letter, if relevant (p. D4). End with a period.

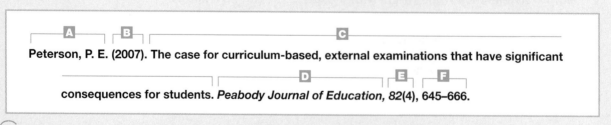

▶ **In This Book** For more APA-style models for citing other types of periodical articles, see pp. 647 and 649.

Spring, include that word in the date. For all journals, whether paginated by issue or by volume, include the volume number (italicized), followed immediately by the issue number in parentheses (not italicized), set off by commas. End with the page number(s).

> Türkel, Y. D., & Tezer, E. (2008, Spring). Parenting styles and learned resourcefulness of Turkish adolescents. *Adolescents, 43*(169), 143–155.

23. *Magazine Article* Include the month in the date. If it's a weekly magazine, include the day. Include the volume number, if there is one, after the magazine title.

> Zimmer, C. (2008, June). What is a species? *Scientific American, 298,* 72–79.

24. *Newspaper Article* Include the specific publication date following the year.

> Borns, P. (2008, June 1). Saving traces of the Jewish diaspora in Barbados. *Boston Sunday Globe,* p. M5.

25. *Newsletter Article* Cite a newsletter article as you would a magazine article.

> Walls, D. E. (2008, Spring). World War I posters go digital. *Nota Bene, 23,* 5.

ELECTRONIC SOURCES

Generally, include all the same elements for electronic sources as you would for print sources. Include any information required to locate the item. Many scholarly publishers are now assigning a digital object identifier (DOI) to journal articles and other documents. A DOI is a unique alphanumeric string assigned by a registration agency. It provides a persistent link to unchanging content on the Internet. When available, substitute the DOI for the URL. If the content is subject to change, include the retrieval date before the DOI or URL. Use the exact URL for open-source material and the home page or menu page URL for subscription-only material or content presented in frames, which make exact URLs unworkable. Break URLs before most punctuation, and avoid punctuation after them so as not to confuse the reader.

26. *Nonperiodical Web Document* To cite a nonperiodical Web document, provide as much of the following information as possible: author's name, date of publication or most recent update (use *n.d.* if there is no date), document title (in italics), and URL for the document.

> Centers for Disease Control and Prevention. (2007, January). *Biosafety in microbiological and biomedical laboratories.* Retrieved from http://www.cdc.gov/od/ohs/biosfty/bmbl5/BMBL_5th_Edition.pdf

If the author of a document is not identified, begin the reference with the title of the document. If the document is from a university program's Web

APA: CITING A NONPERIODICAL WEB DOCUMENT

You will likely need to search the Web site to find some of the citation information you need. For some sites, all of the details may not be available; find as many as you can. Remember that the citation you provide should allow readers to retrace your steps electronically to locate the source.

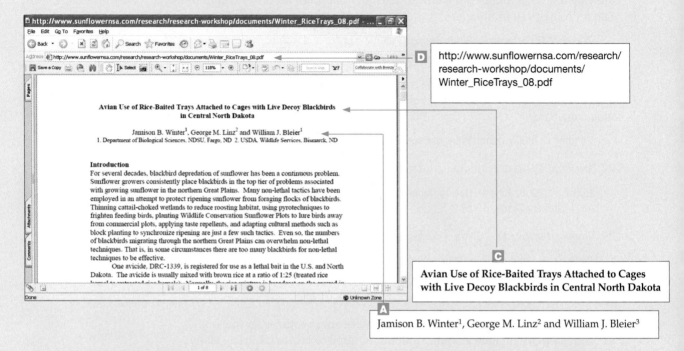

D http://www.sunflowernsa.com/research/research-workshop/documents/Winter_RiceTrays_08.pdf

C Avian Use of Rice-Baited Trays Attached to Cages with Live Decoy Blackbirds in Central North Dakota

A Jamison B. Winter[1], George M. Linz[2] and William J. Bleier[3]

Record the following information:

A **The author.** Give the last name first, followed by a comma and initials for first and middle names. Separate initials with a space (Tufte, E. R.). Separate the names of multiple authors with a comma or commas; use an ampersand (&) before the final author's name.

B **The date of publication or most recent update.** Put the date in parentheses and end with a period (outside the parentheses). If there is no date, use *n.d.*

C **The document title.** Give the full title; include the subtitle (if any), preceded by a colon. Italicize the title and subtitle, capitalizing only the first word of the title, the first word of the subtitle, and any proper nouns. End with a period.

D **The retrieval date and URL.** Include the word *Retrieved* before the date, insert a comma after the year, and include the word *from* before the complete URL.

A   **B**   **C**

Winter, J. B., Linz, G. M., & Bleier, W. J. (2008). *Avian use of rice-baited trays attached to cages with*

D

live decoy blackbirds in central North Dakota. **Retrieved June 1, 2008, from**

http://www.sunflowernsa.com/research/research-workshop/documents/Winter_RiceTrays_08.pdf

▶ **In This Book** For more APA-style models for citing other types of Web sources, see pp. 653–55.

site, identify the host institution and program or department, followed by a colon and the URL for the document.

> *Safety manual.* (2008, April 10). Retrieved April 12, 2008, from Harvard University, Center for Nanoscale Systems Web site: http://www-safety.deas.harvard.edu/manual.html

Journal Articles

27. Article with DOI Assigned

> Burakov, V. S., Butsen, A. V., Bruser, V., Harnisch, F., Misakov, P. Y., & Nevar, E. A., et al. (2008, May). Synthesis of tungsten carbide nanopowder via submerged discharge method. *Journal of Nanoparticle Research, 10*(5), 881–886. doi:10.1007/s11051-007-9314-7

28. Article with No DOI Assigned

> Hossain, A. B. M. S., Salleh, A., Boyce, A. N., Chowdhury, P., & Naqiuddin, M. (2008). Biodiesel fuel production from algae as renewable energy. *American Journal of Biochemistry and Biotechnology 4*(3), 250–254. Retrieved from http://www.scipub.org/fulltext/ajbb/ajbb43250-254.pdf

29. Preprint Version of Article

> Park, J. H., Scheerer, P., Hofmann, K. P., Choe, H., & Ernst, O. P. (2008). Crystal structure of the ligand-free G-protein-coupled receptor opsin. *Nature.* Advance online publication. Retrieved June 15, 2008. doi:10.1038/nature07063

Electronic Books

30. Entire Book   Use "Retrieved from" if the URL leads to the information itself and "Available from" if the URL leads to information on how to obtain the content.

> Einstein, A. (n.d.). *Relativity: The special and general theory.* Available from http://www.gutenberg.org/etext/5001

Dissertations and Theses

31. Dissertation Retrieved from Database   The database name is included in the reference, followed by the accession number, if one is assigned.

> Puzz, T. E. (2008). *Development of a tungsten carbide-nickel braze alloy hardface coating.* Retrieved from ProQuest Dissertations & Theses. (AAT 1451431)

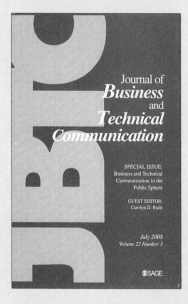

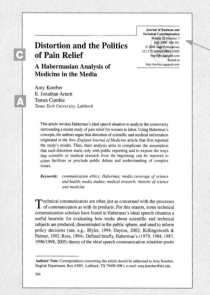

Record the following information:

A **The author.** Give the last name first, followed by a comma and initials for first and middle names. Separate initials with a space (Tufte, E. R.). Separate the names of multiple authors with a comma or commas; use an ampersand (&) before the final author's name.

B **The date of publication.** Put the year in parentheses and end with a period (outside the parentheses). For magazines and newspapers, include the month and, if relevant, the day (2006, May 23).

C **The article title.** Give the full title; include the subtitle (if any), preceded by a colon. Do not underline or italicize the title or put it in quotation marks. Capitalize only the first word of the title, the first word of the subtitle, and any proper nouns. End with a period.

D **The periodical title.** Italicize the periodical title and capitalize all major words. Insert a comma.

E **The volume number and issue number.** For journals, include the volume number (italicized), followed immediately by the issue number in parentheses (not italicized). Insert a comma.

F **Inclusive page numbers.** Give all the numbers in full (316–337, *not* 316–37). For newspapers, include the abbreviation p. for *page* (or pp. for *pages*) and the section letter, if relevant (p. D4). End with a period.

G **The DOI.** If the DOI references a preprint, include the word *Retrieved* before the date, which is followed by a period. End with *doi* followed by a colon, no space, then the DOI. Leave off final punctuation.

Koerber, A., Arnett, E. J., & Cumbie, T. (2008). Distortion and the politics of pain relief: A Habermasian

analysis of medicine in the media. *Journal of Business and Technical Communication, 22*(3),

364–391. doi:10.1172/1050651908315985

In This Book For more APA-style models for citing other types of electronic sources, see pp. 653–55.

Reference Materials

Give the home or index page URL for reference works.

32. Online Encyclopedia

Cross, M. S. (2008). Social history. In E. N. Zalta (Ed.), *The Canadian Encyclopedia*. Retrieved June 20, 2008, from http://www.thecanadianencyclopedia.com

33. Online Dictionary

Conductance. (n.d.). In *Merriam-Webster's online dictionary*. Retrieved June 10, 2008, from http://www.merriam-webster.com/dictionary

34. Wiki

CA:EV revocation checking. (2008, February 5). Retrieved March 28, 2008, from Mozilla Wiki: http://wiki.mozilla.org

Raw Data

35. Data Set

Kee, H., Nicita, A., & Olarreaga, M. (2008). *Global monitoring report 2008: Overall trade restrictiveness indices* [Report and data sets]. Available from http://go.worldbank.org/C5VQJIV3H0

36. Graphic Representation of Data

Centers for Disease Control and Prevention. (2007, September 20). *Reported cases of Lyme disease by year, United States, 1991–2006* [Bar graph]. Retrieved from http://www.cdc.gov/ncidod/dvbid/lyme/ld_UpClimbLymeDis.htm

37. Qualitative Data

Sánchez, R. (Interviewee). (2008). Ramón "Chunky" Sánchez [Audio stream]. Available from StoryCorps: Recording America, Sound Corporate Productions Web site: http://www.storycorps.net/listen/stories/ramon-chunky-sanchez

Gray Literature

38. Technical or Research Report

Moran, R., Rampey, B. D., Dion, G. S., & Donahue, P. L. (2008). *National Indian education study 2007, Part 1. Performance of American Indian and Alaska native students at grades 4 and 8 on NAEP 2007 reading and mathematics assessments* (Report No. NCES 2008–457). Retrieved from National Center for Education Statistics Web site: http://nces.ed.gov/nationsreportcard/pdf/studies/2008457.pdf

Gray literature refers to print or electronic documents published by organizations such as businesses, government agencies, and scientific groups rather than by traditional publishers. Because grey literature is typically not cited in the popular bibliographic sources, it is often difficult to find and access.

39. Presentation Slides

Straneo, F. (2008). *The role of dense water formation regions in the ocean and climate* [PowerPoint slides]. Retrieved from http://earth.geology.yale.edu/~avf5/OceanClimateForum/straneo_yale.pdf

General-Interest Media and Alternative Presses

40. Newspaper Article

Hart, K. (2008, June 14). Twitters from Mars! A ghost-written micro-blog makes NASA's robot lander less alien. *The Washington Post.* Retrieved from http://www.washingtonpost.com

41. Audio Podcast   Include authority, if known; date; episode title; episode or show identifier in brackets, such as *[Show 13]*; show name; and retrieval information.

Cooper, Q. (Presenter). (2008, April 17). Blood brain barrier. *The Material World.* Podcast retrieved from http://www.bbc.co.uk/radio4/science/thematerialworld.shtml

42. Online Magazine Content Not Found in Print Version

Biello, D. (2008, April 3). Aztec math used hearts and arrows [Online exclusive]. *Scientific American.* Retrieved June 12, 2008, from http://www.sciam.com/article.cfm?id=aztec-math-uses-hearts-and-arrows

Online Communities

43. Message Posted to a Newsgroup, Online Forum, or Discussion Group
Use screen name if author's name not available. Provide any identifier for the message in brackets after the subject line or thread name.

Landgrebe, B. (2008, April 2). Non-aqueous consolidants for matte, flaking paintings [Msg 2]. Message posted to Conservation DistList, archived at http://palimpsest.stanford.edu/byform/mailing-lists/cdl/2008/0365.html

44. Weblog Post

Chatham, C. (2008, June 6). The external reality filter: A right-hemispheric, ventral attention network. Message posted to http://scienceblogs.com/developingintelligence/

45. E-mail Message or Real-Time Communication   E-mail messages are not cited in the reference list. Instead, they should be cited in the text as personal communications. (See item 8 on page 643.)

46. Online Posting   If an online posting is not archived, and therefore is not retrievable, cite it as a personal communication and do not include it in the reference list. If the posting can be retrieved from an archive, provide the author's name or screen name, the exact date of the posting, the title or subject line, and any identifier in brackets. Finish with *Message posted to*, followed by the address.

> John. (2008, June 5). Are digital orchestras a sign of the times? [Msg 17]. Message posted to http://pogue.blogs.nytimes.com/2008/06/05/are-digital-orchestras-a-sign-of-the-times/

OTHER SOURCES

47. Technical or Research Report   Include identifying numbers in parentheses after the report title. If appropriate, include the name of the service used to locate the item in parentheses after the publisher.

> Richard, G. A., & Anderson, R. M. (2007, May). *Channel-forming discharge on the Dolores River and Yampa River, Colorado* (Technical Publication No. 44). Denver, CO: Colorado Division of Wildlife.

48. Government Document   For most government agencies, use the abbreviation *U.S.* instead of spelling out *United States*. Include identifying document numbers after the publication title.

> U.S. Department of State. (2007, August). *U.S. counternarcotics strategy for Afghanistan*. Washington, DC: Bureau of International Narcotics and Law Enforcement Affairs.

49. Brochure or Pamphlet   After the title of the document, include the word *Brochure* or *Pamphlet* in brackets.

> Center for Disease Control and Prevention & U.S. Department of Health and Human Services. (2007). *Preventing smoking and exposure to secondhand smoke before, during, and after pregnancy* [Brochure]. Washington, DC: Authors.

50. Article from Conference Proceedings   After the proceedings title, give the page numbers on which the article appears.

> Sasoh, A., Jeung, I., & Choic, J. (2008). Access to space without energy and propellant on board. In *Beamed Energy Propulsion: Fifth International Symposium on Beamed Energy Propulsion* (pp. 37–46). Melville, NY: American Institute of Physics.

51. Lecture or Speech

> Griffin, M. D. (2008, April 17). Building NASA's future. Lecture presented at Johns Hopkins University, Baltimore, MD.

52. Audio Recording   Give the function of the originator or primary contributor in parentheses after the name. Give the medium in brackets after the title.

> Young, J. K. (Lecturer). (2007). *The building blocks of human life: Understanding mature cells and stem cells* [CD]. Prince Frederick, MD: Recorded Books.

53. Motion Picture   Give the names of the primary contributors, such as the producer and director, and follow the film's title with the words *Motion picture* in brackets. List the country in which the film was produced and the studio's name. If the film was not widely distributed, give instead the distributor's name and address in parentheses.

> Epstein, A., Netto, P., & Slotnick, A. (Producers), & Epstein, A. (Director). (2008). *The business of being born* [Motion picture]. United States: New Line Home Entertainment.

54. Television Program   Start with the director, producer, or other principal contributor and the date the program aired. Include the words *Television broadcast* or *Television series* in brackets after the program title.

> Axelrod, D. (Executive Producer), & Angier, J. (Producer). (2007). *WIRED science* [Television series]. Los Angeles: KCET.

For a single episode in a television series, start with the writer and director or other relevant editorial personnel of the episode. Include the words *Television series episode* in brackets after the episode title. Also include information about the series.

> Liota, V. (Producer & Editor). (2007, July 10). Emergence [Television series episode]. In S. Fine (Executive Producer), *NOVA scienceNOW*. Boston: WGBH.

55. Published Interview   If it is not clear from the title, or if there is no title, include the words *Interview with* and the subject's name in brackets.

> Pelusi, N. (2008, February). Grand inquisitor [Interview with Howard Bloom]. *Psychology Today*, 41–42.

56. Personal Interview   Interviews you conduct, whether in person or over the telephone, are considered personal communications and are not included in the reference list. Instead, they should be cited in the text. (See item 8 on page 643.)

57. Personal Correspondence   Personal letters and memos are not included in the reference list. Instead, they should be cited in the text. (See item 8 on page 643.)

58. Unpublished Data   Include a description of the data in brackets.

> Standifer, M. (2007). [Daily temperatures, 2007, Barton Springs municipal pool, Austin, TX]. Unpublished raw data.

Sample APA Reference List

Following is a sample reference list using the APA citation system.

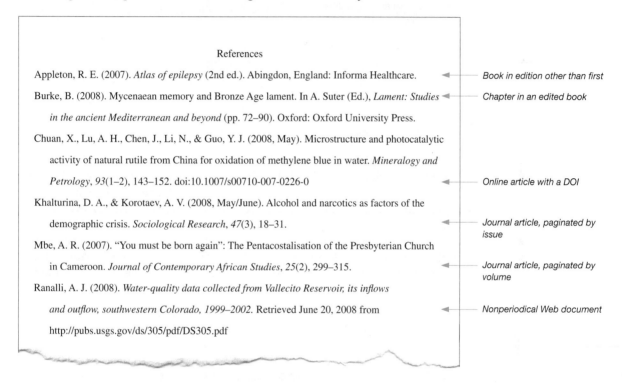

References

Appleton, R. E. (2007). *Atlas of epilepsy* (2nd ed.). Abingdon, England: Informa Healthcare.   ◄——— *Book in edition other than first*

Burke, B. (2008). Mycenaean memory and Bronze Age lament. In A. Suter (Ed.), *Lament: Studies* ◄——— *Chapter in an edited book*

    in the ancient Mediterranean and beyond (pp. 72–90). Oxford: Oxford University Press.

Chuan, X., Lu, A. H., Chen, J., Li, N., & Guo, Y. J. (2008, May). Microstructure and photocatalytic

    activity of natural rutile from China for oxidation of methylene blue in water. *Mineralogy and*

    Petrology, 93(1–2), 143–152. doi:10.1007/s00710-007-0226-0   ◄——— *Online article with a DOI*

Khalturina, D. A., & Korotaev, A. V. (2008, May/June). Alcohol and narcotics as factors of the

    demographic crisis. *Sociological Research, 47*(3), 18–31.   ◄——— *Journal article, paginated by issue*

Mbe, A. R. (2007). "You must be born again": The Pentacostalisation of the Presbyterian Church

    in Cameroon. *Journal of Contemporary African Studies, 25*(2), 299–315.   ◄——— *Journal article, paginated by volume*

Ranalli, A. J. (2008). *Water-quality data collected from Vallecito Reservoir, its inflows*

    and outflow, southwestern Colorado, 1999–2002. Retrieved June 20, 2008 from   ◄——— *Nonperiodical Web document*

    http://pubs.usgs.gov/ds/305/pdf/DS305.pdf

IEEE STYLE

IEEE style consists of two elements: the citation in the text and the bibliography annex (appendix) at the end of the document.

On TechComm Web

For more information, see the IEEE Web site. Click on Links Library for the Appendix on <bedfordstmartins.com/techcomm>.

IEEE Style for Reference List or Bibliography Annex Entries

BOOKS

1. Book by One Author   659
2. Book by Multiple Authors   659
3. Book Issued by an Organization   659
4. Edited Book   661
5. Chapter or Section in an Edited Book   661
6. Book in Edition Other Than First   661

IEEE Style for Reference List or Bibliography Annex Entries

PERIODICALS

7. Journal Article   661

8. Magazine Article   661

9. Newspaper Article   661

ELECTRONIC SOURCES

10. Article in an Online Journal or Magazine   661

11. Thesis or Dissertation   661

12. Web Site   664

13. Government Site   664

OTHER SOURCES

14. Standard   664

15. Scientific or Technical Report   664

16. Paper Published in Conference Proceedings   664

17. Government Document   664

18. Other Media   664

IEEE Textual Citations

In the bibliography annex (appendix) at the end of the document, the cited sources are ordered alphabetically (by author's last name or by standard number) regardless of the type of publication being cited. Then they are numbered, using a combination of a letter designating the annex (e.g., Annex B) and a number designating their alphabetical order. Textual citations refer to this alphanumeric designation (e.g., B1) and are enclosed in brackets. Typically, the first annex, or Annex A, is reserved for standards, and the second, Annex B, is the bibliography. For simplicity, all of the following examples refer to Annex B. The first reference cited in the document should be footnoted as follows:

A recent study by Goldfinkel [B5][2] shows that this is not an efficient solution.

[2]The numbers in brackets correspond to those in the bibliography in Annex B.

The IEEE Reference List or Bibliography Annex

In This Book
For a sample IEEE-style reference list, see p. 665.

The following guidelines will help you prepare an IEEE-style bibliography annex. For additional information on formatting entries, consult the latest edition of *The Chicago Manual of Style*.

- *Arranging Entries.* The entries are arranged in alphabetical order by author, if there is one, or title. Standards are alphabetized by their designation (e.g., IEEE Std 1226.6-1996).

- *Authors.* Names are listed in inverted order (last name, first name). If an editor or translator is used in place of an author, add the abbreviation *ed.* (or *eds.* for *editors*) or *trans.* You may choose to write out first names or use initials; be consistent.

- *Book Titles.* Titles of books should be italicized. In English, the first word and all major words are capitalized. In foreign languages, the first word of the title and subtitle are capitalized, as well as any words that would be capitalized in that language.

- *Publication Information.* Give the place (city) of publication, the publisher's name, and the date (year) of publication. Include only the first city listed when two or more are given. If the city is not well-known, add the abbreviation of the state or province (if Canada) or the country. If the publisher's name indicates the state, no state abbreviation is necessary.

- *Periodical Titles.* Titles of periodicals are italicized. They are not abbreviated, although you can omit an initial *The*.

- *Article Titles.* Titles of articles are placed in quotation marks. The first word is capitalized. The remaining words are lowercase unless they are proper nouns.

- *Electronic Sources.* Generally treat electronic sources as you would the print equivalents. Include a URL. For material other than books or periodicals, include as many of the following pieces of information as you can: author, title of page (in quotation marks), title or owner of the site, and URL. When available, use DOIs or other permanent identifiers.

- *Spacing.* Double-space the entire reference list. Do not add extra spacing between entries.

- *Page Numbers.* If you are giving a range of pages for specific articles in books and periodicals, use the abbreviations *pp.* or *p.* Write numbers in full (152–159, *not* 152–59 or 152–9).

- *Dates.* Follow this format: dd mmm. yyyy (3 Apr. 2007 or Feb. 2008). Do not abbreviate May, June, or July.

BOOKS

1. Book by One Author   Include the last name of the author and the first name or initials (or the name of the organization), the title (in italics), the edition (if applicable), the place of publication (city), the publisher, the year of publication, and the first and last page of reference.

> [B1] Szabo, V. E., *Monstrous Fishes and the Mead-Dark Sea: Whaling in the Medieval North Atlantic*. Boston: Brill, 2008, pp. 198–231.

2. Book by Multiple Authors   List all the authors' names in reverse order.

> [B2] Steriade, M., and Paré, D., *Gating in Cerebral Networks*. Cambridge: Cambridge University Press, 2007, pp. 255–277.

3. Book Issued by an Organization   The organization takes the place of the author.

> [B3] American Library Association (ALA), *Libraries Connect Communities: Public Library Funding and Technology Access Study, 2006–2007*. Chicago: ALA, 2007, pp. 107–110.

IEEE: CITING A BOOK BY ONE AUTHOR

When citing a book, use the information from the title page and the copyright page (on the reverse side of the title page), not from the book's cover or a library catalog.

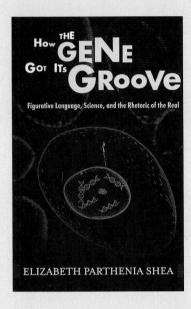

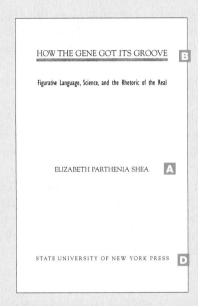

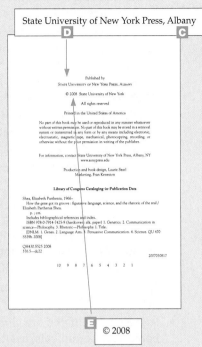

Record the following information:

A The author. Give the last name first, followed by initials for first and middle names. Separate initials with a space (Tufte, E. R.). (You may spell out the first name if you wish.) End with a comma.

B The title. Give the full title; include the subtitle (if any), preceded by a colon. Capitalize the first word of the title and subtitle and all major words. Italicize the full title. End with a period.

C The city of publication. If more than one city is given, use the first one listed. For a city that may be unfamiliar to your readers or confused with another

city, add an abbreviation of the state or province (if Canada) or the country: Sweetwater, TX; London ON; Milan, Italy. Insert a colon.

D The publisher. Give a concise version of the publisher's name. End with a comma.

E The date of publication. Use the publication date, if given. Otherwise, use the copyright date. End with a comma.

F The pages referenced. Give the first and last pages of the material referenced.

[B17] Shea, E. P., *How the Gene Got Its Groove: Figurative Language, Science, and the Rhetoric of the Real.* Albany: State University of New York Press, 2008, pp. 59–78.

▶ In This Book For more IEEE-style models for citing other types of books, see pp. 659 and 661.

4. Edited Book   Include the word *ed.* or *eds.* after the name(s).

[B4] Schiebinger, L., ed., *Gendered Innovations in Science and Engineering*, 4th ed. Stanford, CA: Stanford University Press, 2008, pp. 112–162.

5. Chapter or Section in an Edited Book   Give the author and title of the chapter or section first, followed by the word *in*, the book title, and the book editor. Then give the publication information for the book and the page numbers on which the chapter or section appears.

[B5] Sims, L. D., and Turner, A. J., "Avian influenza in Australia," in *Avian Influenza*, ed. D. E. Swayne. Ames, IA: Blackwell, 2008, pp. 239–250.

6. Book in Edition Other Than First   The edition number follows the title of the book and is preceded by a comma.

[B6] Morrissey, J. F., and Sumich, J. L., *Introduction to the Biology of Marine Life*, 9th ed. Boston: Jones and Bartlett, 2009, pp. 38–155, 302–368.

PERIODICALS

7. Journal Article   List the author's name, the article title, and the journal title, followed by the volume number, issue number, page number(s), and year.

[B7] Haworth, D., "Verify and debug DDR2 memory systems," *Embedded Systems Design*, vol. 20, no. 6, pp. 18–28, 2007.

8. Magazine Article   List the author's name, the article title, and the magazine title, followed by the page number(s) and issue date.

[B8] Fallows, J., "China makes, the world takes," *Atlantic*, pp. 28–33, July/Aug. 2007.

9. Newspaper Article   List the author's name, the article title, and the newspaper name, followed by the section and the date.

[B9] Kang, C., "FCC chief pushes new rules on phone fees," *Washington Post*, sec. D, 13 May 2008.

ELECTRONIC SOURCES

10. Article in an Online Journal or Magazine

[B10] Dingell, C., Johns, W. A., and White, J. W., "To the moon and beyond," *Scientific American*, Sept. 2007. http://www.sciam.com/article.cfm?id=to-the-moon-and-beyond.

11. Thesis or Dissertation

[B11] Puzz, T. E., "Development of a Tungsten Carbide-Nickel Braze Alloy Hardface Coating." Master's thesis, Mississippi State University, 2008.

IEEE: CITING AN ARTICLE FROM A PERIODICAL

Periodicals include journals, magazines, and newspapers. This page gives an example of a citation for a print journal article.

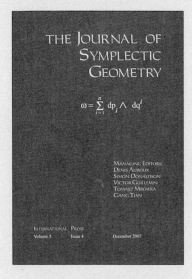

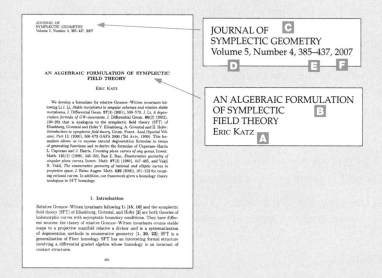

Record the following information:

A   The author. Give the last name first, followed by a comma and initials for first and middle names. Separate initials with a space (Tufte, E. R.). (You may spell out the first name if you wish.) End with a comma.

B   The article title. Give the full title; include the subtitle (if any), preceded by a colon. Capitalize only the first word of the title and proper nouns. End with a comma. Enclose all in quotation marks.

C   The periodical title. Italicize the periodical title; capitalize all major words. Don't abbreviate

elements of the title, but leave off an initial *The*. End with a comma.

D   The volume number and issue number. Include the volume and issue numbers, using the abbreviations *vol.* and *no.* End each with a comma.

E   Inclusive page numbers. Give all the page numbers on which the article appears. End with a comma.

F   The date of publication. Give the year or month and year for a magazine. End with a period.

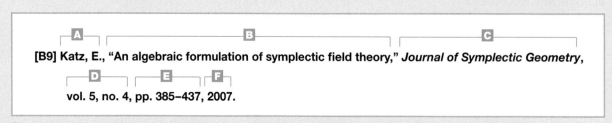

▶ **In This Book** For more IEEE-style models for citing other types of periodical articles, see p. 661.

IEEE: CITING AN ARTICLE FROM A DATABASE

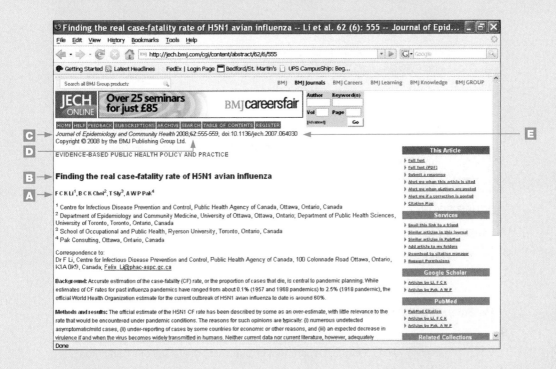

Record the following information:

A **The author.** End with a comma.

B **The article title.** Place the article title in quotation marks and end with a period (unless the title ends with its own punctuation). Capitalize only the first word of the title and proper nouns.

C **The periodical title.** Italicize the periodical title. Don't abbreviate elements of the title, but leave off an initial *The*. End with a comma.

D **The volume number, issue number, pages, and date.** Include the volume and issue numbers, using the abbreviations *vol.* and *no.* End each with a comma. Give all the page numbers on which the article appears. End with a comma. Provide the year. End with a period.

E **Retrieval information.** Include the DOI, beginning with *doi*, a colon, and no space. End with a period.

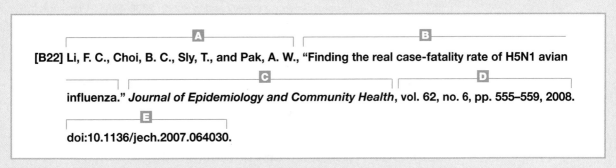

In This Book For more IEEE-style models for citing other types of electronic sources, see pp. 661 and 664.

12. Web Site

[B12] American Institute of Physics, *American Institute of Physics*, 2008. http://www.aip.org.

13. Government Site

[B13] Centers for Disease Control and Prevention, "CDC floods: emergency preparedness and response," *Department of Health and Human Services (US)*. http://emergency.cdc.gov/disasters/floods/.

OTHER SOURCES

14. Standard   Standards should include designation and title.

[B14] IEEE Std C37.110-2007, IEEE Guide for the Application of Current Transformers Used for Protective Relaying Purposes.

15. Scientific or Technical Report

[B15] Mondal, D., and Percival, D. B., *Wavelet analysis of variance or time series with missing values*. Seattle: Department of Statistics, University of Washington, 2007.

16. Paper Published in Conference Proceedings

[B16] Dahiya, H., and Gupta, M., "Strangeness in the nucleon," *International Workshop on Theoretical High Energy Physics*, Roorkee, India, pp. 3–6, 15–20, Mar. 2007.

17. Government Document

[B17] "Documentation of Computer Program INFIL3.0: A Distributed-Parameter Watershed Model to Estimate Net Infiltration Below the Root Zone: U.S. Geological Survey Scientific Investigations Report 2008–5006." Washington, DC: Geological Survey (US), 2008.

18. Other Media   Give a description of the medium in brackets.

[B18] "Rome: Engineering an Empire." [A&E Home Video]. Hosted by Peter Weller. New York City, 2007.

Sample IEEE Reference List or Bibliography Annex

Following is a sample reference list using the IEEE alphanumeric reference system.

Annex B
(informative)

Bibliography

[B1] Appleton, R. E., *Atlas of Epilepsy*, 2d ed. Abingdon, England: Informa Healthcare, 2007, pp. 38–155. ◄——— *Book in edition other than first*

[B2] Burke, B., "Mycenaean memory and Bronze Age lament," in *Lament: Studies in the Ancient Mediterranean and Beyond*, A. Suter, ed. Oxford: Oxford University Press, 2008, pp. 72–90. ◄——— *Chapter in an edited book*

[B3] IEEE Std C37.110-2007, IEEE Guide for the Application of Current Transformers Used for Protective Relaying Purposes. ◄——— *Standard*

[B4] Chuan, X., Lu, A. H., Chen, J., Li, N., and Guo, Y. J., "Microstructure and photocatalytic activity of natural rutile from China for oxidation of methylene blue in water," *Mineralogy and Petrology*, vol. 98, no. 1, pp. 143–152, 2008. doi:10.1007/s00710-007-0226-0, http://www.springerlink.com/content/nw03877m1470m771/fulltext.pdf. ◄——— *Online article with a DOI*

[B5] Mathieson, A. C., Hehre, E. J., Dawes, C. J., and Neefus, C. D., "An historical comparison of seaweed populations from Casco Bay, Maine," *Rhodora*, vol. 110, no. 941, pp. 1–10, 2008. ◄——— *Journal article*

[B6] Schmidt, S., "Arthur C. Clarke, 1917–2008," *Analogsf.com*, June 2008. analogsf.com/0806/Obitclarke.shtml. ◄——— *Article in an online magazine*

MLA STYLE

MLA style consists of two elements: the citation in the text and the list of works cited at the end of the document.

On TechComm Web

For more information, see the MLA Web site. Click on Links Library for the Appendix on <bedfordstmartins.com/techcomm>.

MLA Style for Textual Citations

1. Entire Work   666
2. Specific Page(s)   667
3. Work Without Page Numbers   667
4. Multiple Sources by Same Author   667
5. Source with Multiple Authors   667
6. Source Quoted Within Another Source   668
7. Source Issued by an Organization   668
8. Source with an Unknown Author   668
9. Multiple Sources in One Citation   668
10. Multiple Authors with Same Last Name   668
11. Chapter or Section in an Edited Book   668
12. Multivolume Work   669
13. Entry in a Reference Work   669
14. Electronic Source   669

MLA Style for Works Cited Entries

BOOKS

15. Book by One Author 670
16. Book by Multiple Authors 670
17. Multiple Books by Same Author 672
18. Book Issued by an Organization 672
19. Book by an Unknown Author 672
20. Edited Book 672
21. Chapter or Section in an Edited Book 672
22. Book in Edition Other Than First 673
23. Multivolume Work 673
24. Book That Is Part of a Series 673
25. Translated Book 673
26. Book in a Language Other Than English 673
27. Entry in a Reference Work 673

PERIODICALS

28. Journal Article 673
29. Magazine Article 675
30. Newspaper Article 675
31. Unsigned Article 675
32. Article That Skips Pages 675
33. Review 675

ELECTRONIC SOURCES

34. Entire Web Site 675
35. Short Work from a Web Site 677

36. Online Book 677
37. Article in an Online Periodical 677
38. Article from a Database or Subscription Service 677
39. Dissertation 677
40. CD-ROM 679
41. E-mail Message 679
42. Online Posting 679
43. Other Online Sources 679

OTHER SOURCES

44. Government Document 679
45. Article from Conference Proceedings 680
46. Pamphlet 680
47. Report 680
48. Interview 680
49. Letter or Memo 680
50. Lecture or Speech 681
51. Map or Chart 681
52. Photograph or Work of Art 681
53. Legal Source 681
54. Radio or Television Program 681
55. Film, Video, or DVD 682
56. Advertisement 682

MLA Textual Citations

In MLA style, the textual citation typically includes the name of the source's author and the number of the page being referred to. Textual citations vary depending on the type of information cited, the author's name, and the context of the citation. The following models illustrate a variety of common textual citations; for additional examples, consult the *MLA Style Manual and Guide to Scholarly Publishing.*

1. Entire Work   If you are referring to the whole source, not to a particular page or pages, use only the author's name.

> Harwood's work gives us a careful framework for understanding the aging process and how that affects communication.

2. Specific Page(s)   Immediately following the borrowed material, include a parenthetical reference with the author's name and the page number(s) being referred to. Do not use a comma between the name and the page number, and do not use the abbreviation *p.* or *pp.*

> Each feature evolves independently, so there can't be a steady progression of fossils representing change (Prothero 27).

If your sentence already includes the author's name, include only the page number in the parenthetical notation.

> Prothero explains why we won't find a steady progression of human fossils approaching modern humans, as each feature evolves independently (127).

3. Work Without Page Numbers   Give a section, paragraph, or screen number, if provided. Use *par.* or *pars.* to indicate paragraph numbers. Either spell out or use standard abbreviations for other identifying words. Use a comma after the name if it begins the citation.

> Under the right conditions, humanitarian aid forestalls health epidemics in the aftermath of natural disasters (Bourmah, pars. 3–6).

> Maternal leave of at least three months has a significantly positive effect on the development of attachment in the infant (screen 2).

4. Multiple Sources by Same Author   If you cite two or more sources by the same author, either include the full source title in the text or add a shortened title after the author's name in the parenthetical citation to prevent confusion.

> Chatterjee believes that diversification in investments can take many forms (*Diversification* 13).

> Risk is a necessary component of a successful investment strategy (Chatterjee, *Failsafe* 25).

5. Source with Multiple Authors   For a source written by two or three authors, cite all the names.

> Grendel and Chang assert that . . .

> This phenomenon was verified in the late 1970s (Grendel and Chang 281).

For a source written by four or more authors, list all the authors or only the first author, followed by the abbreviation *et al.* Follow the same format as in the works cited list.

> Studies show that incidences of type 2 diabetes are widespread and rising quickly (Gianarikas et al.).

6. Source Quoted Within Another Source   Give the source of the quotation in the text. In the parenthetical citation, give the author and page number(s) of the source in which you found the quotation, preceded by *qtd. in.*

> Freud describes the change in men's egos as science proved that the earth was not the center of the universe, and that man was descended from animals (qtd. in Prothero 89–90).

Only the source by Prothero will appear in the list of works cited.

7. Source Issued by an Organization   If the author is an organization rather than a person, use the name of the organization.

> In a recent booklet, the Association of Sleep Disorders discusses the causes of narcolepsy (2–3).

> The causes of narcolepsy are discussed in a recent booklet (Assn. of Sleep Disorders 2–3).

8. Source with an Unknown Author   If the source does not identify an author, use a shortened form of the title in your parenthetical citation.

> Multidisciplinary study in academia is becoming increasingly common ("Interdisciplinary" 23).

In a Web document, the author's name is often at the end of the document or in small print on the home page. Do some research before assuming that a Web site does not have an author. Remember that an organization may be the author. (See item 7.)

9. Multiple Sources in One Citation   To refer to two or more sources at the same point, separate the sources with a semicolon.

> Much speculation exists about the origin of this theory (Brady 42; Yao 388).

10. Multiple Authors with Same Last Name   If two or more sources have authors with the same last name, spell out the first names of those authors in the text and use the authors' first initials in the parenthetical citation.

> In contrast, Albert Martinez has a radically different explanation (29).

> The economy's strength may be derived from its growing bond market (J. Martinez 87).

11. Chapter or Section in an Edited Book   Cite the author of the work, not the editor of the anthology. (See item 21 on page 672.)

> Wolburg and Treise note that college binge drinkers include students with both high and low GPAs (4).

12. Multivolume Work   If you use only one volume of a multivolume work, list the volume number in the works cited list only. If you use more than one volume of a multivolume work, indicate the specific volume you are referring to, followed by a colon and the page number, in your parenthetical citation.

> Many religious organizations opposed the Revolutionary War (Hazlitt 2: 423).

13. Entry in a Reference Work   If the entry does not have an author, alphabetize it by the word or term you referenced. You do not need to cite a page number for encyclopedias and dictionaries because they are arranged alphabetically.

> The term *groupism* is important to understand when preparing to communicate with Japanese business counterparts ("Groupism").

14. Electronic Source   When citing electronic sources in your document, follow the same rules as for print sources, providing author names and page numbers, if available. If an author's name is not given, use either the full title of the source in the text or a shortened version of the title in the parenthetical citation. If no page numbers are used, include any other identifying numbers. (See item 3 on page 667.)

> Twenty million books were in print by the early sixteenth century (Rawlins, ch. 3, sec. 2).

The MLA List of Works Cited

A list of works cited provides the information your readers will need to find each source you have cited in the text. It should not include background reading. Following are some guidelines for an MLA-style list of works cited.

▶ **In This Book**

For a sample MLA-style list of works cited, see p. 682.

- *Arranging Entries.* The entries are arranged alphabetically by the author's last name. Two or more works by the same author are arranged alphabetically by title. Works by an organization are alphabetized by the first significant word in the name of the organization.
- *Book Titles.* Titles of books should follow standard capitalization rules and should be italicized. Note that MLA style is *not* to capitalize prepositions of any length.
- *Publication Information.* Shorten the publisher's name. For cities outside the United States, include the province (if Canada) or country, abbreviated, unless the city is well known (such as Tokyo or London).
- *Periodical Titles.* Titles of periodicals should be italicized, and all major words should be capitalized. Omit any initial article.
- *Article Titles.* Titles of articles and other short works should be placed in quotation marks, and all major words should be capitalized.
- *Electronic Sources.* Include as much information as you can about electronic sources, such as author, date of publication, identifying numbers,

and retrieval information. Also, be sure to record the date you retrieved the information, because electronic information changes frequently. If no author is known, start with the title of the Web site. Titles of entire Web sites should be italicized; titles of works within Web sites, such as articles and video clips, should be treated as in print sources. Citations for online sources should include the sponsor or publisher, as well as the date of publication or update. If this information can't be located, use *N.p.* (for *No publisher*) or *n.d.* (for *no date*). Insert the word *Web* before the date of retrieval. Include the URL only if you feel that your reader will be unable to locate the source with a search engine. Place the URL in angle brackets at the end of the entry, after the date of retrieval.

- *Indenting.* Use a hanging indent, with the second and subsequent lines of each entry indented one-half inch.

- *Spacing.* Double-space the entire works cited list. Do not add extra spacing between entries.

- *Page Numbers.* Do not use the abbreviation *p.* or *pp.* when giving page numbers. For a range of pages, give only the last two digits of the second number if the previous digits are identical (for example, 243–47, *not* 243–247 or 243–7). Use a plus sign (+) to indicate that an article continues on subsequent pages interrupted by other articles or advertisements.

- *Dates.* Follow this format: day, month, year, with no commas (20 Feb. 2009). Spell out *May, June,* and *July;* abbreviate all other months by using the first three letters (except *Sept.*) plus a period.

- *Medium.* With a few exceptions, explained below, the last part of any entry will be the medium of publication followed by a period. (See bullet item on electronic sources above.) Examples: *Print; Web; Radio; Television; CD; CD-ROM; Audiocassette; Film; Videocassette; DVD; Performance; Address; MS* (for *manuscript*); *TS* (for *typescript*); *E-mail; PDF file; Microsoft Word file; JPEG file; MP3 file.*

Following are models of works cited list entries for a variety of sources. For further examples of MLA-style citations, consult the *MLA Style Manual and Guide to Scholarly Publishing.*

BOOKS

15. Book by One Author   Include the author's full name, in reverse order, followed by the book title. Next give the location and name of the publisher, followed by the year of publication and medium.

> Prothero, Donald R. *Evolution: What the Fossils Say and Why It Matters.* New York: Columbia UP, 2007. Print.

16. Book by Multiple Authors   For a book by two or three authors, present the names in the sequence in which they appear on the title page. Only the

MLA: CITING A BOOK BY ONE AUTHOR

When citing a book, use the information from the title page and the copyright page (on the reverse side of the title page), not from the book's cover or a library catalog.

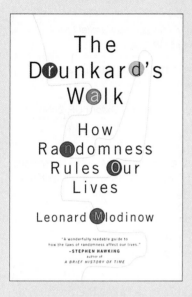

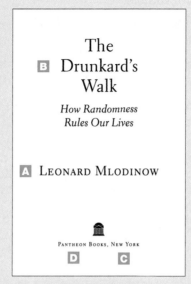

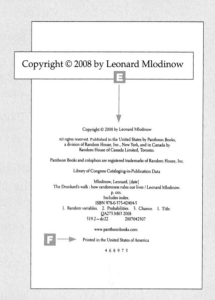

Record the following information:

A **The author.** Give the last name first, followed by a comma, the first name, and the middle initial (if given). Don't include titles such as *MD*, *PhD*, or *Sir*; include suffixes after the name and a comma (Jones, Durham F., Jr.). End with a period.

B **The title.** Give the full title; include the subtitle (if any), preceded by a colon. Italicize the title and subtitle, capitalizing all major words. End with a period.

C **The city of publication.** If more than one city is given, use the first one listed. For a city outside the United States that may be unfamiliar to your readers or confused with another city, add an

abbreviation of the province (if Canada) or country: London, ON; Plymouth, Eng. Insert a colon.

D **The publisher.** Give a shortened version of the publisher's name (*Simon* for *Simon and Schuster*; *Houghton* for *Houghton Mifflin*; *Columbia UP* for *Columbia University Press*). Do not include the words *Press*, *Publisher*, or *Inc.* Insert a comma.

E **The date of publication.** If more than one copyright date is given, use the most recent one. Use *n.d.* if no date is given. End with a period.

F **The medium of publication.** For a book, this would be *Print*.

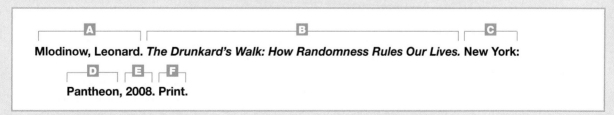

Mlodinow, Leonard. *The Drunkard's Walk: How Randomness Rules Our Lives.* New York: Pantheon, 2008. Print.

In This Book For more MLA-style models for citing other types of books, see pp. 670, 672, and 673.

name of the first author is presented in reverse order. A comma separates the names of the authors.

> Bearzi, Maddalena, and Craig B. Stanford. *Beautiful Minds: The Parallel Lives of Great Apes and Dolphins.* Cambridge: Harvard UP, 2008. Print.

For a book by four or more authors, either name all the authors or use the abbreviation *et al.* after the first author's name.

> Thomas, David N., et al. *The Biology of Polar Regions.* Oxford: Oxford UP, 2008. Print.

17. Multiple Books by Same Author   For the second and subsequent entries by the same author, use three hyphens followed by a period in place of the name. Arrange the entries alphabetically by title.

> Amsel, Philip. *Final Battle: A Tale in Verse and Prose.* Westmount, QC: Services, 2007. Print.

> ---. *Remembrance Road.* Westmount, QC: Services, 2007. Print.

18. Book Issued by an Organization   The organization takes the position of the author.

> Pontifical Institute of Mediaeval Studies. *The Gilson Lectures on Thomas Aquinas.* Toronto: Pontifical Inst. of Mediaeval Studies, 2008. Print.

19. Book by an Unknown Author   If the author of the book is unknown, begin with the title.

> *They Will Know Us by Our Love: Service Ideas for Small Groups.* Loveland, 2007. Print.

20. Edited Book   The book editor's name, followed by *ed.* (or *eds.* if more than one editor), is used in place of the author's name.

> Meyers, Jennifer N., ed. *Trends in Signal Transduction Research.* New York: Nova, 2007. Print.

21. Chapter or Section in an Edited Book   Give the author and title of the article first, followed by the book title and editor. Present the editor's name in normal order, preceded by *Ed.* (for *Edited by*). After the publication information, give the pages on which the article appears.

> Jestice, Phyllis G. "A Great Jewish Conspiracy? Worsening Jewish-Christian Relations and the Destruction of the Holy Sepulcher." *Christian Attitudes toward the Jews in the Middle Ages: A Casebook.* Ed. Michael Frassetto. New York: Routledge, 2007. 25–42. Print.

22. Book in Edition Other Than First   The edition number follows the title of the book.

> Backman, Clifford R. *The Worlds of Medieval Europe*. 2nd ed. New York: Oxford UP, 2009. Print.

23. Multivolume Work   If you use two or more of the volumes, give the total number of volumes before the place of publication (4 *vols.*). If you use only one volume, give the volume number before the place of publication. Give the total number of volumes after the medium, if you wish.

> Darity, William A., ed. *International Encyclopedia of the Social Sciences*. Vol. 7. Detroit: Macmillan, 2008. Print. 9 vols.

24. Book That Is Part of a Series   End the entry with the series name as it appears on the title page (but use common abbreviations, such as *Ser.*), followed by the series number, if any. Note that the medium is placed prior to the series information.

> Bircham, Peter. *A History of Ornithology*. London: Collins, 2007. Print. New Naturalist Libr. Ser. 104.

25. Translated Book   After the title, present the translator's name in normal order, preceded by *Trans.* (for *Translated by*).

> Monzote, Reinaldo F. *From Rainforest to Cane Field in Cuba: An Environmental History since 1492*. Trans. Alex Martin. Chapel Hill: U of North Carolina P, 2008. Print.

26. Book in a Language Other Than English   You may give a translation of the book's title in brackets.

> Trawny, Peter. *Sokrates, oder, Die Geburt der Politischen Philosophie* [*Socrates: Or the Birth of Political Philosophy*]. Würzburg: Königshausen, 2007. Print.

27. Entry in a Reference Work   If the work is well known, you do not need to include the publisher or place of publication.

> "Intracluster Medium." *Cambridge Illustrated Dictionary of Astronomy*. Cambridge: Cambridge UP, 2007. Print.

PERIODICALS

28. Journal Article   List the author's name, the article title (in quotation marks), and the journal title (italicized), followed by the volume number, issue number, year, page number(s), and medium.

> Vleck, William. "Development vs. Terrorism Money: Transfers and EU Financial Regulations in the UK." *British Journal of Politics and International Relations* 10.2 (2008): 286–302. Print.

Periodicals include journals, magazines, and newspapers. This page gives an example of a citation for a print journal article.

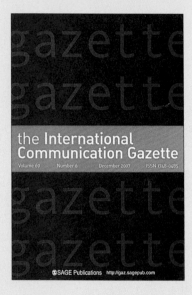

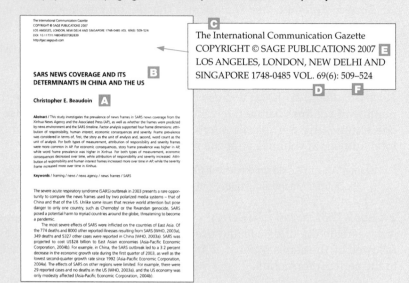

Record the following information:

A **The author.** Give the last name first, followed by a comma, the first name, and the middle initial (if given). Omit titles such as *MD*, *PhD*, or *Sir*; include suffixes after the name and a comma (Jones, Durham F., Jr.). End with a period.

B **The article title.** Give the title; include the subtitle (if any), preceded by a colon. Enclose the full title in quotation marks and capitalize all major words. Insert a period inside the closing quotation mark.

C **The periodical title.** Italicize the title. Omit any initial article and capitalize all major words.

D **The volume number and issue number.** For journals, give the volume number, followed by a period (no space) and then the issue number. Use both volume and issue regardless of whether the journal is paginated by issue or by volume.

E **The date of publication.** For journals, give the year in parentheses, followed by a colon. For monthly magazines, don't use parentheses; give the month and year. For weekly magazines and newspapers, don't use parentheses; give the day, month, and year (in that order). Abbreviate the names of all months except May, June, and July.

F **Inclusive page numbers.** For a range of page numbers 100 and above, give only the last two digits of the second number if the previous digits are identical (for example 243–47, *not* 243–247 or 243–7). Include section letters for newspapers, if relevant. End with a period.

G **The medium of publication.** Print.

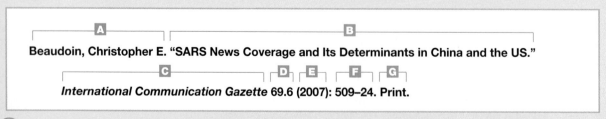

Beaudoin, Christopher E. "SARS News Coverage and Its Determinants in China and the US." *International Communication Gazette* 69.6 (2007): 509–24. Print.

▶ **In This Book** For more MLA-style models for citing other types of periodical articles, see pp. 673 and 675.

29. Magazine Article   List the author's name, the article title (in quotation marks), and the magazine title (italicized), followed by the issue date, page number(s), and medium.

> Marano, Hara E. "The Skinny Sweepstakes." *Psychology Today* Feb. 2008: 88–95. Print.

30. Newspaper Article   List the author's name, the article title (in quotation marks), and the newspaper name (italicized), followed by the issue date, page number(s) (which might include the section letter), and medium. If the newspaper appears in more than one edition, add a comma after the date and cite the edition (for example, *late ed.*). If sections are numbered, add a comma after the date, the word *sec.*, and the section number.

> Stobbe, Mike. "Sleep Habits Linked to Obesity." *Washington Post* 13 May 2008: F3. Print.

31. Unsigned Article   If the author of an article is not indicated, begin with the title. Alphabetize the work by title, ignoring any initial article.

> "Don't Make the Desert Bloom." *Economist* 7–13 June 2008: 60–61. Print.

32. Article That Skips Pages   Give the first page on which the article appears, followed by a plus sign (+) and a period.

> Carr, Nicholas. "Is Google Making Us Stupid?" *Atlantic* July/Aug. 2008: 56+. Print.

33. Review   For a book or film review, give the author of the review and the title of the review (in quotation marks), followed by the words *Rev. of* and the title of the work reviewed (italicized). Insert a comma and the word *by*, then give the name of the author of the work. (Instead of *by*, you might use *ed.*, *trans.*, or *dir.*, depending on the work.) End with the publication information for the periodical in which the review was published.

> Hersch, Matthew H. "Apollo's Stepchildren: New Works on the American Lunar Program." Rev. of *Dark Side of the Moon*, by Gerard J. DeGroot. *Technology and Culture* 49.2 (2008): 449–55. Print.

ELECTRONIC SOURCES

34. Entire Web Site   If you are citing an entire Web site, begin with the name of the author or editor (if given) and the title of the site (italicized). Then give the name of the sponsoring institution or organization (or *N.p.*), the date of publication or most recent update (or *n.d.*), the medium, and your access date. Only if necessary, add the URL in angle brackets at the end, followed by a period.

> Mikkelson, Barbara, and David P. Mikkelson, eds. *Urban Legends Reference Pages*. Snopes.com, 2008. Web. 15 July 2008.

MLA: CITING A SHORT WORK FROM A WEB SITE

You will likely need to search the Web site to find some of the citation information you need. Always include the sponsor/publisher and date of publication/most recent update.

Record the following information:

A **The author.** Give the last name first, followed by a comma, the first name, and the middle initial (if given). Omit titles such as *MD*, *PhD*, or *Sir*; include suffixes after the name and a comma (Jones, Durham F., Jr.). End with a period.

B **The document title.** Give the full title; include the subtitle (if any), preceded by a colon. Enclose the title and subtitle in quotation marks and capitalize all major words. Place a period inside the closing quotation mark.

C **The title of the Web site.** Give the title of the Web site, italicized. If there is no clear title and it is a personal home page, use *Home page* without italicizing it. End with a period.

D **The name of the sponsoring organization.** Look for the sponsor's name at the bottom of the home

page. If you can't identify the sponsor or publisher, use *N.p.* End with a comma.

E **The date of publication or most recent update.** Use the day, month, year format; abbreviate all months except May, June, and July. If you can't identify the date of publication or most recent update, use *n.d.* End with a period.

F **The medium of publication.** *Web*.

G **The retrieval date.** Give the most recent date you accessed the site. Provide a URL only if there is little likelihood that your reader will be able to find the information using a search engine. Give the complete URL, enclosed in angle brackets and followed by a period, after the date. If the URL is very long and complicated, however, give the URL of the site's search page instead.

Leonard, Andrew. "Seeking the Cellphone Future, in Kampala." *Salon.com.*

Salon Media Group, 30 Jan. 2008. Web. 14 Jul. 2008.

▶ **In This Book** For more MLA-style models for citing other types of Web sources, see pp. 675, 677, and 679.

35. Short Work from a Web Site   If you are citing a portion of a Web site, begin with the author, the title of the work (in quotation marks), and the title of the site (italicized). Then include the site's sponsor, the date of publication, the medium, and your access date.

> Friedmann, Susan. "Saving Time and Energy: A 6 Step Process to Adopting New
>   Technology." *MarcommWise*. Klebanoff Assoc., 2008. Web. 15 May 2008.

36. Online Book   Begin with the author's name and the title of the work, along with publication information about the print source. If the book has not been published before, include the online publication date and publisher. Include the medium. End with your access date.

> McDowall, Ian E., and Margaret Dolinsky, eds. *The Engineering Reality of Virtual
>   Reality, 2008*. Bellingham: SPIE, 2008. *SPIE Digital Library*. Web. 5 June 2008.

37. Article in an Online Periodical   Begin with the author's name and include the title of the document, the name of the periodical, and the date of publication. If the periodical is a scholarly journal, include relevant identifying numbers, such as volume, issue, and page numbers (or *n. pag.* if there are no page numbers). For abstracts of articles, include the word *Abstract*, followed by a period, after the page number(s). End with the medium and your access date.

> Filimowicz, Michael. "The Noise of the World." *Janus Head* 10.1 (2007): 25–40. Web.
>   15 Feb. 2008.

For magazine and newspaper articles found online, give the author; the title of the article (in quotation marks); the title of the magazine or newspaper (italicized); the sponsor or publisher of the site (use *N.p.* if there is none); the date of publication; the medium; and your date of access.

> Paulson, Steve. "Buddha on the Brain." *Salon.com*. Salon Media Group, 27 Nov.
>   2006. Web. 18 Jan. 2007.

38. Article from a Database or Subscription Service   After giving the print article information, give the name of the database (italicized), medium (*Web*), and your access date.

> Bapteste, Eric, and Yan Boucher. "Lateral Gene Transfer Challenges Principles of
>   Microbial Systematics." *Trends in Microbiology* 16.5 (2008): 200–07. *ISI Web of
>   Knowledge*. Web. 10 June 2008.

39. Dissertation

> Irawan, Piti. "Appearance of Woven Cloth." Diss. Cornell, 2008. *ProQuest Disserta-
>   tions & Theses*. Web. 15 June 2008.

MLA: CITING AN ARTICLE FROM A DATABASE

Libraries subscribe to services such as LexisNexis, ProQuest, InfoTrac, and EBSCOhost that provide access to databases of electronic texts.

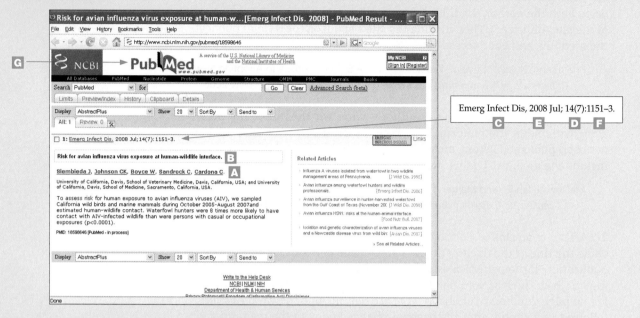

Record the following information:

A **The author.** Give the last name first, followed by a comma, the first name, and the middle initial (if known). For an article by multiple authors, only the name of the first author is presented in reverse order. A comma separates the names of the authors.

B **The article title.** Give the full title; include the subtitle (if any), preceded by a colon. Enclose the title in quotation marks and capitalize all major words.

C **The periodical title.** Italicize the title. Omit any initial article and capitalize all major words.

D **The volume number and issue number (if appropriate).**

E **The date of publication.** For journals, give the year in parentheses. For monthly magazines, don't use parentheses; give the month and year. For weekly magazines and newspapers, don't use parentheses; give the day, month, and year (in that order).

F **Inclusive page numbers.** If only the first page number is given, follow it with a plus sign and a period.

G **The name of the database.** Italicize.

H **The medium of publication.** *Web.*

I **The retrieval date.** Use the day, month, year format. If necessary, add the URL, enclosed in angle brackets and followed by a period.

A

Siembieda, Jennifer, Christine Johnson, Walter Boyce, Christian Sandrock, & Carol Cardona.

B **C**

"Risk for avian influenza virus exposure at human-wildlife interface." *Emerging Infectious*

D **E** **F** **G** **H** **I**

Diseases 14.7 (2008): 1151–3. *PubMed.* Web. 10 June 2008.

In This Book For more MLA-style models for citing other types of electronic sources, see pp. 675, 677, and 679.

40. CD-ROM   Treat a CD-ROM as you would any other source. If a book, treat as a book with CD-ROM as the medium. For an article in a database, include CD-ROM after the page numbers, followed by the database title, the vendor, and the publication date of the database.

> Malchow, Horst, Sergei V. Petrovskii, and Ezio Venturino. *Spatiotemporal Patterns in Ecology and Epidemiology.* Boca Raton: Taylor, 2008. CD-ROM.

41. E-mail Message   Include the author's name and the subject line (if any), then the words *Message to* followed by the name of the recipient (if you, *the author*). End with the date the e-mail was sent and the medium (*E-mail*).

> Lange, Frauke. "Data for Genealogical Project." Message to the author. 26 Dec. 2007. E-mail.

42. Online Posting   List the author's name, the subject line (if any) in quotation marks, the name of the discussion group or newsgroup, the sponsor, the posting date, the medium (*Web*), and your access date. If there is no subject line, use the expression *Online posting* (not in quotation marks) in its place.

> Krycek, Fiona. "Using a Wiki as Your Primary Authoring Tool & Delivery Mechanism." *TECHWR-L*. RayComm, 6 Jan. 2008. Web. 10 June 2008.

43. Other Online Sources   Follow the MLA guidelines, adapting them as appropriate to the electronic medium. The following examples are for a podcast and a blog, respectively. For a podcast, the medium might be *Web*, *MP3 file*, *MPEG-4 file*, *Video file*, and so on. If the blog doesn't have a title (in quotation marks), use the expression *Weblog entry* or *Weblog comment* in its place, not in quotation marks.

> "The Ocean Surface Topography Mission." *NASACast Video*. NASA, 19 June 2008. Web. 20 June 2008.

> Pogue, David. "How to Block Cellphone Spam." *Pogue's Posts.* New York Times, 12 June 2008. Web. 15 June 2008.

OTHER SOURCES

44. Government Document   Give the government name and agency as the author, followed by the publication title, the edition or identifying number (if any), the place and publisher, the date, and the medium.

> United States. Dept. of State. *Soviet-American Relations: The Détente Years, 1962–1972.* Dept. of State Pub. 11438. Washington: GPO, 2008. Print.

For an online government publication, begin with the name of the country and the government agency. Follow with the document title and the name of the author (if known), preceded by the word By. If the author is not known, follow with the agency. Give the date of publication, the report number, the medium, and your access date.

> United States. Geological Survey. *Shear Wave Structure of Umbria and Marche, Italy, Strong Motion Seismometer Sites Affected by the 1997–98 Umbria-Marche, Italy, Earthquake Sequence.* By Robert Kayen, Giuseppe Scasserra, Jonathan P. Stewart, and Giuseppe Lanzo. 2008. Open-File Report 2008-1010. USGS, Earthquake Hazards Program. Web. 12 Feb. 2008.

45. Article from Conference Proceedings   List the author's name, the article title, the proceedings title, and the editor's name(s), followed by the publication information.

> Matthews, Grant J. "Big Bang Cosmology." *The Tenth International Symposium on Origin of Matter and Evolution of Galaxies: From the Dawn of Universe to the Formation of Solar System.* Ed. Takuma Sua, et al. Sapporo: Amer. Inst. of Physics, 2007. 7–14. Print.

46. Pamphlet   Cite a pamphlet as you would a book.

> US Geological Survey. *Facing Tomorrow's Challenges: An Overview.* Denver: Habitat, 2008. Print.

47. Report   Cite a report as you would a book.

> Demirgüç-Kunt, Asli, Thorsten Beck, and Patrick Honohan. *Finance for All? Policies and Pitfalls in Expanding Access.* Washington: World Bank, 2008. Print.

48. Interview   Begin with the name of the person interviewed. If the interview has a title, enclose it in quotation marks; otherwise use the word *Interview*, followed by a period and the bibliographic information for the work in which it was published.

> Nolan, Patrick. Interview. *New Zealand Listener* 3–9 May 2008: 12. Print.

If it is a personal interview, give the interviewee's name, the words *Personal interview*, and the date.

> Youngblood, Adelaide. Personal interview. 5 June 2008.

49. Letter or Memo   If the letter or memo was written to you, give the writer's name, the words *Letter/memo to the author*, and the date it was written. End with the medium (e.g., *MS* for *manuscript* or *TS* for *typescript*).

> Jakobiak, Ursula. Letter to the author. 27 Oct. 2007. MS.

If the letter or memo was written to someone else, give his or her name in place of *the author*.

50. Lecture or Speech   Give the speaker's name, the title of the lecture or speech, and the place and date. If there is no title, use a descriptive label (such as *Lecture* or *Speech*), not enclosed in quotation marks. End with the medium.

> Ginsburg, Ruth B. "Law Should Be Settled and Settled Right." Ahavath Achim Synagogue. Atlanta. 21 Oct. 2007. Address.

51. Map or Chart   Give the author (if known), the title (in quotation marks), the word *Map* or *Chart*, the publication or source (in italics), and the date. Add the medium and, for an online source, the sponsor or publisher and the date of access.

> "Geologic Map of Montana." Map. *Butte: US Geological Survey*, 2007. Print.

52. Photograph or Work of Art   Give the name of the artist; the title of the artwork, italicized; the date of composition; the medium of composition; and the institution and city in which the artwork can be found. For artworks found online, omit the medium of composition and include the title of the Web site on which you found the work, the medium, and your date of access.

> Highsmith, Carol M. *Second Floor Corridor, Library of Congress Thomas Jefferson Building, Washington, DC.* 2007. Prints and Photographs Div., Lib. of Cong., Washington. Library of Congress. Web. 15 June 2008.

53. Legal Source   For a legal case, give the name of the first plaintiff and first defendant, the law report number, the name of the court, the year of the decision, and information about the medium in which you found the case.

> Natl. Assn. of Home Builders v. Defenders of Wildlife. No. 06-340. Supreme Court of the US. 2007. Supreme Court of the United States. Web.

For a legislative act, give the name of the act, the Public Law number, the Statutes at Large volume and page numbers, the date it was enacted, the medium, and the date of access.

> Protect America Act of 2007. Pub. L. 110-55. 5 Stat. 121.552. 5 Aug. 2007. Web. 15 June 2008.

54. Radio or Television Program   Give the title of the episode or segment, if applicable, and the title of the program. Include relevant information about the host, writer, director, or performers. Then give the network, the local station (if any), the broadcast date, and the medium. If on the Web, after the information about the program give the network, the title of the Web site, the medium (*Web*), and your date of access.

> "No More Mr. Nice Guy." *House, M.D.* Fox. WXFT, Boston, 28 Apr. 2008. Television.

> "Nice Work If You Can Get It." *This American Life*. Host Ira Glass. National Public Radio. WBEZ, Chicago, 6 Apr. 2007. Radio.

55. Film, Video, or DVD   Give the title of the film and the name of the director. You may also give the names of major performers (*Perf.*) or the narrator (*Narr.*). Give the distributor, the year of the original release, and the medium (*Film*, *DVD*, or *Videocassette*).

> *The Last King of Scotland*. Dir. Kevin Macdonald. Perf. Forest Whitaker, James McAvoy, and Kerry Washington. 20th Century Fox Home Entertainment, 2007. DVD.

56. Advertisement   Include the name of the product, organization, or service being advertised; the word *Advertisement*; and the publication information. If accessed online, give the source, the date, the medium (*Web*), and your access date.

> Discovery Channel. Advertisement. *Wired* June 2008: 148. Print.

Sample MLA List of Works Cited

Following is a sample list of works cited using the MLA citation system.

Works Cited

Book in edition other than first

Appleton, Richard E. *Atlas of Epilepsy*. 2nd ed. Abingdon, Eng.: Informa Healthcare, 2007. Print.

Chapter in an edited book

Burke, Brendan. "Mycenaean Memory and Bronze Age Lament." *Lament: Studies in the Ancient Mediterranean and Beyond*. Ed. Ann Suter. Oxford: Oxford UP, 2008. 70–92. Print.

Article in an online newspaper

Engel, Mary. "Flu Not Only Culprit in '18," *Chicago Tribune*. Tribune Newspapers, 18 Aug. 2008. Web. 22 Aug. 2008.

Journal article

Mbe, Akoko R. "'You Must Be Born Again': The Pentacostalisation of the Presbyterian Church in Cameroon." *Journal of Contemporary African Studies* 25.2 (2007): 299–315. Print.

Article in an online magazine

Schmidt, Stanley. "Arthur C. Clarke, 1917–2008." *Analog: Science Fiction and Fact*. Dell Magazines, June 2008. Web. 18 June 2008.

Part C: Editing and Proofreading Your Documents

This part of the handbook contains advice on editing your documents for grammar, punctuation, and mechanics.

If your organization or professional field has a style guide with different recommendations about grammar and usage, you should of course follow those guidelines.

Your instructor might use the following abbreviations to refer you to specific topics in Parts C and D of this Appendix.

Abbreviation	Topic	Page Number	Abbreviation	Topic	Page Number
abbr	abbreviation	707	ref	ambiguous pronoun reference	686
adj	adjective (ESL)	688, 722	rep	repeated word (ESL)	724
adv	adverb (ESL)	723	run	run-on sentence	686
agr p/a	pronoun-antecedent agreement	689	sent	sentence part (ESL)	712
agr s/v	subject-verb agreement (ESL)	689, 719	sub	subordinating clause (ESL)	715
art	article (*a, an, the*) (ESL)	721	t	verb tense	690
cap	capitalization	708	vb	verb tense (ESL)	715
comp	comparison of items	688	.	period	696
cond	conditional sentence (ESL)	720	!	exclamation point	696
coor	coordinating clause (ESL)	714	?	question mark	697
cs	comma splice	685	,	comma	691
frag	sentence fragment	684	;	semicolon	695
help	helping verb and main verb (ESL)	718	:	colon	695
inf	infinitive form of the verb (ESL)	718	—	dash	697
-ing	*-ing* form of the verb (ESL)	717	( )	parentheses	698
ital	italics (underlining)	702	-	hyphen	703
num	number	705	'	apostrophe	699
omit	omitted word or words (ESL)	724	" "	quotation marks	700
			. . .	ellipses	701
			< >	angle brackets	703
			[ ]	square brackets	702

GRAMMATICAL SENTENCES

frag   ## Avoid Sentence Fragments

On TechComm Web

For online exercises covering these grammar skills, click on Re:Writing, then Exercise Central on <bedfordstmartins.com/techcomm>.

A sentence fragment is an incomplete sentence, an error that occurs when a sentence is missing either a verb or an independent clause. To correct a sentence fragment, use one of the following two strategies:

1. Introduce a verb.

FRAGMENT   The pressure loss caused by a worn gasket.

This example is a fragment because it lacks a verb. (The word caused *does not function as a verb here; rather, it introduces a phrase that describes the pressure loss.)*

COMPLETE   The pressure loss was caused by a worn gasket.

Pressure loss *has a verb:* was caused.

COMPLETE   We identified the pressure loss caused by a worn gasket.

Pressure loss *becomes the object in a new main clause:* We identified the pressure loss.

FRAGMENT   A plotting program with clipboard plotting, 3-D animation, and FFTs.

COMPLETE   It is a plotting program with clipboard plotting, 3-D animation, and FFTs.

COMPLETE   A plotting program with clipboard plotting, 3-D animation, and FFTs will be released today.

2. Link the fragment (a dependent element) to an independent clause.

FRAGMENT   The article was rejected for publication. Because the data could not be verified.

Because the data could not be verified *is a fragment because it lacks an independent clause: a clause that has a subject and a verb and could stand alone as a sentence. To be complete, it needs more information.*

COMPLETE   The article was rejected for publication because the data could not be verified.

The dependent element is joined to the independent clause that precedes it.

COMPLETE   Because the data could not be verified, the article was rejected for publication.

The dependent element is followed by the independent clause.

FRAGMENT Delivering over 150 horsepower. The two-passenger coupe will cost over $32,000.

COMPLETE Delivering over 150 horsepower, the two-passenger coupe will cost over $32,000.

COMPLETE The two-passenger coupe will deliver over 150 horsepower and cost over $32,000.

CS Avoid Comma Splices

A comma splice is an error that occurs when two independent clauses are joined, or spliced together, by a comma. Independent clauses in a comma splice can be linked correctly in three ways:

1. **Use a comma and a coordinating conjunction (*and*, *or*, *nor*, *but*, *for*, *so*, or *yet*).**

   SPLICE The 909 printer is our most popular model, it offers an unequaled blend of power and versatility.

   CORRECT The 909 printer is our most popular model, for it offers an unequaled blend of power and versatility.

       The coordinating conjunction *for* explicitly states the relationship between the two clauses.

2. **Use a semicolon.**

   SPLICE The 909 printer is our most popular model, it offers an unequaled blend of power and versatility.

   CORRECT The 909 printer is our most popular model; it offers an unequaled blend of power and versatility.

       The semicolon creates a somewhat more distant relationship between the two clauses than the comma-and-coordinating-conjunction link; the link remains implicit.

3. **Use a period or another form of terminal punctuation.**

   SPLICE The 909 printer is our most popular model, it offers an unequaled blend of power and versatility.

   CORRECT The 909 printer is our most popular model. It offers an unequaled blend of power and versatility.

       The two independent clauses are separate sentences. Of the three ways to punctuate the two clauses correctly, this punctuation suggests the most distant relationship between them.

run   Avoid Run-on Sentences

In a run-on sentence (sometimes called a *fused sentence*), two independent clauses appear together with no punctuation between them. A run-on sentence can be corrected in the same three ways as a comma splice:

1. **Use a comma and a coordinating conjunction (*and*, *or*, *nor*, *but*, *for*, *so*, or *yet*).**

   RUN-ON   The 909 printer is our most popular model it offers an unequaled blend of power and versatility.

   CORRECT   The 909 printer is our most popular model, for it offers an unequaled blend of power and versatility.

2. **Use a semicolon.**

   RUN-ON   The 909 printer is our most popular model it offers an unequaled blend of power and versatility.

   CORRECT   The 909 printer is our most popular model; it offers an unequaled blend of power and versatility.

3. **Use a period or another form of terminal punctuation.**

   RUN-ON   The 909 printer is our most popular model it offers an unequaled blend of power and versatility.

   CORRECT   The 909 printer is our most popular model. It offers an unequaled blend of power and versatility.

ref   Avoid Ambiguous Pronoun References

Pronouns must refer clearly to their antecedents—the words or phrases they replace. To correct ambiguous pronoun references, try one of these four strategies:

1. **Clarify the pronoun's antecedent.**

   UNCLEAR   Remove the cell cluster from the medium and analyze it.

              Analyze what: the cell cluster or the medium?

   CLEAR   Analyze the cell cluster after removing it from the medium.

   CLEAR   Analyze the medium after removing the cell cluster from it.

   CLEAR   Remove the cell cluster from the medium. Then analyze the cell cluster.

   CLEAR   Remove the cell cluster from the medium. Then analyze the medium.

2. **Clarify the relative pronoun, such as *which*, introducing a dependent clause.**

   UNCLEAR   She decided to evaluate the program, which would take five months.

              What would take five months: the program or the evaluation?

CLEAR   She decided to evaluate the program, a process that would take five months.

By replacing *which* with *a process that*, the writer clearly indicates that it is the evaluation that will take five months.

CLEAR   She decided to evaluate the five-month program.

By using the adjective *five-month*, the writer clearly indicates that it is the program that will take five months.

3. **Clarify the subordinating conjunction, such as *where*, introducing a dependent clause.**

UNCLEAR   This procedure will increase the handling of toxic materials outside the plant, where adequate safety measures can be taken.

Where can adequate safety measures be taken: inside the plant or outside?

CLEAR   This procedure will increase the handling of toxic materials outside the plant. Because adequate safety measures can be taken only in the plant, the procedure poses risks.

CLEAR   This procedure will increase the handling of toxic materials outside the plant. Because adequate safety measures can be taken only outside the plant, the procedure will decrease safety risks.

Sometimes the best way to clarify an unclear reference is to split the sentence in two, drop the subordinating conjunction, and add clarifying information.

4. **Clarify the ambiguous pronoun that begins a sentence.**

UNCLEAR   Allophanate linkages are among the most important structural components of polyurethane elastomers. They act as cross-linking sites.

What act as cross-linking sites: allophanate linkages or polyurethane elastomers?

CLEAR   Allophanate linkages, which are among the most important structural components of polyurethane elastomers, act as cross-linking sites.

The writer has rewritten part of the first sentence to add a clear nonrestrictive modifier and has combined it with the second sentence.

If you begin a sentence with a demonstrative pronoun that might be unclear to the reader, be sure to follow it immediately with a noun that clarifies the reference.

UNCLEAR   The new parking regulations require that all employees pay for parking permits. These are on the agenda for the next senate meeting.

What are on the agenda: the regulations or the permits?

CLEAR   The new parking regulations require that all employees pay for parking permits. These regulations are on the agenda for the next senate meeting.

comp   Compare Items Clearly

When comparing or contrasting items, make sure your sentence communicates their relationship clearly. A simple comparison between two items often causes no problems: "The X3000 has more storage than the X2500." Simple comparisons, however, can sometimes result in ambiguous statements:

AMBIGUOUS   Trout eat more than minnows.

Do trout eat minnows in addition to other food, or do trout eat more than minnows eat?

CLEAR   Trout eat more than minnows do.

If you are introducing three items, make sure the reader can tell which two are being compared:

AMBIGUOUS   Trout eat more algae than minnows.

CLEAR   Trout eat more algae than they do minnows.

CLEAR   Trout eat more algae than minnows do.

Beware of comparisons in which different aspects of the two items are compared:

ILLOGICAL   The resistance of the copper wiring is lower than the tin wiring.

LOGICAL   The resistance of the copper wiring is lower than that of the tin wiring.

Resistance cannot be logically compared with *tin wiring*. In the revision, the pronoun *that* substitutes for *resistance* in the second part of the comparison.

adj   Use Adjectives Clearly

In general, adjectives are placed before the nouns that they modify: *the plastic washer*. In technical communication, however, writers often need to use clusters of adjectives. To prevent confusion in technical communication, follow two guidelines:

1. **Use commas to separate coordinate adjectives.**
   Adjectives that describe different aspects of the same noun are known as coordinate adjectives.

   portable, programmable CD player

   adjustable, removable housings

   The comma is used instead of the word *and*.

Sometimes an adjective is considered part of the noun it describes: *electric drill*. When one adjective modifies *electric drill*, no comma is required: *a reversible electric drill*. The addition of two or more adjectives, however, creates the traditional coordinate construction: *a two-speed, reversible electric drill*.

2. **Use hyphens to link compound adjectives.**
   A compound adjective is made up of two or more words. Use hyphens to link these elements when compound adjectives precede nouns.

   a variable-angle accessory

   increased cost-of-living raises

   The hyphens prevent *increased* from being read as an adjective modifying *cost*.

   A long string of compound adjectives can be confusing even if you use hyphens appropriately. To ensure clarity, turn the adjectives into a clause or a phrase following the noun.

   UNCLEAR   an *operator-initiated default-prevention* technique

   CLEAR   a technique *initiated by the operator to prevent default*

agr s/v   Maintain Subject-Verb Agreement

The subject and verb of a sentence must agree in number, even when a prepositional phrase comes between them. The object of the preposition may be plural in a singular sentence.

   INCORRECT   The *result* of the tests *are* promising.

   CORRECT   The *result* of the tests *is* promising.

The object of the preposition may be singular in a plural sentence.

   INCORRECT   The *results* of the test *is* promising.

   CORRECT   The *results* of the test *are* promising.

Don't be misled by the fact that the object of the preposition and the verb don't sound natural together, as in *tests is* or *test are*. Here, the noun *test(s)* precedes the verb, but it is not the subject of the verb. As long as the subject and verb agree, the sentence is correct.

agr p/a   Maintain Pronoun-Antecedent Agreement

A pronoun and its antecedent (the word or phrase being replaced by the pronoun) must agree in number. Often an error occurs when the antecedent is a collective noun—one that can be interpreted as either singular or plural, depending on its usage.

INCORRECT	The *company* is proud to announce a new stock option plan for *their* employees.
CORRECT	The *company* is proud to announce a new stock option plan for *its* employees.

Company acts as a single unit; therefore, the singular pronoun is appropriate.

When the individual members of a collective noun are emphasized, however, plural pronouns are appropriate.

CORRECT	The inspection team have prepared their reports.

The use of *their* emphasizes that the team members have prepared their own reports.

t   Use Tenses Correctly

Two verb tenses are commonly used in technical communication: the present tense and the past perfect tense. It is important to understand the specific purpose of each.

1. **The present tense is used to describe scientific principles and recurring events.**

INCORRECT	In 1992, McKay and his coauthors argued that the atmosphere of Mars *was* salmon pink.
CORRECT	In 1992, McKay and his coauthors argued that the atmosphere of Mars *is* salmon pink.

Although the argument was made in the historical past— 1992—the point is expressed in the present tense because the atmosphere of Mars continues to be salmon pink.

When the date of the argument is omitted, some writers express the entire sentence in the present tense.

CORRECT	McKay and his coauthors *argue* that the atmosphere of Mars *is* salmon pink.

2. **The past perfect tense is used to describe the earlier of two events that occurred in the past.**

CORRECT	We *had begun* excavation when the foreman *discovered* the burial remains.

Had begun is the past perfect tense. The excavation began before the burial remains were discovered.

CORRECT	The seminar *had concluded* before I *got* a chance to talk with Dr. Tran.

PUNCTUATION

, Commas

The comma is the most frequently used punctuation mark, as well as the one about whose usage writers most often disagree. Examples of common misuses of the comma are noted within the following guidelines. This section concludes with advice about editing for unnecessary commas.

On TechComm Web

For online exercises covering punctuation, click on Re:Writing, then Exercise Central on <bedfordstmartins.com/ techcomm>.

1. **Use a comma in a compound sentence, to separate two independent clauses linked by a coordinating conjunction (*and*, *or*, *nor*, *but*, *so*, *for*, or *yet*):**

   INCORRECT   The mixture was prepared from the two premixes and the remaining ingredients were then combined.

   CORRECT   The mixture was prepared from the two premixes, and the remaining ingredients were then combined.

2. **Use a comma to separate items in a series composed of three or more elements:**

   The manager of spare parts is responsible for ordering, stocking, and disbursing all spare parts for the entire plant.

   Despite the presence of the conjunction *and*, most technical-communication style manuals require a comma after the second-to-last item. The comma clarifies the separation and prevents misreading.

   CONFUSING   The report will be distributed to Operations, Research and Development and Accounting.

   CLEAR   The report will be distributed to Operations, Research and Development, and Accounting.

3. **Use a comma to separate introductory words, phrases, and clauses from the main clause of the sentence:**

   However, we will have to calculate the effect of the wind.

   To facilitate trade, the government holds a yearly international conference.

   In the following example, the comma actually prevents misreading:

   Just as we finished eating, the rats discovered the treadmill.

   NOTE: Writers sometimes make errors by omitting commas following introductory words, phrases, or clauses. A comma is optional only if the introductory text is brief and cannot be misread.

   CORRECT   First, let's take care of the introductions.

CORRECT	First let's take care of the introductions.
INCORRECT	As the researchers sat down to eat the laboratory rats awakened.
CORRECT	As the researchers sat down to eat, the laboratory rats awakened.

4. Use a comma to separate a dependent clause from the main clause:

Although most of the executive council saw nothing wrong with it, the advertising campaign was canceled.

Most PCs use green technology, even though it is relatively expensive.

▶In This Book
For more about restrictive and nonrestrictive modifiers, see Ch. 10, p. 230.

5. Use commas to separate nonrestrictive modifiers (parenthetical clarifications) from the rest of the sentence:

Jones, the temporary chairman, called the meeting to order.

NOTE: Writers sometimes introduce an error by dropping one of the commas around a nonrestrictive modifier.

INCORRECT	The phone line, which was installed two weeks ago had to be disconnected.
CORRECT	The phone line, which was installed two weeks ago, had to be disconnected.

6. Use a comma to separate interjections and transitional elements from the rest of the sentence:

Yes, I admit that your findings are correct.

Their plans, however, have great potential.

NOTE: Writers sometimes introduce an error by dropping one of the commas around an interjection or a transitional element.

INCORRECT	Our new statistician, however used to work for Konaire, Inc.
CORRECT	Our new statistician, however, used to work for Konaire, Inc.

7. Use a comma to separate coordinate adjectives:

The finished product was a sleek, comfortable cruiser.

The heavy, awkward trains are still being used.

The comma here takes the place of the conjunction *and*.

If the adjectives are not coordinate—that is, if one of the adjectives modifies the combined adjective and noun—do not use a comma:

They decided to go to the first general meeting.

For more about coordinate adjectives, see page 688.

8. **Use a comma to signal that a word or phrase has been omitted from a sentence because it is implied:**

   Smithers is in charge of the accounting; Harlen, the data management; Demarest, the publicity.

   The commas after *Harlen* and *Demarest* show that the phrase *is in charge of* has not been repeated.

9. **Use a comma to separate a proper noun from the rest of the sentence in direct address:**

   John, have you seen the purchase order from United?

   What I'd like to know, Betty, is why we didn't see this problem coming.

10. **Use a comma to introduce most quotations:**

    He asked, "What time were they expected?"

11. **Use a comma to separate towns, states, and countries:**

    Bethlehem, Pennsylvania, is the home of Lehigh University.

    He attended Lehigh University in Bethlehem, Pennsylvania, and the University of California at Berkeley.

    Note that a comma precedes and follows *Pennsylvania*.

12. **Use a comma to set off the year in a date:**

    August 1, 2009, is the anticipated completion date.

    If the month separates the date and the year, you do not need to use commas because the numbers are not next to each other:

    The anticipated completion date is 1 August 2009.

13. **Use a comma to clarify numbers:**

    12,013,104

    NOTE: European practice is to reverse the use of commas and periods in writing numbers: periods signify thousands, and commas signify decimals.

14. **Use a comma to separate names from professional or academic titles:**

    Harold Clayton, PhD

    Marion Fewick, CLU

    Joyce Carnone, PE

NOTE: The comma also follows the title in a sentence:

Harold Clayton, PhD, is the featured speaker.

UNNECESSARY COMMAS

Writers often introduce errors by using unnecessary commas. Do not insert commas in the following situations:

- Commas are not used to link two independent clauses without a coordinating conjunction (known as a "comma splice"):

INCORRECT	All the motors were cleaned and dried after the water had entered, had they not been, additional damage would have occurred.
CORRECT	All the motors were cleaned and dried after the water had entered; had they not been, additional damage would have occurred.
CORRECT	All the motors were cleaned and dried after the water had entered. Had they not been, additional damage would have occurred.

For more about comma splices, see page 691.

- Commas are not used to separate the subject from the verb in a sentence:

INCORRECT	Another of the many possibilities, is to use a "first in, first out" sequence.
CORRECT	Another of the many possibilities is to use a "first in, first out" sequence.

- Commas are not used to separate the verb from its complement:

INCORRECT	The schedules that have to be updated every month are, numbers 14, 16, 21, 22, 27, and 31.
CORRECT	The schedules that have to be updated every month are numbers 14, 16, 21, 22, 27, and 31.

- Commas are not used with a restrictive modifier:

INCORRECT	New and old employees who use the processed order form, do not completely understand the basis of the system.
	The phrase *who use the processed order form* is a restrictive modifier necessary to the meaning: it defines which employees do not understand the system.
CORRECT	New and old employees who use the processed order form do not completely understand the basis of the system.
INCORRECT	A company, that has grown so big, no longer finds an informal evaluation procedure effective.
	The clause *that has grown so big* is a restrictive modifier.
CORRECT	A company that has grown so big no longer finds an informal evaluation procedure effective.

- Commas are not used to separate two elements in a compound subject:

INCORRECT   Recent studies, and reports by other firms confirm our experience.

CORRECT   Recent studies and reports by other firms confirm our experience.

; Semicolons

Semicolons are used in the following instances.

1. Use a semicolon to separate independent clauses not linked by a coordinating conjunction:

The second edition of the handbook is more up-to-date; however, it is also more expensive.

2. Use a semicolon to separate items in a series that already contains commas:

The members elected three officers: Jack Resnick, president; Carol Wayshum, vice president; Ahmed Jamoogian, recording secretary.

Here the semicolon acts as a "supercomma," grouping each name with the correct title.

MISUSE OF SEMICOLONS

Sometimes writers incorrectly use a semicolon when a colon is called for:

INCORRECT   We still need one ingredient; luck.

CORRECT   We still need one ingredient: luck.

: Colons

Colons are used in the following instances.

1. Use a colon to introduce a word, phrase, or clause that amplifies, illustrates, or explains a general statement:

The project team lacked one crucial member: a project leader.

Here is the client's request: we are to provide the preliminary proposal by November 13.

We found three substances in excessive quantities: potassium, cyanide, and asbestos.

The week was productive: 14 projects were completed and another dozen were initiated.

NOTE: The text preceding a colon should be able to stand on its own as a sentence:

INCORRECT   We found: potassium, cyanide, and asbestos.

CORRECT   We found the following: potassium, cyanide, and asbestos.

CORRECT   We found potassium, cyanide, and asbestos.

📌 **In This Book**

For more about constructing lists, see Ch. 10, p. 222.

2. **Use a colon to introduce items in a vertical list if the sense of the introductory text would be incomplete without the list:**

> We found the following:
>
> - potassium
> - cyanide
> - asbestos

3. **Use a colon to introduce long or formal quotations:**

> The president began: "In the last year . . ."

MISUSE OF COLONS

Writers sometimes incorrectly use a colon to separate a verb from its complement:

INCORRECT	The tools we need are: a plane, a level, and a T square.
CORRECT	The tools we need are a plane, a level, and a T square.
CORRECT	We need three tools: a plane, a level, and a T square.

▪ Periods

Periods are used in the following instances.

1. **Use a period at the end of sentences that do not ask questions or express strong emotion:**

> The lateral stress still needs to be calculated.

2. **Use a period after some abbreviations:**

> U.S.A.
>
> etc.

For more about abbreviations, see page 707.

3. **Use a period with decimal fractions:**

> 4.056
>
> $6.75
>
> 75.6 percent

! Exclamation Points

The exclamation point is used at the end of a sentence that expresses strong emotion, such as surprise or doubt.

> The nuclear plant, which was originally expected to cost $1.6 billion, eventually cost more than $8 billion!

In technical documents, which require objectivity and a calm, understated tone, exclamation points are rarely used.

? Question Marks

The question mark is used at the end of a sentence that asks a direct question.

> What did the commission say about effluents?

NOTE: When a question mark is used within quotation marks, no other end punctuation is required.

> She asked, "What did the commission say about effluents?"

MISUSE OF QUESTION MARKS

Do not use a question mark at the end of a sentence that asks an indirect question.

> He wanted to know whether the procedure had been approved for use.

— Dashes

To make a dash, use two uninterrupted hyphens (--). Do not add spaces before or after the dash. Some word-processing programs turn two hyphens into a dash, but with others, you have to use a special character to make a dash; there is no dash key on the keyboard.

Dashes are used in the following instances.

1. **Use a dash to set off a sudden change in thought or tone:**

   > The committee found—can you believe this?—that the company bore full responsibility for the accident.
   >
   > That's what she said—if I remember correctly.

2. **Use a dash to emphasize a parenthetical element:**

   > The managers' reports—all 10 of them—recommend production cutbacks for the coming year.
   >
   > Arlene Kregman—the first woman elected to the board of directors—is the next scheduled speaker.

3. **Use a dash to set off an introductory series from its explanation:**

   > Wet suits, weight belts, tanks—everything will have to be shipped in.

NOTE: When a series follows the general statement, a colon replaces the dash.

Everything will have to be shipped in: wet suits, weight belts, and tanks.

MISUSES OF DASHES

Sometimes writers incorrectly use a dash as a substitute for other punctuation marks:

INCORRECT	The regulations—which were issued yesterday—had been anticipated for months.
CORRECT	The regulations, which were issued yesterday, had been anticipated for months.
INCORRECT	Many candidates applied—however, only one was chosen.
CORRECT	Many candidates applied; however, only one was chosen.

() Parentheses

Parentheses are used in the following instances.

1. Use parentheses to set off incidental information:

Please call me (x3104) when you get the information.

Galileo (1564–1642) is often considered the father of modern astronomy.

The cure rate for lung cancer has almost doubled in the last thirty years (Capron, 1999).

2. Use parentheses to enclose numbers and letters that label items listed in a sentence:

To transfer a call within the office, (1) place the party on HOLD, (2) press TRANSFER, (3) press the extension number, and (4) hang up.

Use both a left and a right parenthesis—not just a right parenthesis—in this situation.

MISUSE OF PARENTHESES

Sometimes writers incorrectly use parentheses instead of brackets to enclose their insertion within a quotation.

INCORRECT	He said, "The new manager (Farnham) is due in next week."
CORRECT	He said, "The new manager [Farnham] is due in next week."

For more about square brackets, see page 702.

, Apostrophes

Apostrophes are used in the following instances.

1. **Use an apostrophe to indicate possession:**

   the manager's goals   the employee's credit union

   the workers' lounge   Charles's T square

   For joint possession, add an apostrophe and an *s* only to the last noun or proper noun:

   Watson and Crick's discovery

   For separate possession, add an apostrophe and an *s* to each of the nouns or pronouns:

   Newton's and Galileo's theories

   NOTE: Do not add an apostrophe or an *s* to possessive pronouns: *his, hers, its, ours, yours, theirs.*

2. **Use an apostrophe to indicate possession when a noun modifies a gerund:**

   We were all looking forward to Bill's joining the company.

   The gerund *joining* is modified by the proper noun *Bill.*

3. **Use an apostrophe to form contractions:**

   I've   shouldn't

   can't   it's

   The apostrophe usually indicates an omitted letter or letters:

   can(no)t = can't

   it (i)s = it's

   NOTE: Some organizations discourage the use of contractions; others have no preference. Find out the policy your organization follows.

4. **Use an apostrophe to indicate special plurals:**

   three 9's

   two different JCL's

   the why's and how's of the problem

   NOTE: For plurals of numbers and abbreviations, some style guides omit the apostrophe: *9s, JCLs.* Because usage varies considerably, check with your organization.

MISUSE OF APOSTROPHES

Writers sometimes incorrectly use the contraction *it's* in place of the possessive pronoun *its*.

INCORRECT	The company does not feel that the problem is it's responsibility.
CORRECT	The company does not feel that the problem is its responsibility.

Quotation Marks

Quotation marks are used in the following instances.

1. **Use quotation marks to indicate titles of short works, such as articles, essays, or chapters:**

   Smith's essay "Solar Heating Alternatives" was short but informative.

2. **Use quotation marks to call attention to a word or phrase used in an unusual way or in an unusual context:**

   A proposal is "wired" if the sponsoring agency has already decided who will be granted the contract.

   NOTE: Do not use quotation marks to excuse poor word choice:

   INCORRECT   The new director has been a real "pain."

3. **Use quotation marks to indicate a direct quotation:**

   "In the future," he said, "check with me before authorizing any large purchases."
   As Breyer wrote, "Morale *is* productivity."

   NOTE: Quotation marks are not used with indirect quotations.

INCORRECT	He said that "third-quarter profits will be up."
CORRECT	He said that third-quarter profits will be up.
CORRECT	He said, "Third-quarter profits will be up."

   Also note that quotation marks are not used with quotations that are longer than four lines; instead, set the quotation in block format. In a word-processed manuscript, a block quotation is usually

   - indented one-half inch from the left-hand margin
   - typed without quotation marks
   - introduced by a complete sentence followed by a colon

   Different style manuals recommend variations on these basic rules; the following example illustrates APA style.

▶ In This Book

For more about quoting sources, see Appendix, Part A, p. 633.

McFarland (1997) writes:

> The extent to which organisms adapt to their environment is still being charted. Many animals, we have recently learned, respond to a dry winter with an automatic birth control chemical that limits the number of young to be born that spring. This prevents mass starvation among the species in that locale. (p. 49)

Hollins (1999) concurs. She writes, "Biological adaptation will be a major research area during the next decade" (p. 2).

USING QUOTATION MARKS WITH OTHER PUNCTUATION

- If the sentence contains a *tag*—a phrase identifying the speaker or writer—a comma separates it from the quotation:

  Wilson replied, "I'll try to fly out there tomorrow."

  "I'll try to fly out there tomorrow," Wilson replied.

  Informal and brief quotations require no punctuation before a quotation mark:

  She asked herself "Why?" several times a day.

- In the United States (unlike most other English-speaking nations), commas and periods at the end of quotations are placed within the quotation marks:

  The project engineer reported, "A new factor has been added."

  "A new factor has been added," the project engineer reported.

- Question marks, dashes, and exclamation points are placed inside quotation marks when they are part of the quoted material:

  He asked, "Did the shipment come in yet?"

- When question marks, dashes, and exclamation points apply to the whole sentence, they are placed outside the quotation marks:

  Did he say, "This is the limit"?

- When a punctuation mark appears inside a quotation mark at the end of a sentence, do not add another punctuation mark.

  INCORRECT   Did she say, "What time is it?"?

  CORRECT   Did she say, "What time is it?"

Ellipses

Ellipses (three spaced periods) indicate the omission of material from a direct quotation.

SOURCE   My team will need three extra months for market research and
               quality-assurance testing to successfully complete the job.

QUOTE   She responded, "My team will need three extra months . . . to
               successfully complete the job."

Insert an ellipsis after a period if you are omitting entire sentences that
follow:

Larkin refers to the project as "an attempt . . . to clarify the issue of compulsory
arbitration. . . . We do not foresee an end to the legal wrangling . . . but perhaps the
report can serve as a definition of the areas of contention."

The writer has omitted words from the source after *attempt* and after
wrangling. After *arbitration*, the writer has inserted an ellipsis after a
period to indicate that a sentence has been omitted.

NOTE: If the author's original statement has ellipses, MLA style recommends
that you insert brackets around an ellipsis that you introduce in a quotation.

Sexton thinks "reuse adoption offers . . . the promise to improve business [. . .]
worldwide."

[ ]   Square Brackets

Square brackets are used in the following instances.

1. Use square brackets around words added to a quotation:

As noted in the minutes of the meeting, "He [Pearson] spoke out against the
proposal."

A better approach would be to shorten the quotation:

The minutes of the meeting note that Pearson "spoke out against the proposal."

**2. Use square brackets to indicate parenthetical information within
parentheses:**

(For further information, see Charles Houghton's *Civil Engineering Today* [1997].)

MECHANICS

On TechComm Web

For online exercises covering
mechanics, click on Re:Writing,
then Exercise Central on
<bedfordstmartins.com/
techcomm>.

ital   Italics

Although italics are generally preferred, you may use underlining in place of
italics. Whichever method you choose, be consistent throughout your document. Italics (or underlining) are used in the following instances.

1. **Use italics for words used as words:**

   In this report, the word *operator* will refer to any individual who is in charge of the equipment, regardless of that individual's certification.

2. **Use italics to indicate titles of long works (books, manuals, and so on), periodicals and newspapers, long films, long plays, and long musical works:**

   See Houghton's *Civil Engineering Today*.

   We subscribe to the *Wall Street Journal*.

   Note that *the* is not italicized or capitalized when the title is used in a sentence.

   NOTE: The MLA style guide recommends that the names of Web sites be italicized.

   The Library of Congress maintains *Thomas*, an excellent site for legislative information.

3. **Use italics to indicate the names of ships, trains, and airplanes:**

   The shipment is expected to arrive next week on the *Penguin*.

4. **Use italics to set off foreign expressions that have not become fully assimilated into English:**

   Grace's *joie de vivre* makes her an engaging presenter.

   Check a dictionary to determine whether a foreign expression has become assimilated.

5. **Use italics to emphasize words or phrases:**

   Do not press the red button.

< > Angle Brackets

Many style guides now advocate using angle brackets around URLs in print documents to set them off from the text.

   Our survey included a close look at three online news sites: the *New York Times* <www.nytimes.com>, the *Washington Post* <www.washingtonpost.com>, and CNN <www.cnn.com>.

You may want to check with your instructor or organization before following this recommendation.

- Hyphens

Hyphens are used in the following instances.

1. **Use hyphens to form compound adjectives that precede nouns:**

   general-purpose register

   meat-eating dinosaur

   chain-driven saw

   NOTE: Hyphens are not used after adverbs that end in -ly.

   newly acquired terminal

   Also note that hyphens are not used when the compound adjective follows the noun:

   The Woodchuck saw is chain driven.

   Many organizations have their own preferences about hyphenating compound adjectives. Check to see if your organization has a preference.
   For more about compound adjectives, see page 689.

2. **Use hyphens to form some compound nouns:**

   once-over

   go-between

   NOTE: There is a trend away from hyphenating compound nouns (*vice president, photomicroscope, drawbridge*); check your dictionary for proper spelling.

3. **Use hyphens to form fractions and compound numbers:**

   one-half

   fifty-six

4. **Use hyphens to attach some prefixes and suffixes:**

   post-1945

   president-elect

5. **Use hyphens to divide a word at the end of a line:**

   We will meet in the pavil-

   ion in one hour.

   Whenever possible, however, avoid such line breaks; they slow the reader down. When you do use them, check the dictionary to make sure you have divided the word between syllables. If you need to break a URL at the end of a line, do not add a hyphen. Instead, break it after a slash or before a period:

<http://www.stc.org/

ethical.asp

num   Numbers

Ways of handling numbers vary considerably. Therefore, in choosing between words and numerals, consult your organization's style guide. Many organizations observe the following guidelines.

1. Technical quantities of any amount are expressed in numerals, especially if a unit of measurement is included:

   3 feet   43,219 square miles

   12 grams   36 hectares

2. Nontechnical quantities of fewer than 10 are expressed in words:

   three persons

   six whales

3. Nontechnical quantities of 10 or more are expressed in numerals:

   300 persons

   12 whales

4. Approximations are written out:

   approximately ten thousand people

   about two million trees

5. Round numbers over nine million are expressed in both words and numerals:

   14 million light-years

   $64 billion

6. Decimals are expressed in numerals:

   3.14

   1,013.065

   Decimals of less than one should be preceded by a zero:

   0.146

   0.006

7. Fractions are written out, unless they are linked to technical units:

   two-thirds of the members

   $3\frac{1}{2}$ hp

8. Time of day is expressed in numerals if A.M. or P.M. is used; otherwise, it is written out:

> 6:10 A.M.
>
> six o'clock
>
> the nine-thirty train

9. Page numbers and titles of figures and tables are expressed in numerals:

> Figure 1
>
> Table 13
>
> page 261

10. Back-to-back numbers are written using both words and numerals:

> six 3-inch screws
>
> fourteen 12-foot ladders
>
> 3,012 five-piece starter units

In general, the technical unit should be expressed with the numeral. If the nontechnical quantity would be cumbersome in words, use the numeral for it instead.

11. Numbers in legal contracts or in documents intended for international readers should be represented in both words and numerals:

> thirty-seven thousand dollars ($37,000)
>
> five (5) relays

12. Street addresses may require both words and numerals:

> 3801 Fifteenth Street

SPECIAL CASES

- A number at the beginning of a sentence should be spelled out:

  > Thirty-seven acres was the size of the lot.

  Many writers would revise the sentence to avoid this problem:

  > The lot was 37 acres.

- Within a sentence, the same unit of measurement should be expressed consistently in either numerals or words:

INCORRECT	On Tuesday the attendance was 13; on Wednesday, eight.
CORRECT	On Tuesday the attendance was 13; on Wednesday, 8.
CORRECT	On Tuesday the attendance was thirteen; on Wednesday, eight.

- In general, months should not be expressed as numbers. In the United States, 3/7/09 means March 7, 2009; in many other countries, it means July 3, 2009. The following forms, in which the months are written out, are preferable:

    March 7, 2009

    7 March 2009

abbr   Abbreviations

Abbreviations save time and space, but you should use them carefully because your readers may not understand them. Many companies and professional organizations provide lists of approved abbreviations.

Analyze your audience to determine whether and how to abbreviate. If your readers include a general audience unfamiliar with your field, either write out the technical terms or attach a list of abbreviations. If you are new to an organization or are publishing in a field for the first time, find out which abbreviations are commonly used. If for any reason you are unsure about a term, write it out.

The following are general guidelines about abbreviations.

1. When an unfamiliar abbreviation is introduced for the first time, the full term should be given, followed by the abbreviation in parentheses. In subsequent references, the abbreviation may be used alone. For long works, the full term and its abbreviation may be written out at the start of major units, such as chapters.

    The heart of the new system is the self-loading cartridge (SLC).

    The cathode-ray tube (CRT) is your control center.

2. To form the plural of an abbreviation, an *s* is added, either with or without an apostrophe, depending on the style of your organization:

    GNPs

    PhD's

    Most unit-of-measurement abbreviations do not take plurals:

    10 in.

    3 qt

3. Most abbreviations in scientific writing are not followed by periods:

    lb

    cos

    dc

If the abbreviation can be confused with another word, however, a period should be used:

in.

Fig.

4. **If no number is used with a measurement, an abbreviation should not be used.**

INCORRECT   How many sq meters is the site?

CORRECT   How many square meters is the site?

cap   Capitalization

For the most part, the conventions of capitalization in general writing apply in technical communication.

1. **Proper nouns, titles, trade names, places, languages, religions, and organizations should be capitalized:**

William Rusham

Director of Personnel

Quick-Fix Erasers

Bethesda, Maryland

Italian

Methodism

Society for Technical Communication

In some organizations, job titles are not capitalized unless they refer to specific persons.

Alfred Loggins, Director of Personnel, is interested in being considered for vice president of marketing.

2. **Headings and labels should be capitalized:**

A Proposal to Implement the Wilkins Conversion System

Mitosis

Table 3

Section One

The Problem

Rate of Inflation, 1995–2005

Figure 6

Proofreading Symbols and Their Meanings

Mark in margin	Instructions	Mark on manuscript	Corrected type
ℯ	Delete	$10 billion dollars	$10 billion
∧	Insert	enviroment	environment
(stet)	Let stand	let it stand	let it stand
(cap)	Capitalize	the english language	the English language
(lc)	Make lowercase	the English Language	the English language
—	Italicize	Technical Communication	*Technical Communication*
(tr)	Transpose	recieve	receive
◡	Close up space	diagnostic ultra sound	diagnostic ultrasound
(sp)	Spell out	(Pres) Smithers	President Smithers
#	Insert space	3amp light	3 amp light
¶	Start paragraph	. . . the results. These results	. . . the results. These results
run in	No paragraph	. . . the results. For this reason,	. . . the results. For this reason,
(sc)	Set in small capitals	Needle-nosed pliers	NEEDLE-NOSED PLIERS
(bf)	Set in boldface	Needle-nosed pliers	**Needle-nosed pliers**
⊙	Insert period	Fig 21	Fig. 21
⋏	Insert comma	the plant which was built	the plant, which was built
=	Insert hyphen	menu driven software	menu-driven software
⊙	Insert colon	Add the following	Add the following:
⋏	Insert semicolon	. . . the plan however, the committee	. . . the plan; however, the committee
⋎	Insert apostrophe	the users preference	the user's preference
❝/❞	Insert quotation marks	Furthermore, she said . . .	"Furthermore," she said . . .
(/)	Insert parentheses	Write to us at the Newark office	Write to us (at the Newark office)
[/]	Insert brackets	President John Smithers	President [John] Smithers
‒N‒	Insert en dash	1984 2001	1984–2001
‒M‒	Insert em dash	Our goal victory	Our goal—victory
⌄	Insert superscript	4,000 ft2	4,000 ft^2
⌃	Insert subscript	H2O	H$_2$O
//	Align	$123.05 $86.95	$123.05 $86.95
[	Move to the left	PVC piping	PVC piping
]	Move to the right	PVC piping	PVC piping
⌐	Move up	PVC piping	PVC piping
⌊⌋	Move down	PVC piping	PVC piping

Part D: Guidelines for Multilingual Writers (ESL)

CULTURAL AND STYLISTIC COMMUNICATION ISSUES

▶ In This Book
For more about communicating across cultures, see Ch. 5, p. 90.

Just as native speakers of English must learn how to communicate with nonnative speakers of English in the United States and abroad, technical communicators whose first language is not English must learn how to communicate with native speakers in the United States.

If you want to communicate effectively with native speakers, you need to understand U.S. culture. Specifically, you need to understand how U.S. readers expect writers to select, organize, and present information and what writers expect from their readers. Beyond readers and writers, speakers and listeners in the United States also have expectations. Indeed, cultural values affect all styles of communication. Of course, no two communicators are exactly alike. Still, if you know how culture affects Western communicators in general, you can analyze your communication task and communicate effectively.

Readers, writers, speakers, and listeners in the United States value the following qualities:

▶ In This Book
For more about claim letters, see Ch. 14, p. 374.

- *Directness.* U.S. audiences expect writers and speakers to get to the point quickly and to communicate information clearly. So when you write a claim letter, for example, clearly state what you want the individual you are addressing to do to correct a situation. Related to directness is *task orientation*. Do not begin a letter with a comment about the weather or family. Instead, communicate immediately about business.

▶ In This Book
For more about writing collaboratively, see Ch. 4.

- *Independence.* In spite of the increasingly significant role of collaborative writing, U.S. audiences still value individualism and people who can work independently. Therefore, when you write a letter to an individual in an organization, be aware that the recipient sees you as one person, too, not merely as a mouthpiece of an organization. Use the pronoun *I* rather than *we*.

- *Time consciousness.* Try to meet deadlines and to arrive on time for appointments. U.S. audiences consider slowness in responding to issues a sign of disrespect.

To become familiar with the U.S. style of communication, study documents, talk to people, and ask for feedback from U.S. readers and listeners. Following are some specific guidelines for applying the preceding general cultural values as you listen, speak, and write to U.S. audiences.

Listening

Speakers in the United States expect you, their audience, to listen actively. They assume that you will ask questions and challenge their points—but not interrupt them unless you are invited to do so. To become a better listener, try the following strategies:

- *Look at the speaker's eyes, or at least at the speaker's face.* Lean forward or nod your head to encourage the speaker. If you avoid looking at the speaker, he or she may think that you are not interested in the message.

- *Do not interrupt the speaker.* Interrupting shows the speaker that you do not value his or her opinion. Give the speaker enough time to complete his or her presentation.

- *Do not become indignant.* Be prepared to hear speakers state clearly what they like and dislike, often without considering other people's personal feelings.

- *Assume that the speaker values your opinion.* Form responses and, at the appropriate time, express your opinions openly.

- *Ask questions.* If you have questions, ask them. If you do not ask questions, the speaker may assume that you not only understand but also agree with the message of the presentation. It is altogether appropriate to ask questions such as these: "Do you mean . . . ?" "Did I understand you to say . . . ?" "Would you repeat . . . ?"

Speaking

As suggested in Chapter 21, U.S. audiences expect speakers to control the situation, keep the audience interested, address listeners directly, and speak with authority. Do not apologize for problems in your content or your fluency. Doing so may diminish your credibility and make the audience think you are wasting their time. To become a better speaker, try the following strategies:

- *Start and end your presentation on time.* If you start late or speak too long, you send the message "Your time is less valuable than mine."

- *Make eye contact and smile.* If you make eye contact with people, you look friendly and confident, and you send the message "You are important."

- *Speak up.* If you speak with your head bowed or in too low a voice, audience members may become distracted or think you are hiding something.

- *Make friendly gestures.* Invite the audience to ask questions. It is appropriate to say "Please feel free to ask me questions at any time" or "If you have questions, I'd be glad to answer them at the conclusion of my talk." Also, try to break the invisible barrier between you and your audience. For example, step away from behind the podium or move toward the audience.

Writing

In the United States, technical writers generally state their claims up front and clearly. They support their claims by presenting the most important information first and by using numerical data. To become a better writer, try the following strategies:

▶ In This Book

For more about claims, see Ch. 8, p. 185. For more about introductions, see Ch. 19, p. 508.

- *State your claims directly.* In most cases, state your purpose directly in the first paragraph of a memo or letter, as well as at the start of any other document and at the start of each section within it.

- *Avoid digressions.* Focus on your task. If a piece of information is interesting but does not help you make your point, do not include it.

▶ In This Book

For more about organizing information, see Ch. 7. For more about writing coherent paragraphs, see Ch. 9.

- *Move from one point to the next systematically.* Use an appropriate pattern of organization, and use transitions and other devices to ensure a smooth flow within a paragraph and between paragraphs.

▶ In This Book

For more about persuasion, see Ch. 8.

- *Use logic and technical information rather than allusion, metaphor, or emotion.* Western readers are persuaded more by numerical data—that is, by statistics, be they raw scores, dollar amounts, or percentages—than by an argument from authority.

▶ In This Book

For more about choosing the right words and phrases, see Ch. 10, p. 233.

- *Use an appropriate level of formality.* Consider your audience, your subject, and your purpose. In the United States, e-mails and memos tend to be less formal than reports and proposals. In most cases, avoid overly formal words, such as *pursuant, aforementioned,* and *heretofore,* in favor of clear, concise writing.

SENTENCE-LEVEL ISSUES

sent   Basic Characteristics of a Sentence

A sentence has five characteristics.

1. **It starts with an uppercase letter and ends with a period, a question mark, or (rarely) an exclamation point attached to the final word.**

    I have a friend.

    Do you have a friend?

    I asked, "Do you have a friend?"

    The question mark is part of the quoted question.

    Did you write, "Ode to My Friend"?

    The question mark is part of the question, not part of the title in quotation marks.

    Yes! You are my best friend!

2. **It has a subject, usually a noun. The subject performs the action(s) mentioned in the sentence or exists in a certain condition according to the rest of the sentence.**

   SUBJECT

   My friend speaks five languages fluently.

   The subject performs an action—*speaks*.

   SUBJECT

   My friend is fluent in five languages.

   The subject exists as (is) a fluent person.

3. **It has a verb, which tells what the subject does or states its existence.**

   VERB

   My friend speaks five languages fluently.

   The verb tells what the subject does.

   VERB

   My friend is fluent in five languages.

   The verb states that the subject exists.

4. **It has a standard word order.**

   The most common sequence in English is subject-verb-object:

   SUBJECT   VERB   OBJECT

   We hired a consulting firm.

   You can add information to the start of the sentence:

   Yesterday we hired a consulting firm.

   or to the end of the sentence:

   Yesterday we hired a consulting firm: *Sanderson & Associates*.

   or in the middle:

   Yesterday we hired *the city's most prestigious* consulting firm: Sanderson & Associates.

   In fact, any element of a sentence can be expanded.

5. **It has an independent clause (a subject and verb that can stand alone—that is, a clause that does not begin with a subordinating word or phrase).**

 In This Book

For more about subordinating
words and phrases, see p. 715.

The following is a sentence:

SUBJECT VERB

The pump failed because of improper maintenance.

The following is also a sentence:

SUBJECT VERB

The pump failed.

But the following is not a sentence because it lacks a subject with a verb and because it begins with a subordinating phrase:

Because of improper maintenance.

An independent clause is required to complete this sentence:

Because of improper maintenance, the pump failed.

coor Linking Ideas by Coordination

One way to connect ideas in a sentence is by coordination. Coordination means that ideas in the sentence are roughly equal in importance. There are three main ways to coordinate ideas.

1. **Use a semicolon (;) to coordinate ideas that are independent clauses:**

   The information for bid was published last week; the proposal is due in less than a month.

2. **Use a comma and a coordinating conjunction (*and, but, or, nor, so, for,* or *yet*) to coordinate two independent clauses:**

   The information for bid was published last week, but the proposal is due in less than a month.

   In this example, *but* clarifies the relationship between the two clauses: the writer hasn't been given enough time to write the proposal.

3. **Use transitional words and phrases to coordinate two independent clauses. You can end the first independent clause with a semicolon or a period. If you use a period, begin the transitional word or phrase with a capital letter.**

   The Pentium 4 chip has already been replaced; *as a result*, it is hard to find a Pentium 4 in a new computer.

   The Pentium 4 chip has already been replaced. *As a result*, it is hard to find a Pentium 4 in a new computer.

▶In This Book

For more about transitional words and phrases, see Ch. 9, p. 206.

sub   Linking Ideas by Subordination

Two ideas can also be linked by subordination—that is, by deemphasizing one of them. There are two basic methods of subordination.

1. **Use a subordinating word or phrase to turn one idea into a subordinate clause.**

after	because	since	until	while
although	before	so that	when	who
as	even though	that	where	whom
as if	if	unless	which	whose

Start with two independent clauses:

> The bridge was completed last year. The bridge already needs repairs.

Then choose a subordinating word and combine the clauses:

> *Although* the bridge was completed last year, it already needs repairs.

Although subordinates the first clause, leaving *it already needs repairs* as the independent clause.

Note that a writer could reverse the order of the ideas:

> The bridge already needs repairs *even though* it was completed last year.

Another way to subordinate one idea is to turn it into a nonrestrictive clause using the subordinating word *which*:

> The bridge, which was completed last year, already needs repairs.

> This version deemphasizes *was completed last year* by turning it into a nonrestrictive clause and emphasizes *already needs repairs* by leaving it as the independent clause.

⏵ **In This Book**

For more about restrictive and nonrestrictive modifiers, see Ch. 10, p. 231.

2. **Turn one of the ideas into a phrase modifying the other.**

> Completed last year, the bridge already needs repairs.

> *Completed last year* was turned into a phrase by dropping the subject and verb from the independent clause. Here the phrase is used to modify *the bridge*.

vb   Verb Tenses

1. **SIMPLE: An action or state that was, is, or will be static or definite**

   SIMPLE PAST (*verb* + *ed* [or irregular past])

   > Yesterday we *subscribed* to a new ecology journal.

⏵ **In This Book**

For more about verb tenses, see Appendix, Part C.

The action of subscribing happened at a specific time. The action of subscribing definitively happened regardless of what happens today or tomorrow.

SIMPLE PRESENT (*VERB* or *VERB* + *s*)

We *subscribe* to three ecology journals every year.

The action of subscribing never changes; it's regular, definite.

SIMPLE FUTURE (*will* + *VERB* or simple present of *be* + *going to* + *VERB*)

We *will subscribe* to the new ecology journal next year.

We *are going to subscribe* to the new ecology journal next year.

The action of subscribing next year (a specific time) will not change; it is definite.

2. PROGRESSIVE: An action in progress (continuing) at a known time

PAST PROGRESSIVE (simple past of *be* + *VERB* + *ing*)

We *were updating* our directory when the power failure occurred.

The action of updating was in progress at a known time in the past.

PRESENT PROGRESSIVE (simple present of *be* + *VERB* + *ing*)

We *are updating* our directory now.

The action of updating is in progress at a known time, this moment.

FUTURE PROGRESSIVE (simple future of *be* + *VERB* + *ing*)

We *will be updating* our directory tomorrow when you arrive.

The action of updating will be in progress at a known time in the future.

3. PERFECT: An action occurring (sometimes completed) at some indefinite time before a definite time

PAST PERFECT (simple past of *have* + *VERB* + *ed* [or irregular past])

We *had* already *written* the proposal when we got your call.

The action of writing began and ended at some indefinite past time before a definite past time.

PRESENT PERFECT (simple present of *have* + *VERB* + *ed* [or irregular past])

We *have written* the proposal and are proud to hand it to you.

The action of writing began at some indefinite past time and is being commented on in the present, a definite time.

FUTURE PERFECT (simple future of *have* + *VERB* + *ed* [or irregular past])

We *will have written* the proposal by the time you arrive.

The action of writing will have begun and ended at some indefinite time in the future before the definite time in the future when you arrive.

4. **PERFECT PROGRESSIVE: An action in progress (continuing) until a known time**

   PAST PERFECT PROGRESSIVE (simple past of *have* + *been* + VERB + *ing*)

   > We *had been working* on the reorganization when the news of the merger became public.

   The action of working continued until a known time in the past.

   PRESENT PERFECT PROGRESSIVE (simple present of *have* + *been* + VERB + *ing*)

   > We *have been working* on the reorganization for over a year.

   The action of working began at some indefinite past time and is continuing in the present, when it is being commented on.

   FUTURE PERFECT PROGRESSIVE (simple future of *have* + *been* + VERB + *ing*)

   > We *will have been working* on the reorganization for over a year by the time you become CEO.

   In the future, the action of working will have been continuing before another future action.

-ing Forming Verbs with *-ing*

English uses the *-ing* form of verbs in three major ways.

1. **As part of a progressive or perfect progressive verb (see numbers 2 and 4 in the previous section):**

   > We are *shipping* the materials by UPS.
   > We have been *waiting* for approval since January.

2. **As a present participle, which functions as an adjective either by itself:**

   > the *leaking* pipe

   or as part of a participial phrase:

   > *Analyzing* the sample, we discovered two anomalies.
   > The sample *containing* the anomalies appears on Slide 14.

3. **As a gerund, which functions as a noun either by itself:**

   > *Writing* is the best way to learn to write.

   or as part of a gerund phrase:

   > The designer tried *inserting* the graphics by hand.

inf   Infinitives

Infinitives consist of the word *to* plus the base form of the verb (*to write, to understand*). An infinitive can be used in three main ways.

1. As a noun:

> The editor's goal for the next year is *to publish* the journal on schedule.

2. As an adjective:

> The company requested the right *to subcontract* the project.

3. As an adverb:

> We established the schedule ahead of time *to prevent* the kind of mistake we made last time.

help   Helping Verbs and Main Verbs

Instead of a one-word verb, many English sentences contain a *verb phrase*.

> The system *meets* code.

This sentence has a one-word verb, *meets*.

> The new system *must meet* all applicable codes.

This sentence has a two-word verb phrase, *must meet*.

> The old system *must have met* all applicable codes.

This sentence has a three-word verb phrase, *must have met*.

In a verb phrase, the verb that carries the main meaning is called the *main verb*. The other words in the verb phrase are called *helping verbs*. The following discussion explains four categories of helping verbs.

1. Modals
There are nine modal verbs: *can, could, may, might, must, shall, should, will,* and *would*. After a modal verb, use the base form of the verb (the form of the verb used after *to* in the infinitive).

BASE FORM

> The system *must meet* all applicable codes.

2. Forms of *do*
After a helping verb that is a form of *do*—*do, does,* or *did*—use the base form of the verb.

BASE FORM

Do we *need* to include the figures for the recovery rate?

3. Forms of *have* plus the past participle

To form one of the perfect tenses (past, present, or future), use a form of *have* as the helping verb plus the past participle of the verb (usually the *-ed* form of the verb or the irregular past).

PAST PERFECT

We *had written* the proposal before learning of the new RFP.

PRESENT PERFECT

We *have written* the proposal according to the instructions in the RFP.

FUTURE PERFECT

We *will have written* the proposal by the end of the week.

4. Forms of *be*

To describe an action in progress, use a form of *be* (*be, am, is, are, was, were, being, been*) as the helping verb and the present participle (the *-ing* form of the verb).

We *are testing* the new graphics tablet.

The company *is considering* flextime.

To create the passive voice, use a form of *be* and the past participle.

The piping *was installed* by the plumbing contractor.

> ▶ **In This Book**
> For more about active and passive voice, see Ch. 10, p. 234.

---

agr s/v   Agreement of Subject and Verb

The subject and the verb in a clause or sentence must agree in number. That is, if the noun is singular, the verb must be singular.

The *valve needs* replacement.

Note the *s* that marks a singular present-tense verb.

If the noun is plural, the verb must be plural.

The *valves need* replacement.

Note the *s* that marks a plural noun.

Here are additional examples of subject-verb agreement.

The new *valve is* installed according to the manufacturer's specifications.

The new *valves are* installed according to the manufacturer's specifications.

When you edit your document for subject-verb agreement, keep in mind the following guidelines.

1. **Make sure the subject and verb agree when information comes between the subject and the verb.**

   The *result* of the tests *is* included in Appendix C.

   The *results* of the test *are* included in Appendix C.

2. **Certain pronouns and quantifiers always require singular verbs. Pronouns that end in *-body* or *-one*—such as *everyone*, *everybody*, *someone*, *somebody*, *anyone*, *anybody*, *no one*, and *nobody*—are singular. In addition, quantifiers such as *something*, *each*, and *every* are singular.**

   SINGULAR   *Everybody is* invited to the preproposal meeting.

   SINGULAR   *Each* of the members *is* asked to submit billable hours by the end of the month.

3. **When the clause or sentence contains a compound subject, the verb must be plural.**

   COMPOUND
   SUBJECT   *The contractor and the subcontractor want* to meet to resolve the difficulties.

4. **When a relative pronoun such as *who*, *that*, or *which* begins a clause, make sure the verb agrees in number with the noun that the relative pronoun refers to.**

   The *numbers* that *are* used in the formula do not agree with the ones we were given at the site.

   Numbers is plural, so the verb in the *that* clause (*are*) is also plural.

   The *number* that *is* used in the formula does not agree with the one we were given at the site.

   Number is singular, so the verb in the *that* clause (*is*) is also singular.

cond   Conditions

The word *if* in English can introduce four main types of conditions.

1. **Conditions of fact**
   Conditions of fact usually—but not always—call for the same verb tense in both clauses. In most cases, use a form of the present tense:

   If rats *eat* as much as they want, they *become* obese.

   If you *see* "Unrecoverable Application Error," the program *has crashed*.

2. **Future prediction**

For prediction, use the present tense in the *if* clause. Use a modal (*can, could, may, might, must, shall, should, will,* or *would*) plus the base form of the verb in the independent clause.

> If we *win* this contract, we *will need* to add three more engineers.

> If this weather *keeps* up, we *may postpone* the launch.

3. **Present-future speculation**

The present-future speculation usage suggests a condition contrary to fact. Use *were* in the *if* clause if the verb is *be*; use the simple past in the *if* clause if it contains another verb. Use a modal plus the base form of the verb in the independent clause.

> If I *were* president of the company, I *would be* much more aggressive.

> If I *took* charge of the company, I *would be* much more aggressive.

The example sentences imply that you are not president of the company and have not taken charge of it.

The past tense in the example *if* clauses shows distance from reality, not distance in time.

4. **Past speculation**

Use the past perfect in the *if* clause. Use a modal plus the present perfect in the independent clause.

> If we *had won* this contract, we *would have needed* to add three engineers.

This sentence implies that the condition is contrary to fact: the contract wasn't won, so the engineers were not needed.

art Articles

Few aspects of English can be as frustrating to the nonnative speaker of English as the correct usage of the articles *a, an,* and *the* before nouns. Although there are a few rules that you should try to learn, remember that there are many exceptions and special cases.

Here is an outline to help you look at nouns and decide whether they may or must take an article—or not. As you will see, to make the decision about an article, you must determine

- whether a noun is proper or common
- for a common noun, whether it is countable or uncountable
- for a countable common noun, whether it is specific or nonspecific, and if it is nonspecific, whether it is singular or plural
- for an uncountable common noun, whether it is specific or nonspecific

Specific in this context means that the writer and the reader can both identify the noun—"which one" it is.

1. Proper nouns

Singular proper nouns usually take no article but occasionally do take *a* or *an*:

James Smith, but not John Smith, contributed to the fund last year.

A Smith will contribute to the fund this year.

The speaker does not know which Smith will make the contribution, so an article is necessary. Assuming that there is only one person with the name *Quitkin*, the sentence "Quitkin will contribute to the fund this year" is clear, so the proper noun takes no article.

Plural proper nouns often, but not always, take *the*:

The Smiths have contributed for the past 10 years.

There are Smiths on the class roster again this year.

2. Countable common nouns

Singular and plural specific countable common nouns take *the*:

The microscope is brand-new.

The microscopes are brand-new.

Singular nonspecific countable common nouns take *a* or *an*:

A microscope will be available soon.

An electron is missing.

Plural nonspecific countable common nouns take no article but must have a plural ending:

Microscope*s* must be available for all students.

3. Uncountable common nouns

Specific uncountable common nouns take *the*:

The research started by Dr. Quitkin will continue.

The subject under discussion is specific research.

Nonspecific uncountable common nouns generally take no article:

Research is always critical.

The subject under discussion is nonspecific—that is, research in general.

adj   Adjectives

Adjectives are modifiers. They modify—that is, describe—nouns and pronouns. Keep in mind four main points about adjectives in English.

1. Adjectives do not take a plural form.

a *complex* project

three *complex* projects

2. Adjectives can be placed either before the nouns they modify or after linking verbs.

> The *critical* need is to reduce the drag coefficient.
>
> The need to reduce the drag coefficient is *critical*.

3. Adjectives of one or two syllables take special endings to create the comparative and superlative forms.

Positive	Comparative	Superlative
big	bigger	biggest
heavy	heavier	heaviest

4. Adjectives of three or more syllables take the word *more* for the comparative form and the words *the most* for the superlative form.

Positive	Comparative	Superlative
qualified	more qualified	the most qualified
feasible	more feasible	the most feasible

adv Adverbs

Like adjectives, adverbs are modifiers. They modify—that is, describe—verbs, adjectives, and other adverbs. Their placement in the sentence is somewhat more complex than the placement of adjectives. Remember five points about adverbs.

1. Adverbs can modify verbs.

> Management terminated the project *reluctantly*.

2. Adverbs can modify adjectives.

> The executive summary was *conspicuously* absent.

3. Adverbs can modify other adverbs.

> The project is going *very* well.

4. Adverbs that describe how an action takes place can appear in different locations in the sentence—at the beginning of a clause, at the end of a clause, right before a one-word verb, and between a helping verb and a main verb.

> *Carefully* the inspector examined the welds.
>
> The inspector examined the welds *carefully*.
>
> The inspector *carefully* examined the welds.
>
> The inspector was *carefully* examining the welds.

NOTE: The adverb should not be placed between the verb and the direct object.

INCORRECT   The inspector examined *carefully* the welds.

5. Adverbs that describe the whole sentence can also appear in different locations in the sentence—at the beginning of the sentence, before an adjective, and at the end of the sentence.

> *Apparently*, the inspection was successful.
>
> The inspection was *apparently* successful.
>
> The inspection was successful, *apparently*.

omit   Omitted Words

Except for imperative sentences, in which the subject *you* is understood (*Get the correct figures*), all sentences in English require a subject.

> *The company* has a policy on conflict of interest.

Do not omit the expletive *there* or *it*.

In This Book

For more about expletives, see Ch. 10, p. 228.

INCORRECT   Are four reasons for us to pursue this issue.

CORRECT   *There* are four reasons for us to pursue this issue.

INCORRECT   Is important that we seek his advice.

CORRECT   *It* is important that we seek his advice.

rep   Repeated Words

1. Do not repeat the subject of a sentence.

INCORRECT   The company we are buying from *it* does not permit us to change our order.

CORRECT   The company we are buying from does not permit us to change our order.

2. In an adjective clause, do not repeat an object.

INCORRECT   The technical communicator does not use the same software that we were writing in *it*.

CORRECT   The technical communicator does not use the same software that we were writing in.

3. In an adjective clause, do not use a second adverb.

INCORRECT   The lab where we did the testing *there* is an excellent facility.

CORRECT   The lab where we did the testing is an excellent facility.

References

Chapter 1: Introduction to Technical Communication

About.com. (2008). *Self-service customer support.* Retrieved January 26, 2008, from http://onlinebusiness.about.com/cs/integration/a/selfsupport.htm

Acer, Inc. (2008). *Products.* Retrieved January 26, 2008, from http://www.acer.ca/public/page115.do?sp=page115&stu10.values=30&UserCtxParam=0&GroupCtxParam=0&dctx1=27&CountryISOCtxParam=CA&LanguageISOCtxParam=en&ctx3=32&ctx4=Canada&crc=3481551221

Apple, Inc. (2008). *iPhone questions and answers.* Retrieved January 26, 2008, from http://www.apple.com/iphone/questionsandanswers.html

Center for Plain Language. (2005). *Plain language.* Retrieved May 10, 2005, from http://www.centerforplainlanguage.org/plainlang.htm

College Entrance Examination Board. (2004). *Writing: A ticket to work . . . or a ticket out: A survey of business leaders.* Retrieved January 25, 2008, from http://www.writingcommission.org/prod_downloads/writingcom/writing-ticket-to-work.pdf

Mikkonen, T., & Taivalsaari, A. (2007). *Web applications—Spaghetti code for the 21st century.* Retrieved January 26, 2008, from http://research.sun.com/techrep/2007/smli_tr-2007-166.pdf

Plain English Network. (2002). *Writing and oral communication skills: Career-boosting assets.* Retrieved August 5, 2002, from http://www.plainlanguage.gov/Summit/writing.htm

Radvision. (2008). *Click to Meet® platform.* Retrieved January 26, 2008, from http://www.radvision.com/Products/Desktop/CTMPlatform/

Segway, Inc. (2006). Segway Personal Transporter [Brochure]. Retrieved January 26, 2008, from http://www.segway.com/downloads/pdfs/2006_Catalog.pdf

Technical Communication. (1990). 37(4), 385.

Xerox Corporation. (2000). *The Document Centre at a glance.* Webster, NY: Author.

Chapter 2: Understanding Ethical and Legal Considerations

Creative Commons. (2007). *Choosing a license.* Retrieved December 27, 2007, from http://creativecommons.org/about/licenses

Donaldson, T. (1991). *The ethics of international business.* New York: Oxford University Press.

Ethics Resource Center. (2007). *Ethics Resource Center's national business ethics survey: An inside view of private sector ethics.* Arlington, VA: Author.

Garmin. (2005). *Garmin G1000 pilot's guide for the Beechcraft 58/G58* [Manual] (p. 9-1). Retrieved January 3, 2008, from http://www8.garmin.com/manuals/G1000:BeechcraftBaron58_G58_PilotsGuide.pdf

Harley-Davidson. (2008). Web site. Retrieved January 10, 2008, from http://www.harley-davidson.com/wcm/Content/Pages/home.jsp?locale=en_US

Helyar, P. S. (1992). Products liability: Meeting legal standards for adequate instructions. *Journal of Technical Writing and Communication, 22*(2), 125–147.

IEEE. (2006). *IEEE code of ethics.* Retrieved January 30, 2008, from http://www.ieee.org/portal/pages/iportals/aboutus/ethics/code.html

Kaptein, M. (2004). Business codes of multinational firms: What do they say? *Journal of Business Ethics, 50*(1), 13–31.

Lipus, T. (2006). International consumer protection: Writing adequate instructions for global audiences. *Journal of Technical Writing and Communication, 36*(1), 75–91.

Murphy, P. (1995). Corporate ethics statements: Current status and future prospects. *Journal of Business Ethics, 14,* 727–740.

Natural Science Industries. (2005). *Rock tumbler.* Retrieved October 5, 2005, from http://www .amazon.com/exec/obidos/tg/detail/-/B00000ISUU/ 104-7612043-2382338?v=glance&s =imaginarium&me=A1PA6795UKMFR9&vi =pictures&img=14#

Safety Label Solutions. (2008). *Other energy hazards.* Retrieved January 3, 2008, from http:// safetylabelsolutions.com/store/page8.html

Sigma Xi. *Honor in science.* (1986). New Haven, CT: Author.

Texas Instruments. (2008). *Ethics.* Retrieved January 3, 2008, from http://www.ti.com/corp/docs/ company/citizen/ethics/index.shtml

U.S. Census Bureau. (2007). *Statistical abstract of the United States: 2008.* Washington, DC: U.S. Government Printing Office.

U.S. Consumer Product Safety Commission. (2007). *U.S. Consumer Product Safety Commission 2007 performance and accountability report.* Retrieved December 27, 2007, from http://www.cpsc.gov/ cpscpub/pubs/reports/2007par.pdf

Velasquez, M. G. (2006). *Business ethics: Concepts and cases* (6th ed.). Upper Saddle River, NJ: Pearson Prentice Hall.

Chapter 3: Writing Technical Documents

MatchWare A/S. (2008). *OpenMind 2 features.* Retrieved February 20, 2008, from http://www.matchware .com/en/products/openmind/features .htm#MultiMaps

Microsoft Corporation. (2007). *Memo, professional theme* [Template]. Retrieved January 30, 2008, from http://office.microsoft.com/enus/templates/ TC010129271033.aspx?CategoryID =CT101172591033

Chapter 4: Writing Collaboratively

Borisoff, D., & Merrill, L. (1987). Teaching the college course in gender differences as barriers to conflict resolution. In L. B. Nadler, M. K. Nadler, & W. R. Todd-Mancillas (Eds.), *Advances in gender and communication research* (pp. 351–361). Lanham, MD: University Press of America.

Chodorow, N. (1978). *The reproduction of mothering: Psychoanalysis and the sociology of gender.* Berkeley: University of California Press.

Duin, A. H., Jorn, L. A., & DeBower, M. S. (1991). Collaborative writing—Courseware and telecommunications. In M. M. Lay & W. M. Karis (Eds.), *Collaborative writing in industry: Investigations in theory and practice* (pp. 146–169). Amityville, NY: Baywood.

Invensys. (2008). *InFusion collaboration wall.* Retrieved February 23, 2008, from http://www.infusioncs .com/template.aspx?PageID=19

Lustig, M. W., & Koester, J. (2006). *Intercultural competence* (5th ed.). New York: Allyn & Bacon.

McMillan, J. R., Clifton, A. K., McGrath, D., & Gale, W. S. (1977). Women's language: Uncertainty or interpersonal sensitivity and emotionality? *Sex Roles, 3,* 545–549.

Skype. (2005). *Skype 2.0 beta.* Retrieved February 23, 2008, from http://share.skype.com/sites/en/ 2005/12/skype_20_beta_free_video_calli.html

Tannen, D. (1990). *You just don't understand.* New York: William Morrow.

Chapter 5: Analyzing Your Audience and Purpose

Accelerating the cure (2007). Michael J. Fox Foundation for Parkinson's Research. Retrieved January 3, 2008, from http://www.michaeljfox.org/ newsletters/Fall%202007%20FINAL.pdf

Apple, Inc. (2008). *CamCamX 1.510.* Retrieved January 3, 2008, from http://www.apple.com/downloads/ macosx/video/camcamx.html

Bathon, G. (1999, May). Eat the way your mama taught you. *Intercom,* 22–24.

Bell, A. H. (1992). *Business communication: Toward 2000.* Cincinnati: South-Western.

Bosley, D. S. (1999). Visual elements in cross-cultural technical communication: Recognition and comprehension as a function of cultural conventions. In C. R. Lovitt and D. Goswami (Eds.), *Exploring the rhetoric of international professional communication: An agenda for teachers and researchers* (pp. 253–276). Amityville, NY: Baywood.

Enäjärvi, M. (2007). The director general's report. In *National Board of Patents and Registration of Finland annual report 2006.* Retrieved January 2, 2008, from http://www.prh.fi/material/attachments/tietoaprhsta/vuosikertomus/5uqlkCkgY/Files/CurrentFile/annualreport2006.pdf

Ford Motor Company. (2007). *Ford teams up with Microsoft to deliver Sync; in-car digital system exclusive to Ford* [Press release]. Retrieved January 4, 2008, from http://media.ford.com/newsroom/release_display.cfm?release=25168

Hoft, N. L. (1995). *International technical communication: How to export information about high technology.* New York: Wiley.

Indian Railways. (2008). *Salient features of Indian Railways.* Retrieved January 2, 2008, from http://www.indianrail.gov.in/index.html

Japanese communication styles. (2002). Retrieved January 22, 2002, from University of California, Los Angeles, Web site: http://www.anderson.ucla.edu/research/japan/mainfrm.htm

Linux.com. (2008). *Forum index.* Retrieved January 3, 2008, from http://www.linux.com/forums/

Lovitt, C. R. (1999). Introduction: Rethinking the role of culture in international professional communication. In C. R. Lovitt and D. Goswami (Eds.), *Exploring the rhetoric of international professional communication: An agenda for teachers and researchers* (pp. 1–13). Amityville, NY: Baywood.

Micron Technology, Inc. (2008). *Pat Otte.* Retrieved January 3, 2008, from http://www.micron.com/about/executives/officers/otte

Monster. (2008). Home page. Retrieved January 3, 2008, from http://www.monster.com/

National Geographic Society. (2008). *Going green quiz.* Retrieved January 3, 2008, from http://green.nationalgeographic.com/environment/global-warming/quiz-going-green.html?nav=FEATURES

Netflix, Inc. (2008). *How it works.* Retrieved January 3, 2008, from http://www.netflix.com/HowItWorks

Shunk, C. (2007, July 4). Live from Dearborn: Microsoft and Ford demo Sync. *Autoblog.* Retrieved January 4, 2008, from http://www.autoblog.com/2007/07/04/video-live-from-dearborn-microsoft-and-ford-demo-sync/

Solomon, S., Qin, D., Manning, M., Marquis, M., Averyt, K., & Tignor, M. M. B., et al. (2007). *Climate change 2007: The physical science basis.* New York: Cambridge University Press.

Sugimoto, T. (2008). *Message from the president.* Retrieved January 2, 2008, from http://www.fdk.co.jp/company_e/message-e.html

Taser International, Inc. (2008). *Law enforcement FAQ's.* Retrieved January 3, 2008, from http://www.taser.com/research/Pages/LawEnforcementFAQs.aspx

Tebeaux, E., and Driskill, L. (1999). Culture and the shape of rhetoric: protocols of international document design. In C. R. Lovitt and D. Goswami (Eds.), *Exploring the rhetoric of international professional communication: An agenda for teachers and researchers* (pp. 211–251). Amityville, NY: Baywood.

U.S. Census Bureau. (2007). *Statistical abstract of the United States: 2008.* Washington, DC: U.S. Government Printing Office.

Chapter 6: Researching Your Subject

CSA Illumina. (2008). *ARTbibliographies Modern abstracts.* Retrieved February 7, 2008, from http://www.csa.com/factsheets/artbm-set-c.php

Del.icio.us. (2008). *Search results for "pesticide."* Retrieved February 7, 2008, from http://del.icio.us/search/?fr=del_icio_us&p=pesticide&type=all

Flickr. (2008). *Iceland.* Retrieved February 7, 2008, from http://www.flickr.com/photos/tags/iceland/

Forbes.com. (2008). *The secret diary of Steve Jobs: Profile page.* Retrieved February 9, 2008, from http://www.blogger.com/profile/15043759939497216186

Managed Care Watch. (2007). *Another life threatening illness misdiagnosed as psychological problem.* Retrieved February 8, 2008, from http://www.kaiserthrive.org/2007/12/08/another-life-threatening-illness-misdiagnosed-as-psychological-problem/

Technorati. (2008). *Carbon offset blogs.* Retrieved February 7, 2008, from http://technorati.com/blogs/tag/carbon+offset

U.S. General Services Administration. (2008). *RSS feeds from USA.gov and Pueblo.* Retrieved February 7, 2008, from http://www.usa.gov/rss/index.shtml

Chapter 7: Organizing Your Information

Apple, Inc. (2008). *MacBook Air User's guide* [PDF] (p. 5). Retrieved February 27, 2008, from http://manuals.info.apple.com/en/MacBook_Air_Users_Guide.pdf

Bergman, M. K. (2004). *The deep Web* [White paper]. Retrieved November 30, 2004, from http://www.brightplanet.com/technology/deepweb.asp

Britt, R. R. (2005). *Drivers on cell phones kill thousands, snarl traffic*. Retrieved January 7, 2008, from http://www.livescience.com/technology/050201_cell_danger.html

Canon U.S.A, Inc. (2008). *Canon PowerShot SX 100 IS digital camera*. Retrieved January 7, 2008, from http://www.usa.canon.com/consumer/controller?act=ModelInfoAct&fcategoryid=144&modelid=15672#BoxContentsAct

Energy Star. (2007). *Dealing with dust in Georgia*. Retrieved January 8, 2008, from http://www.energystar.gov/ia/home_improvement/Case_Georgia2.pdf

Gore, A. (2006). *Cause and effect: A photographic case*. Retrieved January 8, 2008, from http://www.read-the-truth.com/

Invisalign. (2005). *Is Invisalign right for me?* Retrieved June 13, 2005, from http://www.invisalign.com/generalapp/us/en/for/compare.jsp

Metropolitan Museum of Art. (2008). *How Van Gogh made his mark*. Retrieved January 7, 2008, from http://www.metmuseum.org/explore/van_gogh/menu.html

National Highway Traffic Safety Administration. (2007). *Traffic safety facts 2005*. Retrieved March 15, 2008, from http://www-nrd.nhtsa.dot.gov/pdf/nrd-30/NCSA/TSFAnn/TSF2005.pdf

National Weather Service. (2007). *The Saffir-Simpson Hurricane Scale*. Retrieved February 1, 2008, from http://www.nhc.noaa.gov/aboutsshs.shtml

U.S. Consumer Product Safety Commission. (2007). *U.S. Consumer Product Safety Commission 2007 performance and accountability report*. Retrieved December 27, 2007, from http://www.cpsc.gov/cpscpub/pubs/reports/2007par.pdf

Washington State Department of Labor and Industries. (2008). *Steps to a safe workplace*. Retrieved January 7, 2008, from http://www.lni.wa.gov/Safety/Basics/Steps/default.asp

Chapter 8: Communicating Persuasively

General Electric Company. (2008). *Ecomagination*. Retrieved January 11, 2008, from http://ge.ecomagination.com/site/index.html#vision/intro

Honeywell International, Inc. (2008). *Intelligent Analytics* [Video brochure] (p. 2). Retrieved January 11, 2008, from http://www.honeywellvideo.com/products/ias/va/160966.html

Insurance Institute for Highway Safety. (2008). *Scion xD 2008 models*. Retrieved January 11, 2008, from http://www.iihs.org/ratings/rating.aspx?id=867

KentuckyFriedCruelty.com. (2008). *Cruelty capital, USA*. Retrieved January 11, 2008, from http://www.kentuckyfriedcruelty.com/

Microsoft Corporation. (2008). *Employee profile: Corey*. Retrieved January 10, 2008, from http://members.microsoft.com/careers/epdb/profileDetailPage.aspx?profileID=90

NBA Media Ventures, LLC. (2008). *NBA cares*. Retrieved January 12, 2008, from http://www.nba.com/nba_cares/

Thomas, J. (2007). *Web site lets people offer microloans to borrowers worldwide*. Retrieved January 10, 2008, from http://usinfo.state.gov/xarchives/display.html?p=washfile-english&y=2007&m=December&x=200712111708191CJsamohT0.2462274

U.S. Marine Corps. (2008). *Officer candidate's guide*. Retrieved January 11, 2008, from http://officer.marines.com/

Chapter 9: Writing Coherent Documents

Agency for Healthcare Research and Quality. (2002a). *AHRQ focus on research: HIV disease*. Retrieved February 1, 2005, from http://www.ahrq.gov/news/focus/fochiv.htm

Agency for Healthcare Research and Quality. (2002b). *AHRQ focus on research: Healthcare for women*. Retrieved February 1, 2005, from http://www.ahrq.gov/news/focus/fochiv.htm

Benson, P. (1985). Writing visually: Design considerations in technical publications. *Technical Communication, 32*, 35–39.

Cohen, S., & Grace, D. (1994). Engineers and social responsibility: An obligation to do good. *IEEE Technology and Society, 13*, 12–19.

Microsoft Corporation. (2008). *Xbox 360*. Retrieved February 28, 2008, from http://www.xbox.com/en-US/hardware/?WT.svl=nav

Snyder, J. D. (1993). Off-the-shelf bugs hungrily gobble our nastiest pollutants. *Smithsonian, 24*, 66+.

U.S. Agency for International Development. (2005). *FY 2004 performance and accountability report*. Retrieved June 21, 2005, from http://www.usaid.gov/policy/par04/performance.pdf

Williams, J. M. (2006). *Style: Ten lessons in clarity and grace* (9th ed.). New York: Longman.

Chapter 10: Writing Effective Sentences

Chacón, J. A., and Davis, M. (2006). *No one is illegal: Fighting racism and state violence on the U.S.–Mexico border*. Chicago: Haymarket Books.

Fuchsberg, G. (1990, December 7). Well, at least "terminated with extreme prejudice" wasn't cited. *The Wall Street Journal*, p. B1.

National Science Foundation. (2008). Pre-submission information. In *Grant proposal guide* (chap. 1). Retrieved March 12, 2008, from http://www.nsf .gov/pubs/policydocs/pappguide/nsf08_1/gpg_1 .jsp#IA1

Snow, K. (2008). *People First language*. Retrieved March 4, 2008, from http://www .disabilityisnatural.com/peoplefirstlanguage.htm

U.S. Census Bureau. (2006, July 26). *Facts for features: Americans with Disabilities Act* [Press release]. Retrieved March 4, 2008, from http://www.census .gov/Press-Release/www/releases/archives/ facts_for_features_special_editions/006841.html

Userlab, Inc. (2004). *Simplified English*. Retrieved December 22, 2004, from http://www.userlab .com/SE.html

Williams, J. (2003). *Style: Ten lessons in clarity and grace* (7th ed.). New York: Addison-Wesley Educational Publishers.

Chapter 11: Designing Documents and Web Sites

Biggs, J. R. (1980). *Basic typography*. New York: Watson-Guptill.

Blogger. (2008). Home page. Retrieved February 15, 2008, from https://www.blogger.com/start

Carnegie Science Center. (n.d.). *Carnegie Science Center* [Brochure]. Pittsburgh: Author.

Corel Corporation. (2008). Web page. Retrieved February 14, 2008, from http://www.corel.com/ servlet/Satellite/us/en/Content/1150905725000

Discover. (2005, February). Letters, *Discover*, 6.

Gibaldi, J. (1999). *MLA handbook for writers of research papers* (5th ed.). New York: Modern Language Association of America.

Google, Inc. (2008). Site map. Retrieved February 18, 2008, from http://www.google.com/sitemap.html

Gruber, J. (2005). *Public finance and public policy*. New York: Worth.

Haley, A. (1991). All caps: A typographic oxymoron. *U&lc*, *18*(3), 14–15.

Hockenbury, D. H., and Hockenbury, S. E. (2007). *Discovering psychology* (4th ed.). New York: Worth.

Horton, W. (1993). The almost universal language: Graphics for international documents. *Technical Communication*, *40*, 682–693.

Ichimura, M. (2001). Intercultural research in page design and layout for Asian/Pacific audiences. *Proceedings of the STC's 48th Annual Conference*. Retrieved April 9, 2002, from http://www.stc .org/proceedings/ConfProceed/2001/PDFs/ STC48-000122.pdf

Institute of Scientific and Technical Communicators. (2005, Spring). Industry news. *Communicator*, 43.

Internet World Stats. (2008). *Internet world users by language*. Retrieved March 1, 2008, from http://www.internetworldstats.com/stats7.htm

Kerman, J., & Tomlinson, G. (2004). *Listen* (brief 5th ed.). Boston: Bedford/St. Martin's.

Keyes, E. (1993). Typography, color, and information structure. *Technical Communication*, *40*, 638–654.

Kittery Outlets. (2005). *Maine Kittery Outlets & Kittery Trading Post*. Kittery, ME: Author.

Micron Technology, Inc. (2005). *Q-flash Memory: MT28F128J3, MT28F640J3, MT28F320J3* [Data sheet]. Retrieved July 11, 2005, from http://download .micron.com/pdf/datasheets/flash/qflash/ mt28f640j.pdf

Microsoft Corporation. (2001). *Discovering Microsoft Office XP Standard and Professional Version 2002*. Redmond, WA: Author.

Museum of Contemporary Art. (2003). Brochure. Chicago: Author.

Myers, D. G. (2003). *Exploring psychology* (5th ed. in modules). New York: Worth.

Myers, D. G. (2007). *Psychology* (8th ed.). New York: Worth.

National Plant Board. (1999). *Safeguarding American plant resources*. Retrieved November 23, 2005, from http://www.aphis.usda.gov/ppq/safeguarding/ MainReport.pdf

National Science Foundation. (2001). *National Science Foundation guide to programs: FY 2001 NSF funding opportunities* (p. 20). Retrieved October 18, 2002, from http://www.nsf.gov/pubs/2001/nsf013/ nsf013.pdf

Nissan North America, Inc. (2004). *Nissan Murano selection guide* (p. 3). Franklin, TN: Author.

Norman Rockwell Museum. (2005). *Norman Rockwell Museum* [Brochure]. Stockbridge, MA: Author.

Poulton, E. (1968). Rate of comprehension of an existing teleprinter output and of possible alternatives. *Journal of Applied Psychology, 52,* 16–21.

Purves, W. K., Sadava, D., Orians, G. H., & Heller, H. C. (2004). *Life: The science of biology* (7th ed.). Sunderland, MA: Sinauer.

Roark, J. L., Johnson, M. P., Cohen, P. C., Stage, S., Lawson, A., & Hartmann, S. M. (2005). *The American promise: A history of the United States: Vol. 1. To 1877.* Boston: Bedford/St. Martin's.

Sadava, D., Heller, H. C., Orians, G. H., Purves, W. K., & Hillis, D. M. (2008). *Life: The science of biology* (8th ed.). Sunderland, MA: Sinauer.

Silver Council. (2008). *About us.* Retrieved February 18, 2008, from http://www.silvercouncil.org/html/aboutus.htm

Stelzner Consulting. (2008). *Comverse sample* [White paper] (p. 6). Retrieved February 14, 2008, from http://www.stelzner.com/PDF/Comverse-MultiModality.pdf

Sun Microsystems. (1999). *Guide to Web style.* Retrieved September 10, 1999, from http://www.sun.com/styleguide/

U.S. Agency for International Development. (2007). *Bulgaria, 2007* (p. 34). Retrieved February 29, 2008, from http://www.usaid.gov/locations/europe_eurasia/countries/bg/17years.pdf

U.S. Copyright Office. (2008). *Frequently asked questions about copyright.* Retrieved February 18, 2008, from http://www.copyright.gov/help/faq/

U.S. Department of Agriculture. (2002, March 5). *Thermometer usage messages and delivery mechanisms for parents of young children.* Retrieved April 4, 2002, from http://www.fsis.usda.gov/oa/research/rti_thermy.pdf

U.S. General Services Administration. (2008). *Frequently asked questions.* Retrieved February 15, 2008, from http://answers.usa.gov/cgi-bin/gsa_ict.cfg/php/enduser/std_alp.php?p_sid=KTOOiSBh

Valley, J. W. (2005, October). A cool early earth? *Scientific American,* 58–65.

W3 Schools. (2008). *W3 Schools home page.* Retrieved January 13, 2008, from http://www.w3schools.com

Williams, G. A., & Miller, R. B. (2002, May). Change the way you persuade. *Harvard Business Review,* 65–73.

Williams, T., & Spyridakis, J. (1992). Visual discriminability of headings in text. *IEEE Transactions on Professional Communication, 35,* 64–70.

Chapter 12: Creating Graphics

Barnum, C. M., & Carliner, S. (1993). *Techniques for technical communicators.* New York: Macmillan.

Brockmann, R. J. (1990). *Writing better computer user documentation: From paper to hypertext.* New York: Wiley.

Corante. (2005, June 21). *Going global: Translation.* Retrieved July 5, 2005, from http://www.corante.com/goingglobal/archives/cat_translation.php

Deutsch, J. (2007). *Baxter Heparin Sodium Injection 10,000 units/mL and Hep-Lock U/P 10 units/mL.* Retrieved February 22, 2008, from http://www.fda.gov/medWatch/SAFETY/2007/heparin_DHCP_02-06-2007.pdf

Gatlin, P. L. (1988). Visuals and prose in manuals: The effective combination. In *Proceedings of the 35th International Technical Communication Conference* (pp. RET 113–115). Arlington, VA: Society for Technical Communication.

Grimstead, D. (1987). Quality graphics: Writers draw the line. In *Proceedings of the 34th International Technical Communication Conference* (pp. VC 66–69). Arlington, VA: Society for Technical Communication.

Gruber, J. (2007). *Public finance and public policy* (2nd ed.). New York: Worth.

Hockenbury, D. H., and Hockenbury, S. E. (2007). *Discovering psychology* (4th ed.). New York: Worth.

Holmes, N., & Bagby, M. (2002). *USA: An annual report.* Retrieved July 11, 2002, from http://www.understandingusa.com/chaptercc=2&cs=18.html

Horton, W. (1993). The almost universal language: Graphics for international documents. *Technical Communication, 40,* 682–693.

Levie, W. H., & Lentz, R. (1982). Effects of text illustrations: A review of research. *Journal of Educational Psychology, 73,* 195–232.

Morrison, C., & Jimmerson, W. (1989, July). Business presentations for the 1990s. *Video Manager, 4,* 18.

Myers, D. G. (2007). *Psychology* (8th ed.). New York: Worth.

National Aeronautics and Space Administration. (2004). *International Space Station imagery.* Retrieved December 28, 2004, from http://spaceflight.nasa.gov/gallery/images/station/crew-9/html/iss009e05034.html

Purves, W. K., Sadava, D., Orians, G. H., & Heller, H. C. (2004). *Life: The science of biology* (7th ed.). Sunderland, MA: Sinauer.

Sadava, D., Heller, H. C., Orians, G. H., Purves, W. K., & Hillis, D. M. (2008). *Life: The science of biology* (8th ed.). Sunderland, MA: Sinauer.

Townsend, F. F. (2006). *The federal response to Hurricane Katrina: Lessons learned* (p. 6). Retrieved February 27, 2008, from http://www.whitehouse.gov/reports/katrina-lessons-learned.pdf

Tufte, E. R. (1983). *The visual display of quantitative information*. Cheshire, CT: Graphics Press.

USA.gov. (2008). *USA.gov virtual tour: Get it done online.* Retrieved February 22, 2008, from http://www.usa.gov/tutorials/online/done_online_2.html

U.S. Census Bureau. (2007). *Statistical abstract of the United States: 2007* (p. 119). Retrieved March 19, 2008, from http://www.census.gov/prod/www/statistical-abstract.html

U.S. Consumer Product Safety Commission. (1999). *Your used crib could be deadly.* Retrieved August 3, 1999, from http://www.cpsc.gov/cpscpub/pubs/usedcrib.pdf

White, J. V. (1984). *Using charts and graphs: 1000 ideas for visual persuasion.* New York: R. R. Bowker.

White, J. V. (1990). *Color for the electronic age.* New York: Watson-Guptill.

Zimmer, C. (2005, February). Testing Darwin. *Discover*, 29–35.

Chapter 13: Reviewing, Evaluating, and Testing Documents and Web Sites

Computer Systems Odessa Corporation. (2008). *ConceptDraw WebWave.* Retrieved March 6, 2008, from http://www.conceptdraw.com/en/products/webwave/lessons/lesson2.php

Dumas, J. S., & Redish, J. C. (1993). *A practical guide to usability testing.* Norwood, NJ: Ablex.

Frog Design, Inc. (2008). *Dattoos.* Retrieved March 6, 2008, from http://www.frogdesign.com/case-study/dattoos.html

Kantner, L. (1994). The art of managing usability tests. *IEEE Transactions on Professional Communication, 37*, 143–148.

Rubin, J. (1994). *Handbook of usability testing: How to plan, design, and conduct effective tests.* New York: Wiley.

Usability.gov. (2008a). *Videotape release form* [Template]. Retrieved March 5, 2008, from http://www.usability.gov/templates/docs/release.doc

Usability.gov. (2008b). *What is usability?* Retrieved March 5, 2008, from http://www.usability.gov/basics/whatusa.html

Vatrapu, R., & Pérez-Quiñones, M. A. (2006). Culture and international usability testing: The effects of culture in structured interviews. *Journal of Usability Studies, 4*, 156–170.

Xperience Consulting. (2008). Diagram and photograph of usability lab. Retrieved March 8, 2008, from http://www.xperienceconsulting.com/eng/servicios.asp?ap=25#3

Chapter 14: Writing Letters, Memos, and E-mails

Brannen, C., & Wilen, T. (1993). *Doing business with Japanese men: A woman's handbook.* Berkeley, CA: Stone Bridge Press.

Missty/Flickr. (2007). *Baby MacGeek.* Retrieved April 1, 2008, from http://www.flickr.com/photos/missty/1337034307/

Russell, T. (2007). Teens are ditching email—But will work change that? *Epicenter* [Blog]. Retrieved March 12, 2008, from http://blog.wired.com/business/2007/12/teens-are-ditch.html

Chapter 15: Preparing Job-Application Materials

Chong, F. E. (2007). *Felicia E. Chong* [Professional portfolio]. Retrieved March 13, 2008, from http://www.feliciachong.efoliomn.com/

College Entrance Examination Board National Commission on Writing. (2004). *Writing skills necessary for employment, says big business.* Retrieved January 18, 2005, from http://www.writingcommission.org/pr/writing_for_employ.html

ExecuNet. (2006, June 12). *Growing number of job searches disrupted by digital dirt.* Retrieved March 13, 2008, from http://www.execunet.com/m_releases_content.cfm?id=3349

Hansen, K. (2008a). *Tapping the power of keywords to enhance your resume's effectiveness.* Retrieved March 12, 2008, from http://www.quintcareers.com/resume_keywords.html

Hansen, K. (2008b). *The top 10 things you need to know about e-resumes and posting your resume online.* Retrieved March 12, 2008, from http://www.quintcareers.com/e-resumes.html

Isaacs, K. (2004). *How to decide on résumé length.* Retrieved December 30, 2004, from http://resume.monster.com/components/length/

JobWeb.com. (2004). *Job outlook 2005.* Retrieved December 30, 2004, from http://www.jobweb.com/joboutlook/2005outlook/3a.htm

Maxwell, J. (2006). *A job hunter's secret weapon: How to survive a background check and get the job you really want!* Gainesville, VA: Purple Ink Press.

U.S. Department of Labor. (2006, August 25). *News: Document 04-1678* [Press release] (p. 1). Retrieved February 29, 2008, from http://www.bls.gov/news.release/pdf/nlsoy.pdf

Wait, P., & Dizard, W. P., III. (2003, July 21). False credentials, real problems. *Washington Technology, 18*, 8. Retrieved July 20, 2005, from http://www.washingtontechnology.com/news/18_8/federal/21210-1.html

Chapter 16: Writing Proposals

CBD/FBO Online. (2008). *Franklin County WRP tree planting 08.* Retrieved March 17, 2008, from http://cbdweb.com/index.php/search/show/21764263

Newman, L. (2006). *Proposal guide for business and technical professionals* (3rd ed.). Farmington, UT: Shipley.

Ohio Office of Criminal Justice Services. (2003). *Sample grant proposal.* Retrieved March 18, 2008, from http://www.graduate.appstate.edu/gwtoolbox/ocjs_sample_grant.pdf

Pritiken, J., & Turner, M. (2008). *Proposal for feasibility study on music options at Total Gym Fitness.* Unpublished manuscript.

SmartDraw.com. (2004). *Gannt chart and timeline center.* Retrieved April 30, 2002, from http://www.smartdraw.com/tutorials/gantt/tutorial1.htm#what

Thrush, E. (2000, January 20). *Writing for an international audience: Part 1. Communication skills.* Retrieved November 5, 2002, from http://www.suite101.com/article.cfm/5381/32233

U.S. Air Force. (2007). *916th Air Refueling Wing.* Retrieved March 18, 2008, from http://www.916arw.afrc.af.mil/shared/media/photodb/photos/060407-F-1600L-001.jpg

Chapter 17: Writing Informational Reports

National Transportation Safety Board. (2008). *DFW08IA074A.* Retrieved March 19, 2008, from http://www.ntsb.gov/ntsb/brief.asp?ev_id=20080307X00283&key=1

Pritiken, J., & Turner, M. (2008). *Progress report for feasibility study on music options at Total Gym Fitness.* Unpublished manuscript.

Saskatchewan Labour. (2007). *A sample policy on workplace violence.* Retrieved March 19, 2008, from http://fpse1.labour.gov.sk.ca/safety/violence/policy/printpage.htm

Walsham, G. (2001). *Globalization and ICTs: Working across cultures.* Retrieved November 6, 2002, from http://www.jims.cam.ac.uk/research/working_papers/abstract_01/0108.html

Chapter 18: Writing Lab Reports

IEEE. (2007). *General manuscript preparation.* Retrieved February 26, 2008, from http://www.ieee.org/portal/cms_docs_iportals/iportals/publications/authors/transjnl/auinfo07.pdf

Kress, M., & Gifford, G. F. 1984. Fecal coliform release from cattle fecal deposits. *Water Resources Bulletin, 20*(1), 61–66.

National Oceanic and Atmospheric Administration. (2006). *From research to field applications . . . Like bridging Death Valley?* Retrieved February 26, 2008, from http://coastalscience.noaa.gov/news/feature/12012006.html

Thomford, T. (2008). Bile salts enhance lipase digestion of fats. Unpublished document.

Chapter 19: Writing Recommendation Reports

Honold, P. (1999). Learning how to use a cellular phone: Comparison between German and Chinese users. *Technical Communication, 46*(2), 195–205.

Pritiken, J., & Turner, M. (2008). *Completion report for feasibility study on music options at Total Gym Fitness.* Unpublished manuscript.

Trampe. (2008). *Trampe bicycle lift.* Retrieved March 20, 2008, from http://www.trampe.no/english/photogallery.php

Chapter 20: Writing Definitions, Descriptions, and Instructions

AB Volvo. (2007). *MC60B* [Specifications]. Retrieved March 22, 2008, from http://www.volvo.com/constructionequipment/na/en-us/products/skidsteerloaders/MC60B/

Anthro Corporation. (2005). *Anthro IdeaCart* [Assembly instructions] (p. 1). Retrieved October 3, 2005, from http://www.anthro.com/assemblyinstructions/300-5055-00.pdf

Apple, Inc. (2008). *iPhone* [User's guide] (p. 122). Retrieved March 25, 2008, from http://manuals.info.apple.com/en/iPhone_User_Guide.pdf

Brain, M. (2005). *How computer viruses work*. Retrieved June 20, 2005, from http://computer .howstuffworks.com/virus1.htm

Canon U.S.A., Inc. (2002). *MultiPASS C755 Quick Start Guide* [Manual]. Retrieved November 18, 2002, from http://www.usa.canon.com/cpr/pdf/Manuals/ C755_Setup.pdf

Casio Computer. (2008). *Privia PX-800 user's guide* [PDF] (p. E-10). Retrieved March 25, 2008, from http://ftp.casio.co.jp/pub/world_manual/emi/en/ px_800/01_e.pdf

CEMA (Conveyor Equipment Manufacturers Association). 2004. *CEMA safety labels placement guidelines: Palletizers*. Retrieved January 28, 2005, from http://www.cemanet.org/safety/pl1.pdf

Delio, M. (2002, June 4). Read the f***ing story, then RTFM. *Wired News*. Retrieved June 6, 2002, from http://www.wired.com/news/culture/ 0,1284,52901,00.html

Falco, M. (2008, January 14). *New hope may lie in lab-created heart*. Retrieved March 21, 2008, from http://www.cnn.com/2008/HEALTH/01/14/ rebuilt.heart/

Fraternity Insurance and Purchasing Group. (2003). *Risk management* [Manual] (p. 45). Retrieved June 20, 2005, from http://www.fipg.org/media/ FIPGRiskMgmtManual.pdf

Funnel, Inc. (2005). *Selling a medical procedure*. Retrieved March 21, 2008, from http://www .funnelinc.com/funl_tattoff_detail.html

General Electric. (2003). *Installation instructions: Free-standing electric ranges* [Manual 229C4053P545-1 31-10556-1 04-03 JR] (p. 2).

HCS, LLC. (2004). *HCS 2004 safety label catalog*. Retrieved January 28, 2005, from http://www .safetylabel.com/catalogs/view.php?page =0&catalog=1&category=25

Nintendo of America, Inc. (2005). *Nintendo GameCube health and safety precautions* [Manual]. Retrieved February 15, 2005, from http://www.nintendo.com/ consumer/manuals/precautions_gcn_english.jsp

Petzl. (2005). *Petzl sport catalog 2005* (p. 120). Paris: Author.

Quamut. (2008). *How hybrid cars work*. Retrieved March 24, 2008, from http://www.quamut.com/ quamut/buying_a_hybrid_car/page/how_hybrid _cars_work.html

Slide-Lok Garage and Storage Cabinets. (2005). *P2468 pantry cabinet* [Assembly instructions] (p. 2).

Retrieved September 29, 2005, from http://www.slide-lok.com/assembly/ P2468/P2468.pdf

U.S. Congress, Office of Technology Assessment. (1995). *Renewing our energy future* (OTA-ETI-614). Washington, DC: U.S. Government Printing Office.

U.S. Department of Transportation. (2007). *Description of the IVI Technologies and the FOT*. Retrieved February 20, 2008, from http://www.itsdocs.fhwa .dot.gov/JPODOCS/REPTS_TE/14352_files/ 2.0description.htm

U.S. Environmental Protection Agency. (2001). *Global warming*. Retrieved June 25, 2001, from http://www.epa.gov/globalwarming/climate/ index.html

Chapter 21: Making Oral Presentations

Aspmo, K., Berg, T., & Wibetoe, G. (2004, June 16). *Atmospheric mercury depletion events (AMDEs) in polar regions during arctic spring* [Slide presentation]. Retrieved March 26, 2008, from http://www.writing.eng.vt.edu/slides.html/ slide_template.ppt

Reynolds, G. (2006, January 31). *Presentation Zen*. Retrieved March 26, 2008, from http:// presentationzen.blogs.com/ presentationzen/2006/01/contrasts_in_pr.html

Rochester, J. (2004, June 16). *Three primary products of an explosive*. Retrieved March 26, 2008, from http://www.writing.eng.vt.edu/samples/arl2.pdf

Smith, T. C. (1991). *Making successful presentations: A self-teaching guide*. New York: Wiley.

Tufte, E. (2003, September). PowerPoint is evil. *Wired*, 11. Retrieved March 26, 2008, from http://www .wired.com/wired/archive/11.09/ppt2.html.

Chapter 22: Connecting with the Public

American Marketing Association. (2004). *AMA statement of ethics*. Retrieved April 11, 2008, from http://www.marketingpower.com/content435.php

Angel.com. (2008). Can a call be transferred from one agent to another? Retrieved April 12, 2008, from IVR Wiki: http://www.socialtext.net/ivrwiki/ index.cgi?can_a_call_be_transferred_from_one _agent_to_another

Early American History Discussion Board. (2008). *Revolutionary War*. Retrieved May 19, 2008, from http://earlyamericanhistory.net/board/index .php?board=3.0

Federal Trade Commission. (2008). *Avoid ID theft.* Retrieved April 7, 2008, from http://www.ftc.gov/bcp/edu/pubs/consumer/idtheft/idt01.pdf

Johnson, T. (2008, May 6). I'd rather be writing. Retrieved May 21, 2008, from http://www.idratherbewriting.com/2008/05/06/podcast-pushing-your-company-into-the-wikis-blogs-and-social-networks-of-web-20-interview-with-alan-porter-of-webworks/

National Institutes of Health. (2007). International team studies South African plant for HIV/AIDS. *CAM at the NIH*, 14, 1. Retrieved April 8, 2008, from http://nccam.nih.gov/news/newsletter/pdf/2007fall.pdf

National Weather Service, Wichita, Kansas. (2007). *Spotter Newsletter*, 1. Retrieved May 12, 2008, from http://www.crh.noaa.gov/images/ict/newsletter/pdf/Fall2007.pdf

One Touch Global Technologies. (2006). *Instantly connecting documents with workers.* Retrieved April 8, 2008, from http://www.stelzner.com/PDF/OneTouch.pdf

Orlowski, A. (2005, October 18). Wikipedia founder admits to serious quality problems. *The Register.* Retrieved March 24, 2008, from http://www.theregister.co.uk/2005/10/18/wikipedia_quality_problem/

Podcast Networks. (2008). *Hardware.* Retrieved April 23, 2008, from http://www.podcast.net/cat/48

Stephens, T. (2008, March 4). Our next-generation GM hybrid. *FastLane Blog.* Retrieved April 12, 2008, from http://fastlane.gmblogs.com/archives/2008/03/our_nextgenerat_1.html

Selected Bibliography

Technical Communication

Barker, T. (2003). *Writing software documentation: A task-oriented approach* (2nd ed.). New York: Longman.

Barnum, C. (2001). *Usability testing and research.* Boston: Allyn & Bacon.

Brusaw, C. T., Alred, G. J., & Oliu, W. E. (2009). *Handbook of technical writing* (9th ed.). Boston: Bedford/St. Martin's.

Courage, C., & Baxter, K. (2005). *Understanding your users: A practical guide to user requirements: Methods, tools, and techniques.* San Francisco: Morgan Kaufman.

Dumas, J. S., & Redish, J. C. (1993). *A practical guide to usability testing.* Norwood, NJ: Ablex.

Neuliep, J. W. (2006). *Intercultural communication: A contextual approach* (3rd ed.). Thousand Oaks, CA: Sage.

Nielsen, J., & Mack, R. L. (Eds.). (1994). *Usability inspection methods.* New York: Wiley.

Varner, I., & Beamer, L. (2005). *Intercultural communication in the global workplace* (3rd ed.). Boston: McGraw-Hill.

Warren, T. (2006). *Cross-cultural communication: Perspectives in theory and practice.* Amityville, NY: Baywood.

Wieringa, D., Moore, C., & Barnes, V. (1998). *Procedure writing: Principles and practices* (2nd ed.). Columbus, OH: Battelle.

Ethics and Legal Issues

Beauchamp, T. L., Bowie, N. E., & Arnold, D. (2004). *Ethical theory and business* (8th ed.). Upper Saddle River, NJ: Prentice Hall.

Gillespie, T. (2007). *Wired shut: Copyright and the shape of digital culture.* Cambridge, MA: MIT Press.

Litman, J. (2006). *Digital copyright.* Amherst, NY: Prometheus Books.

Markel, M. (2000). *Ethics and technical communication: A synthesis and critique.* Stamford, CT: Greenwood.

Velasquez, M. G. (2006). *Business ethics: Concepts and cases* (6th ed.). Upper Saddle River, NJ: Pearson Prentice Hall.

Wilson, L. (2005). *Fair use, free use and use by permission: How to handle copyrights in all media.* New York: Allworth Press.

Collaborative Writing

Berkun, S. (2005). *The art of project management.* Sebastopol, CA: O'Reilly.

Dinsmore, P. C., & Cabanis-Brewin, J. (Eds.). (2006). *The AMA handbook of project management* (2nd ed.). New York: Amacom.

Duarte, D. L., & Snyder, N. T. (2006). *Mastering virtual teams: Strategies, tools, and techniques that succeed* (3rd ed.). San Francisco: Jossey-Bass.

Ede, L., & Lunsford, A. (1990). *Singular texts/plural authors: Perspectives on collaborative writing.* Carbondale: Southern Illinois University.

Hackos, J. (2007). *Information development: Managing your documentation projects, portfolio, and people.* Indianapolis: Wiley.

Sadowski-Raster, G., Dysters, G., & Sadowski, B. M. (2006). *Communication and cooperation in the virtual workplace: Teamwork in computer-mediated communication.* Northampton, MA: Edward Elgar.

Research Techniques

Fink, A. (2006). *How to conduct surveys: A step-by-step guide* (3rd ed.). Thousand Oaks, CA: Sage.

Gray, D. E. (2004). *Doing research in the real world.* London: Sage.

Harnack, A., & Kleppinger, E. (2003). *Online! A reference guide to using Internet sources* (3rd ed.). Boston: Bedford/St. Martin's.

Rubin, H. J., & Rubin, I. S. (2005). *Qualitative interviewing: The art of hearing data* (2nd ed.). Thousand Oaks, CA: Sage.

Willis, G. B. (2005). *Cognitive interviewing: A tool for improving questionnaire design.* Thousand Oaks, CA: Sage.

Usage and General Writing

The American Heritage guide to contemporary usage and style. (2005). Boston: Houghton Mifflin.

Josephson, D., & Hidden, L. (2005). *Write it right: The ground rules for self-editing like the pros.* Hilton Head Island, SC: Ground Rules Press.

Plotnik, A. (2005). *Spunk & bite: A writer's guide to punchier, more engaging language & style.* New York: Random House Reference.

Rees Cheney, T. A. (2005). *Getting the words right: 39 ways to improve your writing* (2nd ed.). Cincinnati: Writer's Digest Books.

Ritter, R. M. (2005). *New Hart's rules: The handbook of style for writers and editors.* Oxford: Oxford University Press.

Strunk, W., & White, E. B. (1999). *The elements of style.* (4th ed.). Boston: Allyn & Bacon.

Weiss, E. H. (2005). *The elements of international English style: A guide to writing correspondence, reports, technical documents, and Internet pages for a global audience.* Armonk, NY: M. E. Sharpe.

Williams, J. (2006). *Style: The basics of clarity and grace.* (2nd ed.). New York: Pearson Longman.

Handbooks for Grammar and Style

Hacker, D. (2006). *The Bedford handbook* (7th ed.). Boston: Bedford/St. Martin's.

Lunsford, A. A. (2008). *The St. Martin's handbook* (6th ed.). Boston: Bedford/St. Martin's.

Style Manuals

American Psychological Association. (2001). *Publication manual of the American Psychological Association* (5th ed.). Washington, DC: Author.

The Chicago manual of style. (2003). (15th ed.). Chicago: University of Chicago Press.

Coghill, A. M., & Garson, L. R. (2006). *The ACS style guide: Effective communication of scientific information* (3rd ed.). New York: Oxford University Press.

Council of Science Editors, Style Manual Committee. (2006). *Scientific style and format: The CSE manual for authors, editors, and publishers* (7th ed.). Reston, VA: Author.

Microsoft Corporation. (2004). *Microsoft manual of style for technical publications* (3rd ed.). Redmond, WA: Author.

U.S. Government Printing Office style manual 2000. (2000). Washington, DC: United States Government Printing Office. Available from http://www.access.gpo.gov/styleman/2000/browse-sm-00.html

Graphics, Design, and Web Pages

Barnard, M. (2005). *Graphic design as communication.* New York: Routledge.

Eccher, C. (2005). *Professional Web design: Techniques and templates* (2nd ed.). Hingham, MA: Charles River Media.

Farkas, D. K., & Farkas, J. (2002). *Principles of Web design.* New York: Longman.

George-Palilonis, J. (2006). *A practical guide to graphics reporting: Information graphics for print, web & broadcast.* Burlington, MA: Focal Press.

Hill, C. A., & Helmers, M. (Eds.). (2004). *Defining visual rhetorics.* Mahwah, NJ: Erlbaum.

Horton, S. (2006). *Access by design: A guide to universal usability for web designers.* Berkeley, CA: New Riders.

Kostelnick, C., & Roberts, D. D. (1998). *Designing visual language: Strategies for professional communicators.* Needham Heights, MA: Allyn & Bacon.

Kress, G., & van Leeuwen, T. (2006). *Reading images: The grammar of visual design* (2nd ed.). New York: Routledge.

Krug, S. (2006). *Don't make me think: A common sense approach to web usability* (2nd ed.). Berkeley, CA: New Riders.

Lazar, J. (2006). *Web usability: A user-centered design approach.* Boston: Pearson Addison Wesley.

Lupton, E. (2004). *Thinking with type: A critical guide for designers, writers, editors, and students.* New York: Princeton Architectural Press.

MacDonald, M. (2006). *Creating Web sites: The missing manual.* Sebastopol, CA: Pogue Press/O'Reilly.

McWade, J. (2005). *Before and after graphics for business.* Berkeley, CA: Peachpit Press.

Morville, P., & Rosenfeld, L. (2007). *Information architecture for the World Wide Web* (3rd ed.). Sebastopol, CA: O'Reilly.

Nielsen, J., & Loranger, H. (2006). *Prioritizing Web usability*. Berkeley, CA: New Riders.

Parker, R. C. (2006). *Looking good in print* (6th ed.). Scottsdale, AZ: Paraglyph.

Robbins, N. B. (2005). *Creating more effective graphs*. Hoboken, NJ: Wiley-Interscience.

Sutherland, R., & Karg, B. (2004). *Graphic designer's color handbook: Choosing and using color from concept to final output*. Gloucester, MA: Rockport Publishers.

Tufte, E. R. (1983). *The visual display of quantitative information*. Cheshire, CT: Graphics Press.

Tufte, E. R. (1990). *Envisioning information*. Cheshire, CT: Graphics Press.

Tufte, E. R. (1997). *Visualizing explanations*. Cheshire, CT: Graphics Press.

Vaughan, T. (2004). *Multimedia: Making it work* (6th ed.). New York: McGraw-Hill Technology Education.

Wagner, R. (2006). *Web design before and after makeovers*. Hoboken, NJ: Wiley.

White, J. V. (1990). *Color for the electronic age*. New York: Watson-Guptill.

Williams, R. (2006). *The non-designer's type book* (2nd ed.). Berkeley, CA: Peachpit Press.

Williams, R. (2008). *The non-designer's design book: Design and typographic principles for the visual novice* (3rd ed.). Berkeley, CA: Peachpit Press.

Williams, R., & Tollett, J. (2005). *The non-designer's Web book: An easy guide to creating, designing, and posting your own Web site* (3rd ed.). Berkeley, CA: Peachpit Press.

Web 2.0 Applications and White Papers

Brown, M. K., Huettner, B., & James-Tanny, C. (2007). *Managing virtual teams: Getting the most from wikis, blogs, and other collaborative tools*. Plano, TX: Wordware.

Castro, E. (2005). *Publishing a blog with Blogger: Visual quick project guide*. Berkeley, CA: Peachpit Press.

Hill, B. (2006). *Blogging for dummies*. Hoboken, NJ: Wiley.

McElhearn, K., Giles, R., & Herrington, J. D. (2006). *Podcasting pocket guide*. Sebastopol, CA: O'Reilly.

Stelzner, M. A. (2007). *Writing white papers: How to capture readers and keep them engaged*. Poway, CA: WhitePaperSource.

Job-Application Materials

Baron, C. L. (2004). *Designing a digital portfolio*. Indianapolis: New Riders.

Bolles, R. N. (2007). *What color is your parachute 2008: A practical manual for job-hunters and career-changers*. Berkeley, CA: Ten Speed Press.

Greene, B. (2005). *Get the interview every time: Fortune 500 hiring professionals' tips for writing winning résumés and cover letters*. Chicago: Dearborn Trade.

Smith, G. M. (2005). *Gainfully employed: A guide to résumé writing, job hunting, and effective interviewing*. New Orleans: Chatgris Press.

Oral Presentations

Gurak, L. J. (2000). *Oral presentations for technical communication*. Boston: Allyn & Bacon.

Hill, M., & Storey, A. (2000). *SpeakEasy! Oral presentation skills in English for academic and professional use*. Hong Kong: Hong Kong University Press.

Zwickel, S. B., & Pfeiffer, W. S. (2006). *Pocket guide to technical presentations and professional speaking*. Upper Saddle River, NJ: Pearson Prentice Hall.

Proposals and Grants

Freed, R. C., Freed, S., & Romano, J. (2003). *Writing winning business proposals: Your guide to landing the client, making the sale, persuading the boss*. New York: McGraw-Hill.

Miner, J. T., & Miner, L. E. (2005). *Models of proposal planning and writing*. Westport, CT: Praeger.

Pugh, D. G., & Bacon, T. R. (2005). *Powerful proposals: How to give your business the winning edge*. New York: American Management Association.

Wason, S. D. (2004). *Webster's new world grant writing handbook*. Hoboken, NJ: Wiley.

Acknowledgments (continued from page iv):

Figure 1.2, p. 12: Reprinted by permission of Sun Microsystems Laboratories. http://research.sun.com/.

Figure 1.3, p. 13: Reprinted with the permission of Apple Computer, Inc. from www.apple.com/iphone/questionsandanswers.html.

Screenshot, p. 15: Courtesy of Acer America Corporation (Canada).

Case Document 1.1a, p. 17: Hypertension Illustration Clip Art. Courtesy Nova Development Corporation.

Figure 2.1, p. 26: Licensed under Creative Commons Attribution 3.0 License. http://creativecommons.org/licenses.

Figure 2.2, p. 29: Reprinted with permission of Natural Science Industries, Ltd.

Figure 2.3, p. 29: Courtesy of Safety Label Solutions, Inc.

Text, p. 31: Rich Templeton. "Intro" from "The Value and Ethics of TI" by Rich Templeton, President and CEO of Texas Instruments, January 3, 2008. Reprinted by permission of Texas Instruments, Inc.

Figure, p. 34: Copyright © 2008 IEEE, Reprinted with permission of the Institute for Electronics and Electrical Engineering, Inc.

Figure 2.4, p. 38: Copyright © 2008 Garmin Ltd or its subsidiaries. All rights reserved.

Case Study, p. 39: "The Name Game." Adapted from Mike Markel, *Ethics in Technical Communication: A Critique and Synthesis.* Copyright © 2001 by Mike Markel. Reproduced with the permission of Greenwood Publishing Group, Inc., Westport, CT.

Screenshot, p. 41: Reprinted with the permission of MatchWare, Inc.

Figure 4.6, p. 71: Courtesy Skype Technologies S.A., http://share.skype.com/.

Screenshot, p. 80: Courtesy Monster.com.

Figure 5.1, p. 87: Micron Technology, Inc. (2008), http://www.micron.com/about/executives/officers/otte.

Figure 5.2a, p. 89: Courtesy Apple Computer, Inc.

Figure 5.2b, p. 89: Courtesy Taser International, Inc.

Figure 5.2c, p. 90: Courtesy The Michael J. Fox Foundation for Parkinson's Research. www.michaeljfox.org.

Figure 5.3a, p. 91: Reprinted with the permission of Netflix, Inc. All rights reserved.

Figure 5.3b, p. 91: Reprinted with permission of the National Geographic Society.

Figure 5.3c, p. 91: Courtesy Linux.com. www.linux.com/forums.

Table 5.1, p. 94: "Cultural Variables 'Beneath the Surface'" based on "Culture and the Shape of Rhetoric: Protocols of International Document Design" by Elizabeth Tebeaux and Linda Driskill, from *Exploring the Rhetoric of International Professional Communication: An Agenda for Teachers and Researchers,* edited by Carl R. Lovitt. Copyright © 1999 by Baywood Publishing Company, Inc. Adapted with the permission of the publisher.

Text, p. 95: "Japanese Communication Styles." Reprinted with the permission of UCLA Anderson School of Management.

Figure, p. 97: FDK Corporation. "Message from the President." Excerpt from a Japanese electronics company, Toshiharu Sugimoto. Reprinted with permission. www.fdk.co.jp.

Figure 5.4, p. 98: M. Enajarvi. Excerpt from NBPRF, the Director General's report. From the head of the Patent Office in Finland. Reprinted by permission. www.prh.fi.

Figure 5.6, p. 103: From Susan Solomon et al, *Climate Change 2007: The Physical Science Basis.* Used by permission of the IPCC Secretariat.

Figure 5.7, p. 106: Reprinted with the permission of Ford Motor Company.

Figure 5.8, p. 107: © 2008, Weblogs, Inc. Used with permission.

Screenshot, p. 113: Reprinted with the permission of Daniel Lyons.

Figure 6.4, p. 123: Copyright © 2008 by ProQuest Information and Learning. Reprinted by permission.

Figure 6.5, p. 125: Reprinted with the permission of Yahoo!, Inc.

Figure 6.6, p. 126. Reprinted by permission of Technorati. www.technorati.com/.

Figure 6.7, p. 127: Reprinted with the permission of Yahoo!, Inc.

Screenshot, p. 131: Reprinted by permission from Kaiser-Permanente-Thrive-Exposed. www.kaiserthrive.org.

Screenshot, p. 132: Courtney Perkes. "Kaiser to pay $1.8 million in malpractice case." From OCRegister.com, December 7, 2007. Reprinted with the permission of OC Register.

Screenshot, p. 149: Reprinted by permission of Rodale, Inc.

Figure 7.2, p. 154: Reprinted by permission of Apple Computer, Inc.

Figure 7.4, p. 156: Copyright © Metropolitan Museum of Art. Reprinted by permission.

Figure 7.7, p. 161: Copyright © 2005 by BrightPlanet Corp. Used by permission of BrightPlanet Corp., 3510 South First Avenue Circle, Sioux Falls, SD 57105. All rights reserved.

Screenshot, p. 163: Reprinted with the permission of Align Technology, Inc.

Figure 7.9, p. 166: Copyright © 2008 Canon U.S.A., Inc. All rights reserved.

Figure 7.11, p. 170: Reprinted by permission from LiveScience .com.

Photo, p. 176: Reprinted by permission of NBA Media Ventures, LLC.

Figure 8.2, p. 185: Reprinted by permission of PETA.

Figure 8.3, page 190: Copyright © 2008 U.S. Marine Corps. Used with permission.

Figure 8.4, p. 190: Institute for Highway Safety. *Scion xD 2008 model: Side Impact Test with Standard Side Airbags.* Reprinted by permission. www.iihs.org.

Figure 8.6, p. 192: Courtesy General Electric Company.

Figure 8.7, p. 193: Courtesy of Honeywell International, Inc.

Figure 10, p. 221: Justin Akers Chacón and Mike Davis. *No One Is Illegal*, Cover design by Amy Bakin. Copyright 2006 by Haymarket Books. Used by permission of the publisher.

Figure 11.1, p. 255: Used by permission of Nissan North America, Inc.

Figure 11.2, p. 255: Used by permission of Carnegie Science Center, Pittsburgh, PA.

Figure 11.3, p. 256: David Myers. Effective use of repetition as a design element (p. 362). From *Exploring Psychology*, Eighth Edition. Copyright © 2007 by Worth Publishers. Reprinted with the permission of Worth Publishers, Inc.

Figure 11.4, p. 257: David Myers. Effective use of contrast (p. 334). From *Exploring Psychology*, Eighth Edition. Copyright © 2007 by Worth Publishers. Reprinted with the permission of Worth Publishers, Inc.

Table 11.2a, p. 261: Courtesy of Kittery Outlets & Kittery Trading Post, Kittery, ME.

Table 11.2b, p. 261: From *Discover*, February 6, 2005 issue. Copyright © 2005 by Discover. All rights reserved. Used by permission and protected by the Copyright Laws of the United States. The printing, copying, redistribution, or retransmission of the Material without express written permission is prohibited.

Figure 11.6, p. 264: Jonathan Gruber. Queuing (p. 461). From *Public Finance and Public Policy*. Copyright © 2005 by Worth Publishers. Reprinted with the permission of Worth Publishers, Inc.

Figure 11.7, p. 264: Jonathan Gruber. Filtering (p. 95). From *Public Finance and Public Policy*. Copyright © 2005 by Worth Publishers. Reprinted with the permission of Worth Publishers, Inc.

Figure 11.9, p. 265: J. Kerman and G. Tomlinson. Sample Grids Using Picas and Inches. (p. 388). From *Listen*, Brief Fifth Edition. Copyright © 2004 by Bedford/St. Martin's. Used with permission of Bedford/St. Martin's Press.

Figure 11.10a, p. 266: G. A. Williams and R. B. Miller. "Disruptive Change: When Trying Harder Is Part of the Problem" (p. 96). From *Harvard Business Review* (May 2002). Copyright © 2002 by the Harvard Business School Publishing Corporation. Reprinted with the permission of *Harvard Business Review*. All rights reserved.

Figure 11.10b, p. 266: David Myers. From *Exploring Psychology*, Fifth Edition. Copyright © 2003 by Worth Publishers. Reprinted with the permission of Worth Publishers, Inc.

Figure 11.10c, p. 266: Norman Rockwell Museum. 3-panel brochure. (2005). Reprinted with the permission of The Norman Rockwell Museum at Stockbridge, MA.

Figure 11.17, p. 272: W. K. Purves, D. Sadava, G. H. Orians, and H. C. Heller. Line Spacing Used to Distinguish One Section from Another (p. 217). From *Life: The Science of Biology*, Seventh Edition. Copyright © 2004. Reprinted with the permission of Sinauer Associates, Inc., Publishers.

Table 11.3a, p. 276: Institute of Scientific and Technical Communicators. "Industry News" (p. 43). From *Communicator* (Spring 2005). Reprinted with the permission of the Institute of Scientific and Technical Communicators.

Table 11.3b, p. 276: J. W. Valley, "A cool early Earth?" (p. 61). From *Scientific American* (October 2005). Copyright © 2005 by Scientific American, Inc. All rights reserved. This figure includes an illustration by Lucy Reading-Ikkanda, which is reprinted with the permission of the illustrator.

Table 11.3c, p. 276: W. K. Purves, D. Sadava, G. H. Orians, and H. C. Heller. "Screens" (p. 466). From *Life: The Science of Biology*, Seventh Edition. Copyright © 2004. Reprinted with the permission of Sinauer Associates, Inc., Publishers.

Table 11.3d, p. 277: David Myers. "Marginal Glosses" (p. 603). From *Exploring Psychology*, Eighth Edition. Copyright © 2007 by Worth Publishers. Reprinted with the permission of Worth Publishers, Inc.

Table 11.3e, p. 277: J. L. Roark, M. P. Johnson, P. C. Cohen, S. Stage, A. Lawson, and S. M. Hartman. "Pull Quotes." (p. 115). From *The American Promise: A History of the United States, Volume I: To 1877*. Copyright © 2005 by Bedford/St. Martin's. Used with permission of Bedford/St. Martin's Press.

Figure 11.18, p. 279: D. Sadava, H. C. Heller, G. H. Orians, W. K. Purves, & D. M. Hills. "A Two-Column Design" (p. 477). From *The Science of Biology*, Eighth Edition. Copyright © 2008. Reprinted with the permission of Sinauer Associates, Inc., Publishers.

Figure 11.19, p. 280: Stelzner Consulting. "Converse Sample" (white paper, p. 6, February 14, 2008), www.stelzner.com/PDF/Comverse-MultiModality.pdf. Reprinted with permission.

Figure 11.20, p. 281: Don H. Hockenbury and Sandra E. Hockenbury. "A Complex Page Design." From *Discovering Psychology*, Fourth Edition. Copyright © 2007. Reprinted by permission of Worth Publishers, Inc.

Figure 11.22a, p. 284: Copyright © 2008 Corel Corporation. Used by permission.

Figure 11.23b, p. 284. Copyright © 2008 Corel Corporation. Used by permission.

Figure 11.24, p. 286: "Google Site Map." Reprinted by permission of Google, Inc.

Figure 11.26, p. 290: Reprinted by permission of The Silver Council. www.silvercouncil.org.

Figure 11.27, p. 291. Reprinted by permission of Google, Inc.

Figure 11.28, p. 291: Copyright © 2008 Refsnes Data. Used with permission.

Figure, p. 293: Reprinted with permission of Micron Technology, Inc.

Figure 12.3a, p. 307: Carl Zimmer. "Testing Darwin." Excerpt from *Discover*, February 2005, p. 32. Copyright © 2005. Reprinted with permission of the author.

Figure 12.3b, p. 307: W. K. Purves, D. Sadava, G. H. Orians, and H. C. Heller. "Red Algae" excerpt with graph. From *Life: The Science of Biology*, Seventh Edition. Copyright © 2004. Reprinted with the permission of Sinauer Associates, Inc., Publishers.

Figure 12.4, p. 308: David Myers. "Color Used to Establish Patterns." From *Exploring Psychology*, Eighth Edition. Copyright © 2007 by Worth Publishers. Reprinted by permission of Worth Publishers.

Graph, p. 322: Nigel Holmes & Meredith Bagby. "Really young vs. really old" bar graph. Copyright © 2002. Reprinted with the permission of Nigel Holmes.

Figure 12.13, p. 323: David G. Myers. Line graph, p. 132. From *Exploring Psychology*, Eighth Edition. Copyright © 2007 by Worth Publishers. Reprinted with the permission of Worth Publishers, Inc.

Figure 12.14, p. 324: Jonathan Gruber. "Pie Charts," p. 315. From *Public Finance and Public Policy*, Second Edition. Copyright © 2008 by Worth Publishers. Reprinted by permission of Worth Publishers, Inc.

Figure 12.15, p. 326: W. K. Purves, D. Sadava, D. Orians, G. H. Orians, and H. C. Heller. "Diagram." p. 264. From *Life: The Science of Biology*, Seventh Edition. Copyright © 2004 by Worth Publishers. Reprinted by permission of Worth Publishers, Inc.

Figure 12.16, p. 326: D. G. Myers. "Organization Chart," p. 61. From *Exploring Psychology*, Eighth Edition. Copyright © 2007 by Worth Publishers. Reprinted by permission of Worth Publishers, Inc.

Figure 12.19a, p. 328: From W. K. Purves, D. Sadava, G. H. Orians, and H. C. Heller. *Life: The Science of Biology*, Eighth Edition. © 2007 Sinauer Associates, p. 594, fig. 27.14. Reprinted by permission.

Figure 12.19b, p. 328: From Don H. Hockenbury and Sandra E. Hockenbury, *Discovering Psychology,* Fourth Edition. © Worth Publishers, 2007, p. 27, fig. 1.4. Reprinted by permission.

pp. 333–34: From *Technical Communication* 40 (1993): 682–693. Used with permission from the Society for Technical Communication, U.S.A.

Figure 13.2, p. 347: Courtesy of Computer Systems Odessa Corporation, Ltd.

Figure, p. 361: Alamy Laptop A39ECM-L. Copyright © 2008. All rights reserved. Reproduced by permission of Alamy Stock Photography.

Figure, p. 389: "Felicia E. Chong's Professional Portfolio." Copyright © 2007 by Felicia E. Chong. Reprinted with permission. www.feliciachong.efoliomn.com.

Figure 16.3, p. 434: Courtesy of NEPAC, Inc.

Figure 16.5, p. 445: Courtesy SmartDraw.com, San Diego, CA.

Figure 18.2, p. 490: Reprinted with the permission of the Institute for Electronics and Electrical Engineering, Inc.

Figure, pp. 491–95: John Thomford. "Sample Scientific Laboratory Report" (unpublished document, 2008). Adapted with permission. Text, "Lab Report Abstract" and "Executive Summary." Courtesy of George Murgel, Boise State University.

Screenshot, p. 539: Graphic by Funnel.com, 2005.

Figure 20.2, p. 552: Reprinted with the permission of Petzl America.

Figure 20.3, p. 554: John Brogan and S. Venkateswaran. "Diverse Choices for Hybrid and Electric Motor Vehicles," from *Proceedings of the International Conference on Urban EVs.* Copyright © 1992 by the Organization for Economic Cooperation and Development. Reprinted by permission of OECD, Stockholm.

Figure 20.4, p. 555: Excerpt plus graphic from "Hybrid Cars: Gasoline and Electric" from *How Hybrid Cars Work,* www.quamut.com. Copyright © 2008 Barnes & Noble, Inc. Reprinted with permission.

Figure 20.5, p. 556: Copyright © 2007 AB Volvo. Reprinted with permission.

Figure 20.6, p. 557: Victoria Institute of Forensic Medicine Web site. "The Autopsy Process." Reprinted by permission of the Victorian Institute of Forensic Medicine.

Figure 20.7a, p. 560: Courtesy of Slide-Lok.

Figure 20.7b, p. 560: Courtesy of Anthro Corporation.

Figure 20.8, p. 562: Courtesy of Hazard Communications Systems, LLC.

Figure 20.10, p. 563: Courtesy of Conveyor Equipment Manufacturers Association.

Figure 20.11, p. 567: Courtesy of Casio Computer, Ltd.

Figure 20.12, p. 568: Courtesy of General Electric Company.

Figure 20.13, p. 569: Courtesy of Nintendo of America, Inc.

Figure 20.14, p. 570: Courtesy of Apple Computer, Inc.

Figure, p. 571: Copyright © 2002 Canon U.S.A., Inc. All rights reserved.

Figure 21a, p. 578: Reprinted with the permission of Garr Reynolds.

Figure 22a, p. 607: Reprinted with the permission of Tom Johnson. Blog: www.idratherbewriting.com. Twitter: www.twitter.com/tomjohnson. News: www.writerriver.com.

Figure 22.2, p. 614: Courtesy of WhatsTheBigIdea.com, Inc.

Figure 22.4, p. 617: Reprinted with the permission of One Touch Global Technologies.

Figure 22.6, p. 621: Reprinted with permission of www.earlyamericanhistory.net.

Figure 22.7, p. 623: Courtesy of General Motors Corporation.

Figure 22.8, p. 625: Courtesy of Angel.com.

Index

Note: *f* indicates a figure and *t* indicates a table.

abbreviations
    editing and proofreading, 683
    lists of, 517
    for multicultural
        audiences, 98
    periods in, 696, 707–8
    using, 707–8
abstractions, in oral
        presentations, 596
abstract nouns, 241
abstracts
    descriptive, 482, 511–12, 512*f*
    informative, 482, 511, 512, 515
    in lab reports, 480, 491, 496
    in recommendation reports,
        511–12, 521
abstract services, 123, 123*f*
abstract terms, 236
academic research, 114
accessibility, as measure of
        excellence, 14
accessing tools, 263
    color, 261*t*
    dividers, 262*t*
    headers and footers, 262*t*
    icons, 261*t*
    page numbering, 262*t*
    tabs, 262*t*
accident reports, 472, 472*f*
    chronological organizational
        pattern for, 154
    more-important-to-less-
        important organizational
        pattern for, 158
    spatial organizational pattern
        for, 154–56
accomplishments, listing on
        résumé, 401
accountability, 608

accuracy
    of information, 128–29
    as measure of excellence, 12–14
    of print and online sources, 130
acknowledgments
    in collaboration, 38
    in lab reports, 486, 496
    of reviewers, 58
acronyms
    extended definitions of, 547
    for multicultural audiences, 98
action, showing in graphics,
        332–33, 333*f*
action verbs, for résumés, 402–3
active voice
    appropriate use of, 234–36
    for easy-to-translate text, 246
    in lab reports, 484
    for multicultural audiences, 99
    in résumés, 402–3
activity reports, 464. *See also*
        status reports
ad hominem argument, 186*t*
adjective clauses, repeated words
        in, 734
adjectives
    coordinate, 688–89, 692
    guidelines for using, 688–89,
        722–23
    trademarks as, 28
adjustment letters
    "bad news," 351*f*
    "good news," 350*f*
ad populum argument, 187*t*
advance organizers
    defined, 203
    headings used with, 203
    in oral presentations, 583, 595
    to proposals, 448, 449

adverbs, 733–34
advertisements, MLA style for, 682
agendas, for meetings, 61
alignment, in design, 255, 255*f*
Alley, Michael, 584, 585*f*–586*f*
ambiguous words and phrases,
        235, 236, 238
American National Standards
        Institute (ANSI), 561
analogy, 546
analysis section, in lab
        reports, 485
angle brackets, 713
announcements, electronic, 71
antecedents
    pronoun agreement with,
        689–90
    pronoun references to, 686–87
APA style, 637, 640–57
    for reference list entries, 495,
        640, 643–57
    for textual citations, 640, 641–43
APA Style Guide to Electronic
        References, 637
apostrophes, 699–700
appeal to pity, 186*t*
appear and dim animation
        effect, 587
appendices
    data presented in, 141
    definitions in, 549
    for lab reports, 488, 496
    for proposals, 432, 444–47, 452
    for recommendation reports,
        518, 534
approval, management, 104–5
approximation words and
        phrases, 236
archiving of drafts, 346

arguments
  audience analysis and, 177–78
  from authority, 187t
  based on emotions, 184–85, 185f
  circular, 187t
  claim and, 181, 185
  "commonsense," 159, 610
  context of, 177–80
  cultural factors affecting, 191
  defined, 177
  editing and, 345
  ethical constraints, 178
  evidence for, 181
  financial constraints, 180
  format and tone constraints, 180
  identifying elements of, 181
  from ignorance, 186t
  informational constraints,
    179–80
  lab reports and, 479, 480, 485
  legal constraints, 178
  opposing viewpoints in, 184
  personnel constraints, 180
  political constraints, 178–79
  reasoning and, 181
  against the speaker, 186t
  time constraints, 180
  writing, 180–85
articles (*a, an, the*)
  guidelines for using, 721–22
  in instructions, 565
articles (text). *See also* database
    articles; journal articles;
    magazine articles;
    newsletter articles;
    newspaper articles;
    periodical articles
  skimming, 630
articles with DOI, APA reference
    list style for, 652
article titles
  APA reference list style for, 644,
    648, 652
  IEEE reference list style for, 659,
    662, 663
  MLA works cited list style for,
    669, 674, 678
articulation, in oral
    presentations, 599
artworks, MLA works cited style
    for, 681
ASCII text, in résumés, 384, 385
assistance, acknowledging, 38
asynchronous discussions, 70

attention, in oral presentations, 599
audience, 67–78. *See also* readers
  appealing to broader goals
    of, 179f
  attitudes toward subject, 84
  attitudes toward writer, 84
  body language and, 599–600
  collaboration and, 59
  cultural variables and, 81
  design goals and, 254
  design planning and, 257–58
  determining characteristics
    of, 81–85
  ethical communication and, 37
  filler phrases and, 240
  formality level for, 234
  for instructions, 558–59
  interviewing as part of, 86
  jargon and technical knowledge
    of, 237
  learning about, 86–88
  meeting needs of, 99
  multicultural, 7
  multiple, 103
  nervousness and, 597–98
  oral presentation involvement
    of, 595–96, 599
  planning and, 42–43
  planning graphics for, 301–2
  primary, 83, 102
  problem solving by, 7
  proposals and, 437–38
  reading documents written
    by, 88
  revising information for,
    51, 105
  searching on the Internet for
    information about, 86–88, 87f
  secondary, 83, 102
  technical documents and, 6–7
  tertiary, 83
  text created to meet needs of,
    88, 89f–90f
  topic sentences as promise
    to, 209
  verbal and visual techniques to
    meet the needs of, 88, 91f
  writing headings for, 202–3
  writing purpose and, 81
audience analysis, 80–108
  descriptions and, 550
  for informational reports, 460
  information organization
    and, 150–51

  for oral presentations, 579–80,
    581–82
  persuasive writing and,
    177–78, 194
  for proposals, 432
  research and, 115f
  writer's checklists for, 107–8, 194
audience profile sheet, 102, 102f
audio recordings, APA reference
    list style for, 656
authority, argument from, 187t
authors
  APA reference list style for, 645,
    646, 650, 652
  evaluating, for print and online
    sources, 129
  IEEE reference list style for, 658,
    660, 662, 663
  MLA works cited style for, 670,
    671, 676, 678
authors, multiple
  APA citations style for, 642, 643
  APA reference list style for, 645
  IEEE reference list style for, 659
  MLA works cited style for, 670–72
authors, unknown
  APA citation style for, 642–43
  APA reference list style for, 647
  MLA textual citation style for, 668
  MLA works cited style for, 672
author's guides, 489, 490
awards, listing on résumé, 401, 408f
axes, on graphs, 300, 323

background
  in proposals, 447
  in recommendation reports, 509
background checks, 399
back matter
  collaboration pattern and, 58f
  in manuals, 572
  in recommendation reports,
    507, 508t, 516
back-to-back headings, 202, 203
back-to-top links, for Web sites, 285
bandwagon argument, 187t
bar charts (Gantt charts), 444, 445,
    445f, 446, 450, 469
bar graphs
  creating, 317–19
  deviation, 320t
  grouped, 319t
  horizontal, 316f
  100-percent, 319t

bar graphs (*continued*)
proportions in, 317
scale in, 318
for slide presentations, 591*f*
stratum, 320*t*
subdivided, 319*t*
tick marks in, 318
title of, 319
two- vs. three-dimensional, 299, 300*f*
types of, 316*f*, 319, 319*t*–320*t*
uses of, 310*f*
vertical, 316*f*
be, forms of, 719
begging the question, 187*t*
Bell, A. H., 96
bias
in field research, 135
of information in research, 129
in questions on questionnaires, 140
in recommendations report criteria, 505–6
bibliographic information
in note taking, 630
for summaries, 634
bibliography, 518
bibliography annex entries, IEEE style for, 658–65
bindings
document design and, 260
types of, 260*t*
blind copy line, in e-mails, 380*f*
blogs, 622–24
examples of, 607, 623*f*
guidelines for, 622–23
job searches and, 394
research using, 118*f*, 121, 132
uses of, 622
Web site home page for, 291*f*
writer's checklist for, 626
body
collaboration pattern and, 58*f*
of recommendation reports, 507, 508*t*, 508–9
body language, 599–600
body paragraphs, 206
boilerplate, 441, 444
boldface, 269, 275, 515, 572
bond paper, 259
book editions
IEEE reference list style for, 661
MLA works cited style for, 673

book paper, 259–60
books
APA reference list style for, 645–47
IEEE reference list style for, 659–61
MLA works cited style for, 670–73
online, MLA works cited style for, 677
skimming, 630
books in series, MLA works cited style for, 673
book titles
APA reference list style for, 644, 646
IEEE reference list style for, 658–59, 660
MLA works cited style for, 669, 671
boxes
creating, 276*t*, 278
page design and, 276, 281*f*
brackets
angle, 703
square, 702
brainstorming, 44*t*
branching, 45*t*
brochures, 11*f*
APA reference list style for, 655
connecting with the public using, 610, 613–14, 615*f*
defined, 613
examples of information in, 613
fold design of, 613, 614*f*, 615
guidelines for, 614
as a one-way application, 610
partition organizational pattern for, 162
writer's checklist for, 626
budgets
honesty about, in progress reports, 465
in proposals, 432, 438, 439, 443–44, 450, 452
bulleted lists, 222, 223
ineffective, 282
for slide presentations, 587, 591*f*
Tech Tip for creating, 226
bulletin boards, 121
business communication. *See also* technical communication
cultural variables in, 100–101
business life, and private life, 94*f*

capitalization
guidelines for, 708
in lists, 223, 224, 225
page design and, 270
captions
with graphics, 438
with tables, 312*f*
care, 21
career development, 6
case, in page design, 270, 270*f*
cause-and-effect organizational pattern
description of, 167–69, 170*f*
graphics with, 169
guidelines for, 147
kind of information presented using, 153*f*
overstatement in, 169
CD-ROMs, MLA works cited style for, 679
chalkboard, for presentations, 593*t*
change notifications, distribution of, 71
chapters in edited books
APA reference list style for, 647
IEEE reference list style for, 661
MLA textual citations style for, 668
MLA works cited style for, 672
chartjunk, 300*f*
charts
bar (Gantt), 444, 445, 446
MLA works cited style for, 681
network diagrams, 445, 445 (illus.)
pie, 324, 324*f*, 448
white papers with, 616
checklists, 311*f*, 326–27, 327*f*. *See also* writer's checklists
choppy sentences, 227–28
chronological organizational pattern
defined, 154
guidelines for using, 155
kind of information presented using, 152*f*
signposts for, 155
topic sentences and, 208
uses of, 154, 154*f*, 155*f*
writer's checklist for, 171

chronological résumés, 399–405, 381*f*–382*f*
  education, 400–401
  elements of, 399–405
  employment history, 402–4
  identifying information, 399
  interests and activities, 404–5
  for nontraditional students, 410*f*
  objectives, 400
  personal information on, 404
  references for, 409*f*
  summary of qualifications, 400
  for traditional students, 408*f*–409*f*
chunking, in page design, 263, 263*f*, 282
circular argument, 187*t*
circular definitions, 543
citations
  copyright and, 27
  for graphics, 300, 306
  for tables, 314
city of publication
  APA reference list style for, 646
  IEEE reference list style for, 660
  MLA works cited style for, 671
claims
  in arguments, 181, 185
  in presentation graphics, 584, 585*f*–586*f*
  where to present, 185
clarity
  ethical communication using, 37–38
  of graphics for oral presentations, 587
  of information collected in research, 129
  as measure of excellence, 11–12
  of Web page links, 289, 290
  of words and phrases, 234–39
classification, defined, 162
classification organizational pattern, 163*f*
  guidelines for, 165
  kind of information presented using, 153*f*
  logical sequence in, 165
  overlapping in, 165
  writer's checklist for, 171
clichés, 238–39
clip art
  maps, 332, 333*f*
  pictographs, 320

clustering, 45*t*
coated paper, 260
codes of conduct
  abiding by, 36
  analyzing, 34
  characteristics of, 33
  corporate culture and, 32–33
  ethical constraints in persuasive writing and, 178
cognitive walkthroughs, 348
coherence, 198–217
  design and, 214–16
  headers and footers and, 214–15, 215*f*
  headings, 201–3
  incorporating while writing, 199
  lists, 204–6
  outline view for checking, 199, 200*f*
  paragraphs, 206–14
  styles and, 216
  titles, 200–201
  typefaces and, 215
  writer's checklist for, 216–17
collaboration, 8, 51–75
  acknowledging, 38
  advantages of, 59
  agendas, 61, 65
  conducting meetings, 61–67
  culture and, 74
  disadvantages of, 59
  electronic tools for, 67–68
  gender and, 73
  groupware for, 70–71
  interpersonal skills in, 8
  patterns of, 58, 58*f*
  project management and, 60–61
  in proposals, 441
  pulling your weight in, 65
  reviewing documents and, 69
  videoconferencing and, 71–73
  writer's checklist for, 74–75
college catalogs, classification organizational pattern for, 162
college courses, listing on résumé, 400, 401
college placement offices, 393
colons, 695–96
color
  as accessing tool, 261*t*
  contrast and, 308, 308*f*
  creating patterns with, 307, 308*f*

cultural considerations, 309, 334
  for emphasis, 307
  in graphics, 300, 307–9
  in line graphs, 323
  on maps, 333*f*
  page design and, 281*f*
  repetition and, 307
  symbolic meanings for, 309, 309*f*
  text size and, 309
  Web site design and, 287
  of Web site links, 290
Color for the Electronic Age (White), 307
column breaks, 268
columns
  formatting, 268
  multicolumn design, 267, 281*f*
  one-column design, 280*f*
  three-column layout, 281*f*
  two-column layout, 266*f*, 279*f*
commas
  compound, 689
  independent clauses and, 714
  nonrestrictive modifiers with, 231
  quotation marks and, 701
  run-on sentences and, 686
  separating coordinate adjectives, 688–89
  unnecessary, 694–95
  uses of, 691–95
comma splices, 685, 694
comment features, in word processors, 68
"commonsense" arguments, 182, 610
communicating verbs, 104
communication skills
  collaboration and, 59
  diplomatic, 65–67
company research, in job application process, 390–92, 394
comparison and contrast organizational pattern
  description of, 159–60, 161*f*
  ethical issues in, 162, 163
  in extended definitions, 545–46
  guidelines for, 161
  kind of information presented using, 153*f*
  part by part, 160
  whole by whole, 160, 161*f*
  writer's checklist for, 171
comparisons, in tables, 313

completion reports, 501. *See also*
recommendation reports
problem-method-solution
organizational pattern
for, 167
for proposals, 450
for research projects, 436
compliance programs, 31
compound adjectives,
hyphenating, 689, 704
compound nouns, hyphenating, 704
compound sentences, commas
in, 691
compound subjects
commas and, 695
verb agreement with, 720
comprehension, and design
goals, 254
comprehensiveness
of information in research, 129
as measure of excellence, 14
computer presentations, in oral
presentations, 593t
computer skills, listing on
résumés, 405
conciseness
principles of, 239–42
revising for, 243
word phrases changed for,
241, 241t
conclusions
cultural variables and, 150–51
for descriptions, 553–54
for instructions, 566, 570f
for job-application letters, 420
for lab reports, 486, 496
for oral presentations,
583–84, 591f
for progress reports, 466, 470
for recommendation reports,
510, 532
for status reports, 466
for slide presentations, 591f
conditions of fact, and verb tense,
720–21
conference proceedings articles
APA reference list style for, 655
IEEE reference list style for, 664
MLA works cited style for, 680
conflict resolution procedures, 62
consensus, and gender, 73
consistency
coherence and, 199
editing and, 345

styles and, 215
content, and coherence, 199
contractions, 699
contract law, 29
contrast
color and, 308, 308f
design and, 257, 257f
conventions section, in
manuals, 572
convincing verbs, 104
cooperativeness, 189
coordinate adjectives,
688–89, 692
coordinating conjunctions
comma splices and, 685
independent clauses and, 714
run-on sentences and, 686
coordination, linking ideas
by, 714
copy line, in e-mails, 380f
copyright law
dealing with questions in, 27
editing and, 344
ethical communication
and, 36
fair use and, 26, 27
graphics and, 305, 306, 587
legal obligations under, 25–26
copyright page, in manuals, 572
correctness as measure of
excellence, 14–15
correlative constructions, 232–33
correspondence, and cultural
considerations, 382–84
countable common nouns, 732
cover, of recommendation
reports, 511
Creative Commons, 26, 26f
credentials, in proposals, 440,
448, 450
criteria
bias in, 505–6
comparison-and-contrast
organizational pattern
and, 160
establishing, in
recommendation reports,
503–4, 503f
critiquing work of others, 67, 68,
70, 73
cropping photographs, 329, 330f
cross-references, in progress
reports, 468
cross-reference tables, 262t

cultural considerations. *See also*
multicultural audiences
audience and, 81
"beneath the surface" variables,
93, 94f–95f
in business letters, 100–101
collaboration and, 74
communicating across cultures,
90–96, 710–12
considering when writing,
95–96, 97f–98f
distance between business and
private life, 94f
distance between ranks, 94f
individual vs. group focus, 94f
modular documents for,
103, 103f
"on the surface" variables, 92–93
organizational differences in, 93
types of, 92
uncertainty, 95f
U.S. communication style, 710–12
cutaway drawings, 332f

dangling modifiers, 233
dashes
misuse of, 698
quotation marks and, 701
uses of, 697–98
data
experiments and analysis of, 134
field research and analysis
of, 135
honest analysis and reporting
of, 143, 485
presenting in appendices,
141, 452
database articles
IEEE reference list style
for, 663
MLA works cited style for, 678
databases
dissertations on, APA reference
list style for, 651
online, 121, 678
data set, APA reference list style
for, 653
date of publication
APA reference list style for, 646,
648, 650, 652
IEEE reference list style for, 660,
662, 663
MLA works cited style for, 671,
674, 676, 678

dates
    APA reference list style for, 645
    commas in, 693
    cultural variety in expressing, 92
    IEEE reference list style for, 659
    MLA works cited style for, 670
debriefing, in usability testing, 353
decimal fractions, 696
definitions, 540–49. *See also*
        key terms
    analyzing writing situation
        for, 541
    circular, 543
    defined, 540
    extended, 543–47
    in lab reports, 482
    parenthetical, 541–42
    purpose and, 541
    sentence, 542–43
    types of, 541
    uses of, 540
    where to place, 547–49
    writer's checklist for, 573
deliverables, 435–37
    budgeting, 115f
    collaboration and, 62
    defined, 435
    determining information
        needed for, 116f
    honesty in progress reports
        about, 465
    scheduling, 115f
    visualizing, 115f
demonstrations, for primary
        research, 133
demonstrative pronouns, 213–14
density, of screens (design), 277t
dependent clauses
    commas separating, 62
    linking to independent clauses,
        684–85
    pronoun references and, 686–87
descenders, and underlining, 275
descriptions, 549–57
    analyzing writing situation for,
        549–50
    concluding, 553–54
    defined, 540
    detail in, 552–53
    examples, 554–57
    general, 550
    graphics in, 550–51, 554f
    introducing, 550–51
    of mechanisms, 549, 552–53, 555f

nature and scope of, 550
    of objects, 549, 551, 552–53
    part-by-part section, 552
    particular, 550
    process, 549, 552–53, 554, 557f,
        573–74
    specifications, 556
    step-by-step section, 552
    writer's checklists for, 573–74
    writing situation for, 549–50
descriptive abstracts, 482,
        511–12, 512f
design, 253–92. *See also* page
        design; Web page design;
        Web site design
    audience and, 254, 258
    bindings, 260
    brochures, 613, 614f, 615
    coherent, 214–16
    defined, 254
    documents, 259–78
    ethical and legal information
        and, 37
    goals of, 254
    instructions, 558–60
    for multicultural audiences, 99
    newsletters, 611, 613
    page count, 259
    page size, 259
    paper, 259–60
    persuasive writing and, 189–91
    planning, 257
    principles of, 255–57
    readability and, 8
    resources and, 258
    safety information, 561
    writer's checklists for, 292
details
    cultural variables in, 95f
    in descriptions, 552–53
    enlarged details, 552f
    specificity and, 236
deviation bar graphs, 320f
diagrams, 310f, 325, 326f
    in lab reports, 484
dictionaries, online, APA reference
        list style for, 653
diplomatic communication, 65–67
direct costs, for proposals, 444
directives, 459, 461f
    defined, 461
    writer's checklist for, 475
    writing, 461, 462
directness, in U.S. culture, 710

directory search engines, 122
direct quotations, 700–701
disabilities, people with
    people-first approach with, 245
    Web site design for, 287
discriminatory language, 38
discussion boards, 620–21
    participating in, 621
    screen from, 621f
    writer's checklist for, 626
discussion group postings, APA
        reference list style for, 654
discussion section, in lab reports,
        485–86, 495, 496
dissertations
    APA reference list style for, 651
    MLA works cited style for, 677
dividers, as accessing tools, 262t
do, forms of, 718–19
documentation of sources, 518,
        637–82
    functions of, 637
    for graphics, 637
    for paraphrased ideas, 637
    for quotations, 637
document change notifications, 71
document delivery services, 122
document design, 259–78. *See
        also* design
    elements of, 259
    goals of, 254
    instructions and, 558–60
document sections, and
        collaboration pattern, 58f
dot leaders, in tables, 314
double-blind field research, 135
drafting, in writing process,
        42, 47–51
    coherence techniques and, 199
    collaboration pattern and, 58f
    guidelines for, 48
    of informational reports, 460
    of proposals, 432
    styles and, 49, 51
    templates and, 48
drafts
    archiving, 346
    critiquing, 67, 68, 70, 73
    electronic tools for
        collaboration and, 67
drawings. *See also* graphics
    cutaway, 332f
    exploded, 332f
    phantom, 332f

drawings (*continued*)
    showing motion in, 332–33, 333*f*
    uses of, 311*f*, 331
drawing tools, 278, 321
Driskill, L., 93
DVDs, MLA works cited style for, 682

easy-to-read text
    on presentation graphics, 584
    on Web pages, 289
easy-to-see graphics, in oral
        presentation graphics, 584
economic variables, 92
edited books
    APA reference list style for, 647
    IEEE reference list style for, 661
    MLA textual citations style
        for, 668
    MLA works cited style for, 672
editing, 42, 53, 683–709
    abbreviations and, 683
    amount needed, 53
    defined, 53
    grammatical sentences and,
        684–90
    guidelines for, 344–45
    of informational reports, 460
    of instructions, 566
    mechanics of, 702–8
    of proposals, 433
    punctuation and, 691–712
    reviewing and, 342, 344–46
    writer's checklists for, 54, 356
edition number, APA reference list
        style for, 647
education
    in chronological résumés,
        400–401
    cultural variables, 92
    in job-application letters,
        418–19, 420, 421*f*
    of readers, 82
    in résumés, 408*f*, 410*f*
either-or arguments, 187*t*
electronic books, APA reference list
        style for, 651
electronic mailing lists, 121
electronic portfolio, 392
electronic résumés, 407–15
    content of, 412–13
    format of, 407–12, 413–15
    preparing, 413, 414
    scannable, 412, 415, 416*f*
    text, 412, 413

types of, 407–12
Web-based, 412
writer's checklist for, 426
electronic sources
    APA citation style for, 643
    APA reference list style for,
        649–57
    IEEE reference list style for, 659,
        661–64
    MLA textual citations style
        for, 669
    MLA works cited style for,
        669–70, 675–79
electronic tools, in collaboration,
        67–68, 69, 70–71
ellipses
    in quotations, 633–34
    uses of, 701–2
e-mail, 71, 379–81
    cultural considerations,
        382–84
    elements of, 380*f*
    format of, 381*f*–382*f*
    informational reports in form
        of, 459
    MLA works cited style for, 679
    netiquette in, 379, 380–81,
        381*f*–382*f*
    for primary research, 138
    proofreading, 381*f*, 382*f*
    reports, 459, 460
    subject line in, 381*f*, 382*f*
    writer's checklist for, 385
emotions
    appealing to, 184–85, 185*f*
    effective listening and, 61
emphasis
    coherence and, 199
    color for, 307
    editing and, 345
    of new information in
        sentences, 225–26
employers
    ethical obligations to, 23–24
    learning about, 390–92, 394
employment. *See also* job entries
    job search for, 390–92
    trends in, 390, 392
employment history
    explaining gaps in, on
        résumés, 403
    listing nonprofessional
        positions, on résumés, 403
    listing on résumés, 402–4

listing several positions with
        same employer on
        résumés, 404
    in proposals, 439
employment paragraph, in job-
        application letters, 419–20
enclosure line, in job-application
        letters, 417
encyclopedias, 118*f*
    online, APA reference list style
        for, 653
engineering
    importance of articles in, 489
    notebooks kept in, 480
environment, ethical obligations
        to, 24–25
environmental impact
        statements, 169
epitome, 515
equations, 483
equipment, and design, 259
equipment and methods section,
        in lab reports, 483
equipment catalogs, 162
ethics, 19–25
    codes of conduct and, 178
    conflicts in, 22
    corporate culture and, 31–33
    moral standards in, 20–21
    multicultural audiences
        and, 35–36
    obligations of writer in, 22–25
    obligations to employer in, 23
    obligations to the environment
        in, 24–25
    obligations to the public in, 23–24
    passive voice and, 235
    persuasive writing and, 178
    principles for ethical
        communication in, 36–38
    writer's checklist for, 39
ethics notes
    acknowledging reviewers, 53
    burying bad news in
        paragraphs, 208
    collaborative projects, 65
    comparing and contrasting
        fairly, 162, 163
    data analyses and reporting, 143
    euphemisms, 239
    font sizes, 271
    graphics, 300
    informed consent in usability
        testing, 354

ethics notes (*continued*)
  marketing your
    organization, 618
  meeting needs of readers, 99
  persuasive writing honesty, 191
  plagiarism and reuse of
    information and, 28
  résumé honesty, 399
  safety information, 561
  Web page design honesty, 288
ethics office, 36
ethics programs, 31
etymology, 546–47
euphemisms, 239
evaluation. *See also* usability
    evaluations
  factors to be considered
    in, 342–43
  of lab reports, 487–88
  proposals and, 445–47, 449
  relationship among reviewing,
    evaluating, and testing,
    342, 343*f*
evaluation materials
  creating, 62
  group-members evaluation
    form, 64*f*
  for oral presentations, 601
  self-evaluation form, 66*f*
event analysis, 156
evidence
  in arguments, 181, 182, 183
  claim placement and, 185
  "commonsense" arguments, 182
  examples as, 182
  expert testimony as, 182
  kinds of, 182
  lab reports and, 479, 484
  numerical data, 182
examples
  as evidence, 182
  as extended definitions, 544
  persuasive writing with, 610
exclamation points, 696–97, 701
executive overview, 515
executive summary
  in recommendation reports,
    515, 516, 517, 523
  in white papers, 616
expectations of readers
  about documents, 84
  editing and, 344
  about instructions, 558
  planning and, 43

experiments, for primary
    research, 134
expert testimony, 182, 610
expletives, 228–29
exploded drawings, 332*f*
express warranty, 29
extemporaneous presentations,
    579, 596–97
extended definitions, 543–47
  analogy, 546
  comparison and contrast, 545–46
  defined, 543
  etymology, 546–47
  examples, 544, 548
  graphics, 543–44
  negation, 546
  partitioning, 544–45
  principles of operations, 545
external proposals
  defined, 433
  readers' needs in, 437–38
  uses of, 433
extracurricular activities
  listing in job-application
    letters, 418
  listing on résumés, 404–5
eye contact
  in oral presentations, 599
  U.S. communication style
    and, 711
  in videoconferencing, 72

fair-mindedness, 189
fair use, 26, 27
fancy words, plain equivalents of,
    243, 243t
FAQ pages, on Web sites, 285
feasibility reports, 449
  classification organizational
    pattern for, 162
  comparison-and-contrast
    organizational pattern for, 161
  more-important-to-less-
    important organizational
    pattern for, 158
  questions answered by, 501–2
FedBizOpps Web site, 434
feedback statements, 565
field reports, 459, 463*f*
  guidelines for, 464
  writer's checklist for, 475
  writing, 463
field research
  bias in, 135

double-blind, 135
  effect on behavior studied, 135
  as primary research, 135
figures
  defined, 309
  lists of, 513
file sharing, 70
fillers, 240
fill patterns, for pie charts, 324
film
  APA reference list style for, 656
  MLA works cited style for, 682
filtering, and page design, 264, 264*f*
final reports, 179–80, 501. *See also*
    recommendation reports
financial constraints, and
    persuasive writing, 180
findings, in recommendation
    reports, 509
flaming, in e-mail, 381
flowcharts, 167, 169, 311*f*, 327–28,
    328*f*, 504
focus groups, 349
fold design, of brochures, 613,
    614*f*, 615
follow-up letters, after job
    interviews, 425–26
fonts, formatting, 270
footers
  as accessing tools, 262t
  coherent design and, 214–15, 216*f*
  formatting, 514
  for Web sites, 284, 284*f*, 291*f*
footnotes
  placing definitions in, 547
  for tables, 314
formality
  in e-mail, 381
  levels of, 233–34
  U.S. communication style
    and, 712
format
  author's guides on, 490
  of electronic résumés, 413–15
  of e-mail, 381*f*–382*f*
  of headers, 514
  of informational reports, 460
  of proposals, 433
  of recommendation reports, 511
formative evaluation, for
    proposals, 447
forms
  for meeting minutes, 473
  in usability testing, 352

formulas, 482, 483
forwarding e-mail, 381
fractions, 704
frames, in Web site design, 290f
freewriting, 44t
front matter
    collaboration pattern and, 58f
    for manuals, 572
    for recommendation reports,
        507, 508t, 511–16
full justification, 272–75
future, in oral presentations, 584
future perfect progressive tense, 717
future perfect tense, 716, 719
future prediction, and verb
    tense, 721
future progressive tense, 716
future tense, simple, 716

Gantt charts, 445, 446, 450, 469
gender, and collaboration, 73
gender-specific words, 242, 244
general descriptions, 550
general-to-specific organizational
    pattern
    description of, 157
    guidelines for, 157
    kind of information presented
        using, 152f
    uses of, 154f, 157
    writer's checklist for, 171
gerunds, 563, 699, 717
gestures
    cultural considerations, 335, 600
    in oral presentations, 599
    U.S. communication style
        and, 711
glossaries
    for easy-to-translate text, 246
    in manuals, 572
    for nonnative speakers of
        English, 541
    placing definitions in, 541, 547–49
    in recommendation reports,
        516, 518f
glossy paper, 260
goods-and-services proposals,
    436–37
government documents
    APA reference list style for, 655
    IEEE reference list style for, 664
    MLA works cited style for,
        679–80
government publications, 124

government Web sites
    IEEE reference list style for, 664
grade-point averages, listing on
    résumés, 401
grammar checkers, 54
grammatical form, of headings, 203
grammatical sentences, 684–90
grant proposals, 437–38
graphic representation of data,
    APA reference list style
    for, 653
graphics, 297–335. See also
    figures; tables
    accessibility of, 301
    animation in, 587, 589
    balancing clarity and drama
        in, 322
    captions for, 438
    cause-and-effect organizational
        pattern and, 169
    characteristics of effective,
        299–301
    choosing appropriate, 309–35
    chronological organizational
        pattern and, 155
    citing, 300, 306
    classification or partition
        organizational pattern
        and, 164f
    color in, 300, 307–9
    copyright laws affecting, 305,
        306, 587
    creating, 304–6
    cultural considerations and, 99,
        299, 333–35, 600
    defined, 298
    in descriptions, 550–51, 554f
    documentation of, 637
    ease of reading, 584
    editing and, 345
    with enlarged details, 552f
    in Excel, 317
    explaining in text, 301
    extended definitions with,
        543–44
    functions of, 298–99
    honesty of, 300, 485
    information communicated by,
        302, 303f, 304
    inserting in documents, 305
    for instructions, 311f, 325–32,
        560, 565
    integrating with text, 301
    introducing in text, 301

labeling, 300
    in lab reports, 484, 494
    legibility of, 587
    liability law and, 30
    for logical relationships, 298
    in manuals, 573
    master page design in, 588
    modifying, 305
    more-important-to-less-
        important organizational
        pattern and, 158
    for multicultural audiences, 99,
        541, 573
    for numerical information, 298,
        309, 310f
    oral presentations with, 580,
        581–82, 584–93, 585f–586f
    persuasive writing with, 193f
    placement of, 301
    planning, 301–4
    problem-methods-solution
        organizational pattern
        and, 167
    for process descriptions, 298,
        311f, 325–32
    professionally created, 305
    proposals with, 438
    purpose and choice of, 302, 303f
    revising, 306
    saving space with, 299
    sequencing, 333–34
    showing motion in, 332–33, 333f
    simplicity of, 587
    for spatial information, 298,
        329–32
    spatial organizational pattern
        and, 155
    speaking situation and, 587–89
    supported claim in, 584,
        585f–586f
    in technical communication,
        9, 10
    translation costs and, 299, 541
    using existing graphics, 304–5
    visibility of, 587
    for visual information, 311f,
        329–32
    writer's checklist for, 335
graphs
    bar, 299, 300f, 310f, 314, 316f,
        317–19, 319t–320t, 591f
    in lab reports, 484, 494
    line, 310f, 323, 323f
    white papers with, 616

gray literature, APA reference list style for, 653–54
grid lines, in line graphs, 323
group, in sending e-mail, 380f
grouped bar graphs, 319f
group members
    critiquing work of, 67, 68, 70, 73
    evaluation form, 64f
    project management and, 60–61
    tasks for, 62
    videoconferencing with, 71–73
groups
    cultural focus on, 94f
    leaders, 62
    task setting, 62
groupware, 70–71

handbooks, 118f
hand gestures. *See* gestures
handicapped, use of word, 245
handouts, for oral presentations, 592, 592f, 593t
hanging indentation, 225
hasty generalization, 188t
have, forms of, 729
hazardous-product laws, 35
headers
    as accessing tools, 262t
    coherent design and, 214–15, 216f
    formatting, 514
    for Web sites, 284, 285f
headings
    back-to-back, 202, 203
    capitalization of, 718
    coherent, 201–3
    cultural considerations, 150–51, 206
    grammatical form, 203
    informative, 201, 202, 203
    in lab reports, 492
    levels of, 275
    line spacing and, 272f, 273f, 275
    long noun strings in, 203
    organizational pattern and, 152
    page design and, 275
    in recommendation reports, 513
    revision guidelines, 203
    separating with text, 202–3
    skimming, 630
    styles and, 215
    in tables of contents, 513
    writer's checklist for, 216

hearing impairment, Web site design for, 287
helping verbs, 728
help section, in manuals, 570f, 572
Helvetica family of type, 269f
heuristic evaluation, 348–49
highlighting features, in word processors, 68
Hoft, Nancy L., 92
home page
    design of, 291f
    links on, for Web sites, 285
honesty
    in answering questions, 600
    data in lab reports and, 485
    editing and, 344, 345
    in graphics, 300
    in job-application materials, 399
    in marketing your organization, 618
    as measure of excellence, 10
    in oral presentations, 600
    in progress reports, 465
    in proposals, 440
honors, listing on résumés, 401, 408f
horizontal axis, on graphs, 300, 323
horizontal bar graphs, 316f
horizontal rules, 276t
Horton, William, 310, 333
how-to manuals. *See* manuals
how-to titles, in instructions, 563
humor, 246
hyperlinks. *See* links
hyphens
    linking compound adjective with, 689
    in noun strings, 238
    uses of, 703–5

icons, as accessing tools, 261t, 569f
idea generation, 43, 44t–45t
identifying information, in chronological résumés, 399
idioms, 99, 288
IEEE Standards Style Manual, 637–38
IEEE style, 657–65
    for bibliography annex entries, 658–65
    elements in, 657
    for textual citations, 658
IFBs (information for bids), 434, 434f–435f, 441
ignorance, argument from, 186t

illustrations, lists of, 513–15, 515f, 522
imperative mood
    dangling modifiers and, 233
    in instructions, 565
implied warranty, 29, 29f
impromptu presentations, 579
inadequate sampling, 188t
inches, page grids using, 265, 265f
incidental information, setting off, 698
incident reports, 459, 472f
    writer's checklist for, 475
    writing, 472–73
indentation
    APA reference list style for, 644
    hanging, 225
    MLA works cited style for, 670
independence, in U.S. culture, 710
independent clauses
    linking dependent clauses to, 684–85
    semicolons and, 695
    in sentences, 713–14
indexes
    in manuals, 572
    newspaper, 122–23
    periodical, 122
    skimming, 630
indicative abstracts, 511
indicative mood, 233
indirect costs, for proposals, 444
individuals, cultural focus on, 94f
industry standards, in manuals, 572
infinitives, 718
informal language, 233–34
information. *See also* online information
    evaluating, in research, 128–30
    in headings, 201, 202, 203
    new, emphasizing in sentences, 225–26
informational constraints, and persuasive writing, 179–80
informational reports. *See also* reports
    activity reports, 464
    directives, 461–62
    field reports, 463–64
    honesty in, 465
    kinds of, 459
    progress reports, 464–71
    status reports, 464–65
    uses of, 459

informational reports (*continued*)
    writer's checklist for, 475
    writing process, 459–61
information centers, 110
information for bids (IFBs), 434,
    435*f*, 441
information organization, 149–71
    audience analysis and, 150–51
    cause and effect, 153*f*, 167–69,
      170*f*, 171
    chronological, 152*f*, 154, 154*f*, 171
    classification and partition,
      153*f*, 162, 166*f*, 171
    comparison and contrast, 153*f*,
      159–60, 161*f*, 163, 171
    conventional patterns of, 151
    cultural variables and, 150–51
    displaying pattern of, 151–52
    general-to-specific, 152*f*, 154*f*,
      157, 171
    more-important-to-less-
      important, 152*f*, 158,
      159*f*, 171
    multiple patterns in single
      document, 154*f*
    partition, 153*f*, 154*f*, 162, 166*f*
    patterns of, 152–69
    principles of, 150–52
    problem-methods-solution,
      153*f*, 166–67, 171
    spatial, 152*f*, 154–56, 171
information retention, 254
information sources. *See*
    documentation of sources;
    sources
informative abstracts, 482, 511,
    512, 515
informed consent, in usability
    testing, 354, 355
-*ing* verbs, 563, 717
inoffensive language, 242–45
inquiry letters
    primary research using, 138
    when to use for research, 118*f*
inspections, as primary research,
    133–34
Institute of Electrical and
    Electronics Engineers. *See*
    IEEE style
instructions, 558–73
    articles (*a, an, the*) in, 565
    audience for, 58–59
    brief, 562
    conclusions, 563, 566, 570*f*

cultural attitudes toward, 334
defined, 540, 558
designing, 558–60
drafting, 562–66
editing, 566
environment for, 502
feedback statements in, 565
general introductions, 563, 564
general-to-specific
    organizational pattern
    for, 157
graphics for, 311*f*, 325–32,
    560, 565
imperative mood in, 565
liability law and, 29, 30
list of tools and materials in, 568*f*
manuals differentiated
    from, 572
multilingual, 559
numbering, 564–65
organization of, 563
page design in, 559–60, 560*f*, 567*f*
process descriptions vs., 558
proofreading, 566
readers' expectations about, 558
revising, 566
safety information in, 560–62,
    562*f*, 563*f*, 564, 569*f*
samples, 566–70
step-by-step, 563, 564–65
steps in, 565
title, 563
uses of, 558
writer's checklist for, 574
writing process for, 558
interactive sample documents
    analyzing evidence in
      arguments, 183
    ASCII résumés, 414
    coherent paragraphs, 214
    commercial templates, 50
    comparing and contrasting
      honestly, 164
    conciseness and simplicity, 243
    critiquing drafts, 70
    cultural variables in business
      letters, 100–101
    e-mail netiquette, 383
    evaluating information from
      Internet sources, 131–32
    graphics in, 322
    instructions, 571
    integrating graphics and text on
      slides, 594

page design analysis, 283
persuasive directive, 462
intercultural communication. *See*
    cultural considerations;
    multicultural audiences
interests, listing on résumés,
    404–5
interjections, 702
interlibrary loans, 122
internal proposals
    defined, 433
    readers' needs in, 437
    sample, 447–50
    uses of, 433–34
International Organization for
    Standardization (ISO), 561
international proposals, 438
interpersonal conflict, 59
interpersonal skills, 8
interpreters, 594
interviews. *See also* job interviews
    APA reference list style for, 656
    audience analysis using, 86
    choosing respondents for, 136
    concluding, 137–38
    conducting, 137
    MLA works cited style for, 680
    preparing for, 136–37
    presenting data from, 138
    primary research using, 136–38
    transcripts or excerpts of,
      138, 139*f*
    of SMEs and usability experts, in
      usability evaluation, 348
    of users, in usability evaluation,
      347–48
    when to use for research,
      118*f*, 119*f*
introductions
    cultural variables and, 150–51
    in instructions, 563, 564
    in job-application letters, 417
    to lab reports, 482, 491, 496
    to lists, 205
    in oral presentations, 583
    in progress reports, 467
    in proposals, 432, 441, 442, 448,
      449, 452
    in recommendation reports,
      508–9, 524
    skimming, 630
introductory series, 697–98
introductory words, 691–92
invisible writing, 48

issue number
    APA reference list style for,
        648, 652
    IEEE reference list style for,
        662, 663
    MLA works cited style for,
        674, 678
italics, 269, 572, 702–3

Japanese readers, 96
jargon, 98, 237
job advertisements, 393, 418
job-application letters
    concluding paragraph in, 420
    education paragraph in, 418–19,
        420, 421f
    employment paragraph in,
        419–20
    enclosure line in, 417
    extracurricular activities in, 418
    introductory paragraph in,
        417–18
    persuasive writing in,
        191, 192f
    selectivity and development in,
        415–17
    self-confidence in, 418
    unsolicited letters to
        organizations, 394, 418
    writer's checklist for, 426
    writing, 415–22
job-application materials, 389–426
    honesty in, 399
    for international positions, 392
    portfolio for, 392
    preparation process for, 390,
        391f, 392
job boards, 393, 425
job fairs, 390
job hunting, 390–92
    application letter preparation
        in, 391f
    learning about employers and,
        390–92
    methods in, 393–94
    preparing for job interviews in,
        391f, 422–24
    preparing materials for, 392
    résumé writing in, 391f,
        395–415
    self-inventory for, 390
    social-networking sites and,
        394–95
    writer's checklist for, 426

writing interview follow-up
    letters in, 391f, 425–26
writing job-application letters
    for, 415–22
job interviews
    follow-up letters after, 425–26
    preparing for, 422–24
    writer's checklist for, 426
job offers
    letters accepting, 425–26
    letters rejecting, 425
job specialty, collaboration based
    on, 58f
journal articles. See also magazine
    articles; periodical articles
    APA reference list style for,
        651, 652
    classification organizational
        pattern for, 162
    IEEE reference list style for, 661
    MLA works cited style for, 673
    when to use for research, 118f
journal indexes, 122
journalistic questions, 44t
justice, 20
justification
    justified type (full justification),
        272–75
    left justification, 272, 273, 275
    page design and, 272–75
    setting, 274

key terms. See also definitions
    defining for multicultural
        audiences, 541
    in recommendation reports, 509
    repeating, for coherence,
        213, 214
    variation in, 213
keywords
    lab report titles with, 481, 491
    tagged content on Web sites
        using, 124–26, 125f, 126f

labels
    for appendices, 518
    capitalization of, 718
    for graphics, 300
    for photographs, 329
lab reports, 478–95
    abstract in, 482, 491
    acknowledgments in, 486, 486f
    appendices in, 486–88
    basic elements of, 481

conclusion in, 486
discussion section in, 485–86, 494
evaluating, 487–88
formulas in, 482, 483
how to read, 480
introduction to, 482, 491
materials and methods section
    in, 483–84, 492
persuasion and, 479–80
presenting data honestly in, 485
references in, 486, 495
results section in, 484–85, 493
sample, 491–95
science and engineering
    articles and, 488–89
structure of, 481–88
title in, 481, 491
writer's checklist in, 496
writing process for, 480
language
    discriminatory, 38
    effective, in oral presentations,
        594–96
    memorable, in oral
        presentations, 595
    questions on questionnaires
        and, 140
    in Web site design, 288, 291f
language ability, listing on
    résumés, 405
language choice
    for correspondence, 382–84
    cultural considerations and,
        334, 382–84
    for instructions, 559
    for manuals, 572
laser printer paper, 259
lawsuits, liability, 29
layout settings, in word-processing
    programs, 259
leading, in page design, 271
lead-ins, for lists, 205, 224
learning theory, and page design,
    263–64
lectures
    APA reference list style
        for, 655
    MLA works cited style for, 681
left justification, 272, 273, 275
legal cases, MLA works cited style
    for, 681
legal constraints, and persuasive
    writing, 178
legal counsel, and copyright, 27

legal obligations, 20, 25–30
  codes of conduct in, 34
  contract law and, 29
  copyright law and, 25–26
  corporate culture and, 31–33
  editing and, 344
  liability law and, 29, 30
  plagiarism and reuse of
    information and, 28
  trademark law and, 26–27, 28
  writer's checklist for, 39
legibility, of graphics for oral
    presentations, 587
length
  of paragraphs, 209–11, 288
  of sentences, 227–29, 288
letter of transmittal, in
    recommendation reports,
    511, 519
letters, MLA works cited style
    for, 680
liability law
  ethical communication and, 36
  guidelines for abiding by, 30
  legal obligations under, 29, 29f
  multicultural considerations
    in, 35
libraries
  information centers, 119
  online databases in, 121
Likert-scale questions, 140f, 142f
line breaks, hyphenating, 714
line drawings, 331, 332f
line graphs, 323f
  color for, 323
  creating, 323
  grid lines, 323
  horizontal and vertical axes on,
    300, 323
  plotting multiple lines on, 323
  proportions in, 323
  uses of, 310f, 323
line lengths, and page design, 271
line spacing
  for headings, 275
  modifying, 274
  page design and, 271–72,
    272f, 273f
linguistic variables, 92
links
  placing definitions in, 547
  Web page design and, 289, 290
  Web site design and, 285,
    286, 291f

listening
  collaboration and, 8
  in meetings, 61
  U.S. communication style, 721
list of illustrations, in
    recommendation reports,
    513–15, 515f, 522
list of symbols, 517, 518f
list of tables, 513, 522
list of tools and materials, 568f
list of works, 518. *See also*
    references
lists
  advantages of, 204–5
  breaking up, 223
  bulleted, 222, 223, 226,
    587, 591f
  coherent, 204–6
  effective use of, 222–25
  lead-ins for, 205, 224
  for multicultural audiences, 206
  numbered, 158, 223, 226
  paragraph division into, 211
  paragraphs vs., 204, 204f
  parallel structure of, 223–24
  punctuation of, 224
  in résumés, 396
  Tech Tip for, 226
  used instead of paragraphs,
    204–5, 211
  uses of, 204
  writer's checklist for, 247
lists of abbreviations, 517
lists of figures, 513
logical fallacies
  in cause-and-effect
    organizational pattern, 169
  persuasive writing and
    avoiding, 186, 194
  writer's checklist for, 194
logical organization, 199
logical relationships, graphics for,
    298, 310f, 325
logic boxes, 504, 504f
logic trees, 311f, 328–29, 329f
long sentences, 227
loose-leaf binders, 260t
Lord, David, 239
lowercase letters, 270, 270f

magazine articles. *See also* journal
    articles; periodical articles
  APA reference list style for, 649
  IEEE reference list style for, 661

MLA works cited style for, 675
  when to use for research, 118f
main ideas, 61
main points
  in field reports, 463
  in oral presentations, 583
maintenance tips, 566
male-gender words, 242, 244
management approval, 104–5
management overview, 515
management summary, 515
managing projects, 60–61
mandatory language, 569f
mannerisms, 599
manuals
  back matter in, 572
  front matter in, 572
  instructions differentiated
    from, 572
  organization of, 572
  page design in, 569f
  safety information in, 572
  writing, 572–73
maps
  from clip art, 332, 333f
  color on, 333f
  MLA works cited style
    for, 681
  uses of, 311f
marginal glosses
  page design and, 267, 276,
    277t, 280f
  placing definitions in, 547
margins
  page design and, 267f
  purposes of, 266–67
  on résumés, 395
  setting up, 259
  typical widths, 267, 267f
marketing, 618
master page design, 588
materials and methods section,
    in lab reports, 483–84,
    492, 496
materials list of, 568f
matrixes, 505, 505f
measurement units, in tables, 313
mechanics, 702–8
  abbreviations, 707–8
  angle brackets, 703
  capitalization, 708
  hyphens, 703–5
  italics, 702–3
  numbers, 705–7

mechanism descriptions
   defined, 549
   detail in, 552–53
   example of, 555f
   introducing, 551
medium, MLA works cited style
      for, 670
meeting minutes, 459, 474f
   templates for, 473
   writer's checklist for, 475
   writing, 473
meetings
   agenda for, 61, 65
   attendance, 65
   collaboration and, 65
   conducting, 61–67
   critiquing work of others, 67, 68,
      70, 73
   diplomatic communication in,
      65–67
   effective listening, 61
   efficient, 65
   electronic tools for, 67
   face-to-face, 65
   recording decisions made
      in, 65
   summarizing
      accomplishments, 65
   videoconferencing for, 71–73
memorable language, 595
memorized presentations, 579
memos
   comparison and contrast
      organizational pattern
      for, 159
   cultural considerations, 382–84
   general-to-specific
      organizational pattern
      for, 157
   informational reports in form
      of, 459
   MLA works cited style for, 680
   progress reports in form of,
      467–71
   proposals in form of, 447
   writer's checklists for, 385
men
   nonsexist language and
      references to, 242–44
   speech patterns of, 73
methods
   in field reports, 463
   in problem-methods-solution
      organizational pattern, 166

metric system, 92
milestones, 62, 63f
military experience, listing on
      résumés, 405
MILSPEC, 561
minutes. See meeting minutes
misplaced modifiers, 232–33
MLA style, 665–82
   for textual citations, 666–69
   for works cited entries, 669–82
MLA Style Manual and Guide to
      Scholarly Publishing, 638
mobility impairment, and Web site
      design, 287
modal verbs, 718
models, in oral presentations, 593t
moderation, 189
Modern Language Association
      (MLA). See MLA style
modesty, 189
modifiers
   dangling, 233
   effective use of, 230–33
   imperative mood, 233
   indicative mood, 233
   misplaced, 232–33
   nonrestrictive, 231
   relative pronouns in, 231
   restrictive, 231
   squinting, 232
modular documents, 103, 103f
more-important-to-less-important
      organizational pattern, 159f
   defined, 158
   guidelines, 158
   kind of information presented
      using, 153f
   signposts for, 158
   usefulness of, 158
   writer's checklist for, 171
motion, showing in graphics,
      332–33, 333f
motion pictures
   APA reference list style
      for, 656
   MLA works cited style for, 682
motivation, and collaboration, 59
multicultural audiences, 90–96.
      See also cultural
      considerations
   "beneath the surface" variables,
      93, 94f–95f
   collaboration and, 74
   color and, 309, 334

considering cultural variables
      in writing, 95–96, 97f–98f
correspondence, 382–84
definitions, 541
design and, 99
document design and, 99
easy-to-translate text, 246
editing and, 344
ethical communication with,
      35–36
graphics for, 99, 299, 333–35
headings, 206
informational reports, 461
information organization for,
      150–51
international job
      applications, 392
international proposals, 438
interpreters and translators
      for, 594
lists, 206
manuals and, 572–73
modular documents for, 103, 103f
"on the surface" variables, 92–93
oral presentations, 594, 600
persuasive writing and, 189–91
recommendation reports and,
      507–8
research strategies for, 119
revising and, 52–53
usability evaluation and, 349
Web site design for, 287–88
writing definitions for, 541
writing for, 95–96, 97f–98f, 98–99
multilingual writers' (ESL)
      guidelines, 710–24
   adjectives, 722–23
   adverbs, 723–24
   articles, 721–22
   conditions, 720–21
   cultural considerations, 710–12
   helping verbs and main verbs,
      718–19
   infinitives, 718
   -ing form of verbs, 717
   linking ideas by
      coordination, 724
   linking ideas by
      subordination, 715
   omitted words, 724
   repeated words, 724
   sentence characteristics, 712–14
   subject-verb agreement, 719–20
   verb tenses, 715–17

multiple audiences, 103
multiple authors
    APA citations style for, 642, 643
    APA reference list style for, 645
    IEEE reference list style for, 659
    MLA works cited style for, 670–72
multiple-choice questions, 140f
multiple sources in one citation,
        APA citation style for, 643
multivolume works
    APA reference list style for, 647
    MLA textual citations style
        for, 669
    MLA works cited style for, 673

navigation
    design and readability and, 8
    Web site, 285
negation, in extended
        definitions, 546
negative constructions, 237–38
negative space, 265. *See also*
        white space
nervousness
    coping with, 598
    oral presentations and, 597
netiquette, 379, 380–81, 381f–382f
network diagrams, 445, 445 (illus.)
networking sites, 394–95
newsgroup postings, APA reference
        list style for, 654
newsletter articles, APA reference
        list style for, 649
newsletters, 610–11
    design of, 613
    distribution of, 611
    front page of, 611, 612f
    guidelines for, 611
    as a one-way application, 610
    typical news items in, 610–11
    writer's checklist for, 626
newspaper articles
    APA reference list style for,
        649, 654
    IEEE reference list style
        for, 661
    MLA works cited style for, 675
newspapers
    indexes, 122–23
    print vs. online versions
        of, 123
nominalizations, 229, 241
Non-Designer's Design Book, The
        (Williams), 255

non-English books
    APA reference list style
        for, 647
    MLA works cited style for, 673
nonfluencies, in oral
        presentations, 599
nonnative speakers of English,
        Simplified English for,
        245–46, 572
nonprofessional positions, listing
        on résumés, 403
nonrestrictive modifiers, 231, 702
nonsexist language, 242–44
nonverbal communication, 57
notebooks, and lab reports, 480
note taking
    activities in, 631
    bibliographic information in, 631
    electronically, 630
    guidelines for, 630
    paraphrasing, 631–33
    quoting, 633
    summarizing, 634
nouns
    compound, 704
    countable common, 722
    demonstrative pronouns and,
        213–14
    plural, 699, 722
    proper, 693, 708, 722
    in sentence definitions, 543
    in sentences, 713
    trademarks as, 28
    uncountable common, 722
noun strings, 203, 238
numbered lists, 158, 223, 226
numbers
    commas clarifying, 693
    cultural variety in expressing, 92
    guidelines for using, 705–7
    parentheses with, 698
numerical information
    as evidence, 182
    graphics for, 298, 310, 310f

object descriptions
    defined, 549
    detail in, 552–53
    introducing, 551
objective statements
    in chronological résumés, 400
    in skills résumés, 411f
objectivity, and passive voice, 235
objects, in oral presentations, 593t

observations
    for primary research, 133
    usability evaluation using, 348
obvious statements, 240
Occupational Outlook Handbook, 392
Occupational Safety and Health
        Administration (OSHA), 561
ombudspersons, 36, 178
omitted words or phrases, 693, 724
100-percent bar graphs, 319t
online books, MLA works cited
        style for, 677
online catalogs, 120
online communities, APA reference
        list style for, 654
online databases, 121
online dictionaries, APA reference
        list style for, 653
online discussion groups, 118f, 121
    APA reference list style for
        postings to, 654
online encyclopedias, APA
        reference list style for, 653
online forum postings APA
        reference list style for, 654
online information, evaluating
        sources of, 128–30, 131–32
online magazine articles
    APA reference list style for, 654
    online periodical articles, MLA
        reference list style for,
        687, 688
online postings
    APA reference list style for, 655
    MLA works cited style for, 679
opinions, 57
opposing viewpoints, 184
oral presentations, 578–603
    advance organizers in, 595
    answering questions after,
        600–601
    audience analysis for, 579–80,
        581–82
    body language, 599–600
    checklist for, 603
    conclusion, 583–84
    delivering, 597–600
    effective language for, 580,
        594–96
    equipment for, 589
    evaluation form for, 600
    graphics for, 580, 584–93,
        585f–586f
    handouts for, 592, 592f, 593t

oral presentations (*continued*)
    honesty in, 600
    introduction, 583
    length of, 587
    media for, 592–93, 593t
    nervousness during, 597–98
    organization of, 580, 582–84
    preparation process, 580, 581f
    preparation time, 580
    preparing, 580–97
    presentation graphics software
        for, 587, 588, 589–90
    purpose of, 582
    rehearsing, 580, 596–97
    role of, 579–80
    slides for, 585f–586f, 587, 588,
        590f–591f, 594
    speaking notes for, 592, 592f
    speaking situation analysis for,
        580–82
    summaries in, 595
    time budgeting for, 582, 582f
    transitions in, 589, 595
    types of, 579
    U.S. communication style, 721
    voice in, 598
organization. *See also* information
        organization
    editing and, 345
    graphics and, 589
    headings and, 202
    of instructions, 563
    of manuals, 572
    of oral presentations, 582–84
    of progress and status reports,
        465–66
    of proposals, 449
    of recommendation reports,
        509, 512
    of résumés, 396
organizational culture
    cultural variables, 93, 94f
    fluidity of, 93
organizational patterns, 152–69
    cause and effect, 153f, 167–69,
        170f, 171
    chronological and partition,
        152f, 154, 154f, 171
    classification, 153f, 162, 163f,
        165, 171
    comparison and contrast, 153f,
        159–60, 161f, 163, 171
    conventional, 151
    displaying, 151–52

general-to-specific, 152f, 154f,
        157, 171
    more-important-to-less-
        important, 152f, 158, 159f, 171
    multicultural audiences and, 206
    multiple in a single
        document, 154f
    partition, 153f, 154f, 162, 166f
    problem-methods-solution,
        153f, 166–67, 171
    spatial, 152f, 154–56, 171
    supporting information in
        paragraphs and, 209
    topic sentences and, 207–8
    writer's checklist for, 170–71
organization charts, 163, 169, 310f,
        325, 326f
organizations, as sources
    APA citation style for, 642
    APA reference list style for, 645
    IEEE reference list style for, 659
    MLA textual citations style
        for, 668
    MLA works cited style for, 672
orienters to time and space, 226
outline view
    checking for coherence with,
        199, 200f
    editing and, 345
    Tech Tip for using, 46
overhead projectors, 593t
oversimplifying, 188t
overstatement
    in cause-and-effect
        organizational pattern, 169
    in progress and status
        reports, 466
overview
    in manuals, 572
    topic sentence containing, 207

page count, 259
page design, 263–83. *See also* design
    analyzing, 279–82
    boxes and, 281f
    chunking, 263, 263f
    color and, 281f
    complex, 281f
    filtering, 264, 264f
    goals of, 254
    guidelines for, 263–64, 559–60
    for instructions, 558, 560f, 567f
    layout, 263–67
    learning theory and, 263–64

poor design, 282f
    queuing, 264, 264f
    three-column layout, 281f
    two-column layout, 279f
    white space and, 280f
    writer's checklist for, 292
page grids, 265, 266f
    picas and inches in, 265, 265f
    three-panel brochure, 266f
    two-column layout, 266f
    two-page, 266f
page layout, 263–67
    margins and, 266–67
    page grids in, 265, 265f, 266f
    typography and, 268–78
    white space in, 265–67
page numbering, 262t
page numbers
    APA reference list style for,
        644–45
    IEEE reference list style for, 659
    MLA textual citations style
        for, 667
    MLA works cited style for, 670,
        674, 678
    page numbers in documents,
        format of, 514
    page numbers in periodicals, APA
        reference list style for, 648
    page numbers in tables of
        contents, 513
page size, 259
pamphlets
    APA reference list style for, 655
    MLA works cited style for, 680
paper, 259–60
paper size, 259
paragraphs
    body, 206
    coherence of, 206–14
    cultural considerations, 150–51
    demonstrative pronouns in,
        213–14
    dividing into smaller units,
        210–11
    double-spacing between, in
        e-mail, 382f
    editing and, 345
    introductory, for job-application
        letters, 417–18
    length of, 209–11, 288
    lists used instead of, 204–5, 211
    lists vs., 204, 204f
    repeating key words in, 213

paragraphs (*continued*)
  structuring clearly, 207–10
  supporting information in, 209
  topic sentences in, 207–8
  transitional, 207–8, 210
  transitional words and phrases
    in, 211–12, 214t
  writer's checklist for, 217
parallel structure
  for items in a series, 230
  for lists, 223–24
  for proposal tasks, 450
  for sentences, 230
paraphrasing
  APA citation style for, 641
  documentation of, 637
  example of, 632f
  guidelines for, 633
  note taking for, 631–33
  titles in, 201, 633
parentheses, 698
parenthetical comments, 697
parenthetical definitions, 541–42
part-by-part pattern, 160
part-by-part section, in
    descriptions, 552
particular descriptions, 550
partition
  defined, 162
  extended definitions, 544–45
partition organizational
    pattern, 166f
  guidelines for, 164
  kind of information presented
    using, 153f
  uses for, 154f, 162
passive voice
  appropriate use of, 234–36
  in instructions, 565
  in lab reports, 484
  locating with grammar
    checkers, 236
  in résumés, 402–3
past perfect progressive tense, 717
past perfect tense, 690, 716, 719
past progressive tense, 716
past speculation, and verb tense, 721
past tense, 494
  simple, 715–16
patterns. *See also* organizational
    patterns
  creating with color, 307, 308f
  fill, for pie charts, 324
peer reviews, 489

people, graphic portrayal of, 335
people-first approach, 245
perfect binding, 260t
perfect progressive tenses, 716
perfect tenses, 716
periodical articles. *See also* journal
    articles; magazine articles
  APA reference list style for, 648
  MLA works cited style for, 674
  online, MLA works cited style
    for, 677, 678
periodical indexes, 122
periodicals
  APA reference list style for, 644,
    647–49
  IEEE reference list style for,
    661, 662
  MLA works cited style for, 673–75
periodical titles
  APA reference list style for,
    648, 652
  IEEE reference list style for, 659,
    662, 663
  MLA works cited style for, 669,
    674, 678
periods
  in abbreviations, 696, 707–8
  comma splices and, 685
  run-on sentences and, 686
  uses of, 696
persona
  creating, 189
  defined, 189
  writer's checklist for, 194
personal characteristics, of
    readers, 82
personal communication
  APA citation style for, 643
  APA reference list style for, 656
personal constraints, and
    persuasive writing, 180
personal growth, and persuasive
    writing, 178
personal information, on résumés,
    404–5, 410f
personal interviews
  APA reference list style for, 656
  MLA works cited entry for, 680
persuasive writing, 176–94
  audience analysis and, 177–78
  connecting with the public and,
    609–10
  corporate use of, 192f
  crafting an argument, 180–85

cultural variables and,
    189–91, 438
  design and, 189–91
  examples of, 191–93
  graphics and, 189–91, 193f
  job-application letters and,
    191, 192f
  lab reports and, 479–80
  logical fallacies and, 186,
    186t–188t, 194
  photographs in, 190f, 192,
    192f, 193f
  real and expressed purpose
    in, 104
  uses of, 177
  writer's checklist for, 194
phantom drawings, 332f
photocopy paper, 259
photographs
  cropping, 329, 330f
  labeling, 329
  MLA works cited style for, 681
  perspective of, 329
  persuasive communication
    with, 190f, 192, 192f, 193f
  presenting effectively, 329
  scale of, 329
  for slide presentations, 591f
  uses of, 311f
  for visual information, 190f, 329
  white papers with, 616
phrases
  clarity of, 234–39
  conciseness of, 239–42
  formality of, 233–34
  inoffensive language and, 242–45
  in lists, and punctuation, 224
  writer's checklist for, 247
picas, 265, 265f
pictographs, 310f, 320, 321f
"Pictures Please—Presenting
    Information Visually"
    (Horton), 310
pie charts, 310f, 324, 324f, 448
pilot usability tests, 352
pitch, in oral presentations, 599
pity, appeal to, 186t
plagiarism, 28
planning, 42–47
  audience analysis in, 42–43
  collaboration pattern and, 58f
  design and, 257
  generating ideas about subject
    and, 43, 44t–45t

planning (*continued*)
    in project management, 60
    purpose and, 43
    researching additional
        information during, 43–44
    writer's checklist for, 54
plan of work, in proposals, 442–43
plural abbreviations, 707
plural nouns, 699, 722
plural pronouns, and sexist
    language, 244
podcasts
    APA reference list style for, 654
    connecting with the public
        using, 610, 618–19
    defined, 618
    directory, 619, 619*f*
    as a one-way application, 610
    research using, 121
    writer's checklist for, 626
pointers, in oral presentations, 599
points (type size), 270–71
political constraints, and
    persuasive writing, 178–79
political variables, and culture, 92
Porter, Alan, 624
portfolios, for job-application
    materials, 392
positive constructions, 237–38
possession, 700
post hoc reasoning, 188*t*
PowerPoint, 588. *See also*
    presentation slides
precise terms
    formality level and, 234
    in titles, 200–201
    using, 236
prefaces
    for manuals, 572
    skimming, 630
prefixes, 714
preliminary research, for
    proposals, 443
preliminary results, in progress
    and status reports, 466
prepositional phrases, avoiding
    unnecessary, 240–41
preprint articles, APA reference list
    style for, 651
presentation-graphics software,
    587, 588, 589–90
presentation of self, 189
presentations, oral. *See* oral
    presentations

presentation slides, 585*f*–586*f*,
    590*f*–591*f*
    APA reference list style for, 654
    integrating graphics and text
        on, 594
    numbers for, 591*f*
present future speculation, and
    verb tense, 721
present participles, 717
present perfect progressive
    tense, 717
present perfect tense, 716, 719
present progressive tense, 716
present tense, 690, 716
press releases
    articles based on, 107*f*
    defined, 106*f*
    example of, 106*f*
    revising information for a new
        audience, 105, 107*f*
primary audience, 83, 102
primary research, 133–43
    categories of, 133
    defined, 114
    demonstrations, 133
    e-mails, 138
    experiments, 134
    field research, 135
    inquiry letters, 138
    inspections, 133–34
    interviews, 136–38
    observations, 133
    for progress reports, 469
    in proposals, 449
    questionnaires for, 138–43
    in research process, 116*f*
    selecting methods of, 116–19
principal investigators, 443
principles of operation, 545
printable version of Web sites, 286
print media
    evaluating sources of, in
        research, 128–30
    when to use for research,
        118*f*–119*f*
private life, vs. business life, 94*f*
problem-methods-solution
    organizational pattern
    components of, 166
    description of, 166–67, 168*f*
    guidelines for, 167
    kind of information presented
        using, 153*f*
    logical sequence for, 167

problems
    in problem-methods-solution
        organizational pattern, 166
problem-solving method, 502–7
procedures, in lab reports,
    483, 493
process descriptions, 557*f*
    defined, 549
    detail in, 552–53
    example, 554
    graphics for, 298, 311*f*, 325–32
    instructions vs., 558
    introducing, 551
    writer's checklist for, 573–74
product descriptions, 162,
    192, 193*f*
professional appearance, as
    measure of excellence, 14
professional experience, of
    readers, 82
professional growth, 178
professionalism, 439
professional persona, 189
professional placement
    bureaus, 393
profiles, on social-networking
    sites, 395
progressive tenses, 716
progress reports, 459, 464–71
    conclusions of, 466
    Gantt charts in, 469
    honesty in, 465
    organization of, 465–66, 468
    for research projects, 436
    sample, 466–71
    secondary research for, 469
    summaries for, 467
    writer's checklist for, 475
project budgets, 115*f*
project descriptions, as
    proposals, 451
project management, 60–61
project reports, 436, 501. *See also*
    recommendation reports
project schedules
    honesty in progress reports
        about, 465
    research and, 115*f*
pronoun-antecedent agreement,
    689–90
pronouns
    ambiguous references, 686–87
    antecedents, 686–87
    for easy-to-translate text, 246

pronouns (*continued*)
  relative, 686–87
  verb agreement with, 720
proofreading, 42, 53–54
  abbreviations, 683
  defined, 53
  e-mail, 381*f*, 382*f*
  instructions, 566
  of proposals, 433
  reading aloud for, 346
  résumés, 396
  reviewing with, 346
  symbols, 709
  writer's checklists for, 54, 356
proper nouns
  articles and, 722
  capitalization for, 708
  commas separating, 693
proposals, 431–52
  budget information in, 432, 438,
    439, 443–44, 450, 452
  comparison-and-contrast
    organizational pattern
    for, 159
  credentials in, 439, 450
  deliverables, 435–37
  demonstrating
    professionalism, 439
  drafting, 432
  evaluation techniques in,
    445–47, 449
  external, 433
  goods and services, 436–37
  honesty in, 440
  internal, 433–34, 437, 447–50
  international, 438
  introductions, 432, 441, 442,
    448–49, 452
  logistics of, 433–35, 433 (illus.)
  in memo format, 447–50
  more-important-to-less-
    important organizational
    pattern for, 158
  partition organizational pattern
    for, 162
  plan description, 438–39
  plan of work in, 442–43
  problem-methods-solution
    organizational pattern
    for, 166
  progress reports and, 467
  project description in, 451
  proposal tasks in, 449–50
  purpose of, 432

qualifications and experience
  section, 432, 443, 452
readers' needs and, 437–38
references in, 450
research, 436
resources needed for writing,
  440–41
sample internal proposal, 447–50
solicited, 434
statement of purpose in, 447
structure of, 441–47
summaries in, 441, 447, 452
tables in, 444, 444*f*
task schedules, 439, 444, 448,
  449–50
types of, 433
unsolicited, 434, 437–38
writer's checklist for, 452
writing process, 432–33
proposed programs, 432
proprietary information, statement
  of, 511
prototypes, 346–47, 347*f*
proximity, in design, 255, 255*f*
publication date
  APA reference list style for, 646,
    648, 650, 652
  IEEE reference list style for, 660,
    662, 663
  MLA works cited style for, 671,
    674, 676, 678
publication information
  APA reference list style
    for, 644
  IEEE reference list style
    for, 659
  MLA works cited style for, 669
*Publication Manual of the American
  Psychological Association*
  (APA), 637. *See also* APA style
published interviews, APA
  reference list style for, 656
publisher information
  APA reference list style for, 646
  IEEE reference list style for, 660
  MLA works cited style for, 671
publishing bodies, evaluating in
  research, 130
pull quotes, 276, 277t, 616
punctuation, 691–702
  apostrophes, 699–700
  colons, 695–96
  commas, 685, 688–89, 691–95,
    701, 714

dashes, 697–98, 701
ellipses, 633–34, 701–2
exclamation points, 696–97
  of lists, 224
parentheses, 698
periods, 685, 686, 696, 707–8
question marks, 697, 699
quotation marks, 697, 700–701
semicolons, 685, 686, 695, 714
purpose. *See also* writing purpose
  of graphics, 302
  headings and, 202
  in reading documents, 83
  of oral presentations, 582, 583
purpose statements, for progress
  reports, 467

qualifications-and-experience
  section, for proposals, 432,
    443, 452
qualifications summary, in
  chronological résumés, 400
qualifiers, verb agreement
  with, 720
qualifying information, placement
  in sentences, 226
qualitative evaluations, for
  proposals, 445–46
quantitative data, APA reference
  list style for, 653
quantitative evaluations, for
  proposals, 447
question-and-answer sessions,
  600–601
question marks, and quotation
  marks, 697, 701
questionnaires
  administering, 141
  asking effective questions
    on, 140
  common types of questions on,
    140t–141t
  presenting data from, 141–43
  primary research using, 138–43
  problems with data from, 139–40
  progress reports using, 470–71
  testing, 141
  when to use for research, 119*f*
questions
  commonly used on
    questionnaires, 140t–141t
  diplomatic communication
    using, 65–67
  in interviews, 136, 137

questions (*continued*)
    in job interviews, 423
    Likert-scale, 140*f*, 142*f*
    multiple choice, 140*f*
    in oral presentations, 584
    ranking, 140*f*
    short answer, 141*f*, 142*f*
    short essay, 141*f*
    in usability testing, 352–53
queuing, and page design, 264, 264*f*
quotation marks
    question marks and, 697
    uses of, 700–701
quotations
    APA citation style for, 641
    commas introducing, 693
    documentation of, 637
    ellipses in, 633–34
    MLA works cited style for, 668
    note taking for, 631, 633
    in oral presentations, 596

radio programs, MLA works cited
        style for, 681
ranking questions, 140*f*
ranks, distance between, 94*f*
raw data, APA reference list style
        for, 653
readability
    case and, 270
    design and, 8
    typefaces and, 269
readers. *See also* audience
    attitudes toward subject, 84
    attitudes toward writer, 84
    cultural characteristics of, 82
    education of, 82
    expectations of, 43, 84–85
    factors in identifying, 82
    how document will be used
        by, 85
    job responsibilities of, 82
    personal characteristics of, 82
    personal preferences of, 82
    physical environment of, 85
    professional experience of, 82
    reading skills of, 85
reading aloud, in proofreading, 346
reading skill, 85
read-throughs, 438
"real" subjects, in sentences,
        228–29
"real" verbs, in sentences, 229
reasoning, in arguments, 181

recognition, and persuasive
        writing, 178
recommendation reports, 500–535
    abstract in, 511–12, 521
    appendices in, 518, 534
    back matter in, 516–18
    body of, 508–9
    conclusions in, 510, 532
    cover of, 511
    defined, 501
    determine options in, 503*f*, 504–5
    drawing conclusions about
        options in, 503*f*, 506
    establish criteria in, 503–4, 503*f*
    executive summary in, 515, 516,
        517, 523
    formulating recommendations
        in, 503*f*, 506–7
    front matter in, 511–16
    glossary in, 516, 518*f*
    identifying the problem or
        opportunity in, 502–3, 503*f*
    introduction in, 508–9, 524
    as last link in a document
        chain, 501
    letter of transmittal in, 511, 519
    list of illustrations in, 513–15, 522
    list of symbols in, 517
    methods section in, 509, 525–26
    multicultural audiences
        and, 507–8
    problem-solving model
        for, 502–7
    recommendations made in,
        510, 532
    references in, 518, 533
    results section in, 509–10, 527
    sample, 518–34
    studying options in, 503*f*, 505–6
    table of contents in, 512–13, 522
    title page to, 511, 520
    writer's checklist for, 535–36
    writing, 507–18
    writing process for, 502
recommendations
    in recommendation reports,
        509, 510, 519, 532
    in slide presentations, 591*f*
recycled paper, 260
redundant expressions, 240
reference list entries. *See also*
        works cited entries
    APA style for, 640, 643–57
    IEEE style for, 658–65

reference manuals, chronological
        organization of, 154
references
    in lab reports, 486, 488, 490,
        495, 496
    listing on résumés, 405, 406*f*,
        408*f*, 409*f*
    for proposals, 450
    in recommendation reports,
        518, 533
    selecting, 405
    skimming, 630
reference works
    APA reference list style for, 647
    defined, 120
    guides to, 120
    MLA textual citation style for, 669
    MLA works cited style for, 673
registered trademarks, 26, 27, 36
rehearsing, of oral presentations,
        580, 596–97
relationships, and gender, 73
relative pronouns
    clarifying, 686–87
    in modifiers, 231
    verb agreement with, 720
religious variables, 92
relocation willingness, listing on
        résumés, 405
repetition
    color and, 261t, 307
    columns and, 267
    design and, 256*f*, 256
    of key terms, 213, 214
    marginal glosses and, 277t
    of safety information, 562
    of words in sentences, 724
reports. *See also* informational
        reports
    APA reference list style for,
        653, 655
    cause-and-effect organizational
        pattern for, 169
    chronological organizational
        pattern for, 154
    comparison and contrast
        organizational pattern
        for, 159
    defined, 459
    general-to-specific organizational
        pattern for, 157
    IEEE reference list style for, 664
    MLA works cited style for, 680
    modular, 103, 103*f*

reports (*continued*)
    for research projects, 436
    in usability testing, 349, 354
requests for proposals (RFPs),
    434, 441
research, 113–44
    academic vs. workplace, 114
    citing, in proposals, 442–43
    field, 135
    goal of, 114
    guidelines for, 117–18
    for informational reports, 460
    lab reports on, 485–86, 495
    planning and, 43–44
    primary, 114, 116f, 133–43, 449
    secondary, 119–32
    writer's checklist for, 144
research media
    selecting, 117
    for specific research questions,
      118f–119f
research methods
    choosing and describing, 116–19
    data recording, 117
    persistence and, 117
    in recommendation report, 525
    triangulating, 118
research process, 115, 115f–116f
research proposals
    deliverables in, 436
    preliminary research in, 443
    writing, 442–43
research questions, 118f–119f
research reports, APA reference list
    style for, 653, 655
research tools, 117, 120–23
resource links, on Web sites, 286
restrictive modifiers, 231, 694
results
    in field reports, 463
    in lab reports, 484–85, 493, 496
    in recommendation reports,
      509–10, 527
résumé-preparation agencies, 395
résumés, 395–415. *See also*
      chronological résumés; skills
      résumés
    active vs. passive voice in, 402–3
    appearance of, 395–96
    attractive vs. unattractive, 396,
      397f–398f
    chronological, 399–405,
      408f–409f, 410f
    content of, 396–99

design, 395–96
education, 400–401, 408f, 410f
electronic, 407–15
elements of, 399–405
employment history, 402–4
identifying information, 399
interests and activities, 404–5
objectives, 400
paper, 395–407
personal information on,
    404, 410f
posting on job boards, 393
references in, 405, 406f, 408f, 409f
skills, 399, 407, 411f
summary of qualifications
    on, 400
writer's checklist for, 426
writing own vs. using résumé-
    preparation agency, 395
retrieval dates
    APA reference list style for, 650
    IEEE reference list style for, 663
    MLA works cited style for,
      676, 678
reviewing, 342, 343–46
    acknowledging reviewers in, 53
    collaboration and, 69
    critiquing work of others, 67, 68,
      70, 73
    editing and, 344–46
    factors to be considered in,
      342–43
    for multicultural audiences, 99
    proofreading and, 346
    relationship among reviewing,
      evaluating, and testing,
      342, 343f
    revising and, 344
    word-processing features for, 69
review process, for scientific and
    engineering articles, 489
reviews, MLA works cited style
    for, 675
revising, 42, 51–53
    collaboration pattern and, 58f
    defined, 51
    electronic tools for
      collaboration and, 67
    informational reports, 460
    instructions, 566
    major topics to be addressed
      in, 51
    multicultural audiences and,
      52–53

for new au
of proposal, 105
reading by o
reading by th, 52–53
reviewing and ter, 52
writer's checkl 343
revision features, i, 54, 356
    processors, 6
RFPs (requests for p
    434, 441
rights, 20
ring binders, 260t
RSS aggregators
    podcasts and, 618
    on social-bookmarkin
      sites, 128
RSS feeds
    podcasts and, 618
    on social-bookmarking si
      128, 128f
rules
    defined, 276t
    horizontal, 276t
    in page layout, 276, 276t
    in tables, 314
    vertical, 276t
run-on sentences, 696

saddle binding, 260t
safety information
    design of, 37, 38f, 561
    ethics notes, 561
    in instructions, 560–62, 562f,
      563f, 564, 569f
    in manuals, 572
    placement of, 562
    repetition of, 562
    signal words in, 561,
      562f, 569f
salutations, cultural variables
    in, 101
sample documents. *See* interactive
    sample documents
samples, in oral presentations, 593t
sans-serif typefaces, 268, 269f,
    281f, 415
scannable résumés, 412, 415, 416f
schedules. *See* project schedules;
    task schedules; work
    schedules
science
    importance of articles in, 489
    notebooks kept in, 480
scientific method, 481

…EE reference

scientific reports…564
  list style

scope …, 202
  heading…idation reports,
  in reco…
    50
  screen…f, 277t
    design and, 276, 277t
  …ts
  …ng, 331
  …of, 311f, 330, 330f
  …d presentations, 579, 597
  …pages or engines, 86, 285
  …dary audience, 83, 102
…ndary research
  basic research tools in, 121–23
  conducting, 119–32
  defined, 114
  evaluating information in, 128–32
  government information in, 124
  for progress reports, 469
  in research process, 116f
  understanding media in, 120
  Web 2.0 resources in, 124–28
sections in edited books
  APA reference list style for, 647
  IEEE reference list style for, 661
  MLA textual citations style for, 668
  MLA works cited style for, 673
security, and persuasive writing, 177–78
security notices, 511
self-confidence
  in job-application letters, 418
  in oral presentations, 598
self-evaluation form, 66f
self-inventory, for job search, 390
semantic differentials, 140f
semicolons
  comma splices and, 685
  independent clauses and, 714
  misuses of, 695
  run-on sentences and, 686
  uses of, 695
sentence definitions, 542–43
sentences, 221–47
  adjectives in, 688–89, 722–23
  adverbs in, 723–24
  articles in, 721–22
  characteristics of, 712–14
  combining, 227–28

comma splices and, 685, 694
conditions, 720–21
cultural factors in writing, 438
editing and, 345
effective, 221–47
emphasis in, 225–26
fragments, 684–85
grammatical, 684–60
helping and main verbs in, 718–19
infinitives in, 718
-ing verbs in, 717
length of, 98, 227–29, 246, 288
linking ideas by coordination, 714
linking ideas by subordination, 715
lists for, 222–25
long, 227
modifiers in, 230–33
omitted words in, 724
orienters to time and space in, 226
parallel structures in, 230
pronoun-antecedent agreement in, 689–90
pronoun references in, 686–88
qualifying information in, 226
"real" subjects in, 228–29
"real" verbs in, 229
repeated words in, 724
run-on, 686
short, 227–28
structuring, 222–33
subject-verb agreement in, 689, 719–20
verb tenses and, 690, 715–17
writer's checklist for, 247
sequence
  of graphics, 333–34
  of information in lists, 205
series, items in
  commas for, 691
  parallel structure for, 230
  semicolons for, 695
series books, MLA works cited style for, 673
serif typefaces, 268, 269f, 281f
shading, in screens, 277t
shapes, creating with drawing tools, 321
short-answer questions, 141f, 142f
short-essay questions, 141f
short sentences, 227–28

signal words, 561, 562f, 569f
signatures, in e-mails, 380f
simple future tense, 716
simple past tense, 715–16
simple present tense, 716
simple tenses, 715–16
simplicity
  of presentation graphics, 587
  revising for, 243
  in Web page design, 288, 289, 290f
Simplified English, 245–46, 541, 572
site maps, for Web sites, 285, 286f
skills résumés, 399, 407
  education, 411f
  employment section on, 411f
  skills section, 407
  table format for, 411f
skimming, 630
slang, 99
slide projectors, 593t
slides, for presentations, 585f–586f, 590f–591f
  APA reference list style for, 654
  integrating graphics and text on, 594
  numbers for, 591f
Smith, T. C., 584
social-bookmarking sites, 127–28, 128f
social-networking sites, 394–95
social variables, 92
solicited proposals, 434
solution, in problem-methods-solution organizational pattern, 166
sources. See also documentation of sources
  citing on presentation slides, 591f
  indicating, for graphics, 314
  for lab reports, 486
  plagiarism and, 28
  for proposals, 450
  for recommendation reports, 409
space orienters, in sentences, 226
spacing
  APA reference list style for, 644
  IEEE reference list style for, 659
  MLA works cited style for, 670
spatial information, graphics for, 298, 311f, 329–32

spatial organizational pattern, 156f
  description of, 156
  guidelines for, 156
  kind of information presented
    using, 152f
  signposts for, 156
  topic sentences and, 208
  writer's checklist for, 171
speaker's checklist, 603
speaking. *See also* oral presentations
  in videoconferencing, 72
speaking notes, 592, 592f
specifications, in manuals, 556, 572
specificity
  ambiguity and, 236
  approximation, 237
  detail for, 236
  lab report titles and, 481
  precise words, 236
  of recommendations, 510
  questions on questionnaires
    and, 140
  in sentence definitions, 543
  of words and phrases, 234–39
speeches
  APA reference list style
    for, 655
  MLA works cited style for, 681
speed of speaking, in
    presentations, 598
spell checkers, 54
spiral binders, 260t
squinting modifiers, 232
standards, in manuals, 572
statement of proprietary
    information, 511
states, commas with, 693
status reports, 464–65
  conclusions of, 466
  organization of, 465–66
  writer's checklist for, 475
step-by-step instructions, 563,
    564–65
step-by-step section, in
    descriptions, 552
stratum bar graphs, 320f
stub head, in tables, 312f
style guides
  APA style, 637, 640–57
  company-specific, for
    reports, 511
  graphics citation format, 306
  MLA style, 638, 665–82
  for specific disciplines, 638–40

styles
  coherence and, 216
  creating, 216
  definition, 215
  modifying, 216
  using, 49
style sheets, 62
subdivided bar graphs, 319t
subheadings, 513
subject
  analyzing, 115f
  collecting information for
    proposals, 432
  formality level for, 234
  idea generation on, 43,
    44t–45t
  omitting, 734
  "real," of sentences, 228–29
  repeating, 724
  revising and, 51
  titles and, 202
subject lines
  in e-mail, 381f, 382f
  in progress reports, 467
  in proposals, 447
  in recommendation reports, 519
subject-matter experts (SMEs), 52
  usability evaluation and,
    348–49, 348f
subjects
  commas and, 694
  compound, 695
subject-verb agreement, 689,
    719–20
sublists, 223
subordinating conjunctions, 687
subordinating words or phrases, 715
subordination, linking ideas by, 715
subscription service articles, MLA
    works cited style for, 677
suffixes, 704
summaries
  APA citation style for, 641
  in oral presentations, 583, 595
  in progress reports, 467
  in proposals, 441, 447, 448,
    450, 452
  in recommendation reports, 510
summarizing
  example of, 635f, 640f–641f
  guidelines for, 634
  note taking for, 631, 634–35
summary of qualifications, in
    chronological résumés, 400

summative evaluation, for
    proposals, 447
supporting information
  in paragraphs, 209
  in presentation graphics, 584,
    585f–586f
  for topic sentences, 209
supporting letters, in proposals, 444
surveys, in usability evaluation,
    347–48
symbolic meaning of colors,
    309, 309f
symbols
  cultural considerations with, 334
  lists of, 517, 518f
  for proofreading, 781
  trademark, 27, 28, 36
synchronous discussions, 70

table of contents
  creating, 514
  multicultural audiences and, 508
  organizational pattern and, 151
  of recommendation reports,
    512–13, 522
  skimming, 630
  for Web sites, 285, 286f
table-of-contents abstracts, 511
tables
  arrangement of data in, 313–14
  captions for, 312f
  creating, 315
  cross-referencing, 262t
  defined, 309
  dot leaders in, 314
  effective, 313–14
  footnotes in, 314
  information sources, 314
  items being compared, 313
  in lab reports, 484, 494
  lists of, 513, 522
  math presented in, 314
  meeting minute templates
    using, 473
  for oral presentations, 591f
  parts of, 312f
  in proposals, 444, 444f
  rules in, 314
  saving space with, 299
  titles of, 312
  units of measure in, 313–14
  uses of, 310, 310f
  width of, 314
tabs, as accessing tools, 262t

tab stops, 315
tagged content, Web 2.0 resources, 124–26, 125f, 126f
tags, commas with, 701
task pattern, in progress and status reports, 465
tasks, and project management, 69
task schedules, for proposals, 439, 444, 448, 449–50
Tebeaux, Elizabeth, 93
technical communication, 2–15. *See also* business communication
 career development and, 6
 characteristics of, 6–10, 13f
 defined, 4–5
 importance of, 3
 interactive sample document, 9
 measures of excellence in, 10–15
technical communicators
 defined, 5
 ethical obligations of, 22–25
 legal obligations of, 25–30
technical detail, in evaluation research information, 129
technical information, photographs for, 189, 190f
technical reports
 APA reference list style for, 653, 655
 IEEE reference list style for, 664
technological variables, 92
Tech Tips
 appear and dim animation effect, 589
 bar charts (Gantt charts), 446
 boxes, 278
 bulleted lists, 226
 drawing tools, 321
 formatting columns, 268
 formatting fonts, 270
 graphics in Excel, 317
 inserting and modifying graphics, 305
 master page design in PowerPoint, 588
 modifying line spacing, 274
 modifying templates, 47
 numbered lists, 226
 outline view, 46
 page setup, 259
 review features in word processors, 68
 screen shots, 331

styles, 216
tables, 315
tab stops, 315
text boxes, 278
television programs
 APA reference list style for, 656
 MLA works cited style for, 681
templates
 commercial, 48, 50
 company-designed, 48
 for meeting minutes, 473
 for memos, 50
 modifying, 49
 for presentation graphics, 587, 592
 problems using, 48
tenses, 690, 715–17
terminal punctuation
 comma splices and, 685
 run-on sentences and, 686
tertiary audience, 83
testing. *See also* usability tests
 collaboration pattern and, 58f
 factors to be considered in, 342–43
 of questionnaires, 141
 relationship among reviewing, evaluating, and testing, 342, 343f
test plans, in usability testing, 351, 352
Texas Instruments, 31–32
text boxes, 278
text direction, 259
text-only version of Web sites, 286
text paper, 260
text résumés, preparing, 413
textual citations
 APA reference list style for, 640, 641–43
 IEEE style for, 658
 MLA works cited style for, 666–69
theses, APA reference list style for, 651
three-column page layout, 281f
three-dimensional bar graphs, 299, 300f
three-dimensional pie charts, 324
thumbnail sketches, 265, 265f
time budget, for oral presentations, 582, 582f

time-consciousness, in U.S. culture, 710
time constraints, 180, 259–60
time factor, in reviewing, evaluating, and testing, 343
timeliness of information, 130
time orienters, in sentences, 226
time pattern, in progress and status reports, 465
title pages, of recommendation reports, 511, 520
titles (of text)
 for bar graphs, 319
 coherent, 200–201
 for instructions, 563
 for lab reports, 480, 481, 491, 496
 of oral presentations, 583, 590f
 page design and, 275
 paraphrasing and, 201, 633
 for recommendation reports, 520
 for tables, 312
 working, 200
 writer's checklist for, 216
title slides, 583, 590f
tone
 in persuasive writing, 180
 in progress and status reports, 466
 in recommendations, 510
tools and materials, list of, 568f
topical abstracts, 511
topic sentences
 coherence and, 207–8, 214
 organizational pattern and, 152, 207–8
 paragraph structure and, 207–8, 210
 supporting information and, 209
towns, commas with, 703
trademark law, 26–27
trademarks
 defined, 26–27
 ethical communication and, 36
 legal obligations for, 26–27
 in manuals, 572
 protecting, 28
 symbols for, 27, 28, 36
transcripts of interviews, 138, 139f
transitional paragraphs, 207–8, 210
transitional words and phrases
 independent clauses and, 724
 paragraph coherence and, 211–12, 214, 214t
 placement of, 212

transitions, in oral presentations, 589, 595
translated books
  APA reference list style for, 647
  MLA works cited style for, 673
translation
  graphics and, 299, 541
  manuals and, 572
  oral presentations and, 594
  preparing text for, 246
  proposals and, 438
trouble reports, 472
troubleshooting guides, 566, 570*f*
truth
  cultural variables and, 95*f*
  ethical communication and, 36–37
  euphemisms and, 239
turnover lines, in lists, 225, 282*f*
two-dimensional bar graphs, 299, 300*f*
typefaces
  coherent design and, 216
  defined, 268
  serif and sans serif, 268, 269*f*, 281*f*
type families, 269, 269*f*
type size
  color and, 309
  for headings, 275
  page design and, 270–71
  for titles, 275
  using responsibly, 271
  Web site design and, 287
typography
  case, 270, 270*f*
  font formats, 270
  justification, 272–75
  line length, 271
  line spacing, 271–72, 272*f*, 273*f*
  in manuals, 572
  page layout and, 268–78
  typefaces, 268, 269*f*
  type families, 269, 269*f*
  type size, 270–71, 275, 309

uncertainty, 95*f*
uncountable common nouns, 732
underlining
  descenders and, 275
  uses of, 702–3
units of measure, in tables, 313–14
"Universal Language, The: Graphics for International Documents" (Horton), 333

university placement offices, 393
unknown authors
  APA citation style for, 642–43
  APA reference list style for, 647
  MLA textual citation style for, 668
  MLA works cited style for, 672
unpublished data, APA reference list style for, 657
unsigned articles, MLA works cited style for, 675
unsolicited proposals, 434, 437–38
uppercase letters, 270, 270*f*
URLs
  angle brackets for, 703
  APA reference list style for, 650
  MLA works cited style for, 676, 678
usability evaluations, 342, 346–49
  factors covered by, 342
  forms used in, 347–49
  liability law and, 30
  multicultural audiences and, 349
  prototype in, 346–47, 347*f*
  roles in, 347, 348*f*
  usability testing vs., 349
  writer's checklist for, 356
usability experts, 348–49, 348*f*
Usablity.gov, 355
usability labs, 239, 251, 351*f*
usability tests, 342, 349–54
  basic principles of, 350
  conducting, 352–53
  debriefing participants after, 353
  informed consent and, 354
  interpreting and reporting data from, 353–54
  pilot in, 352
  preparing for, 350–52
  purpose of, 350
  test plan in, 351, 352
  test team in, 350
  usability evaluation vs., 349
  writer's checklist for, 356
U.S. communication style, 710–12
Usenet newsgroups, 121
users of a document
  liability law and, 29, 30
  as reviewers, 52

  usability evaluation and, 347–48, 348*f*
  usability testing involving, 350
U.S. government
  goods-and-services proposals to, 436
  RFPs and IFBs issued by, 434
U.S. military, MILSPEC, 561
utility, 21
UV-coated paper, 260

verb phrases, 718
verbs
  action, for résumés, 402–3
  clarifying writing purpose with, 104
  commas and, 694
  communicating, 104
  convincing, 104
  correcting sentence fragments with, 694
  helping and main, 718
  -*ing* verbs, 717
  modal, 718
  nominalized, 229
  "real," in sentences, 229
  in sentences, 713
  subject-verb agreement, 689, 719–20
  trademarks as, 28
verb tenses, 690, 715–17
vertical axis, on graphs, 300, 323
vertical bar graphs, 316*f*
vertical rules, 276t
video
  MLA works cited style for, 682
  Web site design and, 287
videoconferencing, 71–73, 71*f*
  guidelines for, 72
  writer's checklist for, 75
visibility, of presentation graphics, 587
vision impairment, and Web site design, 287
visual aids, 298. *See also* graphics
visual information
  graphics for, 311*f*, 329–32
  photographs for, 329
  readers' needs, interests, and attitudes and, 88, 91*f*
vocabulary, 99, 438
vocalizing, 598
volume, in oral presentations, 598

volume number
APA reference list style for, 648, 652
IEEE reference list style for, 662, 663
MLA works cited style for, 674, 678
volunteer work, listing on résumés, 404

walkthroughs, 348
warnings
design and, 37, 38*f*
labels, 29, 29*f*, 30
warranties
express, 29
implied, 29, 29*f*
Web-based documents
APA reference list style for, 650
manuals, 573
portfolios on, 392
résumés, 412
Weblog posts, APA reference list style for, 654
Weblogs. *See* blogs
Web page design, 288–90
analysis of pages in, 290, 290*f*, 291*f*
clear, informative links on, 289, 290, 291*f*
easy-to-read text on, 289
honesty in, 288
simplicity and, 288, 289
writer's checklist for, 292
Web site design, 284–88
back-to-top links in, 285
extra features, 285–87
FAQs, 285
headers and footers, 284
home page links, 285
links, 285, 286
multicultural audiences and, 287–88
navigation and, 285
printable version, 286
readers with disabilities and, 287
resource links on, 286
search pages or engines, 86, 285
site maps and, 285, 286*f*
table of contents, 285, 286*f*
text-only version, 286
writer's checklist for, 292

Web sites
audience analysis by searching for information on, 86–88
graphics on, 305
IEEE reference list style for, 664
job listings on, 393
MLA works cited style for, 675, 676
newspapers on, 123
periodicals on, 122
social-networking sites on, 394–95
when to use for research, 118*f*, 119*f*
Web 2.0
RSS feeds on, 128, 128*f*
social-bookmarking sites on, 127–28, 128*f*
secondary research using, 121, 124–28
tagged content on, 124–26, 125*f*, 126*f*
when to use for research, 119*f*
WebWorks, 624
whistleblowing, 33
White, Jan V., 307
whiteboards, 71, 71*f*, 72
white papers, 609, 610, 616–18, 617*f*
guidelines for, 616
as a one-way application, 610
writer's checklist for, 626
white space
page design and, 265–67, 280*f*
whole-by-whole pattern, 160, 161*f*
Wikipedia, 132
wikis, 624, 625*f*
APA reference list style for, 653
edits to, 624, 625*f*
participating in, 625
using in research, 132
writer's checklist for, 626
Williams, Joseph, 209
Williams, Robin, 255
women
nonsexist language and references to, 242–44
speech patterns of, 73
word-processing tools
common features, 68
equations, 483
grammar checker, 54
highlighting feature, 68
reviewing features, 68, 69
revision features, 68
spell checkers, 54

styles, 49
templates, 48, 49, 50
words
clarity of, 234–39
conciseness of, 239–42
for easy-to-translate text, 246
formality of, 233–34
inoffensive language, 242–45
precise, 200–201, 234, 236
writer's checklist for, 247
wordy phrases, concise equivalents of, 242, 242*t*
working procedures, for groups, 62
working titles, 200
work made for hire, 26
workplace research, 114. *See also* research
work schedules
collaboration and, 62
form, 63*f*
honesty about, 465
project management and, 60
works cited entries
MLA style for, 669
sample list, 682
writer's checklists
audience analysis, 107–8, 194
blogs, 626
brochures, 626
coherence, 216–17
collaboration, 74–75
definitions, 573
descriptions, 573–74
design, 292
discussion boards, 626
editing, 54, 356
electronic résumés, 426
e-mail, 385
graphics, 335
informational reports, 475
instructions, 574
job-application letters, 426
job-interview follow-up letters, 426
job-interview preparation, 426
letters, 384–85
lists, 247
logical fallacies, 194
memos, 385
newsletters, 626
oral presentations, 603
organizational patterns, 170–71
persona, 194

writer's checklists (*continued*)
   persuasive writing, 194
   podcasts, 626
   proofreading, 54, 356
   proposals, 452
   recommendation reports,
     535–36
   research, 144
   résumés, 426
   revising, 54, 356
   sentences, 247
   usability evaluation, 356
   usability tests, 356
   Web site and page design, 292
   white papers, 626
   wikis, 626
   words and phrases, 247
writing process, 41–51
   collaboration pattern and, 58*f*
   descriptions, 550–51
   drafting and, 47–51
   editing and, 53
   for field reports, 463
   for informational
     reports, 460
   planning and, 42–47
   proofreading and, 53–54
   revising and, 51–53
   steps in, 42
   writer's checklist for, 54
writing purpose
   analyzing, 115*f*
   audience analysis and, 81
   for definitions, 541
   determining, 103–4
   formality level and, 234
   for informational reports, 460
   information organization
     and, 150
   for oral presentations, 582
   planning and, 43
   for proposals, 432
   real and expressed, 104
   for recommendation reports,
     509, 519
   revising and, 51
   titles and, 200
   verbs representing, 104
writing style, U.S., 722

"you attitude," 340–41

INDEX OF FEATURES

Ethics Notes

Distinguishing Plagiarism from Acceptable Reuse of Information 28

Acknowledging Reviewers Responsibly 53

Pulling Your Weight on Collaborative Projects 65

Meeting Your Readers' Needs Responsibly 99

Reporting and Analyzing Data Honestly 143

Comparing and Contrasting Fairly 162

Seeming Honest Versus *Being* Honest in Persuasive Writing 191

Avoiding Burying Bad News in Paragraphs 208

Euphemisms and Truth Telling 239

Using Type Sizes Responsibly 271

Designing Legal and Honest Web Pages 288

Creating Honest Graphics 300

Understanding the Ethics of Informed Consent 354

Writing Honest Business Correspondence 368

Writing Honest Job-Application Materials 399

Writing Honest Proposals 440

Reporting Your Progress Honestly 465

Presenting Data Honestly 485

Presenting Honest Recommendations 507

Protecting Your Readers' Safety 561

Answering Questions Honestly 600

Marketing Your Organization Honestly 618

Tech Tips

How to Use the Outline View 46

How to Modify Templates 49

How to Use the Styles Group 51

How to Use the Review Tab 69

How to Modify and Create Styles 216

How to Create Numbered and Bulleted Lists 226

How to Set Up Pages 259

How to Format Columns 268

How to Format Fonts 270

How to Modify Line Spacing 274

How to Modify Justification 274

How to Create Borders and Screens 278

How to Create Text Boxes 278

How to Insert and Modify Graphics 305

How to Use Tab Stops 315

How to Create Tables 315

How to Create Graphics in Excel 317

How to Use Drawing Tools 321

How to Create Screen Shots 331

How to Create a Gantt Chart 446

How to Format Headers, Footers, and Page Numbers 514

How to Create a Table of Contents 514

How to Create a Master Page Design in PowerPoint 588

How to Set List Items to Appear and Dim During a Presentation 589

Interactive Sample Documents

Studying How Technical Communication Combines Words and Graphics 9

Analyzing a Code of Conduct 34

Identifying the Strengths and Weaknesses of a Commercial Template 50

Critiquing a Draft Clearly and Diplomatically 70

Examining Cultural Variables in a Business Letter 100

Evaluating Information from Internet Sources 131

Comparing and Contrasting Honestly 164

Analyzing Evidence in an Argument 183

Identifying the Elements of a Coherent Paragraph 214

Revising for Conciseness and Simplicity 243

Analyzing a Page Design 283

Balancing Clarity and Drama in Graphics 322

Obtaining Informed Consent 355